VOX

Super-Mini
SPANISH
and
ENGLISH
Dictionary

English-Spanish/Spanish-English

Second Edition

Dictionary Compiled by
The Editors of Spes Editorial, S.L.

North American Edition Prepared by
the Editors of McGraw-Hill

McGraw·Hill

New York   Chicago   San Francisco   Lisbon   London   Madrid   Mexico City
Milan   New Delhi   San Juan   Seoul   Singapore   Sydney   Toronto

The McGraw·Hill Companies

Library of Congress Cataloging-in-Publication Data

Vox super-mini Spanish and English dictionary.— 2nd ed.
      p.   cm.
   ISBN 0-07-145178-1
    1. Spanish language—Dictionaries—English.   2. English language—
Dictionaries—Spanish.

   PC4680.V698   2005
   463'.21—dc22   2004065577

© Spes Editorial, S.L. 2003, 2005
Aribau, 197-199, 3a planta
08021 Barcelona (Spain)
e-mail: vox@vox.es
www.vox.es

    4 5 6 7 8 9 10 11   LBM/LBM   0 9 8 7 6

ISBN 0-07-145178-1

McGraw-Hill books are available at special quantity discounts to use as premiums
and sales promotions, or for use in corporate training programs. For more
information, please write to the Director of Special Sales, Professional Publishing,
McGraw-Hill, Two Penn Plaza, New York, NY 10121-2298. Or contact your local
bookstore.

This book is printed on acid free paper.

Contents

Abbreviations Used in This Dictionary/
    Abreviaturas usadas en el diccionario iv

INGLÉS-ESPAÑOL/ENGLISH-SPANISH
Fonética vi
Diccionario 1-222

SPANISH-ENGLISH/ESPAÑOL-INGLÉS
Key to Pronunciation in Spanish . . . . i-iv
Dictionary 1-211

APPENDICES/APÉNDICES
Monetary Units/Unidades monetarias 213
Weights and Measures/Pesas y medidas 215
Numbers/Numerales 218
Temperature/La temperatura 220
Abbreviations Most Commonly Used in Spanish 222
Maps 226

Abbreviations Used in This Dictionary

abbreviation, acronym	*abbr, abr*	abreviatura, sigla
adjective	*adj*	adjetivo
adverb	*adv*	adverbio
somebody	algn	alguien
architecture	ARCH, ARQ	arquitectura
slang	*arg*	argot
auxiliary	*aux*	auxiliar
commercial	COMM, COM	comercio
computing	COMPUT	informática
conditional	*cond*	conticional
conjunction	*conj*	conjunción
determiner	*det*	determinante
euphemism	*euf, euph*	eufemismo
familiar	*fam*	familiar
figurative	*fig*	uso figurado
finance	FIN	finanzas
formal	*fml*	formal
future	*fut*	futuro
British English	GB	inglés británico
geography	GEOG	geografía
history	HIST	historia
indicative	*ind*	indicativo
computing	INFORM	informática
interjection	*interj*	interjección
invariable	*inv*	invariable
ironic	*iron, irón*	irónico
law	JUR	derecho
mathematics	MATH, MAT	matemáticas
medicine	MED	medicina
music	MUS, MÚS	música

Abreviaturas usadas en el diccionario

noun	*n*	nombre
femenine noun	*nf*	nombre femenino
masculine noun	*nm*	nombre masculino
masc, and fem. noun	*nm,f*	nombre masc. y fem.
masc. or fem. noun	*nm & f*	género ambiguo
plural noun	*npl*	nombre plural
number	*num*	número
pejorative	*pej, pey*	peyorativo
perfect	*perf*	perfecto
person	*pers*	persona
phrase	*phr*	locución
pluperfect	*pluperf*	pluscuamperfecto
politics	POL	política
past participle	*pp*	participio pasado
preposition	*prep*	preposición
present	*pres*	presente
pronoun	*pron*	pronombre
past	*pt*	pasado
somebody	sb	alguien
singular	*sing*	singular
slang	*sl*	argot
sport	SP	deportes
something	*sth*	algo
American English	US	inglés de América
intransitive verb	*vi*	verbo intransitivo
reflexive verb	*vpr*	verbo pronominal
transitive verb	*vt*	verbo transitivo
vulgar	*vulg*	vulgar
see	→	véase
registered trademark	®	marca registrada

Fonética

Todas las entradas inglesas en este diccionario llevan transcripción fonética basada en el sistema de la Asociación Fonética Internacional (AFI). He aquí una relación de los símbolos empleados. El símbolo ' delante de una sílaba indica que es ésta la acentuada.

Las consonantes

[p]	pan [pæn], happy ['hæpɪ], slip [slɪp].
[b]	big [bɪg], habit ['hæbɪt], stab [stæb].
[t]	top [tɒp], sitting ['sɪtɪŋ], bit [bɪt].
[d]	drip [drɪp], middle ['mɪdəl], rid [rɪd].
[k]	card [kɑːd], maker ['meɪkəʳ], sock [sɒk].
[g]	god [gɒd], mugger ['mʌgəʳ], dog [dɒg].
[tʃ]	chap [tʃæp], hatchet ['hætʃɪt], beach [biːtʃ].
[dʒ]	jack [dʒæk], digest [daɪ'dʒest], wage [weɪdʒ].
[f]	wish [wɪʃ], coffee ['kɒfɪ], wife [waɪf].
[v]	very ['verɪ], never ['nevəʳ], give [gɪv].
[θ]	thing [θɪŋ], cathode ['kæθəʊd], filth [fɪlθ].
[ð]	they [ðeɪ], father ['fɑːðəʳ], loathe [ləʊð].
[s]	spit [spɪt], stencil ['stensəl], niece [niːs].
[z]	zoo ['zuː], weasel ['wiːzəl], buzz [bʌz].
[ʃ]	show [ʃəʊ], fascist [fæ'ʃɪst], gush [gʌʃ].
[ʒ]	gigolo ['ʒɪgələʊ], pleasure ['pleʒəʳ], massage ['mæsɑːʒ].
[h]	help [help], ahead [ə'hed].
[m]	moon [muːn], common ['kɒmən], came [keɪm].
[n]	nail [neɪl], counter ['kaʊntəʳ], shone [ʃɒn].
[ŋ]	linger ['fɪŋgəʳ], sank [sæŋk], thing [θɪŋ].
[l]	light [laɪt], illness ['ɪlnəs], bull [bʊl].
[r]	rug [rʌg], merry ['merɪ].
[j]	young [jʌn], university [juːnɪ'veːsɪtɪ], Europe ['jʊərəp].
[w]	want [wɒnt], rewind [riː'waɪnd].
[x]	loch [lɒx].
[']	se llama *"linking r"* y se encuentra únicamente a final de palabra. Se pronuncia sólo cuando la palabra siguiente empieza por una vocal: **mother and father came** ['mʌðər ən 'fɑːðə keɪm].

Las vocales y los diptongos

[iː]   sheep [ʃiːp], sea [siː], scene [siːn], field [fiːld].

[ɪ]   ship [ʃɪp], pity ['pɪtɪ], roses ['rəʊzɪz], babies ['beɪbɪz], college ['kɒlɪdʒ].

[e]   shed [ʃed], instead [ɪn'sted], any ['enɪ], bury ['berɪ], friend [frend].

[æ]   fat [fæt], thank [θæŋk], plait [plæt].

[ɑː]   rather ['rɑːðəʳ], car [kɑːʳ], heart [hɑːt], clerk [klɑːk], palm [pɑːm], aunt [ɑːnt].

[ɒ]   lock [lɒk], wash [wɒʃ], trough [trɒf], because [bɪ'kɒz].

[ɔː]   horse [hɔːs], straw [strɔː], fought [fɔːt], cause [kɔːz], fall [fɔːl], boar [bɔːʳ], door [dɔːʳ].

[ʊ]   look [lʊk], pull [pʊl], woman ['wʊmən], should [ʃʊd].

[uː]   loop [luːp], do [duː], soup [suːp], elude [i'luːd], true [truː], shoe [ʃuː], few [fjuː].

[ʌ]   cub [kʌb], ton [tʌn], young [jʌŋ], flood [flʌd], does [dʌz].

[ɛː]   third [θɛːd], herd [hɛːd], heard [hɛːd], curl [kɛːl], word [wɛːd], journey ['dʒɛːnɪ].

[ə]   actor ['æktəʳ], honour ['ɒnəʳ], about [ə'baʊt].

[ə]   opcional. En algunos casos se pronuncia y en otros se omite: trifle ['traɪfəl].

[eɪ]   cable ['keɪbəl], way [weɪ], plain [pleɪn], freight [freɪt], prey [preɪ], great [greɪt].

[əʊ]   go [gəʊ], toad [təʊd], toe [təʊ], though [ðəʊ], snow [snəʊ].

[aɪ]   lime [laɪm], thigh [θaɪ], height [haɪt], lie [laɪ], try [traɪ], either ['aɪðəʳ].

[aʊ]   house [haʊs], cow [kaʊ].

[ɔɪ]   toy [tɔɪ], soil [sɔɪl].

[ɪə]   near [nɪəʳ], here [hɪəʳ], sheer [ʃɪəʳ], idea [aɪ'dɪə], museum [mjuː'zɪəm], weird [wɪəd], pierce [pɪəs].

[eə]   hare [heəʳ], hair [heəʳ], wear [weəʳ].

[ʊə]   pure [pjʊəʳ], during ['djʊərɪŋ], tourist ['tʊərɪst].

English - Spanish

A

a [eɪ, ə] *det* un, una.

A [eɪ] *abbr* **1** sobresaliente *(calificación)*. **2** la *(nota musical)*.

abandon [ə'bændən] *vt* abandonar.

abattoir ['æbətwɑːʳ] *n* matadero.

abbey ['æbɪ] *n* abadía.

abbreviation [əbriːvɪ'eɪʃən] *n* abreviatura.

abdomen ['æbdəmən] *n* abdomen.

abduct [æb'dʌkt] *vt* raptar, secuestrar.

ability [ə'bɪlɪtɪ] *n* **1** capacidad. **2** talento, aptitud.

able ['eɪbəl] *adj* hábil, capaz. • **to be able to 1** poder. **2** saber: *he was able to drive when he was sixteen*, sabía conducir a los dieciséis años.

abnormal [æb'nɔːməl] *adj* **1** anormal. **2** inusual.

aboard [ə'bɔːd] *adv* a bordo.

abort [ə'bɔːt] *vi* abortar.

abortion [ə'bɔːʃən] *n* aborto *(provocado)*.

about [ə'baʊt] *prep* **1** de, sobre, acerca de. **2** por, en: *he's somewhere about the house*, está por algún rincón de la casa. ► *adv* **1** alrededor de. **2** por aquí, por ahí: *there was nobody about*, no había nadie. • **to be about to...** estar a punto de...

above [ə'bʌv] *prep* **1** por encima de. **2** más de, más que: *above 5,000 people*, más de 5.000 personas. ► *adv* arriba. • **above all** sobre todo.

abridged [ə'brɪdʒd] *adj* abreviado,-a.

abroad [ə'brɔːd] *adv* al extranjero.

absent ['æbsənt] *adj* ausente.

absent-minded [æbsənt'maɪndɪd] *adj* distraído,-a.

absolute ['æbsəluːt] *adj* absoluto,-a.

absorb [əb'zɔːb] *vt* absorber

abstain [əb'steɪn] *vi* abstenerse.

abstract ['æbstrækt] *adj* abstracto,-a. ► *n* resumen, sinopsis.

abundant [ə'bʌndənt] *adj* abundante.

abuse [(*n*) ə'bjuːs, (*vb*) ə'bjuːz] *n* **1** insultos. **2** malos tratos. **3** abuso.

abyss [ə'bɪs] *n* abismo.

academic [ækə'demɪk] *adj* académico,-a. ► *n* profesor, -ra de universidad. ■ **academic year** curso escolar.

academy [ə'kædəmɪ] *n* academia.

accelerate [æk'seləreɪt] *vt-vi*
acelerar.

accelerator [æk'seləreɪtəʳ] *n*
acelerador.

accent ['æksənt] *n* acento.

accept [ək'sept] *vt* aceptar.

access ['ækses] *n* acceso. ▶ *vt*
COMPUT acceder a.

accessory [æk'sesərɪ] *n* **1** accesorio. **2** cómplice.

accident ['æksɪdənt] *n* accidente.

accident-prone ['æksɪdənt-prəʊn] *adj* propenso,-a a los accidentes.

acclaim [ə'kleɪm] *vt* aclamar.

accommodation [əkɒmə'deɪʃən] *n* alojamiento.

accompany [ə'kʌmpənɪ] *vt*
acompañar.

accomplish [ə'kɒmplɪʃ] *vt* lograr, conseguir.

according to [ə'kɔːdɪŋtu] *prep*
según.

accordion [ə'kɔːdɪən] *n* acordeón.

account [ə'kaʊnt] *n* **1** cuenta. **2** relato, versión. **3** importancia. • **on account** a cuenta; **on account of** por, a causa de.

to account for *vi* explicar.

accounting [ə'kaʊntɪŋ] *n* contabilidad.

accumulate [ə'kjuːmjʊleɪt] *vt-vi* acumular(se).

accurate ['ækjʊrət] *adj* exacto,-a, preciso,-a.

accusation [ækjuː'zeɪʃən] *n*
acusación.

accuse [ə'kjuːz] *vt* acusar.

accustom [ə'kʌstəm] *vt* acostumbrar.

accustomed [ə'kʌstəmd] *adj*
acostumbrado,-a. • **to get accustomed to** acostumbrarse a.

ace [eɪs] *n* as.

ache [eɪk] *n* dolor. ▶ *vi* doler.

achieve [ə'tʃiːv] *vt* lograr.

acid ['æsɪd] *n* ácido. ▶ *adj* ácido,-a. ■ **acid rain** lluvia ácida.

acknowledge [ək'nɒlɪdʒ] *vt*
1 reconocer. **2** agradecer.

acknowledgement [ək'nɒlɪdʒmənt] *n* **1** reconocimiento. **2** acuse de recibo.

acne ['æknɪ] *n* acné.

acorn ['eɪkɔːn] *n* bellota.

acoustic [ə'kuːstɪk] *adj* acústico,-a.

acquaint [ə'kweɪnt] *vt* informar, poner al corriente.

acquaintance [ə'kweɪntəns] *n* conocido,-a.

acquire [ə'kwaɪəʳ] *vt* **1** adquirir *(posesiones)*. **2** obtener, conseguir *(información)*.

acquit [ə'kwɪt] *vt* absolver.

acre ['eɪkəʳ] *n* acre.

acrobat ['ækrəbæt] *n* acróbata.

acronym ['ækrənɪm] *n* sigla.

across [ə'krɒs] *prep* **1** a través de: *to swim across a river*, cruzar un río a nado. **2** al otro lado de: *they live across the*

road, viven enfrente. ▶ *adv* de un lado a otro.

act [ækt] *n* **1** acto. **2** número: *tonight's first act is a clown*, el primer número de la noche es un payaso. **3** *(Act of Parliament)* ley. ▶ *vi* actuar. ■ **act of God** fuerza mayor.

acting ['æktɪŋ] *n* actuación. ▶ *adj* en funciones.

action ['ækʃən] *n* acción. ● **out of action** fuera de servicio; **to bring an action against SB** entablar una demanda contra ALGN.

active ['æktɪv] *adj* activo,-a.

activity [æk'tɪvɪtɪ] *n* actividad.

actor ['æktəʳ] *n* actor.

actress ['æktrəs] *n* actriz.

actual ['æktʃʊəl] *adj* **1** real. **2** exacto,-a: *those were her actual words*, esas fueron sus palabras exactas.

actually ['æktjʊəlɪ] *adv* **1** en realidad, de hecho. **2** de verdad: *have you actually seen a ghost?*, ¿de verdad que has visto un fantasma?

acute [ə'kjuːt] *adj* agudo,-a.

ad [æd] *n fam* anuncio.

adamant ['ædəmənt] *adj* firme, inflexible.

adapt [ə'dæpt] *vt-vi* adaptar(se).

adaptor [ə'dæptəʳ] *n* ladrón *(enchufe)*.

add [æd] *vt* añadir. ▶ *vt-vi* sumar.

to add to *vt* aumentar.

to add up *vt-vi* sumar. ▶ *vi fig* cuadrar: *his version doesn't add up*, su versión no cuadra.

adder ['ædəʳ] *n* víbora.

addict ['ædɪkt] *n* adicto,-a.

addition [ə'dɪʃən] *n* adición. ● **in addition to** además de.

additive ['ædɪtɪv] *n* aditivo.

address [ə'dres] *n* **1** dirección. **2** discurso. **3** conferencia. ▶ *vt* dirigirse a. ■ **address book** agenda.

adept [ə'dept] *adj* experto,-a.

adequate ['ædɪkwət] *adj* adecuado,-a, satisfactorio,-a.

adjective ['ædʒɪktɪv] *n* adjetivo.

adjourn [ə'dʒɜːn] *vt* aplazar.

adjust [ə'dʒʌst] *vt* ajustar*(temperatura)*. ▶ *vi* adaptarse.

adjustable [ə'dʒʌstəbəl] *adj* regulable. ■ **adjustable spanner** llave inglesa.

adjustment [ə'dʒʌstmənt] *n* ajuste.

administration [ədmɪnɪs'treɪʃən] *n* administración.

administrator [əd'mɪnɪstreɪtəʳ] *n* administrador,-ra.

admiral ['ædmərəl] *n* almirante.

admiration [ædmɪ'reɪʃən] *n* admiración.

admire [əd'maɪəʳ] *vt* admirar.

admission [əd'mɪʃən] *n* **1** ingreso *(en hospital, institución)*. **2** entrada: *"Admission free"*, "Entrada gratuita".

admit [əd'mɪt] *vt* **1** admitir. **2** ingresar *(en hospital)*.

adolescent [ædə'lesənt] *adj-n* adolescente.

adopt [ə'dɒpt] *vt* adoptar.

adore [ə'dɔː'] *vt* adorar.

adorn [ə'dɔːn] *vt* adornar.

adrift [ə'drɪft] *adj* a la deriva.

adult ['ædʌlt] *adj-n* adulto,-a.

adulterate [ə'dʌltəreɪt] *vt* adulterar.

advance [əd'vɑːns] *n* **1** avance. **2** anticipo, adelanto *(de dinero)*. ▶ *vt* **1** avanzar *(tropas)*. **2** ascender *(empleado)*. **3** adelantar *(reunión)*. **4** anticipar *(dinero)*. ▶ *vi* adelantarse.
• **in advance** por adelantado.

advantage [əd'vɑːntɪdʒ] *n* ventaja.

adventure [əd'ventʃə'] *n* aventura. ▪ **adventure playground** parque infantil.

adverb ['ædvɜːb] *n* adverbio.

adversary ['ædvəsəri] *n* adversario,-a.

adversity [əd'vɜːsɪti] *n* adversidad.

advert ['ædvɜːt] *n fam* anuncio.

advertise ['ædvətaɪz] *vt* anunciar. ▶ *vi* hacer publicidad.

advertisement [əd'vɜːtɪsmənt] *n* anuncio.

advice [əd'vaɪs] *n* consejos.

advise [əd'vaɪz] *vt* aconsejar.
• **to advise against** STH desaconsejar algo.

adviser [əd'vaɪzə'] *n* asesor,-a.

advocate ['ædvəkət] *n* partidario,-a.

aerial ['eərɪəl] *n* antena.

aerodynamic [eərəudaɪ'næmɪk] *adj* aerodinámico,-a.

aeroplane ['eərəpleɪn] *n* avión.

aerosol ['eərəsɒl] *n* aerosol.

aesthetic [iːs'θetɪk] *adj* estético,-a.

affair [ə'feə'] *n* **1** asunto. **2** caso: *the watergate affair*, el caso watergate. **3** lío, aventura *(amorosa)*.

affect [ə'fekt] *vt* afectar.

affection [ə'fekʃən] *n* afecto.

affectionate [ə'fekʃənət] *adj* afectuoso,-a.

affiliated [ə'fɪlɪeɪtɪd] *adj* afiliado,-a.

affirmative [ə'fɜːmətɪv] *adj* afirmativo,-a.

affluent ['æfluənt] *adj* rico,-a, próspero,-a.

afford [ə'fɔːd] *vt* permitirse: *I can't afford to pay £750 for a coat*, no puedo permitirme pagar 750 libras por un abrigo.

afraid [ə'freɪd] *adj* temeroso,-a.
• **to be afraid** tener miedo.

afresh [ə'freʃ] *adv* de nuevo.

after ['ɑːftə'] *prep* **1** después de. **2** detrás de: *the police are after us*, la policía nos está persiguiendo. ▶ *adv* después. ▶ *conj* después de que. • **after all** al fin y al cabo.

after-effect ['ɑːftərɪfekt] *n* efecto secundario.

afternoon [ɑːftə'nuːn] *n* tarde: *good afternoon*, buenas tardes.

after-sales ['ɑːftə'seɪlz] *adj* posventa.

aftershave ['ɑːftəʃeɪv] *n* loción para después del afeitado.

afterwards ['ɑːftəwədz] *adv* después, luego.

again [ə'gen, ə'geɪn] *prep* de nuevo, otra vez.

against [ə'genst, ə'geɪnst] *prep* contra.

age [eɪdʒ] *n* edad. ▶ *vi-vt* envejecer. ● **of age** mayor de edad; **under age** menor de edad.

aged [eɪdʒd] *adj* **1** de … años: *a boy aged ten*, un niño de diez años. **2** viejo,-a, anciano,-a.

agency ['eɪdʒənsi] *n* agencia.

agenda [ə'dʒendə] *n* orden del día.

agent ['eɪdʒənt] *n* agente.

ages ['eɪdʒɪz] *npl* años, siglos: *it's ages since she left*, hace años que se marchó.

aggressive [ə'gresɪv] *adj* agresivo,-a.

agility [ə'dʒɪlɪti] *n* agilidad.

agitate ['ædʒɪteɪt] *vt* agitar.

ago [ə'gəʊ] *adv* hace: *a long time ago*, hace mucho tiempo.

agonize ['ægənaɪz] *vi* atormentarse, angustiarse.

agony ['ægəni] *n* **1** dolor. **2** angustia.

agree [ə'griː] *vi-vt* **1** estar de acuerdo. **2** ponerse de acuerdo, acordar. **3** acceder, consentir: *will he agree to our request?*, ¿accederá a nuestra petición? **4** concordar, encajar: *the two men's stories don't agree*, las historias de los dos hombres no encajan. **5** sentar bien *(comida)*.

agreeable [ə'griːəbəl] *adj* agradable.

agreement [ə'griːmənt] *n* acuerdo.

agriculture ['ægrɪkʌltʃəʳ] *n* agricultura.

ahead [ə'hed] *adv* delante.

aid [eɪd] *n* ayuda, auxilio. ▶ *vt* ayudar, auxiliar.

AIDS [eɪdz] *abbr* SIDA.

ailment ['eɪlmənt] *n* dolencia, achaque.

aim [eɪm] *n* **1** puntería. **2** meta, objetivo. ● **to take aim** apuntar.

to aim at *vt* apuntar a.

to aim to *vt* tener la intención de, proponerse.

air [eəʳ] *n* aire. ▶ *vt* **1** airear. **2** ventilar. ■ **air hostess** azafata.

airbag ['eəbæg] *n* airbag.

air-conditioned [eəkən'dɪʃənd] *adj* con aire acondicionado, climatizado,-a.

aircraft ['eəkrɑːft] *n* avión. ■ **aircraft carrier** portaaviones.

airline ['eəlaɪn] *n* compañía aérea.

airplane ['eəpleɪn] *n* US avión.

airport ['eəpɔːt] *n* aeropuerto.

airsick ['eəsɪk] *adj* mareado,-a *(en el avión)*.

airstrip ['eəstrɪp] *n* pista de aterrizaje.

airtight ['eətaɪt] *adj* hermético,-a.

airy ['eərɪ] *adj* bien ventilado,-a.

aisle [aɪl] *n* **1** pasillo. **2** nave lateral.

alarm [ə'lɑːm] *n* alarma. ► *vt* alarmar. ■ **alarm clock** despertador.

album ['ælbəm] *n* álbum.

alcohol ['ælkəhɒl] *n* alcohol.

alcoholic [ælkə'hɒlɪk] *adj* alcohólico,-a.

ale [eɪl] *n* cerveza.

alert [ə'lɜːt] *adj* alerta. ► *n* alarma, aviso: *bomb alert*, aviso de bomba. ► *vt* alertar.

algae ['ældʒiː] *npl* algas.

alibi ['ælɪbaɪ] *n* coartada.

alien ['eɪlɪən] *adj* **1** extranjero,-a. **2** extraterrestre.

alight [ə'laɪt] *adj* encendido,-a.

to alight on *vt* **1** posarse en. **2** darse cuenta de.

align [ə'laɪn] *vt-vi* alinear(se).

alike [ə'laɪk] *adj* igual. ► *adv* igual, de la misma forma. ● **to look alike** parecerse.

alimony ['ælɪmənɪ] *n* pensión alimenticia.

alive [ə'laɪv] *adj* vivo,-a.

all [ɔːl] *adj* todo,-a, todos,-as. ► *pron* **1** todo, la totalidad. **2** lo único, sólo. **3** todos, todo el mundo. ► *adv* **1** completamente, muy: *you're all dirty!*, ¡estás todo sucio! **2** empatados, iguales: *the score was three all*, empataron a tres. ● **after all** después de todo; **all right 1** bueno,-a. **2** bien: *are you all right?*, ¿estás bien?; **at all** en absoluto; **not at all 1** en absoluto. **2** no hay de qué, de nada: *Thank you very much. –Not at all*, Muchas gracias. –De nada.

allege [ə'ledʒ] *vt* alegar.

alleged [ə'ledʒd] *adj* presunto,-a, supuesto,-a.

allergy ['ælədʒɪ] *n* alergia.

alley ['ælɪ] *n* callejuela, callejón.

alligator ['ælɪgeɪtə'] *n* caimán.

allocate ['æləkeɪt] *vt* asignar.

allow [ə'laʊ] *vt* **1** permitir, dejar. **2** admitir: *dogs are not allowed in*, no se admiten perros. **3** conceder, dar, asignar.

to allow for *vt* tener en cuenta.

allowance [ə'laʊəns] *n* **1** prestación, subsidio, dietas. **2** US paga semanal.

alloy ['ælɔɪ] *n* aleación.

ally ['ælaɪ] *n* aliado,-a. ► *vt-vi* aliar(se).

almond ['ɑːmənd] *n* almendra.

almost ['ɔːlməʊst] *adv* casi.

alone [ə'ləʊn] *adj* solo,-a.

along [ə'lɒŋ] *prep* a lo largo de, por. ► *adv* hacia delante:

she was walking along, iba caminando. • **all along** desde el principio; **along with** junto con; **come along!** iven!, ivenid!

alongside [ə'lɒŋ'saɪd] *prep* al lado de. ▶ *adv* al costado.

aloof [ə'luːf] *adj* distante.

aloud [ə'laʊd] *adv* en voz alta.

alphabet ['ælfəbet] *n* alfabeto.

already [ɔːl'redɪ] *adv* ya.

also ['ɔːlsəʊ] *adv* también.

altar ['ɔːltəʳ] *n* altar.

alter ['ɔːltəʳ] *vt* **1** cambiar, modificar. **2** arreglar *(ropa)*.

alternate [*(adj)* ɔːl'tɜːnət, *(vb)* 'ɔːltɜːneɪt] *adj* alterno,-a. ▶ *vt-vi* alternar(se).

alternative [ɔːl'tɜːnətɪv] *adj* alternativo,-a. ▶ *n* alternativa.

although [ɔːl'ðəʊ] *conj* aunque.

altogether [ɔːltə'geðəʳ] *adv* **1** del todo, completamente. **2** en conjunto, en total. • **in the altogether** en cueros.

always ['ɔːlweɪz] *adv* siempre.

amateur ['æmətəʳ] *adj-n* aficionado,-a.

amaze [ə'meɪz] *vt* asombrar.

amazing [ə'meɪzɪŋ] *adj* asombroso.

ambassador [æm'bæsədəʳ] *n* embajador,-a.

amber ['æmbəʳ] *n* ámbar.

ambience ['æmbɪəns] *n* ambiente.

ambiguous [æm'bɪgjʊəs] *adj* ambiguo,-a.

ambition [æm'bɪʃən] *n* ambición.

ambitious [æm'bɪʃəs] *adj* ambicioso,-a.

ambulance ['æmbjʊləns] *n* ambulancia.

ambush ['æmbʊʃ] *n* emboscada. ▶ *vt* tender una emboscada a.

amend [ə'mend] *vt* enmendar.

amenities [ə'miːnɪtɪz] *npl* servicios, instalaciones.

amiable ['eɪmɪəbəl] *adj* amable.

amid [ə'mɪd] *prep* en medio de, entre.

amidst [ə'mɪdst] *prep* en medio de, entre.

ammonia [ə'məʊnɪ] *n* amoníaco.

ammunition [æmjʊ'nɪʃən] *n* municiones.

amoeba [æ'miːbə] *n* ameba.

among [ə'mʌŋ] *prep* entre.

amongst [ə'mʌŋst] *prep* entre.

amount [ə'maʊnt] *n* cantidad.

to amount to *vt* ascender a.

ampere ['æmpeəʳ] *n* amperio.

amphibian [æm'fɪbɪən] *n* anfibio.

ample ['æmpəl] *adj* **1** abundante. **2** amplio,-a *(habitación)*.

amplifier ['æmplɪfaɪəʳ] *n* amplificador.

amplify ['æmplɪfaɪ] *vt* amplificar.

amputate ['æmpjʊteɪt] *vt* amputar.

amuse [ə'mjuːz] *vt* entretener, divertir.

amusement [ə'mjuːzmənt] *n* diversión, entretenimiento. ■ **amusement park** parque de atracciones.

amusing [ə'mjuːzɪŋ] *adj* divertido,-a.

an [ən, æn] *det* un,-a.

anaemia [ə'niːmɪə] *n* GB anemia.

anaesthesia [ænəs'θiːzɪə] *n* GB anestesia.

anal ['eɪnəl] *adj* anal.

analgesic [ænəl'dʒiːzɪk] *adj* analgésico,-a. ► *n* analgésico.

analyse ['ænəlaɪz] *vt* analizar.

analysis [ə'nælɪsɪs] *n* análisis.

anarchy ['ænəki] *n* anarquía.

anatomy [ə'nætəmɪ] *n* anatomía.

ancestor ['ænsəstəʳ] *n* **1** antepasado. **2** antecesor.

anchor ['æŋkəʳ] *n* ancla. ► *vt-vi* anclar.

anchovy ['æntʃəvɪ] *n* anchoa.

ancient ['eɪnʃənt] *adj* antiguo,-a, histórico,-a.

and [ænd, ənd] *conj* y, e.

anecdote ['ænɪkdəʊt] *n* anécdota.

anemia [ə'niːmɪə] *n* US anemia.

anesthesia [ænəs'θiːzɪə] *n* US anestesia.

angel ['eɪndʒəl] *n* ángel.

anger ['æŋgəʳ] *n* cólera, ira.

angle ['æŋgəl] *n* ángulo.

angler ['æŋgləʳ] *n* pescador,-ra *(de caña)*. ■ **angler fish** rape.

angling ['æŋglɪŋ] *n* pesca *(con caña)*.

angry ['æŋgrɪ] *adj* enfadado,-a.

anguish ['æŋgwɪʃ] *n* angustia.

animal ['ænɪməl] *n* animal.

animate ['ænɪmeɪt] *vt* animar.

ankle ['æŋkəl] *n* tobillo.

annex [(vb) ə'neks(n) 'aneks] *vt* anexar. ► *n* US anexo.

annexe ['æneks] *n* GB anexo.

annihilate [ə'naɪəleɪt] *vt* aniquilar.

anniversary [ænɪ'vɜːsərɪ] *n* aniversario.

announce [ə'naʊns] *vt* anunciar.

announcement [ə'naʊnsmənt] *n* anuncio.

announcer [ə'naʊnsəʳ] *n* presentador,-ra, locutor,-a.

annoy [ə'nɔɪ] *vt* molestar.

anonymous [ə'nɒnɪməs] *adj* anónimo,-a.

anorexia [ænə'reksɪə] *n* anorexia.

another [ə'nʌðəʳ] *adj-pron* otro,-a.

answer ['ɑːnsəʳ] *n* respuesta. ► *vt-vi* responder, contestar.

to answer back *vt-vi* replicar *(con insolencia)*.

to answer for *vt* responder por, responder de.

answering machine ['ɑːnsərɪŋməʃiːn] *n* contestador automático.

ant [ænt] n hormiga. ▪ **ant hill** hormiguero.

antelope ['æntɪləʊp] n antílope.

antenna [æn'tenə] n antena.

anthem ['ænθəm] n himno.

antibiotic [æntɪbaɪ'ɒtɪk] n antibiótico. ▶ adj antibiótico,-a.

antibody ['æntɪbɒdɪ] n anticuerpo.

anticipate [æn'tɪsɪpeɪt] vt **1** esperar: *we anticipate problems*, esperamos problemas. **2** prever: *as anticipated*, de acuerdo con lo previsto.

anticlockwise [æntɪ'klɒkwaɪz] adj en el sentido contrario al de las agujas del reloj.

antifreeze ['æntɪfriːz] n anticongelante.

antique [æn'tiːk] adj antiguo, -a. ▶ n antigüedad. ▪ **antique shop** anticuario, tienda de antigüedades.

antiseptic [æntɪ'septɪk] adj antiséptico,-a. ▶ n antiséptico.

antivirus [æntɪ'vaɪrəs] adj antivirus.

antlers ['æntləʳ] npl cornamenta.

anus ['eɪnəs] n ano.

anvil ['ænvɪl] n yunque.

anxious ['æŋkʃəs] adj ansioso,-a.

any ['enɪ] adj algún,-una, ningún,-una *(con el verbo negativo)*, cualquier,-ra, todo,-a: *any fool knows that*, cualquier

tonto sabe eso. ▶ pron alguno,-a, ninguno,-a *(con el verbo negativo)*, cualquiera: *I asked for some records, but they hadn't got any left*, pedí unos discos pero ya no quedaba ninguno. ▶ adv: *I don't work there any more*, ya no trabajo allí.

anybody ['enɪbɒdɪ] pron alguien, alguno,-a, nadie *(con el verbo negativo)*, cualquiera: *don't tell anybody*, no se lo digas a nadie.

anyhow ['enɪhaʊ] adv **1** en todo caso. **2** bueno, pues. **3** de cualquier forma.

anyone ['enɪwʌn] pron → anybody.

anything ['enɪθɪŋ] pron algo, alguna cosa, nada *(con el verbo negativo)*, cualquier cosa, todo cuanto: *do you want anything else?*, ¿quieres algo más?

anyway ['enɪweɪ] adv → anyhow.

anywhere ['enɪweəʳ] adv **1** (en) algún sitio, a algún sitio. **2** (en) ningún sitio, a ningún sitio *(con el verbo negativo)*. **3** donde sea, en cualquier sitio, a donde sea, a cualquier sitio: *I'd go anywhere with you*, iría a cualquier sitio contigo.

aorta [eɪ'ɔːtə] n aorta.

apart [ə'pɑːt] adv separado,-a. ▪ **apart from** aparte de, excepto, menos.

apartment [ə'pɑ:tmənt] n 1
piso. apartamento.

apathy ['æpəθɪ] n apatía.

ape [eɪp] n simio. ▶ vt imitar.

aperitif [əperɪ'ti:f] n aperitivo.

apiece [ə'pi:s] adv cada uno,-a.

apologize [ə'pɒlədʒaɪz] vi disculparse, pedir perdón.

apology [ə'pɒlədʒɪ] n disculpa.

appal [ə'pɔ:l] vt GB horrorizar.

appall [ə'pɔ:l] vt US horrorizar.

apparatus [æpə'reɪtəs] n equipo, aparatos.

apparent [ə'pærənt] adj 1 evidente. 2 aparente.

appeal [ə'pi:l] n 1 llamamiento. 2 petición, súplica. 3 atractivo. 4 apelación (contra sentencia judicial). ▶ vi 1 pedir, solicitar, suplicar. 2 atraer: **it doesn't appeal to me**, no me atrae. 3 apelar (contra sentencia judicial).

appealing [ə'pi:lɪŋ] adj atractivo.

appear [ə'pɪə'] vi 1 aparecer. 2 parecer: **this appears to be a mistake**, parece que hay un error.

appearance [ə'pɪərəns] n 1 aparición. 2 apariencia, aspecto.

appendicitis [əpendɪ'saɪtɪs] n apendicitis.

appendix [ə'pendɪks] n apéndice.

appetizer ['æpɪtaɪzə'] n aperitivo.

appetizing ['æpɪtaɪzɪŋ] adj apetitoso,-a.

applaud [ə'plɔ:d] vt-vi aplaudir.

applause [ə'plɔ:z] n aplausos.

apple ['æpəl] n manzana. ■ **apple pie** tarta de manzana.

appliance [ə'plaɪəns] n aparato.

applicant ['æplɪkənt] n candidato,-a, solicitante.

application [æplɪ'keɪʃən] n 1 solicitud. 2 aplicación. ■ **application form** impreso de solicitud.

apply [ə'plaɪ] vt aplicar. ▶ vi 1 aplicarse. 2 dirigirse, presentarse, solicitar: **to apply for a job**, solicitar un trabajo.

appointment [ə'pɔɪntmənt] n 1 cita, hora: **I've got an appointment with the doctor**, tengo hora con el médico. 2 nombramiento.

appraise [ə'preɪz] vt valorar.

appreciate [ə'pri:ʃɪeɪt] vt 1 agradecer. 2 entender. 3 valorar, apreciar.

apprehension [æprɪ'henʃən] n 1 detención, captura. 2 aprensión, recelo.

apprehensive [æprɪ'hensɪv] adj aprensivo.

apprentice [ə'prentɪs] n aprendiz,-za.

approach [ə'prəʊtʃ] n 1 aproximación, acercamiento. 2 entrada, acceso (a un lugar). 3 enfoque (de un problema). ▶ vt 1 acercarse a, aproximarse a.

2 enfocar, abordar, dirigirse *(a un problema)*. ■ **approach road** vía de acceso.

appropriate [ə'prəupriət] *adj* apropiado,-a.

approval [ə'pru:vəl] *n* aprobación. ● **on approval** a prueba.

approve [ə'pru:v] *vt* aprobar. **to approve of** *vt* aprobar.

approximate [ə'prɒksɪmət] *adj* aproximado,-a.

apricot ['eɪprɪkɒt] *n* albaricoque.

April ['eɪprɪl] *n* abril. ■ **April Fool's day** el día de los Inocentes *(celebrado el 1 de abril)*.

apron ['eɪprən] *n* delantal.

apt [æpt] *adj* apropiado,-a.

aquarium [ə'kweəriəm] *n* acuario.

Arab ['ærəb] *adj* árabe. ► *n* árabe.

arbitrate ['ɑ:bɪtreɪt] *vt-vi* arbitrar.

arc [ɑ:k] *n* arco.

arcade [ɑ:'keɪd] *n* **1** galería comercial. **2** salón recreativo. ■ **arcade game** videojuego.

arch [ɑ:tʃ] *n* arco.

archaeology [ɑ:kɪ'bləʤɪ] *n* arqueología.

archery ['ɑːtʃərɪ] *n* tiro con arco.

archipelago [ɑ:kɪ'pelɪgəʊ] *n* archipiélago.

architect ['ɑ:kɪtekt] *n* arquitecto,-a.

architecture ['ɑ:kɪtektʃəʳ] *n* arquitectura.

archive ['ɑ:kaɪv] *npl* archivo.

are [ɑ:ʳ, əʳ] *pres* → be.

area ['eərɪə] *n* área.

arena [ə'ri:nə] *n* **1** estadio. **2** ruedo *(de plaza de toros)*.

argue ['ɑ:gju:] *vi* **1** discutir. **2** argüir, argumentar.

argument ['ɑ:gjomənt] *n* **1** discusión, disputa. **2** argumento.

arise [ə'raɪz] *vi* **1** surgir, provenir de. **2** presentarse.

aristocrat ['ærɪstəkræt] *n* aristócrata.

arithmetic [ə'rɪθmətɪk] *n* aritmética.

ark [ɑ:k] *n* arca.

arm [ɑ:m] *n* **1** brazo. **2** manga. **3** arma.

armchair [ɑ:m'tʃeəʳ] *n* sillón.

armour ['ɑ:məʳ] (US **armor**) *n* **1** armadura. **2** blindaje.

armpit ['ɑ:mpɪt] *n* sobaco, axila.

army ['ɑ:mɪ] *n* ejército.

aroma [ə'rəʊmə] *n* aroma.

arose [ə'rəʊz] *pt* → arise.

around [ə'raʊnd] *adv* alrededor. ► *prep* alrededor de.

arouse [ə'raʊz] *vt* despertar.

arrange [ə'reɪnʤ] *vt* **1** arreglar, colocar, ordenar. **2** planear, organizar, concertar.

arrangement [ə'reɪnʤmənt] *n* **1** arreglo *(floral, musical)*. **2** acuerdo, arreglo. ► *npl* **arrangements** planes, preparativos.

arrears [ə'rɪəz] *npl* atrasos.

arrest [ə'rest] n arresto. ► vt arrestar, detener: *to be under arrest*, estar detenido.

arrival [ə'raɪvəl] n llegada.

arrive [ə'raɪv] vi llegar.

arrow ['ærəʊ] n flecha.

arse [ɑːs] n vulg culo.

arson ['ɑːsən] n incendio provocado.

art [ɑːt] n arte. ► npl **arts** letras. ■ **arts and crafts** artes y oficios.

artery ['ɑːtərɪ] n arteria.

artichoke ['ɑːtɪtʃəʊk] n alcachofa.

article ['ɑːtɪkəl] n artículo. ■ **leading article** editorial.

artificial [ɑːtɪ'fɪʃəl] adj artificial.

artisan [ɑːtɪ'zæn] n artesano,-a.

artist ['ɑːtɪst] n artista.

as [æz, əz] prep como. ► conj 1 mientras, cuando: *she sang as she painted*, cantaba mientras pintaba. 2 como, ya que, puesto que: *as the hotel was full, we had to look for another*, como el hotel estaba completo, tuvimos que buscar otro. 3 como: *as you know*, como sabes. • **as ... as** 1 tan ... como: *as big as an elephant*, tan grande como un elefante. 2 tanto como: *he works as little as possible*, trabaja lo mínimo posible; **as for** en cuanto a; **as if** como si; **as of** desde; **as though** como si; **as yet** hasta ahora.

asbestos [æs'bestəs] n amianto.

ascend [ə'send] vt-vi ascender, subir.

ascent [ə'sent] n subida.

ascribe [əs'kraɪb] vt atribuir.

ash¹ [æʃ] n ceniza.

ash² [æʃ] n fresno.

ashamed [ə'ʃeɪmd] adj avergonzado,-a.

ashore [ə'ʃɔːʳ] adv en tierra, a tierra. • **to go ashore** desembarcar.

ashtray ['æʃtreɪ] n cenicero.

aside [ə'saɪd] adv al lado, a un lado. ► n aparte (en teatro).

ask [ɑːsk] vt 1 preguntar. 2 pedir. 3 invitar, convidar: *they asked me to dinner*, me invitaron a cenar.

to ask after vt preguntar por.

to ask for vt pedir.

to ask out vt invitar a salir.

asleep [ə'sliːp] adj-adv dormido,-a: *to fall asleep*, dormirse.

asparagus [æs'pærəgəs] n espárragos.

aspect ['æspekt] n 1 aspecto. 2 orientación (de edificio).

asphalt ['æsfælt] n asfalto.

aspire [əs'paɪəʳ] vi aspirar.

aspirin® ['æspɪrɪn] n aspirina®.

ass [æs] n burro,-a, asno,-a.

assailant [ə'seɪlənt] n agresor,-ra.

assault [ə'sɔːlt] n 1 asalto (militar). 2 agresión (a persona).

assemble [ə'sembəl] vt montar, armar. ► vi reunirse.

assembly [ə'semblɪ] n 1 reunión, asamblea. 2 montaje, ensamblaje. ▪ **assembly hall** salón de actos.

assert [ə'sɜːt] vt 1 afirmar. 2 imponer *(autoridad)*.

assess [ə'ses] vt valorar.

asset ['æset] n ventaja, baza. ► npl **assets** bienes.

assign [ə'saɪn] vt asignar.

assignment [ə'saɪnmənt] n 1 misión. 2 tarea, trabajo.

assist [ə'sɪst] vt ayudar.

assistant [ə'sɪstənt] n ayudante. ▪ **assistant manager** subdirector,-ra.

associate [(n) ə'səʊʃɪət, (vb) ə'səʊʃɪeɪt] n socio,-a. ► vt-vi asociar(se). • **to associate with SB** relacionarse con ALGN.

association [əsəʊsɪ'eɪʃən] n asociación.

assortment [ə'sɔːtmənt] n surtido.

assume [ə'sjuːm] vt 1 suponer. 2 tomar, asumir *(responsabilidad)*. 3 adoptar *(actitud)*.

assurance [ə'ʃʊərəns] n 1 garantía. 2 seguro.

assure [ə'ʃʊə'] vt asegurar.

asthma ['æsmə] n asma.

astonish [əs'tɒnɪʃ] vt asombrar.

astray [ə'streɪ] adj-adv extraviado,-a. • **to go astray** descarriarse.

astrology [əs'trɒlədʒɪ] n astrología.

astronaut ['æstrənɔːt] n astronauta.

astronomy [əs'trɒnəmɪ] n astronomía.

astute [əs'tjuːt] adj astuto,-a, sagaz.

asylum [ə'saɪləm] n 1 asilo, refugio. 2 manicomio.

at [æt, ət] prep 1 a: *at home*, en casa; *at night*, por la noche; *at the beginning/ end*, al principio/final; *at 50 miles an hour*, a 50 millas la hora.

ate [et, eɪt] pt → eat.

atheist ['eɪθɪɪst] n ateo,-a.

athlete ['æθliːt] n atleta.

athletics [æθ'letɪks] n atletismo.

atlas ['ætləs] n atlas.

atmosphere ['ætməsfɪə'] n atmósfera.

atom ['ætəm] n átomo. ▪ **atom bomb** bomba atómica.

atrocity [ə'trɒsɪtɪ] n atrocidad.

attach [ə'tætʃ] vt 1 sujetar. 2 atar. 3 pegar. 4 adjuntar.

attachment [ə'tætʃmənt] n 1 accesorio. 2 archivo adjunto, anexo. 3 cariño, apego.

attack [ə'tæk] n ataque. ► vt atacar.

attain [ə'teɪn] vt lograr.

attempt [ə'tempt] n intento. ► vt intentar.

attend [ə'tend] vt asistir a.

to attend to vt ocuparse de

attendance [ə'tendəns] n 1 asistencia. 2 asistentes.

attention [ə'tenʃən] n atención.

attic ['ætɪk] n desván.

attitude ['ætɪtjuːd] n actitud.

attorney [ə'tɜːnɪ] n US abogado,-a. ■ **Attorney General** GB Fiscal General.

attract [ə'trækt] vt atraer.

aubergine ['əʊbəʒiːn] n berenjena.

auction ['ɔːkʃən] n subasta. ▶ vt subastar.

audience ['ɔːdɪəns] n **1** público, espectadores. **2** audiencia (de TV).

audit ['ɔːdɪt] n auditoría. ▶ vt auditar.

August ['ɔːgəst] n agosto.

aunt [ɑːnt] n tía.

authentic [ɔː'θentɪk] adj auténtico,-a.

author ['ɔːθə'] n autor,-ra.

authority [ɔː'θɒrɪtɪ] n autoridad. • **on good authority** de buena tinta.

authorize ['ɔːθəraɪz] vt autorizar.

automatic [ɔːtə'mætɪk] adj automático,-a.

automaton [ɔː'tɒmətən] n autómata.

automobile ['ɔːtəməbiːl] n automóvil.

autopsy ['ɔːtɒpsɪ] n autopsia.

autoteller ['ɔːtəʊtələ'] n cajero automático.

autumn ['ɔːtəm] n otoño.

auxiliary [ɔːg'zɪljərɪ] adj auxiliar.

available [ə'veɪləbəl] adj disponible.

avalanche ['ævəlɑːnʃ] n alud, avalancha.

avenge [ə'vendʒ] vt vengar.

avenue ['ævənjuː] n avenida.

average ['ævərɪdʒ] n promedio, media. ▶ adj medio,-a. • **on average** por término medio.

aviation [eɪvɪ'eɪʃən] n aviación.

avocado [ævə'kɑːdəʊ] n aguacate.

avoid [ə'vɔɪd] vt evitar.

awake [ə'weɪk] adj despierto,-a. ▶ vt-vi despertar(se).

awaken [ə'weɪkən] vt-vi → awake.

award [ə'wɔːd] n **1** premio. **2** beca. ▶ vt otorgar, conceder.

aware [ə'weə'] adj consciente. • **to be aware of** ser consciente de.

away [ə'weɪ] adv lejos, fuera: **he lives 4 km away**, vive a 4 km de aquí.

awful ['ɔːful] adj horrible.

awkward ['ɔːkwəd] adj **1** torpe (gesto). **2** difícil, complicado,-a. **3** embarazo-so,-a, delicado,-a (situación).

awning ['ɔːnɪŋ] n toldo.

awoke [ə'wəʊk] pt → awake.

awoken [ə'wəʊkən] pp → awake.

ax [æks] n US hacha.

axe [æks] n GB hacha.

axis ['æksɪs] n eje.

axle ['æksəl] n eje.

B

baa [baː] *vi* balar.

B & B [ˈbiːənˈbiː] *abbr (bed and breakfast)* fonda, hotel.

babble [ˈbæbəl] *vt-vi* balbucear.

baby [ˈbeɪbɪ] *n* bebé, niño,-a.

baby-sitter [ˈbeɪbɪsɪtəʳ] *n* canguro.

bachelor [ˈbætʃələʳ] *n* soltero.

back [bæk] *adj* trasero,-a, posterior. ► *n* **1** espalda. **2** lomo *(de animal)*. **3** respaldo *(de silla)*. **4** fondo, parte de atrás. **5** defensa *(en deportes)*. ► *adv* **1** atrás, hacia atrás, hace. **2** de vuelta. ► *vt* **1** apoyar, respaldar. **2** financiar. **3** dar marcha atrás a *(coche)*. ► *vi* retroceder. •**back to front** al revés. ■**back pay** atrasos; **back street** callejuela.

backbone [ˈbækbəʊn] *n* columna vertebral.

background [ˈbækgraʊnd] *n* **1** fondo *(de imagen)*. **2** *fig* origen, formación.

backhand [ˈbækhænd] *n* revés.

backpack [ˈbækpæk] *n* mochila.

backstroke [ˈbækstrəʊk] *n* espalda *(en natación)*.

backup [ˈbækʌp] *n* apoyo. ■ **backup copy** copia de seguridad.

backward [ˈbækwəd] **1** *adj* hacia atrás. **2** atrasado,-a, retrasado. ► *adv* → backwards.

backwards [ˈbækwədz] *adv* **1** hacia atrás. **2** al revés. •**backwards and forwards** de acá para allá.

bacon [ˈbeɪkən] *n* bacon.

bad [bæd] *adj* **1** malo,-a, mal. **2** grave: *a bad accident*, un accidente grave. **3** fuerte *(dolor de cabeza)*. • **to go bad** echarse a perder pudrirse; **to go from bad to worse** ir de mal en peor.

bade [beɪd] *pt* → bid.

badge [bædʒ] *n* **1** insignia. **2** chapa.

badger [ˈbædʒəʳ] *n* tejón.

bad-tempered [ˈbædˈtempəd] *adj*. • **to be bad-tempered** tener mal carácter, estar de mal humor.

bag [bæg] *n* **1** bolsa, saco. **2** bolso.

baggage [ˈbægɪdʒ] *n* equipaje.

baggy [ˈbægɪ] *adj* holgado,-a.

bagpipes [ˈbægpaɪps] *npl* gaita.

bail [beɪl] *n* fianza.

bait [beɪt] *n* cebo.

bake [beɪk] *vt* cocer al horno. ■ **baked beans** alubias cocidas con salsa de tomate.

baker [ˈbeɪkəʳ] *n* panadero,-a.

baker's [ˈbeɪkəz] *n* panadería.

bakery [ˈbeɪkərɪ] *n* panadería.

balance [ˈbæləns] *n* **1** equilibrio. **2** balanza. **3** saldo, balance. ► *vi* mantenerse en equilibrio.

balcony [ˈbælkənɪ] *n* balcón.

bald [bɔːld] *adj* calvo,-a.

ball [bɔːl] *n* **1** pelota, balón, bola. **2** ovillo. **3** baile, fiesta.

ballet ['bæleɪ] *n* ballet. ∎ **ballet dancer** bailarín, bailarina.

balloon [bə'luːn] *n* globo.

ballot ['bælət] *n* **1** votación. **2** papeleta. ∎ **ballot box** urna.

ballpoint pen ['bɔːlpɔɪnt pen] *n* bolígrafo.

ballroom ['bɔːlruːm] *n* sala de baile.

balm [bɑːm] *n* bálsamo.

ban [bæn] *n* prohibición. ► *vt* prohibir.

banana [bə'nɑːnə] *n* plátano.

band [bænd] *n* **1** banda. **2** cinta, tira. **3** raya, franja.

bandage ['bændɪdʒ] *n* venda, vendaje. ► *vt* vendar.

bandit ['bændɪt] *n* bandido,-a.

bandstand ['bændstænd] *n* quiosco de música.

bang [bæŋ] *n* **1** golpe. **2** porrazo, estampido, estallido, portazo. ► *vt-vi* golpear.

banger ['bæŋəʳ] *n* **1** petardo. **2** GB *fam* salchicha.

bangle ['bæŋgəl] *n* pulsera.

banish ['bænɪʃ] *vt* desterrar.

banister ['bænɪstəʳ] *n* barandilla.

bank¹ [bæŋk] *n* banco. ∎ **bank account** cuenta bancaria; **bank holiday** GB día festivo.

bank² [bæŋk] *n* **1** banco *(para sentarse)*. **2** ribera, orilla *(de río)*.

banker ['bæŋkəʳ] *n* banquero,-a.

banknote ['bæŋknəʊt] *n* billete de banco.

bankrupt ['bæŋkrʌpt] *adj* en quiebra, en bancarrota.

banner ['bænəʳ] *n* **1** estandarte. **2** pancarta.

banquet ['bæŋkwɪt] *n* banquete.

baptize [bæp'taɪz] *vt* bautizar.

bar [bɑːʳ] *n* **1** barra. **2** pastilla *(de jabón)*. **3** tableta *(de chocolate)*. **4** bar.

barb [bɑːb] *n* **1** púa. **2** lengüeta.

barbecue ['bɑːbəkjuː] *n* barbacoa.

barber's ['bɑːbəʳs] *n* barbería.

barbiturate [bɑː'bɪtʃərət] *n* barbitúrico.

bare [beəʳ] *adj* **1** desnudo,-a, descubierto,-a. **2** mero,-a: *a bare 10%*, sólo el 10%.

barely ['beəlɪ] *adv* apenas.

bargain ['bɑːgən] *n* **1** trato. **2** ganga. ► *vi* **1** negociar. **2** regatear.

bark¹ [bɑːk] *n* ladrido. ► *vi* ladrar.

bark² [bɑːk] *n* corteza *(de árbol)*.

barley ['bɑːlɪ] *n* cebada.

barmaid ['bɑːmeɪd] *n* camarera.

barman ['bɑːmən] *n* camarero, barman.

barn [bɑːn] *n* granero.

barnacle ['bɑːnəkəl] *n* percebe.

baroque [bə'rɒk] *adj* barroco,-a.

barracks ['bærəks] n cuartel.

barrage ['bærɑ:ʒ] n presa.

barrel ['bærəl] n 1 barril, tonel, cuba. 2 cañón (de fusil).

barren ['bærən] adj estéril.

barricade [bærɪ'keɪd] n barricada

barrier ['bærɪəʳ] n barrera.

barrister ['bærɪstəʳ] n abogado,-a (en tribunales superiores).

barter ['bɑ:təʳ] n trueque.

base [beɪs] n base. ► vt basar.

baseball ['beɪsbɔ:l] n béisbol.

basement ['beɪsmənt] n sótano.

basic ['beɪsɪk] adj básico,-a.

basin ['beɪsən] n 1 cuenco. 2 lavabo. 3 cuenca.

basis ['beɪsɪs] n base: **on a weekly basis**, semanalmente.

basket ['bɑ:skɪt] n cesta, cesto.

basketball ['bɑ:skɪtbɔ:l] n baloncesto.

bass[1] [bæs] n lubina.

bass[2] [beɪs] n bajo (cantante, instrumento).

bassoon [bə'su:n] n fagot.

bat[1] [bæt] n murciélago.

bat[2] [bæt] n bate.

batch [bætʃ] n lote.

bath [bɑ:θ] n 1 baño. 2 bañera. ► vt bañar. ► vi bañarse. ► npl **baths** piscina (pública).

bathe [beɪð] vi bañarse. ► vt lavar (herida).

bathing ['beɪðɪŋ] n baño. ■ **bathing costume** traje de baño, bañador; **bathing suit** traje de baño.

bathrobe ['bɑ:θrəub] n albornoz.

bathroom ['bɑ:θru:m] n cuarto de baño.

bathtub ['bɑ:θtʌb] n bañera.

baton ['bætən] n 1 porra (policía). 2 batuta (música). 3 testigo (carrera de relevos).

batter[1] ['bætəʳ] n rebozado.

batter[2] ['bætəʳ] vt apalear.

battery ['bætərɪ] n batería.

battle ['bætəl] n batalla.

battlements ['bætəlmənts] npl almenas.

battleship ['bætəlʃɪp] n acorazado.

bauble ['bɔ:bəl] n baratija.

baulk [bɔ:k] vt → balk.

bay[1] [beɪ] n bahía, golfo.

bay[2] [beɪ] n laurel.

bay[3] [beɪ] n hueco. ■ **loading bay** cargadero; **parking bay** plaza de parking.

be [bi:] vi 1 ser: **she's clever**, es inteligente. 2 estar: **how are you?**, ¿cómo estás? 3 tener: **I'm cold**, tengo frío. 4 hacer: **it's sunny**, hace sol. ► aux 1 be + pres participle estar: **it is raining**, está lloviendo. 2 be + past participle ser: **he was sacked**, fue despedido, lo despidieron. 3 be + infinitive: **the King is to visit Egypt**, el Rey visitará Egipto. ● **there is/are** hay.

beach [bi:tʃ] n playa. ► vt varar, embarrancar.

bead [biːd] *n* **1** cuenta *(de collar)*. **2** gota *(de sudor)*.

beak [biːk] *n* pico.

beam [biːm] *n* **1** viga. **2** rayo *(de luz)*. ► *vi* sonreír.

bean [biːn] *n* **1** alubia, judía, haba. **2** grano *(de café)*.

bear[1] [beəʳ] *n* oso.

bear[2] [beəʳ] *vt* soportar.

beard [bɪəd] *n* barba.

bearer [ˈbeərəʳ] *n* **1** portador, -ra. **2** titular.

bearing [ˈbeərɪŋ] *n* cojinete.

beast [biːst] *n* bestia, animal.

beat [biːt] *vt* **1** golpear. **2** batir *(huevos, alas, récord)*. **3** vencer, derrotar. ► *vi* latir *(corazón)*. ► *n* **1** latido. **2** ritmo. ► *adj fam* agotado,-a.

beautician [bjuːˈtɪʃən] *n* esteticista.

beautiful [ˈbjuːtɪfʊl] *adj* **1** bonito,-a. **2** maravilloso,-a.

beauty [ˈbjuːtɪ] *n* belleza. ■ **beauty parlour** salón de belleza; **beauty spot 1** lunar. **2** lugar pintoresco.

beaver [ˈbiːvəʳ] *n* castor.

became [bɪˈkeɪm] *pt* → become.

because [bɪˈkɒz] *conj* porque. ► *prep* **because of** a causa de.

become [bɪˈkʌm] *vi* **1** convertirse en. **2** volverse. • **to become of** ser de.

bed [bed] *n* **1** cama. **2** macizo *(de flores)*. **3** lecho, cauce *(de río)*, fondo *(del mar)*.

bed and breakfast [bedən-ˈbrekfəst] *n* fonda, hotel.

bedroom [ˈbedruːm] *n* dormitorio.

bedside [ˈbedsaɪd] *n* cabecera. ■ **bedside table** mesita de noche.

bedspread [ˈbedspred] *n* colcha.

bee [biː] *n* abeja.

beech [biːtʃ] *n* haya.

beef [biːf] *n* carne de vaca.

beefburger [ˈbiːfbɜːgəʳ] *n* hamburguesa.

beefsteak [ˈbiːfsteɪk] *n* bistec.

beehive [ˈbiːhaɪv] *n* colmena.

been [biːn, bɪn] *pp* → be.

beer [bɪəʳ] *n* cerveza.

beetle [ˈbiːtəl] *n* escarabajo.

beetroot [ˈbiːtruːt] *n* remolacha.

before [bɪˈfɔːʳ] *prep* **1** antes de. **2** delante de, ante. ► *conj* antes de + *inf*, antes de que + *subj*: *before you go*, antes de irte, antes de que te vayas. ► *adv* **1** antes. **2** anterior.

beforehand [bɪˈfɔːhænd] *adv* de antemano.

beg [beg] *vi* mendigar. ► *vt* pedir, suplicar, rogar.

began [bɪˈgæn] *pt* → begin.

beggar [ˈbegəʳ] *n* mendigo,-a.

begin [bɪˈgɪn] *vt-vi* empezar, comenzar. • **to begin with** para empezar.

beginner [bɪˈgɪnəʳ] *n* principiante.

beginning [bɪ'gɪnɪŋ] n principio.

begun [bɪ'gʌn] pp → begin.

behave [bɪ'heɪv] vi comportarse, portarse. • **to behave oneself** portarse bien.

behaviour [bɪ'heɪvjə'] (US **behavior**) n conducta, comportamiento.

behead [bɪ'hed] vt decapitar.

behind [bɪ'haɪnd] prep detrás de. ► adv 1 detrás. 2 atrasado,-a: he's behind with his work, va atrasado con el trabajo.

beige [beɪʒ] adj-n beige.

belch [beltʃ] n eructo.

belief [bɪ'liːf] n creencia.

believe [bɪ'liːv] vt-vi creer.

bell [bel] n 1 campana. 2 timbre: to ring the bell, tocar el timbre.

bellboy ['belbɔɪ] n botones.

bellow ['beləʊ] n bramido.

belly ['belɪ] n vientre, barriga. ■ **belly button** fam ombligo.

belong [bɪ'lɒŋ] vi 1 pertenecer. 2 ser socio,-a.

belongings [bɪ'lɒŋɪŋz] npl pertenencias.

below [bɪ'ləʊ] prep debajo de, por debajo de. ► adv abajo. • **below zero** bajo cero.

belt [belt] n 1 cinturón. 2 correa.

bench [bentʃ] n 1 banco (asiento). 2 banquillo.

bend [bend] n curva. ► vt doblar. ► vi 1 doblarse. 2 torcer.

to bend over vi inclinarse.

beneath [bɪ'niːθ] prep bajo, debajo de, por debajo de. ► adv abajo, debajo.

benefit ['benɪfɪt] n 1 beneficio. 2 subsidio. ► vt-vi beneficiar(se).

benign [bɪ'naɪn] adj benigno,-a.

bent [bent] pt-pp → bend.

bequest [bɪ'kwest] n legado.

beret ['bereɪ] n boina.

berry ['berɪ] n baya.

berth [bɜːθ] n 1 amarradero. 2 camarote, litera.

beside [bɪ'saɪd] prep al lado de, junto a.

besides [bɪ'saɪdz] prep 1 además de. 2 excepto. ► adv además.

besiege [bɪ'siːdʒ] vt sitiar.

best [best] adj mejor. ► adv mejor. ► n lo mejor. • **all the best!** ¡que te vaya bien!; **at best** en el mejor de los casos; **to do one's best** esmerarse. ■ **best man** padrino de boda.

bet [bet] n apuesta. ► vt-vi apostar.

betray [bɪ'treɪ] vt traicionar.

better ['betə'] adj mejor. ► adv mejor. ► vt mejorar. • **had better** más vale que + subj: we'd better be going, más vale que nos vayamos, deberíamos irnos; **to get better** mejorar, ponerse mejor. ■ **better half** media naranja.

betting ['betɪŋ] n apuestas.

between [bɪ'twiːn] *prep* entre.
▶ *adv* en medio, entre medio.

beverage ['bevərɪdʒ] *n* bebida.

beware [bɪ'weə'] *vi* tener cuidado.

bewilder [bɪ'wɪldə'] *vt* desconcertar, confundir.

bewitch [bɪ'wɪtʃ] *vt* hechizar.

beyond [bɪ'jɒnd] *prep* más allá de, al otro lado de. ▶ *adv* más allá.

bias ['baɪəs] *n* parcialidad, prejuicio.

bib [bɪb] *n* babero.

biceps ['baɪseps] *n* bíceps.

bicycle ['baɪsɪkəl] *n* bicicleta.

bid [bɪd] *n* **1** puja. **2** intento. **3** oferta. ▶ *vt-vi* pujar.

bidet ['biːdeɪ] *n* bidé.

big [bɪg] *adj* grande, gran.
■ **big brother** hermano mayor; **big game** caza mayor; **big sister** hermana mayor.

bike [baɪk] *n* **1** *fam* bici. **2** *fam* moto.

bikini [bɪ'kiːnɪ] *n* biquini.

bile [baɪl] *n* bilis, hiel.

bill [bɪl] *n* **1** factura, cuenta. **2** proyecto de ley. **3** US billete de banco. **4** cartel, póster.
● **to top the bill** encabezar el reparto. ■ **bill of exchange** letra de cambio.

billboard ['bɪlbɔːd] *n* US valla publicitaria.

billiards ['bɪlɪədz] *n* billar.

billion ['bɪlɪən] *n* **1** billón. **2** mil millones.

bin [bɪn] *n* cubo de la basura, papelera.

bind [baɪnd] *vt* **1** atar. **2** ligar *(salsa)*. **3** obligar. **4** encuadernar.

binder ['baɪndə'] *n* carpeta.

binoculars [bɪ'nɒkjʊləz] *npl* gemelos.

biography [baɪ'ɒgrəfɪ] *n* biografía.

biology [baɪ'ɒlədʒɪ] *n* biología.

birch [bɜːtʃ] *n* abedul.

bird [bɜːd] *n* ave, pájaro. ■ **bird of prey** ave de rapiña.

birdseed ['bɜːdsiːd] *n* alpiste.

bird's-eye view [bɜːdzˌɪ'vjuː] *n* vista aérea.

Biro® ['baɪrəʊ] *n* GB boli.

birth [bɜːθ] *n* nacimiento. ● **to give birth to** dar a luz a. ■ **birth certificate** partida de nacimiento.

birthday ['bɜːθdeɪ] *n* cumpleaños.

birthmark ['bɜːθmɑːk] *n* antojo.

birthplace ['bɜːθpleɪs] *n* lugar de nacimiento.

biscuit ['bɪskɪt] *n* galleta.

bishop ['bɪʃəp] *n* **1** obispo. **2** alfil *(en ajedrez)*.

bison ['baɪsən] *n* bisonte.

bit¹ [bɪt] *n* trozo, pedacito. ● **a bit** un poco, algo.

bit² [bɪt] *n* bit.

bit³ [bɪt] *n* broca.

bit⁴ [bɪt] *pt* → bite.

bitch [bɪtʃ] *n* **1** hembra, perra. **2** *pej* bruja, arpía.

bite [baɪt] *n* **1** mordisco. **2** picadura. **3** mordedura. **4** bocado. ► *vt-vi* **1** morder(se). **2** picar.

bitten [ˈbɪtən] *pp* → bite.

bitter [ˈbɪtəʳ] *adj* amargo,-a *(sabor)*. ► *n* cerveza amarga. ► *npl* **bitters** bíter.

black [blæk] *adj-n* negro,-a. ■ **black coffee** café solo; **black eye** ojo morado.

blackberry [ˈblækbərɪ] *n* mora, zarzamora.

blackboard [ˈblækbɔːd] *n* pizarra.

blackhead [ˈblækhed] *n* espinilla.

blackmail [ˈblækmeɪl] *n* chantaje.

blacksmith [ˈblæksmɪθ] *n* herrero.

bladder [ˈblædəʳ] *n* vejiga.

blade [bleɪd] *n* **1** hoja, filo, cuchilla. **2** pala *(de remo)*. **3** brizna *(de hierba)*.

blame [bleɪm] *n* culpa. ► *vt* culpar, echar la culpa a. ● **to put the blame on** echar la culpa a.

bland [blænd] *adj* soso,-a.

blank [blæŋk] *adj* en blanco. ■ **blank cartridge** cartucho de fogueo.

blanket [ˈblæŋkɪt] *n* manta.

blast [blɑːst] *n* **1** ráfaga *(de aire)*. **2** chorro *(de agua)*. **3** explosión, voladura. ● **at full blast** a todo volumen. ■ **blast furnace** alto horno.

blaze [bleɪz] *n* **1** incendio. **2** fogata, hoguera. ► *vi* **1** arder. **2** brillar con fuerza.

bleach [bliːtʃ] *n* lejía.

bleat [bliːt] *n* balido.

bled [bled] *pt-pp* → bleed.

bleed [bliːd] *vi* sangrar.

bleep [bliːp] *n* pitido.

bleeper [ˈbliːpəʳ] *n* busca.

blend [blend] *n* mezcla ► *vt-vi* mezclarse.

blender [ˈblendəʳ] *n* batidora.

bless [bles] *vt* bendecir.

blew [bluː] *pt* → blow.

blind [blaɪnd] *adj* ciego,-a. ► *n* persiana. ► *vt* cegar.

blink [blɪŋk] *vi* parpadear.

blister [ˈblɪstəʳ] *n* ampolla.

bloc [blɒk] *n* bloque.

block [blɒk] *n* bloque. ► *vt* **1** obstruir, cegar. **2** bloquear. ■ **block letters** mayúsculas.

blond [blɒnd] *adj-n* rubio,-a.

blood [blʌd] *n* sangre. ■ **blood group** grupo sanguíneo; **blood pressure** tensión arterial.

bloodhound [ˈblʌdhaʊnd] *n* sabueso.

bloom [bluːm] *n* flor. ► *vi* florecer.

blossom [ˈblɒsəm] *n* flor. ► *vi* florecer.

blot [blɒt] *n* borrón.

blotch [blɒtʃ] *n* **1** mancha. **2** borrón.

blouse [blaʊz] *n* blusa.

blow[1] [bləʊ] *n* golpe.

blow² [bləʊ] vi **1** soplar *(viento)*. **2** sonar *(silbato)*. **3** fundirse *(fusible)*. ► vt tocar *(cláxon, trompeta, etc)*. • **to blow one's nose** sonarse la nariz.

to blow up vt **1** hacer explotar. **2** hinchar, inflar. **3** ampliar *(foto)*.

blowout [ˈbləʊaʊt] n reventón.

blue [bluː] adj **1** azul. **2** triste, deprimido,-a. **3** verde *(película)*. ► n azul. • **out of the blue** de forma inesperada, como llovido del cielo. ■ **the blues 1** melancolía. **2** el blues *(música)*.

blueberry [ˈbluːbərɪ] n arándano.

bluff [blʌf] n farol.

blunder [ˈblʌndəʳ] n metedura de pata.

blunt [blʌnt] adj **1** desafilado,-a. **2** franco,-a.

blurred [blɜːd] adj borroso,-a.

blush [blʌʃ] n vi ruborizarse.

boar [bɔːʳ] n. ■ **wild boar** jabalí.

board [bɔːd] n **1** tabla, tablero. **2** tablón de anuncios. **3** junta, consejo. ► vt subirse a, embarcar en. • **on board** a bordo. ■ **full board** pensión completa; **half board** media pensión.

boarding [ˈbɔːdɪŋ] n. ■ **boarding card** tarjeta de embarque; **boarding house** casa de huéspedes.

boast [bəʊst] vi jactarse.

boat [bəʊt] n barco, barca.

bobbin [ˈbɒbɪn] n bobina.

bobby [ˈbɒbɪ] n GB *fam* poli.

body [ˈbɒdɪ] n **1** cuerpo. **2** organismo, entidad.

body-building [ˈbɒdɪbɪldɪŋ] n culturismo.

bodyguard [ˈbɒdɪgɑːd] n guardaespaldas.

bodywork [ˈbɒdɪwɜːk] n carrocería.

bog [bɒg] n pantano.

boil¹ [bɔɪl] n furúnculo.

boil² [bɔɪl] vt-vi hervir.

boiler [ˈbɔɪləʳ] n caldera.

boiling [ˈbɔɪlɪŋ] adj hirviente.

bold [bəʊld] adj valiente. ■ **bold type** negrita.

bolt [bəʊlt] n **1** cerrojo, pestillo. **2** perno, tornillo.

bomb [bɒm] n bomba. ► vt bombardear. ■ **bomb scare** amenaza de bomba.

bombshell [ˈbɒmʃel] n obús.

bond [bɒnd] n **1** lazo, vínculo. **2** bono, obligación.

bone [bəʊn] n **1** hueso. **2** espina *(de pescado)*.

bonfire [ˈbɒnfaɪəʳ] n hoguera.

bonnet [ˈbɒnɪt] n **1** gorro, gorra. **2** capó.

bonus [ˈbəʊnəs] n prima.

bony [ˈbəʊnɪ] adj (-**ier**, -**iest**). **1** huesudo,-a. **2** lleno,-a de espinas.

boo [buː] vt-vi abuchear.

booby trap [ˈbuːbɪtræp] n trampa explosiva.

book [bʊk] n libro. ► vt **1** reservar. **2** multar, amonestar.

bookcase ['bʊkkeɪs] n librería, estantería.

booking ['bʊkɪŋ] n reserva. ■ **booking office** taquilla.

booklet ['bʊklət] n folleto.

bookshelf ['bʊkʃelf] n estante. ► npl **bookshelves** librería, estantería.

bookshop ['bʊkʃɒp] n librería.

bookstore ['bʊkstɔːʳ] n librería.

boom¹ [buːm] n estruendo.

boom² [buːm] n fig boom, auge.

boost [buːst] n empuje. ► vt 1 aumentar (ventas). 2 estimular, impulsar (producción).

boot [buːt] n 1 bota. 2 GB maletero. ► vt-vi arrancar (ordenador). ● **to boot** además.

booth [buːð] n 1 cabina. 2 puesto (de mercado).

bootlegger ['buːtlegəʳ] n contrabandista.

border ['bɔːdəʳ] n 1 frontera. 2 borde, margen.

bore¹ [bɔːʳ] pt → bear.

bore² [bɔːʳ] n calibre. ► vt horadar, taladrar.

bore³ [bɔːʳ] n 1 pelmazo,-a. 2 lata.

bored [bɔːd] adj aburrido,-a.

boring ['bɔːrɪŋ] adj aburrido,-a.

born [bɔːn] pp → bear. ● **to be born** nacer.

borne [bɔːn] pp → bear.

borough ['bʌrə] n 1 distrito. 2 municipio.

borrow ['bɒrəʊ] vt tomar prestado,-a, pedir prestado,-a.

boss [bɒs] n jefe,-a.

botany ['bɒtənɪ] n botánica.

botch [bɒtʃ] n chapuza.

both [bəʊθ] adj-pron ambos,-as, los/las dos. ► conj a la vez.

bother ['bɒðəʳ] n molestia. ► vt 1 molestar. 2 preocupar. ► vi molestarse. preocuparse. ● **not to be bothered** no apetecer.

bottle ['bɒtəl] n 1 botella. 2 biberón. ► vt embotellar. ■ **bottle bank** contenedor de vidrio; **bottle opener** abrebotellas.

bottom ['bɒtəm] n 1 fondo (del mar, calle). 2 culo (de botella, trasero). 3 bajo (de vestido). ► adj de abajo.

bought [bɔːt] pt-pp → buy.

bounce [baʊns] n bote. ► vi 1 rebotar. 2 ser rechazado por el banco.

bound¹ [baʊnd] pt-pp → bind.

bound² [baʊnd] adj seguro: *it's bound to happen*, tiene que pasar. ● **bound for** con destino a, con rumbo a.

bound³ [baʊnd] vi saltar.

boundary ['baʊndərɪ] n límite, frontera.

bounds [baʊndz] npl límites.

bouquet [buːˈkeɪ] n 1 ramillete. 2 aroma.

boutique [buːˈtiːk] n boutique.

bow¹ [baʊ] n reverencia.

bow² [bəʊ] n arco. ■ **bow tie** pajarita.

bow³ [baʊ] n proa.

bowel ['baʊəl] *n* intestino.

bowl[1] [bəʊl] *n* **1** bol, tazón. **2** taza *(de váter)*.

bowl[2] [bəʊl] *n* bocha.

bowler ['bəʊlə'] *n* bombín.

bowling ['bəʊlɪŋ] *n* bolos. ■ **bowling alley** bolera.

box[1] [bɒks] *n* **1** caja, cajón, cajetilla, estuche. **2** palco *(en teatro)*. ■ **box office** taquilla.

box[2] [bɒks] *vi* boxear.

boxing ['bɒksɪŋ] *n* boxeo.

boy [bɔɪ] *n* niño, chico, muchacho, joven.

boyfriend ['bɔɪfrend] *n* novio.

brace [breɪs] *n* aparato *(de dientes)*. ► *npl* **braces** tirantes.

bracelet ['breɪslət] *n* pulsera.

bracket ['brækɪt] *n* **1** paréntesis: *in brackets*, entre paréntesis. **2** soporte.

brag [bræg] *vi* fanfarronear.

braid [breɪd] *n* US trenza.

brain [breɪn] *n* cerebro.

brake [breɪk] *n* freno. ► *vt-vi* frenar.

bramble ['bræmbəl] *n* zarza.

branch [brɑːntʃ] *n* **1** rama. **2** sucursal. ► *vi* bifurcarse.

brand [brænd] *n* marca.

brand-new [bræn'njuː] *adj* completamente nuevo.

brandy ['brændɪ] *n* brandy.

brass [brɑːs] *n* **1** latón. **2** instrumentos de metal.

brassiere ['bræzɪə'] *n* sujetador, sostén.

brave [breɪv] *adj* valiente

brawl [brɔːl] *n* reyerta, pelea.

breach [briːtʃ] *n* **1** brecha. **2** incumplimiento *(de contrato)*.

bread [bred] *n* pan.

breadth [bredθ] *n* anchura.

break [breɪk] *n* **1** ruptura. **2** interrupción, pausa, descanso. ► *vt* **1** romper. **2** batir *(récord)*. **3** no cumplir *(promesa)*. **4** comunicar *(noticias)*. ► *vi* **1** romperse. **2** estallar *(tormenta)*.

to break down *vt* **1** echar abajo, derribar. **2** desglosar. ► *vi* averiarse.

to break in *vt* domar. ► *vi* entrar a robar.

to break out *vi* **1** escaparse *(prisioneros)*. **2** estallar *(guerra)*.

to break up *vi* **1** disolverse *(multitud)*. **2** separarse. **3** empezar las vacaciones.

breakdown ['breɪkdaʊn] *n* **1** avería. **2** crisis nerviosa

breakfast ['brekfəst] *n* desayuno. • **to have breakfast** desayunar.

breakwater ['breɪkwɔːtə'] *n* rompeolas.

breast [brest] *n* **1** pecho. **2** pechuga *(de pollo)*.

breaststroke ['brestrəʊk] *n* braza.

breath [breθ] *n* aliento. • **out of breath** sin aliento; **to hold your breath** contener la respiración.

Breathalyser ['breθəlaɪzə'] *n* alcoholímetro.

breathe [briːð] *vt-vi* respirar.
breathing ['briːðɪŋ] *n* respiración.
bred [bred] *pt-pp* → breed.
breed [briːd] *n* raza. ► *vt* criar
breeze [briːz] *n* brisa.
brew [bruː] *n* brebaje. ► *vt* **1** hacer *(cerveza)*. **2** preparar *(té)*. ► *vi* reposar *(té)*.
brewery ['bruːərɪ] *n* cervecería.
bribe [braɪb] *n* soborno.
brick [brɪk] *n* ladrillo.
bricklayer ['brɪkleɪəʳ] *n* albañil.
bride [braɪd] *n* novia *(el día de la boda)*.
bridegroom ['braɪdgruːm] *n* novio *(el día de la boda)*.
bridesmaid ['braɪdzmeɪd] *n* dama de honor.
bridge [brɪdʒ] *n* puente.
bridle ['braɪdəl] *n* brida.
brief [briːf] *adj* breve. ► *n* informe.
briefcase ['briːfkeɪs] *n* maletín, cartera.
briefs [briːfs] *npl* **1** calzoncillos. **2** bragas.
brigade [brɪ'geɪd] *n* brigada.
bright [braɪt] *adj* **1** brillante. **2** despejado *(día)*. **3** vivo,-a *(color)*.
brilliant ['brɪljənt] *adj* **1** brillante. **2** *fam* estupendo,-a.
brim [brɪm] *n* borde.
bring [brɪŋ] *vt* **1** traer. **2** llevar.
to bring about *vt* causar.
to bring back *vt* devolver.
to bring down *vt* derribar.

to bring in *vt* **1** introducir. **2** producir.
to bring on *vt* provocar.
to bring out *vt* sacar.
to bring round *vt* hacer volver en sí.
to bring up *vt* **1** criar, educar. **2** plantear. **3** devolver, vomitar.
bristle ['brɪsəl] *n* cerda.
brittle ['brɪtəl] *adj* quebradizo,-a, frágil.
broad [brɔːd] *adj* ancho,-a, amplio,-a, extenso,-a. ■ **broad bean** haba.
broadcast ['brɔːdkɑːst] emitir, transmitir.
broadcasting ['brɔːdkɑːstɪŋ] *n* **1** radiodifusión. **2** transmisión.
broccoli ['brɒkəlɪ] *n* brécol.
brochure ['brəʊʃəʳ] *n* folleto.
broil [brɔɪl] *vt* US asar a la parrilla.
broke [brəʊk] *pt* → break. ► *adj fam* sin blanca.
broken ['brəʊkən] *pp* → break. ► *adj* **1** roto,-a. **2** chapurreado,-a *(lenguaje)*.
bronchitis [brɒŋ'kaɪtəs] *n* bronquitis.
bronze [brɒnz] *n* bronce.
brooch [brəʊtʃ] *n* broche.
brook [brʊk] *n* arroyo.
broom [bruːm] *n* escoba.
broth [brɒθ] *n* caldo.
brother ['brʌðəʳ] *n* hermano.
brother-in-law ['brʌðərɪnlɔː] *n* cuñado.
brought [brɔːt] *pt-pp* → bring.

brow [braʊ] *n* **1** ceja. **2** frente. **3** cresta, cima.

brown [braʊn] *adj* **1** marrón. **2** castaño,-a *(pelo)*. **3** moreno,-a *(piel)*. **4** integral *(arroz, pan)*.

browse [braʊz] *vi* mirar, hojear. • **to browse the Web** navegar por la Web.

browser ['braʊzə'] *n* navegador *(programa)*.

bruise [bruːz] *n* morado.

brunette [bruːˈnet] *n* morena.

brush [brʌʃ] *n* **1** cepillo. **2** pincel. **3** brocha. **4** maleza. ► *vt* cepillar.

Brussels sprouts ['brʌsəlz] *n pl* coles de Bruselas.

brutal ['bruːtəl] *adj* brutal.

bubble ['bʌbəl] *n* burbuja. ■ **bubble bath** gel de baño; **bubble gum** chicle.

buck [bʌk] *n* US *fam* dólar.

bucket ['bʌkɪt] *n* cubo.

buckle ['bʌkəl] *n* hebilla. ► *vt* abrochar *(con hebilla)*. ► *vi* combarse, doblarse.

bud [bʌd] *n* yema, capullo.

buddy ['bʌdɪ] *n* US *fam* colega.

budgerigar ['bʌdʒərɪgɑː'] *n* periquito.

budget ['bʌdʒɪt] *n* presupuesto. ► *vt-vi* presupuestar.

buffalo ['bʌfələʊ] *n* búfalo.

buffer ['bʌfə'] *n* **1** tope *(para trenes)*. **2** memoria intermedia.

buffet ['bʊfeɪ] *n* **1** bar, cantina. **2** bufet libre. ■ **buffet car** vagón restaurante.

bug [bʌg] *n* **1** bicho. **2** error *(en programa)*.

build [bɪld] *vt* construir. **to build up** *vt-vi* acumular(se).

building ['bɪldɪŋ] *n* edificio. ■ **building site** obra; **building society** sociedad de ahorro para la vivienda.

built [bɪlt] *pt-pp* → build.

built-in [bɪlt'ɪn] *adj* **1** empotrado,-a. **2** incorporado,-a.

bulb [bʌlb] *n* **1** bulbo. **2** bombilla.

bulk [bʌlk] *n* mayor parte. • **in bulk** a granel, al por mayor.

bull [bʊl] *n* toro.

bullet ['bʊlɪt] *n* bala.

bulletin ['bʊlɪtɪn] *n* boletín.

bullfight ['bʊlfaɪt] *n* corrida de toros.

bullfighter ['bʊlfaɪtə'] *n* torero,-a.

bullring ['bʊlrɪŋ] *n* plaza de toros.

bumblebee ['bʌmbəlbiː] *n* abejorro.

bump [bʌmp] *n* **1** chichón. **2** bache *(en carretera)*. **3** choque. ► *vt-vi* chocar.

to bump into *vt* tropezar con.

bumper ['bʌmpə'] *n* parachoques.

bun [bʌn] *n* **1** panecillo, bollo. **2** moño.

bunch [bʌntʃ] *n* **1** manojo. **2** ramo. **3** racimo. **4** grupo.

bundle ['bʌndəl] *n* **1** fardo. **2** haz. **3** fajo.

bung [bʌŋ] n tapón.
bunion ['bʌnjən] n juanete.
bunk [bʌŋk] n litera *(en un barco o tren)*. ■ **bunk bed** litera *(en una habitación)*.
buoy [bɔɪ] n boya.
burden ['bɜːdən] n carga. ▶ vt cargar.
bureaucracy [bjʊəˈrɒkrəsɪ] n burocracia.
burger ['bɜːgə'] n hamburguesa.
burglar ['bɜːglə'] n ladrón,-ona.
burglary ['bɜːglərɪ] n robo.
burial ['berɪəl] n entierro.
burn [bɜːn] n quemadura. ▶ vt quemar. ▶ vi arder, quemarse.
burner ['bɜːnə'] n quemador.
burnt [bɜːnt] pt-pp → burn.
burrow ['bʌrəʊ] n madriguera.
burst [bɜːst] n 1 explosión. 2 reventón. ▶ vt-vi reventar(se).
bury ['berɪ] vt enterrar.
bus [bʌs] n autobús. ■ **bus stop** parada de autobús.
bush [bʊʃ] n arbusto.
business ['bɪznəs] n 1 los negocios. 2 negocio, empresa. 3 asunto.
businessman ['bɪznəsmən] n hombre de negocios, empresario.
businesswoman ['bɪznəswʊmən] n mujer de negocios, empresaria.
bust[1] [bʌst] n busto.
bust[2] [bʌst] vt-vi fam romper, romperse.

busy ['bɪzɪ] adj 1 ocupado,-a. 2 concurrido,-a *(calle)*. 3 que comunica *(teléfono)*.
but [bʌt] conj 1 pero. 2 sino: *not two, but three*, no dos, sino tres. ▶ prep excepto, salvo, menos. • **but for** si no hubiese sido por, si no fuese por.
butane ['bjuːteɪn] n butano.
butcher ['bʊtʃə'] n carnicero,-a.
butler ['bʌtlə'] n mayordomo.
butt [bʌt] n 1 colilla. 2 culata.
butter ['bʌtə'] n mantequilla.
butterfly ['bʌtəflaɪ] n mariposa.
buttock ['bʌtək] n nalga.
button ['bʌtən] n botón. ▶ vt-vi abrocharse.
buttonhole ['bʌtənhəʊl] n ojal.
buy [baɪ] vt comprar.
buyer ['baɪə'] n comprador,-ra.
buzz [bʌz] n
buzzer ['bʌzə'] n timbre.
by [baɪ] prep 1 por. 2 en: *by car/train*, en coche/tren. 3 para: *I need it by ten*, lo necesito para las diez. 4 de: *by day/night*, de día/noche. 5 junto a, al lado de: *sit by me*, siéntate a mi lado. ▶ adv de largo. • **by and by** con el tiempo.
bye [baɪ] interj fam ¡adiós!, ¡hasta luego!
bypass ['baɪpɑːs] n 1 variante *(carretera)*. 2 by-pass.
by-product ['baɪprɒdʌkt] n subproducto, derivado.
byte [baɪt] n byte.

C

cab [kæb] n **1** taxi. **2** cabina.

cabbage ['kæbɪdʒ] n col.

cabin ['kæbɪn] n **1** cabaña. **2** camarote. **3** cabina.

cabinet ['kæbɪnət] n **1** gabinete. **2** armario, vitrina.

cable ['keɪbəl] n cable. ■ **cable car** teleférico; **cable television** televisión por cable.

cache [kæʃ] n **1** alijo. **2** caché.

cactus ['kæktəs] n cactus.

café ['kæfeɪ] n cafetería.

cafeteria [kæfə'tɪərɪə] n autoservicio.

cage [keɪdʒ] n jaula.

cagoule [kə'guːl] n chubasquero.

cake [keɪk] n pastel, tarta.

calculate ['kælkjəleɪt] vt calcular.

calculating ['kælkjəleɪtɪŋ] adj calculador,-ra. ■ **calculating machine** calculadora.

calendar ['kælɪndəʳ] n calendario.

calf[1] [kɑːf] n ternero,-a.

calf[2] [kɑːf] n pantorrilla.

call [kɔːl] n **1** grito. **2** llamada. **3** demanda: *there's not much call for it*, no tiene mucha demanda. **4** visita. ► vt-vi **1** llamar. vi **2** llamar. **3** pasar: *call at the butcher's*, pásate por la carnicería. **4** efectuar parada: *this train calls at Selby and York*, este tren efectúa parada en Selby y York. ● **on call** de guardia. ■ **call box** GB cabina telefónica.

to call for vt pasar a buscar.

to call off vt suspender.

to call on vt visitar.

to call out vt-vi gritar.

caller ['kɔːləʳ] n **1** visita, visitante. **2** persona que llama.

calm [kɑːm] adj **1** en calma *(mar)*. **2** tranquilo,-a *(persona)*. ► vt calmar.

calorie ['kælərɪ] n caloría.

camcorder ['kæmkɔːdəʳ] n videocámara.

came [keɪm] pt → come.

camel ['kæməl] n camello.

camera ['kæmərə] n cámara.

camomile ['kæməmaɪl] n manzanilla.

camouflage ['kæməflɑːʒ] n camuflaje. ► vt camuflar.

camp [kæmp] n campamento. ► vi acampar. ■ **camp bed** cama plegable; **camp site** camping, campamento.

campaign [kæm'peɪn] n campaña.

camper ['kæmpəʳ] n **1** campista. **2** US caravana.

can[1] [kæn] aux **1** poder. **2** saber.

can[2] [kæn] n lata.

canal [kə'næl] n canal.

canary [kə'neərɪ] n canario.

cancel ['kænsəl] vt **1** cancelar *(pedido)*. **2** anular *(contrato)*.

cancer ['kænsə'] *n* cáncer.
candidate ['kændɪdət] *n* candidato,-a.
candle ['kændəl] *n* vela.
candy ['kændɪ] *n* US caramelo.
cane [keɪn] *n* **1** caña. **2** bastón, vara.
canine ['keɪnaɪn] *adj* canino,-a.
canister ['kænɪstə'] *n* bote, lata.
cannon ['kænən] *n* cañón.
cannot ['kænɒt] *aux* → can.
canoe [kə'nuː] *n* canoa.
canopy ['kænəpɪ] *n* dosel.
can't [kɑːnt] *aux* contracción de **can** + **not**.
canteen [kæn'tiːn] *n* cantina.
canvas ['kænvəs] *n* **1** lona. **2** lienzo.
canyon ['kænjən] *n* cañón.
cap [kæp] *n* **1** gorro, gorra. **2** capuchón, chapa, tapa.
capable ['keɪpəbəl] *adj* capaz.
capacity [kə'pæsɪtɪ] *n* capacidad.
cape[1] [keɪp] *n* capa corta.
cape[2] [keɪp] *n* cabo.
caper ['keɪpə'] *n* alcaparra.
capital ['kæpɪtəl] *n* **1** capital. **2** mayúscula.
capitalism ['kæpɪtəlɪzəm] *n* capitalismo.
capricious [kə'prɪʃəs] *adj* caprichoso,-a.
capsize [kæp'saɪz] *vi* volcar.
capsule ['kæpsjuːl] *n* cápsula.
captain ['kæptɪn] *n* capitán.
caption ['kæpʃən] *n* leyenda, pie de foto.

captive ['kæptɪv] *adj-n* cautivo,-a.
captivity [kæp'tɪvɪtɪ] *n* cautiverio, cautividad.
capture ['kæptʃə'] *n* captura. ▶ *vt* capturar.
car [kɑː'] *n* **1** coche, automóvil. **2** vagón, coche *(de ferrocarril)*. ▪ **car park** aparcamiento; **car wash** túnel de lavado.
caramel ['kærəmel] *n* caramelo.
carat ['kærət] *n* quilate.
caravan ['kærəvæn] *n* caravana.
carbon ['kɑːbən] *n* carbono.
carburettor [kɑːbə'retə'] *n* carburador.
carcass ['kɑːkəs] *n* res muerta.
card [kɑːd] *n* **1** carta, naipe. **2** tarjeta, felicitación. **3** ficha. **4** carnet, carné *(de socio)*. **5** cartulina.
cardboard ['kɑːdbɔːd] *n* cartón.
cardiac ['kɑːdɪæk] *adj* cardíaco,-a. ▪ **cardiac arrest** paro cardíaco.
cardigan ['kɑːdɪgən] *n* rebeca.
cardphone ['kɑːdfəʊn] *n* teléfono de tarjeta.
care [keə'] *n* **1** cuidado. **2** asistencia: *health care*, asistencia sanitaria. ▶ *vi* preocuparse: *I don't care*, me tiene sin cuidado. ● **take care!** ¡cuidado!; **to take care of 1** cuidar, cuidar de. **2** ocuparse de.
to care for *vt* cuidar.

career [kə'rɪəʳ] *n* carrera.
careful ['keəful] *adj* cuidadoso,-a. • **to be careful** tener cuidado.
caress [kə'res] *n* caricia. ► *vt* acariciar.
caretaker ['keəteɪkəʳ] *n* conserje.
cargo ['kɑːgəʊ] *n* carga.
caries ['keərɪz] *n* caries.
carnation [kɑː'neɪʃən] *n* clavel.
carol ['kærəl] *n* villancico.
carp [kɑːp] *n* carpa *(pez)*.
carpenter ['kɑːpɪntəʳ] *n* carpintero.
carpet ['kɑːpɪt] *n* moqueta, alfombra.
carriage ['kærɪdʒ] *n* **1** carruaje. **2** vagón, coche *(de ferrocarril)*. ■ **carriage paid** portes pagados.
carriageway ['kærɪdʒweɪ] *n* GB carril.
carrier ['kærɪəʳ] *n* **1** transportista. **2** portador,-ra *(de enfermedad)*. ■ **carrier bag** bolsa *(de plástico o papel)*.
carrot ['kærət] *n* zanahoria.
carry ['kærɪ] *vt* llevar.
to carry on *vt* seguir.
to carry out *vt* llevar a cabo.
carsick ['kɑːsɪk] *adj* mareado,-a *(en un coche)*.
cart [kɑːt] *n* **1** carro. **2** carretilla.
cartilage ['kɑːtɪlɪdʒ] *n* cartílago.
carton ['kɑːtən] *n* **1** envase de cartón. **2** cartón.

cartoon [kɑː'tuːn] *n* **1** caricatura. **2** dibujos animados. **3** historieta, tira cómica.
cartridge ['kɑːtrɪdʒ] *n* **1** cartucho. **2** recambio *(para estilográfica)*.
carve [kɑːv] *vt* **1** tallar. **2** trinchar *(carne)*.
case[1] [keɪs] *n* caso. • **in any case** en cualquier caso; **in case** por si; **in case of** en caso de; **just in case** por si acaso.
case[2] [keɪs] *n* **1** maleta. **2** caja. **3** estuche, funda.
cash [kæʃ] *n* dinero en efectivo. ► *vt* cobrar *(talón)*. • **cash down** al contado; **cash on delivery** contra reembolso. ■ **cash desk** caja; **cash dispenser** cajero automático; **cash register** caja registradora.
cash-and-carry [kæʃən'kærɪ] *n* autoservicio al por mayor.
cashier [kæ'ʃɪəʳ] *n* cajero,-a.
cashmere [kæʃ'mɪəʳ] *n* cachemira.
casino [kə'siːnəʊ] *n* casino.
cask [kɑːsk] *n* tonel, barril.
casserole ['kæsərəʊl] *n* cazuela.
cassette [kə'set] *n* casete. ■ **cassette player/ recorder** casete.
cast [kɑːst] *n* **1** reparto *(de película, etc)*. **2** molde. ► *vt* **1** lanzar. **2** dar el papel de. **3** moldear. • **to be cast away** naufragar. ■ **cast iron** hierro colado.

castle ['kɑːsəl] n 1 castillo. 2 torre (ajedrez).

casual ['kæʒʊəl] adj 1 fortuito,-a, casual (encuentro). 2 informal (ropa).

casualty ['kæʒʊəltɪ] n 1 víctima. 2 baja (soldado). ■ **casualty department** urgencias.

cat [kæt] n gato,-a.

catalogue ['kætəlɒg] (US **catalog**) n GB catálogo.

cataract ['kætərækt] n catarata.

catarrh [kəˈtɑːˈ] n catarro.

catastrophe [kəˈtæstrəfɪ] n catástrofe.

catch [kætʃ] vt coger. ► n 1 parada (de pelota). 2 pesca. 3 cierre, pestillo.

category ['kætəgərɪ] n categoría.

cater ['keɪtəˈ] vt proveer comida.

caterpillar ['kætəpɪləˈ] n oruga.

cathedral [kəˈθiːdrəl] n catedral.

Catholic ['kæθəlɪk] adj-n católico,-a.

cattle ['kætəl] n ganado vacuno.

caught [kɔːt] pt-pp → catch.

cauliflower ['kɒlɪflaʊəˈ] n coliflor.

cause [kɔːz] n causa. ► vt causar.

caution ['kɔːʃən] n 1 precaución. 2 aviso, advertencia.

cautious ['kɔːʃəs] adj prudente.

cavalry ['kævəlrɪ] n caballería.

cave [keɪv] n cueva. ■ **cave painting** pintura rupestre.

cavern ['kævən] n caverna.

caviar ['kævɪɑːˈ] n caviar.

cavity ['kævɪtɪ] n cavidad.

CD ['siːˈdiː] abbr (**compact disc**) disco compacto, CD. ■ **CD player** reproductor de discos compactos.

cease [siːs] vt-vi cesar.

cease-fire ['siːsˈfaɪəˈ] n alto el fuego.

cedar ['siːdəˈ] n cedro.

ceiling ['siːlɪŋ] n techo.

celebrate ['selɪbreɪt] vt-vi celebrar.

celebration [selɪ'breɪʃən] n celebración.

celery ['selərɪ] n apio.

cell [sel] n 1 celda. 2 célula.

cellar ['seləˈ] n 1 sótano. 2 bodega (para vino).

cello ['tʃeləʊ] n violoncelo.

cellophane® ['seləfeɪn] n celofán®.

cellphone ['selfəʊn] n teléfono móvil.

cement [sɪ'ment] n cemento. ■ **cement mixer** hormigonera.

cemetery ['semətrɪ] n cementerio.

censorship ['sensəʃɪp] n censura.

census ['sensəs] n censo.

cent [sent] n centavo, céntimo. ● **per cent** por ciento.

centigrade ['sentɪgreɪd] *adj* centígrado.

centimetre ['sentɪmiːtə^r] (US **centimeter**) *n* centímetro.

central ['sentrəl] *adj* central. ■ **central heating** calefacción central.

centre ['sentə^r] (US **center**) *n* centro. ► *vt-vi* centrar. ■ **centre forward** delantero centro.

century ['sentʃərɪ] *n* siglo.

ceramics [sə'ræmɪks] *npl* cerámica.

cereal ['sɪərɪəl] *n* cereal.

cerebral ['serɪbrəl] *adj* cerebral.

ceremony ['serɪmənɪ] *n* ceremonia.

certain ['sɜːtən] *adj* 1 seguro,-a. 2 cierto,-a, alguno,-a. ● **for certain** con toda seguridad; **to make certain of** asegurarse de.

certificate [sə'tɪfɪkət] *n* certificado.

cesspit ['sespɪt] *n* pozo negro.

chafe [tʃeɪf] *vt* rozar, escoriar.

chain [tʃeɪn] *n* cadena.

chair [tʃeə^r] *n* 1 silla. 2 sillón. ■ **chair lift** telesilla.

chairman ['tʃeəmən] *n* presidente.

chairwoman ['tʃeəwumən] *n* presidenta.

chalet ['ʃæleɪ] *n* chalet, chalé.

chalk [tʃɔːk] *n* tiza.

challenge ['tʃælɪndʒ] *n* reto, desafío. ► *vt* retar, desafiar.

challenger ['tʃælɪndʒə^r] *n* rival.

chamber ['tʃeɪmbə^r] *n* cámara.

chambermaid ['tʃeɪmbəmeɪd] *n* camarera.

chameleon [kə'miːlɪən] *n* camaleón.

champion ['tʃæmpɪən] *n* campeón,-ona.

championship ['tʃæmpɪənʃɪp] *n* campeonato.

chance [tʃɑːns] *n* 1 azar. 2 oportunidad. ● **by chance** por casualidad; **to take a chance** arriesgarse.

chancellor ['tʃɑːnsələ^r] *n* canciller. ■ **Chancellor of the Exchequer** GB ministro,-a de Economía y Hacienda.

change [tʃeɪndʒ] *n* cambio. ► *vt-vi* cambiar. ► *vi* cambiarse de ropa. ● **for a change** para variar; **to change into** convertirse en, transformarse en.

changing ['tʃeɪndʒɪŋ] *adj*. ■ **changing room** vestuario.

channel ['tʃænəl] *n* canal *(cauce de agua)*. ► *vt* canalizar.

chaos ['keɪɒs] *n* caos.

chap [tʃæp] *n fam* tío, tipo.

chapel ['tʃæpəl] *n* capilla.

chapter ['tʃæptə^r] *n* capítulo.

character ['kærəktə^r] *n* 1 carácter. 2 personaje.

characteristic [kærəktə'rɪstɪk] *adj* característico,-a. ► *n* característica.

charcoal ['tʃɑːkəʊl] *n* 1 carbón vegetal. 2 carboncillo.

charge [tʃɑːdʒ] n **1** precio, coste. **2** cargo, acusación *(formal)*. **3** carga. ▶ vt **1** cobrar. **2** acusar *(de delito)*. **3** cargar. • **to be in charge of** estar a cargo de; **to bring a charge against** SB formular una acusación contra ALGN; **to take charge of** hacerse cargo de.

charger ['tʃɑːdʒəʳ] n cargador *(de batería)*.

charity ['tʃærɪti] n caridad.

charm [tʃɑːm] n **1** encanto. **2** amuleto *(de la suerte)*. ▶ vt encantar.

chart [tʃɑːt] n **1** tabla, gráfico, diagrama. **2** carta de navegación. ▪ **the charts** los cuarenta principales.

charter ['tʃɑːtəʳ] n **1** carta, estatutos. **2** flete. ▶ vt fletar. ▪ **charter flight** vuelo chárter.

chase [tʃeɪs] n persecución. ▶ vt perseguir.

chassis ['ʃæsi] n chasis.

chat [tʃæt] n charla. ▶ vi **1** charlar. **2** chatear. ▪ **chat show** programa de entrevistas.

chatter ['tʃætəʳ] n **1** cháchara, parloteo. **2** castañeteo *(de dientes)*. ▶ vi **1** charlar, parlotear. **2** castañetear *(dientes)*.

chauffeur ['ʃəʊfəʳ] n chófer.

cheap [tʃiːp] adj barato,-a.

cheat [tʃiːt] n tramposo,-a. ▶ vi **1** hacer trampa. **2** copiar *(en un examen)*. ▶ vi vt engañar, timar.

check [tʃek] n **1** comprobación, verificación. **2** US → cheque. **3** US nota, cuenta. **4** jaque. ▶ vt **1** comprobar, verificar. **2** dar jaque a.

to check in vi **1** facturar *(en aeropuerto)*. **2** dejar los datos *(en hotel)*.

checkbook ['tʃekbʊk] n talonario de cheques.

checked [tʃekt] adj a cuadros.

checkers ['tʃekəz] npl US damas.

checkmate ['tʃekmeɪt] n jaque mate. ▶ vt dar mate a.

checkout ['tʃekaʊt] n caja.

checkup ['tʃekʌp] n chequeo.

cheek [tʃiːk] n **1** mejilla. **2** fig descaro.

cheekbone ['tʃiːkbəʊn] n pómulo.

cheer [tʃɪəʳ] n viva. ▶ vt-vi vitorear.

to cheer up vt-vi animar(se).

cheerful ['tʃɪəfʊl] adj alegre.

cheers [tʃɪəz] interj **1** ¡salud! **2** ¡gracias! **3** ¡adiós!, ¡hasta luego!

cheese [tʃiːz] n queso.

cheesecake ['tʃiːzkeɪk] n tarta de queso.

cheetah ['tʃiːtə] n guepardo.

chemist ['kemɪst] n **1** químico,-a. **2** GB farmacéutico,-a.

chemistry ['kemɪstri] n química.

chemist's ['kemɪsts] n farmacia.

cheque [tʃek] n cheque, talón.

chequebook ['tʃekbʊk] n talonario de cheques.

cherish ['tʃerɪʃ] vt 1 apreciar, valorar. 2 abrigar *(esperanza)*.

cherry ['tʃerɪ] n cereza.

chess [tʃes] n ajedrez.

chessboard ['tʃesbɔːd] n tablero de ajedrez.

chest [tʃest] n 1 pecho. 2 cofre, arca. ▪ **chest of drawers** cómoda, cajonera.

chestnut ['tʃesnʌt] n 1 castaña *(fruto)*. 2 castaño *(color)*.

chew [tʃuː] vt masticar.

chewing gum ['tʃuːɪŋɡʌm] n chicle.

chicken ['tʃɪkɪn] n 1 pollo *(carne)*. 2 gallina *(ave)*.

chickenpox ['tʃɪkɪnpɒks] n varicela.

chickpea ['tʃɪkpiː] n garbanzo.

chicory ['tʃɪkərɪ] n achicoria.

chief [tʃiːf] n jefe.

chilblain ['tʃɪlbleɪn] n sabañón.

child [tʃaɪld] n 1 niño,-a. 2 hijo, hija. ▪ **only child** hijo,-a único,-a.

childbirth ['tʃaɪldbɜːθ] n parto.

childhood ['tʃaɪldhʊd] n infancia.

children ['tʃɪldrən] npl → child.

chill [tʃɪl] adj frío,-a. ▶ n resfriado. ▶ vt-vi enfriar(se).

chimney ['tʃɪmnɪ] n chimenea.

chimpanzee [tʃɪmpæn'ziː] n chimpancé.

chin [tʃɪn] n barbilla, mentón.

china ['tʃaɪnə] n porcelana.

chip [tʃɪp] n 1 patata frita. 2 chip. 3 astilla, lasca *(de madera)*. 4 ficha *(en casino)*. ▶ vt-vi 1 astillarse *(madera)*. 2 resquebrajarse *(piedra)*. 3 desconcharse *(pintura)*.

chiropodist [kɪ'rɒpədɪst] n podólogo,-a.

chitchat ['tʃɪttʃæt] n fam charla.

chocolate ['tʃɒkələt] n 1 chocolate. 2 bombón.

choice [tʃɔɪs] n elección.

choir ['kwaɪə'] n coro.

choke [tʃəʊk] n estárter. ▶ vi ahogarse.

cholera ['kɒlərə] n cólera.

choose [tʃuːz] vt escoger.

chop [tʃɒp] n chuleta *(carne)*. ▶ vt cortar.

chopsticks ['tʃɒpstɪks] npl palillos chinos.

chord [kɔːd] n acorde.

chorus ['kɔːrəs] n 1 coro. 2 estribillo.

chose [tʃəʊz] pt → choose.

chosen ['tʃəʊzən] pp → choose.

christen ['krɪsən] vt bautizar.

christening ['krɪsənɪŋ] n bautizo.

Christian ['krɪstɪən] adj-n cristiano,-a. ▪ **Christian name** nombre de pila.

Christmas ['krɪsməs] n Navidad. ▪ **Christmas card** tarjeta de Navidad, christmas; **Christmas Eve** Nochebuena.

chronic ['krɒnɪk] adj crónico,-a.

chronicle ['krɒnɪkəl] n crónica.

chronology [krə'nɒlədʒɪ] n cronología.

chuck [tʃʌk] vt 1 tirar *(objeto)*. 2 dejar *(novio, trabajo)*.

chunk [tʃʌŋk] n *fam* cacho.

church [tʃɜːtʃ] n iglesia.

chute [ʃuːt] n tobogán.

cider ['saɪdəʳ] n sidra.

cigar [sɪ'gɑːʳ] n puro.

cigarette [sɪgə'ret] n cigarrillo. ▪ **cigarette case** pitillera; **cigarette holder** boquilla; **cigarette lighter** encendedor.

cinder ['sɪndəʳ] n ceniza.

cinema ['sɪnəmə] n cine.

cinnamon ['sɪnəmən] n canela.

cipher ['saɪfəʳ] n código.

circle ['sɜːkəl] n 1 círculo. 2 anfiteatro *(en teatro)*.

circuit ['sɜːkɪt] n circuito.

circumference [sə'kʌmfərəns] n circunferencia.

circumstance ['sɜːkəmstəns] n circunstancia.

circus ['sɜːkəs] n 1 circo. 2 GB glorieta, rotonda.

cistern ['sɪstən] n cisterna.

citizen ['sɪtɪzən] n ciudadano,-a.

citric ['sɪtrɪk] adj cítrico,-a.

city ['sɪtɪ] n ciudad.

civil ['sɪvəl] adj 1 civil. 2 cortés, educado,-a. ▪ **civil servant** funcionario,-a; **civil service** administración pública.

civilization [sɪvɪlaɪ'zeɪʃən] n civilización.

claim [kleɪm] n 1 reivindicación. 2 derecho. 3 afirmación. ▶ vt 1 afirmar. 2 reclamar.

clam [klæm] n almeja.

clap [klæp] n 1 aplauso. 2 ruido seco. 3 palmada. ▶ vt-vi aplaudir.

clarinet [klærɪ'net] n clarinete.

clash [klæʃ] n 1 choque. 2 estruendo. ▶ vi 1 chocar. 2 coincidir *(fechas)*. 3 desentonar *(colores)*.

class [klɑːs] n clase.

classic ['klæsɪk] adj clásico,-a.

classification [klæsɪfɪ'keɪʃən] n clasificación.

classify ['klæsɪfaɪ] vt clasificar.

classmate ['klɑːsmeɪt] n compañero,-a de clase.

classroom ['klɑːsruːm] n clase.

clause [klɔːz] n 1 cláusula. 2 oración.

clavicle ['klævɪkəl] n clavícula.

claw [klɔː] n 1 garra *(de ave)*. 2 uña *(de gato)*. 3 pinza *(de cangrejo)*.

clay [kleɪ] n arcilla, barro.

clean [kliːn] adj limpio,-a. ▶ vt limpiar.

cleaner's ['kliːnəz] n tintorería.

cleanse [klenz] vt limpiar.

clear [klɪəʳ] adj 1 claro,-a. 2 transparente *(vidrio)*. 3 despejado,-a *(cielo, vista)*. ▶ vt 1 despejar. 2 levantar, recoger *(mesa)*. 3 absolver *(acusado)*. 4 salvar *(obstáculo)*. ● **in the clear** 1 fuera de peligro. 2 fuera de toda sospecha.

to clear up vt 1 aclarar. 2 ordenar, recoger. ▶ vi mejorar, despejarse *(tiempo)*.

clearance ['klɪərəns] n. ▪ **clearance sale** liquidación.

clearing ['klɪərɪŋ] n claro.

cleavage ['kliːvɪdʒ] n escote.

clef [klef] n clave (música).

clerk [klɑːk, US klɜːrk] n 1 oficinista. 2 US dependiente,-a.

clever ['klevər] adj listo,-a.

click [klɪk] n chasquido.

client ['klaɪənt] n cliente.

cliff [klɪf] n acantilado.

climate ['klaɪmət] n clima.

climb [klaɪm] n subida, escalada. ▶ vt 1 subir (escalera). 2 trepar a (árbol). 3 escalar.

clinic ['klɪnɪk] n clínica.

clip¹ [klɪp] n clip, fragmento (de película). ▶ vt recortar (barba).

clip² [klɪp] n 1 clip. 2 pasador.

clippers ['klɪpəz] npl cortaúñas.

cloak [kləʊk] n capa.

cloakroom ['kləʊkruːm] n 1 guardarropa. 2 GB servicios.

clock [klɒk] n reloj.

clod [klɒd] n terrón.

clog [klɒg] n zueco.

cloister ['klɔɪstə'] n claustro.

close¹ [kləʊs] adj 1 cercano,-a. 2 íntimo,-a (amigo). 3 detenido,-a (examen). ▶ adv cerca.

close² [kləʊz] vt-vi cerrar(se). ▪ **close season** temporada de veda.

closet ['klɒzɪt] n US armario.

close-up ['kləʊsʌp] n primer plano.

closing ['kləʊzɪŋ] n cierre.

clot [klɒt] n coágulo.

cloth [klɒθ] n 1 tela. 2 trapo.

clothes [kləʊðz] npl ropa.

cloud [klaʊd] n nube.

cloudy ['klaʊdɪ] adj nublado,-a.

clove¹ [kləʊv] n clavo (especie).

clove² [kləʊv] n diente (de ajo).

clover ['kləʊvə'] n trébol.

clown [klaʊn] n payaso.

club [klʌb] n 1 club, sociedad. 2 palo (de golf). 3 trébol (cartas).

clue [kluː] n pista, indicio.

clumsy ['klʌmzɪ] adj torpe.

cluster ['klʌstə'] n grupo.

clutch [klʌtʃ] n embrague. ▶ vt agarrar.

coach [kəʊtʃ] n 1 autocar. 2 coche (de tren, de caballos). 3 entrenador,-ra. ▶ vt entrenar. ▪ **coach station** estación de autobuses.

coal [kəʊl] n carbón.

coalition [kəʊəˈlɪʃən] n coalición.

coarse [kɔːs] adj basto,-a.

coast [kəʊst] n costa, litoral.

coastguard ['kəʊstgɑːd] n guardacostas.

coastline ['kəʊstlaɪn] n litoral.

coat [kəʊt] n 1 abrigo (prenda). 2 capa (de pintura). 3 pelaje (de animal). ▶ vt cubrir.

cob [kɒb] n mazorca.

cobble ['kɒbəl] n adoquín.

cobweb ['kɒbweb] n telaraña.

cock [kɒk] n gallo.

cockle ['kɒkəl] n berberecho.

cockpit ['kɒkpɪt] n cabina del piloto.

cockroach ['kɒkrəʊtʃ] n cucaracha.

cocktail ['kɒkteɪl] n cóctel.

cocoa ['kəʊkəʊ] n cacao.

coconut ['kəʊkənʌt] n coco.

cocoon [kə'kuːn] n capullo.

cod [kɒd] n bacalao.

code [kəʊd] n 1 código. 2 prefijo (de teléfono). ► vt codificar.

coffee ['kɒfɪ] n café. ■ **coffee shop** cafetería.

coffeepot ['kɒfɪpɒt] n cafetera.

coffin ['kɒfɪn] n ataúd.

coherent [kəʊ'hɪərənt] adj coherente.

cohesion [kəʊ'hiːʒən] n cohesión.

coin [kɔɪn] n moneda.

coincidence [kəʊ'ɪnsɪdəns] n coincidencia.

coke [kəʊk] n refesco de cola.

colander ['kʌləndə'] n colador.

cold [kəʊld] adj frío,-a. ► n 1 frío. 2 resfriado, catarro. ● **to catch a cold** resfriarse. ■ **cold sore** herpes.

collaboration [kəlæbə'reɪʃən] n colaboración.

collapse [kə'læps] n 1 derrumbamiento. 2 fracaso (de plan). 3 colapso (de persona). ► vi derrumbarse.

collapsible [kə'læpsəbəl] adj plegable.

collar ['kɒlə'] n 1 cuello (de camisa). 2 collar (de perro).

collarbone ['kɒləbəʊn] n clavícula.

colleague ['kɒliːg] n colega.

collect [kə'lekt] vt 1 reunir (objetos). 2 coleccionar (sellos). 3 recaudar (impuestos). 4 ir a buscar (persona). ► vi acumularse. ● **to call collect** US llamar a cobro revertido.

collection [kə'lekʃən] n 1 colección (de sellos). 2 colecta (de dinero). 3 recogida (de correo). 4 recaudación (de impuestos).

college ['kɒlɪdʒ] n centro de educación superior.

collide [kə'laɪd] vi chocar.

collision [kə'lɪʒən] n colisión.

colloquial [kə'ləʊkwɪəl] adj coloquial.

cologne [kə'ləʊn] n colonia.

colon¹ ['kəʊlən] n colon.

colon² ['kəʊlən] n dos puntos.

colonel ['kɜːnəl] n coronel.

colonial [kə'ləʊnɪəl] adj colonial.

colony ['kɒlənɪ] n colonia.

colour ['kʌlə'] (US **color**) n color. ► vt colorear, pintar. ■ **colour bar** discriminación racial.

colour-blind ['kʌləblaɪnd] adj daltónico,-a.

colouring ['kʌlərɪŋ] n 1 colorante. 2 colorido.

colt [kəʊlt] n potro.

column ['kɒləm] n columna.

coma ['kəʊmə] n coma.

comb [kəʊm] n peine. ► vt peinar.

combat ['kɒmbæt] n combate.

combination [kɒmbɪ'neɪʃən] *n* combinación.

combine [kəm'baɪn] *vt-vi* combinar(se).

come [kʌm] *vi* **1** venir. **2** llegar.

to come apart *vi* romperse.

to come back *vi* volver.

to come from *vt* ser de.

to come in *vi* **1** entrar: *come in!*, ¡adelante! **2** llegar *(tren)*.

to come off *vi* **1** tener lugar. **2** desprenderse, caerse *(pieza)*. **3** quitarse *(mancha)*.

to come on *vi* progresar.

to come out *vi* salir.

to come round *vi* **1** volver en sí. **2** visitar.

to come up *vi* **1** surgir *(tema)*. **2** acercarse. **3** salir *(sol)*.

comeback ['kʌmbæk] *n fam* reaparición.

comedy ['kɒmədɪ] *n* comedia.

comet ['kɒmɪt] *n* cometa.

comfort ['kʌmfət] *n* **1** comodidad. **2** consuelo.

comfortable ['kʌmfətəbəl] *adj* cómodo,-a. • **to make oneself comfortable** ponerse cómodo,-a.

comic ['kɒmɪk] *adj-n* cómico,-a. ► *n* tebeo, cómic.

comma ['kɒmə] *n* coma.

command [kə'mɑːnd] *n* **1** orden. **2** mando. **3** comando, instrucción. **4** dominio. ► *vt-vi* mandar.

commander [kə'mɑːndəʳ] *n* comandante.

commemorate [kə'meməreɪt] *vt* conmemorar.

comment ['kɒment] *n* comentario. ► *vi* comentar.

commerce ['kɒmɜːs] *n* comercio.

commercial [kə'mɜːʃəl] *adj* comercial. ► *n* anuncio.

commission [kə'mɪʃən] *n* comisión.

commissioner [kə'mɪʃənəʳ] *n* comisario.

commit [kə'mɪt] *vt* cometer. • **to commit oneself** comprometerse.

commitment [kə'mɪtmənt] *n* compromiso.

committee [kə'mɪtɪ] *n* comité, comisión.

commodity [kə'mɒdɪtɪ] *n* producto, artículo.

common ['kɒmən] *adj* común.

communicate [kə'mjuːnɪkeɪt] *vt-vi* comunicar(se).

communiqué [kə'mjuːnɪkeɪ] *n* comunicado.

communism ['kɒmjənɪzəm] *n* comunismo.

community [kə'mjuːnɪtɪ] *n* comunidad.

commute [kə'mjuːt] *vi viajar diariamente de casa al lugar de trabajo.* ► *vt* conmutar.

compact [kəm'pækt] *adj* compacto,-a. ▪ **compact disc** disco compacto.

company ['kʌmpənɪ] *n* compañía.

compare [kəm'peə'] *vt-vi* comparar(se).

compartment [kəm'pɑːtmənt] *n* compartim(i)ento.

compass ['kʌmpəs] *n* 1 brújula. 2 compás.

compatible [kəm'pætɪbəl] *adj* compatible.

compel [kəm'pel] *vt* obligar.

compensate ['kɒmpənseɪt] *vt* compensar.

compere ['kɒmpeə'] *n* GB presentador,-ra.

compete [kəm'piːt] *vi* competir.

competence ['kɒmpɪtəns] *n* competencia.

competent ['kɒmpɪtənt] *adj* competente.

competition [kɒmpə'tɪʃən] *n* 1 competición. 2 competencia.

complain [kəm'pleɪn] *vt* quejarse.

complaint [kəm'pleɪnt] *n* 1 queja. 2 dolencia.

complement ['kɒmplɪmənt] *n* complemento.

complete [kəm'pliːt] *adj* completo,-a. ▶ *vt* completar.

complex ['kɒmpleks] *adj* complejo,-a. ▶ *n* complejo.

complexion [kəm'plekʃən] *n* cutis, tez.

complicate ['kɒmplɪkeɪt] *vt* complicar.

compliment [(n) 'kɒmplɪmənt, (vb) 'kɒmplɪment] *n* cumplido. ▶ *vt* felicitar.

component [kəm'pəunənt] *adj-n* componente.

composed [kəm'pəuzd] *adj* sereno,-a.

composer [kəm'pəuzə'] *n* compositor,-ra.

composition [kɒmpə'zɪʃən] *n* composición.

compost ['kɒmpɒst] *n* abono.

compound ['kɒmpaund] *adj* compuesto,-a. ▶ *n* compuesto.

comprehensive [kɒmprɪ'hensɪv] *adj* 1 completo,-a. 2 amplio,-a. ▪ **comprehensive insurance** seguro a todo riesgo.

compress ['kɒmpres] *n* compresa. ▶ *vt* comprimir.

comprise [kəm'praɪz] *vt* constar de.

compromise ['kɒmprəmaɪz] *n* acuerdo. ▶ *vi* llegar a un acuerdo.

compulsory [kəm'pʌlsəri] *adj* obligatorio,-a.

computer [kəm'pjuːtə'] *n* ordenador. ▪ **computer science** informática.

computing [kəm'pjuːtɪŋ] *n* informática.

con [kɒn] *n* fam

conceal [kən'siːl] *vt* ocultar.

conceit [kən'siːt] *n* vanidad.

conceive [kən'siːv] *vt-vi* concebir.

concentrate ['kɒnsəntreɪt] *vt-vi* concentrar(se).

concentration [kɒnsən'treɪʃən] *n* concentración.

concept ['kɒnsept] *n* concepto.
concern [kən'sɜːn] *n* **1** preocupación. **2** negocio, empresa. ▶ *vt* **1** afectar, concernir. **2** preocupar. **3** tener que ver con. • **as far as I'm concerned** por lo que a mí se refiere; **to whom it may concern** a quien corresponda.
concerning [kən'sɜːnɪŋ] *prep* referente a, sobre, acerca de.
concert ['kɒnsət] *n* concierto. ▪ **concert house** sala de conciertos.
concise [kən'saɪs] *adj* conciso,-a.
conclude [kən'kluːd] *vt-vi* concluir.
conclusion [kən'kluːʒən] *n* conclusión.
concrete ['kɒŋkriːt] *adj* concreto,-a. ▶ *n* hormigón. ▪ **concrete mixer** hormigonera.
condemn [kən'dem] *vt* condenar.
condition [kən'dɪʃən] *n* **1** condición. **2** circunstancia. **3** afección *(médica)*. ▶ *vt* **1** condicionar. **2** acondicionar. • **in bad/good condition** en mal/buen estado; **to be out of condition** no estar en forma.
conditioner [kən'dɪʃənə'] *n* suavizante.
condolences [kən'dəʊlənsɪz] *npl* pésame.
conduct [*(n)* 'kɒndəkt, *(vb)* kən'dʌkt] *n* **1** conducta. **2** dirección. ▶ *vt* **1** dirigir, llevar a

cabo. **2** comportarse. ▶ *vt-vi* dirigir *(orquesta)*.
conductor [kən'dʌktə'] *n* **1** director,-ra *(de orquesta)*. **2** cobrador *(de autobús)*. **3** conductor *(de calor)*.
cone [kəʊn] *n* cono.
confectionery [kən'fekʃənərɪ] *n* dulces.
conference ['kɒnfərəns] *n* congreso. ▪ **conference call** teleconferencia.
confess [kən'fes] *vt-vi* confesar(se).
confidence ['kɒnfɪdəns] *n* **1** confianza. **2** confidencia *(secreto)*.
confirm [kən'fɜːm] *vt* confirmar.
conflict ['kɒnflɪkt] *n* conflicto.
conform [kən'fɔːm] *vi* **1** conformarse. **2** ajustarse.
confusion [kən'fjuːʒən] *n* confusión.
congenial [kən'dʒiːnɪəl] *adj* agradable.
congratulate [kən'grætjəleɪt] *vt* felicitar.
congratulations [kəngrætjə'leɪʃəns] *npl* felicidades.
congress ['kɒŋgres] *n* congreso.
conjunction [kən'dʒʌŋkʃən] *n* conjunción.
conjurer ['kʌndʒərə'] *n* mago,-a, prestidigitador,-ra.
conjuror ['kʌndʒərə'] *n* mago,-a, prestidigitador,-ra.

connect [kə'nekt] vt conectar. ▶ vi enlazar *(vuelos)*.

connection [kə'nekʃən] n conexión.

connoisseur [kɒnə'sɜːʳ] n entendido,-a.

conquer ['kɒŋkəʳ] vt conquistar.

conquest ['kɒŋkwest] n conquista.

conscience ['kɒnʃəns] n conciencia.

conscious ['kɒnʃəs] adj consciente.

consent [kən'sent] n consentimiento. ▶ vi consentir.

consequence ['kɒnsɪkwəns] n consecuencia.

conservation [kɒnsə'veɪʃən] n conservación.

conservative [kən'sɜːvətɪv] adj-n conservador,-ra.

conservatory [kən'sɜːvətrɪ] n 1 invernadero. 2 conservatorio.

consider [kən'sɪdəʳ] vt considerar.

considerable [kən'sɪdərəbəl] adj considerable.

consist [kən'sɪst] vi consistir.

consistent [kən'sɪstənt] adj 1 consecuente. 2 constante.

consolation [kɒnsə'leɪʃən] n consuelo.

console ['kɒnsəʊl] n consola.

consonant ['kɒnsənənt] n consonante.

conspicuous [kəns'pɪkjʊəs] adj llamativo,-a, visible.

conspiracy [kən'spɪrəsɪ] n conspiración.

constable ['kʌnstəbəl] n policía.

constant ['kɒnstənt] adj constante.

constipation [kɒnstɪ'peɪʃən] n estreñimiento.

constituency [kən'stɪtjʊənsɪ] n circunscripción.

constitution [kɒnstɪ'tjuːʃən] n constitución.

constraint [kən'streɪnt] n 1 coacción. 2 limitación.

construction [kən'strʌkʃən] n construcción.

consul ['kɒnsəl] n cónsul.

consulate ['kɒnsjələt] n consulado.

consult [kən'sʌlt] vt-vi consultar.

consume [kən'sjuːm] vt consumir.

consumer [kən'sjuːməʳ] n consumidor,-ra. ▪ **consumer goods** bienes de consumo.

contact ['kɒntækt] n contacto. ▪ **contact lens** lentilla.

contagious [kən'teɪdʒəs] adj contagioso,-a.

contain [kən'teɪn] vt contener.

container [kən'teɪnəʳ] n 1 recipiente. 2 conáiner.

contamination [kəntæmɪ'neɪʃən] n contaminación.

contemporary [kən'tempərərɪ] adj-n contemporáneo,-a.

contempt [kən'tempt] n desprecio, menosprecio. ▪ **con-**

tempt of court desacato a la autoridad.

contend [kən'tend] *vi* **1** luchar. **2** enfrentarse a.

content ['kɒntent] *n* contenido.

contents ['kɒntents] *npl* contenido.

contest ['kɒntest] *n* **1** concurso. **2** contienda.

contestant [kən'testənt] *n* **1** concursante. **2** candidato,-a.

context ['kɒntekst] *n* contexto.

continent ['kɒntɪnənt] *n* continente.

continental [kɒntɪ'nentəl] *adj* **1** continental. **2** GB europeo,-a. ■ **continental breakfast** desayuno continental.

continuation [kəntɪnjʊ'eɪʃən] *n* continuación.

continue [kən'tɪnjuː] *vt-vi* continuar.

contraceptive [kɒntrə'septɪv] *adj* anticonceptivo,-a. ► *n* anticonceptivo.

contract [(*n*) 'kɒntrækt, (*vb*) kən'trækt] *n* contrato. ► *vi* contraerse. ► *vt* contraer *(enfermedad, matrimonio)*.

contradiction [kɒntrə'dɪkʃən] *n* contradicción.

contrary ['kɒntrərɪ] *adj* contrario,a. ● **contrary to** en contra de, al contrario de; **on the contrary** al contrario.

contrast ['kɒntræst] *n* contraste.

contribute [kən'trɪbjuːt] *vt-vi* contribuir. ► *vi* colaborar *(en periódico)*.

contributor [kən'trɪbjətəʳ] *n* **1** contribuyente. **2** colaborador,-ra *(en periódico)*.

control [kən'trəʊl] *n* **1** control. **2** mando. ► *vt* **1** controlar. **2** dominar. ■ **control tower** torre de control.

controller [kən'trəʊləʳ] *n* **1** controlador,-ra. **2** director,-ra de programación.

convenience [kən'viːnɪəns] *n* conveniencia. ■ **convenience food** plato precocinado.

convenient [kən'viːnɪənt] *adj* conveniente.

convent ['kɒnvənt] *n* convento.

convention [kən'venʃən] *n* convención.

conversation [kɒnvə'seɪʃən] *n* conversación.

convert [(*n*) 'kɒnvɜːt, (*vb*) kən'vɜːt] *n* converso,-a. ► *vt-vi* converti(se).

convertible [kən'vɜːtəbəl] *adj* convertible. ► *adj-n* descapotable *(coche)*.

convey [kən'veɪ] *vt* **1** transportar. **2** comunicar *(idea)*.

conveyor belt [kən'veɪəbelt] *n* cinta transportadora.

convict [(*n*) 'kɒnvɪkt, (*vb*) kən'vɪkt] *n* preso,-a. ► *vt* declarar culpable.

conviction [kən'vɪkʃən] *n* **1** convicción. **2** condena.

convince [kənˈvɪns] *vt* convencer.

convoy [ˈkɒnvɔɪ] *n* convoy.

cook [kʊk] *n* cocinero,-ra. ► *vt* cocinar.

cooker [ˈkʊkə'] *n* cocina *(aparato)*.

cookery [ˈkʊkərɪ] *n* cocina *(arte)*.

cookie [ˈkʊkɪ] *n* US galleta.

cool [kuːl] *adj* **1** fresco,-a *(bebida)*. **2** tranquilo,-a *(persona)*. **3** *sl* en la onda. ► *vt* refrescar. ► *vi* enfriarse.

coop [kuːp] *n* gallinero.

cooperation [kəʊɒpəˈreɪʃən] *n* cooperación.

cooperative [kəʊˈɒpərətɪv] *adj* dispuesto,-a a colaborar. ► *n* cooperativa.

coordinate [kəʊˈɔːdɪneɪt] *vt* coordinar.

cop [kɒp] *n fam* poli.

cope [kəʊp] *vi* arreglárselas. **to cope with** *vt* poder con, hacer frente a.

copper [ˈkɒpə'] *n* cobre.

copy [ˈkɒpɪ] *n* copia. ► *vt-vi* copiar.

coral [ˈkɒrəl] *n* coral.

cord [kɔːd] *n* cuerda, cordón.

corduroy [ˈkɔːdərɔɪ] *n* pana.

core [kɔː'] *n* **1** núcleo, centro. **2** corazón *(de manzana)*.

cork [kɔːk] *n* corcho. ■ **cork oak** alcornoque.

corkscrew [ˈkɔːkskruː] *n* sacacorchos.

corn¹ [kɔːn] *n* **1** maíz. **2** cereales. ■ **corn on the cob** mazorca, maíz tierno.

corn² [kɔːn] *n* callo *(dureza)*.

cornea [ˈkɔːnɪə] *n* córnea.

corner [ˈkɔːnə'] *n* esquina, rincón. ■ **corner kick** córner.

cornet [ˈkɔːnɪt] *n* **1** corneta. **2** GB cucurucho.

cornflakes [ˈkɔːnfleɪks] *npl* copos de maíz.

cornstarch [ˈkɔːnstɑːtʃ] *n* harina de maíz, maicena.

corporal [ˈkɔːpərəl] *n* cabo *(militar)*. ► *adj* corporal.

corporation [kɔːpəˈreɪʃən] *n* corporación.

corpse [kɔːps] *n* cadáver.

corpuscle [ˈkɔːpəsəl] *n* glóbulo.

correct [kəˈrekt] *adj* **1** correcto,-a. **2** exacto,-a. **3** formal. ► *vt* corregir.

correction [kəˈrekʃən] *n* corrección.

correspond [kɒrɪsˈpɒnd] *vi* **1** coincidir, corresponderse. **2** escribirse, cartearse.

correspondence [kɒrɪsˈpɒndəns] *n* correspondencia.

corridor [ˈkɒrɪdɔː'] *n* pasillo.

corrosion [kəˈrəʊʒən] *n* corrosión.

corruption [kəˈrʌpʃən] *n* corrupción.

corset [ˈkɔːsɪt] *n* corsé.

cosmetic [kɒzˈmetɪk] *n* cosmético. ■ **cosmetic surgery** cirugía estética.

cost [kɒst] *n* coste, costo, precio. ► *vi* costar, valer. ● **at all costs** a toda costa; **at the cost of** a costa de; **whatever the cost** cueste lo que cueste.

costume [ˈkɒstjuːm] *n* traje, disfraz. ■ **costume jewellery** bisutería.

cosy [ˈkəʊzɪ] *adj* acogedor,-ra.

cot [kɒt] *n* cuna.

cottage [ˈkɒtɪdʒ] *n* casa de campo. ■ **cottage cheese** requesón.

cotton [ˈkɒtən] *n* algodón. ■ **cotton wool** algodón hidrófilo.

couch [kaʊtʃ] *n* canapé, sofá.

couchette [kuːˈʃet] *n* litera.

cough [kɒf] *n* tos. ► *vi* toser. ■ **cough mixture** jarabe para la tos.

could [kʊd, kəd] *pt* → can.

council [ˈkaʊnsəl] *n* 1 ayuntamiento. 2 consejo.

count[1] [kaʊnt] *n* conde.

count[2] [kaʊnt] *n* cuenta, recuento. ► *vt-vi* contar.

to count on *vt* contar con.

countdown [ˈkaʊntdaʊn] *n* cuenta atrás.

counter [ˈkaʊntəʳ] *n* 1 mostrador *(de tienda)*. 2 ficha *(de juego)*.

counterfeit [ˈkaʊntəfɪt] *adj* falso,-a, falsificado,-a. ► *n* falsificación. ► *vt* falsificar.

counterpane [ˈkaʊntəpeɪn] *n* colcha, cubrecama.

counterpart [ˈkaʊntəpaːt] *n* homólogo,-a.

countess [ˈkaʊntəs] *n* condesa.

country [ˈkʌntrɪ] *n* 1 país. 2 campo. 3 tierra, región.

countryside [ˈkʌntrɪsaɪd] *n* 1 campo. 2 paisaje.

county [ˈkaʊntɪ] *n* condado.

coup [kuː] *n* golpe de estado.

couple [ˈkʌpəl] *n* 1 par *(de cosas)*. 2 pareja *(de personas)*. ► *vt* enganchar, conectar.

coupon [ˈkuːpɒn] *n* cupón.

courage [ˈkʌrɪdʒ] *n* valor.

courgette [kʊəˈʒet] *n* calabacín.

courier [ˈkʊərɪəʳ] *n* 1 mensajero,-a. 2 guía turístico,-a.

course [kɔːs] *n* 1 rumbo *(de barco, avión)*. 2 curso *(de río)*. 3 curso. 4 plato. 5 campo *(de golf)*. ● **in due course** a su debido tiempo; **of course** desde luego, por supuesto. ■ **first course** primer plato; **main course** plato principal.

court [kɔːt] *n* 1 tribunal, juzgado. 2 pista *(de tenis)*. 3 patio. 4 corte *(de rey)*.

courteous [ˈkɜːtɪəs] *adj* cortés.

courtyard [ˈkɔːtjaːd] *n* patio.

cousin [ˈkʌzən] *n* primo,-a.

cove [kəʊv] *n* cala, ensenada.

cover [ˈkʌvəʳ] *n* 1 cubierta, funda. 2 tapa *(de cazuela)*. 3 cubierta *(de libro)*, portada *(de revista)*. 4 cobertura *(de seguro)*. ► *vt* 1 cubrir. 2 tapar *(con*

tapa). **3** asegurar *(con seguro).* ●
under cover of al amparo de,
al abrigo de. ▪ **cover charge**
precio del cubierto.
to cover up *vt* tapar.
covet ['kʌvət] *vt* codiciar.
cow [kaʊ] *n* vaca.
coward ['kaʊəd] *n* cobarde.
cowboy ['kaʊbɔɪ] *n* vaquero.
cowshed ['kaʊʃed] *n* establo.
crab [kræb] *n* cangrejo.
crack [kræk] *vt* **1** rajar, agrietar
(suelo). **2** forzar *(caja fuerte).* **3**
cascar *(huevo, nuez).* **4** soltar
(chiste). ▸ *vi* **1** rajarse, agri-
etarse. **2** quebrarse *(voz).* **3**
hundirse *(persona).* **4** crujir. ▸
n **1** raja *(en taza).* **2** grieta *(en
pared).* **3** chasquido *(de látigo).*
cracker ['krækə'] *n* galleta salada.
cradle ['kreɪdəl] *n* cuna.
craft [krɑːft] *n* **1** arte, oficio. **2**
artesanía. **3** embarcación. ▪ **a
pleasure craft** un barco de
recreo.
craftsman ['krɑːftsmən] *n* artesano.
crag [kræg] *n* risco, peñasco.
cramp [kræmp] *n* calambre.
▸ **cramps** *npl* retortijones.
crane [kreɪn] *n* **1** grulla común. **2** grúa.
crash [kræʃ] *vi* estrellarse *(avión,
coche).* ▸ *n* **1** estallido, estrépito
(ruido). **2** accidente. ▪ **a crash
course** curso intensivo.
crate [kreɪt] *n* caja.

crawfish ['krɔːfɪʃ] *n* langosta.
crawl [krɔːl] *vi* arrastrarse
(adulto), gatear *(bebé).* ▸ *n* crol.
crayfish ['kreɪfɪʃ] *n* cangrejo de
río.
craze [kreɪz] *n* manía, moda.
crazy ['kreɪzɪ] *adj fam* loco,-a.
cream [kriːm] *n* crema, nata.
crease [kriːs] *n* arruga.
create [kriːˈeɪt] *vt* crear.
creature ['kriːtʃə'] *n* criatura.
crèche [kreʃ] *n* guardería.
credible ['kredɪbəl] *adj* creíble.
credit ['kredɪt] *n* **1** mérito, reconocimiento. **2** crédito, haber. ▸ *vt* **1** creer, dar crédito a.
2 abonar, ingresar. ▸ *npl* **cred-
its** créditos *(de película).* ● **on
credit** a crédito. ▪ **credit card**
tarjeta de crédito.
creed [kriːd] *n* credo.
creek [kriːk] *n* **1** GB cala. **2** US
riachuelo.
creep [kriːp] *vi* arrastrarse *(insecto),* deslizarse *(animal).*
creeper ['kriːpə'] *n* enredadera.
crème caramel [kremkærə-
'mel] *n* flan.
crept [krept] *pt-pp* → creep.
crescent ['kresənt] *adj* creciente.
crest [krest] *n* cresta.
crevice ['krevɪs] *n* raja, grieta.
crew [kruː] *n* **1** tripulación. **2**
equipo. ▪ **crew cut** pelado al
cero.
crib [krɪb] *n* cuna. ▸ *vt fam* copiar, plagiar.

crick [krɪk] *n* tortícolis.

cricket[1] [ˈkrɪkɪt] *n* grillo *(insecto).*

cricket[2] [ˈkrɪkɪt] *n* críquet.

crime [kraɪm] *n* **1** crimen. **2** delito.

criminal [ˈkrɪmɪnəl] *adj-n* criminal. ■ **criminal record** antecedentes penales.

crinkle [ˈkrɪŋkəl] *vt-vi* arrugar(se).

cripple [ˈkrɪpəl] *n* lisiado,-a, inválido,-a. ► *vt* paralizar.

crisis [ˈkraɪsɪs] *n* crisis.

crisp [krɪsp] *adj* **1** crujiente *(pan).* **2** fresco,-a *(lechuga).* **3** frío,-a y seco,-a *(tiempo).* ► *n* GB patata frita *(de bolsa).*

criterion [kraɪˈtɪərɪən] *n* criterio.

critic [ˈkrɪtɪk] *n* crítico,-a.

critical [ˈkrɪtɪkəl] *adj* crítico,-a.

criticize [ˈkrɪtɪsaɪz] *vt-vi* criticar.

crockery [ˈkrɒkərɪ] *n* loza.

crocodile [ˈkrɒkədaɪl] *n* cocodrilo.

crocus [ˈkrəʊkəs] *n* azafrán.

crook [krʊk] *n* **1** gancho. **2** cayado. **3** *fam* delincuente.

crooked [ˈkrʊkɪd] *adj* **1** torcido,-a. **2** tortuoso,-a *(camino).*

crop [krɒp] *n* **1** cultivo, cosecha. **2** pelado corto.

cross [krɒs] *n* **1** cruz. **2** cruce; *vt* cruzar, atravesar. ► *vi* cruzar(se).

to cross off *vt* borrar, tachar.

to cross out *vt* borrar, tachar.

to cross over *vt* pasar.

crossbar [ˈkrɒsbɑːʳ] *n* travesaño.

crossbow [ˈkrɒsbəʊ] *n* ballesta.

cross-country [krɒsˈkʌntrɪ] *adj-adv* campo través. ■ **cross-country race** cros.

cross-eyed [ˈkrɒsaɪd] *adj* bizco,-a.

crossing [ˈkrɒsɪŋ] *n* **1** cruce *(de carretera).* **2** travesía *(en barco).*

crossroads [ˈkrɒsrəʊdz] *n* encrucijada, cruce.

crossword [ˈkrɒswɜːd] *n* crucigrama.

crotch [krɒtʃ] *n* entrepierna.

crotchet [ˈkrɒtʃɪt] *n* negra *(nota).*

crouch [kraʊtʃ] *vi* agacharse, agazaparse.

crow [krəʊ] *n* cuervo. ■ **crow's-feet** patas de gallo.

crowbar [ˈkrəʊbɑːʳ] *n* palanca.

crowd [kraʊd] *n* **1** multitud, gentío. **2** público. **3** gente.

crowded [ˈkraʊdɪd] *adj* abarrotado,-a.

crown [kraʊn] *n* **1** corona *(de monarca).* **2** copa *(de árbol, sombrero).* ► *vt* coronar.

crucifix [ˈkruːsɪfɪks] *n* crucifijo.

crude [kruːd] *adj* **1** grosero,-a *(chiste).* **2** crudo,-a *(petróleo).*

cruel [ˈkruːəl] *adj* cruel.

cruet [ˈkruːɪt] *n* vinagreras.

cruise [kruːz] *vi* hacer un crucero. ► *n* crucero *(viaje).*

cruiser [ˈkruːzəʳ] *n* crucero *(barco).*

crumb [krʌm] *n* miga.
crumble ['krʌmbəl] *vt* desmigar. ▶ *vi* desmoronarse, deshacerse.
crumple ['krʌmpəl] *vt-vi* arrugar(se).
crunch [krʌntʃ] ▶ *vi* crujir. ▶ *n* crujido.
crusade [kru:'seɪd] *n* cruzada.
crush [krʌʃ] *n* aglomeración, gentío. ▶ *vt* 1 aplastar. 2 triturar.
crust [krʌst] *n* corteza.
crutch [krʌtʃ] *n* muleta.
cry [kraɪ] *vt-vi* gritar. ▶ *vi* llorar. ▶ *n* 1 grito. 2 llanto.
to cry out *vi* gritar.
crypt [krɪpt] *n* cripta.
crystal ['krɪstəl] *n* cristal.
cub [kʌb] *n* cachorro,-a.
cube [kju:b] *n* 1 cubo. 2 terrón *(de azúcar)*. ∎ **cube root** raíz cúbica.
cubic ['kju:bɪk] *adj* cúbico,-a.
cuckoo ['kʊku:] *n* cuco común.
cucumber ['kju:kʌmbəʳ] *n* pepino.
cuddle ['kʌdəl] *vt-vi* abrazar(se). ▶ *n* abrazo.
cue[1] [kju:] *n* 1 señal. 2 pie *(en teatro)*.
cue[2] [kju:] *n* taco *(de billar)*.
cuff [kʌf] *n* puño. ∎ **cuff links** gemelos *(de camisa)*.
cul-de-sac ['kʌldəsæk] *n* calle sin salida.
culminate ['kʌlmɪneɪt] *vt* culminar.

culprit ['kʌlprɪt] *n* culpable.
cultivate ['kʌltɪveɪt] *vt* cultivar.
cultivated ['kʌltɪveɪtɪd] *adj* 1 culto,-a *(persona)*. 2 cultivado,-a *(tierra)*.
culture ['kʌltʃəʳ] *n* cultura.
cumbersome ['kʌmbəsəm] *adj* 1 voluminoso. 2 incómodo,-a.
cumin ['kʌmɪn] *n* comino.
cunning ['kʌnɪŋ] *adj* astuto,-a.
cup [kʌp] *n* 1 taza. 2 copa.
cupboard ['kʌbəd] *n* armario.
curb [kɜ:b] *n* freno, restricción. ▶ *vt* refrenar, contener.
curd [kɜ:d] *n* cuajada. ∎ **curd cheese** requesón.
cure [kjʊəʳ] *vt* curar. ▶ *n* cura.
curfew ['kɜ:fju:] *n* toque de queda.
curious ['kjʊərɪəs] *adj* 1 curioso,-a. 2 extraño.
curl [kɜ:l] *vt-vi* rizar(se). ▶ *n* 1 rizo, bucle. 2 espiral.
currant ['kʌrənt] *n* pasa.
currency ['kʌrənsɪ] *n* moneda.
current ['kʌrənt] *adj* 1 actual *(precio)*. 2 en curso, corriente *(mes)*. 3 común *(idea)*. ▶ *n* corriente. ∎ **current account** cuenta corriente; **current affairs** temas de actualidad.
curriculum [kə'rɪkjələm] *n* 1 plan de estudios. 2 currículum.
curse [kɜ:s] *n* 1 maldición, maleficio. 2 palabrota. ▶ *vt-vi* maldecir.

cursor ['kɜːsə'] n cursor.
curtail [kɜː'teɪl] vt reducir.
curtain ['kɜːtən] n **1** cortina. **2** telón. • **to draw the curtains** correr las cortinas.
curve [kɜːv] n curva.
cushion ['kʊʃən] n cojín, almohadón. ► vt fig amortiguar.
custard ['kʌstəd] n natillas.
custom ['kʌstəm] n costumbre.
customer ['kʌstəmə'] n cliente. ■ **customer services** servicio de atención al cliente.
customs ['kʌstəmz] n aduana. ■ **customs duties** derechos de aduana, aranceles.
cut [kʌt] vt **1** cortar. **2** tallar (piedra, vidrio). **3** dividir. **4** recortar. ► n **1** corte, incisión. **2** parte (ganancias). **3** rebaja, recorte. ■ **cold cuts** fiambres.
to cut down vt **1** talar, cortar. **2** fig reducir: **to cut down on smoking**, fumar menos.
to cut in vi interrumpir.
to cut off vt **1** cortar (electricidad). **2** aislar.
to cut out vt **1** recortar, cortar. **2** eliminar, suprimir.
cute [kjuːt] adj mono,-a, guapo,-a.
cutlery ['kʌtlərɪ] n cubiertos, cubertería.
cutlet ['kʌtlət] n chuleta.
cuttlefish ['kʌtəlfɪʃ] n sepia.
cycle ['saɪkəl] n ciclo. ► vi ir en bicicleta.
cycling ['saɪklɪŋ] n ciclismo.

cyclist ['saɪklɪst] n ciclista.
cyclone ['saɪkləʊn] n ciclón.
cylinder ['sɪlɪndə'] n **1** cilindro. **2** bombona.
cynical ['sɪnɪkəl] adj cínico,-a.
cypress ['saɪprəs] n ciprés.
cyst [sɪst] n quiste.
czar [zɑː'] n zar.

D

dad [dæd] n fam papá.
daddy ['dædɪ] n fam papá.
daffodil ['dæfədɪl] n narciso.
daft [dɑːft] adj fam tonto,-a.
daily ['deɪlɪ] adj diario,-a, cotidiano,-a. ► adv diariamente. ► n diario.
dairy ['deərɪ] n **1** vaquería. **2** lechería.
daisy ['deɪzɪ] n margarita.
dam [dæm] n **1** dique. **2** embalse, presa.
damage ['dæmɪdʒ] vt dañar. ► n daño.
damn [dæm] interj fam ¡maldito,-a sea! ► adj fam maldito,-a.
damp [dæmp] adj húmedo,-a. ► n humedad.
dance [dɑːns] n baile, danza. ► vt-vi bailar.
dancer ['dɑːnsə'] n bailarín,-ina.
dandelion ['dændɪlaɪən] n diente de león.

dandruff ['dændrəf] n caspa.

danger ['deɪndʒəʳ] n peligro.

dare [deəʳ] vi atreverse. • **I dare say...** creo que; **don't you dare!** ini se te ocurra!

dark [dɑːk] adj 1 oscuro,-a. 2 moreno,-a (pelo, piel). ► n 1 oscuridad. 2 anochecer. • **to grow dark** anochecer.

darkness ['dɑːknəs] n oscuridad.

darling ['dɑːlɪŋ] n querido,-a, cariño.

darn [dɑːn] n zurcido. ► vt zurcir.

dart [dɑːt] n dardo.

dartboard ['dɑːtbɔːd] n diana.

dash [dæʃ] n 1 poco, pizca (de sal). 2 chorro (de líquido).

dashboard ['dæʃbɔːd] n salpicadero.

data ['deɪtə] npl datos, información. ■ **data base** base de datos; **data processing** procesamiento de datos.

date¹ [deɪt] n 1 fecha. 2 cita, compromiso. • **out of date** anticuado,-a.

date² [deɪt] n dátil.

dated ['deɪtɪd] adj anticuado,-a.

daughter ['dɔːtəʳ] n hija.

daughter-in-law ['dɔːtərɪnlɔː] n nuera.

daunt [dɔːnt] vt intimidar.

dawn [dɔːn] n amanecer.

day [deɪ] n 1 día. 2 jornada. 3 época, tiempo. • **by day** de día. ■ **day off** día libre.

daybreak ['deɪbreɪk] n alba.

daylight ['deɪlaɪt] n luz de día.

daytime n día.

dazzle ['dæzəl] vt deslumbrar.

dead [ded] adj 1 muerto,-a. 2 sordo,-a (ruido). 3 total, absoluto,-a: *dead silence*, silencio total. ■ **dead end** callejón sin salida.

deadline ['dedlaɪn] n fecha límite, hora límite.

deadlock ['dedlɒk] n punto muerto.

deaf [def] adj sordo,-a.

deaf-and-dumb [defən'dʌm] adj sordomudo,-a.

deal [diːl] n 1 trato, pacto. 2 cantidad: *a great deal of noise*, mucho ruido. ► vt 1 dar, asestar (golpe). 2 repartir (cartas). ► vi comerciar.

to deal with vt 1 tratar con. 2 abordar, ocuparse de (problema). 3 tratar de (tema).

dealer ['diːləʳ] n 1 comerciante. 2 traficante (de drogas).

dealt [delt] pt-pp → deal.

dear [dɪəʳ] adj 1 querido,-a. 2 caro,-a (precio). • **Dear Sir** Muy señor mío, Estimado señor.

death [deθ] n muerte. ■ **death penalty** pena de muerte.

debate [dɪ'beɪt] n debate. ► vt-vi debatir.

debit ['debɪt] n débito. ► vt cargar en cuenta.

debris ['deɪbriː] n escombros.

debt [det] n deuda.

debug [di:'bʌg] *vt* depurar.
debut ['deibju:] *n* estreno.
decade ['dekeid] *n* década.
decadence ['dekədəns] *n* decadencia.
decaffeinated [di:'kæfineitid] *adj* descafeinado,-a.
decay [di'kei] *n* 1 descomposición *(de cuerpo)*. 2 caries *(de diente)*. 3 *fig* decadencia *(de sociedad)*. ► *vi* 1 descomponerse *(cuerpo)*. 2 deteriorarse *(edificio)*. 3 cariarse *(diente)*.
deceased [di'si:st] *adj-n* fallecido,-a.
deceive [di'si:v] *vt* engañar.
December [di'sembə'] *n* diciembre.
decent ['di:sənt] *adj* decente.
deception [di'sepʃən] *n* engaño, mentira.
decide [di'said] *vt-vi* decidirse.
decimal ['desiməl] *adj-n* decimal.
decision [di'siʒən] *n* decisión.
decisive [di'saisiv] *adj* 1 decisivo,-a. 2 decidido,-a *(persona)*.
deck [dek] *n* 1 cubierta *(de barco)*. 2 piso *(de autobús)*. 3 US baraja.
deckchair ['dektʃeə'] *n* tumbona.
declare [di'kleə'] *vt* declarar.
decorate ['dekəreit] *vt* decorar, adornar. ► *vt-vi* pintar, empapelar.
decoration [dekə'reiʃən] *n* 1 decoración. 2 condecoración.

decrease [di'kri:s] *n* disminución. ► *vt-vi* disminuir.
decree [di'kri:] *n* decreto.
dedicate ['dedikeit] *vt* dedicar.
deduce [di'dju:s] *vt* deducir.
deduct [di'dʌkt] *vt* restar.
deed [di:d] *n* 1 acto. 2 hazaña. 3 escritura *(de propiedad)*.
deep [di:p] *adj* hondo,-a, profundo,-a.
deer [diə'] *n* ciervo.
default [di'fɔ:lt] *n* negligencia. ▪ **default settings** valores por defecto.
defeat [di'fi:t] *n* derrota. ► *vt* derrotar.
defect [(n) 'di:fekt, (vb) di'fekt] *n* defecto. ► *vi* desertar.
defence [di'fens] *n* defensa.
defend [di'fend] *vt* defender.
defer [di'fɜ:'] *vt* aplazar.
deficient [di'fiʃənt] *adj* deficiente.
deficit ['defisit] *n* déficit.
define [di'fain] *vt* definir.
definition [defi'niʃən] *n* definición.
definitive [di'finitiv] *adj* definitivo,-a.
deflate [di'fleit] *vt-vi* desinflar(se), deshinchar(se).
deflect [di'flekt] *vt-vi* desviar(se).
defrost [di:'frɒst] *vt-vi* descongelar(se).
defy [di'fai] *vt* desafiar.
degree [di'gri:] *n* 1 grado. 2 título, licenciatura. ● **to some**

degree hasta cierto punto. ■ **honorary degree** doctorado "honoris causa".

delay [dɪ'leɪ] *n* retraso. ► *vt* aplazar.

delegation [delɪ'geɪʃən] *n* delegación.

delete [dɪ'liːt] *vt* borrar.

deliberate [dɪ'lɪbəreɪt] *vt-vi* deliberar.

delicacy ['delɪkəsɪ] *n* 1 delicadeza. 2 manjar *(exquisito)*.

delicate ['delɪkət] *adj* delicado,-a.

delicatessen [delɪkə'tesən] *n* charcutería selecta.

delicious [dɪ'lɪʃəs] *adj* delicioso,-a.

delight [dɪ'laɪt] *n* placer, delicia.

delighted [dɪ'laɪtɪd] *adj* encantado,-a.

deliver [dɪ'lɪvə'] *vt* 1 entregar, *(mercancía)*. 2 dar *(golpe, patada)*. 3 pronunciar *(discurso)*. 4 traer al mundo.

delivery [dɪ'lɪvərɪ] *n* 1 entrega. 2 parto. ■ **delivery man** repartidor.

delude [dɪ'luːd] *vt* engañar.

demand [dɪ'mɑːnd] *n* 1 reclamación, petición. 2 demanda. ► *vt* exigir, reclamar.

democracy [dɪ'mɒkrəsɪ] *n* democracia.

democrat ['deməkræt] *n* demócrata.

demolish [dɪ'mɒlɪʃ] *vt* derribar, demoler.

demon ['diːmən] *n* demonio.

demonstrate ['demənstreɪt] *vt* 1 demostrar. 2 mostrar. ► *vi* manifestarse.

demonstration [demən'streɪʃən] *n* 1 demostración. 2 manifestación.

denial [dɪ'naɪəl] *n* negativa.

denim ['denɪm] *n* tela vaquera.

denounce [dɪ'naʊns] *vt* denunciar.

dense [dens] *adj* denso,-a.

dent [dent] *n* abolladura. ► *vt* abollar.

dentist ['dentɪst] *n* dentista.

deny [dɪ'naɪ] *vt* negar.

deodorant [diː'əʊdərənt] *n* desodorante.

department [dɪ'pɑːtmənt] *n* 1 departamento, sección. 2 ministerio. ■ **department store** grandes almacenes.

departure [dɪ'pɑːtʃə'] *n* 1 partida, marcha *(de persona)*. 2 salida *(de tren, avión)*.

depend [dɪ'pend] *vi* depender. **to depend on** *vt* confiar en.

deplore [dɪ'plɔː'] *vt* deplorar.

deploy [dɪ'plɔɪ] *vt fig* desplegar.

deport [dɪ'pɔːt] *vt* deportar.

deposit [dɪ'pɒzɪt] *n* 1 depósito. 2 yacimiento *(en mina)*. 3 poso *(en vino)*. ► *vt* 1 depositar. 2 ingresar. ■ **deposit account** cuenta de ahorros.

depot ['depəʊ] *n* 1 almacén. 2 depósito.

depress [dɪ'pres] *vt* deprimir.

depression [dɪ'preʃən] *n* depresión.

deprive [dɪ'praɪv] *vt* privar.

depth [depθ] *n* profundidad.

deputy ['depjətɪ] *n* **1** sustituto,-a, suplente. **2** diputado,-a.

derive [dɪ'raɪv] *vt-vi* derivar(se).

derogatory [dɪ'rɒgətərɪ] *adj* despectivo,-a.

descend [dɪ'send] *vt-vi* bajar.

descendant [dɪ'sendənt] *n* descendiente.

descent [dɪ'sent] *n* **1** descenso, bajada. **2** pendiente.

describe [dɪ'skraɪb] *vt* describir.

description [dɪ'skrɪpʃən] *n* descripción.

desert[1] ['dezət] *n* desierto.

desert[2] [dɪ'zɜːt] *vt* abandonar, dejar. ▶ *vi* desertar.

deserve [dɪ'zɜːv] *vt* merecerse.

design [dɪ'zaɪn] *n* diseño. ▶ *vt-vi* diseñar.

desire [dɪ'zaɪə'] *n* deseo. ▶ *vt* desear.

desk [desk] *n* **1** pupitre. **2** escritorio, mesa *(de trabajo)*.

desktop ['desktɒp] *n* escritorio.
■ **desktop computer** ordenador de sobremesa; **desktop publishing** autoedición.

despair [dɪs'peə'] *n* desesperación. ▶ *vi* desesperarse.

despatch [dɪs'pætʃ] *vt-n* → dispatch.

desperate ['despərət] *adj* desesperado,-a.

desperation [despə'reɪʃən] *n* desesperación.

despicable [dɪ'spɪkəbəl] *adj* despreciable.

despise [dɪ'spaɪz] *vt* despreciar.

despite [dɪ'spaɪt] *prep* a pesar de.

dessert [dɪ'zɜːt] *n* postre.

destination [destɪ'neɪʃən] *n* destino.

destiny ['destɪnɪ] *n* destino.

destroy [dɪ'strɔɪ] *vt* destruir.

destruction [dɪ'strʌkʃən] *n* destrucción.

detach [dɪ'tætʃ] *vt* separar.

detail ['diːteɪl] *n* detalle.

detect [dɪ'tekt] *vt* detectar.

detective [dɪ'tektɪv] *n* detective.

detention [dɪ'tenʃən] *n* detención.

detergent [dɪ'tɜːdʒənt] *n* detergente.

determine [dɪ'tɜːmɪn] *vt* determinar.

deterrent [dɪ'terənt] *adj* disuasivo,-a. ▶ *n* fuerza disuasoria.

detest [dɪ'test] *vt* detestar.

detour ['diːtuə'] *n* desvío.

devaluation [diːvæljuː'eɪʃən] *n* devaluación.

develop [dɪ'veləp] *vt* **1** desarrollar. **2** revelar *(carrete)*. ▶ *vi* desarrollarse.

development [dɪ'veləpmənt] *n* **1** desarrollo. **2** revelado *(de carrete)*.

deviate ['diːvɪeɪt] *vi* desviarse.

device [dɪ'vaɪs] n mecanismo, dispositivo.

devil ['devəl] n diablo.

devise [dɪ'vaɪz] vt idear.

devoted [dɪ'vəʊtɪd] adj fiel.

devotion [dɪ'vəʊʃən] n dedicación.

dew [djuː] n rocío.

dexterity [dek'sterɪtɪ] n destreza, habilidad.

diabetes [daɪə'biːtiːz] n diabetes.

diagnosis [daɪəg'nəʊsɪs] n diagnóstico.

diagonal [daɪ'ægənəl] n diagonal.

diagram ['daɪəgræm] n diagrama, esquema, gráfico.

dial ['daɪəl] n 1 esfera (de reloj). 2 dial (de radio). 3 teclado (de teléfono). ► vt marcar. ■ **dialling code** prefijo telefónico; **dialling tone** señal de llamada.

dialect ['daɪəlekt] n dialecto.

dialogue ['daɪəlɒg] (US **dialog**) n diálogo.

diameter [daɪ'æmɪtəʳ] n diámetro.

diamond ['daɪəmənd] n diamante.

diaper ['daɪəpəʳ] n US pañal.

diarrhoea [daɪə'rɪə] n diarrea.

diary ['daɪərɪ] n 1 diario. 2 agenda.

dice [daɪs] n dado.

dictate [dɪk'teɪt] vt dictar. ► vi mandar.

dictation [dɪk'teɪʃən] n dictado.

dictator [dɪk'teɪtəʳ] n dictador,-ra.

dictionary ['dɪkʃənərɪ] n diccionario.

did [dɪd] pt → do.

die [daɪ] vi morir.

to die away vi desvanecerse.

diesel ['diːzəl] n gasóleo.

diet ['daɪət] n dieta, régimen. ● **to go on a diet** ponerse a régimen.

differ ['dɪfəʳ] vi diferir.

difference ['dɪfərəns] n diferencia.

different ['dɪfərənt] adj diferente, distinto,-a.

difficult ['dɪfɪkəlt] adj difícil.

dig [dɪg] vt 1 cavar (hoyo), excavar (túnel). 2 clavar, hincar (con uñas).

to dig out/up vt desenterrar.

digest ['daɪdʒest] n resumen.

digestion [dɪ'dʒestʃən] n digestión.

digestive [daɪ'dʒestɪv] adj digestivo,-a. ■ **digestive tract** aparato digestivo.

dignity ['dɪgnɪtɪ] n dignidad.

dike [daɪk] n US → dyke.

diligence ['dɪlɪdʒəns] n diligencia.

dilute [daɪ'luːt] vt diluir.

dim [dɪm] adj 1 débil, difuso,-a, tenue. 2 oscuro,-a. 3 borroso,-a. 4 fam tonto,-a. ► vt 1 bajar, atenuar. 2 fig difuminar.

dime [daɪm] n US moneda de diez centavos.

dimension [dɪ'menʃən] n dimensión.

dimple ['dɪmpəl] n hoyuelo.

din [dɪn] n alboroto.

dine [daɪn] vi cenar.

diner ['daɪnə'] n 1 comensal. 2 US restaurante barato.

dinghy ['dɪŋgɪ] n bote.

dingy ['dɪndʒɪ] adj 1 sucio,-a, sórdido,-a. 2 deslucido,-a, deslustrado,-a (ropa).

dining car ['daɪnɪŋkɑː'] n coche restaurante.

dining room ['daɪnɪŋruːm] n comedor.

dinner ['dɪnə'] n comida, cena. ● to have dinner cenar. ■ dinner jacket esmoquin; dinner table mesa de comedor.

dinosaur ['daɪnəsɔː'] n dinosaurio.

dip [dɪp] n vt sumergir, bañar.

diploma [dɪ'pləumə] n diploma.

diplomacy [dɪ'pləuməsɪ] n diplomacia.

direct [dɪ'rekt, daɪ'rekt] adj directo,-a. ► vt dirigir.

direction [dɪ'rekʃən, daɪ'rekʃən] n dirección. ► npl directions instrucciones de uso, modo de empleo.

director [dɪ'rektə', daɪ'rektə'] n director,-ra.

directory [dɪ'rektərɪ, daɪ'rektərɪ] n 1 guía telefónica. 2 callejero.

dirt [dɜːt] n suciedad.

dirty ['dɜːtɪ] adj 1 sucio,-a. 2 verde (chiste). ► vt-vi ensuciar(se). ■ dirty trick cochinada; dirty word palabrota.

disabled [dɪs'eɪbəld] adj minusválido,-a, incapacitado,-a.

disadvantage [dɪsəd'vɑːntɪdʒ] n desventaja.

disagree [dɪsə'griː] vi 1 discrepar. 2 sentar mal (comida).

disappear [dɪsə'pɪə'] vi desaparecer.

disappoint [dɪsə'pɔɪnt] vt decepcionar, defraudar.

disaster [dɪ'zɑːstə'] n desastre.

disc [dɪsk] n 1 disco. 2 disquete. ■ disc jockey discjockey.

discard [dɪs'kɑːd] vt desechar.

discern [dɪ'sɜːn] vt discernir.

discharge [(n) 'dɪstʃɑːdʒ, (vb) dɪs'tʃɑːdʒ] n 1 descarga. 2 liberación (de preso). 3 alta (de paciente). ► vt 1 liberar (preso). 2 dar de alta (paciente). 3 licenciar (soldado).

discipline ['dɪsɪplɪn] n disciplina.

disco ['dɪskəu] n fam discoteca.

discolour [dɪs'kʌlə'] (US discolor) vt-vi desteñir(se).

disconnect [dɪskə'nekt] vt desconectar.

discotheque ['dɪskətek] n discoteca.

discount [(n) 'dɪskaunt, (vb) dɪs'kaunt] n descuento. ► vt descontar.

discourage [dɪsˈkʌrɪdʒ] vt **1** desanimar. **2** disuadir.

discover [dɪˈskʌvəʳ] vt descubrir.

discovery [dɪˈskʌvərɪ] n descubrimiento.

discriminate [dɪˈskrɪmɪneɪt] vi discriminar.

discus [ˈdɪskəs] n disco.

discuss [dɪˈskʌs] vt-vi discutir.

discussion [dɪˈskʌʃən] n discusión.

disease [dɪˈziːz] n enfermedad.

disembark [dɪsɪmˈbɑːk] vt-vi desembarcar.

disgrace [dɪsˈgreɪs] n **1** desgracia. **2** escándalo, vergüenza.

disguise [dɪsˈgaɪz] n disfraz. ► vt disfrazar.

disgusting [dɪsˈgʌstɪŋ] adj asqueroso,-a, repugnante.

dish [dɪʃ] n plato, fuente *(para servir)*. • **to do the dishes** lavar los platos.

dishcloth [ˈdɪʃklɒθ] n paño de cocina.

dishevelled [dɪˈʃevəld] adj **1** despeinado,-a *(pelo)*. **2** desarreglado,-a *(aspecto)*.

dishwasher [ˈdɪʃwɒʃəʳ] n lavavajillas.

disinfectant [dɪsɪnˈfektənt] n desinfectante.

disk [dɪsk] n disco. ▪ **disk drive** disquetera.

diskette [dɪsˈket] n disquete.

dislike [dɪsˈlaɪk] n aversión, antipatía. ► vt no gustar.

dislodge [dɪsˈlɒdʒ] vt desalojar.

dismal [ˈdɪzməl] adj triste.

dismantle [dɪsˈmæntəl] vt-vi desmontar(se), desarmar(se).

dismiss [dɪsˈmɪs] vt **1** despedir *(empleado)*. **2** descartar, desechar.

disobey [dɪsəˈbeɪ] vt-vi desobedecer.

disorder [dɪsˈɔːdəʳ] n desorden.

dispatch [dɪsˈpætʃ] n **1** despacho, parte. **2** reportaje *(de corresponsalía)*. **3** envío. ► vt enviar.

dispenser [dɪsˈpensəʳ] n máquina expendedora.

display [dɪˈspleɪ] n **1** exposición *(de artículos)*. **2** exhibición *(de fuerzas)*. **3** visualización *(en pantalla)*. ► vt mostrar, exponer.

disposable [dɪˈspəʊzəbəl] adj desechable.

dispute [(n) ˈdɪspjuːt, (vb) dɪsˈpjuːt] n discusión, disputa. ► vt cuestionar.

disqualify [dɪsˈkwɒlɪfaɪ] vt descalificar.

disrupt [dɪsˈrʌpt] vt trastornar.

dissatisfied [dɪsˈsætɪsfaɪd] adj descontento,-a.

dissident [ˈdɪsɪdənt] adj-n disidente.

dissolve [dɪˈzɒlv] vt-vi disolver(se).

dissuade [dɪˈsweɪd] vt disuadir.

distance ['dɪstəns] n distancia. ► vt distanciar. • **from a distance** desde lejos; **in the distance** a lo lejos.

distinction [dɪ'stɪŋkʃən] n distinción.

distinguish [dɪ'stɪŋgwɪʃ] vt-vi distinguir(se).

distort [dɪ'stɔːt] vt deformar.

distract [dɪ'strækt] vt distraer.

distraction [dɪ'strækʃən] n distracción.

distress [dɪ'stres] n angustia. ► vt afligir. ■ **distress call/signal** señal de socorro.

distribute [dɪ'strɪbjuːt] vt distribuir.

distribution [dɪstrɪ'bjuːʃən] n distribución.

district ['dɪstrɪkt] n distrito. ■ **district council** municipio.

disturb [dɪ'stɜːb] vt molestar.

ditch [dɪtʃ] n 1 zanja, cuneta. 2 acequia (para agua).

dive [daɪv] n 1 zambullida. 2 buceo. 3 picado (pájaro, avión). 4 fam antro. ► vi 1 tirarse de cabeza (al agua). 2 bucear (bajo el agua). 3 bajar en picado (pájaro, avión).

diver ['daɪvə'] n 1 buceador,-ra. 2 saltador,-ra (de trampolín).

diversion [daɪ'vɜːʃən] n 1 desvío, desviación. 2 distracción.

diversity [daɪ'vɜːsɪtɪ] n diversidad.

divert [daɪ'vɜːt] vt 1 desviar. 2 distraer.

divide [dɪ'vaɪd] vt-vi dividir(se).

diving ['daɪvɪŋ] n 1 submarinismo. 2 saltos de trampolín. ■ **diving board** trampolín.

division [dɪ'vɪʒən] n división.

divorce [dɪ'vɔːs] n divorcio. ► vt-vi divorciarse de.

dizzy ['dɪzɪ] adj mareado,-a.

do [duː] aux: **do you smoke?**, ¿fumas?; **I don't want to dance**, no quiero bailar; **you don't smoke, do you?**, no fumas, ¿verdad? ► vt 1 hacer, realizar: **what are you doing?**, ¿qué haces? 2 ser suficiente: **ten packets will do us**, con diez paquetes tenemos suficiente. • **how do you do?** 1 ¿cómo está usted? (saludo). 2 mucho gusto, encantado,-a (respuesta).

to do up vt 1 fam abrocharse, atar. 2 envolver. 3 arreglar, renovar.

dock¹ [dɒk] n 1 muelle (en puerto). 2 banquillo (de los acusados).

dockyard ['dɒkjɑːd] n astillero.

doctor ['dɒktə'] n médico,-a.

document ['dɒkjəmənt] n documento.

documentary [dɒkjə'mentərɪ] adj-n documental.

does [dʌz] 3rd pers sing pres → do.

dog [dɒg] n perro,-a.

do-it-yourself [duːɪtjɔː'self] n bricolaje.

dole [dəʊl] n GB fam subsidio de desempleo. • **to be on the dole** estar en el paro.

doll [dɒl] n muñeca.

dollar ['dɒləʳ] n dólar.

dolphin ['dɒlfɪn] n delfín.

domain [də'meɪn] n dominio.

domestic [də'mestɪk] adj 1 doméstico,-a (animal). 2 nacional (vuelo).

dominate ['dɒmɪneɪt] vt-vi dominar.

domino ['dɒmɪnəʊ] n ficha de dominó. ► npl **dominoes** dominó.

donate [dəʊ'neɪt] vt donar, hacer un donativo de.

done [dʌn] pp → do.

donkey ['dɒŋkɪ] n burro,-a.

donor ['dəʊnəʳ] n donante.

don't [dəʊnt] aux contracción de do + not.

door [dɔːʳ] n puerta. • **to answer the door** abrir la puerta.

doorbell ['dɔːbel] n timbre.

doorman ['dɔːmən] n portero.

door-to-door [dɔːtə'dɔːr] adj a domicilio.

doorway ['dɔːweɪ] n entrada, portal.

dosage ['dəʊsɪdʒ] n posología.

dose [dəʊs] n dosis.

dot [dɒt] n punto.

double ['dʌbəl] adj-adv doble. ► n doble. ► vt-vi doblar(se). ► npl **doubles** dobles. ■ **double bass** contrabajo; **double bed** cama de matrimonio; **double chin** papada; **double room** habitación doble.

double-decker [dʌbəl'dekəʳ] n GB autobús de dos pisos.

doubt [daʊt] n duda. ► vt dudar. • **no doubt** sin duda.

dough [dəʊ] n 1 masa (de pan). 2 fam pasta (dinero).

doughnut ['dəʊnʌt] n rosquilla, donut.

dove[1] [dʌv] n paloma.

dove[2] [dəʊv] pt US → dive.

down[1] [daʊn] prep abajo, hacia abajo. ► adv 1 abajo, hacia abajo, al suelo. 2 estropeado,-a: *the computer is down*, el ordenador está estropeado. ► adj fam deprimido. ■ **down payment** entrada.

down[2] [daʊn] n 1 plumón. 2 vello, pelusa, pelusilla.

downhill [daʊn'hɪl] adv cuesta abajo. ► adj en pendiente.

download ['daʊn'ləʊd] vt bajar, descargar.

downpour ['daʊnpɔːʳ] n chaparrón.

downstairs [daʊn'steəz] adv abajo: *to go downstairs*, bajar la escalera. ► adj en la planta baja, de abajo.

downstream [daʊn'striːm] adv río abajo.

downtown [daʊn'taʊn] US adv al/en el centro de la ciudad. ► adj del centro de la ciudad.

downward ['daʊnwəd] adj 1 descendente. 2 a la baja.

downwards [ˈdaʊnwədz] *adv* hacia abajo.

doze [dəʊz] *n* cabezada.

dozen [ˈdʌzən] *n* docena.

draft [drɑːft] *n* 1 borrador. 2 letra de cambio, giro. 3 US → draught.

draftsman [ˈdrɑːftsmən] *n* US → draughtsman.

drag [dræg] *n fam* calada. ► *vt* 1 arrastrar. 2 rastrear, dragar. • **in drag** vestido de mujer.

dragon [ˈdrægən] *n* dragón.

drain [dreɪn] *n* desagüe, alcantarilla. ► *vt* 1 drenar *(pantano)*. 2 desecar *(lago)*. 3 apurar *(vaso)*. 4 vaciar *(depósito)*. 5 escurrir *(verduras)*. ► *vi* escurrirse.

drainpipe [ˈdreɪnpaɪp] *n* (tubería de) desagüe.

drama [ˈdrɑːmə] *n* 1 drama. 2 teatro, arte dramático.

drank [dræŋk] *pt* → drink.

drastic [ˈdræstɪk] *adj* drástico,-a.

draught [drɑːft] *n* 1 corriente de aire. 2 trago. ► *npl* **draughts** GB damas. • **on draught** a presión, de barril.

draughtsman [ˈdrɑːftsmən] *n* delineante.

draw [drɔː] *n* 1 sorteo. 2 empate. ► *vt* 1 dibujar *(línea, círculo)*. 2 tirar de. 3 correr *(cortinas)*. 4 cobrar *(sueldo)*. 5 extender *(talón)*. 6 sacar *(conclusión)*. • **to draw apart** separarse.

to draw back *vi* retroceder.

to draw in *vi* apartarse.

to draw on *vt* recurrir a.

drawback [ˈdrɔːbæk] *n* inconveniente.

drawer [ˈdrɔːəʳ] *n* cajón.

drawing [ˈdrɔːɪŋ] *n* dibujo. ■ **drawing pin** GB chincheta; **drawing room** sala de estar.

drawn [drɔːn] *pp* → draw.

dreadful [ˈdredfʊl] *adj* espantoso,-a.

dream [driːm] *n* sueño. ► *vt-vi* soñar.

dreamt [dremt] *pt-pp* → dream.

dress [dres] *n* 1 vestido. 2 ropa. ► *vt* 1 vestir. 2 vendar *(herida)*. 3 aliñar *(ensalada)*. ► *vi* vestirse. ■ **dress rehearsal** ensayo general *(con trajes)*.

to dress up *vi* disfrazarse.

dresser [ˈdresəʳ] *n* 1 GB aparador. 2 US tocador.

dressing [ˈdresɪŋ] *n* 1 vendaje. 2 aliño *(de ensalada)*. ■ **dressing gown** bata; **dressing table** tocador.

drew [druː] *pt* → draw.

dribble [ˈdrɪbəl] *n* 1 gotas. 2 baba. ► *vi* 1 gotear *(líquido)*. 2 babear *(bebé)*. ► *vt* driblar, regatear *(en fútbol)*.

drier [ˈdraɪəʳ] *n* → dryer.

drift [drɪft] *n* 1 flujo. 2 montón *(de arena)*. 3 *fig* significado. ► *vi* ir a la deriva.

drill [drɪl] *n* 1 taladro. 2 broca. 3 ejercicio. 4 fresa *(de dentista)*. ► *vt* taladrar.

drink [drɪŋk] *n* bebida, copa. ▸ *vt-vi* beber.

drinking ['drɪŋkɪŋ] *n*. ▪ **drinking water** agua potable.

drip [drɪp] *n* 1 goteo. 2 gota a gota *(de suero)*. ▸ *vi* gotear.

drive [draɪv] *n* 1 paseo en coche. 2 camino de entrada. 3 drive *(golf, tenis)*. 4 transmisión *(en motor)*. 5 tracción *(en coche)*. 6 unidad de disco. ▸ *vt* 1 conducir. 2 llevar, acompañar: *I'll drive you home*, te llevaré a casa. 3 volver: *you drive me mad*, me vuelves loco.

driven ['drɪvən] *pp* → drive.

driver ['draɪvə'] *n* conductor,-ra.

driving ['draɪvɪŋ] *adj*. ▪ **driving licence** carnet, permiso de conducir; **driving school** autoescuela.

drizzle ['drɪzəl] *n* llovizna. ▸ *vi* lloviznar.

dromedary ['drɒmədəri] *n* dromedario.

drone [drəʊn] *n* zángano.

drop [drɒp] *n* 1 gota. 2 pastilla. 3 pendiente, desnivel. 4 caída. ▸ *vt* 1 dejar caer: *he dropped the glass*, se le cayó el vaso. 2 *fam* romper con. 3 abandonar *(hábito)*. 4 no seleccionar, excluir *(de equipo)*. ▸ *vi* 1 caerse *(persona)*. 2 bajar *(precios, voz)*. 3 amainar *(viento)*.

to drop off *vi* 1 *fam* quedarse dormido,-a. 2 disminuir.

to drop out *vi* 1 dejar los estudios. 2 retirarse *(de un partido)*.

dropper ['drɒpə'] *n* cuentagotas.

drought [draʊt] *n* sequía.

drove [drəʊv] *pt* → drive.

drown [draʊn] *vt-vi* ahogar(se).

drug [drʌg] *n* 1 medicamento. 2 droga. ▸ *vt* drogar. • **to be on/take drugs** drogarse. ▪ **drug addict** drogadicto,-a; **drug pusher** traficante de drogas.

drugstore ['drʌgstɔː'] *n* US establecimiento donde se compran medicamentos, periódicos, comida etc.

drum [drʌm] *n* 1 tambor. 2 bidón *(contenedor)*. ▸ *vi* tocar el tambor. ▸ *npl* **drums** batería.

drumstick ['drʌmstɪk] *n* 1 baqueta. 2 muslo *(de pollo)*.

drunk [drʌŋk] *pp* → drink. ▸ *adj-n* borracho,-a.

dry [draɪ] *adj* seco,-a. ▸ *vt-vi* secar(se).

dry-clean [draɪ'kliːn] *vt* limpiar en seco.

dry-cleaners [draɪ'kliːnəz] *n* tintorería.

dryer ['draɪə'] *n* secadora.

dual ['djuːəl] *adj* dual. ▪ **dual carriageway** autovía.

dub [dʌb] *vt* doblar *(película)*.

duchess ['dʌtʃəs] *n* duquesa.

duck [dʌk] *n* pato,-a.

duct [dʌkt] *n* conducto.
due [djuː] *adj* **1** debido,-a *(dinero)*. **2** pagadero,-a. **3** esperado,-a: *the train is due at five*, el tren debe llegar a las cinco. ► *npl* **dues** cuota. • **to be due to** deberse a. ■ **due date** vencimiento.
duel [ˈdjuːəl] *n* duelo.
duet [djuːˈet] *n* dúo.
dug [dʌg] *pt-pp* → dig.
duke [djuːk] *n* duque.
dull [dʌl] *adj* **1** apagado,-a *(color)*. **2** gris *(día)*. **3** sordo,-a *(sonido)*. **4** torpe *(persona)*. **5** pesado,-a *(película)*.
dumb [dʌm] *adj* mudo,-a.
dummy [ˈdʌmɪ] *n* **1** imitación. **2** maniquí. **3** GB chupete.
dump [dʌmp] *n* vertedero, basurero. ► *vt* tirar: *"No dumping"*, "Prohibido tirar basuras".
dune [djuːn] *n* duna.
dungarees [dʌŋgəˈriːz] *n* pantalones de peto, mono.
dungeon [ˈdʌndʒən] *n* mazmorra.
duo [ˈdjuːəʊ] *n* dúo.
duplicate [*(adj)* ˈdjuːplɪkət, *(n)* ˈdjuːplɪkeɪt] *adj* duplicado,-a. ► *n* duplicado. ► *vt* duplicar.
duration [djʊəˈreɪʃən] *n* duración.
during [ˈdjʊərɪŋ] *prep* durante.
dusk [dʌsk] *n* anochecer.
dust [dʌst] *n* polvo. ► *vt* quitar el polvo a.

dustbin [ˈdʌstbɪn] *n* GB cubo de la basura.
duster [ˈdʌstə'] *n* **1** paño, trapo. **2** borrador *(de pizarra)*.
dustman [ˈdʌstmən] *n* GB basurero.
dustpan [ˈdʌstpæn] *n* recogedor.
duty [ˈdjuːtɪ] *n* **1** deber, obligación. **2** impuesto. **3** guardia. • **to be on/off duty** estar/no estar de servicio/guardia.
duty-free [ˈdjuːtɪfriː] *adj* libre de impuestos.
duvet [ˈduːveɪ] *n* edredón.
dwarf [dwɔːf] *n* enano,-a.
dwelling [ˈdwelɪŋ] *n* morada.
dye [daɪ] *n* tinte. ► *vt-vi* teñir(se).
dynamic [daɪˈnæmɪk] *adj* dinámico,-a.
dynasty [ˈdɪnəstɪ] *n* dinastía.
dyslexia [dɪsˈleksɪə] *n* dislexia.

E

each [iːtʃ] *adj* cada. ► *pron* cada uno,-a. • **each other** el/la uno,-a al/la otro,-a: *we love each other*, nos queremos.
eager [ˈiːgə'] *adj* ansioso,-a, impaciente. • **to be eager for SB to do STH** estar deseando que ALGN haga algo.

eagle ['iːgəl] n águila.
ear¹ [ɪəʳ] n 1 oreja. 2 oído.
ear² [ɪəʳ] n espiga *(de trigo)*.
earache ['ɪəreɪk] n dolor de oídos.
eardrum ['ɪədrʌm] n tímpano.
early ['ɜːlɪ] adj-adv temprano,-a.
earn [ɜːn] vt 1 ganar *(dinero)*. 2 merecer(se).
earnings ['ɜːnɪŋz] npl ingresos.
earphones ['ɪəfəʊnz] npl auriculares.
earplug ['ɪəplʌg] n tapón.
earring ['ɪərɪŋ] n pendiente.
earth [ɜːθ] n tierra. ■ the Earth la Tierra.
earthquake ['ɜːθkweɪk] n terremoto.
earthworm ['ɜːθwɜːm] n lombriz.
ease [iːz] n 1 facilidad. 2 tranquilidad. 3 comodidad. ► vt aliviar, calmar. ► vi disminuir. • at ease relajado,-a.
to ease off vi disminuir.
easel ['iːzəl] n caballete.
easily ['iːzɪlɪ] adv 1 fácilmente. 2 con mucho.
east [iːst] n este, oriente. ► adj oriental, del este. ► adv hacia el este.
Easter ['iːstəʳ] n 1 Pascua. 2 Semana Santa.
eastern ['iːstən] adj oriental, del este.
easy ['iːzɪ] adj fácil. • take it easy! ¡tranquilo,-a! ■ easy chair sillón.

easy-going [iːzɪ'gəʊɪŋ] adj tranquilo,-a.
eat [iːt] vt-vi comer.
to eat out vi comer fuera.
eaten ['iːtən] pp → eat.
ebb [eb] n reflujo.
ebony ['ebənɪ] n ébano.
echo ['ekəʊ] n eco.
ecology [ɪ'kɒlədʒɪ] n ecología.
economical [iːkə'nɒmɪkəl] adj barato,-a, económico,-a.
economize [ɪ'kɒnəmaɪz] vi ahorrar.
economy [ɪ'kɒnəmɪ] n economía.
ecosystem ['iːkəʊsɪstəm] n ecosistema.
eczema ['eksɪmə] n eccema.
edge [edʒ] n 1 borde. 2 canto *(de moneda)*. 3 filo *(de navaja)*. • on edge impaciente; to have the edge on/over SB llevar ventaja a ALGN.
edible ['edɪbəl] adj comestible.
edition [ɪ'dɪʃən] n edición.
editor ['edɪtəʳ] n 1 editor,-ra. 2 director,-ra *(de periódico)*.
editorial [edɪ'tɔːrɪəl] adj-n editorial.
educate ['edjʊkeɪt] vt educar.
education [edjʊ'keɪʃən] n educación.
eel [iːl] n anguila.
effect [ɪ'fekt] n efecto. ► vt efectuar. • to come into effect entrar en vigor.
effective [ɪ'fektɪv] adj 1 eficaz *(medicamento)*. 2 efectivo,-a.

effervescent [efə'vesənt] adj
efervescente.

efficiency [ı'fıʃənsı] n 1 efi-
ciencia (de persona). 2 eficacia
(de producto). 3 rendimiento
(de máquina).

effort ['efət] n esfuerzo.

egg [eg] n huevo. ▪ **boiled egg**
huevo pasado por agua; **egg
cup** huevera; **fried egg** huevo
frito; **hard-boiled egg** huevo duro.

eggplant ['egplɑːnt] n berenjena.

egoist ['iːgəʊıst] n egoísta.

eiderdown ['aıdədaʊn] n edredón.

eight [eıt] num ocho.

eighteen [eı'tiːn] num dieciocho.

eighteenth [eı'tiːnθ] adj de-
cimoctavo,-a.

eighth [eıtθ] adj octavo,-a.

eightieth ['eıtıθ] adj octogési-
mo,-a.

eighty ['eıtı] num ochenta.

either ['aıðəʳ, 'iːðəʳ] adj 1 cualquiera. 2 ni el uno/la una ni
el otro/la otra, ninguno,-a: *I
don't like either of them*, no
me gusta ninguno de los dos.
3 cada, los/las dos, ambos,
-as: *with a gun in either
hand*, con una pistola en cada mano. ▶ *conj* o. ▶ *adv* tampoco. ▶ *pron* cualquiera de los
dos.

eject [ı'dʒekt] vt expulsar.

elaborate [ı'læbərət] adj 1 de-
tallado,-a. 2 complicado,-a.

elastic [ı'læstık] adj elástico,-a.

elbow ['elbəʊ] n codo.

elder ['eldəʳ] adj-n mayor.

elderly ['eldəlı] adj mayor, anciano,-a.

eldest ['eldıst] adj mayor.

elect [ı'lekt] vt elegir.

election [ı'lekʃən] n elección.

electric [ı'lektrık] adj eléctrico,
-a. ▪ **electric shock** electro-
choque, descarga eléctrica.

electrical [ı'lektrıkəl] adj eléctrico,-a. ▪ **electrical appliance** electrodoméstico.

electricity [ılek'trısıtı] n electricidad.

electron [ı'lektrɒn] n electrón.

electronic [ılek'trɒnık] adj
electrónico,-a. ▪ **electronic
mail** correo electrónico.

elegant ['elıgənt] adj elegante.

element ['elımənt] n elemento.

elephant ['elıfənt] n elefante.

elevator ['elıveıtəʳ] n US ascensor.

eleven [ı'levən] num once.

eleventh [ı'levənθ] adj undécimo,-a.

eliminate [ı'lımıneıt] vt eliminar.

elk [elk] n alce.

elm [elm] n olmo.

else [els] adv otro, más. ● **or
else** si no: *hurry up or else
you'll be late*, date prisa o
llegarás tarde.

endorse

elsewhere [els'weə'] *adv* en otro sitio.

e-mail ['i:meɪl] *n* correo electrónico. ► *vt* enviar un correo electrónico a.

embankment [ɪm'bæŋkmənt] *n* **1** terraplén. **2** dique *(de río)*.

embark [ɪm'bɑːk] *vt-vi* embarcar(se).

embarrass [ɪm'bærəs] *vt* avergonzar. • **to be embarrassed** sentir vergüenza.

embarrassing [ɪm'bærəsɪŋ] *adj* embarazoso,-a.

embassy ['embəsɪ] *n* embajada.

embrace [ɪm'breɪs] *n* abrazo. ► *vt* abrazar.

embroidery [ɪm'brɔɪdərɪ] *n* bordado.

embryo ['embrɪəʊ] *n* embrión.

emerald ['emərəld] *n* esmeralda.

emerge [ɪ'mɜːdʒ] *vi* emerger.

emergency [ɪ'mɜːdʒənsɪ] *n* **1** emergencia. **2** urgencia *(médica)*. ▪ **emergency exit** salida de emergencia.

emery ['emərɪ] *n* esmeril. ▪ **emery board** lima de uñas.

emigration [emɪ'greɪʃən] *n* emigración.

emission [ɪ'mɪʃən] *n* emisión.

emit [ɪ'mɪt] *vt* emitir.

emotion [ɪ'məʊʃən] *n* emoción.

emperor ['empərə'] *n* emperador.

emphasis ['emfəsɪs] *n* énfasis.

empire ['empaɪə'] *n* imperio.

employ [ɪm'plɔɪ] *vt* emplear.

employee [em'plɔɪiː, emplɔɪ'iː] *n* empleado,-a, trabajador,-ra.

employer [em'plɔɪə'] *n* patrón,-ona.

employment [em'plɔɪmənt] *n* empleo.

empress ['emprəs] *n* emperatriz.

empty ['emptɪ] *adj* **1** vacío,-a. **2** libre. ► *vt-vi* vaciar(se).

enable [ɪ'neɪbəl] *vt* permitir.

enamel [ɪ'næməl] *n* esmalte.

encircle [ɪn'sɜːkəl] *vt* rodear.

enclose [ɪn'kləʊz] *vt* **1** cercar, rodear. **2** adjuntar.

encounter [ɪn'kaʊntə'] *n* encuentro. ► *vt* encontrarse con.

encourage [ɪn'kʌrɪdʒ] *vt* **1** animar. **2** fomentar.

encouraging [ɪn'kʌrɪdʒɪŋ] *adj* alentador,-ra.

encyclopaedia [ensaɪklə'piːdɪə] *n* enciclopedia.

end [end] *n* **1** fin, final. **2** extremo, punta. **3** objeto, objetivo. ► *vt-vi* acabar(se), terminar(se).

endanger [ɪn'deɪndʒə'] *vt* poner en peligro.

ending ['endɪŋ] *n* final.

endive ['endaɪv] *n* endibia.

endless ['endləs] *adj* interminable.

endorse [ɪn'dɔːs] *vt* **1** endosar *(talón)*. **2** aprobar.

endurance [ɪn'djuərəns] n resistencia.

enemy ['enəmɪ] n enemigo,-a.

energy ['enədʒɪ] n energía.

enforce [ɪn'fɔːs] vt hacer cumplir.

engaged [ɪn'geɪdʒd] adj 1 prometido,-a. 2 ocupado,-a (servicio). 3 comunicando (teléfono).

engagement [ɪn'geɪdʒmənt] n 1 petición de mano, noviazgo. 2 compromiso, cita.

engine ['endʒɪn] n 1 motor. 2 máquina, locomotora.

engineer [endʒɪ'nɪər] n 1 ingeniero,-a. 2 US maquinista.

engrave [ɪn'greɪv] vt grabar.

enhance [ɪn'hɑːns] vt realzar.

enjoy [ɪn'dʒɔɪ] vt gozar de, disfrutar de. • **to enjoy oneself** divertirse, pasarlo bien.

enlargement [ɪn'lɑːdʒmənt] n ampliación.

enough [ɪ'nʌf] adj bastante, suficiente. ▶ adv bastante. ▶ pron suficiente. • **that's enough!** ¡ya basta!

enquire [ɪŋ'kwaɪər] vi 1 preguntar. 2 investigar.

enquiry [ɪŋ'kwaɪərɪ] n 1 pregunta. 2 investigación.

enrol [ɪn'rəʊl] vt-vi matricular(se).

entail [ɪn'teɪl] vt suponer.

entangle [ɪn'tæŋgəl] vt enredar.

enter ['entər] vt entrar en. ▶ vi entrar.

enterprise ['entəpraɪz] n empresa.

entertain [entə'teɪn] vt entretener, divertir.

entertainment [entə'teɪnmənt] n entretenimiento.

enthusiasm [ɪn'θjuːzɪæzəm] n entusiasmo.

entice [ɪn'taɪs] vt seducir.

entire [ɪn'taɪər] adj entero,-a.

entrails ['entreɪlz] npl entrañas.

entrance ['entrəns] n entrada.

entrepreneur [ɒntrəprə'nɜːr] n empresario,-a.

entrust [ɪn'trʌst] vt confiar.

entry ['entrɪ] n entrada. • **"No entry"** "Prohibida la entrada".

envelope ['envələʊp] n sobre.

envious ['envɪəs] adj envidioso,-a.

environment [ɪn'vaɪrənmənt] n medio ambiente.

envy ['envɪ] vt envidiar.

epidemic [epɪ'demɪk] n epidemia.

epilepsy ['epɪlepsɪ] n epilepsia.

episode ['epɪsəʊd] n episodio.

equal ['iːkwəl] adj igual. ▶ vt 1 ser igual a, equivaler a. 2 igualar.

equation [ɪ'kweɪʒən] n ecuación.

equator [ɪ'kweɪtər] n ecuador.

equip [ɪ'kwɪp] vt equipar.

equipment [ɪ'kwɪpmənt] n equipo.

equivalent [ɪ'kwɪvələnt] adj-n equivalente.

era ['ɪərə] *n* era.

erase [ɪ'reɪz] *vt* borrar.

eraser [ɪ'reɪzə'] *n* **1** US goma de borrar. **2** borrador *(de pizarra)*.

erosion [ɪ'rəʊʒən] *n* erosión.

erotic [ɪ'rɒtɪk] *adj* erótico,-a.

errand ['erənd] *n* encargo, recado.

erratic [ɪ'rætɪk] *adj* inconstante.

error ['erə'] *n* error.

eruption [ɪ'rʌpʃən] *n* erupción.

escalator ['eskəleɪtə'] *n* escalera mecánica.

escape [ɪ'skeɪp] *n* fuga. ► *vi* escaparse. ► *vt* evitar.

escort [ɪ'skɔːt] *vt* **1** acompañar. **2** escoltar.

especial [ɪ'speʃəl] *adj* especial.

essay ['eseɪ] *n* **1** redacción, trabajo. **2** ensayo.

essence ['esəns] *n* esencia.

essential [ɪ'senʃəl] *adj* esencial.

establish [ɪ'stæblɪʃ] *vt* establecer.

estate [ɪ'steɪt] *n* **1** finca. **2** urbanización. ■ **estate agent** agente inmobiliario,-a; **estate car** GB coche familiar.

estimate [*(n)* 'estɪmət, *(vb)* 'estɪmeɪt] *n* **1** cálculo. **2** presupuesto. ► *vt* calcular.

estuary ['estjʊərɪ] *n* estuario.

eternity [ɪ'tɜːnətɪ] *n* eternidad.

ethic ['eθɪk] *n* ética.

eucalyptus [juːkə'lɪptəs] *n* eucalipto.

euphemism ['juːfəmɪzəm] *n* eufemismo.

euro ['jʊərəʊ] *n* euro.

evade [ɪ'veɪd] *vt* evadir.

evaluate [ɪ'væljʊeɪt] *vt* evaluar.

evaporate [ɪ'væpəreɪt] *vt-vi* evaporar(se).

eve [iːv] *n* víspera, vigilia.

even ['iːvən] *adj* **1** llano,-a, liso,-a *(superficie)*. **2** uniforme *(color)*. **3** igualado,-a *(puntuación)*. **4** par *(número)*. ► *adv* **1** hasta, incluso. **2** siquiera: *not even John was there*, ni siquiera John estaba allí. **3** aún, todavía.● **even if** aunque; **even so** incluso; **even though** aunque.

evening ['iːvnɪŋ] *n* tarde, noche. ● **good evening!** ¡buenas tardes!, ¡buenas noches!

event [ɪ'vent] *n* **1** suceso, acontecimiento. **2** prueba *(deportiva)*. ● **in any event** pase lo que pase; **in the event of** en caso de.

eventually [ɪ'ventʃʊəlɪ] *adv* finalmente.

ever ['evə'] *adv* **1** nunca, jamás. **2** alguna vez. **3** desde. ● **for ever** para siempre; **hardly ever** casi nunca.

evergreen ['evəgriːn] *adj* de hoja perenne. ■ **evergreen oak** encina.

everlasting [evə'lɑːstɪŋ] *adj* eterno,-a.

every ['evrɪ] *adj* cada, todos,-as

everybody ['evrɪbɒdɪ] *pron* todos,-as, todo el mundo.

everyday ['evrɪdeɪ] *adj* diario,-ade todos los días.

everyone ['evrɪwʌn] *pron* → everybody.

everything ['evrɪθɪŋ] *pron* todo.

everywhere ['evrɪweə'] *adv* **1** en/por todas partes. **2** a todas partes.

evidence ['evɪdəns] *n* pruebas. • **to give evidence** prestar declaración.

evident ['evɪdənt] *adj* evidente.

evil ['iːvəl] *adj* malo,-a. ► *n* mal.

evoke [ɪ'vəʊk] *vt* evocar.

evolution [iːvə'luːʃən] *n* evolución.

exact [ɪg'zækt] *adj* exacto,-a.

exaggerate [ɪg'zædʒəreɪt] *vt-vi* exagerar.

exam [ɪg'zæm] *n fam* examen.

examination [ɪgzæmɪ'neɪʃən] *n* **1** examen. **2** reconocimiento, chequeo. **3** interrogatorio.

examine [ɪg'zæmɪn] *vt* examinar.

example [ɪg'zɑːmpəl] *n* ejemplo. • **for example** por ejemplo.

excellent ['eksələnt] *adj* excelente.

except [ɪk'sept] *prep* excepto.

excess [ɪk'ses] *n* exceso.

exchange [ɪks'tʃeɪndʒ] *n* **1** cambio. **2** intercambio. ► *vt* cambiar, intercambiar. ■ **exchange rate** tipo de cambio.

excite [ɪk'saɪt] *vt* **1** entusiasmar. **2** excitar *(sexualmente)*.

exclamation [eksklə'meɪʃən] *n* exclamación. ■ **exclamation mark** signo de admiración.

exclude [ɪk'skluːd] *vt* excluir.

exclusive [ɪk'skluːsɪv] *adj* **1** exclusivo,-a. **2** selecto,-a.

excursion [ɪk'skɜːʒən] *n* excursión.

excuse [(*n*) ɪk'skjuːs, (*vb*) ɪk'skjuːz] *n* disculpa, excusa. ► *vt* perdonar, disculpar. • **excuse me!** ¡perdone!, ¡por favor!

execute ['eksɪkjuːt] *vt* ejecutar.

executive [ɪg'zekjətɪv] *adj-n* ejecutivo,-a.

exempt [ɪg'zempt] *adj* exento,-a, libre. ► *vt* eximir.

exercise ['eksəsaɪz] *n* ejercicio. ■ **exercise book** cuaderno.

exhaust [ɪg'zɔːst] *vt* agotar. ■ **exhaust pipe** tubo de escape.

exhausted [ɪg'zɔːstɪd] *adj* agotado,-a.

exhibit [ɪg'zɪbɪt] *n* objeto en exposición. ► *vt* **1** exponer. **2** mostrar, dar muestras de, manifestar.

exhibition [eksɪ'bɪʃən] *n* exposición.

exile ['eksaɪl] *n* exilio. ► *vt* exiliar.

exist [ɪg'zɪst] *vi* existir.

exit ['eksɪt] *n* salida.

exotic [eg'zɒtɪk] *adj* exótico,-a.

expand [ɪk'spænd] vt-vi ampliar(se).

expansion [ɪk'spænʃən] n expansión.

expect [ɪk'spekt] vt esperar. • **to be expecting** fam estar embarazada.

expedition [ekspɪ'dɪʃən] n expedición.

expel [ɪk'spel] vt expulsar.

expenditure [ɪk'spendɪtʃəʳ] n gasto.

expense [ɪk'spens] n gasto.

expensive [ɪk'spensɪv] adj caro,-a.

experience [ɪk'spɪərɪəns] n experiencia. ► vt experimentar.

experiment [ɪk'sperɪmənt] n experimento.

expert ['ekspɜːt] adj-n experto,-a.

expire [ɪk'spaɪəʳ] vi 1 vencer (contrato). 2 caducar (pasaporte).

expiry [ɪk'spaɪərɪ] n vencimiento. ■ **expiry date** fecha de caducidad.

explain [ɪk'spleɪn] vt-vi explicar.

explanation [eksplə'neɪʃən] n explicación.

explode [ɪk'spləʊd] vi estallar.

explore [ɪk'splɔːʳ] vt explorar.

explosion [ɪk'spləʊʒən] n explosión.

explosive [ɪk'spləʊsɪv] n explosivo.

export [(n) 'ekspɔːt, (vb) ɪk'spɔːt] n exportación. ► vt exportar.

expose [ɪk'spəʊz] vt exponer.

express [ɪk'spres] adj 1 expreso,-a (tren). 2 urgente (correo). ► vt expresar.

expression [ɪk'spreʃən] n expresión.

extend [ɪk'stend] vt extender.

extension [ɪk'stenʃən] n extensión.

extent [ɪk'stent] n extensión, alcance. • **to a certain extent** hasta cierto punto.

external [ek'stɜːnəl] adj externo,-a.

extinct [ɪk'stɪŋkt] adj 1 extinto,-a. 2 extinguido,-a.

extra ['ekstrə] adj-n extra. ■ **extra charge** suplemento; **extra time** prórroga.

extract [ɪk'strækt] vt extraer.

extraordinary [ɪk'strɔːdənrɪ] adj extraordinario,-a.

extravagant [ɪk'strævəgənt] adj 1 derrochador,-ra. 2 exagerado,-a, excesivo,-a.

extreme [ɪk'striːm] adj 1 extremo,-a. 2 excepcional (caso). ► n extremo.

extremity [ɪk'stremɪtɪ] n extremidad.

eye [aɪ] n ojo.

eyebrow ['aɪbraʊ] n ceja.

eyelash ['aɪlæʃ] n pestaña.

eyelid ['aɪlɪd] n párpado.

eyeshadow ['aɪʃædəʊ] n sombra de ojos.

eyewitness ['aɪ'wɪtnəs] n testigo presencial.

F

f ['femɪnɪn] *abbr* fa *(nota)*.
fable ['feɪbəl] *n* fábula.
fabric ['fæbrɪk] *n* tela, tejido.
fabulous ['fæbjələs] *adj* fabuloso,-a.
facade [fə'sɑːd] *n* fachada.
façade [fə'sɑːd] *n* fachada.
face [feɪs] *n* 1 cara. 2 superficie. ▸ *vt* 1 dar a: *the house faces west*, la casa da al oeste. 2 afrontar, enfrentarse con/a. ▸ *vi* mirar hacia. ● **face down** boca abajo; **face up** boca arriba; **to lose face** desprestigiarse. ■ **face cream** crema facial; **face value** valor nominal.
to face up to *vt* afrontar.
facelift ['feɪslɪft] *n* lifting.
facility [fə'sɪlɪti] *n* facilidad. ▸ *npl* **facilities** instalaciones, servicios.
fact [fækt] *n* hecho. ● **in fact** de hecho.
factor ['fæktəʳ] *n* factor.
factory ['fæktərɪ] *n* fábrica.
faculty ['fækəltɪ] *n* facultad.
fade [feɪd] *vt* desteñir.
to fade away *vi* desvanecerse.
fag [fæg] *n* 1 *fam* lata, rollo. 2 GB *fam* pitillo.
fail [feɪl] *n* suspenso. ▸ *vt-vi* 1 fallar. 2 suspender. ▸ *vi* 1 fracasar. 2 quebrar, hacer bancarrota.

failing ['feɪlɪŋ] *n* defecto, fallo. ▸ *prep* a falta de.
failure ['feɪljəʳ] *n* 1 fracaso. 2 quiebra. 3 fallo, avería. 4 negativa.
faint [feɪnt] *adj* 1 débil. 2 pálido,-a. 3 vago,-a.
fair¹ [feəʳ] *adj* 1 justo,-a. 2 considerable: *he has a fair chance of getting the job*, tiene bastantes posibilidades de conseguir el trabajo. 3 rubio,-a, blanco,-a: *fair hair*, pelo rubio. ● **fair enough** de acuerdo. ■ **fair copy** copia en limpio; **fair play** juego limpio.
fair² [feəʳ] *n* feria, mercado.
fairground ['feəgraʊnd] *n* recinto ferial, parque de atracciones.
fairly ['feəlɪ] *adv* 1 justamente. 2 bastante.
fairy ['feərɪ] *n* hada. ■ **fairy tale** cuento de hadas.
faith [feɪθ] *n* fe.
faithful ['feɪθfʊl] *adj* fiel.
faithfully ['feɪθfʊlɪ] *adv* ● **yours faithfully** le saluda atentamente.
fake [feɪk] *n* falsificación. ▸ *adj* falso,-a, falsificado,-a. ▸ *vt* 1 falsificar. 2 fingir.
falcon ['fɔːlkən] *n* halcón.
fall [fɔːl] *n* 1 caída. 2 nevada. 3 US otoño. ▸ *vi* 1 caer, caerse. 2 bajar. ▸ *npl* **falls** cascada. ● **to fall short** no alcanzar; **to fall flat** salir mal.

fastener

to fall back vi retroceder.
to fall down vt-vi caer, caerse.
to fall out vi reñir, enfadarse.
fallen ['fɔːlən] pp → fall.
false [fɔːls] adj falso,-a. ■ **false alarm** falsa alarma; **false bottom** doble fondo; **false start** salida nula; **false teeth** dentadura postiza.
falsify ['fɔːlsɪfaɪ] vt falsificar.
fame [feɪm] n fama.
family ['fæmɪlɪ] n familia. ■ **family film** película apta para todos los públicos; **family name** apellido.
famine ['fæmɪn] n hambre.
famous ['feɪməs] adj famoso,-a.
fan [fæn] n 1 abanico. 2 ventilador (eléctrico). 3 fan. ► vt abanicar, ventilar.
fanatic [fə'nætɪk] adj-n fanático,-a.
fancy ['fænsɪ] n 1 fantasía. 2 capricho. ► adj elegante. ► vt 1 imaginarse, figurarse. 2 apetecer: *I fancy an ice cream*, me apetece un helado. 3 gustar: *my friend fancies you*, le gustas a mi amigo. ■ **fancy dress** disfraz.
fang [fæŋ] n colmillo.
fantastic [fæn'tæstɪk] adj fantástico,-a.
fantasy ['fæntəsɪ] n fantasía.
far [fɑːʳ] adj 1 lejano,-a. 2 opuesto,-a, extremo,-a: *at the far end of the stadium*, en el

otro extremo del estadio. ► adv 1 lejos. 2 mucho: *far better*, mucho mejor. • **as far as** hasta; **far away** lejos; **in so far as ...** en la medida en que ...; **so far 1** hasta ahora. 2 hasta cierto punto.
faraway ['fɑːrəweɪ] adj lejano,-a.
farce [fɑːs] n farsa.
fare [feəʳ] n tarifa, precio del billete/viaje.
farewell [feə'wel] interj ¡adiós! ► n despedida.
farm [fɑːm] n granja. ■ **farm labourer** jornalero,-a agrícola.
farmer ['fɑːməʳ] n agricultor, -ra, granjero,-a.
farming ['fɑːmɪŋ] n agricultura, ganadería. ■ **farming industry** industria agropecuaria.
farmyard ['fɑːmjɑːd] n corral.
fascinate ['fæsɪneɪt] vt fascinar.
fashion ['fæʃən] n 1 moda. 2 modo. • **in fashion** de moda; **out of fashion** pasado,-a de moda.
fashionable ['fæʃənəbəl] adj de moda.
fast[1] [fɑːst] adj 1 rápido,-a. 2 adelantado,-a: *my watch is fast*, mi reloj está adelantado. ► adv rápidamente, deprisa. ■ **fast food** comida rápida.
fast[2] [fɑːst] vi ayunar.
fasten ['fɑːsən] vt 1 sujetar. 2 atar. 3 abrochar.
fastener ['fɑːsənəʳ] n cierre.

fat [fæt] adj gordo,-a. ► n grasa.

fatal ['feɪtəl] adj 1 fatídico. 2 mortal.

fate [feɪt] n destino.

father ['fɑːðəʳ] n padre. ► vt engendrar. ■ **Father Christmas** Papá Noel.

father-in-law ['fɑːðərɪnlɔː] n suegro.

fatten ['fætən] vt 1 cebar. 2 engordar.

faucet ['fɔːsɪt] n US grifo.

fault [fɔːlt] n 1 defecto. 2 culpa. 3 error, falta. 4 falla (geológica). 5 falta (en deporte).

fauna ['fɔːnə] n fauna.

favour ['feɪvəʳ] (US **favor**) n favor. ► vt 1 favorecer. 2 estar a favor de.

favourite ['feɪvərɪt] (US **favorite**) adj-n preferido,-a.

fax [fæks] n fax. ► vt enviar por fax.

fear [fɪəʳ] n miedo, temor. ► vt-vi temer, tener miedo.

feast [fiːst] n 1 festín, banquete. 2 fiesta de guardar.

feat [fiːt] n proeza, hazaña.

feather ['feðəʳ] n pluma.

feature ['fiːtʃəʳ] n 1 rasgo, facción. 2 rasgo, característica. 3 artículo de fondo. ► vt 1 poner de relieve. 2 tener como protagonista. ■ **feature film** largometraje.

February ['februərɪ] n febrero.

fed [fed] pt-pp → feed.

federal ['fedərəl] adj federal.

federation [fedə'reɪʃən] n federación.

fed up [fed'ʌp] adj fam harto,-a.

fee [fiː] n honorarios, cuota, tarifa.

feeble ['fiːbəl] adj débil.

feed [fiːd] n pienso. ► vt alimentar, dar de comer a. ► vi alimentarse.

feel [fiːl] n tacto, sensación. ► vt 1 tocar, palpar. 2 sentir, notar. 3 creer: *I feel I ought to tell her*, creo que debería decírselo. ► vi 1 sentir(se), encontrarse: *do you feel ill?*, ¿te encuentras mal? 2 parecer: *it feels like leather*, parece piel. • **to feel like** apetecer: *I feel like an ice cream*, me apetece un helado.

feeling ['fiːlɪŋ] n 1 sentimiento. 2 sensación.

feet [fiːt] npl → foot.

feign [feɪn] vt fingir.

feline ['fiːlaɪn] adj-n felino,-a.

fell [fel] pt → fall.

fellow ['feləʊ] n fam tipo, tío.

felt¹ [felt] pt-pp → feel.

felt² [felt] n fieltro.

felt-tip pen ['felttɪp'pen] n rotulador.

female ['fiːmeɪl] n 1 hembra. 2 mujer, chica: *a white female*, una mujer blanca. ► adj 1 femenino,-a. 2 mujer: *a female singer*, una cantante. 3 hembra: *a female elephant*, un elefante hembra.

feminine ['femɪnɪn] *adj* femenino,-a. ► *n* femenino.
fence [fens] *n* valla, cerca. ► *vi* practicar la esgrima. ► *vt* cercar.
fencing ['fensɪŋ] *n* esgrima.
fender ['fendəʳ] *n* 1 pantalla. 2 US parachoques.
fennel ['fenəl] *n* hinojo.
ferment [(*n*) 'fɜːmənt, (*vb*) fə'ment] *n* fermento. ► *vt-vi* fermentar.
fern [fɜːn] *n* helecho.
ferret ['ferɪt] *n* hurón.
ferry ['ferɪ] *n* transbordador, ferry. ► *vt-vi* transportar.
fertile ['fɜːtaɪl] *adj* fértil.
fervent ['fɜːvənt] *adj* fervient.
festival ['festɪvəl] *n* 1 festival. 2 fiesta.
fetch [fetʃ] *vt* ir a por.
fetish ['fetɪʃ] *n* fetiche.
feudal ['fjuːdəl] *adj* feudal.
fever ['fiːvəʳ] *n* fiebre.
few [fjuː] *adj-pron* 1 pocos,-as. 2 **a few** unos,-as cuantos,-as, algunos,-as. • **as few as** solamente; **no fewer than** no menos de.
fiancé [fɪ'ænseɪ] *n* prometido.
fiancée [fɪ'ænseɪ] *n* prometida.
fib [fɪb] *n fam* bola.
fibre ['faɪbəʳ] (US **fiber**) *n* fibra.
fibreglass ['faɪbəɡlɑːs] (US **fiberglass**) *n* fibra de vidrio.
fiction ['fɪkʃən] *n* 1 novela, narrativa. 2 ficción.
fictitious [fɪk'tɪʃəs] *adj* ficticio,-a.

fiddle ['fɪdəl] *n* 1 *fam* violín. 2 *fam* estafa, trampa. ► *vi fam* juguetear. ► *vt fam* falsificar.
fidelity [fɪ'delɪtɪ] *n* fidelidad.
field [fiːld] *n* 1 campo. 2 yacimiento.
fierce [fɪəs] *adj* feroz.
fifteen [fɪf'tiːn] *num* quince.
fifteenth [fɪf'tiːnθ] *adj* decimoquinto,-a.
fifth [fɪfθ] *adj* quinto,-a.
fifty ['fɪftɪ] *num* cincuenta.
fig [fɪɡ] *n* higo.
fight [faɪt] *n* lucha, pelea. ► *vt-vi* pelearse, luchar.
to fight back *vi* resistir.
to fight off *vt* rechazar.
figure ['fɪɡəʳ] *n* 1 figura. 2 cifra, número. ► *vi* figurar. ► *vt* US suponer: *I figure she'll come*, supongo que vendrá. ▪ **figure skating** patinaje artístico.
to figure out *vt fam* comprender, explicarse.
file [faɪl] *n* 1 lima. 2 carpeta. 3 archivo, expediente. 4 archivo, fichero. 5 fila. ► *vt* 1 limar. 2 archivar, fichar. ► *vi* desfilar. • **in single file** en fila india.
filing cabinet ['faɪlɪŋkæbɪnət] *n* archivador.
fill [fɪl] *vt* 1 llenar. 2 rellenar. 3 empastar.
to fill in *vt* rellenar.
fillet ['fɪlɪt] *n* filete.
filling ['fɪlɪŋ] *n* empaste. ▪ **filling station** gasolinera.

film

film [fɪlm] *n* película. ▶ *vt* rodar, filmar. ■ **film star** estrella de cine.

filter [ˈfɪltə'] *n* filtro. ▶ *vt-vi* filtrar(se).

filth [fɪlθ] *n* suciedad.

fin [fɪn] *n* aleta.

final [ˈfaɪnəl] *adj* **1** final, último,-a. **2** definitivo,-a. ▶ *n* final. ▶ *npl* **finals** exámenes finales.

finance [ˈfaɪnæns] *vt* financiar. ▶ *n* finanzas.

find [faɪnd] *n* hallazgo. ▶ *vt* **1** encontrar. **2** declarar: *he was found guilty*, lo declararon culpable.

to find out *vt-vi* averiguar. ▶ *vi* enterarse.

fine¹ [faɪn] *adj* **1** bien: *how are you? –fine, thanks*, ¿cómo estás? –bien, gracias. **2** excelente, magnífico: *that's a fine building*, es un edificio magnífico. **3** bueno: *it's a fine day*, hace buen día. ▶ *adv fam* muy bien.

fine² [faɪn] *n* multa. ▶ *vt* multar, poner una multa.

finger [ˈfɪŋgə'] *n* dedo.

fingerprint [ˈfɪŋgəprɪnt] *n* huella digital, huella dactilar.

fingertip [ˈfɪŋgətɪp] *n* punta del dedo, yema del dedo.

finish [ˈfɪnɪʃ] *n* **1** fin, final. **2** acabado. ▶ *vi-vt* acabar, terminar. ● **a close finish** un final muy reñido.

finishing [ˈfɪnɪʃɪŋ] *adj* final. ■ **finishing line** línea de meta.

fir [fɜː'] *n* abeto.

fire [ˈfaɪə'] *n* **1** fuego. **2** incendio. **3** estufa. ▶ *vt* **1** disparar, lanzar. **2** *fam* despedir, echar. ▶ *vi* disparar. ▶ *interj* ¡fuego! ● **to be on fire** estar ardiendo, estar en llamas. ■ **fire engine** coche de bomberos; **fire escape** escalera de incendios; **fire extinguisher** extintor; **fire station** parque de bomberos; **fire hydrant** boca de incendios.

fireman [ˈfaɪəmən] *n* bombero.

fireplace [ˈfaɪəpleɪs] *n* chimenea, hogar.

fireproof [ˈfaɪəpruːf] *adj* a prueba de fuego.

firewood [ˈfaɪəwʊd] *n* leña.

fireworks [ˈfaɪəwɜːks] *npl* fuegos artificiales.

firing [ˈfaɪərɪŋ] *n* tiroteo. ■ **firing squad** pelotón de fusilamiento; **firing range** campo de tiro.

firm¹ [fɜːm] *n* empresa, firma.

firm² [fɜːm] *adj* firme.

first [fɜːst] *adj* primero,-a. ▶ *adv* **1** primero. **2** por primera vez. ▶ *n* **1** primero,-a. **2** sobresaliente. ● **at first** al principio; **first of all** en primer lugar. ■ **first aid** primeros auxilios; **first aid kit** botiquín de primeros auxilios; **first floor 1** GB primer piso. **2** US

planta baja; **first name** nombre de pila; **first degree** licenciatura.
first-class ['fɜːstklɑːs] *adj* de primera clase.
first-rate ['fɜːstreɪt] *adj* excelente.
fiscal ['fɪskəl] *adj* fiscal.
fish [fɪʃ] *n* **1** pez. **2** pescado. ► *vi* pescar. ■ **fish and chips** pescado con patatas; **fish finger** varita de pescado; **fish shop** pescadería.
fisherman ['fɪʃəmən] *n* pescador.
fishing ['fɪʃɪŋ] *n* pesca. ■ **fishing rod** caña de pescar.
fishmonger ['fɪʃmʌŋgəʳ] *n* GB pescadero,-a.
fishmonger's ['fɪʃmʌŋgəz] *n* pescadería.
fist [fɪst] *n* puño.
fistful ['fɪstfʊl] *n* puñado.
fit¹ [fɪt] *n* ataque, acceso.
fit² [fɪt] *vt* **1** ir bien a: *these shoes don't fit me, they're too big*, estos zapatos no me van bien, me quedan grandes. **2** entrar: *this box won't fit in the boot*, esta caja no va a entrar en el maletero. **3** poner, colocar: *the spy fitted a microphone under the table*, el espía puso un micrófono debajo de la mesa. ► *vi* caber. ► *adj* **1** apto,-a, adecuado,-a. **2** en forma.
to fit in *vi* encajar.

fitness ['fɪtnəs] *n* buena forma *(física)*.
fitting ['fɪtɪŋ] *adj fml* apropiado,-a. ► *n* prueba *(de traje, etc)*. ► *npl* **fittings** accesorios. ■ **fitting room** probador.
five [faɪv] *num* cinco.
fix [fɪks] *vt* **1** fijar. **2** arreglar. **3** US preparar: *let me fix you a drink*, te prepararé una copa.
fizzy ['fɪzɪ] *adj* gaseoso,-a, con gas, espumoso,-a.
flag [flæg] *n* bandera.
flagpole ['flægpəʊl] *n* asta, mástil.
flagstone ['flægstəʊn] *n* losa.
flair [fleəʳ] *n* talento, don.
flake [fleɪk] *n* **1** copo. **2** escama. ► *vi* descamarse.
flame [fleɪm] *n* llama.
flamingo [fləˈmɪŋgəʊ] *n* flamenco *(ave)*.
flan [flæn] *n* tarta rellena.
flank [flæŋk] *n* flanco.
flannel ['flænəl] *n* franela.
flap [flæp] *n* **1** solapa. **2** faldón. ► *vt* batir. ► *vi* **1** agitarse. **2** ondear.
flare [fleəʳ] *n* **1** llamarada. **2** bengala. ► *vi* **1** llamear. **2** estallar.
flared [fleəd] *adj* acampanado,-a.
flash [flæʃ] *n* **1** destello. **2** flash *(de cámara, noticia)*. ► *vi* **1** brillar, destellar. **2** pasar como un rayo. ■ **flash of lightning** relámpago.

flashlight ['flæʃlaɪt] *n* linterna.
flask [flæsk] *n* termo.
flat¹ [flæt] *n* GB piso.
flat² [flæt] *adj* **1** llano,-a, plano,-a. **2** desinflado,-a, deshinchado,-a: *a flat tyre*, un neumático deshinchado. **3** descargado,-a: *a flat battery*, una batería descargada. **4** que ha perdido el gas: *this beer's flat!*, ¡esta cerveza no tiene gas! **5** rotundo,-a. ► *n* llanura. ► *adv*: *in ten seconds flat*, en diez segundos justos. ▪ **flat rate** precio fijo; **flat roof** azotea.
flatten ['flætən] *vt* allanar.
flatter ['flætə'] *vt* adular, halagar.
flautist ['flɔːtɪst] *n* flautista.
flavour ['fleɪvə'] (US **flavor**) *n* sabor. ► *vt* condimentar.
flavouring ['fleɪvərɪŋ] (US **flavoring**) *n* condimento.
flea [fliː] *n* pulga.
fleck [flek] *n* mota, punto.
flee [fliː] *vt* huir de. ► *vi* huir.
fleet [fliːt] *n* **1** armada. **2** flota.
flesh [fleʃ] *n* carne.
flew [fluː] *pt* → fly.
flex [fleks] *n* GB cable *(eléctrico)*. ► *vt* doblar, flexionar.
flexible ['fleksəbəl] *adj* flexible.
flick [flɪk] *n* movimiento rápido, coletazo, latigazo. ► *vt* **1** dar. **2** chasquear.
flicker ['flɪkə'] *n* **1** parpadeo. **2** *fig* indicio. ► *vi* parpadear.

flight [flaɪt] *n* **1** vuelo. **2** bandada. **3** tramo: *flight of stairs*, tramo de escalera. **4** huida, fuga.
fling [flɪŋ] *n* **1** lanzamiento. **2** juerga. **3** lío *(amoroso)*. ► *vt* arrojar, tirar, lanzar.
flint [flɪnt] *n* **1** pedernal. **2** piedra.
flip [flɪp] *n* voltereta.
flipper ['flɪpə'] *n* aleta.
flirt [flɜːt] *n* coqueto,-a. ► *vi* flirtear, coquetear.
float [fləʊt] *n* **1** flotador. **2** corcho. **3** carroza. ► *vi* flotar.
flock [flɒk] *n* **1** rebaño, bandada. **2** *fam* tropel.
flood [flʌd] *n* inundación. ► *vt* inundar. ► *vi* desbordarse.
floodlight ['flʌdlaɪt] *n* foco.
floor [flɔː'] *n* **1** suelo. **2** piso, planta: *my flat is on the fourth floor*, mi casa está en el cuarto piso. ● **to give/have the floor** dar/tener la palabra.
floppy ['flɒpɪ] *adj* blando,-a, flexible. ▪ **floppy disk** disquete, disco flexible.
flora ['flɔːrə] *n* flora.
florist ['flɒrɪst] *n* florista. ▪ **florist's** floristería.
flounce [flaʊns] *n* volante *(de vestido)*.
flour [flaʊə'] *n* harina.
flourish ['flʌrɪʃ] *n* ademán, gesto. ► *vt* ondear, agitar. ► *vi* florecer.

flourishing ['flʌrɪʃɪŋ] *adj* floreciente, próspero,-a.

flow [fləʊ] *n* **1** flujo. **2** corriente: *the flow of traffic*, la circulación del tráfico. ► *vi* **1** fluir, manar. **2** circular: *traffic is flowing*, el tráfico circula con fluidez. **3** correr, fluir. • **to flow into** desembocar en. ■ **flow chart** diagrama de flujo, organigrama.

flower ['flaʊə'] *n* flor. ► *vi* florecer. ■ **flower bed** parterre.

flowerpot ['flaʊəpɒt] *n* maceta, tiesto.

flown [fləʊn] *pp* → fly.

flu [fluː] *n* gripe.

fluency ['fluːənsɪ] *n* fluidez.

fluent ['fluːənt] *adj* fluido,-a, suelto,-a: *she's fluent in French*, habla el francés con fluidez.

fluff [flʌf] *n* pelusa, lanilla.

fluffy ['flʌfɪ] *adj* mullido,-a.

fluid ['fluːɪd] *adj* fluido,-a. ► *n* fluido, líquido.

fluke [fluːk] *n fam* chiripa.

flung [flʌŋ] *pt-pp* → fling.

fluorescent [fluə'resənt] *adj* fluorescente.

flurry ['flʌrɪ] *n* ráfaga: *a flurry of rain*, un chaparrón.

flush [flʌʃ] *n* rubor. ► *vt* **1** limpiar con agua. **2** *fig* hacer salir. ► *vi* ruborizarse. • **to flush the lavatory** tirar de la cadena *(del wáter).*

flute [fluːt] *n* flauta.

flutter ['flʌtə'] *n* **1** agitación. **2** aleteo. **3** parpadeo. ► *vi* **1** ondea. **2** revolotea.

fly¹ [flaɪ] *vi* **1** volar. **2** ondear. **3** irse volando: *he flew down the stairs*, bajó la escalera volando. ► *vt* **1** pilotar *(avión).* **2** izar. ► *npl* **flies** bragueta.

fly² [flaɪ] *n* mosca.

flying ['flaɪɪŋ] *n* **1** aviación. **2** vuelo. ► *adj* **1** volante. **2** rápido,-a. ■ **flying saucer** platillo volante.

flyover ['flaɪəʊvə'] *n* GB paso elevado.

foal [fəʊl] *n* potro,-a.

foam [fəʊm] *n* espuma. ■ **foam rubber** gomaespuma.

focus ['fəʊkəs] *n* foco. ► *vt* enfocar. ► *vi* centrarse. • **in focus** enfocado,-a; **out of focus** desenfocado,-a.

foetus ['fiːtəs] *n* feto.

fog [fɒg] *n* niebla. ► *vt-vi* empañar.

foggy ['fɒgɪ] *adj* de niebla.

foglamp ['fɒglæmp] *n* faro antiniebla.

foil [fɔɪl] *n* papel de aluminio.

fold¹ [fəʊld] *n* redil, aprisco.

fold² [fəʊld] *n* pliegue. ► *vt* doblar, plegar. ► *vi* doblarse, plegarse.

folder ['fəʊldə'] *n* carpeta.

folding ['fəʊldɪŋ] *adj* plegable: *a folding bed*, una cama plegable.

foliage ['fəʊlɪdʒ] *n fml* follaje.

folk [fəʊk] *adj* popular. ▶ *npl* **1** gente: *country folk*, gente del campo. **2 folks** *fam* familia. ▪ **folk music** música popular; **folk song** canción popular.

folklore ['fəʊklɔːʳ] *n* folclor.

follow ['fɒləʊ] *vt-vi* seguir. ▶ *vt* perseguir. ▶ *vi* deducirse: *it follows that he's innocent*, se deduce que es inocente.

follower ['fɒləʊəʳ] *n* seguidor,-ra, discípulo,-a.

following ['fɒləʊɪŋ] *adj* siguiente. ▶ *n* seguidores. ▶ *prep* tras.

fond [fɒnd] *adj* **1** cariñoso,-a. **2** ser aficionado,-a: *he's fond of photography*, le gusta mucho la fotografía. • **to be fond of** SB tenerle cariño a ALGN.

fondle ['fɒndəl] *vt* acariciar.

font [fɒnt] *n* pila bautismal.

food [fuːd] *n* comida, alimento. ▪ **food poisoning** intoxicación alimenticia.

foodstuffs ['fuːdstʌfs] *npl* alimentos, comestibles, productos alimenticios.

fool [fuːl] *n* tonto,-a. ▶ *vt* engañar: *you can't fool me!*, ¡a mí no me engañas! ▶ *vi* bromear: *it wasn't true, I was just fooling*, no era verdad, sólo bromeaba. • **to make a fool of** poner en ridículo a; **to play the fool** hacer el tonto.

foolish ['fuːlɪʃ] *adj* estúpido,-a.

foot [fʊt] *n* **1** pie. **2** pata. • **on foot** a pie.

football ['fʊtbɔːl] *n* fútbol. ▪ **football pools** quinielas.

footballer ['fʊtbɔːləʳ] *n* futbolista.

footnote ['fʊtnəʊt] *n* nota a pie de página.

footpath ['fʊtpɑːθ] *n* sendero, camino.

footprint ['fʊtprɪnt] *n* huella, pisada.

footstep ['fʊtstep] *n* paso, pisada.

footwear ['fʊtweəʳ] *n* calzado.

for [fɔːʳ] *prep* **1** para: *it's for you*, es para ti. **2** por: *do it for me*, hazlo por mí. **3** por, durante: *for two weeks*, durante dos semanas. **4** para, hacia: *her feelings for him*, sus sentimientos hacia él. **5** desde hace: *I have lived in Spain for twenty years*, vivo en España desde hace veinte años. **6** como: *what do they use for fuel?*, ¿qué utilizan como combustible? **7** de: *"T" for Tony*, "T" de Toni. **8 for +** *object + inf*: *it's time for you to go*, es hora de que te marches. ▶ *conj* ya que. • **what for?** ¿para qué?

forbade [fɔːˈbeɪd] *pt* → forbid.

forbid [fəˈbɪd] *vt* prohibir

forbidden [fəˈbɪdn] *pp* → forbid.

former

force [fɔːs] *n* fuerza. ► *vt* forzar. • **by force** a/por la fuerza; **to come into force** entrar en vigor.

forceps ['fɔːseps] *npl* fórceps.

ford [fɔːd] *n* vado. ► *vt* vadear.

forearm ['fɔːrɑːm] *n* antebrazo.

forecast ['fɔːkɑːst] *n* pronóstico, previsión. ► *vt* pronosticar.

forefinger ['fɔːfɪŋgə'] *n* dedo índice.

foreground ['fɔːgraʊnd] *n* primer plano.

forehead ['fɒrɪd, 'fɔːhed] *n* frente.

foreign ['fɒrɪn] *adj* **1** extranjero,-a. **2** exterior: *foreign policy*, política exterior. **3** ajeno, -a. ■ **foreign exchange** divisas; **Foreign Office** GB Ministerio de Asuntos Exteriores; **foreign currency** divisa.

foreigner ['fɒrɪnə'] *n* extranjero,-a.

foreman ['fɔːmən] *n* capataz.

foremost ['fɔːməʊst] *adj* principal. ► *adv* en primer lugar.

forerunner ['fɔːrʌnə'] *n* precursor,-ra.

foresee [fɔː'siː] *vt* prever.

foresight ['fɔːsaɪt] *n* previsión.

forest ['fɒrɪst] *n* bosque, selva.

foretell [fɔː'tel] *vt* presagiar, pronosticar.

foretold [fɔː'təʊld] *pt-pp* → foretell.

forever [fə'revə'] *adv* **1** siempre. **2** para siempre.

foreword ['fɔːwɜːd] *n* prólogo.

forfeit ['fɔːfɪt] *n* **1** pena, multa. **2** prenda.

forgave [fə'geɪv] *pt* → forgive.

forge [fɔːdʒ] *n* fragua. ► *vt* **1** falsificar. **2** forjar, fraguar.

forgery ['fɔːdʒərɪ] *n* falsificación.

forget [fə'get] *vt* olvidar, olvidarse de. • **forget it!** ¡olvídalo!, ¡déjalo!; **to forget oneself** perder el control.

forgive [fə'gɪv] *vt* perdonar.

forgot [fə'gɒt] *pt* → forget.

forgotten [fə'gɒtən] *pp* → forget.

fork [fɔːk] *n* **1** tenedor. **2** horca, horquilla. **3** bifurcación.

form [fɔːm] *n* **1** forma. **2** impreso, formulario. **3** curso: *I'm in the third form*, hago tercero. ► *vt-vi* formar(se). • **off form** en baja forma; **on form** en forma. ■ **form of address** tratamiento.

formal ['fɔːməl] *adj* **1** formal. **2** de etiqueta.

format ['fɔːmæt] *n* formato. ► *vt* formatear.

former ['fɔːmə'] *adj* **1** primer, -a: *the former case*, el primer caso. **2** antiguo,-a, ex-: *the former champion*, el excampeón. ► *pron* **the former** aquél, aquélla.

formula ['fɔːmjələ] n fórmula.

forsake [fəˈseɪk] vt 1 fml abandonar. 2 renunciar a.

fort [fɔːt] n fuerte, fortaleza.

forth [fɔːθ] adv en adelante. • **and so forth** y así sucesivamente.

forthcoming [fɔːθˈkʌmɪŋ] adj próximo,-a.

fortieth ['fɔːtɪəθ] adj cuadragésimo,-a.

fortify ['fɔːtɪfaɪ] vt 1 fortificar. 2 fig fortalecer.

fortnight ['fɔːtnaɪt] n GB quincena, dos semanas.

fortress ['fɔːtrəs] n fortaleza.

fortunate ['fɔːtʃənət] adj afortunado,-a.

fortune ['fɔːtʃən] n 1 fortuna. 2 suerte.

fortune-teller ['fɔːtʃəntelə'] n adivino,-a.

forty ['fɔːtɪ] num cuarenta.

forward ['fɔːwəd] adv 1 hacia adelante. 2 en adelante. ► adj 1 hacia adelante. 2 delantero,-a, frontal: *a forward position*, una posición delantera. 3 adelantado,-a: *forward planning*, planificación anticipada. ► n delantero,-a. ► vt remitir: *please forward*, remítase al destinatario. • **to put the clock forward** adelantar el reloj.

forwards ['fɔːwədz] adv → forward.

fossil ['fɒsəl] n fósil.

foster ['fɒstə'] adj adoptivo,-a. ■ **foster child** hijo,-a adoptivo,-a.

fought [fɔːt] pt-pp → fight.

foul [faul] adj asqueroso,-a. ► n falta (en deporte).

found¹ [faund] vt fundar.

found² [faund] pt-pp → find.

foundation [faunˈdeɪʃən] n 1 fundación. 2 fundamento, base. ► npl **foundations** cimientos.

foundry ['faundrɪ] n fundición.

fountain ['fauntən] n fuente. ■ **fountain pen** pluma estilográfica.

four [fɔː'] num cuatro. • **on all fours** a gatas.

fourteen [fɔːˈtiːn] num catorce.

fourteenth [fɔːˈtiːnθ] adj decimocuarto,-a.

fourth [fɔːθ] adj cuarto,-a.

fowl [faul] n ave de corral.

fox [fɒks] n zorro,-a.

foxy ['fɒksɪ] adj fam astuto,-a.

foyer ['fɔɪeɪ, 'fɔɪə'] n vestíbulo.

fraction ['frækʃən] n fracción.

fracture ['fræktʃə'] n fractura. ► vt-vi fracturar(se).

fragile ['frædʒaɪl] adj frágil.

fragment ['frægmənt] n fragmento.

frame [freim] n 1 armazón, armadura. 2 cuadro (de bici). 3 montura (de gafas). 4 marco (de ventana). 5 fotograma. ► vt 1 enmarcar. ■ **frame of mind** estado de ánimo.

frogman

framework ['freɪmwɜːk] *n* armazón, estructura.
franchise ['fræntʃaɪz] *n* franquicia.
frank [fræŋk] *adj* franco,-a.
frantic ['fræntɪk] *adj* frenético,-a.
fraud [frɔːd] *n* fraude.
fray [freɪ] *vi* deshilacharse, desgastarse.
freak [friːk] *n* **1** monstruo. **2** *sl* fanático,-a: *a film freak*, un fanático del cine. ► *adj* insólito,-a.
freckle ['frekəl] *n* peca.
free [friː] *adj* **1** libre. **2** gratuito,-a. ► *adv* **1** gratis. **2** suelto,-a. ► *vt* **1** poner en libertad. **2** soltar.
freedom ['friːdəm] *n* libertad.
freelance ['friːlɑːns] *adj* autónomo,-a, freelance.
freestyle ['friːstaɪl] *n* estilo libre.
freeway ['friːweɪ] *n* US autopista.
freeze [friːz] *n* **1** helada. **2** congelación *(de precios)*. ► *vt-vi* congelar(se).
freezer ['friːzə'] *n* congelador.
freight [freɪt] *n* **1** transporte. **2** carga, flete. ■ **freight train** tren de mercancías.
frenzy ['frenzɪ] *n* frenesí.
frequency ['friːkwənsɪ] *n* frecuencia.
frequent ['friːkwənt] *adj* frecuente.

fresco ['freskəu] *n* fresco.
fresh [freʃ] *adj* fresco,-a. ■ **fresh water** agua dulce.
freshen ['freʃən] *vt-vi* refrescar(se).
fret [fret] *vi* preocuparse.
friar ['fraɪə'] *n* fraile.
friction ['frɪkʃən] *n* fricción.
Friday ['fraɪdɪ] *n* viernes.
fridge [frɪdʒ] *n* nevera, frigorífico.
fried [fraɪd] *adj* frito,-a.
friend [frend] *n* amigo,-a.
friendly ['frendlɪ] *adj* **1** simpático,-a. **2** acogedor,-ra. ■ **friendly game/match** partido amistoso.
friendship ['frendʃɪp] *n* amistad.
frieze [friːz] *n* friso.
frigate ['frɪgət] *n* fragata.
fright [fraɪt] *n* **1** susto. **2** miedo.
frighten ['fraɪtən] *vt* asustar.
frightened ['fraɪtənd] *adj* asustado,-a. ● **to be frightened** tener miedo.
fringe [frɪndʒ] *n* **1** fleco. **2** flequillo.
frisk [frɪsk] *vt* registrar, cachear.
fritter ['frɪtə'] *n* buñuelo.
frivolous ['frɪvələs] *adj* frívolo,-a.
fro [frəu] *phr.* **to and fro** de un lado para otro.
frog [frɒg] *n* rana.
frogman ['frɒgmən] *n* hombre rana.

from [frɒm] *prep* **1** de: *the train from London to Edinburgh*, el tren de Londres a Edimburgo. **2** de, desde: *from January to June*, desde enero hasta junio. **3** según, por: *from experience*, por experiencia. • **from now on** a partir de ahora.

front [frʌnt] *n* **1** parte delantera. **2** frente. **3** principio. **4** fachada. ► *adj* **1** delantero,-a, de delante. **2** primero. ► *vi* dar: *the window fronts onto the sea*, la ventana da al mar. • **in front of** delante de. ■ **front door** puerta principal, puerta de entrada.

frontier ['frʌntɪə'] *n* frontera.

frost [frɒst] *n* **1** escarcha. **2** helada. ► *vi* **to frost over** helarse, escarcharse.

froth [frɒθ] *n* espuma.

frown [fraʊn] *n* ceño. ► *vi* fruncir el ceño.

froze [frəʊz] *pt* → freeze.

frozen ['frəʊzən] *pp* → freeze.

fruit [fruːt] *n* **1** fruta. **2** fruto. ■ **fruit dish** frutero; **fruit machine** máquina tragaperras; **fruit salad** macedonia.

frustrate [frʌ'streɪt] *vt* frustrar.

fry [fraɪ] *vt-vi* freír, freírse.

frying pan ['fraɪɪŋpæn] *n* sartén.

fudge [fʌdʒ] *n* dulce hecho con azúcar, leche y mantequilla.

fuel [fjʊəl] *n* combustible, carburante.

fugitive ['fjuːdʒɪtɪv] *adj-n* fugitivo,-a.

fulfil [fʊl'fɪl] *vt* **1** cumplir. **2** realizar, efectuar. **3** satisfacer.

full [fʊl] *adj* **1** lleno,-a. **2** completo,-a. ► *adv* justo, de lleno. ■ **full moon** luna llena; **full stop** punto y seguido.

full-time [fʊl'taɪm] *adj* de jornada completa. ► *adv* a jornada completa.

fume [fjuːm] *vi* echar humo. ► *npl* **fumes** humos.

fumigate ['fjuːmɪgeɪt] *vt* fumigar.

fun [fʌn] *n* diversión. ► *adj* divertido,-a. • **in/for fun** en broma; **to have fun** divertirse, pasarlo bien; **to make fun of** reírse de.

function ['fʌŋkʃən] *n* **1** función. **2** acto, ceremonia. ► *vi* funcionar.

fund [fʌnd] *n* fondo. ► *vt* patrocinar.

fundamental [fʌndə'mentəl] *adj* fundamental.

funeral ['fjuːnərəl] *n* entierro, funerales. ■ **funeral procession** cortejo fúnebre; **funeral parlor** US funeraria.

funfair ['fʌnfeə'] *n* GB feria, parque de atracciones.

fungus ['fʌŋgəs] *n* hongo.

funnel ['fʌnəl] *n* **1** embudo. **2** chimenea *(de barco)*.

funny ['fʌnɪ] *adj* **1** gracioso,-a, divertido,-a. **2** raro,-a, extraño,-a, curioso,-a.

fur [fɜːʳ] *n* **1** pelo, pelaje. **2** piel. ▪ **fur coat** abrigo de pieles.

furious ['fjʊərɪəs] *adj* furioso,-a.

furnace ['fɜːnəs] *n* horno.

furnish ['fɜːnɪʃ] *vt* amueblar.

furnishings ['fɜːnɪʃɪŋz] *npl* **1** muebles, mobiliario. **2** accesorios.

furniture ['fɜːnɪtʃəʳ] *n* mobiliario, muebles. ● **a piece of furniture** un mueble. ▪ **furniture van** camión de mudanzas.

further ['fɜːðəʳ] *adj-adv* → far. ▶ *adj* **1** nuevo,-a: *until further notice*, hasta nuevo aviso. **2** adicional: *we need further information*, necesitamos más información. ▶ *adv* más.

furthermore [fɜːðə'mɔːʳ] *adv fml* además.

furthest ['fɜːðɪst] *adj-adv* → far.

fury ['fjʊərɪ] *n* furia, furor.

fuse [fjuːz] *n* **1** fusible, plomo. **2** mecha, espoleta. ▶ *vt-vi* **1** fusionar(se). **2** fundir(se).

fusion ['fjuːʒən] *n* fusión.

fuss [fʌs] *n* alboroto, jaleo. ● **to make a fuss** quejarse.

fussy ['fʌsɪ] *adj* quisquilloso,-a.

future ['fjuːtʃəʳ] *adj* futuro,-a. ▶ *n* futuro.

fuzz [fʌz] *n* pelusa.

fuzzy ['fʌzɪ] *adj* **1** rizado,-a, crespo,-a. **2** borroso,-a.

G

gabardine ['gæbədiːn] *n* gabardina.

gadget ['gædʒɪt] *n* aparato, chisme.

gaffe [gæf] *n* metedura de pata.

gag [gæg] *n* **1** mordaza. **2** chiste, broma.

gage [geɪdʒ] *n* US → gauge.

gain [geɪn] *n* ganancia, beneficio. ▶ *vt* **1** lograr. **2** engordar. **3** aumentar. ▶ *vi* adelantarse *(reloj)*.

gait [geɪt] *n* porte, andares.

gal [gæl] *abbr* (**gallon**) galón.

galaxy ['gæləksɪ] *n* galaxia.

gale [geɪl] *n* vendaval.

gallery ['gælərɪ] *n* **1** galería. **2** galería, gallinero *(en teatro)*.

galley ['gælɪ] *n* galera.

gallon ['gælən] *n* galón.

gallop ['gæləp] *n* galope. ▶ *vi* galopar.

gallows ['gæləʊz] *n* horca.

gamble ['gæmbəl] *vi* jugar. ▶ *vt* apostar, jugarse.

gambling ['gæmblɪŋ] *n* juego. ▪ **gambling den** casa de juego.

game [geɪm] *n* **1** juego. **2** partido *(de tenis, fútbol, etc)*. **3** partida *(de cartas, ajedrez)*. **4** caza. ▪ **game reserve** coto de caza.

gammon ['gæmən] *n* jamón.

gander ['gændəʳ] *n* ganso.

gang 82

gang [gæŋ] *n* **1** banda *(de delincuentes)*. **2** pandilla *(de amigos)*. **3** cuadrilla, brigada *(de obreros)*.

gangrene ['gæŋgriːn] *n* gangrena.

gangster ['gæŋstəʳ] *n* gángster.

gangway ['gæŋweɪ] *n* **1** pasillo. **2** pasarela *(en barco)*.

gaol [dʒeɪl] *n* cárcel.

gap [gæp] *n* **1** abertura, hueco. **2** espacio. **3** blanco. **4** intervalo.

garage ['gærɑːʒ, 'gærɪdʒ] *n* **1** garaje. **2** taller mecánico. **3** gasolinera.

garbage ['gɑːbɪdʒ] *n* basura.

garden ['gɑːdən] *n* jardín.

gardener ['gɑːdənəʳ] *n* jardinero,-a.

gardening ['gɑːdənɪŋ] *n* jardinería.

gargle ['gɑːgəl] *vi* hacer gárgaras.

garlic ['gɑːlɪk] *n* ajo.

garment ['gɑːmənt] *n* prenda de vestir.

garnish ['gɑːnɪʃ] *n* guarnición. ► *vt* guarnecer.

garrison ['gærɪsən] *n* guarnición *(militar)*.

garrulous ['gærələs] *adj* locuaz.

garter ['gɑːtəʳ] *n* liga.

gas [gæs] *n* **1** gas. **2** US gasolina. ■ **gas chamber** cámara de gas; **gas mask** máscara antigás; **gas station** gasolina.

gash [gæʃ] *n* raja, corte. ► *vt* rajar, cortar.

gasoline ['gæsəliːn] *n* US gasolina.

gastronomy [gæs'trɒnəmɪ] *n* gastronomía.

gate [geɪt] *n* **1** puerta, verja. **2** puerta de embarque.

gateau ['gætəʊ] *n* pastel.

gatecrash ['geɪtkræʃ] *vt-vi fam* colarse.

gateway ['geɪtweɪ] *n* puerta.

gather ['gæðəʳ] *vt* **1** juntar, reunir *(personas)*. **2** recoger, coger *(flores, fruta)*. **3** recaudar *(impuestos)*. ► *vi* **1** reunirse *(personas)*. **2** acumularse *(nubes)*.

gauge [geɪdʒ] *n* **1** indicador. **2** medida estándar. **3** calibre. ► *vt* **1** medir, calibrar. **2** *fig* juzgar.

gaunt [gɔːnt] *adj* demacrado,-a.

gauze [gɔːz] *n* gasa.

gave [geɪv] *pt* → give.

gay [geɪ] *adj* **1** alegre. **2** vistoso,-a *(aspecto)*. **3** gay, homosexual. ► *n* gay, homosexual.

gaze [geɪz] *vi* mirar fijamente.

gazelle [gə'zel] *n* gacela.

gazette [gə'zet] *n* gaceta.

gear [gɪəʳ] *n* **1** engranaje. **2** marcha, velocidad: *reverse gear*, marcha atrás. **3** *fam* efectos personales, ropa, cosas, equipo. ■ **gear lever** palanca de cambio.

gearbox ['gɪəbɒks] *n* caja de cambios.

geese [giːs] *npl* → goose.

gelatine ['dʒelətiːn] *n* gelatina.

gem [dʒem] *n* gema.

gen [dʒen] *n fam* información.

gender ['dʒendə'] *n* género.

gene [dʒiːn] *n* gen.

general ['dʒenərəl] *adj-n* general. • **in general** por lo general. ▪ **general practitioner** médico,-a de cabecera; **the general public** el público.

generate ['dʒenəreɪt] *vt* generar.

generation [dʒenə'reɪʃən] *n* generación.

generous ['dʒenərəs] *adj* generoso,-a.

genetic [dʒə'netɪk] *adj* genético,-a.

genial ['dʒiːnɪəl] *adj* simpático,-a, afable.

genital ['dʒenɪtəl] *adj* genital.

genius ['dʒiːnɪəs] *n* genio.

genre ['ʒɑːnrə] *n* género.

gent [dʒent] *n* **1** *fam* caballero. **2 gents** servicio de caballeros.

gentle ['dʒentəl] *adj* **1** amable *(persona)*. **2** suave *(brisa)*. **3** manso,-a *(animal)*.

gentleman ['dʒentəlmən] *n* caballero.

genuine ['dʒenjʊɪn] *adj* **1** genuino,-a. **2** sincero,-a *(sentimiento)*.

geography [dʒɪ'ɒgrəfi] *n* geografía.

geology [dʒɪ'blədʒɪ] *n* geología.

geometry [dʒɪ'ɒmətrɪ] *n* geometría.

geranium [dʒə'reɪnɪəm] *n* geranio.

germ [dʒɜːm] *n* germen.

gerund ['dʒerənd] *n* gerundio.

gesture ['dʒestʃə'] *n* ademán, gesto. ▶ *vi* hacer gestos, hacer un ademán.

get [get] *vt* **1** obtener, conseguir. **2** recibir. **3** traer. **4** coger. **5** persuadir, convencer. **6** preparar, hacer. **7** *fam* entender. **8** comprar. **9** buscar, recoger. ▶ *vi* **1** ponerse, volverse: *to get better*, mejorar; *to get tired*, cansarse. **2** ir: *how do you get there?*, cómo se va hasta allí? **3** llegar: *we got to Edinburgh at six o'-clock*, llegamos a Edimburgo a las seis. **4** llegar a: *I never got to see that film*, nunca llegué a ver esa película.

to get along *vi* arreglárselas.

to get along with *vt* llevarse (bien) con.

to get away *vi* escaparse.

to get back *vi* volver, regresar. ▶ *vt* recuperar.

to get down *vi* bajarse.

to get in *vi* **1** llegar. **2** entrar.

to get into *vt* subir a *(coche)*.

to get off *vt* **1** quitar. **2** bajarse de *(coche)*. ▶ *vi* **1** bajarse *(de coche)*. **2** salir *(de viaje)*.

to get on vt 1 subir(se) a (vehículo). 2 montar (bicicleta). ▶ vi 1 llevarse bien. 2 seguir.

to get out vt 1 sacar (objeto). 2 quitar (mancha). ▶ vi salir: *get out of here!*, ¡sal de aquí!

to get over vt 1 recuperarse de. 2 salvar (obstáculo).

to get through vi conseguir hablar (por teléfono).

to get up vt-vi levantar(se).

getaway ['getəweɪ] n fuga.

gherkin ['gɜːkɪn] n pepinillo.

ghost [gəʊst] n fantasma.

giant ['dʒaɪənt] n gigante,-a.

gift [gɪft] n regalo, obsequio.

gild [gɪld] vt dorar.

gills [gɪlz] npl agallas.

gin [dʒɪn] n ginebra.

ginger ['dʒɪndʒəʳ] n jengibre.

gipsy ['dʒɪpsɪ] n gitano,-a.

giraffe [dʒɜːrɑːf] n jirafa.

girdle ['gɜːdəl] n faja.

girl [gɜːl] n chica, muchacha, joven, niña.

girlfriend ['gɜːlfrend] n 1 novia. 2 US amiga, compañera.

giro ['dʒaɪrəʊ] n giro.

give [gɪv] vt dar. ▶ vi dar de sí, ceder. • **to give way** 1 ceder. 2 ceder el paso. ■ **give and take** toma y daca.

to give back vt devolver.

to give in vi ceder, rendirse. ▶ vt entregar (deberes).

to give up vt dejar: *to give up smoking*, dejar de fumar. ▶ vi rendirse, entregarse.

glacier ['glæsɪəʳ, 'gleɪʃəʳ] n glaciar.

glad [glæd] adj feliz, contento, -a. • **to be glad** alegrarse; **to be glad to do STH** tener mucho gusto en hacer algo.

glamour ['glæməʳ] (US **glamor**) n 1 atractivo. 2 encanto.

glance [glɑːns] n vistazo, mirada. ▶ vi echar un vistazo. • **at first glance** a primera vista; **to take a glance** echar un vistazo.

gland [glænd] n glándula.

glass [glɑːs] n 1 vidrio, cristal. 2 vaso, copa. ▶ npl **glasses** gafas.

glaze [gleɪz] n vidriado (cerámica). ▶ vt vidriar, esmaltar (cerámica). ■ **double glazing** doble acristalamiento.

gleam [gliːm] n destello. ▶ vi relucir, brillar.

glen [glen] n cañada.

glide [glaɪd] vi 1 planear. 2 deslizarse.

glider ['glaɪdəʳ] n planeador.

glimpse [glɪmps] n visión fugaz. ▶ vt vislumbrar.

global ['gləʊbəl] adj global.

globe [gləʊb] n 1 globo. 2 globo terrestre.

gloomy ['gluːmɪ] adj 1 lóbrego,-a, oscuro (lugar). 2 tristón,-ona, melancólico,-a (voz). 3 pesimista, poco prometedor (pronóstico).

glory ['glɔːrɪ] n gloria.

gone

glossary ['glɒsəri] *n* glosario.

glossy ['glɒsɪ] *adj* brillante.

glove [glʌv] *n* guante.

glow [gləʊ] *n* **1** luz suave: *the red glow of the fire*, la suave luz roja del fuego. **2** rubor.

glucose ['glu:kəʊz] *n* glucosa.

glue [glu:] *n* cola, pegamento. ► *vt* encolar, pegar.

glutton ['glʌtən] *n* glotón,-ona.

glycerine [glɪsə'rɪn] *n* glicerina.

gnat [næt] *n* mosquito.

gnaw [nɔ:] *vt* roer.

go [gəʊ] *vi* **1** ir. **2** marcharse, irse, salir. **3** desaparecer. **4** ir, funciona. **5** volverse, ponerse, quedarse: *he's gone deaf*, se ha vuelto sordo. **6** terminarse, acabars. **7** pasar. ► *vt* hacer: *it goes tick-tock*, hace tic-tac. ► *n* **1** energía, empuje. **2** turno: *it's my go now*, ahora me toca a mí. **3** intento. • **to be going to do STH** ir a hacer algo; **to have a go at SB** criticar a ALGN; **to make a go of STH** tener éxito en algo.

to go away *vi* marcharse.

to go back *vi* volver.

to go by *vi* pasar.

to go down *vi* **1** bajar. **2** deshincharse *(neumático)*.

to go in *vi* entrar.

to go off *vi* **1** irse, marcharse. **2** estallar *(bomba)*. **3** sonar *(alarma)*. **4** apagarse *(luz)*. **5** estropearse *(comida)*.

to go on *vi* **1** seguir. **2** pasar, suceder.

to go out *vi* **1** salir. **2** apagarse *(luz)*.

to go up *vi* **1** subir. **2** estallar.

goal [gəʊl] *n* **1** meta, portería. **2** gol, tanto. **3** fin, objeto.

goalkeeper ['gəʊlki:pəʳ] *n* portero, guardameta.

goat [gəʊt] *n* cabra.

goblet ['gɒblət] *n* copa.

god [gɒd] *n* dios.

godchild ['gɒdtʃaɪld] *n* ahijado,-a.

goddaughter ['gɒddɔ:təʳ] *n* ahijada.

goddess ['gɒdəs] *n* diosa.

godfather ['gɒdfɑ:ðəʳ] *n* padrino.

godmother ['gɒdmʌðəʳ] *n* madrina.

godparents ['gɒdpeərənts] *npl* padrinos.

godson ['gɒdsʌn] *n* ahijado.

goggles ['gɒgəls] *npl* gafas para natación.

gold [gəʊld] *n* oro. ► *adj* **1** de oro. **2** dorado.

golden ['gəʊldən] *adj* **1** de oro. **2** dorado,-a.

goldfish ['gəʊldfɪʃ] *n* pez de colores.

goldsmith ['gəʊldsmɪθ] *n* orfebre.

golf [gɒlf] *n* golf. ▪ **golf club 1** palo de golf. **2** club de golf; **golf course** campo de golf.

gone [gɒn] *pp* → go.

good [gʊd] *adj* bueno,-a. ► *interj* ¡bien! ► *n* bien. ► *npl* **goods 1** bienes. **2** género, artículos. ● **as good as** prácticamente, como; **a good deal** bastante; **for good** para siempre; **to be good at** STH tener facilidad para algo, ser bueno en algo; **to do good** hacer bien.

goodbye [gʊdˈbaɪ] *n* adiós. ► *interj* ¡adiós! ● **to say goodbye to** despedirse de.

good-for-nothing [ˈgʊdfənʌθɪŋ] *adj-n* inútil.

good-looking [gʊdˈlʊkɪŋ] *adj* guapo,-a.

goodwill [gʊdˈwɪl] *n* buena voluntad.

goose [guːs] *n* ganso, oca. ● **goose pimples** carne de gallina.

gooseberry [ˈgʊzbrɪ, ˈguːsbərɪ] *n* grosella espinosa.

gooseflesh [ˈguːsfleʃ] *n* piel de gallina.

gorge [gɔːdʒ] *n* desfiladero.

gorgeous [ˈgɔːdʒəs] *adj* espléndido,-a.

gorilla [gəˈrɪlə] *n* gorila.

go-slow [gəʊˈsləʊ] *n* huelga de celo.

gospel [ˈgɒspəl] *n* evangelio.

gossip [ˈgɒsɪp] *n* **1** cotilleo. **2** cotilla. ► *vi* cotillear. ■ **gossip column** crónica de sociedad.

got [gɒt] *pt-pp* → get.

gout [gaʊt] *n* gota.

govern [ˈgʌvən] *vt* gobernar.

government [ˈgʌvənmənt] *n* gobierno.

gown [gaʊn] *n* **1** vestido largo. **2** toga *(de juez)*. **3** bata *(de médico)*.

grab [græb] *vt* asir, coger.

grace [greɪs] *n* gracia.

graceful [ˈgreɪsfʊl] *adj* elegante.

grade [greɪd] *n* **1** grado. **2** clase, categoría. **3** US pendiente, cuesta. **4** US nota, calificación. **5** US clase.

gradual [ˈgrædjʊəl] *adj* gradual.

graduate [(*n*) ˈgrædjʊət, (*vb*) ˈgrædjʊeɪt] *n* graduado,-a, licenciado,-a. ► *vt* graduar. ► *vi* graduarse.

graffiti [grəˈfiːtɪ] *npl* pintadas, grafiti.

graft [grɑːft] *n* injerto. ► *vt* injertar.

grain [greɪn] *n* **1** grano. **2** cereales. **3** veta *(en madera)*.

gram [græm] *n* gramo.

grammar [ˈgræmə] *n* gramática. ■ **grammar school** GB instituto de enseñanza secundaria.

gramme [græm] *n* gramo.

granary [ˈgrænərɪ] *n* granero.

grand [grænd] *adj* **1** grandioso,-a, espléndido,-a. **2** *fam* fenomenal, estupendo,-a. ■ **grand piano** piano de cola; **grand total** total.

grandchild ['græntʃaɪld] n nieto,-a.

granddaughter ['grændɔːtə'] n nieta.

grandfather ['grændfɑːðə'] n abuelo.

grandmother ['grænmʌðə'] n abuela.

grandparents ['grændpeərənts] npl abuelos.

grandson ['grændsʌn] n nieto.

grandstand ['grændstænd] n tribuna.

granite ['grænɪt] n granito.

grant [grɑːnt] n **1** beca. **2** subvención. ► vt **1** conceder. **2** reconocer, admitir. • **to take STH for granted** dar algo por sentado.

grape [greɪp] n uva.

grapefruit ['greɪpfruːt] n pomelo.

grapevine ['greɪpvaɪn] n vid.

graph [grɑːf] n diagrama. ■ **graph paper** papel cuadriculado.

graphic ['græfɪk] adj gráfico,-a.

graphite ['græfaɪt] n grafito.

grasp [grɑːsp] ► vt **1** asir, agarrar. **2** comprender. • **to have a good grasp of** dominar.

grass [grɑːs] n hierba.

grasshopper ['grɑːshɒpə'] n saltamontes.

grate[1] [greɪt] vt rallar.

grate[2] [greɪt] n rejilla, parrilla.

grateful ['greɪtfʊl] adj agradecido,-a.

grater ['greɪtə'] n rallador.

gratify ['grætɪfaɪ] vt complacer, satisfacer.

gratis ['grætɪs, 'grɑːtɪs] adv gratis.

gratitude ['grætɪtjuːd] n gratitud.

gratuity [grə'tjuːɪtɪ] n propina.

grave[1] [greɪv] n tumba.

grave[2] [greɪv] adj grave.

gravel ['grævəl] n grava.

graveyard ['greɪvjɑːd] n cementerio.

gravity ['grævɪtɪ] n gravedad.

gravy ['greɪvɪ] n salsa (de carne).

gray [greɪ] adj US → grey.

graze [greɪz] n roce, rasguño. ► vt rozar. ► vi pacer, pastar.

grease [griːs] n grasa. ► vt engrasar.

great [greɪt] adj **1** grande, gran. **2** fam estupendo,-a, fantástico,-a.

greed [griːd] n **1** codicia, avaricia. **2** gula, glotonería.

green [griːn] adj **1** verde. **2** novato,-a. ► n **1** verde. **2** green (en golf). ► npl **greens** verduras. • **to be green with envy** morirse de envidia. ■ **green bean** judía verde.

greengrocer's ['griːngrəʊsə'] n verdulería.

greenhouse ['griːnhaʊs] n invernadero. ■ **greenhouse effect** efecto invernadero.

greet [griːt] vt **1** saludar, recibir (persona). **2** acoger, recibir (propuesta).

greeting ['gri:tɪŋ] *n* saludo.
■ **greetings card** tarjeta de felicitación; **greetings from...** recuerdos de...

gremlin ['gremlɪn] *n* duende.

grenade [grə'neɪd] *n* granada.

grew [gru:] *pt* → grow.

grey [greɪ] *adj* 1 gris. 2 cano,-a *(pelo)*. ► *n* gris.

greyhound ['greɪhaʊnd] *n* galgo.

grid [grɪd] *n* reja, parrilla.

grief [gri:f] *n* dolor, pena.

grill [grɪl] *n* 1 parrilla. 2 parrillada: **mixed grill**, parrillada de carne. ► *vt* asar a la parrilla.

grille [grɪl] *n* rejilla.

grim [grɪm] *adj* 1 terrible. 2 lúgubre *(lugar)*. 3 severo,-a, muy serio,-a *(persona)*.

grimace ['grɪməs] *n* mueca. ► *vi* hacer una mueca.

grind [graɪnd] *vt* 1 moler. 2 afilar *(cuchillo)*.

grinder ['graɪndə'] *n* molinillo.

grip [grɪp] *vt* asir, agarra. ► *n* 1 asimiento, apretón. 2 adherencia *(sujección de neumático)*.

grizzly bear [grɪzlɪ'beə'] *n* oso pardo.

groan [grəʊn] *n* gemido, quejido *(de dolor)*. ► *vi* 1 gemir, quejarse *(de dolor)*. 2 crujir *(puerta)*.

grocer ['grəʊsə'] *n* tendero,-a.

grocer's ['grəʊsəz] *n* tienda de comestibles.

groceries ['grəʊsərɪz] *npl* comestibles.

groin [grɔɪn] *n* ingle.

groom [gru:m] *n* novio.

groove [gru:v] *n* 1 ranura. 2 surco.

gross [grəʊs] *adj* bruto,-a *(peso, cantidad)*.

ground¹ [graʊnd] *n* 1 tierra, suelo. 2 terreno. 3 campo *(de fútbol, batalla)*. ► *npl* **grounds** 1 razón, motivo. 2 posos.
■ **ground floor** planta baja.

ground² [graʊnd] *pt-pp* → grind.

group [gru:p] *n* grupo. ► *vt* agrupar.

grove [grəʊv] *n* arboleda.

grow [grəʊ] *vi* crecer. ► *vt* 1 cultivar *(planta)*. 2 dejarse crecer *(pelo, bigote)*.

to grow up *vi* criarse, crecer.

grown [grəʊn] *pp* → grow.

grown-up ['grəʊnʌp] *adj-n* adulto,-a, persona mayor.

growth [grəʊθ] *n* crecimiento.

grub [grʌb] *n* larva.

grudge [grʌdʒ] *n* resentimiento, rencor.

grumble ['grʌmbəl] *n* queja.

grunt [grʌnt] *n* gruñido. ► *vi* gruñir.

guarantee [gærən'ti:] *n* garantía. ► *vt* garantizar.

guard [gɑ:d] *n* 1 guardia. 2 jefe de tren. ► *vt* 1 guardar, proteger. 2 vigilar. ● **on guard**

de guardia; **to stand guard** montar guardia. ▪ **guard dog** perro guardián.

guerrilla [gəˈrɪlə] n guerrillero,-a.

guess [ges] vt-vi **1** adivinar. **2** fam suponer. ► n conjetura: **have a guess!**, ¡a ver si lo adivinas!

guest [gest] n **1** invitado,-a. **2** cliente,-a, huésped,-a.

guesthouse [ˈgesthaʊs] n casa de huéspedes, pensión.

guide [gaɪd] n guía. ► vt guiar.

guidebook [ˈgaɪdbʊk] n guía.

guideline [ˈgaɪdlaɪn] n pauta, directriz.

guilty [ˈgɪltɪ] adj culpable.

guinea [ˈgɪnɪ] n. ▪ **guinea pig** conejillo de Indias.

guitar [gɪˈtɑːʳ] n guitarra.

guitarist [gɪˈtɑːrɪst] n guitarrista.

gulf [gʌlf] n golfo.

gull [gʌl] n gaviota.

gullible [ˈgʌlɪbəl] adj crédulo,-a.

gulp [gʌlp] n trago.

gum¹ [gʌm] n encía.

gum² [gʌm] n goma, pegamento.

gun [gʌn] n arma de fuego. ▪ **gun dog** perro de caza.

gunman [ˈgʌnmən] n pistolero.

gunpoint [ˈgʌnpɔɪnt] phr. **at gunpoint** a punta de pistola.

gunpowder [ˈgʌnpaʊdəʳ] n pólvora.

gunshot [ˈgʌnʃɒt] n disparo.

gust [gʌst] n ráfaga, racha.

gut [gʌt] n intestino, tripa. ► npl **guts 1** entrañas, vísceras. **2** fam agallas.

gutter [ˈgʌtəʳ] n **1** cuneta, alcantarilla (en calle). **2** canalón, desagüe (en tejado). ▪ **gutter press** prensa amarilla.

guy [gaɪ] n fam tipo, tío.

guzzle [ˈgʌzəl] vt zamparse.

gym [dʒɪm] n **1** fam gimnasio. **2** gimnasia. ▪ **gym shoes** zapatillas de deporte.

gymnastics [dʒɪmˈnæstɪks] n gimnasia.

gynaecology [gaɪnɪˈkɒlədʒɪ] n ginecología.

gypsy [ˈdʒɪpsɪ] adj-n gitano,-a.

H

habit [ˈhæbɪt] n hábito.

habitat [ˈhæbɪtæt] n hábitat.

habitual [həˈbɪtʃʊəl] adj habitual.

hack [hæk] vt COMPUT piratear.

had [hæd] pt-pp → have.

haddock [ˈhædək] n eglefino.

haemorrhage [ˈhemərɪdʒ] n hemorragia.

haemorrhoids [ˈhemərɔɪdz] npl hemorroides.

hag [hæg] n bruja, arpía.

haggle ['hægəl] vi regatear.

hail[1] [heɪl] vt llamar.

hail[2] [heɪl] n granizo. ► vi granizar.

hair [heəʳ] n cabello, pelo.

haircut ['heəkʌt] n corte de pelo.

hairdresser ['heədresəʳ] n peluquero,-a. ■ **hairdresser's** peluquería.

hairdryer ['heədraɪəʳ] n secador de pelo.

hairpiece ['heəpiːs] n peluquín.

hairpin ['heəpɪn] n horquilla.

hairspray ['heəspreɪ] n laca.

hairstyle ['heəstaɪl] n peinado.

hake [heɪk] n merluza.

half [hɑːf] n 1 mitad: *the second half*, la segunda mitad. 2 medio: *a kilo and a half*, un kilo y medio. ► adj medio,-a. ► adv medio, a medias. ► pron mitad. **half past** y media: *it's half past two*, son las dos y media.

half-time [hɑːfˈtaɪm] n descanso (en partido).

halfway [hɑːfˈweɪ] adv a mitad de camino.

hall [hɔːl] n 1 vestíbulo, entrada. 2 sala (de conciertos). ■ **hall of residence** colegio mayor.

hallo [həˈləʊ] interj → hello.

hallucination [həluːsɪˈneɪʃən] n alucinación.

halo ['heɪləʊ] n halo, aureola.

halt [hɔːlt] n alto, parada. ► vt-vi parar(se), cesar.

ham [hæm] n jamón.

hamburger ['hæmbɜːgəʳ] n hamburguesa.

hammer ['hæməʳ] n martillo.

hammock ['hæmək] n hamaca.

hand [hænd] n 1 mano. 2 trabajador,-ra, operario,-a. 3 tripulante (de barco). 4 manecilla (de reloj). 5 letra, caligrafía. ► vt dar, entregar. ● **at first hand** de primera mano; **at hand** a mano; **by hand** a mano; **hands up!** ¡manos arriba!; **on the one hand** por una parte; **on the other hand** por otra parte; **to hold hands** estar cogidos,-as de la mano; **to lend a hand** echar una mano.

to hand in vt entregar.

to hand out vt repartir.

to hand over vt entregar.

handbag ['hændbæg] n bolso.

handball ['hændbɔːl] n balonmano.

handbook ['hændbʊk] n manual.

handbrake ['hændbreɪk] n freno de mano.

handcuff ['hændkʌf] vt esposar. ► npl **handcuffs** esposas.

handful ['hændfʊl] n puñado.

handicap ['hændɪkæp] n 1 discapacidad, minusvalía. 2 desventaja, obstáculo. 3 hándicap. ► vt obstaculizar.

handicapped ['hændɪkæpt] *adj* minusválido,-a.

handicraft ['hændɪkrɑːft] *n* artesanía.

handkerchief ['hæŋkətʃiːf] *n* pañuelo.

handle ['hændəl] *n* **1** pomo *(de puerta)*. **2** tirador *(de cajón)*. **3** asa *(de taza)*. **4** mango *(de cuchillo)*. ► *vt* **1** manejar. **2** tratar *(gente, problema)*.

handlebar ['hændəlbɑːʳ] *n* manillar.

handmade [hænd'meɪd] *adj* hecho,-a a mano.

handout ['hændaʊt] *n* **1** folleto. **2** nota de prensa. **3** limosna.

handshake ['hændʃeɪk] *n* apretón de manos.

handsome ['hænsəm] *adj* guapo,-a.

handwritten [hænd'rɪtən] *adj* escrito,-a a mano.

handy ['hændɪ] *adj* **1** práctico,-a, útil. **2** a mano.

hang [hæŋ] *vt-vi* colgar.

to hang about/ around *vi* **1** esperar. **2** perder el tiempo.

to hang out *vt* tender.

to hang up *vt-vi* colgar *(teléfono)*.

hangar ['hæŋəʳ] *n* hangar.

hanger ['hæŋəʳ] *n* percha.

hang-glider ['hæŋglaɪdəʳ] *n* ala delta.

hangover ['hæŋəʊvəʳ] *n* resaca.

happen ['hæpən] *vi* ocurrir.

happiness ['hæpɪnəs] *n* felicidad.

happy ['hæpɪ] *adj* **1** feliz, alegre. **2** contento,-a: *happy birthday!*, ¡feliz cumpleaños!

harass ['hærəs] *vt* acosar.

harbour ['hɑːbəʳ] (US **harbor**) *n* puerto.

hard [hɑːd] *adj* **1** duro,-a *(material)*. **2** difícil *(pregunta, tema)*. ► *adv* fuerte, duro. ■ **hard court** pista rápida; **hard disk** disco duro; **hard shoulder** arcén.

hardly ['hɑːdlɪ] *adv* **1** apenas. **2** casi.

hardware ['hɑːdweəʳ] *n* **1** artículos de ferretería. **2** hardware, soporte físico. ■ **hardware store** ferretería.

hare [heəʳ] *n* liebre.

haricot bean [hærɪkəʊ'biːn] *n* alubia.

harm [hɑːm] *n* mal, daño, perjuicio. ► *vt* dañar, perjudicar, hacer daño.

harmony ['hɑːmənɪ] *n* armonía.

harp [hɑːp] *n* arpa.

harpoon [hɑː'puːn] *n* arpón.

harvest ['hɑːvɪst] *n* cosecha. ► *vt* cosechar.

has [hæz] *3rd pers sing pres* → have.

hash [hæʃ] *n* picadillo.

haste [heɪst] *n* prisa.

hat [hæt] *n* sombrero.

hatch [hætʃ] *n* escotilla.

hate [heɪt] *n* odio. ► *vt* odiar.

haughty ['hɔːtɪ] *adj* arrogante.

haul [hɔːl] *n* **1** botín. **2** redada *(de peces)*. ► *vt* tirar de, arrastrar.

haulage ['hɔːlɪdʒ] *n* transporte.

haunted ['hɔːntɪd] *adj* encantado,-a.

have [hæv] *vt* **1** tener. **2** comer, beber, fumar: *to have lunch*, comer. **3** tomar: *to have a bath*, bañarse. **4** hacer, mandar: *he had the house painted*, hizo pintar la casa. ► *aux* haber. • **have got** GB tener; **to have just** acabar de.

to have on *vt* llevar puesto, -a *(prenda)*.

haversack ['hævəsæk] *n* mochila.

hawk [hɔːk] *n* halcón.

hay [heɪ] *n* heno.

hay-fever ['heɪfiːvə'] *n* fiebre del heno, alergia.

hazard ['hæzəd] *n* riesgo, peligro. ► *vt* aventurar.

haze [heɪz] *n* neblina.

hazelnut ['heɪzəlnʌt] *n* avellana.

he [hiː] *pron* él. ► *adj* macho: *a he bear*, un oso macho.

head [hed] *n* **1** cabeza. **2** cabezal *(de casete)*. **3** cabecera *(de cama, mesa)*. ► *vt* **1** encabezar *(procesión)*. **2** cabecear. **3** dirigir *(organización)*. • **heads or tails?** ¿cara o cruz?

to head for *vt* dirigirse hacia.

headache ['hedeɪk] *n* dolor de cabeza.

header ['hedə'] *n* cabezazo.

headlamp ['hedlæmp] *n* faro.

headland ['hedlənd] *n* cabo.

headlight ['hedlaɪt] *n* faro.

headline ['hedlaɪn] *n* titular.

headphones ['hedfəʊnz] *npl* auriculares.

headquarters ['hedkwɔːtəz] *npl* **1** sede, oficina principal. **2** cuartel general.

heal [hiːl] *vt-vi* curar(se).

health [helθ] *n* salud.

healthy ['helθɪ] *adj* **1** sano,-a. **2** saludable.

heap [hiːp] *n* montón.

hear [hɪə'] *vt-vi* oír.

heart [hɑːt] *n* corazón. ► *npl* **hearts** corazones. • **by heart** de memoria; **to lose heart** desanimarse. ■ **heart attack** ataque al corazón.

heartbeat ['hɑːtbiːt] *n* latido del corazón.

heartless ['hɑːtləs] *adj* cruel.

heat [hiːt] *n* **1** calor. **2** calefacción. **3** eliminatoria *(en deporte)*. ► *vt-vi* calentar(se). • **on heat** en celo.

heater ['hiːtə'] *n* estufa, calefactor.

heather ['heðə'] *n* brezo.

heating ['hiːtɪŋ] *n* calefacción.

heaven ['hevən] *n* cielo.

heavy ['hevɪ] *adj* **1** pesado,-a. **2** fuerte *(lluvia, golpe)*. • **to be**

a **heavy smoker** fumar mucho.

heavyweight ['hevɪweɪt] *n* peso pesado.

hectare ['hektɑːʳ] *n* hectárea.

hedge [hedʒ] *n* seto.

hedgehog ['hedʒhɒg] *n* erizo.

heel [hiːl] *n* **1** talón. **2** tacón.

height [haɪt] *n* **1** altura. **2** altitud.

heir [eəʳ] *n* heredero.

heiress ['eəres] *n* heredera.

held [held] *pt-pp* → hold.

helicopter ['helɪkɒptəʳ] *n* helicóptero.

hell [hel] *n* infierno.

hello [he'ləʊ] *interj* **1** ¡hola! **2** ¡diga!, ¡dígame! *(por teléfono)*.

helm [helm] *n* timón.

helmet ['helmɪt] *n* casco.

help [help] *n* ayuda. ▸ *interj* ¡socorro! ▸ *vt* ayuda. • **help yourself** sírvete tú mismo, -a; **I can't help it** no lo puedo evitar.

helping ['helpɪŋ] *n* ración.

hem [hem] *n* dobladillo.

hemp [hemp] *n* cáñamo.

hen [hen] *n* gallina.

hence [hens] *adv* **1** por eso. **2** de aquí a.

hepatitis [hepə'taɪtəs] *n* hepatitis.

her [hɜːʳ] *pron* **1** la *(complemento - directo)*; le, se *(- indirecto)*. **2** ella *(después de preposición)*. ▸ *adj* su, sus, de ella.

herb [hɜːb] *n* hierba.

herd [hɜːd] *n* **1** manada *(de ganado)*. **2** rebaño *(de cabras)*.

here [hɪəʳ] *adv* aquí. • **here you are** aquí tienes.

heritage ['herɪtɪdʒ] *n* herencia.

hero ['hɪərəʊ] *n* héroe.

heroin ['herəʊɪn] *n* heroína *(droga)*.

heroine ['herəʊɪn] *n* heroína.

herring ['herɪŋ] *n* arenque.

hers [hɜːz] *pron* (el) suyo, (la) suya, (los) suyos, (las) suyas.

herself [hɜː'self] *pron* se, ella misma. • **by herself** sola.

hesitate ['hezɪteɪt] *vi* dudar.

hi [haɪ] *interj* ¡hola!

hiccough ['hɪkʌp] *n* hipo. ▸ *vi* tener hipo.

hiccup ['hɪkʌp] *n* hipo. ▸ *vi* tener hipo.

hid [hɪd] *pt-pp* → hide.

hidden ['hɪdən] *pp* → hide.

hide [haɪd] *vt-vi* esconder(se).

hide [haɪd] *n* piel, cuero.

hierarchy ['haɪərɑːkɪ] *n* jerarquía.

high [haɪ] *adj* **1** alto,-a. **2** agudo,-a *(voz)*. **3** fuerte *(viento)*. ■ **high court** tribunal supremo; **high jump** salto de altura; **high school** instituto de enseñanza secundaria; **high street** calle mayor; **high tide** pleamar.

high-heeled ['haɪ'hiːld] *adj* de tacón alto.

highlight ['haɪlaɪt] *vt* hacer resaltar, poner de relieve.

highly ['haɪlɪ] *adv* muy.

Highness ['haɪnəs] *n* Alteza.

highway ['haɪweɪ] *n* US autovía. ■ **Highway Code** GB código de la circulación.

hijack ['haɪdʒæk] *n* secuestro. ► *vt* secuestrar.

hike [haɪk] *n* excursión. ► *vi* ir de excursión.

hill [hɪl] *n* colina.

hilt [hɪlt] *n* empuñadura.

him [hɪm] *pron* **1** lo *(complemento - directo)*; le, se *(- indirecto)*. **2** él *(después de preposición)*.

himself [hɪm'self] *pron* se, sí mismo. ● **by himself** solo.

hinder ['hɪndə'] *vt-vi* entorpecer, estorbar.

hinge [hɪndʒ] *n* bisagra.

hint [hɪnt] *n* **1** insinuación, indirecta. **2** consejo. **3** pista, indicio. ► *vt* insinuar. ► *vi* lanzar indirectas.

hip [hɪp] *n* cadera.

hippie ['hɪpɪ] *adj-n fam* hippie.

hippo(potamus) [hɪpə'pɒtəməs] *n* hipopótamo.

hippy ['hɪpɪ] *adj-n fam* hippie.

hire ['haɪə'] *n* alquiler. ► *vt* **1** alquilar. **2** contratar. ● **on hire purchase** a plazos.

his [hɪz] *adj* **1** su, sus. **2** de él. ► *pron* (el) suyo, (la) suya, (los) suyos, (las) suyas.

history ['hɪstərɪ] *n* historia.

hit [hɪt] *n* **1** golpe. **2** éxito. **3** visita *(a página web)*. ► *vt* golpear, pegar.

hitchhike ['hɪtʃhaɪk] *vi* hacer autoestop.

hive [haɪv] *n* colmena.

hoarding ['hɔːdɪŋ] *n* valla.

hoarse [hɔːs] *adj* ronco,-a.

hobby ['hɒbɪ] *n* afición, hobby.

hockey ['hɒkɪ] *n* hockey.

hog [hɒg] *n* cerdo.

hoist [hɔɪst] *n* **1** grúa. **2** montacargas. ► *vt* **1** levantar. **2** izar *(bandera)*.

hold [həʊld] *n* bodega *(de barco, avión)*. ► *vt* **1** aguantar, sostener, agarrar *(con la mano)*. **2** dar cabida a, tener capacidad para. **3** celebrar *(reunión)*. **4** mantener *(conversación)*.

to hold on *vi* esperar, no colgar *(por teléfono)*.

to hold up *vt* **1** atracar, asaltar. **2** levantar *(mano)*.

holder ['həʊldə'] *n* poseedor,-ra, titular *(de pasaporte)*.

hold-up ['həʊldʌp] *n* atraco.

hole [həʊl] *n* agujero, hoyo.

holiday ['hɒlɪdeɪ] *n* **1** fiesta. **2** vacaciones.

hollow ['hɒləʊ] *adj* hueco,-a. ► *n* hueco.

holly ['hɒlɪ] *n* acebo.

holy ['həʊlɪ] *adj* santo,-a, sagrado,-a.

home [həʊm] *n* hogar, casa. ■ **home help** asistenta; **Home Office** Ministerio del Interior; **home page** página inicial.

homeland ['həʊmlænd] *n* patria.

homeless ['həʊmləs] *adj* sin techo, sin hogar.

home-made ['həʊm'meɪd] *adj* casero,-a.

homework ['həʊmwɜːk] *n* deberes.

honest ['ɒnɪst] *adj* honrado,-a.

honey ['hʌnɪ] *n* miel.

honeymoon ['hʌnɪmuːn] *n* luna de miel.

honour ['ɒnəʳ] (US **honor**) *n* honor.

hood [hʊd] *n* **1** capucha. **2** capota *(de coche)*. **3** US capó *(de coche)*.

hoof [huːf] *n* **1** pezuña. **2** casco *(de caballo)*.

hook [hʊk] *n* **1** gancho. **2** anzuelo *(para pescar)*. ► *vt* enganchar. • **off the hook 1** descolgado,-a *(teléfono)*. **2** a salvo *(persona)*.

hoop [huːp] *n* aro.

hoot [huːt] *n* bocinazo. ► *vi* tocar la bocina.

hooter ['huːtəʳ] *n* bocina.

hoover ['huːvə'] *n* aspiradora. ► *vt-vi* pasar la aspiradora (por).

hope [həʊp] *n* esperanza. ► *vt-vi* esperar.

hopeless ['həʊpləs] *adj* imposible, desesperado,-a, inútil.

horizon [hə'raɪzən] *n* horizonte.

horn [hɔːn] *n* **1** asta, cuerno. **2** bocina, cláxon.

horoscope ['hɒrəskəʊp] *n* horóscopo.

horror ['hɒrə'] *n* horror. ■ **horror film** película de terror.

hors d'oeuvre [ɔː'dɜːvʳ] *n* entremés.

horse [hɔːs] *n* caballo.

horsepower ['hɔːspaʊəʳ] *n* caballo *(de vapor)*.

horseshoe ['hɔːsʃuː] *n* herradura.

hose [həʊz] *n* manguera.

hospital ['hɒspɪtəl] *n* hospital.

host [həʊst] *n* **1** anfitrión, -ona. **2** presentador, -ra.

hostage ['hɒstɪdʒ] *n* rehén.

hostel ['hɒstəl] *n* **1** hostal, albergue. **2** residencia *(en universidad)*.

hostess ['həʊstəs] *n* **1** anfitriona. **2** azafata *(de avión, programa)*. **3** camarera.

hostile ['hɒstaɪl] *adj* hostil.

hot [hɒt] *adj* **1** caliente. **2** caluroso,-a, cálido,-a *(día, tiempo)*. **3** picante *(comida)*. • **to be hot 1** tener calor. ■ **hot dog** perrito caliente.

hotchpotch ['hɒtʃpɒtʃ] *n fam* revoltijo.

hotel [həʊ'tel] *n* hotel.

hound [haʊnd] *n* perro de caza.

hour [aʊəʳ] *n* **1** hora. **2** horario. • **on the hour** a la hora en punto.

house [haʊs] *n* casa.

housewife ['haʊswaɪf] *n* ama de casa.

housework ['haʊswɜːk] *n* tareas de la casa.

housing ['haʊzɪŋ] n vivienda. ■ **housing development/estate** urbanización.

how [haʊ] adv 1 cómo. 2 qué: *how beautiful you look!*, !qué guapa estás! ● **how about...?** ¿qué tal si...?; **how are you?** ¿cómo estás?; **how much** cuánto,-a; **how many** cuántos,-as.

however [haʊ'evə'] conj sin embargo, no obstante.

howl [haʊl] n aullido. ► vi aullar.

hub [hʌb] n cubo (de rueda).

hug [hʌg] n abrazo. ► vt abrazar.

huge [hju:dʒ] adj enorme.

hull [hʌl] n casco (de barco).

hullo [hʌ'ləʊ] interj → hello.

human ['hju:mən] adj humano,-a. ► n humano. ■ **human being** ser humano.

humanity [hju:'mænɪtɪ] n humanidad.

humble ['hʌmbəl] adj humilde. ► vt humillar.

humid ['hju:mɪd] adj húmedo,-a.

humiliate [hju:'mɪlɪeɪt] vt humillar.

humility [hju:'mɪlɪtɪ] n humildad.

hummingbird ['hʌmɪŋbɜːd] n colibrí.

humour ['hju:mə'] (US **humor**) n humor.

hump [hʌmp] n giba, joroba.

hundred ['hʌndrəd] adj cien, ciento. ► n cien, ciento.

hundredth ['hʌndrədθ] adj-n centésimo,-a.

hung [hʌŋ] pt-pp → hang.

hunger ['hʌŋgə'] n hambre.

hungry ['hʌŋgrɪ] adj hambriento,-a. ● **to be hungry** tener hambre.

hunt [hʌnt] n caza. ► vt-vi cazar. ● **to hunt for** buscar.

hunter ['hʌntə'] n cazador.

hunting ['hʌntɪŋ] n caza.

hurdle ['hɜːdəl] n valla.

hurl [hɜːl] vt lanzar, arrojar.

hurricane ['hʌrɪkən, 'hʌrɪkeɪn] n huracán.

hurry ['hʌrɪ] n prisa. ► vt meter prisa a. ► vi darse prisa. ● **to be in a hurry** tener prisa. **to hurry up** vi darse prisa.

hurt [hɜːt] n daño, dolor. ► vt herir, hacer daño. ► vi doler. ● **to get hurt** hacerse daño.

husband ['hʌzbənd] n marido, esposo.

hush [hʌʃ] n quietud.

husk [hʌsk] n cáscara.

hut [hʌt] n 1 cabaña. 2 cobertizo.

hutch [hʌtʃ] n conejera.

hyaena [haɪ'i:nə] n hiena.

hydrant ['haɪdrənt] n boca de riego.

hydraulic [haɪ'drɔ:lɪk] adj hidráulico,-a.

hydrofoil ['haɪdrəfɔɪl] n hidroala.

hydrogen ['haɪdrədʒən] *n* hidrógeno.
hydroplane ['haɪdrəpleɪn] *n* hidroavión.
hyena [haɪ'i:nə] *n* hiena.
hygiene ['haɪdʒi:n] *n* higiene.
hymn [hɪm] *n* himno.
hypermarket ['haɪpəmɑ:kɪt] *n* hipermercado.
hyphen ['haɪfən] *n* guión.
hypnotize ['hɪpnətaɪz] *vt* hipnotizar.
hypocrite ['hɪpəkrɪt] *n* hipócrita.
hypothesis [haɪ'pɒθəsɪs] *n* hipótesis.
hysteria [hɪ'stɪərɪə] *n* histeria.

I

I [aɪ] *pron* yo.
ice [aɪs] *n* 1 hielo. 2 helado. ▪ **ice cube** cubito; **ice lolly** polo; **ice rink** pista de (patinaje sobre) hielo.
iceberg ['aɪsbɜ:g] *n* iceberg.
ice-cream ['aɪskri:m] *n* helado.
ice-skate ['aɪsskeɪt] *vi* patinar sobre hielo. ► *n* patín de hielo.
ice-skating ['aɪskeɪtɪŋ] *n* patinaje sobre hielo.
icicle ['aɪsɪkəl] *n* carámbano.
idea [aɪ'dɪə] *n* idea.
identify [aɪ'dentɪfaɪ] *vt* identificar.

identity [aɪ'dentɪtɪ] *n* identidad. ▪ **identity card** carnet de identidad.
ideology [aɪdɪ'ɒlədʒɪ] *n* ideología.
idiom ['ɪdɪəm] *n* locución.
idiot ['ɪdɪət] *n* idiota.
idle ['aɪdəl] *adj* perezoso,-a.
idol ['aɪdəl] *n* ídolo.
if [ɪf] *conj* 1 si: *if you want*, si quieres. 2 aunque: *a clever if rather talkative child*, un niño inteligente aunque demasiado hablador. • **if only** ojalá, si.
igloo ['ɪglu:] *n* iglú.
ignition [ɪg'nɪʃən] *n* 1 ignición. 2 encendido *(de motor)*. ▪ **ignition key** llave de contacto.
ignorant ['ɪgnərənt] *adj* ignorante.
ignore [ɪg'nɔ:'] *vt* ignorar.
ill [ɪl] *adj* enfermo,-a.
illegal [ɪ'li:gəl] *adj* ilegal.
illiterate [ɪ'lɪtərət] *adj-n* 1 analfabeto,-a. 2 inculto,-a.
illness ['ɪlnəs] *n* enfermedad.
illuminate [ɪ'lu:mɪneɪt] *vt* iluminar.
illusion [ɪ'lu:ʒən] *n* ilusión.**illustration** [ɪləs'treɪʃən] *n* 1 ilustración. 2 ejemplo.
image ['ɪmɪdʒ] *n* imagen.
imagination [ɪmædʒɪ'neɪʃən] *n* imaginación.
imagine [ɪ'mædʒɪn] *vt* imaginar.
imitate ['ɪmɪteɪt] *vt* imitar.

imitation [ɪmɪ'teɪʃən] n imitación.

immediate [ɪ'miːdɪət] adj inmediato,-a.

immense [ɪ'mens] adj inmenso,-a.

immerse [ɪ'mɜːs] vt sumergir.

immigrant ['ɪmɪɡrənt] adj inmigrante. ▶ n inmigrante.

immobile [ɪ'məʊbaɪl] adj inmóvil.

immunity [ɪ'mjuːnɪtɪ] n inmunidad.

impact ['ɪmpækt] n impacto.

impassive [ɪm'pæsɪv] adj impasible, imperturbable.

imperative [ɪm'perətɪv] adj esencial, imprescindible. ▶ n imperativo.

imperfect [ɪm'pɜːfekt] adj defectuoso,-a. ▶ n imperfecto (tiempo verbal).

imperial [ɪm'pɪərɪəl] adj imperial.

impersonal [ɪm'pɜːsənəl] adj impersonal.

impertinent [ɪm'pɜːtɪnənt] adj impertinente.

implant ['ɪmplɑːnt] vt implantar.

implausible [ɪm'plɔːzəbəl] adj inverosími.

implement [(n) 'ɪmpləmənt, (vb) 'ɪmplɪment] n instrumento, utensilio. ▶ vt llevar a cabo, poner en práctica.

implicate ['ɪmplɪkeɪt] vt implicar.

implicit [ɪm'plɪsɪt] adj 1 implícito,-a. 2 absoluto,-a, incondicional.

implore [ɪm'plɔːr] vt implorar.

impolite [ɪmpə'laɪt] adj maleducado,-a.

import ['ɪmpɔːt] n 1 artículo de importación. 2 importación. ▶ vt importar.

importance [ɪm'pɔːtəns] n importancia.

important [ɪm'pɔːtənt] adj importante.

impossible [ɪm'pɒsɪbəl] adj imposible.

impress [ɪm'pres] vt 1 impresionar. 2 subrayar, recalcar.

impression [ɪm'preʃən] n 1 impresión. 2 imitación.

impressive [ɪm'presɪv] adj impresionante.

imprisonment [ɪm'prɪzənmənt] n 1 encarcelamiento. 2 cárcel.

improve [ɪm'pruːv] vt mejorar. ▶ vi mejorar, mejorarse.

improvement [ɪm'pruːvmənt] n 1 mejora, mejoría. 2 reforma.

improvise ['ɪmprəvaɪz] vt-vi improvisar.

impulse ['ɪmpʌls] n impulso.

impulsive [ɪm'pʌlsɪv] adj impulsivo,-a.

in [ɪn] prep 1 en: *in May*, en mayo; *in the box*, en la caja. 2 en, vestido,-a de: *the man in black*, el hombre vestido de negro. **3** por: *in the afternoon*, por la tarde. **4** al: *in doing that*, al hacer eso. **5** de: *the biggest in the world*, el más grande del mundo. ► *adv* **1** dentro. **2** en casa: *is Judith in?*, ¿está Judith? **3** de moda: *short skirts are in*, las faldas cortas están de moda. • **in so far as** en lo que, hasta donde; **in all** en total.

inaccurate [ɪn'ækjərət] *adj* inexacto,-a.

inadequate [ɪn'ædɪkwət] *adj* **1** insuficiente. **2** inepto,-a, incapaz *(persona)*.

inaugural [ɪ'nɔːgjʊrəl] *adj* inaugural.

inaugurate [ɪ'nɔːgjʊreɪt] *vt* **1** inaugurar *(edificio)*. **2** investir *(presidente)*.

incapacity [ɪnkə'pæsɪti] *n* incapacidad.

incense ['ɪnsens] *n* incienso.

incentive [ɪn'sentɪv] *n* incentivo.

incessant [ɪn'sesənt] *adj* incesante.

inch [ɪntʃ] *n* pulgada.

incidence ['ɪnsɪdəns] *n* **1** índice *(frecuencia)*. **2** incidencia *(efecto)*.

incident ['ɪnsɪdənt] *n* incidente.

incidental [ɪnsɪ'dentəl] *adj* accesorio,-a, secundario,-a.

incinerate [ɪn'sɪnəreɪt] *vt* incinerar.

incision [ɪn'sɪʒən] *n* incisión.

incisive [ɪn'saɪsɪv] *adj* incisivo,-a.

incisor [ɪn'saɪzəʳ] *n* incisivo *(diente)*.

incite [ɪn'saɪt] *vt* incitar.

inclination [ɪnklɪ'neɪʃən] *n* inclinación.

incline [ɪn'klaɪn] *vt-vi* inclinar(se).

include [ɪn'kluːd] *vt* incluir.

including [ɪn'kluːdɪŋ] *prep* incluso, inclusive, incluido.

incoherent [ɪnkəʊ'hɪərənt] *adj* incoherente.

income ['ɪnkʌm] *n* ingresos, renta. ▪ **income tax** impuesto sobre la renta; **income tax return** declaración de la renta.

incoming ['ɪnkʌmɪŋ] *adj* entrante, nuevo,-a.

incompetent [ɪn'kɒmpətənt] *adj* incompetente, inepto,-a.

inconclusive [ɪnkən'kluːsɪv] *adj* no concluyente.

incongruous [ɪn'kɒŋgrʊəs] *adj* incongruente.

inconsiderate [ɪnkən'sɪdərət] *adj* desconsiderado,-a.

inconsistent [ɪnkən'sɪstənt] *adj* contradictorio,-a.

inconspicuous [ɪnkən'spɪkjʊəs] *adj* que pasa desapercibido,-a.

inconvenient [ɪnkən'viːnɪənt] *adj* **1** mal situado,-a *(lugar)*. **2** inoportuno,-a *(momento)*.

incorporate [ɪn'kɔːpəreɪt] *vt* incorporar.

increase [(n) 'ɪnkriːs, (vb) ɪn-'kriːs] n aumento. ► vt-vi aumentar, subir.

incredible [ɪn'kredɪbəl] adj increíble.

incur [ɪn'kɜːr] vt **1** incurrir en (críticas). **2** contraer (deuda).

indeed [ɪn'diːd] adv **1** en efecto, efectivamente. **2** realmente, de veras: *thank you very much indeed*, muchísimas gracias.

indefinite [ɪn'defɪnət] adj indefinido,-a.

indemnity [ɪn'demnɪti] n indemnización.

independence [ɪndɪ'pendəns] n independencia.

independent [ɪndɪ'pendənt] adj independiente.

in-depth [ɪn'depθ] adj exhaustivo,-a, a fondo.

index ['ɪndeks] n índice. ► vt poner un índice a, catalogar. ▪ **index finger** dedo índice.

indicate ['ɪndɪkeɪt] vt indicar.

indicative [ɪn'dɪkətɪv] adj indicativo,-a. ► n indicativo.

indicator ['ɪndɪkeɪtər] n **1** indicador. **2** intermitente (de coche).

indigenous [ɪn'dɪdʒənəs] adj indígena.

indignant [ɪn'dɪgnənt] adj **1** indignado,-a (persona). **2** de indignación (mirada).

indistinct [ɪndɪ'stɪŋkt] adj **1** vago,-a (recuerdo). **2** borroso,-a, poco definido,-a (forma).

individual [ɪndɪ'vɪdjʊəl] adj **1** individual. **2** particular, personal (estilo). ► n individuo.

indoor ['ɪndɔːr] adj **1** interior, de estar por casa (ropa). **2** cubierto,-a (pista de tenis). ▪ **indoor football** fútbol sala; **indoor pool** piscina cubierta.

indoors [ɪn'dɔːz] adv dentro.

indulgent [ɪn'dʌldʒənt] adj indulgente.

industrial [ɪn'dʌstrɪəl] adj industrial. ▪ **industrial estate** polígono industrial.

industrious [ɪn'dʌstrɪəs] adj trabajador,-ra, aplicado,-a.

industry ['ɪndəstrɪ] n industria.

inedible [ɪn'edəbəl] adj no comestible.

inequality [ɪnɪ'kwɒlətɪ] n desigualdad.

inexpensive [ɪnɪk'spensɪv] adj barato,-a, económico,-a.

infantry ['ɪnfəntrɪ] n infantería.

infect [ɪn'fekt] vt **1** infectar. **2** contagiar.

infection [ɪn'fekʃən] n **1** infección. **2** contagio.

infectious [ɪn'fekʃəs] adj infeccioso,-a, contagioso,-a.

inferior [ɪn'fɪərɪər] adj inferior. ► n inferior.

infertile [ɪn'fɜːtaɪl] adj estéril.

infest [ɪn'fest] vt infestar.

infiltrate ['ɪnfɪltreɪt] vt infiltrarse en.

infinite ['ɪnfɪnət] adj infinito,-a.

infinitive [ɪnˈfɪnɪtɪv] *n* infinitivo.

infirm [ɪnˈfɜːm] *adj* débil, enfermizo,-a.

infirmary [ɪnˈfɜːmərɪ] *n* **1** hospital. **2** enfermería.

inflammable [ɪnˈflæməbəl] *adj* inflamable.

inflammation [ɪnfləˈmeɪʃən] *n* inflamación.

inflation [ɪnˈfleɪʃən] *n* inflación.

influence [ˈɪnfluəns] *n* influencia. ▶ *vt* influir en.

influenza [ɪnfluˈenzə] *n* gripe.

inform [ɪnˈfɔːm] *vt* informar.

information [ɪnfəˈmeɪʃən] *n* información.

infuriate [ɪnˈfjuərɪeɪt] *vt* enfurecer.

ingenious [ɪnˈdʒiːnɪəs] *adj* ingenioso,-a.

ingrained [ɪnˈɡreɪnd] *adj* **1** incrustado,-a *(suciedad)*. **2** arraigado,-a *(costumbre)*.

ingredient [ɪnˈɡriːdɪənt] *n* ingrediente.

inhabitant [ɪnˈhæbɪtənt] *n* habitante.

inherit [ɪnˈherɪt] *vt* heredar.

inheritance [ɪnˈherɪtəns] *n* herencia.

initial [ɪˈnɪʃəl] *adj-n* inicial.

initiate [ɪˈnɪʃɪeɪt] *vt* iniciar.

injection [ɪnˈdʒekʃən] *n* inyección.

injure [ˈɪndʒəʳ] *vt* herir.

injury [ˈɪndʒərɪ] *n* herida, lesión. ■ **injury time** tiempo de descuento *(en partido)*.

ink [ɪŋk] *n* tinta.

inkjet printer [ˈɪŋkdʒetˈprɪntəʳ] *n* impresora de chorro de tinta.

inland [*(adj)* ˈɪnlənd, *(adv)* ɪnˈlænd] *adj* de tierra adentro. ▶ *adv* tierra adentro.

inlet [ˈɪnlet] *n* **1** cala, ensenada. **2** entrada *(de río, mar)*.

inn [ɪn] *n* **1** posada, fonda, mesón. **2** taberna.

inner [ˈɪnəʳ] *adj* interior.

innocent [ˈɪnəsənt] *adj-n* inocente.

innovation [ɪnəˈveɪʃən] *n* innovación.

inpatient [ˈɪnpeɪʃənt] *n* paciente hospitalizado,-a.

input [ˈɪnput] *n* **1** entrada, inversión *(de dinero)*. **2** input, entrada *(de datos)*.

inquire [ɪnˈkwaɪəʳ] *vt* preguntar. • **"Inquire within"** "Razón aquí".

inquiry [ɪnˈkwaɪərɪ] *n* **1** pregunta. **2** investigación. • **"Inquiries"** "Información".

inquisitive [ɪnˈkwɪzɪtɪv] *adj* curioso,-a.

insane [ɪnˈseɪn] *adj* demente, loco,-a.

insect [ˈɪnsekt] *n* insecto.

insert [ɪnˈsɜːt] *vt* insertar.

inside [ɪnˈsaɪd] *n* interior. ▶ *adj* interior, interno,-a. ▶ *adv* **1** dentro *(posición)*. **2** adentro *(movimiento)*. ▶ *prep* dentro de. • **inside out** de dentro afuera, al revés, del revés.

insight ['ɪnsaɪt] *n* **1** perspicacia, penetración. **2** idea.

insinuate [ɪn'sɪnjʊeɪt] *vt* insinuar.

insist [ɪn'sɪst] *vi* insistir.

insomnia [ɪn'sɒmnɪə] *n* insomnio.

inspection [ɪn'spekʃən] *n* **1** inspección. **2** registro *(a equipaje)*. **3** revista *(a tropas)*.

inspector [ɪn'spektə'] *n* **1** inspector,-ra. **2** revisor,-ra *(en tren)*.

inspiration [ɪnspɪ'reɪʃən] *n* inspiración.

install [ɪn'stɔːl] *vt* instalar.

instalment [ɪn'stɔːlmənt] *n* **1** plazo *(de pago)*. **2** fascículo *(de libro)*. **3** episodio *(de serie)*.

instance ['ɪnstəns] *n* ejemplo, caso. • **for instance** por ejemplo.

instant ['ɪnstənt] *n* instante. ► *adj* **1** inmediato,-a. **2** instantáneo,-a *(café)*.

instead [ɪn'sted] *adv* en cambio. • **instead of** en vez de.

instep ['ɪnstep] *n* empeine.

instinct ['ɪnstɪŋkt] *n* instinto.

institute ['ɪnstɪtjuːt] *n* instituto.

institution [ɪnstɪ'tjuːʃən] *n* institución.

instruction [ɪn'strʌkʃən] *n* instrucción.

instrument ['ɪnstrəmənt] *n* instrumento.

insulate ['ɪnsjəleɪt] *vt* aislar.

insult [*(n)* 'ɪnsʌlt, *(vb)* ɪn'sʌlt] *n* insulto. ► *vt* insultar.

insurance [ɪn'ʃʊərəns] *n* seguro. ■ **insurance policy** póliza de seguro.

insure [ɪn'ʃʊə'] *vt* asegurar.

intake ['ɪnteɪk] *n* consumo.

integral ['ɪntɪgrəl] *adj-n* integral.

integrity [ɪn'tegrɪtɪ] *n* integridad.

intellectual [ɪntə'lektjʊəl] *adj-n* intelectual.

intelligence [ɪn'telɪdʒəns] *n* inteligencia.

intelligent [ɪn'telɪʒənt] *adj* inteligente.

intend [ɪn'tend] *vt* tener la intención de, proponerse.

intense [ɪn'tens] *adj* **1** intenso,-a. **2** muy serio,-a *(persona)*.

intensive [ɪn'tensɪv] *adj* intensivo,-a. ■ **intensive care** cuidados intensivos.

intention [ɪn'tenʃən] *n* intención.

interactive [ɪntər'æktɪv] *adj* interactivo,-a.

interchange ['ɪntətʃeɪndʒ] *n* **1** intercambio. **2** enlace.

intercom ['ɪntəkɒm] *n* interfono.

interest ['ɪntrəst] *n* interés. ► *vt* interesar. ■ **interest rate** tipo de interés.

interface ['ɪntəfeɪs] *n* interfaz.

interference [ɪntə'fɪərəns] *n* interferencia.

interior [ɪn'tɪərɪə'] *adj-n* interior.

interjection [ɪntə'dʒekʃən] n
1 interjección. 2 comentario.

interlude ['ɪntəluːd] n 1 intermedio, descanso. 2 interludio *(en música)*.

intermediate [ɪntə'miːdɪət] adj intermedio,-a.

intermission [ɪntə'mɪʃən] n intermedio, descanso.

internal [ɪn'tɜːnəl] adj interior, interno,-a. ▪ **internal flight** vuelo nacional.

international [ɪntə'næʃənəl] adj internacional.

Internet ['ɪntənet] n Internet.

interplay ['ɪntəpleɪ] n interacción.

interpret [ɪn'tɜːprət] vt interpretar. ▶ vi hacer de intérprete.

interrogation [ɪntərə'geɪʃən] n interrogatorio.

interrogative [ɪntə'rɒgætɪv] adj interrogativo,-a.

interrupt [ɪntə'rʌpt] vt-vi interrumpir.

interval ['ɪntəvəl] n 1 intervalo. 2 descanso, intermedio *(en teatro, etc)*.

intervention [ɪntə'venʃən] n intervención.

interview ['ɪntəvjuː] n entrevista. ▶ vt entrevistar.

interviewer ['ɪntəvjuːəʳ] n entrevistador,-ra.

intestine [ɪn'testɪn] n intestino.

intimacy ['ɪntɪməsɪ] n intimidad.

intimate ['ɪntɪmət] adj íntimo,-a.

into ['ɪntʊ] prep 1 en, dentro de. 2 dividido entre.

intonation [ɪntə'neɪʃən] n entonación.

intoxicated [ɪn'tɒksɪkeɪtɪd] adj ebrio,-a.

intranet ['ɪntrənet] n intranet.

intransitive [ɪn'trænsɪtɪv] adj intransitivo,-a.

intrigue [ɪn'triːg] n intriga.

introduce [ɪntrə'djuːs] vt 1 introducir. 2 presentar.

introduction [ɪntrə'dʌkʃən] n 1 introducción. 2 presentación.

intruder [ɪn'truːdəʳ] n intruso,-a.

intuition [ɪntjuː'ɪʃən] n intuición.

invade [ɪn'veɪd] vt invadir.

invaluable [ɪn'væljʊəbəl] adj inestimable.

invasion [ɪn'veɪʒən] n invasión.

invent [ɪn'vent] vt inventar.

invention [ɪn'venʃən] n 1 invento *(cosa)*. 2 invención *(acción)*.

inventor [ɪn'ventəʳ] n inventor,-ra.

inventory ['ɪnvəntrɪ] n inventario.

inversion [ɪn'vɜːʒən] n inversión.

invert [ɪn'vɜːt] vt invertir.

inverted [ɪn'vɜːtɪd] adj invertido,-a. ▪ **inverted commas** comillas.

invest [ɪn'vest] vt-vi invertir.

investigation [ɪnvestɪ'geɪʃən] *n* investigación.

investment [ɪn'vestmənt] *n* inversión.

invitation [ɪnvɪ'teɪʃən] *n* invitación.

invite [ɪn'vaɪt] *vt* invitar.

inviting [ɪn'vaɪtɪŋ] *adj* tentador,-ra, atractivo,-a.

invoice ['ɪnvɔɪs] *n* factura. ► *vt* facturar.

involve [ɪn'vɒlv] *vt* **1** involucrar. **2** afectar a. **3** suponer.

inward ['ɪnwəd] *adj* interior. ► *adv* hacia adentro.

inwards ['ɪnwədz] *adv* hacia adentro.

iris ['aɪrɪs] *n* **1** iris *(del ojo)*. **2** lirio.

iron ['aɪən] *n* **1** hierro. **2** plancha. ► *vt* planchar.

ironic [aɪ'rɒnɪk] *adj* irónico,-a.

ironmonger ['aɪənmʌŋgəʳ] *n* ferretero,-a.

ironmonger's ['aɪənmʌŋgəz] *n* ferretería.

irony ['aɪrəni] *n* ironía.

irrational [ɪ'ræʃənəl] *adj* irracional.

irregular [ɪ'regjələʳ] *adj* irregular.

irrelevant [ɪ'relɪvənt] *adj* irrelevante.

irresistible [ɪrɪ'zɪstəbəl] *adj* irresistible.

irresponsible [ɪrɪ'spɒnsəbəl] *adj* irresponsable.

irrigate ['ɪrɪgeɪt] *vt* regar.

irritate ['ɪrɪteɪt] *vt* irritar.

irritating ['ɪrɪteɪtɪŋ] *adj* irritante, molesto,-a.

irritation [ɪrɪ'teɪʃən] *n* irritación.

is [ɪz] *3rd pers sing pres* → be.

island ['aɪlənd] *n* isla.

isle [aɪl] *n* isla.

isolate ['aɪsəleɪt] *vt* aislar.

isolation [aɪsə'leɪʃən] *n* aislamiento.

issue ['ɪʃuː] *n* **1** asunto, tema. **2** edición *(de libro)*. **3** número *(de revista)*. **4** emisión *(de sellos, acciones)*. **5** expedición *(de pasaporte)*. ► *vt* **1** publicar *(libro)*. **2** emitir *(sellos, acciones)*. **3** expedir *(pasaporte)*.

isthmus ['ɪsməs] *n* istmo.

it [ɪt] *pron* **1** él, ella, ello *(sujeto)*. **2** lo, la *(complemento - directo)*; le *(- indirecto)*. **3** él, ella, ello *(después de preposición)*.

italics [ɪ'tælɪks] *npl* cursiva.

itch [ɪtʃ] *n* picazón, picor. ► *vi* picar: *my leg itches*, me pica la pierna.

item ['aɪtəm] *n* **1** artículo, cosa. **2** asunto *(en agenda)*. **3** partida *(en factura)*. **4** noticia.

itinerary [aɪ'tɪnərəri] *n* itinerario.

its [ɪts] *adj* su, sus.

itself [ɪt'self] *pron* **1** se *(reflexivo)*. **2** sí, sí mismo,-a *(después de preposición)*. ● **by itself** solo.

ivory ['aɪvəri] *n* marfil.

ivy ['aɪvi] *n* hiedra.

J

jab [dʒæb] *n* pinchazo, inyección. ▶ *vt* pinchar, clavar.

jabber ['dʒæbəˈ] *vi-vt* farfullar.

jack [dʒæk] *n* 1 gato *(para coche)*. 2 jota, sota.

jackal ['dʒækɔːl] *n* chacal.

jacket ['dʒækɪt] *n* 1 chaqueta, americana. 2 cazadora. 3 sobrecubierta *(de libro)*.

jack-knife ['dʒæknaɪf] *n* navaja.

jackpot ['dʒækpɒt] *n* premio gordo.

jade [dʒeɪd] *n* jade.

jaguar ['dʒægjʊəˈ] *n* jaguar.

jail [dʒeɪl] *n* cárcel, prisión. ▶ *vt* encarcelar.

jam¹ [dʒæm] *n* mermelada.

jam² [dʒæm] *n* 1 aprieto, apuro. 2 atasco. ▶ *vt* 1 atestar, apiñar. 2 embutir, meter. ▶ *vi* atascarse, bloquearse.

janitor ['dʒænɪtəˈ] *n* portero.

January ['dʒænjʊərɪ] *n* enero.

jar [dʒɑːˈ] *n* tarro, pote.

jargon ['dʒɑːgən] *n* jerga.

jasmin ['dʒæzmɪn] *n* jazmín.

jaundice ['dʒɔːndɪs] *n* ictericia.

jaunt [dʒɔːnt] *n* excursión.

javelin ['dʒævəlɪn] *n* jabalina.

jaw [dʒɔː] *n* mandíbula.

jazz [dʒæz] *n* jazz.

jealous ['dʒeləs] *adj* celoso,-a.
• **to be jealous of** SB tener celos de ALGN.

jealousy ['dʒeləsɪ] *n* celos.

jeans [dʒiːnz] *npl* vaqueros.

jeep® [dʒiːp] *n* jeep®.

jeer [dʒɪəˈ] *vi* 1 burlarse. 2 abuchear. ▶ *n* 1 burla. 2 abucheo.

jelly ['dʒelɪ] *n* 1 jalea. 2 gelatina.

jellyfish ['dʒelɪfɪʃ] *n* medusa.

jerk [dʒɜːk] *n* 1 tirón, sacudida. 2 *fam* imbécil. ▶ *vt* sacudir, tirar de.

jerkin ['dʒɜːkɪn] *n* chaleco.

jersey ['dʒɜːzɪ] *n* jersey, suéter.

jet [dʒet] *n* 1 reactor, jet. 2 chorro.

jet-lag ['dʒetlæg] *n* jet-lag.

jet-set ['dʒetset] *n* jetset.

jetty ['dʒetɪ] *n* malecón.

Jew [dʒuː] *n* judío.

jewel ['dʒuːəl] *n* 1 joya, alhaja. 2 piedra preciosa.

jeweller ['dʒuːələˈ] *n* joyero, -a. ▪ **jeweller's** joyería.

jewellery ['dʒuːəlrɪ] *n* joyas.

Jewish ['dʒuːɪʃ] *adj* judío,-a.

jigsaw ['dʒɪgsɔː] *n* rompecabezas.

jingle ['dʒɪŋgəl] *n* 1 tintineo. 2 melodía *(de anuncio)*. ▶ *vi* tintinear.

jinx [dʒɪŋks] *n* gafe.

job [dʒɒb] *n* trabajo.

jobless ['dʒɒbləs] *adj* parado,-a, sin trabajo.

jockey ['dʒɒkɪ] *n* jockey.

jog [dʒɒg] *n* trote. ▶ *vt* empujar, sacudir. ▶ *vi* hacer footing, correr. • **to go for a jog** hacer footing.

jogging ['dʒɒgɪŋ] *n* footing.

join [dʒɔɪn] *vt* **1** juntar, unir. **2** reunirse con. **3** acompañar. **4** alistarse *(en ejército)*; ingresar *(en policía)*. **5** hacerse socio,-a *(de un club)*. **6** afiliarse a *(partido)*. ► *vi* confluir *(ríos)*.

joiner ['dʒɔɪnə'] *n* carpintero.

joint [dʒɔɪnt] *n* **1** junta, juntura, unión. **2** articulación *(de rodilla, cadera)*. ► *adj* conjunto,-a. ■ **joint venture** empresa conjunta.

joke [dʒəʊk] *n* **1** chiste. **2** broma. ► *vi* bromear.

joker ['dʒəʊkə'] *n* **1** bromista. **2** comodín.

jolly ['dʒɒlɪ] *adj* alegre.

jolt [dʒəʊlt] *n* **1** sacudida. **2** sorpresa, susto. ► *vt* sacudir. ► *vi* dar una sacudida.

jotter ['dʒɒtə'] *n* GB bloc.

journal ['dʒɜːnəl] *n* **1** revista, publicación *(especializada)*. **2** diario.

journalism ['dʒɜːnəlɪzəm] *n* periodismo.

journalist ['dʒɜːnəlɪst] *n* periodista.

journey ['dʒɜːnɪ] *n* **1** viaje. **2** trayecto.

joy [dʒɔɪ] *n* gozo, alegría.

joyful ['dʒɔɪfʊl] *adj* alegre.

joystick ['dʒɔɪstɪk] *n* joystick.

judge [dʒʌdʒ] *n* juez, jueza. ► *vt-vi* juzgar.

judgement ['dʒʌdʒmənt] *n* juicio, fallo.

jug [dʒʌg] *n* jarro.

juggler ['dʒʌglə'] *n* malabarista.

juice [dʒuːs] *n* jugo; zumo.

jukebox ['dʒuːkbɒks] *n* máquina de discos.

July [dʒuː'laɪ] *n* julio.

jump [dʒʌmp] *n* salto. ► *vt-vi* saltar. ► *vi* dar un salto.

jumper ['dʒʌmpə'] *n* **1** GB jersey. **2** US pichi.

jump-suit ['dʒʌmpsuːt] *n* mono.

junction ['dʒʌŋkʃən] *n* **1** salida, acceso *(en autopista)*. **2** cruce.

June [dʒuːn] *n* junio.

jungle ['dʒʌŋgəl] *n* jungla.

juniper ['dʒuːnɪpə'] *n* enebro.

junk¹ [dʒʌŋk] *n* trastos. ■ **junk food** comida basura; **junk mail** propaganda.

junk² [dʒʌŋk] *n* junco.

jury ['dʒʊərɪ] *n* jurado.

just¹ [dʒʌst] *adj* justo,-a.

just² [dʒʌst] *adv* **1** exactamente, justo. **2** solamente. **3** justo ahora. **4** justo. • **just now** ahora mismo.

justice ['dʒʌstɪs] *n* justicia.

justify ['dʒʌstɪfaɪ] *vt* justificar.

jute [dʒuːt] *n* yute.

juvenile ['dʒuːvɪnaɪl] *adj* **1** juvenil. **2** infantil. ► *n* menor.

juxtapose ['dʒʌkstəpəʊz] *vt* yuxtaponer.

K

kangaroo [kæŋgə'ruː] *n* canguro.

karate [kə'rɑːtɪ] *n* kárate.

kayak ['kaɪæk] *n* kayac.

keel [kiːl] *n* quilla.

keen [kiːn] *adj* **1** entusiasta, muy aficionado,-a. **2** agudo,-a *(mente)*. **3** penetrante *(mirada)*. **4** cortante *(viento)*. **5** fuerte *(competencia)*. ● **keen on** aficionado,-a a.

keep [kiːp] *vt* **1** guardar. **2** retener, entretener. **3** tener *(tienda, negocio)*. **4** llevar *(cuentas, diario)*. **5** cumplir *(promesa)*. **6** acudir a, no faltar a *(cita)*. **7** mantener. **8** criar *(gallinas, cerdos)*. ► *vi* **1** seguir, continuar. **2** conservarse bien ● **to keep** STH **to oneself** guardar algo para sí.

to keep on *vi* seguir, continuar.

keg [keg] *n* barril.

kennel ['kenəl] *n* perrera, caseta para perros.

kept [kept] *pt-pp* → keep.

kerb [kɜːb] *n* bordillo.

kernel ['kɜːnəl] *n* **1** semilla *(de nuez, fruta)*. **2** *fig* núcleo.

ketchup ['ketʃəp] *n* ketchup, catsup.

kettle ['ketəl] *n* hervidor.

key [kiː] *n* **1** llave *(de cerradura)*. **2** clave *(de misterio)*. **3** tecla *(de teclado)*. **4** soluciones, respuestas *(de ejercicios)*. ► *adj* clave. ► *vt* teclear. ■ **key ring** llavero.

keyboard ['kiːbɔːd] *n* teclado.

keyhole ['kiːhəʊl] *n* ojo de la cerradura.

kick [kɪk] *n* **1** puntapié, patada. **2** coz. **3** emoción, sensación. ► *vt* **1** dar un puntapié a, dar una patada a. **2** dar coces a.

to kick out *vt* echar.

kick-off ['kɪkɒf] *n* saque inicial *(en fútbol, rugby)*.

kid¹ [kɪd] *n* **1** cabrito *(animal)*. **2** cabritilla *(piel)*. **3** *fam* niño,-a, chico,-a.

kid² [kɪd] *vt* tomar el pelo a. ► *vi* estar de broma: *you must be kidding!*, ¡debes de estar de broma!

kidnap ['kɪdnæp] *vt* secuestrar.

kidney ['kɪdnɪ] *n* riñón.

kill [kɪl] *vt* matar.

killer ['kɪlə'] *n* asesino,-a.

kilo ['kiːləʊ] *n* kilo.

kilogram ['kɪləgræm] *n* kilogramo.

kilometre [kɪ'lɒmɪtə'] (US **kilometer**) *n* kilómetro.

kilt [kɪlt] *n* falda escocesa.

kin [kɪn] *n* parientes, familia.

kind [kaɪnd] *adj* simpático,-a, amable. ► *n* tipo, género, clase. ● **a kind of** una especie de; **to be so kind as to** tener la bondad de.

kindergarten ['kɪndəgæːtən] *n* jardín de infancia.

king [kɪŋ] *n* rey.

kingdom ['kɪŋdəm] *n* reino.

kiosk ['kiːɒsk] *n* **1** quiosco. **2** cabina telefónica.

kiss [kɪs] *n* beso. ► *vt-vi* besar(se).

kit [kɪt] *n* **1** equipo. **2** petate. **3** maqueta, kit.

kitchen ['kɪtʃɪn] *n* cocina.

kite [kaɪt] *n* cometa.

kitty ['kɪti] *n fam* bote *(de dinero)*.

kiwi ['kiːwiː] *n* kiwi.

knapsack ['næpsæk] *n* mochila.

knead [niːd] *vt* amasar.

knee [niː] *n* rodilla.

kneecap ['niːkæp] *n* rótula.

kneel [niːl] *vi* arrodillarse.

knelt [nelt] *pt-pp* → kneel.

knew [njuː] *pt* → know.

knickers ['nɪkəz] *npl* bragas.

knick-knack ['nɪknæk] *n* chuchería.

knife [naɪf] *n* cuchillo.

knight [naɪt] *n* **1** caballero. **2** caballo *(ajedrez)*.

knit [nɪt] *vt* tejer. ► *vi* hacer punto, tricotar.

knitting ['nɪtɪŋ] *n* punto.

knob [nɒb] *n* **1** pomo *(de puerta)*. **2** tirador *(de cajón)*. **3** botón *(de radio)*.

knock [nɒk] *n* golpe. ► *vt* golpear. ► *vi* llamar.

to knock down *vt* **1** derribar *(edificio)*. **2** atropellar.

to knock out *vt* dejar sin conocimiento, dejar fuera de combate *(en boxeo)*.

to knock over *vt* volcar *(vaso)*, atropellar *(persona)*.

knockout ['nɒkaʊt] *n* K.O., fuera de combate.

knot [nɒt] *n* nudo. ► *vt* anudar.

know [nəʊ] *vt-vi* **1** conocer. **2** saber. ● **as far as I know** que yo sepa.

know-how ['nəʊhaʊ] *n* conocimiento práctico.

knowledge ['nɒlɪdʒ] *n* conocimiento(s).

known [nəʊn] *pp* → know.

knuckle ['nʌkəl] *n* nudillo.

KO ['keɪ'əʊ] *abbr* **(knockout)** fuera de combate, KO.

koala [kəʊ'ɑːlə] *n* koala.

L

label ['leɪbəl] *n* etiqueta. ► *vt* etiquetar.

laboratory [lə'bɒrətəri] *n* laboratorio.

labour ['leɪbə'] (US **labor**) *n* **1** trabajo. **2** mano de obra.

labourer ['leɪbərə'] (US **laborer**) *n* peón, obrero,-a.

lace [leɪs] *n* **1** cordón *(de zapato)*. **2** encaje.

lack [læk] *n* falta, carencia. ► *vt* faltar, carecer de.

lacquer ['lækə'] *n* laca.

lad [læd] *n* muchacho, chaval.

ladder ['lædə'] *n* **1** escalera de mano. **2** carrera *(en medias)*.

ladle ['leɪdəl] *n* cucharón.

lady ['leɪdɪ] *n* señora, dama.

ladybird ['leɪdɪbɜːd] *n* mariquita.

lager ['lɑːgə'] *n* cerveza rubia.

lagoon [lə'guːn] *n* laguna.

laid [leɪd] *pt-pp* → lay.

lain [leɪn] *pp* → lie.

lair [leə'] *n* guarida.

lake [leɪk] *n* lago.

lamb [læm] *n* cordero.

lame [leɪm] *adj* cojo,-a.

lamp [læmp] *n* lámpara.

lamp-post ['læmppəʊst] *n* farola.

lampshade ['læmpʃeɪd] *n* pantalla *(de lámpara)*.

lance [lɑːns] *n* lanza.

land [lænd] *n* tierra. ► *vi* aterrizar. ► *vt-vi* desembarcar.

landing ['lændɪŋ] *n* **1** aterrizaje *(de avión)*. **2** descansillo, rellano *(en escalera)*. **3** desembarco *(de personas)*.

landlady ['lændleɪdɪ] *n* **1** propietaria, casera *(de vivienda)*. **2** dueña *(de pensión)*.

landlord ['lændlɔːd] *n* **1** propietario, casero *(de vivienda)*. **2** dueño *(de pensión)*.

landscape ['lændskeɪp] *n* paisaje.

landslide ['lændslaɪd] *n* desprendimiento de tierras.

lane [leɪn] *n* **1** camino. **2** carril *(de autopista)*. **3** calle *(en atletismo, natación)*.

language ['læŋgwɪdʒ] *n* **1** lenguaje. **2** lengua, idioma.

lantern ['læntən] *n* linterna.

lap¹ [læp] *n* regazo, rodillas.

lap² [læp] *n* **1** vuelta *(de carrera)*. **2** etapa *(de viaje)*.

lapel [lə'pel] *n* solapa.

lapse [læps] *n* **1** lapso *(de tiempo)*. **2** lapsus.

laptop ['læptɒp] *n* ordenador portátil.

lard [lɑːd] *n* manteca de cerdo.

large [lɑːdʒ] *adj* grande, gran. ● **at large** suelto,-a.

lark [lɑːk] *n* alondra.

larynx ['lærɪŋks] *n* laringe.

lash [læʃ] *n* **1** latigazo, azote. **2** pestaña.

last [lɑːst] *adj* **1** último,-a. **2** pasado,-a: *last night*, anoche. ► *adv* **1** por última vez. **2** en último lugar. ► *n* el/la último,-a. ► *vt-vi* durar. ● **at last** al fin, por fin; **last but one** penúltimo,-a.

latch [lætʃ] *n* pestillo.

late [leɪt] *adj* **1**: *in the late afternoon*, a media tarde. **2** difunto,-a. ► *adv* tarde. ● **to be late** llegar tarde; **to get late** hacerse tarde.

later ['leɪtə'] *adj* posterior *(fecha, edición)*. ► *adv* **1** más tarde. **2** después, luego.

latest ['leɪtɪst] *adj* último,-a.

lather ['lɑːðəʳ] *n* espuma.
laugh [lɑːf] *n* risa. ► *vi* reír, reírse. • **to laugh at** reírse de
launch [lɔːntʃ] *n* lanzamiento. ► *vt* lanzar.
launder ['lɔːndəʳ] *vt* **1** lavar y planchar *(ropa)*. **2** blanquear *(dinero)*.
launderette [lɔːndəˈret] *n* lavandería automática.
laundry ['lɔːndrɪ] *n* **1** lavandería. **2** colada.
laurel ['lɒrəl] *n* laurel.
lavatory ['lævətərɪ] *n* servicios, aseo *(público)*.
lavender ['lævɪndəʳ] *n* lavanda.
lavish ['lævɪʃ] *adj* generoso,-a.
law [lɔː] *n* **1** ley. **2** derecho *(carrera)*.
lawn [lɔːn] *n* césped.
lawyer ['lɔːjəʳ] *n* abogado,-a.
lay [leɪ] *vt* **1** poner, colocar. **2** poner *(huevos)*.
lay³ [leɪ] *pt* → lie.
lay-by ['leɪbaɪ] *n* área de descanso.
layer ['leɪəʳ] *n* capa, estrato.
layout ['leɪaʊt] *n* diseño.
lazy ['leɪzɪ] *adj* perezoso,-a.
lead¹ [led] *n* **1** plomo *(metal)*. **2** mina *(de lápiz)*.
lead² [liːd] *n* **1** delantera, cabeza. **2** correa *(de perro)*. **3** papel principal. ► *vt* **1** llevar, conducir *(sendero, guía)*. **2** liderar. ► *vi* **1** ir primero,-a. **2** tener el mando. **3** conducir *(camino)*.

leader ['liːdəʳ] *n* líder.
leadership ['liːdəʃɪp] *n* liderazgo.
lead-free ['ledfriː] *adj* sin plomo.
leaf [liːf] *n* hoja.
leaflet ['liːflət] *n* folleto.
league [liːg] *n* liga.
leak [liːk] *n* **1** escape, fuga. **2** gotera.
lean [liːn] *vi* **1** apoyarse. **2** inclinarse *(curva, pendiente)*.
to lean out *vt-vi* asomar(se).
leant [lent] *pt-pp* → lean.
leap [liːp] *n* salto, brinco. ► *vi* saltar, brincar. ■ **leap year** año bisiesto.
leapt [lept] *pt-pp* → leap.
learn [lɜːn] *vt-vi* aprender.
learner ['lɜːnəʳ] *n* estudiante.
learnt [lɜːnt] *pt-pp* → learn.
lease [liːs] *n* *vt* arrendar.
leash [liːʃ] *n* correa.
least [liːst] *adj* más mínimo,-a, menor. ► *adv* menos. • **at least** por lo menos.
leather ['leðəʳ] *n* piel, cuero.
leave¹ [liːv] *vt* **1** dejar *(gen)*. **2** salir de *(lugar)*. ► *vi* salir, marcharse, irse. • **to be left** quedar.
lecture ['lektʃəʳ] *n* **1** conferencia. **2** clase *(en universidad)*.
lecturer ['lektʃərəʳ] *n* **1** conferenciante. **2** profesor,-ra *(universitario)*.
led [led] *pt-pp* → lead.
leech [liːtʃ] *n* sanguijuela.

leek [liːk] *n* puerro.

left¹ [left] *adj* izquierdo,-a. ► *n* izquierda. ► *adv* a la izquierda, hacia la izquierda.

left² [left] *pt-pp* → leave.

left-handed [left'hændɪd] *adj* zurdo,-a.

left-luggage office [left-'lʌgɪdʒ ɒfɪs] *n* consigna.

leftover *adj* sobrante.

leg [leg] *n* **1** pierna. **2** pata. **3** muslo *(de pollo)*.

legal ['liːgəl] *adj* lega.

legend ['ledʒənd] *n* leyenda.

leggings ['legɪŋgz] *npl* mallas.

legitimate [lɪ'dʒɪtɪmət] *adj* legítimo,-a.

leisure ['leʒəʳ] *n* ocio.

lemon ['lemən] *n* limón.

lemonade [lemə'neɪd] *n* limonada.

lend [lend] *vt* dejar, prestar.

length [leŋθ] *n* **1** largo, longitud. **2** duración.

lens [lenz] *n* **1** lente *(de gafas)*. **2** objetivo *(de cámara)*.

lent [lent] *pt-pp* → lend.

Lent [lent] *n* Cuaresma.

lentil ['lentɪl] *n* lenteja.

leopard ['lepəd] *n* leopardo.

leotard ['liːətɑːd] *n* malla.

leprosy ['leprəsɪ] *n* lepra.

less [les] *adj-adv-prep* menos.

lesson ['lesən] *n* lección, clase.

let [let] *vt* **1** dejar. **2** arrendar, alquilar: *"To let"*, "Se alquila". ► *aux*: **let's go!**, ¡vamos!

to let in *vt* dejar entrar.

to let out *vt* **1** dejar salir, soltar. **2** alquilar.

letter ['letəʳ] *n* **1** letra. **2** carta. ■ **letter box** buzón.

lettuce ['letɪs] *n* lechuga.

level ['levəl] *adj* **1** llano,-a. **2** nivelado,-a. **3** empatado,-a. ► *vt* nivelar. ■ **level crossing** paso a nivel.

lever ['liːvəʳ] *n* palanca.

levy ['levɪ] *n* recaudación. ► *vt* recaudar.

liability [laɪə'bɪlɪtɪ] *n* responsabilidad. ► *npl* **liabilities** COMM pasivo.

liar ['laɪəʳ] *n* mentiroso,-a.

liberal ['lɪbərəl] *adj* liberal.

liberate ['lɪbəreɪt] *vt* liberar.

liberty ['lɪbətɪ] *n* libertad.

library ['laɪbrərɪ] *n* biblioteca.

lice [laɪs] *npl* → louse.

licence ['laɪsəns] *n* licencia.

license ['laɪsəns] *vt* autorizar.

lick [lɪk] *n* lamedura, lametón. ► *vt* lamer.

licorice ['lɪkərɪs] *n* regaliz.

lid [lɪd] *n* tapa, tapadera.

lie¹ [laɪ] *n* mentira: **to tell lies**, decir mentiras. ► *vi* mentir.

lie² [laɪ] *vi* **1** acostarse, tumbarse. **2** estar situado,-a, encontrarse.

to lie back *vi* recostarse.

to lie down *vi* acostarse.

lie-down ['laɪdaʊn] *n* siesta.

lieutenant [lef'tenənt] *n* teniente.

life [laɪf] *n* vida. • **for life** para toda la vida. ■ **life belt** salvavidas; **life imprisonment** cadena perpetua; **life jacket** chaleco salvavidas; **life sentence** cadena perpetua.

life-boat ['laɪfbəʊt] *n* bote salvavidas.

lifeguard ['laɪfgɑːd] *n* socorrista.

lifestyle ['laɪfstaɪl] *n* estilo de vida.

lifetime ['laɪftaɪm] *n* vida.

lift [lɪft] *n* GB ascensor. ► *vt-vi* levantar.• **to give SB a lift** llevar a ALGN en coche.

light¹ [laɪt] *n* **1** luz. **2** fuego *(para cigarrillo)*. ► *vt-vi* encender(se). ► *vt* iluminar, alumbrar. ► *adj* claro,-a. ■ **light bulb** bombilla.

light² [laɪt] *adj* ligero,-a.

lighter ['laɪtə'] *n* encendedor.

lighthouse ['laɪthaʊs] *n* faro.

lighting ['laɪtɪŋ] *n* **1** iluminación. **2** alumbrado.

lightning ['laɪtənɪŋ] *n* rayo, relámpago.

like¹ [laɪk] *adj* semejante, parecido,-a. ► *prep* como. • **like this** así.

like² [laɪk] *vt* gustar: *I like wine*, me gusta el vino. • **as you like** como quieras.

likeable ['laɪkəbəl] *adj* simpático,-a, agradable.

likelihood ['laɪklɪhʊd] *n* probabilidad.

likely ['laɪklɪ] *adj* probable.

lily ['lɪlɪ] *n* lirio, azucena.

limb [lɪmb] *n* miembro.

lime¹ [laɪm] *n* cal.

lime² [laɪm] *n* lima *(fruto)*.

lime³ [laɪm] *n* tilo *(árbol)*.

limit ['lɪmɪt] *n* límite. ► *vt* limitar.

limited ['lɪmɪtɪd] *adj* limitado, -a. ■ **limited company** sociedad anónima.

limp¹ [lɪmp] *n* cojera. ► *vi* cojear.

limp² [lɪmp] *adj* flojo,-a.

limpet ['lɪmpɪt] *n* lapa.

line¹ [laɪn] *n* **1** línea. **2** raya *(en papel)*. **3** cuerda, cordel. **4** sedal *(de pesca)*. **5** US cola. **6** tendedero. ► *vt* alinear.

line² [laɪn] *vt* forrar.

lined² [laɪnd] *adj* forrado,-a.

linen ['lɪnɪn] *n* **1** lino. **2** ropa blanca.

liner ['laɪnə'] *n* transatlántico.

linesman ['laɪnzmən] *n* juez de línea.

lingerie ['lɑːnʒərɪː] *n* lencería.

lining ['laɪnɪŋ] *n* forro.

link [lɪŋk] *vt* unir, conectar. ► *n* **1** eslabón *(de cadena)*. **2** enlace, conexión. ► *npl* **links** campo de golf.

linkage ['lɪŋkɪdʒ] *n* conexión.

lion ['laɪən] *n* león.

lioness ['laɪənəs] *n* leona.

lip [lɪp] *n* labio.

lipstick ['lɪpstɪk] *n* pintalabios, lápiz de labios.

liqueur [lɪˈkjʊəʳ] n licor.
liquid [ˈlɪkwɪd] adj líquido,-a.
► n líquido.
liquor [ˈlɪkəʳ] n alcohol, bebida alcohólica.
liquorice [ˈlɪkərɪs] n regaliz.
list [lɪst] n lista. ► vt hacer una lista de.
listen [ˈlɪsən] vi escuchar.
listener [ˈlɪsənəʳ] n oyente.
lit [lɪt] pt-pp → light.
literal [ˈlɪtərəl] adj literal.
literature [ˈlɪtərɪtʃəʳ] n literatura.
litre [ˈliːtəʳ] (US **liter**) n litro.
litter [ˈlɪtəʳ] n **1** basura, papeles. **2** camada.
little [ˈlɪtəl] adj **1** pequeño,-a. **2** poco,-a. ► pron poco. ► adv poco.
live¹ [lɪv] vt-vi vivir.
live² [laɪv] adj **1** vivo,-a. **2** en directo (programa, transmisión).
to live on vt vivir de, alimentarse de. ► vi sobrevivir.
lively [ˈlaɪvlɪ] adj animado,-a.
liven up [laɪvənˈʌp] vt-vi animar(se).
liver [ˈlɪvəʳ] n hígado.
livestock [ˈlaɪvstɒk] n ganado.
living [ˈlɪvɪŋ] adj vivo,-a. ► n medio de vida: **what do you do for a living?**, ¿cómo te ganas la vida? ■ **living room** sala de estar.
lizard [ˈlɪzəd] n lagarto (grande), lagartija (pequeño).

llama [ˈlɑːmə] n llama.
load [ləʊd] n carga. ► vt-vi cargar. ● **loads of...** montones de…
loaf [ləʊf] n pan, barra.
loan [ləʊn] n préstamo. ► vt prestar.
loathe [ləʊð] vt detestar.
lobby [ˈlɒbɪ] n **1** vestíbulo. **2** POL grupo de presión.
lobe [ləʊb] n lóbulo.
lobster [ˈlɒbstəʳ] n bogavante. ■ **spiny lobster** langosta.
local [ˈləʊkəl] adj local.
loch [lɒk] n lago.
lock¹ [lɒk] n **1** cerradura (de puerta). **2** esclusa (en canal). ► vt cerrar con llave.
lock² [lɒk] n mecha, mechón.
locker [ˈlɒkəʳ] n taquilla, armario.
locksmith [ˈlɒksmɪθ] n cerrajero.
locomotive [ləʊkəˈməʊtɪv] n locomotora.
locust [ˈləʊkəst] n langosta.
lodge [lɒdʒ] vi alojarse, hospedarse. ► vt presentar (queja).
lodging [ˈlɒdʒɪŋ] n alojamiento.
loft [lɒft] n desván.
log [lɒg] n **1** tronco (para fuego). **2** COMPUT registro. ► vt registrar, anotar.
to log in/log on vi COMPUT entrar (en sistema).
to log off/log out vi COMPUT salir (del sistema).

logical ['lɒdʒɪkəl] *adj* lógico,-a.

loin [lɔɪn] *n* **1** lomo *(de cerdo)*. **2** solomillo *(de ternera)*.

lollipop ['lɒlɪpɒp] *n* **1** piruleta, pirulí. **2** polo.

loneliness ['ləʊnlɪnəs] *n* soledad.

lonely ['ləʊnlɪ] *adj* solitario,-a.

long[1] [lɒŋ] *adj* largo,-a. ► *adv* **1** mucho, mucho tiempo. **2 no longer, not any longer**: *she doesn't work here any longer*, ya no trabaja aquí. ● **as long as** mientras, con tal de que; **so long** hasta la vista. ■ **long jump** salto de longitud.

long[2] [lɒŋ] *vi* **to long for** anhelar.

long-distance [lɒŋ'dɪstəns] *adj* **1** de larga distancia *(llamada)*. **2** de fondo *(corredor)*.

longing ['lɒŋɪŋ] *n* **1** ansia, anhelo. **2** nostalgia.

longitude ['lɒndʒɪtjuːd] *n* longitud.

long-playing [lɒŋ'pleɪɪŋ] *adj* de larga duración.

long-range [lɒŋ'reɪndʒ] *adj* **1** de largo alcance *(distancia)*. **2** a largo plazo *(tiempo)*.

long-sighted [lɒŋ'saɪtɪd] *adj* hipermétrope.

loo [luː] *n fam* wáter, servicio.

look [lʊk] *vi* **1** mirar. **2** parecer: *it looks easy*, parece fácil. ► *n* **1** mirada, vistazo. **2** aspecto, apariencia.

to look after *vt* **1** ocuparse de. **2** cuidar.

to look at *vt* mirar.

to look for *vt* buscar.

to look forward to *vt* esperar *(con ansia)*.

to look like *vt* **1** parecer: *what does Sarah look like?*, ¿cómo es Sarah? **2** parecerse a: *he looks like his father*, se parece a su padre.

lookalike ['lʊkəlaɪk] *n* doble.

lookout ['lʊkaʊt] *n* **1** vigía. **2** atalaya.

loop [luːp] *n* **1** lazo. **2** curva. **3** COMPUT bucle.

loose [luːs] *adj* **1** suelto,-a. **2** flojo,-a. ► *vt* soltar.

loosen ['luːsən] *vt-vi* soltar(se), aflojar(se).

loot [luːt] *n* botín.

lop [lɒp] *vt* podar.

lord [lɔːd] *n* **1** señor. **2** lord. ● **the Lord's Prayer** el padrenuestro.

lorry ['lɒrɪ] *n* camión.

lose [luːz] *vt-vi* **1** perder. **2** atrasarse *(reloj)*.

loser ['luːzəʳ] *n* perdedor,-a.

loss [lɒs] *n* pérdida.

lost [lɒst] *pt-pp* → lose. ► *adj* perdido,-a. ● **to get lost** perderse. ■ **lost property** objetos perdidos.

lot [lɒt] *n* **1** US solar, terreno. **2** lote *(en subasta)*. **3** cantidad: *a lot*, mucho, muchísimo.

lotion ['ləʊʃən] *n* loción.

lottery ['lɒtərɪ] n lotería.
loud [laʊd] adj **1** fuerte (sonido). **2** alto,-a (voz). ► adv fuerte, alto.
loudspeaker [laʊd'spi:kə'] n altavoz.
lounge [laʊndʒ] n salón, sala de estar.
louse [laʊs] n piojo.
love [lʌv] n **1** amor. **2** cero (en tenis). ► vt **1** amar, querer. **2** gustar: *I love fish*, me encanta el pescado. • **to be in love with** estar enamorado,-a de.
lovely ['lʌvlɪ] adj encantador, -ra.
low [ləʊ] adj bajo,-a. ► adv bajo. ▪ **low tide** bajamar.
lower ['ləʊə'] adj inferior. ► vt bajar.
low-necked [ləʊ'nekt] adj escotado,-a.
loyal ['lɔɪəl] adj leal, fiel.
lozenge ['lɒzɪndʒ] n rombo.
lubricant ['lu:brɪkənt] n lubricante.
luck [lʌk] n suerte.
lucky ['lʌkɪ] adj afortunado, -a, con suerte. • **to be lucky** tener suerte. ▪ **lucky charm** amuleto.
luggage ['lʌgɪdʒ] n equipaje. ▪ **luggage rack** portaequipajes.
lull [lʌl] n momento de calma. ► vt adormecer, arrullar.
lullaby ['lʌləbaɪ] n canción de cuna, nana.

lumberjack ['lʌmbədʒæk] n leñador.
lump [lʌmp] n **1** pedazo, trozo. **2** terrón (de azúcar). **3** bulto (en cuerpo). **4** grumo (en salsa).
lunar ['lu:nə'] adj lunar.
lunch [lʌntʃ] n comida. ► vi comer.
luncheon ['lʌntʃən] n fml almuerzo.
lung [lʌŋ] n pulmón.
lurch [lɜ:tʃ] n bandazo. ► vi **1** dar bandazos. **2** tambalearse.
lure [ljʊə'] n **1** señuelo. **2** fig atractivo. ► vt atraer.
lurid ['ljʊərɪd] adj **1** chillón, -ona (color). **2** horripilante, espeluznante (detalles).
lush [lʌʃ] adj exuberante.
lust [lʌst] n lujuria.
lute [lu:t] n laúd.
luxury ['lʌkʃərɪ] n lujo.
lynch [lɪntʃ] vt linchar.
lynx [lɪŋks] n lince.
lyric ['lɪrɪk] adj lírico,-a. ► npl **lyrics** letra (de canción).

M

mac [mæk] n impermeable.
macabre [mə'ka:brə] adj macabro,-a.
macaroni [mækə'rəʊnɪ] n macarrones.

machine [mə'ʃiːn] *n* máquina, aparato. ■ **machine gun** ametralladora.

mackerel ['mækrəl] *n* caballa.

mackintosh ['mækɪntɒʃ] *n* impermeable.

mad [mæd] *adj* 1 loco,-a. 2 furioso,-a, muy enfadado,-a *(persona)*.

madam ['mædəm] *n fml* señora.

madden ['mædən] *vt* enfurecer.

made [meɪd] *pt-pp* → make.

madness ['mædnəs] *n* locura.

magazine [mægə'ziːn] *n* revista.

maggot ['mægət] *n* larva.

magic ['mædʒɪk] *n* magia. ▶ *adj* mágico,-a.

magician [mə'dʒɪʃən] *n* mago,-a.

magnet ['mægnət] *n* imán.

magnetic [mæg'netɪk] *adj* magnético,-a. ■ **magnetic tape** cinta magnetofónica.

magnify ['mægnɪfaɪ] *vt* aumentar, ampliar..

magnifying glass ['mægnɪfaɪɪŋglɑːs] *n* lupa.

magnitude ['mægnɪtjuːd] *n* magnitud.

mahogany [mə'hɒgənɪ] *n* caoba.

maid [meɪd] *n* 1 criada, sirvienta. 2 camarera *(en hotel)*. ■ **maid of honour** dama de honor.

maiden ['meɪdən] ▶ *adj* 1 soltera. 2 inaugural. ■ **maiden name** apellido de soltera.

mail [meɪl] *n* correo. ▶ *vt* US echar al buzón. ■ **mail order** venta por correo.

mailbox ['meɪlbɒks] *n* US buzón.

mailman ['meɪlmæn] *n* US cartero.

main [meɪn] *adj* principal. ▶ *n* 1 tubería principa. 2 red eléctrica. ■ **main beam** viga maestra; **main office** oficina central; **main street** calle mayor.

maintain [meɪn'teɪn] *vt* mantener.

maintenance ['meɪntənəns] *n* 1 mantenimiento. 2 pensión alimenticia.

maisonette [meɪzə'net] *n* dúplex.

maize [meɪz] *n* maíz.

majesty ['mædʒəstɪ] *n* majestad.

major ['meɪdʒəʳ] *adj* principal. ▶ *n* comandante.

majority [mə'dʒɒrɪtɪ] *n* mayoría.

make [meɪk] *vt* 1 hacer. 2 ganar: *how much do you make a year?*, ¿cuánto ganas al año? ▶ *n* marca.

to make up *vt* 1 inventar. 2 hacer, preparar *(cama, paquete)*. 3 maquillar. ▶ *vi* maquillarse.

manure

maker ['meɪkəʳ] n fabricante.

make-up ['meɪkʌp] n **1** maquillaje. **2** composición. ▪ **make-up remover** desmaquillador.

malaria [məˈleərɪə] n malaria.

male [meɪl] adj-n macho. ► adj **1** varón. **2** masculino,-a. ▪ **male chauvinism** machismo.

malfunction [mælˈfʌnkʃən] n funcionamiento defectuoso.

malice ['mælɪs] n malicia.

malignant [məˈlɪgnənt] adj maligno,-a.

malt [mɔːlt] n malta.

mammal ['mæməl] n mamífero.

mammoth ['mæməθ] n mamut.

man [mæn] n hombre. ► vt **1** tripular (nave). **2** servir.

manage ['mænɪdʒ] vt **1** dirigir (negocio). **2** administrar (propiedad). ► vi **1** poder. **2** arreglárselas. **3** conseguir.

management ['mænɪdʒmənt] n dirección, administración, gestión.

manager ['mænɪdʒəʳ] n **1** director,-ra, gerente (de empresa). **2** administrador,-ra (de propiedad). **3** entrenador (de deportista).

manageress [mænɪdʒəˈres] n directora, gerente.

mane [meɪn] n **1** crin (de caballo). **2** melena (de león).

mango ['mæŋgəʊ] n mango.

manhood ['mænhʊd] n madurez.

mania ['meɪnɪə] n manía.

manicure ['mænɪkjʊəʳ] n manicura.

manipulate [məˈnɪpjʊleɪt] vt manipular.

mankind [mænˈkaɪnd] n el género humano.

manly ['mænlɪ] adj viril.

man-made [mænˈmeɪd] adj **1** artificial. **2** sintético,-a.

manner ['mænəʳ] n manera, modo. ► npl **manners** modales. • **in this manner** de esta manera, así; **to be bad manners** ser de mala educación.

mannerism ['mænərɪzəm] n peculiaridad.

manoeuvre [məˈnuːvəʳ] (US **maneuver**) n maniobra. ► vt-vi maniobrar.

manor ['mænəʳ] n señorío. ▪ **manor house** casa solariega.

manpower ['mænpaʊəʳ] n mano de obra.

mansion ['mænʃən] n mansión.

manual ['mænjʊəl] adj-n manual.

manufacture [mænjʊˈfæktʃəʳ] n fabricación, manufactura. ► vt **1** fabricar, manufacturar.

manufacturer [mænjʊˈfæktʃərəʳ] n fabricante.

manure [məˈnjʊəʳ] n abono, estiércol.

many ['menɪ] *adj-pron* muchos,-as. ● **as many ... as** tantos,-as ... como; **how many?** ¿cuántos,-as?; **not many** pocos,-as; **too many** demasiados,-as.

map [mæp] *n* **1** mapa *(de país, región)*. **2** plano *(de ciudad)*.

maple ['meɪpəl] *n* arce.

marathon ['mærəθən] *n* maratón.

marble ['mɑːbəl] *n* **1** mármol. **2** canica.

march [mɑːtʃ] *n* marcha. ► *vi* marchar, caminar.

to march past *vi* desfilar.

March [mɑːtʃ] *n* marzo.

mare [meəʳ] *n* yegua.

margarine [mɑːdʒəˈriːn] *n* margarina.

margin ['mɑːdʒɪn] *n* margen.

marginal ['mɑːdʒɪnəl] *adj* marginal.

marine [məˈriːn] *adj* marino, -a, marítimo,-a. ► *n* soldado de infantería de marina.

marionette [mærɪəˈnet] *n* marioneta.

marital ['mærɪtəl] *adj* matrimonial. ■ **marital status** estado civil.

maritime ['mærɪtaɪm] *adj* marítimo,-a.

mark [mɑːk] *n* **1** marca, señal. **2** mancha. **3** nota. ► *vt* **1** marcar. **2** corregir, puntuar. ● **on your marks!** ¡preparados!

marker ['mɑːkəʳ] *n* rotulador.

market ['mɑːkɪt] *n* mercado.

marketing ['mɑːkɪtɪŋ] *n* márketing, mercadotecnia.

marmalade ['mɑːməleɪd] *n* mermelada *(de cítricos)*.

marquee [mɑːˈkiː] *n* carpa.

marriage ['mærɪdʒ] *n* **1** matrimonio. **2** boda.

married ['mærɪd] *adj* casado,-a. ● **to get married** casarse.

marrow ['mærəʊ] *n* **1** tuétano, médula. **2** calabacín.

marry ['mærɪ] *vt-vi* casar(se).

marsh [mɑːʃ] *n* **1** pantano, ciénaga. **2** marisma.

marshal ['mɑːʃəl] *n* **1** mariscal. **2** US jefe,-a de policía.

martial ['mɑːʃəl] *adj* marcial.

martyr ['mɑːtəʳ] *n* mártir.

marvellous ['mɑːvələs] *adj* maravilloso,-a.

mascara [mæˈskɑːrə] *n* rímel.

mascot ['mæskɒt] *n* mascota.

masculine ['mɑːskjʊlɪn] *adj* masculino,-a. ► *n* masculino.

mash [mæʃ] *vt* triturar. ► *n fam* puré de patatas.

mask [mɑːsk] *n* **1** máscara. **2** mascarilla. ■ **masked ball** baile de disfraces.

mason ['meɪsən] *n* albañil.

mass[1] [mæs] *n* masa. ● **to mass produce** fabricar en serie. ■ **mass media** medios de comunicación de masas; **mass production** fabricación en serie.

mass² [mæs] n misa.

massacre ['mæsəkə'] n masacre.

massage ['mæsɑːʒ] n masaje. ► vt dar masajes a.

massive ['mæsɪv] adj **1** macizo,-a, sólido,-a. **2** enorme.

mast [mɑːst] n mástil.

master ['mɑːstə'] n **1** señor, amo, dueño. **2** maestro. ► vt dominar. ▪ **master key** llave maestra.

masterpiece ['mɑːstəpiːs] n obra maestra.

mat [mæt] n **1** alfombrilla, felpudo. **2** salvamanteles.

match¹ [mætʃ] n cerilla.

match² [mætʃ] n partido. ► vt-vi hacer juego (con).

matchbox ['mætʃbɒks] n caja de cerillas.

mate¹ [meɪt] n mate (en ajedrez).

mate² [meɪt] n **1** compañero, -a, colega. **2** pareja (persona), macho, hembra (animal). ► vt-vi aparear(se).

material [mə'tɪərɪəl] adj-n material.

maternity [mə'tɜːnɪti] n maternidad. ▪ **maternity leave** baja por maternidad.

mathematics [mæθə'mætɪks] n matemáticas.

matt [mæt] adj mate.

matter ['mætə'] n **1** materia. **2** asunto, cuestión. ► vi importar. • **as a matter of fact** en realidad; **it's a matter of ...** es cuestión de ...; **no matter ...**: *I never win, no matter what I do*, nunca gano, haga lo que haga; **the matter**: *what's the matter?*, ¿qué pasa?

mattress ['mætrəs] n colchón.

mature [mə'tʃʊə'] adj maduro,-a. ► vt-vi madurar.

maximum ['mæksɪməm] adj máximo,-a. ► n máximo.

may [meɪ] aux poder: *he may come*, es posible que venga, puede que venga; *may I go?*, ¿puedo irme?

May [meɪ] n mayo.

maybe ['meɪbiː] adv quizá, quizás, tal vez.

mayonnaise [meɪə'neɪz] n mayonesa, mahonesa.

mayor [meə'] n alcalde.

maze [meɪz] n laberinto.

me [miː] pron **1** me, mí. **2** yo: *it's me!*, ¡soy yo! • **with me** conmigo.

meadow ['medəʊ] n prado.

meagre ['miːgə'] (US **meager**) adj escaso,-a.

meal [miːl] n comida.

mean¹ [miːn] adj tacaño,-a.

mean² [miːn] vt **1** querer decir, significar. **2** querer, tener intención de: *I didn't mean to do it*, lo hice sin querer.

mean³ [miːn] n media.

meaning ['miːnɪŋ] n sentido, significado.

means [miːnz] *npl* medios, recursos económicos. • **by all means!** inaturalmente!; **by no means** de ninguna manera. ▪ **means of transport** medio de transporte.

meant [ment] *pt-pp* → mean.

meantime ['miːntaɪm] *phr.* **in the meantime** mientras tanto.

meanwhile ['miːnwaɪl] *adv* mientras tanto, entretanto.

measles ['miːzəlz] *n* sarampión. ▪ **German measles** rubeola.

measure ['meʒəʳ] *n* **1** medida. **2** MUS compás. ▶ *vt* medir.

measurement ['meʒəmənt] *n* **1** medición. **2** medida.

meat [miːt] *n* carne.

meatball ['miːtbɔːl] *n* albóndiga.

mechanic [mɪ'kænɪk] *n* mecánico,-a.

mechanism ['mekənɪzəm] *n* mecanismo.

medal ['medəl] *n* medalla.

meddle ['medəl] *vi* entrometerse.

media ['miːdɪə] *npl* medios de comunicación.

medical ['medɪkəl] *adj* médico,-a. ▶ *n fam* chequeo. ▪ **medical record** historial médico.

medicine ['medsɪn] *n* **1** medicina. **2** medicamento.

mediocre [miːdɪ'əʊkəʳ] *adj* mediocre.

medium ['miːdɪəm] *n* medio. ▶ *adj* mediano,-a.

meet [miːt] *vt* **1** encontrar, encontrarse con *(por casualidad)*. **2** reunirse con, verse con. **3** conocer. ▶ *vi* **1** encontrarse. **2** reunirse, verse. • **pleased to meet you!** iencantado,-a de conocerle!

meeting ['miːtɪŋ] *n* **1** reunión. **2** POL mítin. **3** encuentro. ▪ **meeting point** lugar de encuentro.

megaphone ['megəfəʊn] *n* megáfono.

mellow ['meləʊ] *adj* **1** maduro,-a *(fruta)*. **2** añejo,-a *(vino)*. **3** suave *(color, voz)*.

melody ['melədɪ] *n* melodía.

melon ['melən] *n* melón.

melt [melt] *vt-vi* **1** derretir(se) *(hielo, nieve)*. **2** fundir(se) *(metal)*.

member ['membəʳ] *n* **1** miembro. **2** socio,-a *(de club)*.

memorandum [memə'rændəm] *n* memorándum.

memory ['memərɪ] *n* **1** memoria. **2** recuerdo.

men [men] *npl* → man.

menace ['menəs] *n* amenaza.

mend [mend] *n* remiendo. ▶ *vt* **1** reparar, arreglar. **2** remendar *(ropa)*.

menstruation [menstrʊ'eɪʃən] *n* menstruación.

menswear ['menzweəʳ] *n* ropa de caballero.

mental ['mentəl] *adj* mental.

mention ['menʃən] *n* mención. ► *vt* mencionar.

menu ['menjuː] *n* **1** carta *(en restaurante)*. **2** COMPUT menú.

merchandise ['mɜːtʃəndaɪz] *n* mercancías, géneros.

merchant ['mɜːtʃənt] *n* comerciante.

mercy ['mɜːsɪ] *n* misericordia, compasión. • **at the mercy of** a la merced de.

mere [mɪəʳ] *adj* mero,-a.

merge [mɜːdʒ] *vt* unir, empalmar *(carreteras)*. ► *vt-vi* fusionar(se) *(empresas)*.

merger ['mɜːdʒəʳ] *n* fusión.

meringue [məˈræŋ] *n* merengue.

merit ['merɪt] *n* mérito. ► *vt* merecer.

mermaid ['mɜːmeɪd] *n* sirena.

merry ['merɪ] *adj* alegre. • **merry Christmas!** ¡feliz Navidad!

merry-go-round ['merɪgəʊraʊnd] *n* tiovivo, caballitos.

mesh [meʃ] *n* malla.

mess [mes] *n***1** desorden, lío.

to mess about/around *vi* gandulear..

to mess up *vt* **1** *fam* desordenar *(habitación)*. **2** estropear *(planes)*.

message ['mesɪdʒ] *n* mensaje.

messenger ['mesɪndʒəʳ] *n* mensajero,-a.

met [met] *pt-pp* → meet.

metabolism [meˈtæbəlɪzəm] *n* metabolismo.

metal ['metəl] *n* metal. ► *adj* metálico,-a, de metal.

meteorite ['miːtɪəraɪt] *n* meteorito.

meter¹ ['miːtəʳ] *n* US → metre.

meter² ['miːtəʳ] *n* contador.

method ['meθəd] *n* método.

metre ['miːtəʳ] (US **meter**) *n* metro.

mew [mjuː] *n* maullido.

mezzanine ['mezəniːn] *n* entresuelo.

miaow [mɪˈaʊ] *vi* maullar.

mice [maɪs] *npl* → mouse.

microbe ['maɪkrəʊb] *n* microbio.

microchip ['maɪkrəʊtʃɪp] *n* microchip.

microphone ['maɪkrəfəʊn] *n* micrófono.

microprocessor [maɪkrəʊˈprəʊsesəʳ] *n* microprocesador.

microscope ['maɪkrəskəʊp] *n* microscopio.

microwave ['maɪkrəʊweɪv] *n* microonda, microondas.

midday [mɪdˈdeɪ] *n* mediodía.

middle ['mɪdəl] *adj* del medio, central. ► *n* **1** medio, centro *(de habitación)*. **2** mitad. ■ **middle age** mediana edad; **middle class** clase media.

middleman ['mɪdəlmən] *n* intermediario.

midnight ['mɪdnaɪt] *n* medianoche.

midway ['mɪdweɪ] *adv* a medio camino.

midwife ['mɪdwaɪf] *n* comadrona.

might [maɪt] *aux* → may.

migraine ['maɪgreɪn] *n* jaqueca, migraña.

migrate [maɪ'greɪt] *vi* emigrar.

mild [maɪld] *adj* **1** apacible *(persona)*. **2** suave *(clima)*.

mile [maɪl] *n* milla.

milestone ['maɪlstəʊn] *n* hito.

military ['mɪlɪtərɪ] *adj* militar.

milk [mɪlk] *n* leche. ▪ **milk chocolate** chocolate con leche; **milk shake** batido.

mill [mɪl] *n* **1** molino. **2** molinillo *(de café)*. **3** fábrica. ► *vt* moler.

millimetre ['mɪlɪmiːtə'] (US **millimeter**) *n* milímetro.

million ['mɪljən] *n* millón.

mime [maɪm] *n* **1** mímica. **2** mimo *(persona)*.

mimic ['mɪmɪk] *vt* imitar.

mince [mɪns] *n* GB carne picada. ► *vt* picar.

mind [maɪnd] *n* mente. ► *vt* **1** hacer caso de. **2** cuidar. **3** tener cuidado con. ► *vt-vi* importar. ▪ **never mind** no importa, da igual; **to change one's mind** cambiar de opinión; **to have** STH **in mind** estar pensando en algo; **to make up one's mind** decidirse.

mine¹ [maɪn] *n* mina.

mine² [maɪn] *pron* (el) mío, (la) mía, (los) míos, (las) mías.

miner ['maɪnə'] *n* minero,-a.

mineral ['mɪnərəl] *adj* mineral. ► *n* mineral.

minimum ['mɪnɪməm] *adj* mínimo,-a. ► *n* mínimo.

minister ['mɪnɪstə'] *n* **1** ministro,-a. **2** pastor,-ra *(cura)*.

ministry ['mɪnɪstrɪ] *n* **1** ministerio. **2** sacerdocio.

mink [mɪŋk] *n* visón.

minor ['maɪnə'] *adj* de poca importancia. ► *n* menor de edad.

minority [maɪ'nɒrɪtɪ] *n* minoría. ► *adj* minoritario,-a.

mint¹ [mɪnt] *vt* acuñar.

mint² [mɪnt] *n* menta.

minus ['maɪnəs] *prep* menos: **minus five degrees**, cinco grados bajo cero.

minute¹ ['mɪnɪt] *adj* diminuto,-a.

minute² ['mɪnɪt] *n* minuto. ▪ **minute hand** minutero.

miracle ['mɪrəkəl] *n* milagro.

mirage [mɪ'rɑːʒ] *n* espejismo.

mirror ['mɪrə'] *n* espejo; retrovisor *(de coche)*.

miscarriage [mɪs'kærɪdʒ] *n* aborto *(espontáneo)*.

miscellaneous [mɪsɪ'leɪnɪəs] *adj* diverso,-a, variado,-a.

mischievous ['mɪstʃɪvəs] *adj* travieso,-a.

misdemeanour [mɪsdɪ'miːnə'] (US **misdemeanor**) *n* **1** fechoría. **2** delito menor.

miserable ['mɪzərəbəl] *adj* **1** triste. **2** desagradable *(tiempo)*. **3** miserable.

misery ['mɪzərɪ] *n* **1** tristeza, desdicha. **2** miseria.

misfire [mɪs'faɪə'] *vi* fallar.

misfortune [mɪs'fɔːtʃən] *n* infortunio, desgracia.

mishap ['mɪshæp] *n* percance.

misjudge [mɪs'dʒʌdʒ] *vt* juzgar mal.

mislaid [mɪs'leɪd] *pt-pp* → mislay.

mislay [mɪs'leɪ] *vt* extraviar.

mislead [mɪs'liːd] *vt* engañar.

misled [mɪs'led] *pt-pp* → mislead.

misprint ['mɪsprɪnt] *n* errata.

miss¹ [mɪs] *n* señorita.

miss² [mɪs] *n* fallo. ► *vt-vi* fallar. ► *vt* **1** perder: *he missed the train*, perdió el tren. **2** no entender. **3** echar de menos, añorar. **4** echar en falta. ► *vi* faltar.

missile ['mɪsaɪl] *n* misil. ■ **missile launcher** lanzamisiles.

missing ['mɪsɪŋ] *adj* **1** perdido,-a *(objeto)*. **2** desaparecido, -a *(persona)*.

mission ['mɪʃən] *n* misión.

missionary ['mɪʃənərɪ] *n* misionero,-a.

mistake [mɪs'teɪk] *n* error. ► *vt* **1** entender mal. **2** confundir. • **by mistake** por error, por equivocación; **to make a mistake** equivocarse.

mister ['mɪstə'] *n* señor.

mistletoe ['mɪzəltəʊ] *n* muérdago.

mistook [mɪs'tʊk] *pt* → mistake.

mistreat [mɪs'triːt] *vt* maltratar.

mistress ['mɪstrəs] *n* ama, señora *(de casa)*.

mistrust [mɪs'trʌst] *n* desconfianza, recelo. ► *vt* desconfiar de.

misunderstand [mɪsʌndə'stænd] *vt-vi* entender mal.

misunderstanding [mɪsʌndə'stændɪŋ] *n* malentendido.

misunderstood [mɪsʌndə'stʊd] *pt-pp* → misunderstand.

misuse [(*n*) mɪs'juːs, (*vb*) mɪs'juːz] *n* **1** mal uso. **2** abuso *(de poder)*. ► *vt* **1** emplear mal. **2** abusar de *(de poder)*.

mitten ['mɪtən] *n* manopla.

mix [mɪks] *n* mezcla. ► *vt-vi* mezclar(se).

mixed [mɪkst] *adj* **1** variado,-a. **2** mixto,-a *(de ambos sexos)*.

mixer ['mɪksə'] *n* batidora.

mixture ['mɪkstʃə'] *n* mezcla.

moan [məʊn] *n* gemido, quejido. ► *vi* gemir.

moat [məʊt] *n* foso.

mobile ['məʊbaɪl] *adj-n* móvil. ■ **mobile home** caravana, remolque; **mobile phone** móvil, teléfono móvil.

moccasin ['mɒkəsɪn] *n* mocasín.

mock [mɒk] *adj* **1** falso, de imitación. **2** de prueba, simulado,-a. ► *vt-vi* burlarse (de).
mockery ['mɒkərɪ] *n* burla.
model ['mɒdəl] *n* modelo. ■ **model home** casa piloto.
modem ['məʊdəm] *n* módem.
moderate ['mɒdərət] *adj* moderado,-a. ► *vt-vi* moderar(se).
modern ['mɒdən] *adj* **1** moderno,-a.
modest ['mɒdɪst] *adj* modesto,-a.
modify ['mɒdɪfaɪ] *vt* modificar.
module ['mɒdjuːl] *n* módulo.
moist [mɔɪst] *adj* húmedo,-a.
moisture ['mɔɪstʃəʳ] *n* humedad.
mold [məʊld] *n* US → mould.
mole¹ [məʊl] *n* lunar.
mole² [məʊl] *n* topo *(animal)*.
molecule ['mɒləkjuːl] *n* molécula.
molest [məˈlest] *vt* **1** hostigar, acosar. **2** agredir sexualmente.
moment ['məʊmənt] *n* momento. • **just a moment** un momento.
monarchy ['mɒnəkɪ] *n* monarquía.
monastery ['mɒnəstərɪ] *n* monasterio.
Monday ['mʌndɪ] *n* lunes.
money ['mʌnɪ] *n* dinero. ■ **money order** giro postal.

moneybox ['mʌnɪbɒks] *n* hucha.
monitor ['mɒnɪtəʳ] *n* monitor.
monk [mʌŋk] *n* monje.
monkey ['mʌŋkɪ] *n* mono. ■ **monkey wrench** llave inglesa.
monopoly [məˈnɒpəlɪ] *n* monopolio.
monotonous [məˈnɒtənəs] *adj* monótono,-a.
monster ['mɒnstəʳ] *n* monstruo.
month [mʌnθ] *n* mes.
monthly ['mʌnθlɪ] *adj* mensual. ► *adv* mensualmente. ■ **monthly instalment** mensualidad.
monument ['mɒnjʊmənt] *n* monumento.
moo [muː] *n* mugido.
mood [muːd] *n* humor. • **to be in the mood for** tener ganas de.
moon [muːn] *n* luna. ■ **moon landing** alunizaje.
moonlight ['muːnlaɪt] *n* luz de luna, claro de luna.
moor [mʊəʳ] *n* páramo.
Moor [mʊəʳ] *n* moro,-a.
mop [mɒp] *n* fregona.
moped ['məʊped] *n* ciclomotor.
moral ['mɒrəl] *adj* moral. ► *n* moraleja.
more [mɔːʳ] *adj-adv* más. • ... **any more** ya no ...; **more or less** más o menos.

moreover [mɔːˈrəʊvəʳ] *adv fml* además.

morgue [mɔːg] *n* depósito de cadáveres.

morning [ˈmɔːnɪŋ] *n* mañana. • **good morning!** ¡buenos días!; **tomorrow morning** mañana por la mañana.

morphine [ˈmɔːfiːn] *n* morfina.

morsel [ˈmɔːsəl] *n* bocado.

mortal [ˈmɔːtəl] *adj-n* mortal.

mortar [ˈmɔːtəʳ] *n* mortero.

mortgage [ˈmɔːgɪdʒ] *n* hipoteca. ▶ *vt* hipotecar. ■ **mortgage loan** préstamo hipotecario.

mosaic [məˈzeɪɪk] *adj* mosaico.

mosque [mɒsk] *n* mezquita.

mosquito [məsˈkiːtəʊ] *n* mosquito.

moss [mɒs] *n* musgo.

most [məʊst] *adj* **1** más. **2** la mayoría. ▶ *adv* más. ▶ *pron* **1** la mayor parte. **2** la mayoría.

mostly [ˈməʊstlɪ] *adv* principalmente.

motel [məʊˈtel] *n* motel.

moth [mɒθ] *n* **1** mariposa nocturna. **2** polilla.

mother [ˈmʌðəʳ] *n* madre. ■ **mother tongue** lengua materna.

motherhood [ˈmʌðəhʊd] *n* maternidad.

mother-in-law [ˈmʌðərɪnlɔː] *n* suegra.

motif [məʊˈtiːf] *n* motivo.

motion [ˈməʊʃən] *n* movimiento. • **in slow motion** a cámara lenta. ■ **motion picture** película.

motive [ˈməʊtɪv] *n* motivo.

motor [ˈməʊtəʳ] *n* motor. ■ **motor racing** carreras de coches.

motorbike [ˈməʊtəbaɪk] *n fam* moto.

motorboat [ˈməʊtəbəʊt] *n* lancha motora.

motorcycle [ˈməʊtəsaɪkəl] *n* motocicleta.

motorist [ˈməʊtərɪst] *n* automovilista.

motorway [ˈməʊtəweɪ] *n* GB autopista.

motto [ˈmɒtəʊ] *n* lema.

mould[1] [məʊld] *n* moho.

mould[2] [məʊld] *n* molde. ▶ *vt* moldear, modelar .

mount [maʊnt] *n* montura. ▶ *vt* **1** montar a *(caballo)*. **2** montar en *(bicicleta)*. **3** enmarcar *(foto)*.

mountain [ˈmaʊntən] *n* montaña. ■ **mountain bike** bicicleta de montaña; **mountain range** cordillera, sierra.

mourn [mɔːn] *vt* **1** llorar la muerte de. **2** echar de menos.

mourning [ˈmɔːnɪŋ] *n* luto.

mouse [maʊs] *n* ratón.

moustache [məsˈtɑːʃ] *n* bigote.

mouth [maʊθ] *n* **1** boca. **2** desembocadura *(de río)*.

mouthful ['maʊθfʊl] n bocado.

move [muːv] n movimiento. ► vt-vi mover(se).

movement ['muːvmənt] n movimiento.

movie ['muːvɪ] n US película.

mow [məʊ] vt segar, cortar.

mower ['məʊəʳ] n cortacésped.

much [mʌtʃ] adj mucho,-a. ► adv-pron mucho. • **how much?** ¿cuánto?

mud [mʌd] n barro, lodo.

muddle ['mʌdəl] n lío.

mudguard ['mʌdgaːd] n guardabarros.

mug [mʌg] n 1 taza. 2 jarra.

mule [mjuːl] n mulo,-a.

multiple ['mʌltɪpəl] adj múltiple.

multiply ['mʌltɪplaɪ] vt-vi multiplicar(se).

mum [mʌm] n GB fam mamá.

mumps [mʌmps] n paperas.

murder ['mɜːdəʳ] n asesinato. ► vt asesinar.

murderer ['mɜːdərəʳ] n asesino,-a.

murmur ['mɜːməʳ] n murmullo. ► vt-vi murmurar.

muscle ['mʌsəl] n músculo.

muse [mjuːz] n musa.

museum [mjuːˈzɪəm] n museo.

mushroom ['mʌʃrʊm] n seta, hongo, champiñón.

music ['mjuːzɪk] n música. ■ **music hall** teatro de variedades; **music score** partitura; **music stand** atril.

musical ['mjuːzɪkəl] adj-n musical.

musician [mjuːˈzɪʃən] n músico,-a.

mussel ['mʌsəl] n mejillón.

must¹ [mʌst] aux 1 deber, tener que. 2 deber de. ► n fam cosa imprescindible.

must² [mʌst] n mosto.

mustard ['mʌstəd] n mostaza.

mute [mjuːt] adj-n mudo,-a.

mutiny ['mjuːtɪnɪ] n motín.

mutton ['mʌtən] n carne de oveja.

mutual ['mjuːtʃʊəl] adj mutuo,-a.

muzzle ['mʌzəl] n 1 hocico. 2 bozal.

my [maɪ] adj mi, mis.

myopia [maɪˈəʊpɪə] n miopía.

myself [maɪˈself] pron 1 me. 2 mí. • **by myself** yo mismo, -a, yo solo,-a.

mystery ['mɪstərɪ] n misterio.

myth [mɪθ] n mito.

mythology [mɪˈθɒlədʒɪ] n mitología.

N

nail [neɪl] n 1 uña. 2 clavo. ► vt clavar. ■ **nail file** lima de uñas; **nail varnish** esmalte de uñas; **nail varnish remover** quitaesmaltes.

naive [naˈiːv] *adj* ingenuo,-a.

naked [ˈneɪkɪd] *adj* desnudo,-a.

name [neɪm] *n* nombre.

nanny [ˈnænɪ] *n* niñera.

nap [næp] *n* siesta.

nape [neɪp] *n* nuca, cogote.

napkin [ˈnæpkɪn] *n* servilleta.

nappy [ˈnæpɪ] *n* pañal.

narcotic [nɑːˈkɒtɪk] *adj* narcótico,-a. ► *n* narcótico.

narrate [nəˈreɪt] *vt* narrar.

narrow [ˈnærəʊ] *adj* estrecho,-a. ► *vt-vi* estrechar(se).

narrow-minded [nærəʊˈmaɪndɪd] *adj* estrecho,-a de miras.

nasal [ˈneɪzəl] *adj* nasal.

nasty [ˈnɑːstɪ] *adj* 1 desagradable, asqueroso,-a. 2 malo,-a.

nation [ˈneɪʃən] *n* nación.

national [ˈnæʃnəl] *adj* nacional.

nationality [næʃəˈnælɪtɪ] *n* nacionalidad.

nationalize [ˈnæʃnəˈlaɪz] *vt* nacionalizar.

nationwide [ˈneɪʃənwaɪd] *adj* a escala nacional.

native [ˈneɪtɪv] *adj* 1 natal. 2 originario,-a. 3 materno. ► *n* nativo,-a.

natural [ˈnætʃərəl] *adj* natural.

nature [ˈneɪtʃəʳ] *n* naturaleza.

naught [nɔːt] *n* nada.

naughty [ˈnɔːtɪ] *adj* 1 travieso,-a. 2 atrevido,-a.

nausea [ˈnɔːzɪə] *n* náusea.

nautical [ˈnɔːtɪkəl] *adj* náutico,-a.

naval [ˈneɪvəl] *adj* naval.

nave [neɪv] *n* nave.

navel [ˈneɪvəl] *n* ombligo.

navigate [ˈnævɪgeɪt] *vt* navegar por.

navigation [nævɪˈgeɪʃən] *n* navegación.

navy [ˈneɪvɪ] *n* armada. ■ **navy blue** azul marino.

near [nɪəʳ] *adj* 1 cercano,-a. 2 próximo,-a. ► *adv* 1 cerca. 2 a punto de. ► *prep* cerca de.

nearby [ˈnɪəbaɪ] *adj* cercano,-a. ► *adv* cerca.

nearly [ˈnɪəlɪ] *adv* casi.

neat [niːt] *adj* 1 ordenado,-a. 2 pulcro,-a. 3 claro,-a. 4 solo,-a.

necessary [ˈnesɪsərɪ] *adj* necesario,-a.

necessity [nɪˈsesɪtɪ] *n* necesidad.

neck [nek] *n* cuello.

necklace [ˈnekləs] *n* collar.

neckline [ˈneklaɪn] *n* escote.

nectar [ˈnektəʳ] *n* néctar.

née [neɪ] *adj* de soltera.

need [niːd] *n* necesidad. ► *vt* 1 necesitar. 2 tener que. ► *aux* tener que: *you needn't do it if you don't want to*, no tienes que hacerlo si no quieres.● **in need** necesitado; **to be in need of** necesitar.

needle [ˈniːdəl] *n* aguja.

needless [ˈniːdləs] *adj* innecesario,-a. ● **needless to say** huelga decir.

negation [nɪˈgeɪʃən] n negación.

negative [ˈnegətɪv] adj negativo,-a. ► n 1 negativa. 2 negativo (de foto).

neglect [nɪˈglekt] n descuido. ► vt descuida.

neglectful [nɪˈglektfʊl] adj negligente, descuidado,-a.

negligée [ˈneglɪdʒeɪ] n salto de cama.

negligent [ˈneglɪdʒənt] adj negligente.

negotiate [nɪˈgəʊʃɪeɪt] vt-vi negociar.

negotiation [nɪgəʊʃɪˈeɪʃən] n negociación.

negro [ˈniːgrəʊ] adj-n negro,-a.

neighbour [ˈneɪbəʳ] (US **neighbor**) n vecino,-a.

neighbourhood [ˈneɪbəhʊd] (US **neighborhood**) n vecindad.

neither [ˈnaɪðəʳ, ˈniːðəʳ] adj-pron ninguno de los dos, ninguna de las dos. ► adv-conj 1 ni. 2 tampoco: I can't swim. –Neither can I, No sé nadar. –Yo tampoco. • neither ... nor... ni ... ni ...

neon [ˈniːɒn] n neón.

nephew [ˈnevjuː] n sobrino.

nerve [nɜːv] n 1 nervio. 2 valor. 3 descaro: you've got a nerve!, ¡qué cara tienes!

nervous [ˈnɜːvəs] adj nervioso,-a. ■ **nervous breakdown** depresión nerviosa.

nest [nest] n nido. ► vi anidar.

nestle [ˈnesəl] vi acomodarse.

net¹ [net] n 1 red. 2 **the Net** la Red. ► vt coger con red. ■ **Net user** internauta.

net² [net] adj neto,-a.

netball [ˈnetbɔːl] n baloncesto femenino.

netting [ˈnetɪŋ] n malla.

nettle [ˈnetəl] n ortiga. ► vt irritar.

network [ˈnetwɜːk] n red.

neurotic [njʊˈrɒtɪk] adj-n neurótico,-a.

neuter [ˈnjuːtəʳ] adj neutro,-a. ► n neutro.

neutral [ˈnjuːtrəl] adj 1 neutro,-a. 2 POL neutral. ► n punto muerto.

never [ˈnevəʳ] adv nunca, jamás.

never-ending [nevəˈrendɪŋ] adj interminable.

nevertheless [nevəðəˈles] adv sin embargo.

new [njuː] adj nuevo,-a. • **as good as new** como nuevo; **new to STH** nuevo en algo. ■ **New Year** Año Nuevo; **New Year's Eve** Nochevieja.

newborn [ˈnjuːbɔːn] adj recién nacido,-a.

newcomer [ˈnjuːkʌməʳ] n recién llegado,-a.

newly [ˈnjuːlɪ] adv recién, recientemente.

newlywed [ˈnjuːlɪwed] n recién casado,-a.

news [nju:z] *n* noticias. • **to break the news to** SB dar la noticia a ALGN. ■ **a piece of news** una noticia; **news bulletin** boletín informativo.

newsagent ['nju:zeɪdʒənt] *n* vendedor,-ra de periódicos. ■ **newsagent's** quiosco de periódicos.

newsflash ['nju:zflæʃ] *n* noticia de última hora.

newsgroup ['nju:zgru:p] *n* grupo de noticias.

newsletter ['nju:zletə'] *n* hoja informativa.

newspaper ['nju:speɪpə'] *n* diario, periódico.

newt [nju:t] *n* tritón.

next [nekst] *adj* **1** próximo,-a. **2** de al lado: *he lives next door*, vive en la casa de al lado. ► *adv* luego, después. • **next to** al lado de. ■ **next of kin** pariente(s) más cercano(s).

nibble ['nɪbəl] *n* **1** mordisco. **2** bocadito. ► *vt-vi* mordisquear.

nice [naɪs] *adj* **1** amable, simpático,-a. **2** agradable. **3** bonito,-a, guapo,-a.

niche [ni:ʃ] *n* nicho.

nick [nɪk] *n* mella, muesca.

nickel ['nɪkəl] *n* **1** níquel. **2** US moneda de cinco centavos.

nickname ['nɪkneɪm] *n* apodo. ► *vt* apodar.

niece [ni:s] *n* sobrina.

night [naɪt] *n* noche. • **good night** buenas noches *(despedida)*; **last night** anoche.

nightclub ['naɪtklʌb] *n* club nocturno.

nightdress ['naɪtdres] *n* camisón.

nightgown ['naɪtgaʊn] *n* camisón.

nightingale ['naɪtɪŋgeɪl] *n* ruiseñor.

nightmare ['naɪtmeə'] *n* pesadilla.

nil [nɪl] *n* nada, cero.

nimble ['nɪmbəl] *adj* ágil.

nine [naɪn] *num* nueve.

nineteen [naɪn'ti:n] *num* diecinueve.

nineteenth [naɪn'ti:nθ] *adj* decimonoveno,-a.

ninety ['naɪntɪ] *num* noventa.

ninth [naɪnθ] *adj* noveno,-a.

nip [nɪp] *n* **1** pellizco. **2** mordisco. ► *vt-vi* **1** pellizcar. **2** mordisquear.

nipple ['nɪpəl] *n* **1** pezón. **2** tetilla.

nit [nɪt] *n* liendre.

nite [naɪt] *n* US → night.

no [nəʊ] *adv* no. ► *adj* **1** ninguno,-a, ningún: *I have no time*, no tengo tiempo. **2** no: *he's no friend of mine*, no es amigo mío.

noble ['nəʊbəl] *adj* noble. ► *n* noble.

nobody ['nəʊbədɪ] *pron* nadie.

nod [nɒd] n **1** saludo (con la cabeza). **2** señal de asentimiento. ► vi **1** saludar (con la cabeza). **2** asentir (con la cabeza).

noise [nɔɪz] n ruido, sonido.

noisy ['nɔɪzɪ] adj ruidoso,-a.

nomad ['nəʊmæd] adj-n nómada.

nominal ['nɒmɪnəl] adj **1** nominal. **2** simbólico,-a (precio).

nominate ['nɒmɪneɪt] vt **1** nombrar. **2** proponer.

nonchalant ['nɒnʃələnt] adj **1** despreocupado. **2** impasible.

nonconformist [nɒnkən'fɔːmɪst] adj-n inconformista.

none [nʌn] pron **1** ninguno,-a. **2** nadie. **3** nada.

nonexistent [nɒnɪg'zɪstənt] adj inexistente.

nonplussed [nɒn'plʌst] adj perplejo,-a.

nonsense ['nɒnsəns] n tonterías.

nonsmoker [nɒn'sməʊkəʳ] n no fumador,-ra.

nonstick [nɒn'stɪk] adj antiadherente.

nonstop [nɒn'stɒp] adj directo,-a: *a nonstop flight*, un vuelo directo. ► adv sin parar.

noodle ['nuːdəl] n fideo.

noon [nuːn] n mediodía.

no-one ['nəʊwʌn] pron nadie.

nor [nɔːʳ] conj **1** ni. **2** tampoco: *nor do I*, yo tampoco.

norm [nɔːm] n norma.

normal ['nɔːməl] adj normal.

north [nɔːθ] n norte. ► adj del norte:. ► adv al norte.

northern ['nɔːðən] adj del norte, septentrional.

nose [nəʊz] n **1** nariz,. **2** hocico, morro. **3** olfato.

nosey ['nəʊzɪ] adj fam curioso,-a.

nostalgia [nɒ'stældʒɪə] n nostalgia.

nostril ['nɒstrɪl] n fosa nasal.

not [nɒt] adv no.

notation [nəʊ'teɪʃən] n notación.

notch [nɒtʃ] n muesca. ► vt hacer muescas en.

note [nəʊt] vt **1** notar, observar. **2** apuntar, anotar. ► n **1** nota. **2** billete. • **to note down** apuntar, tomar nota.

notebook ['nəʊtbʊk] n libreta, cuaderno.

notepaper ['nəʊtpeɪpəʳ] n papel de cartas.

nothing ['nʌθɪŋ] pron nada. • **for nothing 1** gratis, gratuitamente. **2** en vano, en balde; **if nothing else** al menos; **nothing but** tan sólo.

notice ['nəʊtɪs] n **1** letrero. **2** anuncio. **3** aviso. ► vt notar, fijarse en, darse cuenta de. • **to take no notice of** no hacer caso de; **until further notice** hasta nuevo aviso.

noticeboard ['nəʊtɪsbɔːd] n tablón de anuncios.

notify ['nəʊtɪfaɪ] *vt* notificar.
notion ['nəʊʃən] *n* noción.
notwithstanding [nɒtwɪθ-'stændɪŋ] *adv* no obstante. ► *prep* a pesar de.
nougat ['nuːgɑː] *n* turrón blando.
nought [nɔːt] *n* cero.
noun [naʊn] *n* nombre.
nourish ['nʌrɪʃ] *vt* nutrir.
novel ['nɒvəl] *n* novela.
novelty ['nɒvəltɪ] *n* novedad.
November [nəʊ'vembəʳ] *n* noviembre.
now [naʊ] *adv* **1** ahora. **2** hoy en día, actualmente.• **from now on** de ahora en adelante; **now and then** de vez en cuando.
nowadays ['naʊədeɪz] *adv* hoy día, hoy en día.
nowhere ['nəʊweəʳ] *adv* ninguna parte.
noxious ['nɒkʃəs] *adj* nocivo,-a.
nozzle ['nɒzəl] *n* boquilla.
nuance [njuː'ɑːns] *n* matiz.
nuclear ['njuːklɪəʳ] *adj* nuclear.
nucleus ['njuːklɪəs] *n* núcleo.
nude [njuːd] *adj* desnudo,-a. ► *n* desnudo.
nugget ['nʌgɪt] *n* pepita.
nuisance ['njuːsəns] *n* **1** molestia, fastidio, lata. **2** pesado,-a.
null [nʌl] *adj* nulo,-a.
numb [nʌm] *adj* entumecido,-a. ► *vt* entumecer.
number ['nʌmbəʳ] *n* número.

numberplate ['nʌmbəpleɪt] *n* GB placa de la matrícula.
nun [nʌn] *n* monja.
nunnery ['nʌnərɪ] *n* convento *(de monjas)*.
nurse [nɜːs] *n* **1** enfermero,-a. **2** niñera.
nursery ['nɜːsrɪ] *n* guardería.
nut [nʌt] *n* **1** fruto seco. **2** tuerca. **3** *fam* chalado,-a.
nutcracker ['nʌtkrækəʳ] *n* cascanueces.
nutmeg ['nʌtmeg] *n* nuez moscada.
nutritious [njuː'trɪʃəs] *adj* nutritivo,-a.
nutshell ['nʌtʃel] *n* cáscara.
nylon ['naɪlɒn] *n* nilón, nailon.

O

O [əʊ] *n* cero.
oak [əʊk] *n* roble.
oar [ɔːʳ] *n* remo.
oarsman ['ɔːzmən] *n* remero.
oasis [əʊ'eɪsɪs] *n* oasis.
oath [əʊθ] *n* juramento.
oats [əʊt] *npl* avena.
obedient [ə'biːdɪənt] *adj* obediente.
obese [əʊ'biːs] *adj* obeso,-a.
obey [ə'beɪ] *vt* obedecer.
object ['ɒbdʒɪkt] *n* objeto.
objective [əb'dʒektɪv] *adj* objetivo,-a. ► *n* objetivo.

obligation [ɒblɪ'ɡeɪʃən] n obligación.
oblige [ə'blaɪdʒ] vt 1 obligar. 2 hacer un favor a.
oblivion [ə'blɪvɪən] n olvido.
obscene [ɒb'siːn] adj obsceno,-a.
obscure [əbs'kjʊəʳ] adj oscuro,-a.
observatory [əb'zɜːvətrɪ] n observatorio.
observe [əb'zɜːv] vt observar.
obsess [əb'ses] vt obsesionar.
obstacle ['ɒbstəkəl] n obstáculo.
obstinate ['ɒbstɪnət] adj obstinado,-a.
obstruct [əb'strʌkt] vt obstruir.
obtain [əb'teɪn] vt obtener.
obvious ['ɒbvɪəs] adj obvio,-a.
occasion [ə'keɪʒən] n ocasión.
occult ['ɒkʌlt] adj oculto,-a.
occupant ['ɒkjʊpənt] n ocupante (de silla, vehículo).
occupation [ɒkjʊ'peɪʃən] n 1 ocupación. 2 pasatiempo.
occupy ['ɒkjʊpaɪ] vt ocupar.
occur [ə'kɜːʳ] vi ocurrir.
ocean ['əʊʃən] n océano.
o'clock [ə'klɒk] adv: it's one o'clock, es la una.
October [ɒk'təʊbəʳ] n octubre.
octopus ['ɒktəpəs] n pulpo.
odd [ɒd] adj 1 extraño,-a, raro,-a. 2 impar. 3: thirty odd, treinta y pico, trenta y tantos.

odds [ɒdz] npl probabilidades.
odour ['əʊdəʳ] (US **odor**) n olor.
oesophagus [iː'sɒfəɡəs] (US **esophagus**) n esófago.
of [ɒv, unstressed əv] prep de:.
off [ɒf] prep 1 de. 2 cerca. 3: there's a button off your coat, a tu abrigo le falta un botón. ► adv 1: he ran off, se fue corriendo. 2: two days off, dos días libres. ► adj 1 ausente, de baja. 2 apagado,-a (aparato). 3 malo,-a, pasado,-a, agrio,-a.
offence [ə'fens] n 1 ofensa. 2 infracción, delito.
offend [ə'fend] vt ofender.
offensive [ə'fensɪv] adj ofensivo,-a. ► n ofensiva.
offer ['ɒfəʳ] n oferta. ► vt ofrecer. • **on offer** de oferta.
office ['ɒfɪs] n 1 despacho, oficina. 2 cargo. • **in office** en el poder; **to take office** tomar posesión del cargo. ■ **office hours** horas de oficina; **office worker** oficinista.
officer ['ɒfɪsəʳ] n 1 oficial (militar). 2 agente, policía.
official [ə'fɪʃəl] adj oficial. ► n funcionario,-a.
off-key [ɒf'kiː] adj desafinado,-a.
off-licence ['ɒflaɪsəns] n GB tienda de bebidas alcohólicas.
off-line ['ɒflaɪn] adj COMPUT desconectado,-a.

offshoot ['ɒfʃuːt] n vástago, retoño *(de planta, árbol)*.

offside [ɒf'saɪd] *adj-adv* fuera de juego.

offspring ['ɔːfsprɪŋ] n descendiente.

often ['ɒfən] *adv* a menudo. • **how often…?** ¿cada cuánto…?

oil [ɔɪl] n **1** aceite. **2** petróleo. **3** óleo, pintura al óleo. ▪ **oil rig** plataforma petrolífera; **oil slick** marea negra; **oil tanker** petrolero; **oil well** pozo petrolífero.

oilcloth ['ɔɪlklɒθ] n hule.

oilfield ['ɔɪfiːld] n yacimiento petrolífero.

ointment ['ɔɪntmənt] n ungüento.

okay [əʊ'keɪ] *interj* ¡vale!, ¡de acuerdo! ▶ *adj-adv* **1** bien. **2** vale, de acuerdo. ▶ n visto bueno.

old [əʊld] *adj* viejo,-a. • **how old are you?** ¿cuántos años tienes?; **to be… years old** tener… años. ▪ **old age** vejez.

old-fashioned [əʊld'fæʃənd] *adj* anticuado,-a.

olive ['ɒlɪv] n aceituna, oliva. ▪ **olive oil** aceite de oliva.

omelette ['ɒmlət] n US tortilla.

omit [əʊ'mɪt] vt omitir.

on [ɒn] *prep* **1** en. **2** sobre. **3**: *on Sunday*, el domingo; *he got on the bus*, se subió al autobús; *he's on the phone*, está al teléfono. ▶ *adv* **1** conectado, -a, encendido,-a *(luz, aparato)*. **2** abierto,-a *(grifo)*. **3** puesto,-a. • **and so on** y así sucesivamente; **on and off** de vez en cuando; **on and on** sin parar.

once [wʌns] *adv* **1** una vez. **2** antes, anteriormente. ▶ *conj* una vez que. • **at once 1** enseguida. **2** a la vez. **3** de una vez; **once and for all** de una vez para siempre; **once upon a time** érase una vez.

one [wʌn] *adj* un, una. ▶ *num* uno. ▶ *pron* uno,-a. • **one another** el uno al otro.

oneself [wʌn'self] *pron* uno,-a mismo,-a, sí mismo,-a. • **by oneself** solo.

one-way ['wʌnweɪ] *adj* **1** de sentido único *(calle)*. **2** de ida *(billete)*.

onion ['ʌnɪən] n cebolla.

on-line ['ɒn'laɪn] *adj* COMPUT en línea.

onlooker ['ɒnlʊkəʳ] n espectador,-ra.

only ['əʊnlɪ] *adj* único,-a. ▶ *adv* sólo, solamente, únicamente. ▶ *conj* pero. • **if only** ojalá; **only just** apenas.

onto ['ɒntʊ] *prep* sobre.

onwards ['ɒnwədz] *adv* adelante, hacia adelante.

opaque [əʊ'peɪk] *adj* opaco,-a.

open ['əʊpən] *adj* abierto,-a. ▶ *vt-vi* abrir(se). ▪ **open season** temporada de caza.

open-air ['əʊpəneəˈ] *adj* al aire libre.

opener ['əʊpənəˈ] *n* abridor.

opening ['əʊpənɪŋ] *n* abertura. ■ **opening hours** horario de apertura; **opening night** noche de estreno.

open-minded [əʊpənˈmaɪndɪd] *adj* tolerante, abierto.

opera ['ɒpərə] *n* ópera. ■ **opera house** ópera.

operate ['ɒpəreɪt] *vt* hacer funcionar. ► *vi* operar. ■ **operating theatre** quirófano.

operation [ɒpəˈreɪʃən] *n* operación.

operator ['ɒpəreɪtəˈ] *n* 1 operador,-a, telefonista. 2 operario,-a.

opinion [əˈpɪnɪən] *n* opinión.

opponent [əˈpəʊnənt] *n* adversario,-a.

opportunity [ɒpəˈtjuːnɪti] *n* oportunidad.

oppose [əˈpəʊz] *vt* oponerse a.

opposite ['ɒpəzɪt] *adj* 1 de enfrente. 2 opuesto,-a, contrario,-a. ► *prep* enfrente de, frente a. ► *adv* enfrente.

opposition [ɒpəˈzɪʃən] *n* oposición.

oppress [əˈpres] *vt* oprimir.

opt [ɒpt] *vi* optar.

optical ['ɒptɪkəl] *adj* óptico,-a.

optician [ɒpˈtɪʃən] *n* óptico, -a. ■ **optician's** óptica.

optimist ['ɒptɪmɪst] *n* optimista.

optimistic [ɒptɪˈmɪstɪk] *adj* optimista.

option ['ɒpʃən] *n* opción.

or [ɔːˈ] *conj* 1 o. 2 ni. ● **or else** de lo contrario, si no.

oral ['ɔːrəl] *adj* oral. ► *n* examen oral.

orange ['ɒrɪndʒ] *n* naranja. ■ **orange blossom** azahar.

orbit ['ɔːbɪt] *n* órbita.

orchard ['ɔːtʃəd] *n* huerto.

orchestra ['ɔːkɪstrə] *n* orquesta.

orchid ['ɔːkɪd] *n* orquídea.

order ['ɔːdəˈ] *n* 1 orden. 2 pedido. ► *vt* 1 ordenar. 2 pedir. ● **in order to** para, a fin de; "**Out of order**" "No funciona".

ordinal ['ɔːdɪnəl] *adj* ordinal. ► *n* ordinal.

ordinary ['ɔːdɪnəri] *adj* normal, corriente. ■ **ordinary chart** organigrama.

oregano [ɒrɪˈgaːnəʊ] *n* orégano.

organ ['ɔːgən] *n* órgano.

organism ['ɔːgənɪzəm] *n* organismo.

organization [ɔːgənaɪˈzeɪʃən] *n* organización. ■ **organization chart** organigrama.

organize ['ɔːgənaɪz] *vt-vi* organizar(se).

orientation [ɔːrɪenˈteɪʃən] *n* orientación.

origin ['ɒrɪdʒɪn] *n* origen.

original [əˈrɪdʒɪnəl] *adj-n* original.

orphan ['ɔːfən] n huérfano,-a.

ostrich ['ɒstrɪtʃ] n avestruz.

other ['ʌðəʳ] adj-pron otro,-a.
• **other than** aparte de, salvo; **the others** los demás.

otherwise ['ʌðəwaɪz] adv **1** de otra manera. **2** por lo demás. ► conj si no, de lo contrario.

otter ['ɒtəʳ] n nutria.

ought [ɔːt] aux deber.

ounce [aʊns] n onza.

our ['aʊəʳ] adj nuestro,-a, nuestros,-as.

ours ['aʊəz] pron (el) nuestro, (la) nuestra, (los) nuestros, (las) nuestras.

ourselves [aʊə'selvz] pron **1** nos. **2** nosotros,-as mismos, -as. • **by ourselves** solos.

out [aʊt] adv **1** fuera, afuera. **2** equivocado,-a. **3**: *white socks are out*, los calcetines blancos ya no se llevan. **4** apagado,-a *(luz)*. **5** fuera, eliminado,-a *(jugador)*. **6** despedido,-a. ► prep **out of 1** fuera de. **2** de: *made out of wood*, hecho,-a de madera. **3** sin: *we're out of tea*, se nos ha acabado el té. **4** de cada: *eight women out of ten*, ocho de cada diez mujeres.

outboard ['aʊtbɔːd] adj fueraborda.

outbreak ['aʊtbreɪk] n **1** estallido *(de guerra)*. **2** comienzo *(de hostilidades)*. **3** brote *(de epidemia)*.

outburst ['aʊtbɜːst] n explosión.

outcast ['aʊtkɑːst] n marginado,-a.

outcome ['aʊtkʌm] n resultado.

outdated [aʊt'deɪtɪd] adj anticuado,-a.

outdoor [aʊt'dɔːʳ] adj al aire libre. ► adv **outdoors** fuera.

outer ['aʊtəʳ] adj exterior.

outfit ['aʊtfɪt] n **1** conjunto, traje. **2** equipo, grupo.

outgoing [aʊt'gəʊɪŋ] adj **1** saliente, cesante. **2** sociable.

outing ['aʊtɪŋ] n salida, excursión.

outlaw ['aʊtlɔː] n forajido,-a, proscrito,-a. ► vt prohibir.

outlay ['aʊtleɪ] n desembolso.

outlet ['aʊtlet] n **1** salida. **2** desagüe.

outline ['aʊtlaɪn] n **1** contorno. **2** resumen, esbozo. ► vt **1** perfilar. **2** resumi.

outlook ['aʊtlʊk] n **1** vista. **2** punto de vista.

outlying ['aʊtlaɪɪŋ] adj alejado,-a, remoto.

outnumber [aʊt'nʌmbəʳ] vt exceder en número.

outpatient ['aʊtpeɪʃənt] n paciente externo,-a.

output ['aʊtpʊt] n **1** producción, rendimiento. **2** COMPUT salida.

outrage ['aʊtreɪdʒ] n indignación. ► vt ultrajar, atropellar.

outright [ˈaʊtraɪt] *adj* absoluto,-a.

outside [(n) aʊtˈsaɪd, (prep) ˈaʊtsaɪd] *n* exterior. ► *prep* fuera de. ► *adv* fuera, afuera. ► *adj* exterior.

outsider [aʊtˈsaɪdə^r] *n* forastero,-a.

outskirts [ˈaʊtskɜːts] *npl* afueras.

outstanding [aʊtˈstændɪŋ] *adj* destacado,-a.

outward [ˈaʊtwəd] *adj* 1 externo,-a. 2 de ida *(viaje)*. ► *adv* **outward** a **outwards** hacia fuera, hacia afuera.

outwit [aʊtˈwɪt] *vt*

oval [ˈəʊvəl] *adj* oval, ovalado,-a. ► *n* óvalo.

ovary [ˈəʊvəri] *n* ovario.

oven [ˈʌvən] *n* horno.

over [ˈəʊvə^r] *adv: come over here*, ven aquí; *over there*, allí; *he fell over*, se cayó. ► *adj* acabado,-a. ► *prep* 1 encima de, por encima de. 2 más de. 3 al otro lado de. 5 durante. 6 por. • **over and over again** una y otra vez; **over here** aquí; **over there** allí.

overall [(adj) ˈəʊvərɔːl, (adv) əʊvəˈrɔːl] *adj* global, total. ► *adv* 1 en total. 2 en conjunto. ► *npl* **overalls** mono.

overboard [ˈəʊvəbɔːd] *adv* por la borda.

overcame [əʊvəˈkeɪm] *pt* → overcome.

overcast [ˈəʊvəkɑːst] *adj* cubierto,-a, nublado,-a.

overcoat [ˈəʊvəkəʊt] *n* abrigo.

overcome [əʊvəˈkʌm] *vt* 1 vencer, superar. 2 abrumar.

overdose [ˈəʊvədəʊs] *n* sobredosis.

overexposed [əʊvərɪkˈspəʊʒd] *adj* sobreexpuesto,-a.

overflow [(n) ˈəʊvəfləʊ (vb) əʊvəˈfləʊ] *vi* desbordarse.

overhaul [(n) ˈəʊvəhɔːl, (vb) əʊvəˈhɔːl] *n* revisión general. ► *vt* repasar, revisar.

overheat [əʊvəˈhiːt] *vi* recalentarse.

overjoyed [əʊvəˈdʒɔɪd] *adj* encantadísimo,-a.

overland [ˈəʊvəlænd] *adj-adv* por tierra.

overlap [əʊvəˈlæp] *vi* superponerse.

overleaf [əʊvəˈliːf] *adv* al dorso, a la vuelta.

overlook [əʊvəˈlʊk] *vt* 1 pasar por alto, no notar. 2 hacer la vista gorda a, disculpar, dejar pasar. 3 dar a, tener vistas a.

overnight [əʊvəˈnaɪt] *adj* de una noche. ► *adv* por la noche. • **to stay overnight** pasar la noche.

overran [əʊvəˈræn] *pt* → overrun.

overrate [əʊvəˈreɪt] *vt* sobrevalorar.

overrule [əʊvəˈruːl] *vt* desautorizar, anular.

overrun [əʊvəˈrʌn] *vt* invadir. ▶ *vi* durar más de lo previsto.

overseas [əʊvəˈsiːz] *adj* de ultramar, del extranjero. ▶ *adv* en ultramar, en el extranjero.

oversee [əʊvəˈsiː] *vt* supervisar.

overshadow [əʊvəˈʃædəʊ] *vt fig* eclipsar, ensombrecer.

oversight [ˈəʊvəsaɪt] *n* descuido.

oversleep [əʊvəˈsliːp] *vi* dormirse, quedarse dormido.

overstep [əʊvəˈstep] *vt* sobrepasar, pasar de.

overt [ˈəʊvɜːt, əʊˈvɜːt] *adj* declarado,-a, abierto,-a.

overtake [əʊvəˈteɪk] *vt* adelantar.

overthrow [əʊvəˈθrəʊ] *vt* derribar, derrocar.

overtime [ˈəʊvətaɪm] *n* horas extraordinarias, horas extra.

overture [ˈəʊvətjʊə'] *n* obertura.

overturn [əʊvəˈtɜːn] *vt-vi* volcar.

overweight [əʊvəˈweɪt] *adj* demasiado gordo,-a. • **to be overweight** tener exceso de peso.

overwhelm [əʊvəˈwelm] *vt* **1** arrollar, aplastar. **2** *fig* abrumar.

overwhelming [əʊvəˈwelmɪŋ] *adj* aplastante, arrollador,-ra.

overwork [əʊvəˈwɜːk] *vi* trabajar demasiado. ▶ *vt* hacer trabajar demasiado.

overwrought [əʊvəˈrɔːt] *adj* muy nervioso,-a.

ovulation [ɒvjʊˈleɪʃən] *n* ovulación.

ovum [ˈəʊvəm] *n* óvulo.

owe [əʊ] *vt* deber.

owing [ˈəʊɪŋ] *adj* que se debe. • **owing to** debido a, a causa de.

owl [aʊl] *n* búho, mochuelo, lechuza.

own [əʊn] *adj* propio,-a: *he has his own car*, tiene su propio coche. ▶ *pron*: *my/your/his own*, lo mío/ tuyo/ suyo; *a room of my own*, una habitación para mí solo. ▶ *vt* poseer, ser dueño,-a de, tener. • **on one's own** solo, sin ayuda: *can you do it on your own?*, ¿puedes hacerlo solo?

to own up *vi* confesar.

owner [ˈəʊnə'] *n* dueño,-a, propietario,-a, poseedor,-ra.

ownership [ˈəʊnəʃɪp] *n* propiedad, posesión.

ox [ɒks] *n* buey.

oxide [ˈɒksaɪd] *n* óxido.

oxidize [ˈɒksɪdaɪz] *vt-vi* oxidar(se).

oxygen [ˈɒksɪdʒən] *n* oxígeno. ▪ **oxygen mask** máscara de oxígeno.

oyster [ˈɔɪstə'] *n* ostra.

oz [aʊns, ˈaʊnsɪz] *abbr (ounce)* onza.

ozone [ˈəʊzəʊn] *n* ozono. ▪ **ozone layer** capa de ozono.

P

pace [peɪs] *n* **1** paso. **2** marcha, ritmo.

pacemaker ['peɪsmeɪkəʳ] *n* **1** liebre *(en carrera)*. **2** marcapasos.

pacific [pə'sɪfɪk] *adj* pacífico,-a.

pacify ['pæsɪfaɪ] *vt* pacificar, apaciguar.

pack [pæk] *n* **1** paquete. **2** baraja. **3** banda *(de ladrones)*. ▶ *vt* **1** empaquetar. **2** hacer *(maleta)*. **3** apretar.

package ['pækɪdʒ] *n* paquete. ▪ **package tour** viaje organizado.

packaging ['pækɪdʒɪŋ] *n* embalaje.

packet ['pækɪt] *n* paquete.

pact [pækt] *n* pacto.

pad [pæd] *n* **1** almohadilla. **2** taco, bloc *(de papel)*.

paddle ['pædəl] *n* pala *(para remar)*. ▶ *vt-vi* remar con pala.

padlock ['pædlɒk] *n* candado. ▶ *vt* cerrar con candado.

pagan ['peɪgən] *adj-n* pagano,-a.

page¹ [peɪdʒ] *n* página.

paid [peɪd] *pt-pp* → pay.

pain [peɪn] *n* dolor. • **on pain of** so pena de.

painful ['peɪnfʊl] *adj* doloroso,-a.

painkiller ['peɪnkɪləʳ] *n* calmante, analgésico.

painless ['peɪnləs] *adj* indoloro,-a.

paint [peɪnt] *n* pintura. ▶ *vt-vi* pintar.

paintbrush ['peɪntbrʌʃ] *n* **1** brocha. **2** pincel.

painter ['peɪntəʳ] *n* pintor,-ra.

painting ['peɪntɪŋ] *n* **1** pintura. **2** cuadro.

pair [peəʳ] *n* **1** par. **2** pareja.

pajamas [pə'dʒæməz] *npl* US pijama.

pal [pæl] *n fam* camarada.

palace ['pæləs] *n* palacio.

palate ['pælət] *n* paladar.

pale [peɪl] *adj* pálido,-a.

palm [pɑːm] *n* palma *(de la mano)*.

palm² [pɑːm] *n* palmera.

paltry ['pɔːltrɪ] *adj* mísero,-a, mezquino,-a.

pamper ['pæmpəʳ] *vt* mimar.

pamphlet ['pæmflət] *n* **1** folleto *(publicitario)*. **2** panfleto *(político)*.

pan [pæn] *n* cazo, olla.

pancake ['pænkeɪk] *n* crepe.

pancreas ['pæŋkrɪəs] *n* páncreas.

panda ['pændə] *n* oso panda, panda.

panel ['pænəl] *n* panel.

panic ['pænɪk] *n* pánico.

panther ['pænθəʳ] *n* pantera.

panties ['pæntɪz] *npl* bragas.

pantry ['pæntrɪ] *n* despensa.

pants [pænts] *npl* **1** calzoncillos. **2** bragas. **3** US pantalones.

partition

paper ['peɪpəʳ] *n* papel.► *vt* empapelar. • **on paper** por escrito.

paperclip ['peɪpəklɪp] *n* clip.

paperweight ['peɪpəweɪt] *n* pisapapeles.

paperwork ['peɪpəwɜːk] *n* papeleo.

par [pɑːʳ] *n* par *(en golf)*.

parachute ['pærəʃuːt] *n* paracaídas.

parade [pəˈreɪd] *n* desfile. ► *vi* desfilar.

paradise ['pærədaɪs] *n* paraíso.

paragraph ['pærəgrɑːf] *n* párrafo.

parakeet ['pærəkiːt] *n* periquito.

parallel ['pærəlel] *adj* paralelo,-a. ► *n* **1** paralelo. **2** paralela.

paralysis [pəˈrælɪsɪs] *n* parálisis.

parasite ['pærəsaɪt] *n* parásito,-a.

parasol [pærəˈsɒl] *n* sombrilla.

parcel ['pɑːsəl] *n* paquete.

parchment ['pɑːtʃmənt] *n* pergamino.

pardon ['pɑːdən] *n* perdón. ► *vt* perdonar. • **I beg your pardon** le ruego me disculpe, perdón; **pardon?** ¿perdón?, ¿cómo dice?

pare [peəʳ] *vt* **1** pelar *(fruta)*. **2** cortar *(uñas)*.

parent ['peərənt] *n* padre, madre. ► *npl* **parents** padres.

parenthesis [pəˈrenθəsɪs] *n* paréntesis.

parish ['pærɪʃ] *n* parroquia.

park [pɑːk] *n* parque. ► *vt-vi* aparcar.

parking ['pɑːkɪŋ] *n* aparcamiento. • **"No parking"** "Prohibido aparcar". ■ **parking lot** US aparcamiento; **parking meter** parquímetro; **parking place** sitio para aparcar.

parliament ['pɑːləmənt] *n* parlamento.

parlour ['pɑːləʳ] (US **parlor**) *n* salón.

parole [pəˈrəʊl] *n* libertad condicional. • **on parole** en libertad condicional.

parquet ['pɑːkeɪ] *n* parqué.

parrot ['pærət] *n* loro.

parsley ['pɑːslɪ] *n* perejil.

parson ['pɑːsən] *n* párroco.

part [pɑːt] *n* **1** parte. **2** pieza *(de máquina)*. **3** papel *(en obra, etc)*. ► *vt-vi* separar(se).

partial ['pɑːʃəl] *adj* parcial.

participate [pɑːˈtɪsɪpeɪt] *vi* participar.

participle ['pɑːtɪsɪpəl] *n* participio.

particle ['pɑːtɪkəl] *n* partícula.

particular [pəˈtɪkjʊləʳ] *adj* particular. ► *npl* **particulars** detalles, datos.

parting ['pɑːtɪŋ] *n* **1** despedida. **2** raya *(en pelo)*.

partition [pɑːˈtɪʃən] *n* **1** partición. **2** tabique.

partner ['pɑːtnəʳ] *n* **1** compañero,-a. **2** socio,-a *(en negocio)*. **3** pareja *(en deporte)*. **4** cónyuge.

part-time [pɑːt'taɪm] *adj* de media jornada. ► *adv* a tiempo parcial.

party ['pɑːtɪ] *n* **1** fiesta. **2** partido *(político)*. **3** parte *(en contrato, etc)*.

pass [pɑːs] *n* **1** pase. **2** aprobado. ► *vt-vi* **1** pasar. **2** aprobar.

to pass by *vi* pasar cerca.

to pass out *vi* desmayarse.

passage ['pæsɪdʒ] *n* **1** pasaje. **2** paso *(de vehículo, tiempo)*.

passenger ['pæsɪndʒəʳ] *n* pasajero,-a.

passer-by [pɑːsə'baɪ] *n* transeúnte.

passion ['pæʃən] *n* pasión.

passive ['pæsɪv] *adj* pasivo,-a. ► *n* voz pasiva.

passport ['pɑːspɔːt] *n* pasaporte.

password ['pɑːswɜːd] *n* contraseña.

past [pɑːst] *adj* **1** pasado,-a. **2** último,-a. ► *adv* por delante. ► *n* pasado. ► *prep* **1** más allá de. **2** por delante de. **3** y: *five past six*, las seis y cinco. ■ **past participle** participio pasado; **past tense** pasado.

pasta ['pæstə] *n* pasta.

paste [peɪst] *n* **1** pasta. **2** engrudo; cola. ► *vt* pegar.

pastel ['pæstəl] *n* pastel.

pastime ['pɑːstaɪm] *n* pasatiempo.

pastry ['peɪstrɪ] *n* **1** masa. **2** pastel, pasta.

pasture ['pɑːstʃəʳ] *n* pasto.

pasty ['pæstɪ] *n* empanada.

patch [pætʃ] *n* parche.

pâté ['pæteɪ] *n* paté.

patent ['peɪtənt] *adj-n* patente. ► *vt* patentar. ■ **patent leather** charol.

paternity [pə'tɜːnɪtɪ] *n* paternidad.

path [pɑːθ] *n* camino, sendero.

pathway ['pɑːθweɪ] *n* camino, sendero.

patience ['peɪʃəns] *n* paciencia.

patient ['peɪʃənt] *adj* paciente. ► *n* paciente.

patio ['pætɪəʊ] *n* patio.

patrimony ['pætrɪmənɪ] *n* patrimonio.

patriot ['peɪtrɪət] *n* patriota.

patrol [pə'trəʊl] *n* patrulla. ► *vi-vt* patrullar. ■ **patrol car** coche patrulla.

patron ['peɪtrən] *adj*. ■ **patron saint** patrón,-ona.

pattern ['pætən] *n* **1** modelo. **2** patrón *(en costura)*. **3** dibujo, diseño *(en tela)*.

pause [pɔːz] *n* pausa.

pavement ['peɪvmənt] *n* acera.

pavillion [pə'vɪlɪən] *n* pabellón.

paw [pɔː] *n* **1** pata *(de animal)*. **2** garra, zarpa *(de tigre)*.

pawn[1] [pɔːn] *n* peón.

pawn[2] [pɔːn] vt empeñar.

pay [peɪ] n paga, sueldo. ► vt-ví pagar. ▪ **pay phone** teléfono público.

to pay back vt devolver.

payment ['peɪmənt] n pago.

payroll ['peɪrəʊl] n nómina.

payslip ['peɪslɪp] n nómina.

pea [piː] n guisante.

peace [piːs] n paz.

peach [piːtʃ] n melocotón.

peacock ['piːkɒk] n pavo real.

peak [piːk] n 1 cima, pico (de montaña). 2 visera (de gorra). ► adj máximo,-a. ▪ **peak hour** hora punta; **peak period** período de tarifa máxima; **peak season** temporada alta.

peanut ['piːnʌt] n cacahuete.

pear [peəʳ] n pera.

pearl [pɜːl] n perla.

peasant ['pezənt] n campesino,-a.

pebble ['pebəl] n guijarro.

peck [pek] vt picotear.

pedagogy ['pedəgɒdʒɪ] n pedagogía.

pedal ['pedəl] n pedal. ► vi pedalear.

peddler ['pedləʳ] n vendedor, -ra ambulante.

pedestrian [pɪ'destrɪən] n peatón. ▪ **pedestrian crossing** paso de peatones; **pedestrian precinct** zona peatonal.

pediatrician [piːdɪə'trɪʃən] n pediatra.

peel [piːl] n piel. ► vt pelar.

peep [piːp] n ojeada, vistazo. **peep-hole** ['piːphəʊl] n mirilla.

peg [peg] n 1 pinza (de colgar ropa). 2 percha, colgador.

pelican ['pelɪkən] n pelícano.

pellet ['pelɪt] n perdigón.

pelvis ['pelvɪs] n (pl **pelvises**) pelvis.

pen[1] [pen] n 1 bolígrafo. 2 pluma.

pen[2] [pen] n corral.

penalty ['penəltɪ] n 1 pena. 2 penalti. ▪ **penalty area** área de castigo. **pence** [pens] npl → penny.

pencil ['pensəl] n lápiz. ▪ **pencil case** plumier, estuche; **pencil sharpener** sacapuntas.

penetrate ['penɪtreɪt] vt penetrar.

penguin ['peŋgwɪn] n pingüino. **peninsula** [pə'nɪnsjʊlə] n península.

penis ['piːnɪs] n pene.

penknife ['pennaɪf] n 1 cortaplumas. 2 navaja.

penny ['penɪ] n 1 GB penique. 2 US centavo.

pension ['penʃən] n pensión.

pensioner ['penʃənəʳ] n jubilado,-a, pensionista.

penthouse ['penthaʊs] n ático.

people ['piːpəl] npl gente, personas.

pepper ['pepəʳ] n 1 pimienta. 2 pimiento.

peppermint ['pepəmɪnt] *n* menta.

per [pɜː'] *prep* por.

percentage [pə'sentɪdʒ] *n* porcentaje.

perception [pə'sepʃən] *n* percepción.

perch [pɜːtʃ] *n* perca.

percolator ['pɜːkəleɪtə'] *n* cafetera de filtro.

perfect ['pɜːfɪkt] *adj* perfecto,-a.

perfection [pə'fekʃən] *n* perfección.

perform [pə'fɔːm] *vt* 1 hacer. 2 interpretar *(música)*. 3 representar *(obra de teatro)*. ► *vi* actuar *(actor)*.

performance [pə'fɔːməns] *n* 1 ejecución. 2 interpretación, actuación *(de cantante, actor)*. 3 representación *(de obra)*. 4 rendimiento *(de alumno)*.

performer [pə'fɔːmə'] *n* intérprete.

perfume ['pɜːfjuːm] *n* perfume.

perhaps [pə'hæps] *adv* quizá, quizás, tal vez.

period ['pɪərɪəd] *n* 1 período. 2 clase. 3 US punto final.

peripheral [pə'rɪfərəl] *n* COMPUT unidad periférica.

perishable ['perɪʃəbəl] *adj* perecedero,-a.

permanent ['pɜːmənənt] *adj* permanente.

permission [pə'mɪʃən] *n* permiso.

permit ['pɜːmɪt] *vt* permitir.

perpendicular [pɜːpən'dɪkjulə'] *adj-n* per-pendicular.

persecution [pɜːsɪ'kjuːʃən] *n* persecución.

persist [pə'sɪst] *vi* persistir.

person ['pɜːsən] *n* persona.

personal ['pɜːsənəl] *adj* personal. ■ **personal computer** ordenador personal; **personal organizer** agenda personal.

personnel [pɜːsə'nel] *n* personal.

perspective [pə'spektɪv] *n* perspectiva.

perspiration [pɜːspɪ'reɪʃən] *n* transpiración, sudor.

persuade [pə'sweɪd] *vt* persuadir, convencer.

perversion [pə'vɜːʃən] *n* 1 perversión. 2 tergiversación.

pervert [pə'vɜːt] *vt* 1 pervertir. 2 tergiversar *(verdad, etc)*.

pessimism ['pesɪmɪzəm] *n* pesimismo.

pessimist ['pesɪmɪst] *n* pesimista.

pest [pest] *n* 1 insecto nocivo, plaga. 2 *fam* pelma.

pester ['pestə'] *vt* molestar.

pet [pet] *n* animal doméstico.

petal ['petəl] *n* pétalo.

petition [pə'tɪʃən] *n* petición

petrol ['petrəl] *n* gasolina. ■ **petrol pump** surtidor de gasolina; **petrol station** gasolinera; **petrol tank** depósito de gasolina.

petticoat ['petɪkəʊt] *n* **1** enaguas. **2** combinación.

petty ['petɪ] *adj* **1** insignificante. **2** mezquino,-a. ▪ **petty cash** dinero para gastos menores.

phantom ['fæntəm] *n* fantasma.

pharmacy ['fɑːməsɪ] *n* farmacia.

phase [feɪz] *n* fase.

pheasant ['fezənt] *n* faisán.

phenomenon [fɪ'nɒmɪnən] *n* fenómeno.

philosopher [fɪ'lɒsəfə'] *n* filósofo,-a.

philosophy [fɪ'lɒsəfɪ] *n* filosofía.

phobia ['fəʊbɪə] *n* fobia.

phone [fəʊn] *n-vt-vi fam* → telephone. ▪ **phone book** listín telefónico; **phone box** cabina telefónica.

phonecard ['fəʊnkɑːd] *n* tarjeta telefónica.

phonetics [fə'netɪks] *n* fonética.

photo ['fəʊtəʊ] *n fam* foto.

photocopier ['fəʊtəʊkɒpɪə'] *n* fotocopiadora.

photocopy ['fəʊtəʊkɒpɪ] *n* fotocopia. ▶ *vt* fotocopiar.

photograph ['fəʊtəgrɑːf] *n* fotografía. ▶ *vt-vi* fotografiar.

photographer [fə'tɒgrəfə'] *n* fotógrafo,-a.

photography [fə'tɒgrəfɪ] *n* fotografía.

phrasal verb [freɪzəl'vɜːb] *n* verbo con partícula.

phrase [freɪz] *n* frase.

physical ['fɪzɪkəl] *adj* físico,-a. ▪ **physical education** educación física.

physician [fɪ'zɪʃən] *n* médico,-a.

physicist ['fɪzɪsɪst] *n* físico,-a.

physics ['fɪzɪks] *n* física.

physiology [fɪzɪ'blədʒɪ] *n* fisiología.

physiotherapy [fɪzɪəʊ'θerəpɪ] *n* fisioterapia.

pianist ['pɪənɪst] *n* pianista.

piano [pɪ'ænəʊ] *n* piano.

pick [pɪk] *vt* **1** escoger, elegir. **2** coger *(flores, fruta)*. **3** forzar *(cerradura)*.

to pick on *vt* meterse con.

to pick out *vt* **1** escoger. **2** distinguir.

to pick up *vt* **1** coger, recoger. **2** ir a buscar. **3** captar *(emisora de radio)*. **4** aprender *(lengua)*.

picket ['pɪkɪt] *n* piquete.

pickle ['pɪkəl] *n* **1** encurtido, escabeche. **2** aprieto. ▶ *vt* encurtir, escabechar.

pickpocket ['pɪkpɒkɪt] *n* carterista.

pick-up ['pɪkʌp] *n* **1** brazo del tocadiscos. **2** furgoneta.

picnic ['pɪknɪk] *n* merienda, picnic. ▶ *vi* ir de picnic.

picture ['pɪktʃə'] *n* **1** pintura, cuadro. **2** dibujo. **3** fotogra-

fía. **4** película. **5** imagen. ▶ *vt*
1 pintar, retratar. **2** imaginar,
imaginarse. • **to take a picture** hacer una foto.

picturesque [pɪktʃə'resk] *adj*
pintoresco,-a.

pie [paɪ] *n* **1** pastel, tarta
(dulce). **2** pastel, empanada
(salado).

piece [piːs] *n* **1** trozo, pedazo. **2** pieza. **3** moneda. • **to take to pieces** desmontar;
in one piece 1 sano y salvo
(persona). **2** intacto,-a *(objeto)*.

pier [pɪəʳ] *n* muelle.

pierce [pɪəs] *vt* perforar.

pig [pɪg] *n* cerdo,-a.

pigeon ['pɪdʒɪn] *n* paloma.

pigeonhole ['pɪdʒɪnhəʊl] *n*
casilla.

piglet ['pɪglət] *n* cochinillo.

pigment ['pɪgmənt] *n* pigmento.

pigsty ['pɪgstaɪ] *n* pocilga.

pigtail ['pɪgteɪl] *n* trenza.

pile [paɪl] *n* montón, pila.

pile-up ['paɪlʌp] *n* choque en
cadena.

piles ['paɪlz] *npl* hemorroides.

pilgrim ['pɪlgrɪm] *n* peregrino,-a.

pill [pɪl] *n* píldora, pastilla.

pillar ['pɪləʳ] *n* pilar, columna.

pillow ['pɪləʊ] *n* almohada.

pilot ['paɪlət] *adj-n* piloto. ▶ *vt*
pilotar.

pimple ['pɪmpəl] *n* grano.

pin [pɪn] *n* **1** alfiler. **2** clavija.

pinafore ['pɪnəfɔːʳ] *n* delantal.

pincers ['pɪnsəz] *npl* **1** tenazas.
2 pinzas *(de cangrejo)*.

pinch [pɪntʃ] *n* **1** pellizco. **2**
pizca. ▶ *vt* **1** pellizcar. **2** apretar *(zapatos)*.

pine [paɪn] *n* pino. ■ **pine
cone** piña; **pine nut** piñón.

pineapple ['paɪnæpəl] *n* piña.

ping-pong ['pɪŋpɒŋ] *n* tenis
de mesa, pimpón.

pink [pɪŋk] *adj-n* rosa. ▶ *n*
clavel.

pint [paɪnt] *n* pinta.

pioneer [paɪə'nɪəʳ] *n* pionero,-a.

pipe [paɪp] *n* **1** tubería, cañería
(de agua, gas). **2** pipa *(para fumar)*. ▶ *npl* **pipes** gaita.

pipeline ['paɪplaɪn] *n* **1** tubería. **2** gasoducto. **3** oleoducto.

pirate ['paɪərət] *n* pirata.

pistol ['pɪstəl] *n* pistola.

piston ['pɪstən] *n* pistón.

pit[1] [pɪt] *n* **1** hoyo, foso. **2** mina.

pit[2] [pɪt] *n* US hueso *(de fruta)*.

pitch [pɪtʃ] *n* **1** MUS tono. **2**
campo, terreno *(de juego)*. ▶
vt **1** tirar, lanzar. **2** plantar,
armar *(tienda de campaña)*.

pitcher[1] ['pɪtʃəʳ] *n* **1** GB cántaro. **2** US jarro.

pitcher[2] ['pɪtʃəʳ] *n* US lanzador,-ra *(de béisbol)*.

pitchfork ['pɪtʃfɔːk] *n* horca.

pity ['pɪti] *n* pena, lástima.

pivot ['pɪvət] *n* pivote, eje.

pizza ['piːtsə] *n* pizza.

placard ['plækɑːd] n pancarta.
placate [plə'keɪt] vt aplacar.
place [pleɪs] n **1** lugar, sitio. **2** asiento, sitio. **3** plaza (en escuela, etc). ▶ vt colocar, poner, situar. ● **in place of** en vez de.
placenta [plə'sentə] n placenta.
plague [pleɪg] n plaga.
plain [pleɪn] adj **1** claro,-a. **2** sencillo,-a. **3** liso,-a (tejido). **4** sin leche (chocolate). ▶ n llanura. ● **to make STH plain** dejar algo bien claro. ■ **plain yoghurt** yogur natural.
plaintiff ['pleɪntɪf] n demandante.
plait [plæt] n trenza.
plan [plæn] n **1** plan. **2** plano. ▶ vt planear, planificar.
plane¹ [pleɪn] n **1** plano. **2** avión.
plane² [pleɪn] n cepillo.
plane³ [pleɪn] n plátano (árbol).
planet ['plænət] n planeta.
plank [plæŋk] n tablón, tabla.
plant [plɑːnt] n planta. ▶ vt plantar. ■ **plant pot** maceta, tiesto.
plaque [plæk] n placa.
plasma ['plæzmə] n plasma.
plaster ['plɑːstə'] n **1** yeso. **2** MED escayola. **3** esparadrapo, tirita®. ▶ vt enyesar. ■ **plaster cast** escayola.
plastic ['plæstɪk] adj plástico,-a. ▶ n plástico.
plasticine® ['plæstɪsiːn] n plastilina®.

plate [pleɪt] n **1** plato. **2** placa.
plateau ['plætəʊ] n meseta.
platform ['plætfɔːm] n **1** plataforma. **2** andén.
platoon [plə'tuːn] n pelotón.
play [pleɪ] n **1** juego. **2** obra de teatro. ▶ vt-vi **1** jugar. **2** tocar: he plays the piano, toca el piano. ▶ vt **1** interpretar. **2** jugar a: she plays tennis, juega al tenis. **3** jugar contra (equipo, adversario). **4** poner (disco). ■ **play on words** juego de palabras.
player ['pleɪə'] n **1** jugador,-ra. **2** actor, actriz. **3** músico,-a: a piano player, un pianista.
playground ['pleɪgraʊnd] n patio de recreo.
playing field ['pleɪɪŋfiːld] n campo de juego.
playmate ['pleɪmeɪt] n compañero,-a de juego.
play-off ['pleɪɒf] n partido de desempate.
playtime ['pleɪtaɪm] n recreo.
plea [pliː] n petición, súplica.
plead [pliːd] vi suplicar. ▶ vt alegar. ● **to plead guilty** declararse culpable; **to plead not guilty** declararse inocente.
pleasant ['plezənt] adj **1** agradable (tiempo). **2** simpático,-a, amable (persona).
please [pliːz] vt-vi agradar, gustar. ▶ interj por favor. ● **as you please** como quieras.

pleased [pli:zd] *adj* contento, -a, satisfecho,-a. ● **pleased to meet you!** ¡encantado,-a!, ¡mucho gusto!; **to be pleased to do** STH alegrarse de hacer algo.

pleasure ['pleʒəʳ] *n* placer. ● **it's my pleasure** de nada, no hay de qué.

pleat [pli:t] *n* pliegue.

pledge [pledʒ] *n* **1** promesa. **2** prenda, señal.

plenty ['plentɪ] *n* abundancia. ► *pron* **1** muchos,-as. **2** de sobra.

pliers ['plaɪəz] *npl* alicates.

plot [plɒt] *n* **1** complot. **2** trama, argumento.

plot² [plɒt] *n* parcela, terreno.

plough [plaʊ] *n* arado. ► *vt-vi* arar.

plow [plaʊ] *n-vt-vi* US → plough.

pluck [plʌk] *vt* **1** arrancar *(flor)*. **2** desplumar *(ave)*. ● **to pluck one's eyebrows** depilarse las cejas.

plug [plʌg] *n* **1** tapón. **2** enchufe, clavija *(macho)*, toma *(hembra)*. **3** bujía.

to plug in *vt-vi* enchufar(se).

plughole ['plʌghəʊl] *n* desagüe.

plum [plʌm] *n* ciruela.

plumber ['plʌməʳ] *n* fontanero,-a.

plural ['plʊərəl] *adj-n* plural.

plus [plʌs] *prep* más. ► *conj* además de que. ► *n* ventaja.

plywood ['plaɪwʊd] *n* contrachapado.

pneumonia [njuː'məʊnɪə] *n* neumonía, pulmonía.

poach [pəʊtʃ] *vt* **1** hervir. **2** escalfar *(huevos)*.

pocket ['pɒkɪt] *n* bolsillo. ■ **pocket money** dinero de bolsillo.

pod [pɒd] *n* vaina.

poem ['pəʊəm] *n* poema.

poet ['pəʊət] *n* poeta.

poetry ['pəʊətrɪ] *n* poesía.

point [pɔɪnt] *n* **1** punta. **2** punto. **3** coma: *5 point 66*, cinco coma sesenta y seis. **4** sentido. ► *vi* indicar, señalar. ► *vt* apuntar. ● **on the point of** a punto de; **there's no point in...** no vale la pena...

point-blank [pɔɪnt'blæŋk] *adj* a quemarropa.

poison ['pɔɪzən] *n* veneno. ► *vt* envenenar.

poker ['pəʊkəʳ] *n* póquer.

polar ['pəʊləʳ] *adj* polar. ■ **polar bear** oso polar.

pole¹ [pəʊl] *n* **1** palo, poste. **2** pértiga. ■ **pole vault** salto con pértiga.

pole² [pəʊl] *n* polo.

polemic [pə'lemɪk] *adj* polémico,-a. ► *n* polémica.

police [pə'li:s] *npl* policía. ■ **police station** comisaría de policía.

policeman [pə'li:smən] *n* policía, guardia.

policewoman [pə'liːswʊmən] n mujer policía.

policy ['pɒlɪsɪ] n 1 política. 2 póliza (de seguros).

polish ['pɒlɪʃ] n 1 cera (para muebles). 2 betún (para zapatos). 3 esmalte (para uñas). ► vt 1 sacar brillo a. 2 pulir.

polite [pə'laɪt] adj cortés, educado,-a.

politician [pɒlɪ'tɪʃən] n político,-a.

politics ['pɒlɪtɪks] n política.

poll [pəʊl] n 1 votación. 2 encuesta, sondeo.

pollen ['pɒlən] n polen.

pollution [pə'luːʃən] n contaminación.

polo ['pəʊləʊ] n polo. ■ **polo neck** cuello alto.

pomegranate ['pɒmɪɡrænət] n granada (fruta).

pomp [pɒmp] n pompa.

pond [pɒnd] n estanque.

pony ['pəʊnɪ] n poni.

ponytail ['pəʊnɪteɪl] n cola de caballo.

pool¹ [puːl] n 1 charco. 2 estanque. 3 piscina.

pool² [puːl] n 1 fondo común. 2 billar americano. ► npl **the pools** las quinielas.

poor [pʊəʳ] adj pobre.

popcorn ['pɒpkɔːn] n palomitas (de maíz).

pope [pəʊp] n papa.

poplar ['pɒpləʳ] n álamo.

poppy ['pɒpɪ] n amapola.

popular ['pɒpjʊləʳ] adj popular.

populate ['pɒpjʊleɪt] vt poblar.

population [pɒpjʊ'leɪʃən] n población.

porcelain ['pɔːsəlɪn] n porcelana.

porch [pɔːtʃ] n pórtico.

porcupine ['pɔːkjʊpaɪn] n puerco espín.

pore [pɔːʳ] n poro.

pork [pɔːk] n carne de cerdo. ■ **pork chop** chuleta de cerdo.

porridge ['pɒrɪdʒ] n gachas de avena.

port¹ [pɔːt] n puerto (de mar).

port² [pɔːt] n babor.

port³ [pɔːt] n oporto (vino).

portable ['pɔːtəbəl] adj portátil.

portal ['pɔːtəl] n COMPUT portal.

porter ['pɔːtəʳ] n 1 portero,-a. 2 mozo.

portfolio [pɔːt'fəʊlɪəʊ] n 1 carpeta. 2 POL cartera.

portion ['pɔːʃən] n porción, ración.

portrait ['pɔːtreɪt] n retrato.

pose [pəʊz] n pose. ► vt plantear (problema). 2 representar (amenaza). ► vi posar (como modelo).

position [pə'zɪʃən] n 1 sitio, posición. 2 postura, actitud. 3 puesto, empleo. ► vt colocar.

positive ['pɒzɪtɪv] adj 1 positivo,-a. 2 seguro,-a.

possess [pə'zes] *vt* poseer, tener. apoderarse de.

possibility [pɒsɪ'bɪlɪtɪ] *n* posibilidad.

possible ['pɒsɪbəl] *adj* posible.

post¹ [pəʊst] *n* poste.

post² [pəʊst] *n* puesto. ► *vt* destinar.

post³ [pəʊst] *n* correo. ► *vt* **1** echar al correo *(carta)*. **2** poner *(anuncio)*. ■ **post office** oficina de correos; **post office box** apartado de correos.

postage ['pəʊstɪdʒ] *n* franqueo, porte.

postal ['pəʊstəl] *adj* postal.

postbox ['pəʊstbɒks] *n* buzón.

postcard ['pəʊstkɑːd] *n* tarjeta postal, postal.

postcode ['pəʊstkəʊd] *n* código postal.

poster ['pəʊstə'] *n* póster.

posterior [pɒ'stɪərɪə'] *adj* posterior.

postman ['pəʊstmən] *n* cartero.

postmark ['pəʊstmɑːk] *n* matasellos.

postpone [pəs'pəʊn] *vt* posponer.

postscript ['pəʊstskrɪpt] *n* posdata.

posture ['pɒstʃə'] *n* postura.

postwoman ['pəʊstwʊmən] *n* cartera.

pot [pɒt] *n* **1** pote, tarro. **2** bote *(de pintura)*. **3** tetera. **4** cafetera. **5** olla. **6** maceta.

potato [pə'teɪtəʊ] *n* patata.

potent ['pəʊtənt] *adj* potente.

pothole ['pɒthəʊl] *n* **1** cueva. **2** bache *(de carretera)*.

pottery ['pɒtərɪ] *n* **1** alfarería. **2** cerámica.

potty ['pɒtɪ] *n* orinal *(de niño)*.

poultry ['pəʊltrɪ] *n* aves de corral.

pound¹ [paʊnd] *n* libra.

pound² [paʊnd] *n* **1** perrera. **2** depósito municipal *(de coches)*.

pour [pɔː'] *vt* verter, echar. ► *vi* llover a cántaros.

poverty ['pɒvətɪ] *n* pobreza.

powder ['paʊdə'] *n* polvo.

power ['paʊə'] *n* **1** fuerza. **2** poder, capacidad. **3** corriente *(eléctrica)*. **4** energía. **5** potencia. ■ **power cut** apagón; **power station** central eléctrica.

powerful ['paʊəfʊl] *adj* poderoso,-a.

practical ['præktɪkəl] *adj* práctico,-a.

practice ['præktɪs] *n* **1** práctica. **2** consulta *(de médico)*. **3** bufete *(de abogados)*. ► *vt-vi* US → practise.

practise ['præktɪs] *vt-vi* **1** practicar. **2** ejercer *(profesión)*. ► *vi* entrenar *(deportes)*.

practitioner [præk'tɪʃənə'] *n* médico,-a.

prairie ['preərɪ] *n* pradera.

praise [preɪz] *n* alabanza, elogio. ► *vt* alabar.

pram [præm] *n* GB cochecito de niño.

prank [præŋk] *n* travesura, broma.

prawn [prɔːn] *n* gamba.

pray [preɪ] *vi* orar, rezar.

prayer [preəʳ] *n* oración, plegaria. ∎ **prayer book** misal.

preach [priːtʃ] *vt-vi* predicar.

precaution [prɪˈkɔːʃən] *n* precaución.

precede [prɪˈsiːd] *vt-vi* preceder.

precious [ˈpreʃəs] *adj* precioso,-a. ∎ **precious stone** piedra preciosa.

precipice [ˈpresɪpɪs] *n* precipicio.

precise [prɪˈsaɪs] *adj* preciso,-a.

precision [prɪˈsɪʒən] *n* precisión.

precocious [prɪˈkəʊʃəs] *adj* precoz.

precooked [priːˈkʊkt] *vt* precocinado,-a.

predator [ˈpredətəʳ] *n* depredador.

predicament [prɪˈdɪkəmənt] *n* apuro, aprieto.

predict [prɪˈdɪkt] *vt* predecir.

predictable [prɪˈdɪktəbəl] *adj* previsible.

prediction [prɪˈdɪkʃən] *n* predicción.

predominate [prɪˈdɒmɪneɪt] *vi* predominar.

pre-empt [priːˈempt] *vt* adelantarse a.

prefabricated [priːˈfæbrɪkeɪtɪd] *adj* prefabricado,-a.

preface [ˈprefəs] *n* prefacio.

prefer [prɪˈfɜːʳ] *vt* preferir.

preference [ˈprefərəns] *n* preferencia.

prefix [ˈpriːfɪks] *n* prefijo.

pregnancy [ˈpregnənsɪ] *n* embarazo. ∎ **pregnancy test** prueba del embarazo.

pregnant [ˈpregnənt] *adj-n* embarazada.

prehistoric [priːhɪˈstɒrɪk] *n* prehistórico,-a.

prejudice [ˈpredʒədɪs] *n* prejuicio.

prejudicial [predʒəˈdɪʃəl] *adj* perjudicial.

prelude [ˈpreljuːd] *n* preludio.

premature [preməˈtjʊəʳ] *adj* prematuro,-a.

premier [ˈpremɪəʳ] *adj* primero,-a. ▶ *n* primer,-ra ministro,-a.

première [ˈpremɪeəʳ] *n* estreno.

premise [ˈpremɪs] *n* premisa. ▶ *npl* **premises** local.

premium [ˈpriːmɪəm] *n* prima.

preoccupy [priːˈɒkjʊpaɪ] *vt* preocupar.

prepaid [priːˈpeɪd] *adj* pagado,-a por adelantado.

preparation [prepəˈreɪʃən] *n* **1** preparación. **2** preparado. ▶ *npl* **preparations** preparativos.

prepare [prɪˈpeəʳ] *vt-vi* preparar(se).

preposition [prepə'zıʃən] *n* preposición.

prerogative [prı'rɒgətıv] *n* prerrogativa.

preschool [priːˈskuːl] *adj* preescolar.

prescribe [prısˈkraıb] *vt* **1** prescribir. **2** recetar.

prescription [prısˈkrıpʃən] *n* receta médica. • **on prescription** con receta médica.

presence ['prezəns] *n* presencia.

present¹ ['prezənt] *adj* **1** presente. **2** actual. ► *n* presente). • **at present** actualmente; **for the present** por ahora.

present² ['prezənt] *n* regalo. ► *vt* presentar.

presenter [prı'zentə'] *n* **1** locutor,-ra. **2** presentador,-ra.

presently ['prezəntlı] *adv* **1** GB pronto, dentro de poco. **2** US ahora.

preservation [prezə'veıʃən] *n* conservación, preservación.

preservative [prı'zɜːvətıv] *n* conservante.

preserve [prı'zɜːv] *n* **1** conserva *(de fruta, verdura)*. **2** confitura. **3** coto, vedado.

preside [prı'zaıd] *vi* presidir.

president ['prezıdənt] *n* presidente,-a.

press [pres] *n* **1** prensa. **2** imprenta. ► *vt* **1** pulsar, apretar *(botón)*. **2** prensar *(uvas, olivas)*. **3** planchar *(ropa)*. **4** pre-

sionar *(persona)*. ► *vi* apretar. ▪ **press briefing** rueda de prensa; **press release** comunicado de prensa.

pressing ['presıŋ] *adj* urgente.

press-up ['presʌp] *n* flexión.

pressure ['preʃə'] *n* presión.

prestige [pres'tiːʒ] *n* prestigio.

presume [prı'zjuːm] *vt-vi* suponer.

pretend [prı'tend] *vt-vi* **1** aparentar, fingir. **2** pretender. ► *vi* pretender.

pretentious [prı'tenʃəs] *adj* pretencioso,-a.

pretext ['priːtekst] *n* pretexto.

pretty ['prıtı] *adj* bonito,-a, mono,-a. ► *adv* bastante. • **pretty much** más o menos.

prevail [prı'veıl] *vi* **1** predominar, imperar. **2** prevalecer.

prevent [prı'vent] *vt* impedir, evitar.

preview ['priːvjuː] *n* preestreno.

previous ['priːvıəs] *adj* previo,-a.

prey [preı] *n* presa.

price [praıs] *n* precio.

prick [prık] *n* pinchazo. ► *vt* pinchar.

prickle ['prıkəl] *n* pincho, espina.

pride [praıd] *n* orgullo.

priest [priːst] *n* sacerdote.

primary ['praımərı] *adj* **1** principal. **2** primario,-a.

prime [praɪm] *adj* **1** primero,-a. **2** selecto,-a, de primera. ■ **Prime Minister** primer,-a ministro,-a; **prime time** franja de mayor audiencia.

primitive ['prɪmɪtɪv] *adj* primitivo,-a.

prince [prɪns] *n* príncipe.

princess ['prɪnses] *n* princesa.

principal ['prɪnsɪpəl] *adj* principal. ► *n* director,-ra *(de colegio)*; rector,-ra *(de universidad)*.

principle ['prɪnsɪpəl] *n* principio.

print [prɪnt] *n* **1** huella. **2** copia *(fotografía)*. **3** estampado *(de tela)*. ► *vt* **1** imprimir. **2** sacar una copia de *(fotografía)*. **3** estampar *(tela)*. ● **in print** en catálogo; **out of print** descatalogado,-a.

printer ['prɪntəʳ] *n* impresora.

print-out ['prɪntaʊt] *n* copia impresa.

prior ['praɪəʳ] *adj* anterior, previo,-a. .

priority [praɪˈɒrɪtɪ] *n* prioridad.

prison ['prɪzən] *n* prisión.

prisoner ['prɪzənəʳ] *n* **1** preso,-a. **2** prisionero,-a.

privacy ['praɪvəsɪ] *n* intimidad.

private ['praɪvət] *adj* privado,-a. ► *n* soldado raso. ■ **private eye** detective privado.

privilege ['prɪvɪlɪdʒ] *n* privilegio.

prize[1] [praɪz] *n* premio.

probability [prɒbəˈbɪlɪtɪ] *n* probabilidad.

probation [prəˈbeɪʃən] *n* libertad condicional.

probe [prəʊb] *n* sonda.

problem ['prɒbləm] *n* problema.

procedure [prəˈsiːdʒəʳ] *n* procedimiento.

proceed [prəˈsiːd] *vi* **1** continuar, proseguir. **2** proceder.

process ['prəʊses] *n* proceso. ► *vt* **1** procesar. **2** revelar.

proclaim [prəˈkleɪm] *vt* proclamar.

prodigious [prəˈdɪdʒəs] *adj* prodigioso,-a.

produce [*(vb)* prəˈdjuːs, *(n)* 'prɒdjuːs] *vt* producir. ► *n* productos *(agrícolas)*.

product ['prɒdʌkt] *n* producto.

production [prəˈdʌkʃən] *n* producción. ■ **production line** cadena de producción.

profession [prəˈfeʃən] *n* profesión.

professional [prəˈfeʃənəl] *adj-n* profesional.

professor [prəˈfesəʳ] *n* GB catedrático,-a de universidad.

proficiency [prəˈfɪʃənsɪ] *n* competencia.

profile ['prəʊfaɪl] *n* perfil.

profit ['prɒfɪt] *n* ganancia, beneficio.

program ['prəʊgræm] *n* US programa. ► *vt* US programar.

programme ['prəʊgræm] *n* GB programa. ► *vt* GB programar.

progress [*(n)* 'prəʊgres, *(vb)* prəʊ'gres] *n* progreso. ► *vi* progresar. • **in progress** en curso.

prohibit [prə'hɪbɪt] *vt* prohibir.

prohibition [prəʊɪ'bɪʃən] *n* prohibición.

project [*(n)* 'prɒdʒekt, *(vb)* prə'dʒekt] *n* proyecto. ► *vt* proyectar.

projectile [prə'dʒektaɪl] *n* proyectil.

projector [prə'dʒektə^r] *n* proyector.

prologue ['prəʊlɒg] (US **prolog**) *n* prólogo.

promenade [prɒmə'nɑːd] *n* paseo marítimo.

prominent ['prɒmɪnənt] *adj* prominente.

promise ['prɒmɪs] *n* promesa. ► *vt-vi* prometer.

promote [prə'məʊt] *vt* **1** promover. **2** promocionar.

promotion [prə'məʊʃən] *n* promoción.

prompt [prɒmpt] *adj* **1** inmediato, -a, rápido,-a *(servicio, acción)*. **2** puntual *(persona)*. ► *adv* en punto. ► *vt* **1** inducir, impulsar, incitar. **2** apuntar *(en teatro)*.

prompter ['prɒmptə^r] *n* apuntador,-ra.

prone [prəʊn] *adj* boca abajo. • **prone to** propenso,-a a.

prong [prɒŋ] *n* diente, punta.

pronoun ['prəʊnaʊn] *n* pronombre.

pronounce [prə'naʊns] *vt* pronunciar.

pronunciation [prənʌnsɪ'eɪʃən] *n* pronunciación.

proof [pruːf] *n* **1** prueba. **2** graduación *(alcohólica)*.

prop [prɒp] *n* puntal *(objeto)*

propaganda [prɒpə'gændə] *n* propaganda.

propeller [prə'pelə^r] *n* hélice.

proper ['prɒpə^r] *adj* **1** adecuado,-a *(procedimiento)*. **2** correcto,-a *(respuesta, conducta)*. ■ **proper noun** nombre propio.

property ['prɒpətɪ] *n* propiedad.

prophet ['prɒfɪt] *n* profeta.

proportion [prə'pɔːʃən] *n* proporción. • **out of proportion** desproporcionado,-a.

proposal [prə'pəʊzəl] *n* propuesta.

propose [prə'pəʊz] *vt* **1** proponer *(sugerencia)*. **2** pensar, tener la intención de. ► *vi* pedir la mano, declararse.

propriety [prə'praɪətɪ] *n* **1** corrección. **2** conveniencia.

propulsion [prə'pʌlʃən] *n* propulsión.

prose [prəʊz] *n* prosa.

prosecute ['prɒsɪkjuːt] *vt* procesar.

prosecution [prɒsɪ'kjuːʃən] *n* proceso, juicio.

prosecutor ['prɒsɪkjuːtəʳ] *n* fiscal, abogado,-a de la acusación.

prospect ['prɒspekt] *n* **1** perspectiva. **2** probabilidad.

prospectus [prə'spektəs] *n* prospecto.

prosperous ['prɒspərəs] *adj* próspero,-a.

prostate ['prɒsteɪt] *n* próstata.

prostitute ['prɒstɪtjuːt] *n* prostituta.

protect [prə'tekt] *vt* proteger.

protection [prə'tekʃən] *n* protección.

protein ['prəutiːn] *n* proteína.

protest [(n) 'prəutest, (vb) prə'test] *n* protesta. ► *vt-vi* protestar.

protocol ['prəutəkɒl] *n* protocolo.

prototype ['prəutətaɪp] *n* prototipo.

protrude [prə'truːd] *vi* sobresalir.

proud [praud] *adj* orgulloso,-a.

prove [pruːv] *vt* probar, demostrar. ► *vi* resultar. • **to prove** SB **right** demostrar que ALGN tiene razón; **to prove** SB **wrong** demostrar que ALGN está equivocado,-a.

proverb ['prɒvɜːb] *n* proverbio.

provide [prə'vaɪd] *vt* proporcionar, suministrar.

provided [prə'vaɪdɪd] *conj.* **provided (that)** siempre que.

province ['prɒvɪns] *n* provincia.

provision [prə'vɪʒən] *n* **1** suministro, provisión. **2** disposición.

provisional [prə'vɪʒənəl] *adj* provisional.

provoke [prə'vəuk] *vt* provocar.

prow [prau] *n* proa.

proxy ['prɒksɪ] *n* representante, apoderado,-a. • **by proxy** por poderes.

prudent ['pruːdənt] *adj* prudente.

prudish ['pruːdɪʃ] *adj* remilgado,-a.

prune¹ [pruːn] *n* ciruela pasa.

prune² [pruːn] *vt* podar.

psychiatry [saɪ'kaɪətrɪ] *n* psiquiatría.

psychology [saɪ'kɒledʒɪ] *n* psicología.

pub [pʌb] *n* bar, pub.

puberty ['pjuːbətɪ] *n* pubertad.

public ['pʌblɪk] *adj* público,-a. ► *n* público. ■ **public holiday** fiesta nacional; **public school** colegio privado *(en GB)*, colegio público *(en EEUU)*; **public servant** funcionario,-a.

publicity [pʌ'blɪsɪtɪ] *n* publicidad.

publish ['pʌblɪʃ] *vt* publicar.

publisher ['pʌblɪʃəʳ] *n* **1** editor,-ra. **2** editorial.

pudding ['pudɪŋ] *n* **1** budín, pudín. **2** GB postre.

puddle ['pʌdəl] *n* charco.

pull [pʊl] *n* **1** tirón. **2** atracción. ► *vt* tirar de. ► *vi* tirar.

pulley ['pʊlɪ] *n* polea.

pullover ['pʊləʊvəʳ] *n* jersey.

pulp [pʌlp] *n* pulpa.

pulse [pʌls] *n* **1** pulsación. **2** pulso.

pumice stone ['pʌmɪsstəʊn] *n* piedra pómez.

pump [pʌmp] *n* **1** bomba *(de aire, líquido)*. **2** surtidor *(de gasolina)*. ► *vt* bombear .

pumpkin ['pʌmpkɪn] *n* calabaza.

pun [pʌn] *n* juego de palabras.

punch[1] [pʌntʃ] *n* puñetazo.

punch[2] [pʌntʃ] *n* ponche.

punch[3] [pʌntʃ] *vt* **1** perforar. **2** picar *(billete)*.

punctual ['pʌŋktjʊəl] *adj* puntual.

punctuation [pʌŋktjʊ'eɪʃən] *n* puntuación. ▪ **punctuation mark** signo de puntuación.

puncture ['pʌŋktʃəʳ] *n* pinchazo. ► *vt-vi* pinchar(se).

punish ['pʌnɪʃ] *vt* castigar.

punishment ['pʌnɪʃmənt] *n* castigo.

pup [pʌp] *n* cría, cachorro,-a.

pupil[1] ['pjuːpɪl] *n* alumno,-a.

pupil[2] ['pjuːpɪl] *n* pupila.

puppet ['pʌpɪt] *n* títere.

puppy ['pʌpɪ] *n* cachorro,-a.

purchase ['pɜːtʃəs] *n* compra. ► *vt* comprar.

pure ['pjʊəʳ] *adj* puro,-a.

purée ['pjʊəreɪ] *n* puré.

purity ['pjʊərɪtɪ] *n* pureza.

purple ['pɜːpəl] *adj* púrpura.

purpose ['pɜːpəs] *n* propósito. ● **on purpose** a propósito.

purr [pɜːʳ] *n* ronroneo.

purse [pɜːs] *n* **1** GB monedero. **2** US bolso.

pursue [pə'sjuː] *vt* **1** perseguir. **2** proseguir.

pursuit [pə'sjuːt] *n* persecución.

purveyor [pɜː'veɪəʳ] *n* proveedor,-ra.

pus [pʌs] *n* pus.

push [pʊʃ] *n* empujón. ► *vt-vi* empujar. ► *vt* pulsar, apretar *(botón)*.

pushchair ['pʊʃtʃeəʳ] *n* cochecito de niño.

put [pʊt] *vt* poner, colocar.

to put aside *vt* **1** ahorrar, guardar *(dinero)*. **2** dejar a un lado *(trabajo)*.

to put away *vt* guardar.

to put forward *vt* **1** proponer *(plan)*. **2** adelantar *(reloj)*.

to put off *vt* aplazar.

to put on *vt* **1** encender *(luz, radio)*. **2** ponerse *(ropa)*. **3** ganar *(peso, velocidad)*.

to put out *vt* apagar

to put up *vt* **1** levantar *(mano)*. **2** armar *(tienda de campaña)*. **4** construir.

puzzle ['pʌzəl] *n* rompecabezas.

pyjamas [pə'dʒɑːməz] *npl* pijama.

pylon ['paɪlən] *n* torre *(de tendido eléctrico)*.

pyramid ['pɪrəmɪd] *n* pirámide.

Q

quail [kweɪl] *n* codorniz.

quaint [kweɪnt] *adj* pintoresco,-a.

quake [kweɪk] *n fam* terremoto.

qualification [kwɒlɪfɪ'keɪʃən] *n* 1 requisito *(para empleo)*. 2 diploma, título.

qualified ['kwɒlɪfaɪd] *adj* cualificado,-a.

qualify ['kwɒlɪfaɪ] *vt* capacitar. ► *vi* 1 obtener el título. 2 clasificarse.

quality ['kwɒlɪtɪ] *n* 1 calidad. 2 cualidad.

quantity ['kwɒntɪtɪ] *n* cantidad.

quarantine ['kwɒrəntiːn] *n* cuarentena.

quarrel ['kwɒrəl] *n* riña, pelea. ► *vi* reñir, pelear.

quarter ['kwɔːtə'] *n* 1 cuarto, cuarta parte: *a quarter past five*, las cinco y cuarto.

quarterfinal [kwɔːtə'faɪnəl] *n* cuarto de final.

quartz [kwɔːts] *n* cuarzo.

quay [kiː] *n* muelle.

queen [kwiːn] *n* reina.

quench [kwentʃ] *vt* 1 saciar *(sed)*. 2 apagar *(fuego)*.

query ['kwɪərɪ] *n* pregunta.

quest [kwest] *n* búsqueda.

question ['kwestʃən] *n* 1 pregunta. 2 cuestión, problema. ► *vt* 1 hacer preguntas a, interrogar. 2 cuestionar. ■ **question mark** interrogante.

questionnaire [kwestʃə'neə'] *n* cuestionario.

queue [kjuː] *n* cola. ► *vi* hacer cola.

quick [kwɪk] *adj* rápido,-a. ► *adv* rápido, rápidamente.

quiet ['kwaɪət] *adj* 1 callado,-a: *be quiet!*, ¡cállate! 2 tranquilo,-a *(lugar)*.

quilt [kwɪlt] *n* edredón.

quince [kwɪns] *n* membrillo.

quirk [kwɜːk] *n* manía.

quit [kwɪt] *vt* dejar.

quite [kwaɪt] *adv* 1 bastante. 2 completamente.

quiver ['kwɪvə'] *n* temblor.

quiz [kwɪz] *n* concurso *(televisivo, etc)*.

quota ['kwəʊtə] *n* cuota.

quotation [kwəʊ'teɪʃən] *n* 1 cita *(de libro)*. 2 cotización.■ **quotation marks** comillas.

quote [kwəʊt] *n* cita. ► *vt* 1 citar. 2 cotizar.

quotient ['kwəʊʃənt] *n* cociente.

R

rabbit ['ræbɪt] *n* conejo.

rabies ['reɪbiːz] *n* rabia.

raccoon [rə'kuːn] *n* mapache.

race¹ [reɪs] *n* raza.

race² [reɪs] *n* carrera.

racecourse ['reɪskɔːs] *n* GB hipódromo.

racist ['reɪsɪst] *adj-n* racista.

rack [ræk] *n* **1** estante. **2** baca *(de coche)*. **3** rejilla *(en tren)*. **4** escurreplatos.

racket¹ ['rækɪt] *n* raqueta.

racket² ['rækɪt] *n* alboroto.

radar ['reɪdɑːʳ] *n* radar..

radiation [reɪdɪ'eɪʃən] *n* radiación.

radiator ['reɪdɪeɪtəʳ] *n* radiador.

radical ['rædɪkəl] *adj-n* radical.

radio ['reɪdɪəʊ] *n* radio.

radioactive [reɪdɪəʊ'æktɪv] *adj* radiactivo,-a.

radish ['rædɪʃ] *n* rábano.

radius ['reɪdɪəs] *n* radio.

raffle ['ræfəl] *n* rifa. ► *vt-vi* rifar, sortear.

raft [rɑːft] *n* balsa.

rafter ['rɑːftəʳ] *n* viga.

rag [ræg] *n* **1** harapo. **2** trapo.

rage [reɪdʒ] *n* rabia. ► *vi* **1** rabiar. • **to be all the rage** hacer furor.

raid [reɪd] *n* **1** incursiónrazia. **2** redada. **3** atraco, asalto.

rail [reɪl] *n* **1** barra. **2** barandilla. **3** raíl, carril, riel. • **by rail** por ferrocarril.

railings ['reɪlɪŋz] *npl* verja.

railway ['reɪlweɪ] *n* ferrocarril. ▪ **railway line** vía férrea; **railway station** estación de ferrocarril.

rain [reɪn] *n* lluvia. ► *vi* llover. ▪ **rain forest** selva tropical.

rainbow ['reɪnbəʊ] *n* arco iris.

raincoat ['reɪnkəʊt] *n* impermeable.

raindrop ['reɪndrɒp] *n* gota de lluvia.

rainy ['reɪnɪ] *adj* lluvioso,-a.

raise [reɪz] *vt* **1** levantar. **2** subir, aumentar *(precios, temperatura)*. **3** criar, educar *(niños)*. **4** plantear *(asunto, problema)*. **5** recaudar, conseguir *(fondos)*.

raisin ['reɪzən] *n* pasa.

rake [reɪk] *n* rastrillo.

rally ['rælɪ] *n* **1** POL mitin. **2** rally.

ram [ræm] *n* carnero.

ramble ['ræmbəl] *n* excursión.

ramp [ræmp] *n* rampa.

ran [ræn] *pt* → run.

ranch [rɑːntʃ] *n* rancho.

rancid ['rænsɪd] *adj* rancio,-a.

random ['rændəm] *adj* fortuito,-a. • **at random** al azar.

rang [ræŋ] *pp* → ring.

range [reɪndʒ] *n* **1** gama, surtido. **2** alcance *(de misil, telescopio)*. **3** cordillera, sierra.

rank [ræŋk] *n* **1** fila. **2** grado *(militar)*. **3** categoría

ranking ['ræŋkɪŋ] *n* ranking.

ransom ['rænsəm] *n* rescate. ► *vt* rescatar.

rap [ræp] *n* rap *(música)*.

rape[1] [reɪp] *n* violación. ► *vt* violar.

rape[2] [reɪp] *n* colza.

rapid ['ræpɪd] *adj* rápido,-a.

rare [reə'] *adj* **1** raro,-a. **2** poco hecho,-a *(carne)*.

rascal ['rɑːskəl] *n* pillo.

rash[1] [ræʃ] *n* sarpullido.

rash[2] [ræʃ] *adj* imprudente.

rasher ['ræʃə'] *n* loncha.

raspberry ['rɑːzbəri] *n* frambuesa.

rat [ræt] *n* rata.

rate [reɪt] *n* **1** tasa, índice, tipo. **2** velocidad, ritmo. **3** tarifa, precio. • **at any rate** de todos modos. ▪ **rate of exchange** tipo de cambio.

rather ['rɑːðə'] *adv* bastante. • **I would rather** preferiría; **rather than** en vez de, mejor que.

ratings ['reɪtɪŋs] *npl* índice de audiencia.

ratio ['reɪʃɪəʊ] *n* razón, relación.

ration ['ræʃən] *n* ración.

rational ['ræʃənəl] *adj* racional.

rattle ['rætəl] *n* **1** sonajero. **2** traqueteo.

rattlesnake ['rætəlsneɪk] *n* serpiente de cascabel.

rave [reɪv] *vi n* juerga.

raven ['reɪvən] *n* cuervo.

ravine [rə'viːn] *n* barranco.

raw [rɔː] *adj* **1** crudo,-a. **2** bruto,-a. ▪ **raw material** materia prima.

ray[1] [reɪ] *n* rayo *(de luz)*.

ray[2] [reɪ] *n* raya *(pez)*.

razor ['reɪzə'] *n* **1** navaja de afeitar. **2** maquinilla de afeitar. ▪ **razor blade** cuchilla de afeitar.

reach [riːtʃ] *n* alcance. ► *vt* **1** alcanzar, llegar a. **2** contactar. ► *vi* llegar. • **within reach of** al alcance de; **out of reach** fuera del alcance.

react [rɪ'ækt] *vi* reaccionar.

reaction [rɪ'ækʃən] *n* reacción.

read [riːd] *vt* **1** leer. **2** estudiar *(en universidad)*. ► *vi* **1** poner *(cartel, anuncio)*. • **to read back** volver a leer, releer; **to read out** leer en voz alta.

reader ['riːdə'] *n* lector,-ra.

reading ['riːdɪŋ] *n* lectura.

ready ['redɪ] *adj* preparado,-a.

ready-made [redɪ'meɪd] *adj* hecho,-a, confeccionado,-a.

real [rɪəl] *adj* real. ► *adv fam* muy. ▪ **real estate** bienes inmuebles.

reality [rɪ'ælɪtɪ] *n* realidad.

realize ['rɪəlaɪz] *vt* **1** darse cuenta de. **2** realizar.

reap [riːp] *vt* cosechar.

rear [rɪə'] *adj* trasero,-a, de atrás. ► *n* parte de atrás.

rearrange [riːəˈreɪndʒ] *vt* **1** colocar de otra manera. **2** volver a concertar *(reunión)*.

rear-view [ˈrɪəvjuː] *adj.* ■ **rear-view mirror** retrovisor.

reason [ˈriːzən] *n* razón. ▶ *vi* razonar.

reasonable [ˈriːzənəbəl] *adj* razonable.

reassure [riːəˈʃʊəʳ] *vt* tranquilizar.

rebate [ˈriːbeɪt] *n* devolución, reembolso.

rebel [ˈrebəl, rɪˈbel] *adj-n* rebelde. ▶ *vi* rebelarse.

rebellion [rɪˈbeliən] *n* rebelión.

rebound [*(n)* ˈriːbaʊnd, *(vb)* rɪˈbaʊnd] *n* rebote. ▶ *vi* rebotar.

rebuild [riːˈbɪld] *vt* reconstruir.

rebuke [rɪˈbjuːk] *vt* reprender.

recall [rɪˈkɔːl] *vt* recordar.

receipt [rɪˈsiːt] *n* recibo. ▶ *npl* **receipts** recaudación *(en taquilla)*.

receive [rɪˈsiːv] *vt* recibir.

receiver [rɪˈsiːvəʳ] *n* **1** receptor. **2** auricular *(de teléfono)*.

recent [ˈriːsənt] *adj* reciente.

reception [rɪˈsepʃən] *n* recepción. ■ **reception desk** recepción.

receptionist [rɪˈsepʃənɪst] *n* recepcionista.

recess [ˈriːses] *n* **1** hueco. **2** descanso.

recession [rɪˈseʃən] *n* recesión.

rechargeable [riːˈtʃɑːdʒəbəl] *adj* recargable.

recipe [ˈresəpɪ] *n* receta.

reciprocal [rɪˈsɪprəkəl] *adj* recíproco,-a.

recital [rɪˈsaɪtəl] *n* recital.

reckless [ˈrekləs] *adj* **1** precipitado,-a. **2** temerario,-a.

reckon [ˈrekən] *vt-vi* contar. ▶ *vt* creer, considerar.

reclaim [rɪˈkleɪm] *vt* reclamar.

recline [rɪˈklaɪn] *vt-vi* reclinar(se).

recognize [ˈrekəgnaɪz] *vt* reconocer.

recollect [rekəˈlekt] *vt* recordar.

recommend [rekəˈmend] *vt* recomendar.

reconsider [riːkənˈsɪdəʳ] *vt* reconsiderar.

reconstruct [riːkənsˈtrʌkt] *vt* reconstruir.

record [*(n)* ˈrekɔːd, *(vb)* rɪˈkɔːd] *n* **1** registro, documento. **2** historial, expediente. **3** disco *(música)*. **4** récord, marca. ▶ *vt* **1** hacer constar. **2** anotar. **3** grabar. ● **off the record** confidencialmente; **to beat the record** batir el récord. ■ **record player** tocadiscos.

recorder [rɪˈkɔːdəʳ] *n* flauta dulce.

recount [ˈriːkaʊnt] *n* recuento.

recover [rɪˈkʌvəʳ] *vt-vi* recuperar(se).

recovery [rɪˈkʌvərɪ] *n* recuperación.

recruit [rɪˈkruːt] *n* recluta. ▶ *vt* reclutar.

rectangle ['rektæŋgəl] *n* rectángulo.

rectify ['rektɪfaɪ] *vt* rectificar.

recycle [riː'saɪkəl] *vt* reciclar.

red [red] *adj* **1** rojo,-a. **2** pelirrojo,-a *(pelo).* ► *n* rojo. • **to be in the red** estar en números rojos. ■ **red tape** papeleo burocrático; **red wine** vino tinto.

redeem [rɪ'diːm] *vt* rescatar.

reduce [rɪ'djuːs] *vt-vi* reducir(se).

redundancy [rɪ'dʌndənsɪ] *n* despido.

redundant [rɪ'dʌndənt] *adj* **1** redundante. **2** despedido,-a. • **to be made redundant** ser despedido,-a.

reed [riːd] *n* **1** caña, junco. **2** lengüeta *(de instrumento).*

reef [riːf] *n* arrecife.

reek [riːk] *vi* apestar.

reel [riːl] *n* carrete.

refer [rɪ'fɜːr] *vi* **1** referirse. **2** consultar.

referee [refə'riː] *n* árbitro.

reference ['refərəns] *n* referencia. ■ **reference book** libro de consulta.

referendum [refə'rendəm] *n* referéndum.

refill [*(n)* 'riːfɪl, *(vb)* riː'fɪl] *n* recambio. ► *vt* rellenar.

refine [rɪ'faɪn] *vt* refinar.

refinery [rɪ'faɪnərɪ] *n* refinería.

reflect [rɪ'flekt] *vt* reflejar. ► *vi* reflexionar.

reflection [rɪ'flekʃən] *n* **1** reflejo. **2** reflexión.

reflex ['riːfleks] *adj* reflejo.

reflexive [rɪ'fleksɪv] *adj* reflexivo,-a.

reform [rɪ'fɔːm] *n* reforma. ► *vt* reformar.

refrain [rɪ'freɪn] *n* estribillo.

refresh [rɪ'freʃ] *vt* refrescar.

refreshment [rɪ'freʃmənt] *n* refresco, refrigerio.

refrigerator [rɪ'frɪdʒəreɪtər] *n* frigorífico, nevera.

refuge ['refjuːdʒ] *n* refugio.

refugee [refjuː'dʒiː] *n* refugiado,-a.

refund [*(n)* 'riːfʌnd, *(vb)* riː'fʌnd] *n* reembolso. ► *vt* reembolsar.

refusal [rɪ'fjuːzəl] *n* negativa.

refuse[1] ['refjuːs] *n* basura.

refuse[2] [rɪ'fjuːz] *vi* negarse.

regain [rɪ'geɪn] *vt* recobrar.

regard [rɪ'gɑːd] *vt* considerar. ► *n* respeto. ► *npl* **regards** recuerdos. • **as regards...** en lo que se refiere a...; **with regard to** con respecto a;.

regarding [rɪ'gɑːdɪŋ] *prep* respecto a, en relación con.

regime [reɪ'ʒiːm] *n* régimen.

regiment ['redʒɪmənt] *n* regimiento.

region ['riːdʒən] *n* región.

register ['redʒɪstər] *n* registro, lista. ► *vi* **1** registrarse *(en hotel).* **2** matricularse *(para clases).* **3** inscribirse. ► *vt* **1**

certificar *(carta)*. **2** inscribir en el registro *(boda, nacimiento)*. ■ **registered post** correo certificado.

registration [redʒɪs'treɪʃən] *n* **1** registro. **2** matriculación. ■ **registration number** matrícula.

regret [rɪ'gret] *n* pesar. ► *vt* **1** lamentar. **2** arrepentirse de.

regular ['regjʊlə'] *adj* **1** regular. **2** habitual *(cliente)*. **3** normal.

regulate ['regjʊleɪt] *vt* regular.

rehearsal [rɪ'hɜːsəl] *n* ensayo.

rehearse [rɪ'hɜːs] *vt* ensayar.

reign [reɪn] *n* reinado. ► *vi* reinar.

reimburse [riːɪm'bɜːs] *vt* reembolsar.

rein [reɪn] *n* rienda.

reindeer ['reɪndɪə'] *n* reno.

reinforce [riːɪn'fɔːs] *vt* reforzar. ■ **reinforced concrete** hormigón armado.

reinstate [riːɪn'steɪt] *vt* readmitir.

reject [rɪ'dʒekt] *vt* rechazar.

relapse [rɪ'læps] *n* **1** recaída. **2** reincidencia. ► *vi* **1** recaer. **2** reincidir.

relate [rɪ'leɪt] *vt* **1** relatar, contar. **2** relacionar. ► *vi* **1** estar relacionado,-a. **2** identificarse, entenderse.

relation [rɪ'leɪʃən] *n* **1** relación. **2** pariente,-a.

relationship [rɪ'leɪʃənʃɪp] *n* relación.

relative ['relətɪv] *adj* relativo, -a. ► *n* pariente,-a.

relax [rɪ'læks] *vt-vi* relajar(se).

relay ['riːleɪ] *n* **1** relevo. **2** relé.

release [rɪ'liːs] *n* **1** liberación. **2** estreno *(de película)*. **3** disco recién salido. ► *vt* **1** poner en libertad. **2** estrenar *(película)*. **3** sacar *(disco)*.

relevant ['reləvənt] *adj* pertinente.

reliable [rɪ'laɪəbəl] *adj* **1** de fiar *(persona)*. **2** fidedigno,-a *(noticia)*. **3** seguro,-a *(máquina)*.

relieve [rɪ'liːv] *vt* aliviar.

religion [rɪ'lɪdʒən] *n* religión.

reluctant [rɪ'lʌktənt] *adj* reacio,-a.

rely [rɪ'laɪ] *vi* **rely on** confiar en, contar con.

remain [rɪ'meɪn] *vi* quedar(se). ► *npl* **remains** restos.

remark [rɪ'mɑːk] *n* comentario. ► *vt* comentar.

remarkable [rɪ'mɑːkəbəl] *adj* notable, extraordinario,-a.

remedy ['remədɪ] *n* remedio. ► *vt* remediar.

remember [rɪ'membə'] *vt* recordar, acordarse de.

remind [rɪ'maɪnd] *vt* recordar.

remit [rɪ'mɪt] *vt* remitir.

remittance [rɪ'mɪtəns] *n* giro.

remorse [rɪ'mɔːs] *n* remordimiento.

remote [rɪ'məʊt] *adj* remoto,-a. ■ **remote control** mando a distancia.

remove [rɪ'muːv] vt quitar. ► vi trasladarse, mudarse.

renew [rɪ'njuː] vt renovar.

renovate ['renəveɪt] vt restaurar.

renown [rɪ'naʊn] n fama.

rent¹ [rent] n alquiler. ► vt alquilar.

rental ['rentəl] n alquiler.

repair [rɪ'peəʳ] n reparación. ► vt reparar, arreglar.

repayment [riː'peɪmənt] n devolución, reembolso.

repeat [rɪ'piːt] n repetición. ► vt repetir.

repetition [repə'tɪʃən] n repetición.

replace [rɪ'pleɪs] vt **1** devolver a su sitio. **2** reemplazar.

replay [(n) 'riːpleɪ, (vb) riː'pleɪ] n **1** repetición. **2** partido de desempate. ► vt repetir.

reply [rɪ'plaɪ] n respuesta. ► vi responder.

report [rɪ'pɔːt] n inform. ► vt informar sobre. ► vi presentarse.

reporter [rɪ'pɔːtəʳ] n reportero,-a, periodista.

represent [reprɪ'zent] vt representar.

repression [rɪ'preʃən] n represión.

repressive [rɪ'presɪv] adj represivo,-a.

reprieve [rɪ'priːv] n indulto.► vt indultar.

reprimand ['reprɪmaːnd]vt reprender.

reprisal [rɪ'praɪzəl] n represalia.

reproach [rɪ'prəʊtʃ] n reproche. ► vt reprochar.

reproduce [riːprə'djuːs] vt-vi reproducir(se).

reproduction [riːprə'dʌkʃən] n reproducción.

reptile ['reptaɪl] n reptil.

republic [rɪ'pʌblɪk] n república.

reputable ['repjʊtəbəl] adj **1** acreditado,-a. **2** de confianza.

reputation [repjʊ'teɪʃən] n reputación.

request [rɪ'kwest] n solicitud, petición. ► vt pedir, solicitar.

require [rɪ'kwaɪəʳ] vt requerir.

requirement [rɪ'kwaɪəmənt] n requisito.

rescue ['reskjuː] n rescate. ► vt rescatar.

research [rɪ'sɜːtʃ] n investigación. ► vt-vi investigar.

resemble [rɪ'zembəl] vt parecerse a.

resent [rɪ'zent] vt ofenderse.

reservation [rezə'veɪʃən] n reserva.

reserve [rɪ'zɜːv] n reserva. ► vt reservar.

reservoir ['rezəvwaːʳ] n embalse.

reshuffle [riː'ʃʌfəl] n remodelación.

residence ['rezɪdəns] n residencia.

resident ['rezɪdənt] adj-n residente.

residential [resɪ'denʃəl] *adj* residencial.

residue ['rezɪdjuː] *n* residuo.

resign [rɪ'zaɪn] *vt-vi* dimitir. • **to resign oneself to STH** resignarse a algo.

resignation [rezɪg'neɪʃən] *n* **1** dimisión. **2** resignación.

resin ['rezɪn] *n* resina.

resist [rɪ'zɪst] *vt* resistir.

resistance [rɪ'zɪstəns] *n* resistencia.

resistant [rɪ'zɪstənt] *adj* resistente.

resolution [rezə'luːʃən] *n* resolución.

resolve [rɪ'zɒlv] *vt* resolver.

resort [rɪ'zɔːt] *n* lugar de vacaciones.

resource [rɪ'zɔːs] *n* recurso.

respect [rɪ'spekt] *n* respeto. ► *vt* respetar.

respective [rɪ'spektɪv] *adj* respectivo,-a.

respond [rɪ'spɒnd] *vi* responder.

response [rɪ'spɒns] *n* respuesta.

responsibility [rɪspɒnsɪ'bɪlɪtɪ] *n* responsabilidad.

rest[1] [rest] *n* descanso. ► *vt-vi* **1** descansar. **2** apoyar(se).

rest[2] [rest] *n* resto.

restaurant ['restərɒnt] *n* restaurante.

restore [rɪ'stɔːʳ] *vt* restaurar.

restrain [rɪ'streɪn] *vt* contener.

restrict [rɪ'strɪkt] *vt* restringir.

restriction [rɪ'strɪkʃən] *n* restricción.

result [rɪ'zʌlt] *n* resultado. **to result in** *vt* tener como resultado.

resume [rɪ'zjuːm] *vt-vi* reanudar(se).

résumé ['rezjuːmeɪ] *n* resumen.

retail ['riːteɪl] *n* venta al por menor. ■ **retail price** precio de venta al público.

retailer ['riːteɪləʳ] *n* detallista.

retain [rɪ'teɪn] *vt* retener.

retaliation [rɪtælɪ'eɪʃən] *n* represalias.

retch [retʃ] *vi* tener arcadas.

retina ['retɪnə] *n* retina.

retire [rɪ'taɪəʳ] *vt* jubilar. ► *vi* **1** jubilarse. **2** retirarse.

retired [rɪ'taɪəd] *adj* jubilado,-a.

retirement [rɪ'taɪəmənt] *n* jubilación.

retort [rɪ'tɔːt] *n* réplica.

retreat [rɪ'triːt] *n* retirada. ► *vi* retirarse.

retrieve [rɪ'triːv] *vt* recuperar.

return [rɪ'tɜːn] *n* **1** vuelta, regreso. **2** devolución. ► *vi* volver, regresar. ► *vt* devolver. • **in return for** a cambio de. ■ **return ticket** billete de ida y vuelta.

reunite [riːjuː'naɪt] *vt-vi* reunir(se).

reveal [rɪ'viːl] *vt* revelar.

revenge [rɪ'vendʒ] *n* venganza. ► *vt* vengar.

revenue ['revənjuː] *n* ingresos.
reverence ['revərəns] *n* reverencia.
reverse [rɪ'vɜːs] *adj* inverso,-a.
► *n* **1** reverso *(de moneda)*. **2** revés. **3** marcha atrás. ► *vt* **1** invertir. **2** volver al revés. **3** revocar *(decisión)*. ► *vi* dar marcha atrás. ■ **reverse gear** marcha atrás.
review [rɪ'vjuː] *n* **1** revista. **2** examen. **3** crítica. ► *vt* **1** pasar revista a *(tropas)*. **2** examinar. **3** hacer una crítica *(de libro, película)*.
reviewer [rɪ'vjuːəʳ] *n* crítico,-a.
revise [rɪ'vaɪz] *vt* **1** revisar. **2** corregir. ► *vt-vi* repasar.
revision [rɪ'vɪʒən] *n* **1** revisión. **2** repaso *(para examen)*.
revival [rɪ'vaɪvəl] *n* reestreno, reposición.
revolt [rɪ'vəʊlt] *n* revuelta. ► *vi* sublevarse. ► *vt* repugnar.
revolting [rɪmɑrɪ'vəʊltɪŋ] *adj* repugnante.
revolution [revə'luːʃən] *n* revolución.
reward [rɪ'wɔːd] *n* recompensa. ► *vt* recompensar.
rewind [riː'waɪnd] *vt* rebobinar.
rheumatism ['ruːmətɪzəm] *n* reumatismo, reuma.
rhinoceros [raɪ'nɒsərəs] *n* rinoceronte.
rhyme [raɪm] *n* rima.
rhythm ['rɪðəm] *n* ritmo.

rib [rɪb] *n* costilla.
ribbon ['rɪbən] *n* cinta.
rice [raɪs] *n* arroz. ■ **rice pudding** arroz con leche.
rich [rɪtʃ] *adj* **1** rico,-a. **2** fuerte, pesado,-a *(comida)*.
ricochet ['rɪkəʃeɪ] *n* rebote. ► *vi* rebotar.
rid [rɪd] *vt* librar. ● **to get rid of** deshacerse de.
ridden ['rɪdən] *pp* → ride.
riddle ['rɪdəl] *n* **1** acertijo, adivinanza. **2** enigma.
ride [raɪd] *n* paseo, vuelta. ► *vi* montar a caballo. ► *vt* montar *(a caballo, en moto, bicicleta)*.
rider ['raɪdəʳ] *n* **1** jinete, amazona. **2** ciclista. **3** motorista.
ridiculous [rɪ'dɪkjʊləs] *adj* ridículo,-a.
riding ['raɪdɪŋ] *n* equitación.
rife [raɪf] *adj* abundante.
rifle ['raɪfəl] *n* rifle, fusil.
rig [rɪg] *n* plataforma petrolífera.
right [raɪt] *adj* **1** derecho,-a *(mano)*. **2** correcto,-a. **3** justo,-a. ► *adv* **1** a la derecha, hacia la derecha. **2** bien: *he spelt her name right*, escribió bien su nombre. **3** inmediatamente. ► *n* **1** derecha. **2** derecho. **3** bien.. ● **all right!** ¡bien!, ¡vale!; **right away** en seguida; **right now** ahora mismo; **to be right** tener razón. ■ **right angle** ángulo recto.

right-hand [ˈraɪthænd] *adj* derecho,-a.

rigid [ˈrɪdʒɪd] *adj* rígido,-a.

rigour [ˈrɪgə] (US **rigor**) *n* rigor.

rim [rɪm] *n* **1** borde, canto. **2** llanta.

rind [raɪnd] *n* corteza.

ring¹ [rɪŋ] *n* **1** anillo. **2** anilla. **3** círculo *(de personas)*. **4** pista. **5** ring, cuadrilátero. ■ **ring road** carretera de circunvalación.

ring² [rɪŋ] *n* **1** tañido; toque *(de campana)*. **2** llamada *(de teléfono, al timbre)*. ► *vi* **1** tañer, repicar *(campana)*. **2** sonar *(teléfono, timbre)*. ► *vt* **1** llamar *(por teléfono)*. **2** tocar *(timbre)*.

rink [rɪŋk] *n* pista de patinaje.

rinse [rɪns] *vt* aclarar.

riot [ˈraɪət] *n* **1** disturbio. **2** motín. ► *vi* amotinarse.

rip [rɪp] *n* rasgadura. ► *vt-vi* rasgar.

ripe [raɪp] *adj* maduro,-a.

rip-off [ˈrɪpɒf] *n fam* timo.

rise [raɪz] *n* **1** ascenso, subida. **2** aumento *(de sueldo)*. **3** subida, cuesta *(en montaña)*. ► *vi* **1** ascender, subir. **2** aumentar *(precios)*. **3** levantarse *(de la cama)*. **4** salir *(sol, luna)*. **5** alzarse *(voz)*. ● **to give rise to** dar origen a.

risk [rɪsk] *n* riesgo, peligro. ► *vt* arriesgar.

risky [ˈrɪskɪ] *adj* arriesgado,-a.

rite [raɪt] *n* rito.

ritual [ˈrɪtjʊəl] *adj-n* ritual.

rival [ˈraɪvəl] *adj-n* competidor,-ra, rival. ► *vt* competir con, rivalizar con.

rivalry [ˈraɪvəlrɪ] *n* rivalidad.

river [ˈrɪvə] *n* río.

river-bed [ˈrɪvəbed] *n* lecho.

riverside [ˈrɪvəsaɪd] *n* ribera.

rivet [ˈrɪvɪt] *n* remache. ► *vt* remachar.

road [rəʊd] *n* **1** carretera. **2** camino. ■ **road sign** señal de tráfico.

roadway [ˈrəʊdweɪ] *n* calzada.

roam [rəʊm] *vi* vagar.

roar [rɔːʳ] *n* **1** bramido. **2** rugido *(de león)*. **3** estruendo *(de tráfico)*. ► *vi* rugir, bramar.

roast [rəʊst] *adj* asado,-a. ► *n* asado. ► *vt* **1** asar *(carne)*. **2** tostar *(café, nueces)*.

rob [rɒb] *vt* **1** robar. **2** atracar *(banco)*.

robber [ˈrɒbəʳ] *n* **1** ladrón,-ona. **2** atracador,-ra *(de banco)*.

robbery [ˈrɒbərɪ] *n* **1** robo. **2** atraco *(de banco)*.

robe [rəʊb] *n* bata.

robot [ˈrəʊbɒt] *n* robot.

rock [rɒk] *n* **1** roca. **2** rock *(música)*. ► *vt-vi* mecer(se). ● **on the rocks** con hielo *(bebida)*.

rocker [ˈrɒkəʳ] *n* balancín.

rocket [ˈrɒkɪt] *n* cohete.

rocking-chair [ˈrɒkɪŋtʃeəʳ] *n* mecedora.

rod [rɒd] *n* **1** vara. **2** barra.

rode [rəud] *pt* → ride.

role [rəul] *n* papel.

roll [rəul] *n* **1** rollo. **2** lista. **3** bollo, panecillo. ► *vt* **1** hacer rodar. **2** enroscar. **3** liar *(cigarrillo).* ► *vi* **1** rodar. **2** enroscarse.

roller ['rəulə'] *n* **1** rodillo. **2** rulo. ■ **roller coasting** montaña rusa; **roller skating** patinaje sobre ruedas.

roller-skate ['rəuləskeit] *vi* patinar sobre ruedas.

romance [rəu'mæns] *n* **1** novela romántica. **2** idilio.

romantic [rəu'mæntik] *adj* romántico,-a.

roof [ru:f] *n* **1** tejado. **2** cielo *(de boca).* **3** techo *(de coche).*

roof-rack ['ru:fræk] *n* baca.

rook [ruk] *n* **1** grajo. **2** torre *(en ajedrez).*

room [ru:m] *n* **1** cuarto, habitación. **2** espacio, sitio. ● **to take up room** ocupar sitio.

roomy ['ru:mi] *adj* espacioso,-a, amplio,-a.

rooster ['ru:stə'] *n* gallo.

root [ru:t] *n* raíz.

rope [rəup] *n* cuerda.

rosary ['rəuzəri] *n* rosario.

rose[1] [rəuz] *n* rosa.

rose[2] [rəuz] *pt* → rise.

rosé ['rəuzei] *n* vino rosado.

rosemary ['rəuzməri] *n* romero.

rot [rɒt] *vt-vi* pudrir(se).

rotate [rəu'teit] *vi* girar. ► *vt-vi* *fig* alternar.

rotten ['rɒtən] *adj* podrido,-a.

rouge [ru:ʒ] *n* colorete.

rough [rʌf] *adj* **1** áspero,-a, basto,-a *(superficie).* **2** desigual *(suelo).* **3** agitado,-a *(mar).* **4** rudo,-a, tosco,-a *(persona, modales).* **10** aproximado,-a *(presupuesto).* ■ **rough copy** borrador; **rough sea** marejada; **rough version** borrador.

roughly ['rʌfli] *adv* aproximadamente.

roulette [ru:'let] *n* ruleta.

round [raund] *adj* redondo,-a. ► *n* **1** círculo. **2** ronda. **3** asalto *(de boxeo).* ► *adv* por ahí. ► *prep* **1** alrededor de. **2** a la vuelta de.

roundabout ['raundəbaut] *adj* indirecto,-a. ► *n* **1** tiovivo. **2** rotonda.

rouse [rauz] *vt-vi* despertar(se). ► *vt* provocar.

route [ru:t] *n* ruta.

routine [ru:'ti:n] *n* rutina.

row[1] [rau] *n* **1** riña, pelea. **2** jaleo, ruido

row[2] [rəu] *n* fila, hilera. ● **in a row** en fila.

row[3] [rəu] *vt-vi* remar.

rowing ['rəuiŋ] *n* remo.

royal ['rɔiəl] *adj* real.

royalty ['rɔiəlti] *n* realeza. ► *npl* **royalties** derechos .

rub [rʌb] *vt* frotar, restregar. ► *vi* rozar.

to rub out *vt* borrar.

rubber ['rʌbəʳ] *n* **1** caucho, goma. **2** goma de borrar. ▪ **rubber ring** flotador.
rubbish ['rʌbɪʃ] *n* basura.
rubble ['rʌbəl] *n* escombros.
rubella [ru:'belə] *n* rubeola, rubéola.
ruby ['ru:bɪ] *n* rubí.
rucksack ['rʌksæk] *n* mochila.
rudder ['rʌdəʳ] *n* timón.
rude [ru:d] *adj* maleducado,-a.
rug [rʌg] *n* alfombrilla.
rugby ['rʌgbɪ] *n* rugby.
ruin [ru:ɪn] *n* ruina. ▶ *vt* **1** arruinar. **2** estropear.
rule [ru:l] *n* **1** regla, norma. **2** gobierno. **3** reinado. ▶ *vt-vi* **1** gobernar. **2** reinar.
ruler ['ru:ləʳ] *n* **1** gobernante. **2** regla.
rum [rʌm] *n* ron.
ruminant ['ru:mɪnənt] *adj-n* rumiante.
rumour ['ru:məʳ] (US **rumor**) *n* rumor. ▶ *vt* rumorear.
rump [rʌmp] *n* ancas.
rumpus ['rʌmpəs] *n fam* jaleo, escándalo.
run [rʌn] *vi* **1** correr. **2** funcionar (aparato, organización). **3** presentarse (a elecciones). **4** durar. **5** circular (autobús, tren). **6** desteñirse (color). ▶ *vt* **1** correr en. **2** llevar (en coche, moto). **3** dirigir (organización). **4** hacer funcionar (aparato). **5** ejecutar (macro, programa). ▶ *n* **1** carrera. **2** viaje, paseo.

3 racha. **4** pista (de esquí). **5** carrera (en media). ▪ **in the long run** a la larga.
to run after *vt* perseguir.
to run away *vi* escaparse.
to run into *vt* **1** chocar con (coche). **2** tropezar con (persona).
to run out *vi* acabarse.
runaway ['rʌnəweɪ] *adj-n* fugitivo,-a.
rung [rʌŋ] *n* escalón. ▶ *pp* → ring.
runner ['rʌnəʳ] *n* corredor,-ra.
runner-up [rʌnəʳ'ʌp] *n* subcampeón,-ona.
running ['rʌnɪŋ] *n* **1** atletismo. **2** organización. ▶ *adj* **1** corriente (agua). **2** continuo,-a. ▪ **running costs** gastos de mantenimiento.
runny ['rʌnɪ] *adj* blando,-a, líquido,-a.
run-of-the-mill [rʌnəvðə'mɪl] *adj* corrien-te y moliente.
runway ['rʌnweɪ] *n* pista de aterrizaje.
rupture ['rʌptʃəʳ] *n* ruptura.
rural ['rʊərəl] *adj* rural.
rush [rʌʃ] *n* prisa. ▶ *vt* **1** apresurar, dar prisa a. **2** llevar rápidamente. ▶ *vi* apresurarse. ▪ **rush hour** hora punta.
rust [rʌst] *n* óxido. ▶ *vt-vi* oxidar(se).
rustic ['rʌstɪk] *adj* rústico,-a.
rut [rʌt] *n* surco.
rye [raɪ] *n* centeno.

S

sabotage ['sæbətɑːʒ] n sabotaje. ► vt sabotear.

sack [sæk] n saco. ► vt fam despedir a. • **to get the sack** fam ser despedido,-a.

sacred ['seɪkrəd] adj sagrado,-a.

sacrifice ['sækrɪfaɪs] n sacrificio. ► vt sacrificar.

sad [sæd] adj triste.

saddle ['sædəl] n 1 silla (de montar). 2 sillín (de bicicleta).

sadness ['sædnəs] n tristeza.

safe [seɪf] adj 1 a salvo. 2 seguro,-a. ► n caja fuerte.

safety ['seɪftɪ] n seguridad. ■ **safety belt** cinturón de seguridad; **safety pin** imperdible.

said [sed] pt-pp → say.

sail [seɪl] n vela. ► vi navegar. • **to set sail** zarpar.

sailing ['seɪlɪŋ] n vela (deporte). ■ **sailing boat** velero.

sailor ['seɪlə'] n marinero.

saint [seɪnt] n san, santo,-a.

sake [seɪk] n bien. • **for the sake of** por, por el bien de.

salad ['sæləd] n ensalada. ■ **salad bowl** ensaladera; **salad dressing** aliño, aderezo.

salary ['sælərɪ] n salario.

sale [seɪl] n 1 venta. 2 liquidación, rebajas. 3 subasta. • **for sale** en venta; **on sale** 1 a la venta. 2 rebajado,-a.

salesclerk ['seɪlzklɑːk] n dependiente,-a.

salesman ['seɪlzmən] n 1 vendedor. 2 dependiente. 3 representante, viajante.

saleswoman ['seɪlzwʊmən] n 1 vendedora. 2 dependienta. 3 representante, viajante.

saliva [sə'laɪvə] n saliva.

salmon ['sæmən] n salmón.

salon ['sælɒn] n salón.

salt [sɔːlt] n sal. ■ **salt beef** cecina; **salt pork** tocino.

salty ['sɔːltɪ] adj salado,-a.

salute [sə'luːt] n saludo.

same [seɪm] adj mismo,-a. ► pron **the same** lo mismo. ► adv igual, del mismo modo. • **all the same** a pesar de todo.

sample ['sɑːmpəl] n muestra. ► vt probar, catar (vino).

sanction ['sæŋkʃən] n sanción. ► vt sancionar.

sanctuary ['sæŋktjʊərɪ] n santuario.

sand [sænd] n arena. ■ **sand dune** duna.

sandal ['sændəl] n sandalia.

sandpaper ['sændpeɪpə'] n papel de lija. ► vt lijar.

sandwich ['sænwɪdʒ] n sandwich, emparedado.

sang [sæŋ] pt → sing.

sanitary ['sænɪtərɪ] adj 1 sanitario,-a. 2 higiénico,-a. ■ **sanitary towel** compresa.

sank [sæŋk] pt → sink.

sap [sæp] *n* savia.

sapphire ['sæfaɪə'] *n* zafiro.

sardine [saː'diːn] *n* sardina.

sash [sæʃ] *n* faja.

sat [sæt] *pt-pp* → sit.

satchel ['sætʃəl] *n* cartera.

satellite ['sætəlaɪt] *n* satélite. ■ **satellite dish aerial** antena parabólica.

satisfaction [sætɪs'fækʃən] *n* satisfacción.

satisfy ['sætɪsfaɪ] *vt* satisfacer.

Saturday ['sætədɪ] *n* sábado.

sauce [sɔːs] *n* salsa. ■ **sauce boat** salsera.

saucepan ['sɔːspən] *n* **1** cazo, cacerola. **2** olla.

saucer ['sɔːsə'] *n* platillo.

sauna ['sɔːnə] *n* sauna.

sausage ['sɒsɪdʒ] *n* salchicha.

savage ['sævɪdʒ] *adj-n* salvaje.

save [seɪv] *vt* **1** salvar *(vida)*. **2** guardar *(comida, fuerzas)*. **3** ahorrar *(dinero)*. **4** archivar *(en un ordenador)*. **5** evitar. **6** parar *(pelota)*. ► *vi* ahorrar.

saving ['seɪvɪŋ] *n* ahorro. ► *npl* **savings** ahorros. ■ **savings account** cuenta de ahorros; **savings bank** caja de ahorros.

savour ['seɪvə'] (US **savor**) *n* sabor. ► *vt* saborear.

savoury ['seɪvərɪ] (US **savory**) *adj* salado,-a. ► *n* canapé, entremés.

saw[1] [sɔː] *n* sierra. ► *vt-vi* serrar.

saw[2] [sɔː] *pt* → see.

sawdust ['sɔːdʌst] *n* serrín.

sawn [sɔːn] *pp* → saw.

saxophone ['sæksəfəʊn] *n* saxofón.

say [seɪ] *vt* decir. ● **it is said that ...** dicen que ..., se dice que ...; **that is to say** es decir.

saying ['seɪɪŋ] *n* dicho, decir.

scab [skæb] *n* postilla.

scaffold ['skæfəʊld] *n* **1** andamio. **2** patíbulo.

scald [skɔːld] *vt* escaldar.

scale[1] [skeɪl] *n* escama.

scale[2] [skeɪl] *n* balanza.

scale[3] [skeɪl] *n* escala. ■ **scale model** maqueta.

scalp [skælp] *n* cuero cabelludo.

scalpel ['skælpəl] *n* bisturí.

scampi ['skæmpɪ] *n* gambas a la gabardina.

scan [skæn] *vt* examinar. ► *n* ecografía.

scandal ['skændəl] *n* escándalo.

scar [skaː'] *n* cicatriz.

scarce [skeəs] *adj* escaso,-a.

scarcely ['skeəslɪ] *adv* apenas.

scare [skeə'] *vt-vi* asustar(se).

scarecrow ['skeəkrəʊ] *n* espantapájaros.

scarf [skaːf] *n* **1** pañuelo. **2** bufanda.

scarlet ['skaːlət] *adj-n* escarlata. ■ **scarlet fever** escarlatina.

scary ['skeərɪ] *adj* espeluznante

scatter ['skætə'] *vt-vi* **1** dispersar(se). **2** esparcir.

scenario [sɪ'nɑːrɪəʊ] *n* **1** guión. **2** perspectiva, panorama.

scene [siːn] *n* **1** escena. **2** escenario. **3** vista, panorama. • **behind the scenes** entre bastidores.

scent [sent] *n* **1** olor, fragancia. **2** perfume. **3** pista, rastro.

schedule ['ʃedjuːl, 'skedjuːl] *n* **1** programa. **2** lista. **3** US horario. ► *vt* programar, fijar. • **on schedule** a la hora prevista. ■ **scheduled flight** vuelo regular.

scheme [skiːm] *n* **1** plan, programa. **2** intriga, ardid.

scholarship ['skɒləʃɪp] *n* beca.

school [skuːl] *n* escuela, colegio, instituto. ■ **school book** libro de texto.

science ['saɪəns] *n* ciencia. ■ **science fiction** ciencia ficción.

scientific [saɪən'tɪfɪk] *adj* científico,-a.

scientist ['saɪəntɪst] *n* científico,-a.

scissors ['sɪzəz] *npl* tijeras.

scoff[1] [skɒf] *vi* mofarse.

scoff[2] [skɒf] *vt fam* zamparse.

scold [skəʊld] *vt* reñir.

scoop [skuːp] *n* exclusiva.

scooter ['skuːtə'] *n* Vespa®.

scope [skəʊp] *n* **1** alcance. **2** posibilidades.

scorch [skɔːtʃ] *vt* chamuscar.

score [skɔːʳ] *n* **1** tanteo, puntuación *(en golf, naipes)*. **2** resultado. **3** partitura, música *(de película)*. ► *vt-vi* marcar *(gol, etc)*. ► *vi* obtener una puntuación. ► *vt* lograr, conseguir.

scoreboard ['skɔːbɔːd] *n* marcador.

scorn [skɔːn] *n* desprecio. ► *vt* despreciar.

scorpion ['skɔːpɪən] *n* escorpión.

scoundrel ['skaʊndrəl] *n* canalla.

scout [skaʊt] *n* explorador,-ra.

scowl [skaʊl] *n* ceño fruncido. ► *vi* fruncir el ceño.

scramble ['skræmbəl] *n* lucha. ► *vi* **1** trepar. **2** pelearse. ► *vt* revolver, mezclar. ■ **scrambled eggs** huevos revueltos.

scrap [skræp] *vt* desechar. ► *n* trozo, pedazo. ► *npl* **scraps** restos, sobras *(de comida)*. ■ **scrap metal** chatarra; **scrap paper** papel borrador.

scrape [skreɪp] *vt* **1** rascar. **2** rasparse.

scratch [skrætʃ] *n* rasguño, arañazo. ► *vt* **1** arañar. **2** rascar.

scream [skriːm] *n* grito. ► *vt-vi* gritar, chillar.

screen [skriːn] *n* **1** biombo. **2** pantalla *(de cine, televisión)*. ► *vt* **1** proteger. **2** examinar. **3** proyectar *(película)*. ■ **screen saver** protector de pantalla.

screw [skru:] n tornillo. ► vt atornillar.

screwdriver ['skru:draɪvəʳ] n destornillador.

scribble ['skrɪbəl] n garabatos. ► vt-vi garabatear.

script [skrɪpt] n guión.

scrounge [skraʊndʒ] vi gorronear. ► vt gorronear.

scrub [skrʌb] n 1 maleza. 2 fregado. ► vt fregar.

scruff [skrʌf] n cogote.

scruffy ['skrʌfɪ] adj desaliñado,-a.

scrupulous ['skru:pjʊləs] adj escrupuloso,-a.

scrutinize ['skru:tɪnaɪz] vt escudriñar.

scuba diving ['sku:bədaɪvɪŋ] n submarinismo.

sculptor ['skʌlptəʳ] n escultor,-ra.

sculptress ['skʌlptrəs] n escultora.

sculpture ['skʌlptʃəʳ] n escultura.

scum [skʌm] n espuma

sea [si:] n mar. ■ **sea lion** león marino; **sea trout** trucha de mar, reo.

seafood ['si:fu:d] n mariscos.

seafront ['si:frʌnt] n paseo marítimo.

seagull ['si:gʌl] n gaviota.

sea-horse ['si:hɔ:s] n caballito de mar.

seal[1] [si:l] n foca.

seal[2] [si:l] n sello. ► vt sellar.

seam [si:m] n 1 costura. 2 juntura, junta.

search [sɜ:tʃ] n 1 búsqueda. 2 registro (de edificio, persona). ► vi buscar. ► vt registrar. ■ **search engine** buscador; **search warrant** orden de registro.

seasick ['si:sɪk] adj mareado,-a.

seaside ['si:saɪd] n playa, costa. ■ **seaside resort** centro turístico en la costa.

season ['si:zən] n 1 estación (del año). 2 temporada (para deporte, etc). ► vt sazonar. ● **in season 1** en sazón (fruta). 2 en celo (animal). 3 en temporada alta (turismo); **out of season 1** fuera de temporada (fruta). 2 en temporada baja (turismo). ■ **season ticket** abono.

seat [si:t] n 1 asiento. 2 localidad (en teatro, etc). 3 escaño. ► vt sentar(se). ● **to take a seat** sentarse. ■ **seat belt** cinturón de seguridad.

seaweed ['si:wi:d] n alga.

second[1] ['sekənd] adj-n segundo,-a. ► adv segundo. ► vt secundar. ► npl **seconds** artículos defectuosos. ■ **second name** apellido.

second[2] ['sekənd] n segundo.

secondary ['sekəndərɪ] adj secundario,-a. ■ **secondary school** escuela de enseñanza secundaria.

second-hand ['sekəndhænd] *adj* de segunda mano.

secret ['si:krət] *adj* secreto,-a. ► *n* secreto.

secretary ['sekrətərı] *n* secretario,-a. ■ **Secretary of State** **1** ministro,-a con cartera *(en GB)*. **2** ministro,-a de Asuntos Exteriores *(en EEUU)*.

secrete [sɪ'kri:t] *vt* secretar.

sect [sekt] *n* secta.

section ['sekʃən] *n* sección.

sector ['sektə] *n* sector.

secure [sɪ'kjʊəʳ] *adj* seguro,-a.

security [sɪ'kjʊərɪtɪ] *n* seguridad. ► *npl* **securities** COMM valores.

sedative ['sedətɪv] *adj-n* sedante.

seduce [sɪ'dju:s] *vt* seducir.

see[1] [si:] *vt-vi* **1** ver. **2** procurar. **3** acompañar. **4** entender. • **let's see** a ver, vamos a ver; **see you later!** ¡hasta luego!.

to see off *vt* despedirse de.

to see out *vt* acompañar hasta la puerta.

seed [si:d] *n* **1** semilla *(de planta)*. **2** pepita *(de fruta)*. **3** cabeza de serie *(tenis)*.

seek [si:k] *vt* **1** buscar. **2** solicitar.

seem [si:m] *vi* parecer.

seen [si:n] *pp* → see.

seesaw ['si:sɔ:] *n* balancín.

see-through ['si:θru:] *adj* transparente.

segment ['segmənt] *n* segmento.

seize [si:z] *vt* **1** agarrar, coger. **2** incautar, embargar. **3** tomar, apoderarse de.

seldom ['seldəm] *adv* rara vez.

select [sɪ'lekt] *vt* seleccionar. ► *adj* selecto,-a.

selection [sɪ'lekʃən] *n* selección.

self [self] *n* yo.

self-conscious [self'kɒnʃəs] *adj* cohibido,-a, tímido,-a.

self-defence [selfdɪ'fens] *n* autodefensa. • **in self-defence** en defensa propia.

self-employed [selfɪm'plɔɪd] *adj* autónomo,-a.

selfish ['selfɪʃ] *adj* egoísta.

self-portrait [self'pɔ:treɪt] *n* autorretrato.

self-service [self'sɜ:vɪs] *n* autoservicio.

sell [sel] *vt-vi* vender.

to sell off *vt* liquidar.

to sell out *vt* agotarse.

sell-by date ['selbaɪdeɪt] *n* fecha de caducidad.

seller ['seləʳ] *n* vendedor,-ra.

Sellotape® ['seləteɪp] *n* Celo®, cinta adhesiva.

semester [sɪ'mestəʳ] *n* semestre.

semicolon [semɪ'kəʊlən] *n* punto y coma.

semidetached [semɪdɪ'tætʃt] *adj* adosado,-a. ► *n* casa adosada.

semifinal [semɪˈfaɪnəl] n semifinal.

senate [ˈsenət] n senado.

senator [ˈsenətəʳ] n senador,-ra.

send [send] vt enviar, mandar.

sender [ˈsendəʳ] n remitente.

senior [ˈsiːnɪəʳ] adj 1 mayor (por edad). 2 superior (por rango). ► n 1 mayor (por edad). 2 superior (por rango). ■ **senior citizen** persona de la tercera edad.

sensation [senˈseɪʃən] n sensación.

sense [sens] n sentido. ► vt sentir, percibir. • **to make sense** tener sentido, ser sensato,-a.

sensibility [sensɪˈbɪlɪti] n sensibilidad.

sensible [ˈsensɪbəl] adj sensato,-a.

sensitive [ˈsensɪtɪv] adj 1 sensible. 2 confidencial.

sent [sent] pt-pp → send.

sentence [ˈsentəns] n 1 frase. 2 sentencia, fallo. ► vt condenar.

sentry [ˈsentri] n centinela.

separate [(vb) ˈsepəreɪt, (adj) ˈsepərət] vt-vi separar(se).► adj 1 separado,-a. 2 distinto,-a.

September [səpˈtembəʳ] n septiembre, setiembre.

sequence [ˈsiːkwəns] n 1 secuencia. 2 sucesión, serie.

serene [səˈriːn] adj sereno,-a.

sergeant [ˈsɑːdʒənt] n sargento.

serial [ˈsɪərɪəl] n serial. ■ **serial number** número de serie.

series [ˈsɪəriːz] n serie.

serious [ˈsɪərɪəs] adj 1 serio,-a. 2 grave (accidente).

servant [ˈsɜːvənt] n criado,-a.

serve [sɜːv] vt-vi servir. ► vt cumplir (condena). ► n saque (en tenis).

service [ˈsɜːvɪs] n 1 servicio. 2 revisión, puesta a punto (de coche). 3 oficio (religioso). • **in service** en funcionamiento; **out of service** fuera de servicio. ■ **service station** estación de servicio.

serviette [sɜːvɪˈet] n GB servilleta.

session [ˈseʃən] n sesión.

set[1] [set] n 1 juego. 2 conjunto. 3 set (tenis). 4 aparato (televisor, radio).

set[2] [set] n plató (de televisión). ► adj 1 fijo,-a (cantidad). 2 listo,-a. ► vt 1 poner, colocar,. 2 fijar (fecha). 3 marcar (pelo). ► vi 1 ponerse (sol). 2 cuajar (líquido). 3 endurecerse (cemento). • **to set (oneself) up** establecerse. ■ **set lunch** menú del día.

to set back vt 1 apartar. 2 retrasar.

to set off vi salir, ponerse en camino. ► vt 1 hacer estallar *(bomba)*. **2** hacer saltar *(alarma)*.

to set out *vi* **1** partir, salir. **2** proponerse, pretender. ► *vt* disponer, exponer.

to set up *vt* **1** levantar *(monumento)*. **2** montar *(tienda de campaña, negocio)*. **3** planear, convocar.

setback ['setbæk] *n* revés.

settee [se'tiː] *n* sofá.

setting ['setɪŋ] *n* **1** escenario *(de película)*. **2** ajuste *(de máquina)*.

settle ['setəl] *vt* **1** acordar *(precio)*. **2** resolver *(disputa)*. ► *vi* **1** posarse *(pájaro, polvo)*. **2** afincarse, establecerse. **3** calmarse.

to settle down *vi* **1** instalarse, afincarse. **2** sentar la cabeza.

settlement ['setəlmənt] *n* **1** poblado, colonia. **2** acuerdo. **3** pago.

seven ['sevən] *num* siete.

seventeen [sevən'tiːn] *num* diecisiete.

seventeenth [sevən'tiːnθ] *adj* decimoséptimo,-a.

seventh ['sevənθ] *adj-n* séptimo,-a.

seventy ['sevəntɪ] *num* setenta.

several ['sevərəl] *adj-pron* varios,-as.

severe [sɪ'vɪəʳ] *adj* **1** severo, -a. **2** grave *(enfermedad)*.

sew [səʊ] *vt-vi* coser.

sewage ['sjuːɪdʒ] *n* aguas residuales.

sewer [sjʊəʳ] *n* alcantarilla.

sewing ['səʊɪŋ] *n* costura. ■ **sewing machine** máquina de coser.

sewn [səʊn] *pp* → sew.

sex [seks] *n* sexo.

shabby ['ʃæbɪ] *adj* raído,-a.

shack [ʃæk] *n* choza.

shade [ʃeɪd] *n* **1** sombra. **2** pantalla *(de lámpara)*. **3** matiz *(de color)*. ► *vt* dar sombra.

shadow ['ʃædəʊ] *n* sombra.

shady ['ʃeɪdɪ] *adj* **1** a la sombra *(lugar)*. **2** *fam* sospechoso,-a *(persona)*.

shaft [ʃɑːft] *n* **1** mango. **2** eje.

shake [ʃeɪk] *n* **1** sacudida. **2** batido *(bebida)*. ► *vt* sacudir. ► *vi* temblar.

shall [ʃæl, unstressed ʃəl] *aux* **1** *indica un tiempo futuro*: *I shall go tomorrow*, iré mañana. **2** *indica ofrecimiento*: *shall I close the window?*, ¿cierro la ventana? **3** *indica una sugerencia*: *shall we go to the cinema?*, ¿vamos al cine? **4** *indica una promesa*: *you shall have everything you want, my dear*, tendrás todo lo que desees, cariño. **5** *uso enfático, una orden*: *you shall stop work immediately*, debes parar de trabajar enseguida.

shallow ['ʃæləʊ] *adj* poco profundo,-a.

shame [ʃeɪm] *n* **1** vergüenza. **2** lástima, pena.

shampoo [ʃæm'puː] *n* champú.

shandy ['ʃændɪ] *n* GB clara.

shape [ʃeɪp] *n* forma, figura. ► *vt* modelar.• **out of shape** en baja forma.

share [ʃeəʳ] *n* **1** parte. **2** acción *(en bolsa)*. ► *vt-vi* compartir. ► *vt* repartir.

shareholder ['ʃeəhəʊldəʳ] *n* accionista.

shark [ʃɑːk] *n* tiburón.

sharp [ʃɑːp] *adj* **1** afilado,-a *(cuchillo)*. **2** puntiagudo,-a *(palo)*. **3** agudo,-a *(dolor, persona)*. **4** cerrado,-a *(curva)*. ► *adv* en punto.

sharpen ['ʃɑːpən] *vt* **1** afilar *(cuchillo)*. **2** sacar punta a *(lápiz)*.

sharpener ['ʃɑːpənəʳ] *n* sacapuntas *(para lápices)*.

shatter ['ʃætəʳ] *vi* romperse, hacerse añicos.

shave [ʃeɪv] *n* afeitado. ► *vt-vi* afeitar(se).

shaver ['ʃeɪvəʳ] *n* máquina de afeitar.

shaving ['ʃeɪvɪŋ] *n* afeitado. ■ **shaving brush** brocha de afeitar; **shaving foam** espuma de afeitar.

shawl [ʃɔːl] *n* chal.

she [ʃiː] *pron* ella.

shear [ʃɪəʳ] *vt* esquilar.

shed¹ [ʃed] *n* cobertizo.

shed² [ʃed] *vt* **1** derramar *(lágrimas)*. **2** quitarse *(ropa)*.

sheep [ʃiːp] *n* oveja.

sheet [ʃiːt] *n* **1** sábana. **2** hoja *(de papel)*. **3** lámina *(de metal)*.

shelf [ʃelf] *n* estante. ► *npl* **shelves** estantería.

shell [ʃel] *n* **1** cáscara *(de huevo, nuez)*. **2** vaina *(de guisante)*. **3** caparazón *(de tortuga)*. **4** concha *(de caracola)*. **5** obús, proyectil.

shellfish ['ʃelfɪʃ] *n* marisco.

shelter ['ʃeltəʳ] *n* refugio. ► *vt* proteger.

shepherd ['ʃepəd] *n* pastor.

sherry ['ʃerɪ] *n* jerez.

shield [ʃiːld] *n* escudo.

shift [ʃɪft] *n* **1** cambio. **2** turno *(de trabajo)*. ► *vt* cambiar(se) de sitio.

shilling ['ʃɪlɪŋ] *n* chelín.

shin [ʃɪn] *n* espinilla.

shine [ʃaɪn] *n* brillo, lustre. ► *vi* brillar.

shingles ['ʃɪŋɡəlz] *npl* herpes.

shiny ['ʃaɪnɪ] *adj* brillante.

ship [ʃɪp] *n* barco, buque.

shipwreck ['ʃɪprek] *n* naufragio.

shipyard ['ʃɪpjɑːd] *n* astillero.

shirt [ʃɜːt] *n* camisa.

shit [ʃɪt] *n vulg* mierda.

shiver ['ʃɪvəʳ] *n* escalofrío. ► *vi* **1** tiritar. **2** temblar.

shock [ʃɒk] *n* **1** choque. **2** golpe, conmoción. **3** susto. **4** shock. ► *vt* escandalizar.

shocking ['ʃɒkɪŋ] *adj* escandaloso,-a, chocante.

shoe [ʃuː] *n* **1** zapato. **2** herradura. ■ **shoe polish** betún; **shoe shop** zapatería.

shoehorn ['ʃuːhɔːn] *n* calzador.

shoelace ['ʃuːleɪs] *n* cordón.

shoemaker ['ʃuːmeɪkəʳ] *n* zapatero,-a.

shone [ʃɒn] *pt-pp* → shine.

shook [ʃʊk] *pt* → shake.

shoot [ʃuːt] *n* **1** brote, retoño. **2** rodaje *(de película)*. ▶ *vt* **1** pegar un tiro a. **2** disparar. **3** rodar *(película)*. **4** chutar *(pelota)*. ▶ *vi* disparar. ■ **shooting star** estrella fugaz.

to shoot down *vt* **1** derribar. **2** matar a tiros.

shop [ʃɒp] *n* tienda. ▶ *vi* hacer compras, ir de compras. ■ **shop assistant** dependiente,-a; **shop window** escaparate.

shoplifting ['ʃɒplɪftɪŋ] *n* hurto *(en tiendas)*.

shopping ['ʃɒpɪŋ] *n* compras. ■ **shopping arcade** galerías comerciales; **shopping centre** centro comercial.

shore [ʃɔːʳ] *n* orilla, costa.

shorn [ʃɔːn] *pp* → shear.

short [ʃɔːt] *adj* **1** corto,-a. **2** bajo,-a *(estatura, persona)*. **3** seco,-a, brusco,-a *(modales)*. ▶ *n* cortometraje. ▶ *npl* **shorts** pantalón corto. ● **in short** en

pocas palabras; **for short** para abreviar; **to be short of** andar mal de. ■ **short circuit** cortocircuito; **short cut** atajo; **short story** cuento, relato.

shortage ['ʃɔːtɪdʒ] *n* escasez.

shorten ['ʃɔːtən] *vt-vi* acortar(se).

shortly ['ʃɔːtlɪ] *adv* en breve. ● **shortly after** poco después; **shortly before** poco antes.

short-sighted [ʃɔːt'saɪtɪd] *adj* miope.

shot[1] [ʃɒt] *n* **1** tiro, disparo. **2** intento. **3** trago. **4** foto. **5** toma *(en cine)*.

shot[2] [ʃɒt] *pt-pp* → shoot.

shotgun ['ʃɒtɡʌn] *n* escopeta.

should [ʃʊd] *aux* **1** debe. **2** deber de.

shoulder ['ʃəʊldəʳ] *n* **1** hombro *(de persona)*. **2** espalda *(de carne)*. ■ **shoulder blade** omoplato, omóplato.

shout [ʃaʊt] *n* grito. ▶ *vt-vi* gritar.

shove [ʃʌv] *n* empujón. ▶ *vt-vi* empujar.

shovel ['ʃʌvəl] *n* pala.

show [ʃəʊ] *n* **1** espectáculo, función. **2** programa *(televisivo, de radio)*. **3** exposición, feria. **4** demostración, muestra. ▶ *vt* **1** mostrar. **2** exponer. **3** indicar, marcar, señalar. **4** demostrar. ▶ *vt-vi* poner *(película)*. ■ **show business** el mundo del espectáculo.

to show off *vi* presumir.

to show up *vi fam* presentarse, aparecer.

shower ['ʃauəʳ] *n* 1 ducha. 2 chaparrón. ▶ *vi* ducharse.

shown [ʃəun] *pp* → show.

showroom ['ʃəurum] *n* sala de exposiciones.

shrank [ʃræŋk] *pt* → shrink.

shrapnel ['ʃræpnəl] *n* metralla.

shred [ʃred] *n* jirón.

shrimp [ʃrimp] *n* camarón, gamba.

shrink [ʃriŋk] *vt-vi* encoger(se).

shrivel ['ʃrivəl] *vi* marchitarse.

shroud [ʃraud] *n* mortaja.

shrub [ʃrʌb] *n* arbusto.

shrug [ʃrʌg] *vi* encogerse de hombros.

shrunk [ʃrʌŋk] *pp* → shrink.

shuffle ['ʃʌfəl] *vt* barajar. ▶ *vi* andar arrastrando los pies.

shut [ʃʌt] *vt-vi* cerrar(se).

to shut down *vt-vi* cerrar(se).

to shut up *vi fam* callar(se).

shutdown ['ʃʌtdaun] *n* cierre.

shutter ['ʃʌtəʳ] *n* 1 postigo, contraventana. 2 obturador.

shuttle ['ʃʌtəl] *n* 1 puente aéreo *(de avión)*. 2 servicio regular *(de bus, tren)*. 3 transbordador espacial.

shy [ʃai] *adj* tímido,-a.

shyness ['ʃainəs] *n* timidez.

sick [sik] *adj* 1 enfermo,-a. 2 mareado,-a. ▪ **sick leave** baja por enfermedad.

sickness ['siknəs] *n* 1 enfermedad. 2 náusea, mareo.

side [said] *n* 1 lado. 2 costado *(de persona)*. • **side by side** juntos,-as. ▪ **side dish** guarnición; **side effect** efecto secundario; **side street** bocacalle.

sideboard ['saidbɔːd] *n* aparador.

sideburns ['saidbɜːnz] *npl* patillas.

sidelight ['saidlait] *n* luz de posición.

sideline ['saidlain] *n* línea de banda.

sidewalk ['saidwɔːk] *n* US acera.

sideways ['saidweiz] *adj* 1 lateral *(movimiento)*. 2 de soslayo *(mirada)*. ▶ *adv* 1 de lado *(movimiento)*. 2 de soslayo *(mirada)*.

siege [siːdʒ] *n* sitio.

sieve [siv] *n* 1 tamiz *(para harina)*. 2 criba *(para granos)*. 3 colador *(para líquidos)*.

sigh [sai] *n* suspiro. ▶ *vi* suspirar.

sight [sait] *n* 1 vista. 2 mira *(de escopeta)*. ▶ *npl* **sights** atracciones. • **at first sight** a primera vista.

sightseeing ['saitsiːiŋ] *n* visita turística, turismo.

sign [sain] *n* 1 signo. 2 señal, gesto. 3 letrero. ▶ *vt-vi* firmar.

to sign in *vi* firmar el registro.

signal ['sɪgnəl] *n* señal.

signature ['sɪgnɪtʃəʳ] *n* firma.

significant [sɪg'nɪfɪkənt] *adj* significativo,-a.

signpost ['saɪnpəʊst] *n* señal indicadora, poste indicador.

silence ['saɪləns] *n* silencio.

silent ['saɪlənt] *adj* silencioso,-a.

silhouette [sɪluː'et] *n* silueta.

silk [sɪlk] *n* seda.

silkworm ['sɪlkwɜːm] *n* gusano de la seda

sill [sɪl] *n* alféizar, antepecho.

silly ['sɪlɪ] *adj* tonto,-a.

silver ['sɪlvəʳ] *n* plata. ■ **silver foil** papel de plata.

similar ['sɪmɪləʳ] *adj* similar.

simmer ['sɪməʳ] *vt-vi* cocer(se) a fuego lento.

simple ['sɪmpəl] *adj* simple.

simplify ['sɪmplɪfaɪ] *vt* simplificar.

sin [sɪn] *n* pecado. ▶ *vi* pecar.

since [sɪns] *adv* desde entonces. ▶ *prep* desde. ▶ *conj* **1** desde que. **2** ya que, puesto que.

sincere [sɪn'sɪəʳ] *adj* sincero,-a.

sincerely [sɪn'sɪəlɪ] *adv* sinceramente. ● **yours sincerely** atentamente *(en carta)*.

sing [sɪŋ] *vt-vi* cantar..

singer ['sɪŋəʳ] *n* cantante.

single ['sɪŋgəl] *adj* **1** solo,-a. **2** único,-a. **3** individual *(cama)*. **4** soltero,-a. ▶ *n* **1** GB billete de ida. **2** single *(disco)*. ▶ *npl*

singles individuales. ■ **single bed** cama individual; **single parent** madre soltera, padre soltero; **single room** habitación individual.

singular ['sɪŋgjʊləʳ] *adj-n* singular.

sinister ['sɪnɪstəʳ] *adj* siniestro,-a.

sink [sɪŋk] *n* **1** fregadero. **2** US lavabo. ▶ *vi* **1** hundirse *(barco)*. **2** ponerse *(sol, luna)*. **3** bajar, descender.

sinner ['sɪnəʳ] *n* pecador,-ra.

sip [sɪp] *n* sorbo.

sir [sɜːʳ] *n* **1** *fml* señor. **2** sir. ● **Dear Sir** muy señor mío.

siren ['saɪərən] *n* sirena.

sirloin ['sɜːlɔɪn] *n* solomillo.

sister ['sɪstəʳ] *n* hermana.

sister-in-law ['sɪstərɪnlɔː] *n* cuñada.

sit [sɪt] *vi* sentarse.

to sit down *vi* sentarse.

site [saɪt] *n* emplazamiento.

situation [sɪtjʊ'eɪʃən] *n* situación. ■ **"Situations vacant"** "Ofertas de trabajo".

six [sɪks] *adj-n* seis.

sixteen [sɪks'tiːn] *adj* dieciséis. ▶ *n* dieciséis.

sixteenth [sɪks'tiːnθ] *adj-n* decimosexto,-a.

sixth [sɪksθ] *adj-n* sexto,-a.

sixty ['sɪkstɪ] *adj-n* sesenta.

size [saɪz] *n* **1** tamaño. **2** talla *(de prenda)*. **3** número *(de zapatos)*.

skate [skeɪt] n patín. ► vi patinar.

skateboard ['skeɪtbɔːd] n monopatín.

skating ['skeɪtɪŋ] n patinaje. ■ **skating rink** pista de patinaje.

skeleton ['skelɪtən] n esqueleto. ■ **skeleton key** llave maestra.

sketch [sketʃ] n 1 boceto. 2 esquema. 3 sketch. ► vt bosquejar.

ski [skiː] n esquí. ► vi esquiar. ■ **ski lift** telesquí, telesilla; **ski resort** estación de esquí.

skid [skɪd] n patinazo. ► vi patinar.

skier ['skɪə'] n esquiador,-ra.

skiing ['skɪɪŋ] n esquí.

skill [skɪl] n habilidad.

skilled [skɪld] adj 1 especializado,-a. 2 hábil.

skim [skɪm] vt desnatar.

skin [skɪn] n 1 piel. 2 capa (de pintura). 3 nata.

skip[1] [skɪp] n salto. ► vi saltar. ■ **skipping rope** comba.

skip[2] [skɪp] n contenedor.

skirt [skɜːt] n falda. ■ **skirting board** GB zócalo, rodapié.

skittle ['skɪtəl] n bolo. ► npl **skittles** bolo.

skull [skʌl] n cráneo.

sky [skaɪ] n cielo.

skylight ['skaɪlaɪt] n tragaluz.

skyscraper ['skaɪskreɪpə'] n rascacielos.

slack [slæk] adj flojo,-a.

slacken ['slækən] vi 1 aflojarse. 2 reducirse, disminuir.

slam [slæm] n portazo. ► vt cerrar de golpe.

slang [slæŋ] n argot, jerga.

slap [slæp] n 1 palmadita (en la espalda). 2 bofetada.

slash [slæʃ] n 1 tajo. 2 cuchillada, navajazo. 3 barra oblicua.

slate [sleɪt] n pizarra.

slaughter ['slɔːtə'] n matanza. ► vt masacrar.

slave [sleɪv] n esclavo,-a.

sledge [sledʒ] n trineo.

sleep [sliːp] n sueño. ► vt-vi dormir.• **to go to sleep** irse a dormir.

sleeping ['sliːpɪŋ] adj. ■ **sleeping bag** saco de dormir; **sleeping car** coche-cama.

sleepwalker ['sliːpwɔːkə'] n sonámbulo,-a.

sleet [sliːt] n aguanieve. ► vi caer aguanieve.

sleeve [sliːv] n 1 manga. 2 funda (de disco).

sleigh [sleɪ] n trineo.

slice [slaɪs] n 1 rebanada (de pan). 2 loncha (de jamón). 3 tajada (de carne). 4 rodaja (de limón). 5 porción (de pastel). ► vt cortar a rebanadas/lonchas etc.

slide [slaɪd] n 1 resbalón. 2 tobogán. 3 diapositiva. 4 portaobjetos (de microscopio). ► vi 1 deslizarse. 2 resbalar.

snap

slight [slaɪt] *adj* ligero,-a.

slightly ['slaɪtlɪ] *adv* un poco.

slim [slɪm] *adj* **1** delgado,-a. ► *vi* adelgazar.

sling [slɪŋ] *n* cabestrillo.

slip[1] [slɪp] *n* **1** resbalón. **2** combinación *(prenda femenina)*. ► *vi* esbalar.

slip[2] [slɪp] *n* **1** papelito. **2** ficha.

slipper ['slɪpəʳ] *n* zapatilla.

slippery ['slɪpərɪ] *adj* resbaladizo,-a

slit [slɪt] *n* abertura.

slogan ['sləʊgən] *n* eslogan.

slope [sləʊp] *n* cuesta *(de montaña)*. ► *vi* inclinarse.

slot [slɒt] *n* **1** abertura. **2** ranura. **3** muesca. ■ **slot machine** distribuidor automático, tragaperras.

slow [sləʊ] *adj* **1** lento,-a. **2** atrasado,-a *(reloj)*.

to slow down *vi* reducir la velocidad.

slug [slʌg] *n* babosa.

slum [slʌm] *n* **1** barrio bajo. **2** chabola, tugurio.

slump [slʌmp] *n* crisis económica.

sly [slaɪ] *adj* **1** astuto,-a,. **2** furtivo,-a *(mirada)*.

smack [smæk] *n* bofetada, cachete. ► *vt* dar una bofetada a.

small [smɔːl] *adj* pequeño,-a. ■ **small ads** anuncios por palabras; **small change** cambio, suelto.

smallpox ['smɔːlpɒks] *n* viruela.

smart [smɑːt] *adj* **1** elegante. **2** US listo,-a.

smash [smæʃ] *n* smash, mate *(en tenis)*. ► *vt* romper. ■ **smash hit** gran éxito, exitazo.

smashing ['smæʃɪŋ] *adj* GB *fam* fenomenal.

smear [smɪəʳ] *n* mancha. ► *vt* **1** untar. **2** manchar.

smell [smel] *n* **1** olfato. **2** olor. ► *vt-vi* oler.

smelt[1] [smelt] *vt* fundir.

smelt[2] [smelt] *pt-pp* → smell.

smile [smaɪl] *n* sonrisa. ► *vi* sonreír.

smog [smɒg] *n* smog.

smoke [sməʊk] *n* humo. ► *vt-vi* fumar. ► *vt* ahumar. • **"No smoking"** "Prohibido fumar".

smoked [sməʊkt] *adj* ahumado,-a.

smoker ['sməʊkəʳ] *n* fumador,-ra.

smooth [smuːð] *adj* **1** liso,-a, llano,-a. **2** sin grumos *(líquido)*. **3** suave *(vino)*. ► *vt* alisar.

snack [snæk] *n* tentempié. • **to have a snack** picar algo. ■ **snack bar** cafetería, bar.

snail [sneɪl] *n* caracol.

snake [sneɪk] *n* serpiente.

snap [snæp] *n* foto. ► *vt* **1** partir *(en dos)*. **2** chasquear *(los dedos)*.

snapshot ['snæpʃɒt] n foto instantánea.

sneakers ['sniːkrz] npl US zapatillas de deporte.

sneeze [sniːz] n estornudo. ▶ vi estornudar.

sniff [snɪf] vt-vi oler, olfatear.

snip [snɪp] vt cortar.

sniper ['snaɪpəʳ] n francotirador,-ra.

snob [snɒb] n esnob, snob.

snore [snɔːʳ] n ronquido. ▶ vi roncar.

snorkel ['snɔːkəl] n tubo de bucear.

snout [snaʊt] n hocico.

snow [snəʊ] n nieve. ▶ vi nevar.

snowfall ['snəʊfɔːl] n nevada.

snowflake ['snəʊfleɪk] n copo de nieve.

snowman ['snəʊmæn] n muñeco de nieve.

so [səʊ] adv 1 tan, tanto,-a: *she's so tired that...*, está tan cansada que.. 2 mucho: *I miss you so*, te echo mucho de menos. 3 así: *Mary is there –So it is*, Mary está allí –Así es. 4 que sí, que no: *I guess so*, supongo que sí; *I don't think so*, creo que no. 5 también: *I went to the demonstration and so did David*, fui a la manifestación y David también. ▶ conj 1 así que, por lo tanto. 2 para. • **and so on** y así suce-

sivamente; **if so** en ese caso; **not so... as...** no tan... como...; **or so** más o menos; **so (that) ...** para (que) ...; **so what?** fam ¿y qué?

soak [səʊk] vt 1 poner en remojo. 2 empapar.

soap [səʊp] n jabón. ▶ vt enjabonar. ■ **soap opera** telenovela, culebrón.

sob [sɒb] n sollozo. ▶ vi sollozar.

sober ['səʊbəʳ] adj sobrio,-a.

so-called ['səʊkɔːld] adj llamado,-a.

soccer ['sɒkəʳ] n fútbol.

sociable ['səʊʃəbəl] adj sociable.

social ['səʊʃəl] adj social. ■ **social security** seguridad social; **social worker** asistente,-a social.

socialism ['səʊʃəlɪzəm] n socialismo.

socialize ['səʊʃəlaɪz] vi relacionarse, alternar.

society [sə'saɪətɪ] n sociedad.

sociology [səʊsɪ'blədʒɪ] n sociología.

sock [sɒk] n calcetín.

socket ['sɒkɪt] n 1 cuenca (del ojo). 2 enchufe.

soda ['səʊdə] n soda. ■ **soda water** soda, sifón.

sofa ['səʊfə] n sofá.

soft [sɒft] adj 1 blando,-a (cojín). 2 suave (música). ■ **soft drink** refresco.

soften ['sɒfən] *vt-vi* **1** ablandar(se). **2** suavizar(se).

software ['sɒftweəʳ] *n* software.

soil [sɔıl] *n* tierra. ► *vt* ensuciar, manchar.

solar ['səʊləʳ] *adj* solar.

sold [səʊld] *pt-pp* → sell.

solder ['sɒldəʳ] *n* soldadura. ► *vt* soldar.

soldier ['səʊldʒəʳ] *n* soldado.

sole¹ [səʊl] *n* **1** planta *(del pie)*. **2** suela *(de zapato)*.

sole² [səʊl] *n* lenguado *(pez)*.

sole³ [səʊl] *adj* único,-a.

solicitor [sə'lısıtəʳ] *n* **1** abogado,-a. **2** notario,-a.

solid ['sɒlıd] *adj* **1** sólido,-a. **2** macizo,-a. ► *n* sólido.

solidarity [sɒlı'dærıtı] *n* solidaridad.

solitary ['sɒlıtərı] *adj* **1** solitario,-a. **2** solo,-a.

solitude ['sɒlıtjuːd] *n* soledad.

solo ['səʊləʊ] *n* solo.

solution [sə'luːʃən] *n* solución.

solve [sɒlv] *vt* resolver.

some [sʌm] *adj* **1** unos,-as, algunos,-as *(con sust pl)*. **2** un poco *(de) (con sust sing)*. **3** cierto,-a, alguno,-a. **4** bastante. ► *pron* **1** algunos,-as, unos, -as. **2** algo, un poco.

somebody ['sʌmbədı] *pron* alguien.

somehow ['sʌmhaʊ] *adv* **1** de algún modo. **2** por alguna razón.

someone ['sʌmwʌn] *pron* → somebody.

something ['sʌmθıŋ] *n* algo.

sometime ['sʌmtaım] *adv* un día, algún día. ► *adj* antiguo, -a, ex-.

sometimes ['sʌmtaımz] *adv* a veces, de vez en cuando.

somewhat ['sʌmwɒt] *adv* algo, un tanto.

somewhere ['sʌmweəʳ] *adv* en alguna parte, a alguna parte. ► *pron* un lugar, un sitio.

son [sʌn] *n* hijo.

song [sɒŋ] *n* canción.

son-in-law ['sʌnınlɔː] *n* yerno.

soon [suːn] *adv* pronto. • **as soon as** en cuanto; **soon afterwards** poco después.

sooner ['suːnəʳ] *adv* más temprano. • **no sooner...** nada más...; **sooner or later** tarde o temprano; **the sooner the better** cuanto antes mejor.

soot [sʊt] *n* hollín.

soothe [suːð] *vt* **1** calmar *(nervios)*. **2** aliviar *(dolor)*.

soprano [sə'prɑːnəʊ] *n* soprano.

sore [sɔːʳ] *adj* dolorido,-a. *fam* enfadado,-a. ► *n* llaga.

sorrow ['sɒrəʊ] *n* pena, pesar.

sorry ['sɒrı] *interj* ¡perdón!, ¡disculpe! • **to be sorry** sentirlo.

sort [sɔːt] *n* clase, tipo. ► *vt* clasificar. • **all sorts of** todo tipo de.

so-so ['səʊsəʊ] *adv fam* así así.

sought [sɔːt] *pt-pp* → seek.

soul [səʊl] *n* alma.

sound[1] [saʊnd] *n* sonido. ► *vi* sonar.

sound[2] [saʊnd] *adj* **1** sano,-a. **2** en buen estado. **3** razonable. **4** robusto,-a.

soundproof ['saʊndpruːf] *adj* insonorizado,-a.

soundtrack ['saʊndtræk] *n* banda sonora.

soup [suːp] *n* **1** sopa, caldo. ■ **soup plate** plato hondo, plato sopero; **soup spoon** cuchara sopera.

sour ['saʊəʳ] *adj* ácido,-a, agrio,-a.

source [sɔːs] *n* fuente.

south [saʊθ] *n* sur. ► *adj* del sur. ► *adv* hacia el sur, al sur.

southern ['sʌðən] *adj* del sur.

souvenir [suːvəˈnɪəʳ] *n* recuerdo.

sovereign ['sɒvrɪn] *adj-n* soberano,-a.

sow[1] [saʊ] *n* cerda, puerca.

sow[2] [səʊ] *vt* sembrar.

space [speɪs] *n* espacio. ■ **space shuttle** transbordador espacial.

spacecraft ['speɪskrɑːft] *n* nave espacial.

spaceship ['speɪsʃɪp] *n* nave espacial.

spacious ['speɪʃəs] *adj* espacioso,-a, amplio,-a.

spade[1] [speɪd] *n* pala.

spade[2] [speɪd] *n* pica *(naipes)*.

span [spæn] *n* **1** lapso *(de tiempo)*. **2** envergadura *(de alas)*. **3** luz *(de arco)*.

spank [spæŋk] *vt* zurrar.

spanner ['spænəʳ] *n* llave de tuerca.

spare [speəʳ] *adj* **1** de sobra, libre. **2** de recambio, de repuesto. ► *n* recambio. ■ **spare room** habitación de invitados; **spare time** tiempo libre.

spark [spɑːk] *n* chispa. ■ **spark plug** bujía.

sparrow ['spærəʊ] *n* gorrión.

spasm ['spæzəm] *n* espasmo.

spat [spæt] *pt-pp* → spit.

speak [spiːk] *vi-vt* hablar. ► *vt* decir. • **so to speak** por así decirlo.

to speak out *vi* hablar claro.

speaker ['spiːkəʳ] *n* **1** persona que habla. **2** interlocutor,-ra. **3** conferenciante. **4** altavoz.

spear [spɪəʳ] *n* **1** lanza. **2** arpón.

special ['speʃəl] *adj* especial. ■ **special delivery** correo urgente.

specialist ['speʃəlɪst] *n* especialista.

species ['spiːʃiːz] *n* especie.

specific [spəˈsɪfɪk] *adj* específico,-a.

specify ['spesɪfaɪ] *vt* especificar.

specimen ['spesɪmən] *n* espécimen, muestra, ejemplar.

speck [spek] n 1 mota *(de polvo)*. 2 pizca.

spectacle ['spektəkəl] n espectáculo. ► npl **spectacles** gafas.

spectacular [spek'tækjulə'] adj espectacular.

spectator [spek'teitə'] n espectador,-ra.

speculate ['spekjuleit] vi especular.

sped [sped] pt-pp → speed.

speech [spi:tʃ] n 1 habla. 2 pronunciación. 3 discurso

speed [spi:d] n velocidad. ► vi 1 ir corriendo. 2 exceder el límite de velocidad. ■ **speed limit** límite de velocidad. **to speed up** vt-vi acelerar.

speedometer [spi'dɒmitə'] n velocímetro.

spell[1] [spel] n hechizo.

spell[2] [spel] n período, temporada.

spell[3] [spel] vt-vi deletrear. ► vt fig significar.

spelling ['speliŋ] n ortografía. ■ **spelling mistake** falta de ortografía.

spelt [spelt] pt-pp → spell.

spend [spend] vt 1 gastar *(dinero)*. 2 pasar.

spent [spent] pt-pp → spend.

sperm [spɜːm] n esperma.

sphere [sfiə'] n esfera.

spice [spais] n especia. ► vt sazonar, condimentar.

spicy ['spaisi] adj picante.

spider ['spaidə'] n araña. ■ **spider's web** telaraña.

spike [spaik] n 1 punta. 2 pincho. 3 clavo.

spill [spil] n derrame. ► vt-vi derramar(se), verter(se).

spin [spin] n 1 vuelta. 2 centrifugado *(de lavadora)*. 3 efecto *(de pelota)*. ► vt 1 dar vueltas (a). 2 centrifugar.

spinach ['spinidʒ] n espinacas.

spin-dryer [spin'draiə'] n secadora.

spine [spain] n 1 espina dorsal. 2 lomo *(de libro)*.

spiral ['spaiərəl] n espiral. ■ **spiral staircase** escalera de caracol.

spire [spaiə'] n aguja.

spirit[1] ['spirit] n alcohol. ► npl **spirits** licores.

spirit[2] ['spirit] n espíritu. ► npl **spirits** humor, moral. • **to be in high spirits** estar animado,-a; **to be in low spirits** estar desanimado,-a.

spit[1] [spit] n asador, espetón.

spit[2] [spit] n esputo. ► vt-vi escupir.

spite [spait] n. • **in spite of** a pesar de.

splash [splæʃ] n 1 chapoteo. 2 salpicadura. ► vt salpicar, rociar. ► vi chapotear.

splendid ['splendid] adj espléndido.

splinter ['splintə'] n astilla.

split [splɪt] n 1 grieta (en madera). 2 desgarrón (en tela). 3 división. ▶ adj 1 partido,-a. 2 dividido,-a. ▶ vt-vi 1 agrietar(se). 2 partir(se). 3 rajar(se), rasgar(se).

to split up vt partir, dividir. ▶ vi separarse (pareja).

spoil [spɔɪl] vt 1 echar a perder. 2 malcriar.

spoke¹ [spəʊk] pt → speak.

spoke² [spəʊk] n radio (de rueda).

spoken ['spəʊkən] pp → speak.

spokesman ['spəʊksmən] n portavoz.

sponge [spʌndʒ] n esponja. ■ **sponge cake** bizcocho.

sponsor ['spɒnsəʳ] n patrocinador,-ra. ▶ vt patrocinar.

spontaneous [spɒn'teɪnɪəs] adj espontáneo,-a.

spool [spuːl] n carrete, bobina.

spoon [spuːn] n cuchara.

spoonful ['spuːnfʊl] n cucharada.

sport [spɔːt] n deporte.

sportsman ['spɔːtsmən] n deportista.

sportswear ['spɔːtsweəʳ] n ropa deportiva.

sportswoman ['spɔːtswʊmən] n deportista.

spot [spɒt] n 1 lunar. 2 mancha. 3 grano (en cara). 4 sitio, lugar. 5 aprieto, apuro. 6 spot (publicitario). ▶ vt 1 darse cuenta de. 2 notar.

spotlight ['spɒtlaɪt] n foco.

spouse [spaʊz] n cónyuge.

spout [spaʊt] n 1 pico (de jarra). 2 surtidor (de fuente).

sprain [spreɪn] n torcedura. ▶ vt torcerse.

sprang [spræŋ] pt → spring.

spray [spreɪ] n 1 espuma (del mar). 2 spray. ■ **spray can** aerosol.

spread [spred] ▶ vt-vi 1 extender(se). 2 desplegar(se) (alas). 3 propagar(se). ▶ vt untar (mantequilla).

spreadsheet ['spredʃiːt] n hoja de cálculo.

spree [spriː] n juerga.

spring [sprɪŋ] n 1 primavera. 2 manantial, fuente. 3 muelle. 4 ballesta (de coche). ▶ vi saltar. ■ **spring onion** cebolleta; **spring roll** rollito de primavera.

springboard ['sprɪŋbɔːd] n trampolín.

sprinkle ['sprɪŋkəl] vt rociar.

sprinkler ['sprɪŋkələʳ] n aspersor.

sprint [sprɪnt] n esprin. ▶ vi esprintar.

sprout [spraʊt] n brote. ▶ vi brotar.

sprung [sprʌŋ] pp → spring.

spun [spʌn] pt-pp → spin.

spur [spɜːʳ] n espuela.

spurt [spɜːt] n chorro.

spy [spaɪ] n espía. ▶ vi espiar.

squad [skwɒd] n brigada.

squadron ['skwɒdrən] n escuadrón.

square [skweə'] n 1 cuadrado. 2 cuadro (en tela). 3 casilla (en tablero). 4 plaza. ► adj cuadrado,-a. ► vt-vi cuadrar. ► vt elevar al cuadrado. ■ **square brackets** corchetes.

squash[1] [skuɒʃ] n 1 zumo. 2 squash. ► vt aplastar.

squash[2] [skuɒʃ] n calabaza.

squat [skwɒt] adj rechoncho,-a. ► vi 1 agacharse. 2 ocupar ilegalmente.

squatter ['skwɒtə'] n okupa.

squeak [skwiːk] n 1 chillido (de animal). 2 chirrido (de neumático). ► vi 1 chillar (animal). 2 chirriar (neumático).

squeeze [skwiːz] n 1 apretón (de manos). 2 aprieto. ► vt 1 apretar. 2 exprimir (limón).

squid [skwɪd] n calamar.

squint [skwɪnt] n bizquera.

squirrel ['skwɪrəl] n ardilla.

stab [stæb] n puñalada. ► vt-vi apuñalar. ■ **stab of pain** punzada de dolor.

stability [stə'bɪlɪtɪ] n estabilidad.

stable[1] ['steɪbəl] adj estable.

stable[2] ['steɪbəl] n cuadra, establo.

stack [stæk] n montón, pila.

stadium ['steɪdɪəm] n estadio.

staff [stɑːf] n personal.

stage [steɪdʒ] n 1 etapa. 2 escenario. • **on stage** en escena.

stagger ['stægə'] vi tambalearse.

stain [steɪn] n mancha. ► vt-vi manchar(se). ■ **stain remover** quitamanchas.

stainless ['steɪnləs] adj inoxidable. ■ **stainless steel** acero inoxidable.

stair [steə'] n escalón, peldaño. ► npl **stairs** escalera.

staircase ['steəkeɪs] n escalera.

stake[1] [steɪk] n 1 apuesta. 2 intereses. ► vt apostar.

stake[2] [steɪk] n estaca, palo.

stalemate ['steɪlmeɪt] n tablas (en ajedrez).

stalk[1] [stɔːk] n 1 tallo (de planta). 2 rabillo (de fruta).

stalk[2] [stɔːk] vt acechar.

stall [stɔːl] n 1 puesto (de mercado). 2 caseta (de feria). ► npl **stalls** platea.

stammer ['stæmə'] n tartamudeo. ► vi tartamudear.

stamp [stæmp] n 1 sello, timbre. 2 tampón. ► vt sellar.

stand [stænd] n 1 postura. 2 pie (de lámpara). 3 puesto (de mercado). 4 pabellón (de feria). 5 plataforma. 6 tribuna. ► vi 1 estar de pie, ponerse de pie. 2 estar, encontrarse. 3 seguir en pie (oferta). 4 estar. ► vt fam aguantar: **I can't stand him**, no lo aguanto.

to stand for vt 1 significar. 2 defender, representar.

to stand out vi destacar.

to stand up vi ponerse de pie.

standard ['stændəd] n 1 nivel. 2 criterio. 3 norma. 4 patrón. ► adj normal, estándar.

standby ['stændbaɪ] n sustituto,-a. • **to be on standby** estar en lista de espera.

stank [stæŋk] pt → stink.

staple[1] ['steɪpəl] n producto básico.

staple[2] ['steɪpəl] n grapa.

stapler ['steɪpələ'] n grapadora.

star [staː'] n estrella. ► adj estelar. ► vi protagonizar.

starboard ['staːbəd] n estribor.

starch [staːtʃ] n almidón, fécula.

stare [steə'] n mirada fija. ► vi mirar fijamente.

starfish ['staːfɪʃ] n estrella de mar.

start [staːt] n 1 principio. 2 salida (de carrera). ► vt-vi 1 empezar. 2 arrancar (coche).

to start up vt-vi arrancar.

starter ['staːtə'] n 1 juez de salida. 2 motor de arranque. • **for starters** 1 para empezar. 2 como primer plato.

starvation [staːˈveɪʃən] n hambre, inanición.

starve [staːv] vi 1 pasar hambre. 2 tener mucha hambre.

state [steɪt] n estado. ► vt exponer.

statement ['steɪtmənt] n declaración, afirmación.

statesman ['steɪtsmən] n estadista, hombre de Estado.

station ['steɪʃən] n 1 estación (de autobuses, tren). 2 emisora (de radio). 3 canal (de TV).

stationery ['steɪʃənərɪ] n artículos de escritorio.

statistics [stəˈtɪstɪks] n estadística.

statue ['stætjuː] n estatua.

status ['steɪtəs] n 1 estado. 2 estatus.

stave [steɪv] n pentagrama.

stay [steɪ] n estancia. ► vi 1 quedarse, permanecer. 2 alojarse (en hotel).

to stay in vi quedarse en casa.

to stay on vi quedarse.

to stay up vi no acostarse.

steady ['stedɪ] adj 1 firme, estable. 2 constante (movimiento).

steak [steɪk] n bistec, filete.

steal [stiːl] vt-vi robar.

steam [stiːm] n vapor. ► vt cocer al vapor.■ **steam engine** máquina de vapor; **steam iron** plancha de vapor.

steamer ['stiːmə'] n → steamship.

steamroller ['stiːmrəʊlə'] n apisonadora.

steamship ['stiːmʃɪp] n buque de vapo.

steel [stiːl] n acero.■ **steel wool** estropajo de aluminio.

steep[1] [stiːp] adj 1 empinado,-a, escarpado,-a (colina). 2 fig excesivo,-a (precio).

steep² [stiːp] *vt* remojar.
steeple ['stiːpəl] *n* chapitel.
steer [stɪəʳ] *vt* conducir.
steering ['stɪərɪŋ] *n* dirección.
■ **steering wheel** volante.
stem [stem] *n* **1** tallo *(de planta)*. **2** pie *(de vaso)*.
step [step] *n* **1** paso. **2** escalón, peldaño. ► *vi* dar un paso, andar.
to step aside *vi* apartarse.
stepbrother ['stepbrʌðəʳ] *n* hermanastro.
stepchild ['steptʃaɪld] *n* hijastro,-a.
stepdaughter ['stepdɔːtəʳ] *n* hijastra.
stepfather ['stepfɑːðəʳ] *n* padrastro.
stepladder ['steplædəʳ] *n* escalera de mano.
stepmother ['stepmʌðəʳ] *n* madrastra.
stepsister ['stepsɪstəʳ] *n* hermanastra.
stepson ['stepsʌn] *n* hijastro.
stereo ['sterɪəʊ] *adj* estereofónico,-a.
sterile ['steraɪl] *adj* estéril. esterilizado,-a.
sterling ['stɜːlɪŋ] *n* libra esterlina.
stern [stɜːn] *n* popa.
stew [stjuː] *n* estofado, guisado. ► *vt* estofar, guisar.
steward ['stjuːəd] *n* **1** camarero *(de barco)*. **2** auxiliar de vuelo *(de avión)*.

stewardess ['stjuːədes] *n* **1** camarera *(de barco)*. **2** azafata *(de avión)*.
stick¹ [stɪk] *n* **1** palo. **2** bastón *(para caminar)*.
stick² [stɪk] *vt* **1** clavar, hincar *(punta)*. **2** pegar *(con pegamento)*. ► *vi* atrancarse.
sticker ['stɪkəʳ] *n* **1** etiqueta adhesiva. **2** pegatina.
stiff [stɪf] *adj* rígido,-a, tieso,-a.
● **to feel stiff** tener agujetas.
still [stɪl] *adj* **1** quieto,-a. **2** tranquilo,-a *(lago)*. **3** sin gas *(agua)*. ► *adv* **1** todavía, aún. **2** aun así. **3** sin embargo.
■ **still life** ART naturaleza muerta, bodegón.
stimulate ['stɪmjʊleɪt] *vt* estimular.
stimulus ['stɪmjʊləs] *n* estímulo.
sting [stɪŋ] *n* **1** aguijón *(de avispa)*. **2** picadura *(herida)*. ► *vt-vi* picar.
stingy ['stɪndʒɪ] *adj* tacaño,-a.
stink [stɪŋk] *n* peste, hedor. ► *vi* apestar, heder.
stipulate ['stɪpjʊleɪt] *vt* estipular.
stir [stɜːʳ] *vt* remover .
stirrup ['stɪrəp] *n* estribo.
stitch [stɪtʃ] *n* **1** puntada *(al coser)*. **2** punto. ► *vt* **1** coser. **2** suturar.
stock [stɒk] *n* **1** reserva. **2** COMM existencias. **3** capital social. **4** ganado. **5** caldo. ●**to**

be out of stock estar agotado,-a. ■ **stock exchange** bolsa; **stock market** bolsa de valores.

stockbroker ['stɒkbrəʊkəʳ] n corredor,-ra de bolsa.

stocking ['stɒkɪŋ] n media.

stole[1] [stəʊl] pt → steal.

stole[2] [stəʊl] n estola.

stolen ['stəʊlən] pp → steal.

stomach ['stʌmək] n estómago.

stone [stəʊn] n 1 piedra. 2 hueso (de cereza, aceituna).

stood [stʊd] pt-pp → stand.

stool [stuːl] n taburete.

stop [stɒp] n 1 parada, alto. 2 punto (signo de puntuación). ► vt 1 parar. 2 impedir, evitar. 3 poner fin a (injusticia). 4 dejar de: *stop smoking!*, ideja de fumar! ► vi 1 pararse. 2 terminar. ► interj ¡pare!, ¡alto! ■ **stop sign** señal de stop.

stopover ['stɒpəʊvəʳ] n escala (de avión).

stopper ['stɒpəʳ] n tapón.

stopwatch ['stɒpwɒtʃ] n cronómetro.

storage ['stɔːrɪdʒ] n almacenamiento.

store [stɔːʳ] n tienda, almacén. ► vt almacenar.

storey ['stɔːrɪ] n piso, planta.

stork [stɔːk] n cigüeña.

storm [stɔːm] n tormenta.

story ['stɔːrɪ] n historia, cuento.

stout [staʊt] n cerveza negra.

stove [stəʊv] n 1 estufa. 2 cocina, hornillo.

straight [streɪt] adj 1 recto,-a. 2 liso,-a (pelo). 3 seguido,-a. 4 solo,-a (bebida). ► adv 1 en línea recta. 2 directamente.► n recta (en carrera). ● **straight ahead** todo recto.

straightaway [streɪtəˈweɪ] adv en seguida.

straightforward [streɪtˈfɔːwəd] adj franco,-a, honrado,-a.

strain [streɪn] n 1 presión, tensión. 2 torcedura. ► vt 1 estirar (cuerda). 2 torcerse (músculo). 3 forzar (vista, voz).

strait [streɪt] n GEOG estrecho.

strand [strænd] n 1 hebra, hilo. 2 mechón.

strange [streɪndʒ] adj extraño,-a.

stranger ['streɪndʒəʳ] n extraño,-a.

strangle ['stræŋgəl] vt estrangular.

strap [stræp] n 1 correa (de reloj). 2 tirante (de vestido).

strategy ['strætədʒɪ] n estrategia.

straw [strɔː] n paja.

strawberry ['strɔːbərɪ] n fresa.

stray [streɪ] vi perderse.

streak ['striːk] n 1 raya, lista. 2 fig racha (de suerte).

stream [striːm] n 1 arroyo. 2 corriente. ► vi 1 manar. 2 fig desfilar (gente).

streamer ['stri:mə^r] n serpentina.

street [stri:t] n calle.

streetlamp ['stri:tlæmp] n farola.

strength [streŋθ] n fuerza. ■ **strength of will** fuerza de voluntad.

strengthen ['streŋθən] vt-vi fortalecer(se).

stress [stres] n 1 estrés. 2 acento. ► vt 1 recalcar, subrayar. 2 acentuar.

stretch [stretʃ] n 1 extensión. 2 tramo (de terreno). 3 intervalo (de tiempo). ► vt-vi 1 extender(se) (terreno). 2 estirar(se).

to stretch out vt 1 estirar (piernas). 2 alargar (mano). ► vi 1 estirarse. 2 alargarse.

stretcher ['stretʃə^r] n camilla.

strict [strɪkt] adj estricto,-a.

stride [straɪd] n zancada.

strike [straɪk] n huelga. ► vt 1 pegar, golpear. 2 chocar contra. ► vi 1 atacar. 2 hacer huelga. 3 dar la hora. • **to be on strike** estar en huelga.

striker ['straɪkə^r] n 1 huelguista. 2 delantero,-a (en fútbol).

string [strɪŋ] n 1 cuerda, cordón. 2 ristra (de ajos, mentiras). 3 serie (de acontecimientos).

strip^1 [strɪp] n 1 tira. 2 franja (de tierra).

strip^2 [strɪp] vi desnudarse.

stripe [straɪp] n raya.

stroke [strəʊk] n 1 golpe. 2 brazada (en natación). 3 campanada. ► vt acariciar.

stroll [strəʊl] n paseo. ► vi pasear, dar un paseo.

strong [strɒŋ] adj fuerte. ► adv fuerte.

struck [strʌk] pt-pp → strike.

structure ['strʌktʃə^r] n estructura. ► vt estructurar.

struggle ['strʌgəl] n lucha. ► vi luchar.

stub [stʌb] n 1 colilla (de cigarrillo). 2 resguardo.

stubble ['stʌbəl] n 1 rastrojo. 2 barba (incipiente).

stubborn ['stʌbən] adj terco,-a.

stuck [stʌk] pt-pp → stick.

stud^1 [stʌd] n tachuela.

stud^2 [stʌd] n semental.

student ['stju:dənt] n estudiante.

studio ['stju:dɪəʊ] n estudio. ■ **studio flat** estudio.

study ['stʌdɪ] n estudio. ► vt-vi estudiar.

stuff [stʌf] n 1 fam cosas, trastos. 2 cosa. ► vt rellenar. 1 disecar. 2 atiborrar. • **to stuff oneself** fam hartarse de comida.

stuffing ['stʌfɪŋ] n relleno.

stuffy ['stʌfɪ] adj cargado,-a, mal ventilado,-a.

stumble ['stʌmbəl] vi tropezar.

stun [stʌn] vt aturdir.

stung [stʌŋ] pt-pp → sting.

stunk [stʌŋk] *pt-pp* → stink.
stunning ['stʌnɪŋ] *adj* 1 pasmoso. 2 estupendo,-a.
stuntman ['stʌntmæn] *n* doble, especialista.
stuntwoman ['stʌntwumən] *n* doble, especialista.
stupid ['stju:pɪd] *adj-n* tonto,-a.
stutter ['stʌtə'] *n* tartamudeo. ► *vi* tartamudear.
style [staɪl] *n* estilo.
stylish ['staɪlɪʃ] *adj* elegante.
subdue [səb'dju:] *vt* someter, dominar.
subject [(*n-adj*) 'sʌbdʒekt, (*vb*) səb'dʒekt] *n* 1 tema. 2 asignatura. 3 súbdito. 4 sujeto. ► *adj* sujeto,-a.
subjunctive [səb'dʒʌŋktɪv] *adj* subjuntivo,-a. ► *n* subjuntivo.
sublet [sʌb'let] *vt-vi* realquilar.
submarine [sʌbmə'ri:n] *n* submarino.
submerge [səb'mɜ:dʒ] *vt-vi* sumergir(se).
submit [səb'mɪt] *vt* someter. ► *vi* someterse.
subordinate [(*adj-n*) sə'bɔ:dɪnət, (*vb*) sə'bɔ:dɪneɪt] *adj-n* subordinado,-a. ► *vt* subordinar.
subscribe [səb'skraɪb] *vi* 1 subscribirse (*a revista*). 2 suscribir (*opinión*).
subscriber [səb'scraɪbə'] *n* 1 subscriptor,-ra (*de revista*). 2 abonado,-a (*de servicio*).

subscription [səb'skɪpʃən] *n* 1 subscripción (*de revista*). 2 abono (*de servicio*).
subsidize ['sʌbsɪdaɪz] *vt* subvencionar.
subsidy ['sʌbsɪdɪ] *n* subsidio.
substance ['sʌbstəns] *n* sustancia.
substitute ['sʌbstɪtju:t] *n* substituto,-a. ► *vt* sustituir.
subtle ['sʌtəl] *adj* sutil.
subtract [səb'trækt] *vt* restar.
suburb ['sʌbɜ:b] *n* barrio periférico, barrio residencial. ■ **the suburbs** las afueras.
subway ['sʌbweɪ] *n* 1 GB paso subterráneo. 2 US metro.
succeed [sək'si:d] *vi* tener éxito.
success [sək'ses] *n* éxito.
successful [sək'sesful] *adj* que tiene éxito.
successive [sək'sesɪv] *adj* sucesivo,-a.
such [sʌtʃ] *adj* 1 tal, semejante. 2 tan … como, tanto, -a … que. ► *adv* muy, mucho,-a, tan, tanto,-a.
suck [sʌk] *n* *vt-vi* chupar.
sudden ['sʌdən] *adj* repentino,-a.
suddenly ['sʌdənlɪ] *adv* de repente, de pronto.
sue [su:] *vt-vi* demandar.
suede [sweɪd] *n* ante, gamuza.
suffer ['sʌfə'] *vt-vi* sufrir.
sufficient [sə'fɪʃənt] *adj* suficiente.

suffix ['sʌfɪks] *n* sufijo.

suffocate ['sʌfəkeɪt] *vt-vi* asfixiar(se).

sugar ['ʃʊgəʳ] *n* azúcar. ■ **sugar bowl** azucarero.

sugarbeet ['ʃʊgəbiːt] *n* remolacha azucarera.

suggest [sə'dʒest] *vt* **1** sugerir. **2** implicar.

suggestion [sə'dʒestʃən] *n* sugerencia.

suicide ['sjuːɪsaɪd] *n* suicidio. ● **to commit suicide** suicidarse.

suit [sjuːt] *n* **1** traje. **2** pleito. **3** palo *(de naipes).* ► *vt* **1** convenir a. **2** sentar bien.

suitable ['sjuːtəbəl] *adj* conveniente.

suitcase ['suːtkeɪs] *n* maleta.

suite [swiːt] *n* suite.

sultry ['sʌltrɪ] *adj* bochornoso,-a.

sum [sʌm] *n* suma.

summarize ['sʌməraɪz] *vt* resumir.

summary ['sʌmərɪ] *n* resumen.

summer ['sʌməʳ] *n* verano.

summit ['sʌmɪt] *n* cumbre.

sun [sʌn] *n* sol.

sunbathe ['sʌnbeɪð] *vi* tomar el sol.

Sunday ['sʌndeɪ] *n* domingo.

sunflower ['sʌnflaʊəʳ] *n* girasol.

sung [sʌŋ] *pp →* sing.

sunglasses ['sʌnglɑːsɪz] *npl* gafas de sol.

sunk [sʌŋk] *pp →* sink.

sunlight ['sʌnlaɪt] *n* luz del sol.

sunny ['sʌnɪ] *adj* soleado,-a.

sunrise ['sʌnraɪz] *n* salida del sol, amanecer.

sunset ['sʌnset] *n* puesta del sol.

sunshine ['sʌnʃaɪn] *n* luz del sol.

sunstroke ['sʌnstrəʊk] *n* insolación.

suntan ['sʌntæn] *n* bronceado.

superb [suː'pɜːb] *adj* estupendo,-a.

superficial [suːpə'fɪʃəl] *adj* superficial.

superintendent [suːpərɪn'tendənt] *n* inspector,-ra.

superior [suː'pɪərɪəʳ] *adj* superior. ► *n* superior,-ra.

superlative [suː'pɜːlətɪv] *adj* superlativo,-a. ► *n* superlativo.

supermarket [suːpə'mɑːkɪt] *n* supermercado.

supernatural [suːpə'nætʃərəl] *adj* sobrenatural.

superstitious [sjuːpə'stɪʃəs] *adj* supersticioso,-a.

supervise ['suːpəvaɪz] *vt* supervisar.

supper ['sʌpəʳ] *n* cena.

supplement [(n) 'sʌplɪmənt, (vb) 'sʌplɪment] *n* suplemento.

supplier [sə'plaɪəʳ] *n* proveedor,-ra.

supply [sə'plaɪ] *vt* **1** suministrar, abastecer. ► *n* suministro.

▶ *npl* **supplies** provisiones. • **supply and demand** la oferta y la demanda.

support [sə'pɔːt] *n* apoyo. ▶ *vt* **1** sostener *(peso)*. **2** apoyar *(causa)*.

supporter [sə'pɔːtə'] *n* **1** POL partidiario,-a. **2** seguidor,-ra.

suppose [sə'pəʊz] *vt* suponer. • **I suppose so/not** supongo que sí/no.

suppository [sə'pɒzɪtərɪ] *n* supositorio.

suppress [sə'pres] *vt* **1** suprimir *(texto)*. **2** reprimir *(sentimientos, revuelta)*.

supreme [suː'priːm] *adj* supremo,-a.

surcharge ['sɜːtʃɑːdʒ] *n* recargo.

sure [[ʃʊə'] *adj* seguro,-a, cierto,-a. ▶ *adv* **1** claro. **2** seguro. **3** de verdad.

surf [sɜːf] *n* **1** oleaje. **2** espuma. ▶ *vi* hacer surf. • **to surf the Net** navegar por Internet.

surface ['sɜːfəs] *n* superficie.

surgeon ['sɜːdʒən] *n* cirujano,-a.

surgery ['sɜːdʒərɪ] *n* **1** cirugía. **2** GB consultorio, consulta.

surname ['sɜːneɪm] *n* apellido.

surplus ['sɜːpləs] ▶ *n* **1** excedente. **2** superávit.

surprise [sə'praɪz] *n* sorpresa. ▶ *vt* sorprender.

surprising [sə'praɪzɪŋ] *adj* sorprendente.

surrender [sə'rendə'] *n* rendición. ▶ *vt-vi* rendir(se).

surround [sə'raʊnd] *vt* rodear.

surroundings [sə'raʊndɪŋs] *npl* alrededores.

survey ['sɜːveɪ] *n* **1** sondeo *(de opinión)*. **2** encuesta, estudio *(de tendencias)*.

survive [sə'vaɪv] *vt-vi* sobrevivir (a).

survivor [sə'vaɪvə'] *n* superviviente.

suspect [(*adj-n*) 'sʌspekt, (*vb*) sə'spekt] *adj-n* sospechoso,-a. ▶ *vt* sospechar.

suspend [sə'spend] *vt* suspender *(partido)*.

suspender [sə'spendə'] *n* liga. ▶ *npl* **suspenders** tirantes.

suspense [səs'spens] *n* suspense.

suspension [sə'spenʃən] *n* suspensión *(de partido)*. expulsión *(de alumno)*.

suspicion [sə'spɪʃən] *n* sospecha.

suspicious [sə'spɪʃəs] *adj* **1** sospechoso,-a. **2** desconfiado,-a.

sustain [sə'steɪn] *vt* sostener.

swallow[1] ['swɒləʊ] *n* **1** trago *(de bebida)*. **2** bocado *(de comida)*. ▶ *vt-vi* tragar(se).

swallow[2] ['swɒləʊ] *n* golondrina *(ave)*.

swam [swæm] *pt* → swim.

swamp [swɒmp] *n* pantano, ciénaga.

swan [swɒn] *n* cisne.

swap [swɒp] *vt-vi fam* intercambiar, cambiar.

swarm [swɔːm] *n* enjambre.

swear [sweəʳ] *vt-vi* jurar. ► *vi* decir palabrotas.

swearword ['sweəwɜːd] *n* palabrota, taco.

sweat [swet] *n* sudor. ► *vt-vi* sudar.

sweater ['swetəʳ] *n* suéter.

sweep [swiːp] *n* **1** barrido. **2** redada *(de policía).* ► *vt-vi* barrer.

sweeper ['swiːpəʳ] *n* barrendero,-a.

sweet [swiːt] *adj* dulce. ► *n* **1** caramelo, golosina. **2** postre.
■ **sweet potato** boniato.

sweeten ['swiːtən] *vt* endulzar.

swelling ['swelɪŋ] *n* hinchazón.

swept [swept] *pt-pp* → sweep.

swim [swɪm] *n* baño. ► *vi* nadar.

swimmer ['swɪməʳ] *n* nadador,-ra.

swimming ['swɪmɪŋ] *n* natación. ■ **swimming baths** piscina *(pública)*; **swimming costume** bañador; **swimming pool** piscina; **swimming trunks** bañador.

swimsuit ['swɪmsuːt] *n* bañador, traje de baño.

swindle ['swɪndəl] *n* estafa, timo. ► *vt* estafar, timar.

swing [swɪŋ] *n* columpio. ► *vt-vi* **1** balancear(se). **2** columpiar(se).

switch [swɪtʃ] *n* interruptor. ► *vt* cambiar de.

to switch off *vt* apagar .

to switch on *vt* encender.

sword [sɔːd] *n* espada.

swordfish ['sɔːdfɪʃ] *n* pez espada.

swore [swɔːʳ] *pt* → swear.

sworn [swɔːn] *pp* → swear.

swum [swʌm] *pp* → swim.

swung [swʌŋ] *pt-pp* → swing.

syllable ['sɪləbəl] *n* sílaba.

syllabus ['sɪləbəs] *n* plan de estudios.

symbol ['sɪmbəl] *n* símbolo.

sympathize ['sɪmpəθaɪz] *vi* **1** compadecerse. **2** comprender.

sympathy ['sɪmpəθɪ] *n* **1** compasión. **2** pésame. **3** comprensión.

symphony ['sɪmfənɪ] *n* sinfonía.

symptom ['sɪmptəm] *n* síntoma.

synonym ['sɪnənɪm] *n* sinónimo.

syntax ['sɪntæks] *n* sintaxis.

synthesis ['sɪnθəsɪs] *n* síntesis.

synthetic [sɪn'θetɪk] *adj* sintético,-a.

syringe ['sɪrɪndʒ] *n* jeringuilla.

syrup ['sɪrəp] *n* **1** jarabe. **2** almíbar.

system ['sɪstəm] *n* sistema.

tab 194

T

tab [tæb] *n* **1** lengüeta. **2** etiqueta *(en ropa)*.

table ['teɪbəl] *n* **1** mesa. **2** tabla, cuadro. ■ **table football** futbolín; **table tennis** tenis de mesa.

tablecloth ['teɪbəlklɒθ] *n* mantel.

tablespoon ['teɪbəlspuːn] *n* cucharón.

tablet ['tæblət] *n* pastilla.

tabloid ['tæblɔɪd] *n* periódico.

tact [tækt] *n* tacto.

tactics ['tæktɪks] *npl* táctica.

tadpole ['tædpəʊl] *n* renacuajo.

tag [tæg] *n* etiqueta.

tail [teɪl] *vt* seguir. ► *n* cola. ► *npl* **tails** cruz *(de moneda)*.

tailor ['teɪlə'] *n* sastre,-a.

take [teɪk] *vt* **1** tomar, coger. **2** llevar. **3** requerir, necesitar. **4** apuntar, anotar. **5** ocupar. **6** llevar, tardar.

to take away *vt* **1** llevarse. **2** quitar, sacar. **3** restar.

to take back *vt* **1** devolver. **2** retractarse.

to take down *vt* apuntar.

to take off *vt* quitarse *(ropa)*. ► *vi* despegar *(avión)*.

to take out *vt* invitar a salir.

takeaway ['teɪkəweɪ] *n* establecimiento que vende comida para llevar.

taken ['teɪkən] *pp* → take.

takeoff ['teɪkɒf] *n* despegue.

talcum powder ['tælkəmpaʊdə'] *n* polvos de talco.

tale [teɪl] *n* cuento.

talent ['tælənt] *n* talento. ■ **talent scout** cazatalentos.

talk [tɔːk] *vt-vi* hablar. ► *n* conversación. ■ **talk show** programa de entrevistas.

talkative ['tɔːkətɪv] *adj* hablador,-ra.

tall [tɔːl] *adj* alto,-a.

tambourine [tæmbə'riːn] *n* pandereta.

tame [teɪm] *vt* domar.

tampon ['tæmpɒn] *n* tampón.

tan [tæn] *n* bronceado. ► *vi* ponerse moreno,-a.

tangent ['tændʒənt] *n* tangente.

tangerine [tændʒəriːn] *n* mandarina.

tank [tæŋk] *n* **1** depósito. **2** tanque.

tanker ['tæŋkə'] *n* **1** buque cisterna. **2** petrolero. **3** camión cisterna.

tantrum ['tæntrəm] *n* rabieta.

tap[1] [tæp] *n* grifo.

tap[2] [tæp] *n* golpecito.

tape [teɪp] *n* cinta. ► *vt* grabar. ■ **tape measure** cinta métrica; **tape recorder** magnetófono, grabadora.

tapestry ['tæpəstrɪ] *n* tapiz.

tar [tɑː'] *n* alquitrán.

target ['tɑːgɪt] *n* blanco, objetivo.

tariff ['tærɪf] *n* tarifa.

tarmac ['tɑːmæk] *n* asfalto.

tart [tɑːt] *n* tarta, pastel.

task [tɑːsk] *n* tarea, labor.

taste [teɪst] *n* sabor, gusto. ▶ *vt* **1** probar *(comida)*. **2** catar *(vino)*. ▶ *vi* saber.

tasteless ['teɪstləs] *adj* **1** de mal gusto. **2** insípido,-a, soso,-a.

tattoo [tə'tuː] *n* tatuaje. ▶ *vt* tatuar.

taught [tɔːt] *pt-pp* → teach.

tavern ['tævən] *n* taberna.

tax [tæks] *n* impuesto. ▶ *vt* gravar. ▪ **tax free** libre de impuestos; **tax return** declaración de la renta.

taxi ['tæksɪ] *n* taxi. ▪ **taxi driver** taxista.

taxpayer ['tækspeɪəʳ] *n* contribuyente.

tea [tiː] *n* **1** té. **2** merienda. **3** cena.

teach [tiːtʃ] *vt* **1** enseñar. **2** dar clases de *(asignatura)*.

teacher ['tiːtʃəʳ] *n* maestro,-a, profesor,-ra.

teaching ['tiːtʃɪŋ] *n* enseñanza.

teacup ['tiːkʌp] *n* taza de té.

team [tiːm] *n* equipo.

teapot ['tiːpɒt] *n* tetera.

tear¹ [tɪəʳ] *n* lágrima. ▪ **tear gas** gas lacrimógeno.

tear² [teəʳ] *n* rotura, siete. ▶ *vt* rasgar.

tease [tiːz] *vt* burlarse.

teaspoon ['tiːspuːn] *n* cucharilla.

teat [tiːt] *n* **1** teta. **2** tetina *(de botella)*.

technical ['teknɪkəl] *adj* técnico,-a.

technique [tek'niːk] *n* técnica.

technology [tek'nɒlədʒɪ] *n* tecnología.

teddy bear ['tedɪbeəʳ] *n* osito de peluche.

teenager ['tiːneɪdʒəʳ] *n* adolescente *(de 13 a 19 años)*.

tee-shirt ['tiːʃɜːt] *n* camiseta.

teeth [tiːθ] *npl* → tooth.

teetotaller [tiː'təʊtləʳ] *n* abstemio,-a.

telegram ['telɪgræm] *n* telegrama.

telegraph ['telɪgrɑːf] *n* telégrafo.

telephone ['telɪfəʊn] *n* teléfono. ▶ *vt-vi* llamar por teléfono. ▪ **telephone box** cabina telefónica; **telephone directory** guía telefónica; **telephone operator** telefonista.

telephoto lens [telɪfəʊtəʊ'lenz] *n* teleobjetivo.

telescope ['telɪskəʊp] *n* telescopio.

television ['telɪvɪʒən] *n* televisión. ▪ **television set** televisor.

telex ['teleks] *n* télex.

tell [tel] *vt* **1** decir. **2** contar *(historia)*. ▶ *vi* saber.

to tell off *vt* echar una bronca a, reñir.

teller ['teləʳ] *n* cajero,-a.

telling-off [telɪŋ'ɒf] *n fam* bronca.

telly ['telɪ] *n fam* tele.

temper ['tempəʳ] *n* temperamento. ▶ *vt* templar. • **to lose one's temper** enfadarse.

temperature ['tempərətʃəʳ] *n* temperatura. • **to have a temperature** tener fiebre.

tempest ['tempəst] *n* tempestad.

temple ['tempəl] *n* **1** templo. **2** sien.

temporary ['tempərərɪ] *adj* temporal.

tempt [tempt] *vt* tentar.

temptation [temp'teɪʃən] *n* tentación.

ten [ten] *adj* diez. ▶ *n* diez.

tenacity [tə'næsɪtɪ] *n* tenacidad.

tenant ['tenənt] *n* inquilino,-a.

tend [tend] *vi* tender a, tener tendencia a. ▶ *vt* cuidar.

tendency ['tendənsɪ] *n* tendencia.

tender¹ ['tendəʳ] *adj* tierno,-a.

tender² ['tendəʳ] *n* oferta.

tendon ['tendən] *n* tendón.

tenement ['tenəmənt] *n* casa de vecinos.

tennis ['tenɪs] *n* tenis. ■ **tennis court** pista de tenis.

tenor ['tenəʳ] *n* tenor.

tense [tens] *adj* tenso,-a. ▶ *n* tiempo *(de verbo)*.

tension ['tenʃən] *n* tensión.

tent [tent] *n* tienda de campaña.

tentacle ['tentəkəl] *n* tentáculo.

tenth [tenθ] *adj-n* décimo,-a.

tepid ['tepɪd] *adj* tibio,-a.

term [tɜːm] *vt* calificar de. ▶ *n* **1** trimestre. **2** período, plazo. **3** término. ▶ *npl* **terms 1** condiciones. **2** relaciones.

terminal ['tɜːmɪnəl] *adj-n* terminal.

terminate ['tɜːmɪneɪt] *vt-vi* terminar.

terminus ['tɜːmɪnəs] *n* terminal.

termite ['tɜːmaɪt] *n* termita.

terrace ['terəs] *n* terraza.

terrain [tə'reɪn] *n* terreno.

terrible ['terɪbəl] *adj* terrible.

terrific [tə'rɪfɪk] *adj* fabuloso,-a.

terrify ['terɪfaɪ] *vt* aterrar.

territory ['terɪtərɪ] *n* territorio.

terror ['terəʳ] *n* terror.

terrorism ['terərɪzəm] *n* terrorismo.

test [test] *n* **1** prueba. **2** examen, test. ▶ *vt* probar, poner a prueba. ■ **test tube** tubo de ensayo.

testament ['testəmənt] *n* testamento.

testicle ['testɪkəl] *n* testículo.

testify ['testɪfaɪ] *vt-vi* testificar.

testimony ['testɪmənɪ] *n* testimonio.

tetanus ['tetənəs] *n* tétanos.

text [tekst] *n* texto.

textbook ['tekstbʊk] *n* libro de texto.

textile ['tekstaɪl] *adj* textil. ▶ *n* textil, tejido.

texture ['tekstʃə'] *n* textura.

than [ðæn] *conj* **1** que. **2** de.

thank [θæŋk] *vt* agradecer. ► *npl* **thanks** gracias. • **thanks to** gracias a; **thank you** gracias.

thankful ['θæŋkfʊl] *adj* agradecido,-a.

that [ðæt] *adj* ese, esa, aquel, aquella. ► *pron* **1** ése, ésa, aquél, aquélla. **2** eso, aquello. **3** que *(relativo)*. ► *conj* que. • **that is** es decir.

thaw [θɔː] *n* deshielo. ► *vt-vi* deshelar(se).

the [ðə] *det* el, la, los, las.

theatre ['θɪətə'] (US **theater**) *n* **1** teatro. **2** quirófano.

theft [θeft] *n* robo, hurto.

their [ðeə'] *adj* su, sus.

theirs [ðeəz] *pron* (el) suyo, (la) suya, (los) suyos, (las) suyas.

them [ðem] *pron* **1** los, las *(comp directo)*. **2** les *(comp indirecto)*. **3** ellos, ellas *(con preposición)*.

theme [θiːm] *n* tema. ▪ **theme park** parque temático.

themselves [ðəm'selvz] *pron* **1** ellos mismos, ellas mismas *(sujeto)*. **2** se.

then [ðen] *adv* **1** entonces. **2** luego, después. **3** en ese caso. • **then again** también.

theology [θɪ'blədʒɪ] *n* teología.

theory ['θɪərɪ] *n* teoría.

therapy ['θerəpɪ] *n* terapia.

there [ðeə'] *adv* allí, allá, ahí. • **there is/are** hay; **there was/were** había; **there you are** ahí tienes.

thereabouts [ðeərə'baʊts] *adv* por ahí.

thereafter [ðeə'ræftə'] *adv* a partir de entonces.

thereby ['ðeəbaɪ] *adv* de ese modo.

therefore ['ðeəfɔː'] *adv* por lo tanto.

thermal ['θɜːməl] *adj* termal.

thermometer [θe'mɒmɪtə'] *n* termómetro.

thermos® ['θɜːmɒs] *n* termo. También **thermos flask**.

these [ðiːz] *adj* estos,-as. ► *pron* éstos,-as.

thesis ['θiːsɪs] *n* tesis.

they [ðeɪ] *pron* ellos,-as.

thick [θɪk] *adj* **1** grueso,-a. **2** espeso,-a. **3** poblado,-a *(barba)*.

thief [θiːf] *n* ladrón,-ona.

thigh [θaɪ] *n* muslo.

thimble ['θɪmbəl] *n* dedal.

thin [θɪn] *adj* **1** delgado,-a, flaco,-a *(persona)*. **2** fino,-a *(rebanada, material)*. **3** ralo,-a *(pelo, vegetación)*. **4** claro,-a, poco espeso,-a *(líquido)*.

thing [θɪŋ] *n* cosa. • **the thing is …** el caso es que …

think [θɪŋk] *vt - vi* pensar.

third [θɜːd] *adj* tercero,-a. ▪ **Third World** Tercer Mundo.

thirst [θɜːst] *n* sed.

thirsty ['θɜːstɪ] *adj* sediento,-a.
• **to be thirsty** tener sed.
thirteen [θɜː'tiːn] *adj-n* trece.
thirteenth [θɜː'tiːnθ] *adj - n* decimotercero,-a.
thirty ['θɜːtɪ] *adj-n* treinta.
this [ðɪs] *adj* este, esta. ► *pron* éste, ésta, esto.
thistle ['θɪsəl] *n* cardo.
thong [θɒŋ] *n* correa.
thorn [θɔːn] *n* espina, pincho.
thorough ['θʌrə] *adj* **1** a fondo *(investigación)*. **2** cuidadoso,-a, minucioso,-a *(persona)*.
those [ðəʊz] *adj* esos,-as, aquellos,-as. ► *pron* ésos,-as, aquéllos,-as.
though [ðəʊ] *conj* **1** aunque, si bien. **2** pero. ► *adv* sin embargo.
thought [θɔːt] *ptpp* → think.
► *n* **1** pensamiento. **2** idea.
thoughtful ['θɔːtfʊl] *adj* **1** pensativo,-a. **2** considerado,-a.
thousand ['θaʊzənd] *adj-n* mil.
thrash [θræʃ] *vt* dar una paliza a.
thread [θred] *n* **1** hilo. **2** rosca *(de tornillo)*. ► *vt* **1** enhebrar *(aguja)*. **2** ensartar *(cuentas)*.
threat [θret] *n* amenaza.
threaten ['θretən] *vt - vi* amenazar.
three [θriː] *adj-n* tres.
threshold ['θreʃəʊld] *n* umbral.
threw [θruː] *pt* → throw.
thrifty ['θrɪftɪ] *adj* frugal.

thrill [θrɪl] *n* emoción.
thriller ['θrɪlə'] *n* novela de suspense, película de suspense.
thrive [θraɪv] *vi* **1** crecer *(planta)*. **2** prosperar *(industria)*.
throat [θrəʊt] *n* garganta.
throb [θrɒb] *n* latido, palpitación. ► *vi* latir, palpitar.
throne [θrəʊn] *n* trono.
through [θruː] *prep* **1** por. **2** durante todo,-a. **3** hasta el final de. ► *adv* **1** de un lado a otro. **2** hasta el final. ► *adj* directo,-a. • **to be through with** haber acabado con.
throughout [θruː'aʊt] *prep* **1** por, en todo,-a. **2** durante todo,-a, a lo largo de. ► *adv* **1** por todas partes, en todas partes. **2** completamente. **3** todo el tiempo.
throve [θrəʊv] *pt* → thrive.
throw [θrəʊ] *n* lanzamiento.
► *vt* tirar, lanzar.
to throw away *vt* **1** tirar *(basura)*. **2** desaprovechar *(oportunidad)*
to throw up *vi* vomitar.
thru [θruː] *prep-adv* US → through.
thrush [θrʌʃ] *n* tordo.
thrust [θrʌst] *n* **1** empuje. **2** estocada *(de espada)*.
thumb [θʌm] *n* pulgar.
thumbtack ['θʌmtæk] *n* US chincheta.
thump [θʌmp] *n* golpe. ► *vt* golpear.

thunder ['θʌndə'] *n* trueno. ►
vi tronar.

thunderstorm ['θʌndəstɔːm]
n tormenta.

Thursday ['θɜːzdɪ] *n* jueves.

thus [ðʌs] *adv* así.

thyme [taɪm] *n* tomillo.

tic [tɪk] *n* tic.

tick¹ [tɪk] *n* garrapata.

tick² [tɪk] *n* 1 tictac *(ruido)*. 2
marca, señal.

to tick off *vt* marcar.

ticket ['tɪkɪt] *n* 1 billete *(de bus,
etc)*. 2 entrada *(de cine, etc)*. 3
etiqueta, resguardo. 4 *fam*
multa. ▪ **ticket collector** revisor,-ra; **ticket machine**
máquina expendedora de billetes; **ticket office** taquilla.

tickle ['tɪkəl] *vt* hacer cosquillas a. ► *vi* tener cosquillas.

tide [taɪd] *n* marea.

tidy ['taɪdɪ] *adj* 1 ordenado,-a
(habitación, persona). 2 arreglado,-a *(aspecto)*.

to tidy up *vt* 1 ordenar, arreglar *(habitación)*. 2 arreglar,
acicalar *(persona*.

tie [taɪ] *n* 1 corbata. 2 lazo,
vínculo. 3 empate. ► *vt* atar,
hacer *(nudo)*. ► *vi* empatar.

tier [tɪə'] *n* 1 grada, fila *(de
asientos)*. 2 piso *(de pastel)*.

tiger ['taɪɡə'] *n* tigre.

tight [taɪt] *adj* 1 apretado,-a.
2 tenso,-a *(cuerda)*. 3 ajustado,-a, ceñido,-a *(ropa)*. ► *adv*
con fuerza.

tighten ['taɪtən] *vt* 1 apretar.
2 tensar *(cuerda)*.

tightrope ['taɪtrəʊp] *n* cuerda
floja.

tights [taɪts] *npl* 1 panties,
medias. 2 leotardos.

tile [taɪl] *n* 1 azulejo *(de pared)*.
2 baldosa *(de suelo)*. 3 teja *(de
tejado)*.

till [tɪl] *prep* hasta. ► *conj* hasta
que. ► *n* caja registradora.

tilt [tɪlt] *n* inclinación, ladeo.
► *vt-vi* inclinar(se).

timber ['tɪmbə'] *n* 1 madera
(de construcción). 2 viga.

time [taɪm] *n* 1 tiempo. 2 rato. 3 hora: *what time is it?*,
¿qué hora es? 4 vez: *two at a
time*, de dos en dos. ► *vt* 1
cronometrar. 2 fijar la hora
de. ► *prep* **times** por, multi-
plicado por. ● **at any time** en
cualquier momento; **at times**
a veces; **for the time being**
de momento; **from time to
time** de vez en cuando; **it's
about time** ya va siendo
hora; **on time** puntualmen-
te; **to have a good time** divertirse, pasarlo bien; **to tell
the time** decir la hora.

timetable ['taɪmteɪbəl] *n* horario.

timid ['tɪmɪd] *adj* tímido,-a.

tin [tɪn] *n* 1 estaño. 2 lata,
bote. ▪ **tin opener** abrelatas.

tinkle ['tɪŋkəl] *n* tintineo.

tiny ['taɪnɪ] *adj* diminuto,-a.

tip¹ ['tɪp] n extremo, punta.

tip² ['tɪp] n **1** propina. **2** consejo. ► vt dar una propina a.

tiptoe ['tɪptəʊ] vi ir de puntillas. • **on tiptoe** de puntillas.

tire¹ ['taɪəʳ] vt-vi cansar(se).

tire² ['taɪəʳ] n US neumático.

tired ['taɪəd] adj cansado,-a.

tireless ['taɪələs] adj incansable.

tissue ['tɪʃuː] n pañuelo de papel.

title ['taɪtəl] n título.

to [tʊ, unstressed tə] prep **1** a. **2** hacia, a. **3** a, hasta. **4** menos. **5** para, a fin de.

toad [təʊd] n sapo.

toadstool ['təʊdstuːl] n seta venenosa.

toast [təʊst] n **1** pan tostado: *a piece of toast*, una tostada. **2** brindis. ► vt **1** tostar *(pan)*. **2** brindar por. • **to drink a toast to** hacer un brindis por, brindar por.

toaster ['təʊstəʳ] n tostador.

tobacco [təˈbækəʊ] n tabaco.

tobacconist [təˈbækənɪst] n estanquero,-a. ■ **tobacconist's** estanco.

toboggan [təˈbɒgən] n trineo.

today [təˈdeɪ] n hoy. ► adv **1** hoy. **2** hoy en día.

toe [təʊ] n dedo del pie.

together [təˈgeðəʳ] adv junto, juntos,-as. • **all together** todos,-as juntos,-as; **together with** junto con.

toilet ['tɔɪlət] n **1** váter, lavabo *(en casa)*. **2** servicios *(públicos)*. **3** aseo, arreglo personal. ■ **toilet bag** neceser; **toilet paper** papel higiénico.

token ['təʊkən] n ficha.

told [təʊld] ptpp → tell.

tolerate ['tɒləreɪt] vt tolerar.

toll [təʊl] n **1** peaje. **2** número.

tomato [təˈmɑːtəʊ] n tomate.

tomb [tuːm] n tumba.

tombstone ['tuːmstəʊn] n lápida.

tomorrow [təˈmɒrəʊ] adv mañana. ► n mañana.

ton [tʌn] n tonelada.

tone [təʊn] n tono.

tongs [tɒŋz] npl pinzas.

tongue [tʌŋ] n lengua. ■ **tongue twister** trabalenguas.

tonic ['tɒnɪk] adj tónico,-a.

tonight [təˈnaɪt] adv-n esta noche.

tonne [tʌn] n tonelada.

tonsil ['tɒnsəl] n amígdala.

too [tuː] adv **1** demasiado, mucho. **2** también. • **too many** demasiados,-as; **too much** demasiado,-a.

took [tʊk] pt → take.

tool [tuːl] n herramienta.

tooth [tuːθ] n diente, muela.

toothache ['tuːθeɪk] n dolor de muelas.

toothbrush ['tuːθbrʌʃ] n cepillo de dientes.

toothpaste ['tuːθpeɪst] n pasta de dientes.

top [tɒp] n 1 parte superior, parte de arriba. 2 tapón *(de botella)*. 3 top, blusa. ► *adj* de arriba, superior, más alto,-a.

topic ['tɒpɪk] n tema, asunto.

topical ['tɒpɪkəl] *adj* de actualidad.

torch [tɔːtʃ] n 1 antorcha. 2 linterna.

tore [tɔːʳ] *pt* → tear.

torn [tɔːn] *pp* → tear.

tornado [tɔːˈneɪdəʊ] n tornado.

torpedo [tɔːˈpiːdəʊ] n torpedo.

tortoise ['tɔːtəs] n tortuga.

torture ['tɔːtʃə] n tortura. ► *vt* torturar.

total ['təʊtəl] *adj* - n total. ► *vt-vi* sumar.

touch [tʌtʃ] n 1 toque. 2 tacto. ► *vt-vi* tocar(se). ► *vt* conmover. •**to get in touch with** ponerse en contacto con; **to keep in touch** mantenerse en contacto.

touchdown ['tʌtʃdaʊn] n 1 aterrizaje. 2 amerizaje. 3 ensayo *(en rugby)*.

tough [tʌf] *adj* 1 fuerte *(persona)*. 2 duro,-a. ■ **tough luck** mala suerte.

toupee ['tuːpeɪ] n peluquín.

tour [tʊə] n 1 viaje. 2 visita *(de edificio)*. 3 gira. ► *vt* 1 recorrer *(país)*. 2 visitar *(edificio)*.

tourism ['tʊərɪzəm] n turismo.

tourist ['tʊərɪst] n turista. ■ **tourist office** oficina de turismo.

tournament ['tʊənəmənt] n torneo.

tow [təʊ] *vt* remolcar.

towards [təˈwɔːdz] *prep* 1 hacia. 2 para con *(actitud, responsabilidad)*. 3 para. También **toward**.

towel ['taʊəl] n toalla.

tower ['taʊəʳ] n torre.

town [taʊn] n 1 ciudad. 2 pueblo. ■ **town council** ayuntamiento; **town hall** ayuntamiento.

toxic ['tɒksɪk] n tóxico,-a.

toy [tɔɪ] n juguete.

toyshop ['tɔɪʃɒp] n juguetería.

trace [treɪs] n indicio, rastro.

track [træk] n 1 pista, huellas. 2 camino, senda. 3 pista, calle *(atletismo)*. 4 circuito *(de carreras)*. 5 vía *(de ferrocarril)*. ► *vt* seguir la pista de.

tracksuit ['træksuːt] n chándal.

tractor ['træktəʳ] n tractor.

trade [treɪd] n 1 oficio. 2 negocio. 3 comercio. ► *vi* comerciar. ► *vt* cambiar. ■ **trade union** sindicato obrero.

trademark ['treɪdmɑːk] n marca registrada.

trading ['treɪdɪŋ] n comercio. ■ **trading estate** polígono comercial.

tradition [trəˈdɪʃən] n tradición.

traffic ['træfɪk] n tráfico. ► *vi* traficar. ■ **traffic jam** embotellamiento, atasco; **traffic light** semáforo.

tragedy ['trædʒədɪ] n tragedia.

tragic ['trædʒɪk] adj trágico,-a.

trail [treɪl] n 1 rastro, pista. 2 camino, sendero. 3 estela.

trailer ['treɪlə'] n 1 remolque. 2 tráiler, avance (película).

train [treɪn] n 1 tren. 2 cola (de vestido). ► vt-vi 1 entrenar(se). 2 formar(se). ■ **train station** estación de tren.

trainee [treɪ'niː] n aprendiz,-za.

trainer ['treɪnə'] n 1 entrenador,-ra. 2 zapatilla (de deporte).

training ['treɪnɪŋ] n 1 formación. 2 entrenamiento.

traitor ['treɪtə'] n traidor,-ra.

tram [træm] n tranvía.

tramp [træmp] n vagabundo,-a.

trampoline ['træmpəliːn] n cama elástica.

trance [trɑːns] n trance.

transatlantic [trænzət'læntɪk] adj transatlántico,-a.

transcript ['trænskrɪpt] n transcripción.

transfer [(n) 'trænsfɜː', (vb) træns'fɜː'] n 1 transferencia (de dinero). 2 traslado (de empleado). 3 traspaso (de bienes, poderes). ► vt 1 transferir (dinero). 2 traspasar (bienes, poderes). ► vi hacer trasbordo.

transform [træns'fɔːm] vt-vi transformar(se).

transfusion [træns'fjuːʒən] n transfusión.

transitive ['trænsɪtɪv] adj transitivo,-a.

translate [træns'leɪt] vt traducir.

translation [træns'leɪʃən] n traducción.

translator [træns'leɪtə'] n traductor,-ra.

transmit [trænz'mɪt] vt transmitir.

transparent [træns'peərənt] adj transparente.

transplant ['trænsplɑːnt] n trasplante.

transport [(n) 'trænspɔːt, (vb) træns'pɔːt] n transporte. ► vt transportar.

trap [træp] n trampa. ► vt atrapar.

trash [træʃ] n US basura.

travel ['trævəl] n viajes. ► vi 1 viajar. 2 ir, circular. ■ **travel agency** agencia de viajes.

traveller ['trævələ'] n 1 viajero,-a. 2 viajante. ■ **traveller's cheque** cheque de viaje.

travel-sick ['trævəlsɪk] adj mareado,-a.

tray [treɪ] n bandeja.

treacherous ['tretʃərəs] adj 1 traidor,-ra, traicionero,-a. 2 muy peligroso,-a.

treason ['triːzən] n traición.

treasure ['treʒə'] n tesoro.

treat [triːt] vt 1 tratar. 2 convidar, invitar. 3 darse el gusto, permitirse el lujo.

treatment ['triːtmənt] n 1 tratamiento. 2 trato, conducta.

treaty ['triːtɪ] n tratado.

tree [triː] n árbol.

trek [trek] n **1** viaje. **2** caminata *(a pie)*. ► vi caminar.

tremble ['trembəl] vi temblar, estremecerse.

trench [trentʃ] n **1** zanja. **2** trinchera.

trend [trend] n tendencia.

trespass ['trespəs] vi entrar ilegalmente. • **"No trespassing"** "Prohibido el paso".

trestle ['tresəl] n caballete.

trial ['traɪəl] n **1** proceso, juicio. **2** prueba. • **on trial** a prueba. ■ **trial run** ensayo.

triangle ['traɪæŋgəl] n triángulo.

tribe [traɪb] n tribu.

tribunal [traɪˈbjuːnəl] n tribunal.

tributary ['trɪbjʊtərɪ] n afluente.

trick [trɪk] n truco. ► vt engañar.

trill [trɪl] n trino. ► vt - vi trinar.

trim [trɪm] adj bien arreglado, -a. ► n recorte *(de pelo)*. ► vt **1** recortar *(pelo, bigote)*. **2** decorar.

trinket ['trɪŋkɪt] n baratija.

trip [trɪp] n **1** viaje. **2** excursión. ► vi tropezar.

tripe [traɪp] n callos *(plato)*.

triple ['trɪpəl] adj triple.

tripod ['traɪpɒd] n trípode.

triumph ['traɪəmf] n triunfo. ► vi triunfar.

trivial ['trɪvɪəl] adj trivial.

trolley ['trɒlɪ] n carro, carrito.

trombone [trɒmˈbəʊn] n trombón.

troop [truːp] n grupo, banda *(de gente)*.► npl **troops** tropas.

trophy ['trəʊfɪ] n trofeo.

tropic ['trɒpɪk] n trópico.

tropical ['trɒpɪkəl] adj tropical.

trot [trɒt] n trote. ► vi trotar.

trotter ['trɒtə'] n manita *(de cerdo)*.

trouble ['trʌbəl] n **1** problema. **2** preocupación. **3** molestia. ► vt **1** preocupar. **2** molestar. ► vi molestarse.

trough [trɒf] n abrevadero.

trousers ['traʊzəz] npl pantalón.

trousseau ['truːsəʊ] n ajuar.

trout [traʊt] n trucha.

truant ['truːənt] phr. • **to play truant** hacer novillos.

truce [truːs] n tregua.

truck [trʌk] n **1** GB vagón. **2** US camión.

true [truː] adj verdadero,-a. • **it's true** es verdad.

truffle ['trʌfəl] n trufa.

truly ['truːlɪ] adv verdaderamente. • **yours truly** atentamente.

trumpet ['trʌmpɪt] n trompeta.

truncheon ['trʌntʃən] n porra.

trunk [trʌŋk] n **1** tronco. **2** baúl. **3** trompa. **4** US maletero. ► npl **trunks** bañador. ■ **trunk call** llamada interurbana.

trust [trʌst] n confianza, fe. ► vt confiar en, fiarse de.

truth [truːθ] *n* verdad.

try [traɪ] *n* **1** intento. **2** ensayo *(en rugby)*. ► *vt - vi* intentar. ► *vt* probar *(comida)*.

T-shirt ['tiːʃɜːt] *n* camiseta.

tub [tʌb] *n* **1** tina. **2** bañera, baño. **3** tarrina.

tube [tjuːb] *n* **1** tubo. **2** GB metro.

Tuesday ['tjuːzdɪ] *n* martes.

tuft [tʌft] *n* **1** mechón. **2** mata.

tug [tʌg] *vt* tirar de.

tuition [tjʊˈɪʃən] *n* enseñanza.

tulip ['tjuːlɪp] *n* tulipán.

tumble ['tʌmbəl] *n*. ▪ **tumble dryer** secadora.

tumbler ['tʌmbələ'] *n* vaso.

tumour ['tjuːmə'] (US **tumor**) *n* tumor.

tuna ['tjuːnə] *n* atún, bonito.

tundra ['tʌndrə] *n* tundra.

tune [tjuːn] *n* melodía. ► *vt* **1** afinar *(piano, etc)*. **2** poner a punto *(motor)*. **3** sintonizar *(radio, etc)*. ● **in tune** afinado,-a; **out of tune** desafinado,-a.

tunnel ['tʌnəl] *n* túnel.

turbot ['tɜːbət] *n* rodaballo.

tureen [təˈriːn] *n* sopera.

turf [tɜːf] *n* césped.

turkey ['tɜːkɪ] *n* pavo.

turn [tɜːn] *n* **1** vuelta. **2** curva. **3** turno. ► *vt* **1** girar, dar la vuelta a. **2** doblar *(esquina)*. **3** pasar *(página)*. ► *vi* **1** girar, dar vueltas. **2** volverse, dar la vuelta *(persona)*. **3** torcer. **4** hacerse, ponerse, volverse.

to turn back *vi* volver(se).

to turn down *vt* bajar *(radio, etc)*.

to turn into *vt* convertir.

to turn off *vt* **1** desconectar *(electricidad)*. **2** apagar *(luz, gas)*. **3** cerrar *(agua)*. **4** parar *(máquina)*.

to turn on *vt* **1** conectar *(electricidad)*. **2** encender *(luz)*. **3** abrir *(gas, grifo)*. **4** poner en marcha *(máquina)*.

to turn up *vi* aparecer.

turnip ['tɜːnɪp] *n* nabo.

turnover ['tɜːnəʊvə'] *n* volumen de negocio.

turnpike ['tɜːnpaɪk] *n* US autopista de peaje.

turpentine ['tɜːpəntaɪn] *n* trementina, aguarrás.

turtle ['tɜːtəl] *n* tortuga.

tusk [tʌsk] *n* colmillo.

tutor ['tjuːtə'] *n* **1** profesor,-ra particular. **2** tutor,-ra.

tuxedo [tʌkˈsiːdəʊ] *n* US esmoquin.

twelfth [twelfθ] *adj - n* duodécimo,-a.

twelve [twelv] *num* doce.

twentieth ['twentɪəθ] *adj - n* vigésimo,-a.

twenty ['twentɪ] *num* veinte.

twice [twaɪs] *adv* dos veces.

twilight ['twaɪlaɪt] *n* crepúsculo.

twin [twɪn] *n* gemelo,-a. ▪ **twin room** habitación con dos camas.

twist [twɪst] n 1 recodo, vuelta *(de carretera)*. 2 torcedura. 4 twist *(baile)*. ► vt 1 torcer. 2 girar *(tapa)*. ► vi torcerse *(tobillo)*.

two [tuː] adj - n dos.

type [taɪp] n 1 tipo, clase. 2 letra, carácter.

typewriter ['taɪpraɪtə'] n máquina de escribir.

typhoon [taɪ'fuːn] n tifón.

typical ['tɪpɪkəl] adj típico,-a.

typist ['taɪpɪst] n mecanógrafo,-a.

tyranny ['tɪrənɪ] n tiranía.

tyrant ['taɪərənt] n tirano,-a.

tyre ['taɪə'] (US **tire**) n neumático, llanta.

U

udder ['ʌdə'] n ubre.

ugly ['ʌglɪ] adj feo,-a.

ulcer ['ʌlsə'] n úlcera.

umbrella [ʌm'brelə] n paraguas.

umpire ['ʌmpaɪə'] n árbitro. ► vt arbitrar.

unable [ʌn'eɪbəl] adj incapaz.

unanimous [juː'nænɪməs] adj unánime.

unavailable [ʌnə'veɪləbəl] adj no disponible.

unaware [ʌnə'weə'] adj inconsciente.

unbalanced [ʌn'bælənst] adj desequilibrado,-a.

unbeatable [ʌn'biːtəbəl] adj 1 invencible, insuperable *(rival)*. 2 inmejorable *(precio)*.

unbelievable [ʌnbɪ'liːvəbəl] adj increíble.

unbiassed [ʌn'baɪəst] adj imparcial.

unbutton [ʌn'bʌtən] vt desabrochar, desbotonar.

uncertain [ʌn'sɜːtən] adj 1 incierto,-a, dudoso,-a *(futuro)*. 2 indeciso,-a *(persona)*.

uncle ['ʌnkəl] n tío.

uncommon [ʌn'kɒmən] adj 1 poco común. 2 insólito,-a.

unconscious [ʌn'kɒnʃəs] adj inconsciente.

uncouth [ʌn'kuːθ] adj tosco,-a.

uncover [ʌn'kʌvə'] vt 1 destapar, descubrir. 2 revelar.

under ['ʌndə'] prep 1 bajo, debajo de. 2 menos de. ► adv abajo, debajo.

underclothes ['ʌndəkləʊðz] npl ropa interior.

undercoat ['ʌndəkəʊt] n primera mano *(de pintura)*.

undercover [ʌndə'kʌvə'] adj clandestino,-a, secreto,-a.

underdeveloped [ʌndədɪ'veləpt] adj subdesarrollado,-a.

underdone [ʌndə'dʌn] adj poco hecho,-a.

underestimate [ʌndər'estɪmeɪt] vt subestimar, infravalorar.

undergo [ʌndə'gəʊ] *vt* **1** experimentar, sufrir *(cambio, dificultas)*. **2** hacer, someterse a *(operación)*.

undergraduate [ʌndə'grædjʊət] *n* estudiante universitario,-a no licenciado,-a.

underground [*(adj)* 'ʌndəgraʊnd, *(n)* ʌndə'graʊnd] *adj* **1** subterráneo. **2** *fig* clandestino,-a. ▶ *n* **1** metro. **2** resistencia, movimiento clandestino. ▶ *adv* **1** bajo tierra. **2** en secreto.

undergrowth ['ʌndəgrəʊθ] *n* maleza.

underline [ʌndə'laɪn] *vt* subrayar.

underneath [ʌndə'niːθ] *prep* debajo de. ▶ *adv* debajo. ▶ *n* parte inferior.

underpants ['ʌndəpænts] *npl* calzoncillos, eslip.

underpass ['ʌndəpæs] *n* paso subterráneo.

underskirt ['ʌndəskɜːt] *n* enagua.

understand [ʌndə'stænd] *vt* entender, comprender.

understanding [ʌndə'stændɪŋ] *n* **1** entendimiento, comprensión. **2** acuerdo, arreglo.

understood [ʌndə'stʊd] *pt-pp* → understand.

undertake [ʌndə'teɪk] *vt* **1** emprender. **2** asumir. **3** comprometerse.

undertook [ʌndə'tʊk] *pt* → undertake.

underwater [ʌndə'wɔːtə'] *adj* submarino,-a.

underwear ['ʌndəwɜːə'] *n* ropa interior.

underwent [ʌndə'went] *pt* → undergo.

undid [ʌn'dɪd] *pt* → undo.

undo [ʌn'duː] *vt* **1** deshacer *(nudo)*. **2** desabrochar *(botón)*. **3** abrir *(paquete)*.

undress [ʌn'dres] *vt-vi* desnudar(se), desvestir(se).

uneasy [ʌn'iːzɪ] *adj* intranquilo,-a, inquieto,-a.

unemployed [ʌnɪm'plɔɪd] *adj* desempleado,-a.

unemployment [ʌnɪm'plɔɪmənt] *n* paro, desempleo. ■ **unemployment benefit** subsidio de desempleo.

unequal [ʌn'iːkwəl] *adj* desigual.

uneven [ʌn'iːvən] *adj* **1** desigual. **2** irregular *(superficie)*. **3** lleno,-a de baches *(carretera)*.

unexpected [ʌnɪk'spektɪd] *adj* inesperado,-a.

unfamiliar [ʌnfə'mɪlɪə'] *adj* desconocido,-a.

unfasten [ʌn'fɑːsən] *vt* **1** desabrochar *(botón)*. **2** desatar *(nudo)*. **3** abrir *(puerta)*.

unfit [ʌn'fɪt] *adj* **1** inadecuado,-a. **2** desentrenado,-a.

unfold [ʌn'fəʊld] *vt-vi* desplegar(se), abrir(se).

unforeseen [ʌnfɔː'siːn] *adj* imprevisto,-a.

unhappy [ʌn'hæpɪ] *adj* infeliz, triste.

unhurt [ʌn'hɜːt] *adj* ileso,-a.

unidentified [ʌnaɪ'dentɪfaɪd] *adj* no identificado,-a.

unification [juːnɪfɪ'keɪʃən] *n* unificación.

uniform ['juːnɪfɔːm] *adj-n* uniforme.

unify ['juːnɪfaɪ] *vt* unificar.

union ['juːnɪən] *n* 1 unión. 2 sindicato.

unique [juː'niːk] *adj* único,-a.

unisex ['juːnɪseks] *adj* unisex.

unit ['juːnɪt] *n* unidad.

unite [juː'naɪt] *vt-vi* unir(se).

universe ['juːnɪvɜːs] *n* universo.

university [juːnɪ'vɜːsɪtɪ] *n* universidad.

unjust [ʌn'dʒʌst] *adj* injusto,-a.

unkind [ʌn'kaɪnd] *adj* 1 poco amable *(persona)*. 2 cruel.

unknown [ʌn'nəʊn] *adj* desconocido,-a.

unless [ən'les] *conj* a menos que, a no ser que, si no.

unlike [ʌn'laɪk] *adj* diferente. ► *prep* a diferencia de.

unlikely [ʌn'laɪklɪ] *adj* improbable, poco probable.

unload [ʌn'ləʊd] *vt* descargar.

unlock [ʌn'lɒk] *vt* abrir.

unmanned [ʌn'mænd] *adj* no tripulado,-a.

unnoticed [ʌn'nəʊtɪst] *adj* inadvertido,-a, desapercibido,-a.

unoccupied [ʌn'ɒkjʊpaɪd] *adj* 1 deshabitado,-a *(casa)*. 2 de-

socupado,-a *(persona)*. 3 vacante *(empleo)*.

unofficial [ʌnə'fɪʃəl] *adj* extraoficial, oficioso,-a.

unpack [ʌn'pæk] *vt* 1 desempaquetar, desembalar. 2 deshacer *(maleta)*.

unpleasant [ʌn'plezənt] *adj* desagradable.

unplug [ʌn'plʌg] *vt* desenchufar.

unpublished [ʌn'pʌblɪʃt] *adj* inédito,-a.

unreadable [ʌn'riːdəbəl] *adj* ilegible.

unreal [ʌn'rɪəl] *adj* irreal.

unreasonable [ʌn'riːzənəbəl] *adj* 1 poco razonable. 2 desmesurado,-a, excesivo.

unreliable [ʌnrɪ'laɪəbəl] *adj* 1 de poca confianza *(persona)*. 2 poco fiable *(máquina)*.

unrest [ʌn'rest] *n* 1 malestar, intranquilidad. 2 disturbios.

unripe [ʌn'raɪp] *adj* verde, inmaduro,-a.

unroll [ʌn'rəʊl] *vt-vi* desenrollar(se).

unsafe [ʌn'seɪf] *adj* inseguro,-a.

unscrew [ʌn'skruː] *vt* 1 desatornillar. 2 desenroscar.

unskilled [ʌn'skɪld] *adj* 1 no cualificado,-a *(obrero)*. 2 no especializado,-a *(trabajo)*.

unspeakable [ʌn'spiːkəbəl] *adj* indecible.

unstable [ʌn'steɪbəl] *adj* inestable.

unsteady [ʌn'stedɪ] *adj* inseguro,-a, inestable.

unsuccessful [ʌnsək'sesfʊl] *adj* fracasado,-a, sin éxito.

unsuitable [ʌn'suːtəbəl] *adj* **1** poco apropiado,-a *(persona)*. **2** inoportuno, inconveniente.

untidy [ʌn'taɪdɪ] *adj* **1** desordenado,-a *(habitación)*. **2** desaliñado,-a *(persona)*.

untie [ʌn'taɪ] *vt* desatar.

until [ən'tɪl] *prep* hasta. ► *conj* hasta que.

untrue [ʌn'truː] *adj* **1** falso,-a. **2** infiel.

unveil [ʌn'veɪl] *vt* revelar.

unwell [ʌn'wel] *adj* indispuesto,-a.

unwilling [ʌn'wɪlɪŋ] *adj* reacio,-a, poco dispuesto,-a.

unwind [ʌn'waɪnd] *vt* desenrollar(se).

unwise [ʌn'waɪz] *adj* imprudente, poco aconsejable.

unworthy [ʌn'wɜːðɪ] *adj* indigno,-a.

unwound [ʌn'waʊnd] *pt-pp* → unwind.

unwrap [ʌn'ræp] *vt* desenvolver, abrir.

up [ʌp] *adv* **1** arriba, hacia arriba. **2** levantado,-a. **3** hacia. **4** más alto,-a. **5** acabado,-a.► *prep* **1** *to go up the stairs*, subir la escalera. **2** en lo alto de: *up a tree*, en lo alto de un árbol. ► *vt fam* subir, aumentar. ● **up to** hasta; **it's up**

to you *fam* es cosa tuya; **up and down** de arriba a abajo, de un lado al otro. ■ **ups and downs** altibajos.

update [*(n)* 'ʌpdeɪt, *(vb)* ʌp'deɪt] *n* actualización. ► *vt* actualizar.

upgrade [ʌp'greɪd] *vt* **1** ascender *(persona)*. **2** mejorar. **3** actualizar. ► *n* actualización.

uphill [ʌp'hɪl] *adv* cuesta arriba.

upholstery [ʌp'həʊlstərɪ] *n* tapicería, tapizado.

upkeep ['ʌpkiːp] *n* mantenimiento.

upon [ə'pɒn] *prep* → on.

upper ['ʌpə'] *adj* superior, de arriba. ■ **upper case** mayúsculas, caja alta; **upper class** clase alta.

uppermost ['ʌpəməʊst] *adj* **1** más alto,-a. **2** *fig* principal.

upright ['ʌpraɪt] *adj* derecho, -a, vertical.

uprising [ʌp'raɪzɪŋ] *n* sublevación, rebelión.

upset [ʌp'set] *adj* disgustado,-a, ofendido,-a. ► *vt* **1** disgustar. **2** desbaratar *(planes)*. **3** volcar *(barco)*. **4** derramar *(recipiente)*. ► *n* revés.

upside down [ʌpsaɪd'daʊn] *adv* al revés.

upstairs [*(adv)* ʌp'steəz, *(n)* 'ʌpsteəz] *adv* **1** en el piso de arriba *(situación)*. **2** al piso de arriba *(movimiento)*. ► *adj* de arriba.

up-to-date [ˌʌptə'deɪt] *adj* al día, actualizado.

upward ['ʌpwəd] *adj* hacia arriba, ascendente. ► *adv* hacia arriba.

upwards ['ʌpwədz] *adv* hacia arriba.

urban ['ɜːbən] *adj* urbano,-a.

urge [ɜːdʒ] ► *vt* encarecer.

urgency ['ɜːdʒənsɪ] *n* urgencia.

urgent ['ɜːdʒənt] *adj* urgente.

urn [ɜːn] *n* urna.

us [ʌs, unstressed əz] *pron* nos, nosotros,-as.

usage ['juːzɪdʒ] *n* uso.

use [(n) juːs, (vb) juːz] *n* uso. ► *vt* usar, utilizar. • **used to** soler, acostumbrar *(se refiere solo al pasado)*: **he used to get up early**, solía levantarse temprano. • **"Not in use"** "No funciona"; **out of use** en desuso; **what's the use of …?** ¿de qué sirve … ?

used [juːst] *adj* usado,-a. • **to be used to STH** estar acostumbrado,-a a algo; **to get used to STH** acostumbrarse a algo.

useful ['juːsfʊl] *adj* útil.

useless ['juːsləs] *adj* inútil.

user ['juːzə'] *n* usuario,-a.

usher ['ʌʃə'] *n* **1** ujier. **2** acomodador,-ra.

usual ['juːʒʊəl] *adj* usual, habitual, normal. • **as usual** como de costumbre, como siempre.

usually ['juːʒʊəlɪ] *adv* normalmente.

utensil [juːˈtensəl] *n* utensilio. • **kitchen utensils** batería de cocina.

utility [juːˈtɪlɪtɪ] *n* **1** utilidad. **2** empresa de servicio público.

utilize ['juːtɪlaɪz] *vt* utilizar.

utmost ['ʌtməʊst] *adj* sumo,-a.

utopia [juːˈtəʊpɪə] *n* utopía.

utter ['ʌtə'] *adj* absoluto,-a, total. ► *vt* pronunciar, articular.

U-turn ['juːtɜːn] *n* cambio de sentido, giro de 180 grados

V

vacancy ['veɪkənsɪ] *n* **1** vacante *(puesto de trabajo)*. **2** habitación libre. • **"No vacancies"** "Completo".

vacant ['veɪkənt] *adj* **1** vacío. **2** vacante. **3** libre.

vacate [və'keɪt] *vt* **1** dejar vacante. **2** desocupar.

vacation [və'keɪʃən] *n* vacaciones.

vaccinate ['væksɪneɪt] *vt* vacunar.

vaccine ['væksiːn] *n* vacuna.

vacuum ['vækjʊəm] *n* vacío. ► *vt* pasar la aspiradora por. ▪ **vacuum cleaner** aspiradora; **vacuum flask** termo.

vacuum-packed ['vækjuəmpækt] *adj* envasado,-a al vacío.

vagina [və'dʒaɪnə] *n* vagina.

vague [veɪg] *adj* vago,-a, indefinido,-a.

valid ['vælɪd] *adj* 1 válido,-a.

valley ['vælɪ] *n* valle.

valuable ['væljuəbəl] *adj* valioso,-a. ► *npl* **valuables** objetos de valor.

value ['vælju:] *n* valor. ► *vt* 1 valora.

valve [vælv] *n* válvula.

vampire ['væmpaɪə'] *n* vampiro.

van [væn] *n* 1 camioneta, furgoneta. 2 GB furgón.

vandalism ['vændəlɪzəm] *n* vandalismo.

vanguard ['vænɡɑːd] *n* vanguardia.

vanish ['vænɪʃ] *vi* desaparecer.

vanity ['vænɪtɪ] *n* vanidad.

vapour ['veɪpə'] (US **vapor**) *n* vapor, vaho.

variable ['veərɪəbəl] *adj* variable. ► *n* variable.

variation [veərɪ'eɪʃən] *n* variación.

varied ['veərɪd] *adj* variado,-a.

variety [və'raɪətɪ] *n* variedad.
  ■ **variety show** espectáculo de variedades.

various ['veərɪəs] *adj* varios, -as.

varnish ['vɑːnɪʃ] *n* barniz. ► *vt* barnizar.

vary ['veərɪ] *vt-vi* variar.

vase [vɑːz] *n* jarrón, florero.

vast [vɑːst] *adj* vasto,-a, inmenso,-a.

vat [væt] *n* tina, cuba.

VAT [væt, 'viː'eɪ'tiː] *abbr (value added tax)* IVA.

vault [vɔːlt] *n* 1 bóveda. 2 cámara acorazada *(de banco)*. 3 panteón, cripta *(de iglesia)*.

veal [viːl] *n* ternera.

vegetable ['vedʒɪtəbəl] *adj* vegetal. ► *n* hortaliza, verdura, legumbre.

vegetarian [vedʒɪ'teərɪən] *adj-n* vegetariano,-a.

vegetation [vedʒɪ'teɪʃən] *n* vegetación.

vehicle ['viːəkəl] *n* vehículo.

veil [veɪl] *n* velo.

vein [veɪn] *n* vena.

velocity [və'lɒsɪtɪ] *n* velocidad.

velvet ['velvɪt] *n* terciopelo.

vending machine ['vendɪŋməʃiːn] *n* máquina expendedora.

vengeance [vendʒəns] *n* venganza.

vent [vent] *n* abertura, respiradero.

ventilate ['ventɪleɪt] *vt* ventilar.

ventilator ['ventɪleɪtə'] *n* ventilador.

venture ['ventʃə'] *n* empresa arriesgada, aventura. ► *vt-vi* arriesgar(se).

venue ['venju:] *n* lugar.

veranda [və'rændə] *n* veranda, terraza.

verb [vɜːb] *n* verbo.

verge [vɜːdʒ] *n* borde, margen.

verify ['verɪfaɪ] *vt* verificar.

vermin ['vɜːmɪn] *n* **1** alimaña. **2** bichos, sabandijas.

verruca [vəˈruːkə] *n* verruga.

versatile ['vɜːsətaɪl] *adj* versátil.

verse [vɜːs] *n* **1** estrofa, versículo. **2** verso, poesía.

version ['vɜːʒən] *n* versión.

versus ['vɜːsəs] *prep* contra.

vertebra ['vɜːtɪbrə] *n* vértebra.

vertical ['vɜːtɪkəl] *adj* vertical.

vertigo ['vɜːtɪgəʊ] *n* vértigo.

very ['verɪ] *adv* **1** muy. **2** mucho.

vessel ['vesəl] *n* nave.

vest [vest] *n* **1** camiseta *(interior)*. **2** US chaleco.

vet [vet] *n fam* veterinario,-a. ► *vt* GB investigar, examinar.

veteran ['vetərən] *adj-n* veterano,-a.

veterinarian [vetərɪˈneərɪən] *n* US veterinario,-a.

veterinary ['vetərɪnərɪ] *adj* veterinario,-a.

veto ['viːtəʊ] *n* veto. ► *vt* vetar.

via ['vaɪə] *prep* vía, por vía de, por.

viaduct ['vaɪədʌkt] *n* viaducto.

vibrate [vaɪˈbreɪt] *vi* vibrar.

vice [vaɪs] *n* vicio.

vice versa [vaɪsˈvɜːsə] *adv* viceversa.

vicinity [vɪˈsɪnɪtɪ] *n* vecindad.

vicious ['vɪʃəs] *adj* **1** cruel. **2** violento,-a, brutal.

victim ['vɪktɪm] *n* víctima.

victory ['vɪktərɪ] *n* victoria.

video ['vɪdɪəʊ] *n* vídeo. ▪ **video camera** videocámara; **video cassette** videocasete; **video game** videojuego; **video shop** videoclub; **video recorder** vídeo.

videotape ['vɪdɪəʊteɪp] *vt* grabar en vídeo. ► *n* cinta de vídeo.

view [vjuː] *n* **1** vista, panorama. **2** parecer, opinión. ► *vt* mirar, ver. ● **in my view** en mi opinión; **in view of** en vista de.

viewer ['vjuːəʳ] *n* telespectador,-ra.

viewpoint ['vjuːpɔɪnt] *n* punto de vista.

vigour ['vɪgəʳ] (US **vigor**) *n* vigor.

villa ['vɪlə] *n* chalet.

village ['vɪlɪdʒ] *n* pueblo.

villain ['vɪlən] *n* malo,-a.

vinaigrette [vɪnəˈgret] *n* vinagreta.

vindicate ['vɪndɪkeɪt] *vt* reivindicar.

vine [vaɪn] *n* vid, parra.

vinegar ['vɪnɪgəʳ] *n* vinagre.

vineyard ['vɪnjɑːd] *n* viña, viñedo.

vintage ['vɪntɪdʒ] *n* cosecha. ▪ **vintage wine** vino añejo.

vinyl ['vaɪnəl] *n* vinilo.

violate ['vaɪəleɪt] *vt* violar.
violence ['vaɪələns] *n* violencia.
violent ['vaɪələnt] *adj* violento,-a.
violet ['vaɪələt] *n* violeta.
violin [vaɪə'lɪn] *n* violín.
viper ['vaɪpə'] *n* víbora.
virgin ['vɜːdʒɪn] *adj* virgen. ► *n* virgen.
virtual ['vɜːtjʊəl] *adj* virtual. ■ **virtual reality** realidad virtual.
virtue ['vɜːtjuː] *n* virtud.
virus ['vaɪərəs] *n* virus. ■ **virus checker** antivirus.
visa ['viːzə] *n* visado.
visible ['vɪzɪbəl] *adj* visible.
vision ['vɪʒən] *n* visión, vista.
visit ['vɪzɪt] *n* visita. ► *vt* visitar. ● **to pay a visit** visitar.
visitor ['vɪzɪtə'] *n* **1** visita. **2** visitante.
visor ['vaɪzə'] *n* visera.
visual ['vɪzjʊəl] *adj* visual. ■ **visual display unit** pantalla.
vital ['vaɪtəl] *adj* vital.
vitality [vaɪ'tælɪtɪ] *n* vitalidad.
vitamin ['vɪtəmɪn] *n* vitamina.
vivid ['vɪvɪd] *adj* **1** vivo,-a, intenso,-a. **2** gráfico,-a.
vixen ['vɪksən] *n* zorra.
vocabulary [və'kæbjʊlərɪ] *n* vocabulario.
vocal ['vəʊkəl] *adj* vocal.
vocation [vəʊ'keɪʃən] *n* vocación.
vodka ['vɒdkə] *n* vodka.

vogue [vəʊg] *n* boga, moda. ● **to be in vogue** estar de moda.
voice [vɔɪs] *n* voz. ■ **voice mail** buzón de voz.
volcano [vɒl'keɪnəʊ] *n* volcán.
volley ['vɒlɪ] *n* volea. ► *vi* volear.
volleyball ['vɒlɪbɔːl] *n* balonvolea, voleibol.
volt [vəʊlt] *n* voltio.
voltage ['vəʊltɪdʒ] *n* voltaje.
voluble ['vɒljʊbəl] *adj* locuaz, hablador,-ra.
volume ['vɒljuːm] *n* volumen.
voluntary ['vɒləntərɪ] *adj* voluntario,-a. ■ **voluntary organization** organización benéfica.
volunteer [vɒlən'tɪə'] *n* voluntario,-a. ► *vt-vi* ofrecerse (voluntario) para hacer algo.
vomit ['vɒmɪt] *n* vómito. ► *vt-vi* vomitar.
vote [vəʊt] *n* **1** voto. **2** votación. ► *vt-vi* votar.
voter ['vəʊtə'] *n* votante.
voucher ['vaʊtʃə'] *n* vale, bono.
vow [vaʊ] *n* promesa solemne, voto.
vowel ['vaʊəl] *n* vocal.
voyage ['vɔɪdʒ] *n* viaje.
voyager ['vɔɪədʒə'] *n* viajero,-a.
vulgar ['vʌlgə'] *adj* vulgar.
vulnerable ['vʌlnərəbəl] *adj* vulnerable.
vulture ['vʌltʃə'] *n* buitre.
vulva ['vʌlvə] *n* vulva.

W

wafer ['weɪfəʳ] *n* **1** barquillo, galleta, oblea. **2** hostia.

waffle ['wɒfəl] *n* gofre.

wag [wæg] *n* meneo. ▸ *vt-vi* menear(se).

wage [weɪdʒ] *n* sueldo.

wager ['weɪdʒəʳ] *n* apuesta.

wagon ['wægən] *n* **1** carro, carromato. **2** vagón *(de tren)*.

waist [weɪst] *n* cintura, talle.

waistcoat ['weɪskəʊt] *n* chaleco.

wait [weɪt] *n* espera. ▸ *vi* esperar.

waiter ['weɪtəʳ] *n* camarero.

waiting ['weɪtɪŋ] *n* espera. ■ **waiting list** lista de espera; **waiting room** sala de espera.

waitress ['weɪtrəs] *n* camarera.

wake [weɪk] *n* velatorio. ▸ *vt* despertar.

to wake up *vt-vi* despertar(se).

waken ['weɪkən] *vt-vi* despertar(se).

walk [wɔːk] *n* paseo, caminata. ▸ *vi* andar, caminar. ▸ *vt* **1** pasear *(perro)*. **2** acompañar *(persona)*. ● **to go for a walk** dar un paseo.

to walk out *vi* **1** marcharse. **2** ir a la huelga.

walkie-talkie [wɔːkɪˈtɔːkɪ] *n* walkie-talkie.

walking stick ['wɔːkɪŋstɪk] *n* bastón.

Walkman® ['wɔːkmən] *n* Walkman®.

wall [wɔːl] *n* **1** muro *(exterior)*. **2** pared *(interior)*.

wallet ['wɒlɪt] *n* cartera.

wallpaper ['wɔːlpeɪpəʳ] *n* papel pintado. ▸ *vt* empapelar.

wally ['wɒlɪ] *n fam* inútil, imbécil.

walnut ['wɔːlnʌt] *n* nuez. ■ **walnut tree** nogal.

walrus ['wɔːlrəs] *n* morsa.

waltz [wɔːls] *n* vals.

wand [wɒnd] *n* varita.

wander ['wɒndəʳ] *vi* vagar.

want [wɒnt] *vt* **1** querer. **2** *fam* necesitar.

wanted ['wɒntɪd] *adj* **1** necesario,-a: *"Boy wanted"*, "Se necesita chico". **2** buscado,-a: *"Wanted"*, "Se busca".

war [wɔːʳ] *n* guerra.

ward [wɔːd] *n* **1** sala *(de hospital)*. **2** GB distrito electoral.

warden ['wɔːdən] *n* vigilante, guardián,-ana.

wardrobe ['wɔːdrəʊb] *n* **1** armario *(ropero)*, guardarropa. **2** vestuario.

warehouse ['weəhaʊs] *n* almacén.

warfare ['wɔːfeəʳ] *n* guerra.

warm [wɔːm] *adj* **1** caliente. **2** tibio,-a, templado,-a. **3** cálido,-a *(clima)*. **4** de abrigo *(ropa)*. ▸ *vt* calentar.

to warm up *vt* calentar. ► *vi*
1 calentarse. 2 hacer ejercicios de calentamiento.
warmth [wɔːmθ] *n* calor.
warn [wɔːn] *vt* avisar, advertir, prevenir.
warning [wɔːnɪŋ] *n* aviso, advertencia.
warrant [wɒrənt] *n* orden judicial. ► *vt* justificar.
warranty [wɒrəntɪ] *n* garantía.
warrior [wɒrɪəʳ] *n* guerrero,-a.
wart [wɔːt] *n* verruga.
was [wɒz] *pt* → be.
wash [wɒʃ] *vt* 1 lavar, lavarse.
to wash up *vt-vi* fregar *(platos)*.
washbasin [wɒʃbeɪsən] *n* lavabo.
washer [wɒʃəʳ] *n* 1 arandela.
2 lavadora.
washing [wɒʃɪŋ] *n* 1 lavado.
2 colada. • **to do the washing** hacer la colada. ■ **washing machine** lavadora.
washing-up [wɒʃɪŋʌp] *n* 1 fregado. 2 platos. • **to do the washing up** fregar los platos, lavar los platos. ■ **washing-up liquid** lavavajillas.
washroom [wɒʃruːm] *n* US servicios, lavabo.
wasp [wɒsp] *n* avispa.
waste [weɪst] *n* 1 desperdicio. 2 derroche *(de dinero)*. 3 desechos. ► *vt* 1 desperdiciar, malgastar *(comida, oportunidad)*. 2 despilfarrar, derrochar *(dinero)*.

watch [wɒtʃ] *n* reloj *(de pulsera)*. ► *vt* 1 mirar, ver *(televisión, película)*. 2 observar. 3 vigilar. 4 tener cuidado con. •
watch out! ¡ojo!, ¡cuidado!
watchdog [wɒtʃdɒg] *n* perro guardián.
watchman [wɒtʃmən] *n* vigilante.
water [wɔːtəʳ] *n* agua. ► *vt* regar. ► *vi* 1 llorar *(ojos)*. 2 hacerse agua *(boca)*. ■ **water bottle** cantimplora; **water lily** nenúfar; **water polo** waterpolo.
to water down *vt* aguar.
watercolour [wɔːtəkʌləʳ] (US **watercolor**) *n* acuarela.
watercress [wɔːtkres] *n* berro.
waterfall [wɔːtəfɔːl] *n* cascada.
watermelon [wɔːtəmelən] *n* sandía.
watermill [wɔːtəmɪl] *n* molino de agua.
waterproof [wɔːtəpruːf] *adj* impermeable.
water-skiing [wɔːtəskiːɪŋ] *n* esquí acuático.
watertight [wɔːtətaɪt] *adj* hermético,-a.
watt [wɒt] *n* vatio.
wave [weɪv] *n* 1 ola *(de mar)*. 2 onda. ► *vt* 1 agitar. 2 marcar, ondular *(pelo)*.
wavelength [weɪvleŋθ] *n* longitud de onda.
wavy [weɪvɪ] *adj* ondulado,-a.

wax [wæks] *n* cera. ► *vt* encerar.

way [weɪ] *n* 1 camino. 2 dirección. 3 manera, modo. • **by the way** a propósito; **on the way** por el camino; **the right way round** bien puesto; **the wrong way round** al revés; **to get out of the way** apartarse del camino, quitarse de en medio; **to give way** ceder el paso; **to lose one's way** perderse; **to stand in the way of** obstruir el paso.

we [wiː, unstressed wɪ] *pron* nosotros,-as.

weak [wiːk] *adj* débil.

weakness ['wiːknəs] *n* debilidad.

wealth [welθ] *n* riqueza.

wealthy ['welθɪ] *adj* rico,-a.

weapon ['wepən] *n* arma.

wear [weəʳ] *n* 1 uso. 2 desgaste, deterioro. 3 ropa. ► *vt* 1 llevar puesto,-a. 2 vestir, ponerse *(ropa)*. 3 calzar *(zapatos)*. 4 desgastar.

weary ['wɪərɪ] *adj* cansado,-a.

weasel ['wiːzəl] *n* comadreja.

weather ['weðəʳ] *n* tiempo. ■ **weather forecast** pronóstico del tiempo.

weathercock ['weðəkɒk] *n* veleta.

weave [wiːv] *n* tejido. ► *vt-vi* tejer.

web [web] *n* 1 telaraña. 2 *fig* red. 3 Internet. ■ **web page** página web.

website ['websaɪt] *n* sitio web.

wedding ['wedɪŋ] *n* boda. ■ **wedding dress** vestido de novia; **wedding ring** alianza.

wedge [wedʒ] *n* cuña, calce.

Wednesday ['wenzdɪ] *n* miércoles.

week [wiːk] *n* semana.

weekday ['wiːkdeɪ] *n* día laborable.

weekend ['wiːkend] *n* fin de semana.

weekly ['wiːklɪ] *adj* semanal. ► *adv* semanalmente. ► *n* semanario.

weep [wiːp] *vi* llorar.

weigh [weɪ] *vt* pesar.

weight [weɪt] *n* 1 peso. 2 pesa. • **to lose weight** perder peso; **to put on weight** engordar.

weightlifting ['weɪtlɪftɪŋ] *n* halterofilia.

weir [wɪəʳ] *n* presa *(de río)*.

weird [wɪəd] *adj* raro,-a.

welcome ['welkəm] *adj* bienvenido,-a. ► *n* bienvenida. ► *vt* dar la bienvenida a. • **you're welcome** de nada, no hay de qué.

weld [weld] *n* soldadura. ► *vt* soldar.

welfare ['welfeəʳ] *n* bienestar.

well[1] [wel] *adj-adv* bien. ► *interj* bueno • **as well** también; **as well as** además de; **just as well** menos mal; **pretty well** casi.

well[2] [wel] *n* pozo.

well-being [wel'biːɪŋ] n bienestar.

well-built [wel'bɪlt] adj fornido,-a.

wellington ['welɪŋtən] n bota de goma.

well-known [wel'nəʊn] adj conocido,-a, famoso,-a.

well-meaning [wel'miːnɪŋ] adj bien intencionado,-a.

well-off [wel'ɒf] adj rico,-a.

well-timed [wel'taɪmd] adj oportuno,-a.

well-to-do [weltə'duː] adj acomodado,-a.

went [went] pt → go.

wept [wept] pt-pp → weep.

were [wɜːʳ] pt → be.

west [west] n oeste, occidente. ► adj del oeste, occidental. ► adv al oeste, hacia el oeste.

western ['westən] adj del oeste. ► n western,.

wet [wet] adj 1 mojado,-a. 2 húmedo,-a. 3 lluvioso,-a (tiempo). ► vt humedecer. • "Wet paint" "Recién pintado".

whale [weɪl] n ballena.

wharf [wɔːf] n muelle.

what [wɒt] adj 1 qué (preguntas). 2 qué, menudo (exclamaciones). ► pron 1 qué (preguntas). 2 lo que (subordinadas): **that's what he said**, eso es lo que dijo.

whatever [wɒt'evəʳ] adj 1 cualquiera que. 2 en absoluto. ► pron (todo) lo que.

whatsoever [wɒtsəʊ'evəʳ] adj → whatever.

wheat [wiːt] n trigo.

wheel [wiːl] n 1 rueda. 2 volante.■ **wheel clamp** cepo.

wheelbarrow ['wiːlbærəʊ] n carretilla de mano.

wheelchair ['wiːltʃeəʳ] n silla de ruedas.

when [wen] adv cuándo. ► pron cuando.

whenever [wen'evəʳ] conj cuando quiera que, siempre que. ► adv 1 cuando sea. 2 cuándo.

where [weəʳ] adv 1 dónde, adónde. 2 en cualquier parte, donde sea. ► pron donde.

whereabouts [(n) 'weərəbaʊts, (adv) weərə'baʊts] n paradero. ► adv dónde, adónde.

whereas [weər'æz] conj mientras que.

whereby [weə'baɪ] adv por el/la/lo cual.

wherever [weər'evəʳ] adv dónde, adónde. ► conj dondequiera que.

whether ['weðəʳ] conj si.

which [wɪtʃ] adj qué. ► pron 1 cuál, cuáles (en interrogativas). 2 que (en subordinadas). 3 el/la/lo que, el/la/lo cual (con preposición), los/las que, los/las cuales. 4 el/la cual, los/las cuales. 5 lo que/cual.

whichever [wɪtʃ'evəʳ] adj (no importa) el/la/los/las que. ►

pron cualquiera, el/la/los/las que.

while [waɪl] *n* rato, tiempo. ▶ *conj* **1** mientras. **2** aunque. **3** mientras que. • **for a while** un rato; **once in a while** de vez en cuando.

whilst [waɪlst] *conj* → while.

whim [wɪm] *n* antojo.

whip [wɪp] *n* látigo, fusta. ▶ *vt* **1** azotar. **2** batir, montar *(nata, etc)*. ▪ **whipped cream** nata montada.

whirlpool [ˈwɜːlpuːl] *n* remolino.

whisk [wɪsk] *n* **1** batidor. **2** batidora *(eléctrica)*. ▶ *vt* montar *(nata, claras)*.

whisker [ˈwɪskə] *n* pelo *(de bigote)*. ▶ *npl* **whiskers 1** patillas *(de persona)*. **2** bigotes *(de gato)*.

whiskey [ˈwɪskɪ] *n* whisky, güisqui.

whisky [ˈwɪskɪ] *n* whisky, güisqui.

whisper [ˈwɪspə] *n* susurro. ▶ *vt-vi* susurrar.

whistle [ˈwɪsəl] *n* **1** silbato. **2** silbido, pitido. ▶ *vt-vi* silbar.

white [waɪt] *adj* blanco,-a. ▶ *n* **1** blanco *(color)*. **2** clara *(de huevo)*. ▪ **white coffee** café con leche.

white-collar [waɪtˈkɒlə] *adj* administrativo,-a.

whitewash [ˈwaɪtwɒʃ] *n* cal. ▶ *vt* encalar.

who [huː] *pron* **1** quién, quiénes *(en interrogativas directas e indirectas)*. **2** que *(en subordinadas-objeto)*.

whoever [huːˈevə] *pron* **1** quien. **2** quienquiera que, cualquiera que.

whole [həʊl] *adj* **1** entero,-a. **2** intacto,-a. ▶ *n* conjunto, todo. • **as a whole** en conjunto.

wholemeal [ˈhəʊlmiːl] *adj* integral.

wholesale [ˈhəʊlseɪl] *adj-adv* COMM al por mayor.

whom [huːm] *pron* **1** *fml* a quién, a quiénes *(en interrogativas)*. **2** a quien, a quienes *(en subordinadas)*.

whose [huːz] *pron* de quién, de quiénes. ▶ *adj* **1** de quién, de quiénes. **2** cuyo,-a, cuyos,-as.

why [waɪ] *adv* por qué.

wick [wɪk] *n* mecha.

wicked [ˈwɪkɪd] *adj* malo,-a.

wicker [ˈwɪkə] *n* mimbre.

wide [waɪd] *adj* **1** ancho,-a. **2** amplio,-a. • **wide open** abierto,-a de par en par.

widow [ˈwɪdəʊ] *n* viuda.

widower [ˈwɪdəʊə] *n* viudo.

width [wɪdθ] *n* ancho.

wife [waɪf] *n* esposa, mujer.

wig [wɪg] *n* peluca.

wild [waɪld] *adj* **1** salvaje. **2** silvestre, campestre *(planta)*.

wildcat [ˈwaɪldkæt] *n* gato montés.

wildlife ['waɪldlaɪf] *n* fauna.

will[1] [wɪl] *aux* **1** *se usa para formar el futuro de los verbos*: *she will be here tomorrow*, estará aquí mañana. **2** *indica voluntad*: *the car won't start*, el coche no arranca. **3** *indica insistencia*: *he will leave the door open*, es que no hay manera de que cierre la puerta. **4** poder: *this phone will accept credit cards*, este teléfono acepta tarjetas de crédito. **5** *indica una suposición*: *it won't rain, will it?*, ¿no lloverá, ¿verdad?

will[2] [wɪl] *n* **1** voluntad. **2** testamento.

willing ['wɪlɪŋ] *adj* complaciente. • **willing to do STH** dispuesto,-a a hacer algo.

willow ['wɪləʊ] *n* sauce.

willpower ['wɪlpaʊə'] *n* fuerza de voluntad.

win [wɪn] *n* victoria, éxito. ► *vt-vi* ganar.

wind[1] [wɪnd] *n* **1** viento, aire. **2** gases, flato. ■ **wind instrument** instrumento de viento; **wind power** energía eólica.

wind[2] [waɪnd] *vt* **1** envolver. **2** arrollar, enrollar. **3** dar cuerda a *(reloj)*. **4** dar vueltas a *(palanca)*. ► *vi* serpentear.

to wind up [waɪnd'ʌp] *vt* dar cuerda a *(reloj)*.

windmill ['wɪndmɪl] *n* molino de viento.

window ['wɪndəʊ] *n* **1** ventana. **2** ventanilla *(de vehículo)*. **3** escaparate *(de tienda)*.

windpipe ['wɪndpaɪp] *n* tráquea.

windscreen ['wɪndskriːn] *n* parabrisas.

wind-shield ['wɪndʃiːld] *n* US parabrisas.

wine [waɪn] *n* vino.

wing [wɪŋ] *n* **1** ala. **2** aleta *(de coche)*. **3** banda *(fútbol)*. ► *npl* **wings** bastidores.

wink [wɪŋk] *n* guiño.

winner ['wɪnə'] *n* ganador,-ra.

winning ['wɪnɪŋ] *adj* ganador,-ra. ► *npl* **winnings** ganancias.

winter ['wɪntə'] *n* invierno.

wipe [waɪp] *vt* **1** limpiar, pasar un trapo a. **2** secar.

to wipe out *vt* borrar.

wiper ['waɪpə'] *n* limpiaparabrisas.

wire ['waɪə'] *n* **1** alambre. **2** cable. **3** US telegrama.

wisdom ['wɪzdəm] *n* **1** sabiduría. **2** prudencia, juicio. ■ **wisdom tooth** muela del juicio.

wise [waɪz] *adj* **1** sabio,-a. **2** prudente.

wish [wɪʃ] *n* deseo. ► *vt-vi* desear. • **I wish to ...** quisiera ...; **(with) best wishes** muchos recuerdos.

wit [wɪt] *n* agudeza, ingenio.

witch [wɪtʃ] *n* bruja. ■ **witch doctor** hechicero.

with [wɪð] *prep* con.

withdraw [wɪð'drɔː] *vt-vi* retirar(se).

withdrawal [wɪð'drɔːəl] *n* retirada.

withdrawn [wɪð'drɔːn] *pp* → withdraw.

withdrew [wɪð'druː] *pt* → withdraw.

wither ['wɪðəʳ] *vt-vi* marchitar(se).

within [wɪ'ðɪn] *prep* **1** dentro de. **2** al alcance de. **3** a menos de. **4** antes de. ► *adv* dentro.

without [wɪ'ðaʊt] *prep* sin.

withstand [wɪð'stænd] *vt* resistir, aguantar.

witness ['wɪtnəs] *n* testigo. ► *vt* presenciar.

witty ['wɪti] *adj* ingenioso,-a.

wizard ['wɪzəd] *n* brujo.

woke [wəʊk] *pt* → wake.

woken ['wəʊkən] *pp* → wake.

wolf [wʊlf] *n* lobo.

woman ['wʊmən] *n* mujer.

womb [wuːm] *n* útero.

won [wʌn] *pt-pp* → win.

wonder ['wʌndəʳ] *n* **1** maravilla. **2** admiración, asombro. ► *vi* preguntarse.

wonderful ['wʌndəfʊl] *adj* maravilloso,-a.

wood [wʊd] *n* **1** madera. **2** bosque.

wooden ['wʊdən] *adj* de madera.

woodpecker ['wʊdpekəʳ] *n* pájaro carpintero.

woodwork ['wʊdwɜːk] *n* carpintería.

wool [wʊl] *n* lana.

woollen ['wʊlən] *adj* de lana.

word [wɜːd] *n* palabra. • **in a word** en pocas palabras; **in other words** en otras palabras, o sea; **to have words with SB** discutir con ALGN. ■ **word processor** procesador de textos.

wore [wɔːʳ] *pt* → wear.

work [wɜːk] *vt-vi* trabajar. ► *vi* **1** funcionar *(máquina, plan)*. **2** surtir efecto *(medicamento)*. ► *n* **1** trabajo. **2** obra. ► *npl* **works 1** fábrica. **2** mecanismo. • **out of work** parado,-a. ■ **work of art** obra de arte.

to work out *vt* **1** calcular. **2** planear *(plan)*. **3** solucionar *(problema)*. ► *vi* salir bien.

worker ['wɜːkəʳ] *n* trabajador,-ra.

workforce ['wɜːkfɔːs] *n* mano de obra.

working ['wɜːkɪŋ] *adj* de trabajo, laboral.

workout ['wɜːkaʊt] *n* entrenamiento.

workshop ['wɜːkʃɒp] *n* taller.

worktop ['wɜːktɒp] *n* encimera.

world [wɜːld] *n* mundo.

worldwide ['wɜːldwaɪd] *adj* mundial, universal.

worm [wɜːm] *n* gusano, lombriz.

worn [wɔːn] *pp* → wear.

worn-out [wɔːn'aʊt] *adj* **1** gastado,-a *(ropa, neumático).* **2** rendido,-a *(persona).*

worried ['wʌrɪd] *adj* preocupado,-a.

worry ['wʌrɪ] *n* preocupación. ► *vt-vi* preocupar(se).

worse [wɜːs] *adj-adv* peor. ► *n* lo peor. • **to get worse** empeorar.

worst [wɜːst] *adj-adv* peor. ► *n* lo peor.

worth [wɜːθ] *n* valor. ► *adj* que vale. • **to be worth** valer.

worthless ['wɜːθləs] *adj* **1** sin valor *(objeto).* **2** despreciable *(persona).*

worthwhile [wɜːθ'waɪl] *adj* que vale la pena.

worthy ['wɜːðɪ] *adj* digno,-a.

would [wʊd] *aux* **1** *(condicional):* *she would tell you if she knew,* te lo diría si lo supiese. **2** *(disponibilidad):* *he wouldn't help me,* se negó a ayudarme. **3** *(suposición):* *that would have been Jim,* ese debió de ser Jim. **4** soler: *we would often go out together,* solíamos salir juntos. • **would like** querer.

wound[1] [wuːnd] *n* herida. ► *vt* herir.

wound[2] [waʊnd] *pt-pp* → wind.

wounded ['wuːndɪd] *adj* herido,-a.

wove [wəʊv] *pt* → weave.

woven ['wəʊvən] *pp* → weave.

wrap [ræp] *vt* envolver.

wrapping ['ræpɪŋ] *n* envoltorio. ▪ **wrapping paper** papel de envolver.

wreath [riːθ] *n* corona.

wreck [rek] *n* **1** naufragio. **2** barco naufragado. **3** restos *(de coche).*

wrench [rentʃ] *n* llave inglesa.

wrestle ['resəl] *vi* luchar.

wrestler ['reslər] *n* luchador,-ra.

wrestling ['reslɪŋ] *n* lucha.

wretched ['retʃɪd] *adj* **1** desgraciado,-a. **2** *fam* horrible.

wrinkle ['rɪŋkəl] *n* arruga. ► *vt-vi* arrugar(se).

wrist [rɪst] *n* muñeca.

wristwatch ['rɪstwɒtʃ] *n* reloj de pulsera.

write [raɪt] *vt-vi* escribir. ► *vt* extender *(cheque).*

to write back *vi* contestar.

to write down *vt* anotar.

writer ['raɪtər] *n* escritor,-ra.

writing ['raɪtɪŋ] *n* **1** escritura. **2** letra. ► *npl* **writings** obras. ▪ **writing desk** escritorio; **writing paper** papel de cartas.

written ['rɪtən] *pp* → write. ► *adj* escrito,-a.

wrong [rɒŋ] *adj* **1** equivocado,-a. **2** malo,-a. ► *adv* mal. • **to be in the wrong** no tener razón, tener la culpa; **to be wrong** estar equivocado,-a,

equivocarse; **to go wrong 1** equivocarse *(persona)*. **2** estropearse *(máquina)*.
wrote [rəʊt] *pt* → write.
wrought [rɔːt] *adj* forjado,-a.

X

xenophobia [zenəˈfəʊbɪə] *n* xenofobia.
X-ray [ˈeksreɪ] *n* **1** rayo X. **2** radiografía. ▶ *vt* radiografiar.
xylophone [ˈzaɪləfəʊn] *n* xilófono.

Y

yacht [jɒt] *n* yate.
yard [jɑːd] *n* **1** patio. **2** US jardín. **3** yarda.
yarn [jɑːn] *n* hilo.
yawn [jɔːn] *n* bostezo. ▶ *vi* bostezar.
yeah [jeə] *adv fam* sí.
year [jɪəˈ] *n* **1** año. **2** curso.
yeast [jiːst] *n* levadura.
yell [jel] *n* grito, alarido. ▶ *vi* gritar, dar alaridos.
yellow [ˈjeləʊ] *adj* amarillo,-a. ▶ *n* amarillo. ■ **yellow press** prensa amarilla.

yes [jes] *adv* sí. ▶ *n* sí.
yesterday [ˈjestədɪ] *adv* ayer.
yet [jet] *adv* **1** todavía, aún: *the taxi hasn't arrived yet*, aún no ha llegado el taxi. **2** ya: *has the taxi arrived yet?*, ¿ya ha llegado el taxi? ▶ *conj* no obstante, sin embargo.
yew [juː] *n* tejo.
yield [jiːld] *n* **1** rendimiento. **2** cosecha. ▶ *vt* **1** producir, dar. **2** rendir. ▶ *vi* rendirse, ceder.
yoga [ˈjəʊgə] *n* yoga.
yoghurt [ˈjɒgət] *n* yogur.
yoke [jəʊk] *n* yugo. ▶ *vt* uncir.
yolk [jəʊk] *n* yema.
you [juː] *pron* **1** tú, vosotros, -as. **2** usted, ustedes. **3** se *(sujeto - impersonal)*. **4** ti *(complemento)*. **5** te *(antes del verbo)*. **6** vosotros,-as *(plural)*. **7** os *(antes del verbo)*. **8** usted *(complemento)*. **9** le *(antes del verbo)*. **10** ustedes *(plural)*. **11** les *(antes del verbo)*. **12** *(complemento - impersonal)*: *you never know*, nunca se sabe.
young [jʌŋ] *adj* joven.
your [jɔːˈ] *adj* **1** tu, tus, vuestro,-a, vuestros,-as. **2** su, sus.
yours [jɔːz] *pron* **1** (el) tuyo, (la) tuya, (los) tuyos, (las) tuyas, (el) vuestro, (la) vuestra, (los) vuestros, (las) vuestras. **2** (el) suyo, (la) suya, (los) suyos, (las) suyas.

yourself [jɔːˈself] *pron* **1** te, tú mismo,-a. **2** se, usted mismo,-a.

yourselves [jɔːˈselvz] *pron* **1** os, vosotros,-as mismos,-as. **2** se, ustedes mismos,-as.

youth [juːθ] *n* **1** juventud. **2** joven. ■ **youth hostel** albergue de juventud.

yo-yo® [ˈɪəʊɪəʊ] *n* yoyo, yoyó.

Z

zeal [ziːl] *n* celo, entusiasmo.

zealous [ˈzeləs] *adj* celoso,-a, entusiasta.

zebra [ˈziːbrə, ˈzebrə] *n* cebra. ■ **zebra crossing** paso de peatones, paso de cebra.

zenith [ˈzenɪθ] *n* cenit.

zeppelin [ˈzepəlɪn] *n* zepelín.

zero [ˈzɪərəʊ] *n* cero.

zest [zest] *n* entusiasmo.

zigzag [ˈzɪgzæg] *n* zigzag. ► *vt* zigzaguear.

zip [zɪp] *n* cremallera. ► *vi* como un rayo. ■ **zip code** US código postal.

to zip up *vt* cerrar con cremallera.

zipper [ˈzɪpr] *n* US cremallera.

zodiac [ˈzəʊdɪæk] *n* zodiaco, zodíaco.

zombie [ˈzɒmbɪ] *n* zombi.

zone [zəʊn] *n* zona.

zoo [zuː] *n* zoo, zoológico.

zoological [zʊəˈlɒdʒɪkəl] *adj* zoológico,-a.

zoology [zʊˈɒlədʒɪ] *n* zoología.

zoom [zuːm] *n* **1** zumbido. **2** zoom, teleobjetivo. ► *vt-vi* pasar zumbando. ■ **zoom lens** teleobjetivo.

Key to Pronunciation in Spanish

VOWELS

Letter	Approximate sound
a	Like *a* in English *far, father*, e.g., **casa, mano**.
e	When stressed, like *a* in English *pay*, e.g., **dedo**. When unstressed, it has a shorter sound like in English *bet, net*, e.g., **estado, decidir**.
i	Like *i* in English *machine* or *ee* in *feet*, e.g., **fin**.
o	Like *o* in English *obey*, e.g., **mona, poner**.
u	Like *u* in English *rule* or *oo* in *boot*, e.g., **atún**. It is silent in **gue** and **gui**, e.g., **guerra, guisado**. If it carries a diaeresis (**ü**), it is pronounced (see Diphthongs), e.g., **bilingüe**. It is also silent in **que** and **qui**, e.g., **querer, quinto**.
y	When used as a vowel, it sounds like the Spanish **i**, e.g., **y, rey**.

DIPHTHONGS

Diph.	Approximate sound
ai, ay	Like *i* in English *light*, e.g., **caigo, hay**.
au	Like *ou* in English *sound*, e.g., **cauto, paular**.
ei, ey	Like *ey* in English *they* or *a* in *ale*, e.g., **reina, ley**.
eu	Like the *a* in English *pay* combined with the sound of *ew* in English *knew*, e.g., **deuda, feudal**.
oi, oy	Like *oy* in English *toy*, e.g., **oiga, soy**.
ia, ya	Like *ya* in English *yarn*, e.g., **rabia, raya**.
ua	Like *wa* in English *wand*, e.g., **cuatro, cual**.
ie, ye	Like *ye* in English *yet*, e.g., **bien, yeso**.
ue	Like *wa* in English *wake*, e.g., **buena, fue**.
io, yo	Like *yo* in English *yoke*, without the following sound of *w* in this word, e.g., **región, yodo**.

Diph.	Approximate sound
uo	Like *uo* in English *quote*, e.g., **cuota, oblicuo**.
iu, yu	Like *yu* in English *Yule*, e.g., **ciudad, triunfo**.
ui	Like *wee* in English *week*, e.g., **ruido**.

TRIPHTHONGS

Triph.	Approximate sound
iai	Like *ya* in English *yard* combined with the *i* in *fight*, e.g., **estudiáis**.
iei	Like the English word *yea*, e.g., **estudiéis**.
uai, uay	Like *wi* in English *wide*, e.g., **averiguáis, guay**.
uei, uey	Like *wei* in English *weigh*, e.g., **amortigüéis**.

CONSONANTS

Letter	Approximate sound
b	Generally like the English *b* in *boat, bring, obsolete*, when it is at the beginning of a word or preceded by *m*, e.g., **baile, bomba**. Between two vowels and when followed by *l* or *r*, it has a softer sound, almost like the English *v* but formed by pressing both lips together, e.g., **acaba, haber, cable**.
c	Before *a, o, u*, or a consonant, it sounds like the English *c* in *coal*, e.g., **casa, saco**. Before *e* or *i*, it is pronounced like the English *s* in *six* in American Spanish and like the English *th* in *thin* in Castillian Spanish, e.g., **cerdo, cine**. If a word contains two *c*s, the first is pronounced like *c* in *coal*, and the second like *s* or *th* accordingly, e.g., **acción**.
ch	Like *ch* in English *cheese* or *such*, e.g., **chato**.
d	Generally like *d* in English *dog* or *th* in English *this*, e.g., **dedo, digo**. When ending a syllable, it is pronounced like the English *th*, e.g., **usted**.
f	Like *f* in English *fine, life*, e.g., **final**.

Letter	Approximate sound
g	Before *a, o,* and *u;* the groups *ue* and *ui;* or a consonant, it sounds like *g* in English *gain,* e.g., **gato, guitar, digno.** Before *e* or *i,* like a strongly aspirated English *h,* e.g., **general.**
h	Always silent, e.g., **hoyo, historia.**
j	Like *h* in English *hat,* e.g., **joven, reja.**
k	Like *c* in English *coal,* e.g., **kilo.** It is found only in words of foreign origin.
l	Like *l* in English *lion,* e.g., **libro, límite.**
ll	In some parts of Spain and Spanish America, like the English *y* in *yet;* generally in Castillian Spanish, like the *lli* in English *million;* e.g., **castillo, silla.**
m	Like *m* in English *map,* e.g., **moneda, tomo.**
n	Like *n* in English *nine,* e.g., **nuevo, canto.**
ñ	Like *ni* in English *onion* or *ny* in English *canyon,* e.g., **cañón, paño.**
p	Like *p* in English *parent,* e.g., **pipa, pollo.**
q	Like *c* in English *coal.* This letter is only used in the combinations *que* and *qui* in which the *u* is silent, e.g., **queso, aquí.**
r	At the beginning of a word and when preceded by *l, n,* or *s,* it is strongly trilled, e.g., **roca.** In all other positions, it is pronounced with a single tap of the tongue, e.g., **era, padre.**
rr	Strongly trilled, e.g., **carro, arriba.**
s	Like *s* in English *so,* e.g., **cosa, das.**
t	Like *t* in English *tip* but generally softer, e.g., **toma.**
v	Like *v* in English *mauve,* but in many parts of Spain and the Americas, like the Spanish b, e.g., **variar.**
x	Generally like *x* in English *expand,* e.g., **examen.** Before a consonant, it is sometimes pronounced like *s* in English *so,* e.g., **excepción, extensión.** In the word **México,** and in other place names of that country, it is pronounced like the Spanish *j.*

Letter	Approximate sound
y	When used as a consonant between vowels or at the beginning of a word, like the *y* in English *yet*, e.g., **yate**, **yeso**, **hoyo**.
z	Like Spanish c when it precedes e or i, e.g., **azul**.

Español - Inglés

A

a *prep* **1** *(dirección)* to: *girar a la derecha*, to turn (to the) right. **2** *(destino)* to, towards. **3** *(distancia)* away. **4** *(lugar)* at, on. **5** *(tiempo)* at: *a los tres días*, three days later; *estamos a 30 de mayo*, it's the thirtieth of May. **6** *(modo, manera)*: *a ciegas*, blindly; *a pie*, on foot. **7** *(instrumento)*: *escrito a mano*, handwritten; *escrito a máquina*, typewritten. **8** *(precio)* a: *a 3 euros el kilo*, three euros a kilo. **9** *(medida)* at. **10** *(complemento directo, no se traduce)*: *vi a Juana*, I saw Juana. **11** *(complemento indirecto)* to: *te lo di a ti*, I gave it to you. **12** *verbo + a + inf*: *aprender a nadar*, to learn (how) to swim.

abadía *nf (edificio)* abbey.

abajo *adv* **1** *(situación)* below, down. **2** *(en una casa)* downstairs. **3** *(dirección)* down, downward. • **hacia arriba** upwards.

abandonar *vt* **1** *(desamparar)* to abandon. **2** *(lugar)* to leave.

abanico *nm* fan.

abarrotado,-a *adj* packed.

abastecer *vt* to supply.

abastecimiento *nm* suply.

abatir *vt* **1** *(derribar)* to bring down. **2** *(matar)* to shoot.

abdomen *nm* abdomen.

abecedario *nm* alphabet.

abedul *nm* birch tree.

abeja *nf* bee.

abeto *nm* fir tree.

abierto,-a *adj* **1** *(puerta, boca, ojos)* open. **2** *(grifo)* on, running. **3** *(sincero)* frank.

abismo *nm* abyss.

abogado,-a *nm,f* lawyer.

abollar *vt* to dent.

abonado,-a *nm,f (a teléfono, revista)* subscriber; *(a teatro etc)* season-ticket holder.

abonar *vt* **1** *(pagar)* to pay. **2** *(tierra)* to fertilize. ▶ *vpr* **abonarse** *(a revista)* to subscribe; *(a teatro)* to buy a season ticket.

abono *nm* **1** *(pago)* payment. **2** *(para tierra)* fertilizer. **3** *(a revista)* subscription; *(a teatro, tren, etc)* season-ticket.

aborrecer *vt* to abhor, hate.

aborto *nm (voluntario)* abortion; *(espontáneo)* miscarriage.

abrasar *vt (quemar)* to burn. ▶ *vi (comida, etc)* to be boiling hot.

abrazar *vt* to embrace.

abrazo *nm* hug, embrace.

abrebotellas *nm* bottle opener.

abrelatas *nm* GB tin-opener; US can-opener.

abreviatura *nf* abbreviation.

abridor *nm* opener.

abrigarse *vpr* to wrap oneself up.

abrigo *nm* coat, overcoat.

abril *nm* April.

abrir *vt* **1** *(gen)* to open. **2** *(luz)* to switch on, turn on. **3** *(grifo, gas)* to turn on.

abrochar(se) *vt-vpr* to do up, fasten: **abróchense los cinturones**, please fasten your seatbelts.

ábside *nm* apse.

absoluto,-a *adj* absolute. • **en absoluto** not at all.

absolver *vt* to acquit.

absorber *vt* to absorb.

abstemio,-a *nm,f* teetotaller.

abstenerse *vpr* **1** *(en votación)* to abstain. **2** *(de hacer algo)* to refrain *(de,* from).

abstracto,-a *adj* abstract.

absurdo,-a *adj* absurd.

abuchear *vt* to boo.

abuela *nf* grandmother.

abuelo *nm* grandfather. ► *nm pl* **abuelos** grandparents.

abultar *vi* to be bulky.

abundancia *nf* abundance, plenty.

abundante *adj* abundant, plentiful.

aburrido,-a *adj* **1** *(con ser)* boring, tedious: **es un libro muy aburrido**, it's a very boring book. **2** *(con estar)* bored: **estoy aburrido**, I'm bored.

aburrir *vt* to bore. ► *vpr* **aburrirse** to get bored.

abusar *vi* **abusar de 1** *(persona)* to take advantage of; *(autoridad, paciencia)* to abuse. **2** *(sexualmente)* to sexually abuse.

abuso *nm* **1** *(uso excesivo)* abuse, misuse. **2** *(injusticia)* injustice.

acá *adv* *(lugar)* here, over here: **de acá para allá**, to and fro, up and down.

acabar *vt* **1** *(gen)* to finish. **2** *(consumir)* to use up, run out of. ► *vi* **acabar por** + *inf* **acabar** + *ger* to end up: **acabarás comprando el vestido**, you'll end up buying the dress. ► *vpr* **acabarse** *(terminarse)* to end, finish; *(no quedar)* to run out. • **acabar con** to destroy, put an end to; **acabar de** to have just.

acacia *nf* acacia.

academia *nf* **1** *(institución)* academy. **2** *(escuela)* school.

acampada *nf* camping.

acampar *vi* to camp.

acantilado *nm* cliff.

acariciar *vt (persona)* to caress, fondle; *(animal)* to stroke.

acaso *adv* **1** *(en preguntas):* **¿acaso no me crees?**, don't you believe me? **2** *fml (quizá)* perhaps, maybe: **acaso necesite tu ayuda**, I might need your help. • **por si acaso** just in case.

acatarrarse *vpr* to catch a cold.

acceder *vi* **1** *(consentir)* to consent, agree. **2** *(tener entrada)* to enter. **3** INFORM to access.

acceso *nm* **1** *(entrada)* access, entry. **2** *(carretera)* approach road.

accesorio *nm* accessory.

accidentado,-a *nm,f* casualty, accident victim.

accidente *nm* **1** *(percance)* accident. **2** *(del terreno)* unevenness. ■ **accidente aéreo** plane crash; **accidente de coche** car crash.

acción *nf* **1** *(gen)* action. **2** *(acto)* act, deed. **3** *(en bolsa)* share.

accionar *vt* **1** *(manivela)* to pull. **2** *(pieza mecánica)* to operate; *(alarma etc)* to set off.

accionista *nmf* shareholder, stockholder.

acecho ● **al acecho** in wait.

aceite *nm* oil. ■ **aceite de oliva** olive oil.

aceitera *nf* oil bottle.

aceituna *nf* olive. ■ **aceituna rellena** stuffed olive.

acelerador *nm* accelerator.

acelerar *vt* to accelerate.

acelga *nf* chard.

acento *nm* **1** *(gráfico)* accent, written accent; *(tónico)* stress. **2** *(regional, etc)* accent.

acentuar *vt* **1** *(palabra, letra)* to accent. **2** *(resaltar)* to emphasize, stress.

aceptable *adj* acceptable.

aceptar *vt* to accept, receive.

acequia *nf* irrigation ditch.

acera *nf* GB pavement; US sidewalk.

acerca de *prep* about, concerning.

acercar *vt* to bring closer. ► *vpr* **acercarse** to come closer.

acero *nm* steel.

acertante *nmf* winner.

acertar *vt* **1** *(repuesta)* to get right. **2** *(adivinanza)* to guess.

achaque *nm* ailment.

acidez *nf* *(de fruta, vinagre)* sourness; *(en química)* acidity. ■ **acidez de estómago** heartburn.

ácido,-a *adj* **1** *(sabor)* sharp, tart. **2** acidic. ► *nm* **ácido** acid.

acierto *nm* **1** *(solución correcta)* right answer. **2** *(decisión adecuada)* wise decision.

aclaración *nf* explanation.

aclarar *vt* **1** *(cabello, color)* to lighten. **2** *(enjuagar)* to rinse. **3** *(explicar)* to explain.

acogedor,-ra *adj* *(lugar)* cosy, warm.

acoger *vt* *(recibir)* to receive; *(invitado)* to welcome.

acomodador,-ra *nm,f* *(hombre)* usher; *(mujer)* usherette.

acomodarse *vpr* to make oneself comfortable.

acompañamiento *nm* *(guarnición)* accompaniment.

acompañante *nmf* companion.

acompañar *vt (ir con)* to go with, come with. • **le acompaño en el sentimiento** please accept my condolences.

aconsejar *vt* to advise.

acontecimiento *nm* event, happening.

acordar *vt* to agree. ► *vpr* **acordarse** to remember.

acordeón *nm* accordion.

acortar *vt* to shorten.

acostar *vpr* to go to bed. • **acostarse con ALGN** to sleep with SB.

acostumbrado,-a *adj* 1 *(persona)* accustomed, used to. 2 *(hecho)* usual, customary.

acostumbrar(se) *vi-vpr.* • **acostumbrar a hacer algo** to be in the habit of doing STH. • **acostumbrarse a algo** to get used to STH.

acreedor,-ra *nm,f* creditor.

acrílico,-a *adj* acrylic.

acróbata *nmf* acrobat.

acta *nf* 1 *(de reunión)* minutes. 2 *(certificado)* certificate.

actitud *nf* attitude.

activar *vt* to activate.

actividad *nf* activity.

activo,-a *adj* active. ► *nm* **activo** assets.

acto *nm* 1 *(acción)* act. 2 *(ceremonia)* ceremony. 3 *(de obra teatral)* act. • **acto seguido** immediately afterwards; **en el acto** at once.

actor *nm* actor.

actriz *nf* actress.

actuación *nf* 1 *(interpretación)* performance. 2 *(comportamiento)* behaviour.

actual *adj* 1 *(de este momento)* present, current. 2 *(moderno)* up-to-date.

actualidad *nf* 1 *(momento presente)* present time, present. 2 *(hechos)* current affairs.

actualizar *vt* 1 *(poner al día)* to bring up to date. 2 *(programa)* to upgrade; *(página de Internet)* to refresh.

actualmente *adv (hoy en día)* nowadays; *(ahora)* at present.

actuar *vi (gen)* to act; *(cantante, bailarín)* to perform.

acuarela *nf* watercolour.

acuario *nm* aquarium.

acuático,-a *adj* aquatic, water.

acudir *vi (ir)* to go; *(venir)* to come.

acueducto *nm* aqueduct.

acuerdo *nm* agreement. • **¡de acuerdo!** all right!, O.K.!; **estar de acuerdo** to agree.

acusación *nf (inculpación)* accusation; *(en derecho)* charge.

acusar *vt (culpar)* to accuse; *(en derecho)* to charge.

acústico,-a *adj* acoustic.

adaptación *nf* adaptation.

adaptar(se) *vt-vpr* to adapt.

adecuado,-a *adj* adequate, suitable.

adelantado,-a *adj* **1** *(desarrollado)* developed. **2** *(reloj)* fast. • **por adelantado** in advance.

adelantamiento *nm* overtaking.

adelantar *vt* **1** *(mover adelante)* to move forward. **2** *(reloj)* to put forward. **3** *(pasar adelante)* to pass; *(vehículo)* to overtake. **4** *(dinero)* to pay in advance. ► *vi (reloj)* to be fast. ► *vpr* **adelantarse 1** *(llegar temprano)* to be early. **2** *(reloj)* to gain, be fast.

adelante *adv* forward. ► *interj* come in! • **en adelante** from now on; **hacia adelante** forwards; **más adelante** later on.

adelanto *nm* **1** *(avance)* advance. **2** advance payment.

adelgazar *vi (perder peso)* to lose weight; *(con régimen)* to slim.

además *adv* **1** *(por añadidura)* besides. **2** *(también)* also. • **además de** besides.

adentro *adv* inside.

aderezar *vt (condimentar)* to season; *(ensalada)* to dress.

adicto,-a *nm,f* addict.

adiós *nm* goodbye.

adivinanza *nf* riddle.

adivinar *vt* to guess.

adjetivo *nm* adjective.

adjudicar *vt* to award. ► *vpr* **adjudicarse** *(victoria)* to win.

administración *nf* **1** *(de empresa)* administration, management. **2** *(de medicamento)* administering. ▪ **administración de lotería** lottery office.

administrar *vt* **1** *(organizar)* to manage. **2** *(proporcionar)* to give.

administrativo,-a *nm,f (funcionario)* official; *(de empresa, banco)* office worker.

admirable *adj* admirable.

admiración *nf* **1** *(estima)* admiration. **2** *(signo)* exclamation mark.

admirar *vt* **1** *(estimar)* to admire. **2** *(sorprender)* to amaze, surprise.

admisión *nf* admission. • **"Reservado el derecho de admisión"** "The management reserves the right to refuse admission".

admitir *vt* **1** *(dar entrada a, reconocer)* to admit. **2** *(aceptar)* to accept.

adobar *vt* to marinate.

adolescente *adj-nmf* adolescent.

adonde *adv* where.

adónde *adv* where.

adoptar *vt* to adopt.

adoquín *nm (piedra redonda)* cobble; *(piedra cuadrada)* paving stone.

adorar *vt* to adore, worship.

adornar *vt* to decorate.

adorno *nm* decoration. • **de adorno** decorative.

adosado,-a *adj*: *casas adosadas*, semidetached houses.

adquirir *vt (comprar)* to buy, get.

adrede *adv* on purpose.

aduana *nf* customs *pl*.

aduanero,-a *nm,f* customs officer.

adulto,-a *adj-nm,f* adult.

adverbio *nm* adverb.

adversario,-a *nm,f* adversary, opponent.

advertencia *nf* **1** *(aviso)* warning. **2** *(consejo)* advice.

advertir *vt* **1** *(avisar)* to warn. **2** *(aconsejar)* to advise.

aéreo,-a *adj* **1** *(vista, fotografía)* aerial. **2** *(tráfico)* air.

aeropuerto *nm* airport.

aerosol *nm* aerosol, spray.

afán *nm* **1** *(anhelo)* eagerness. **2** *(esfuerzo)* hard work.

afección *nf (enfermedad)* complaint, illness.

afectar *vt* **1** *(concernir)* to affect. **2** *(impresionar)* to move.

afecto *nm* affection.

afeitado *nm* shave, shaving.

afeitar(se) *vt-vpr* to shave.

afición *nf* **1** *(inclinación)* liking. **2** *(pasatiempo)* hobby.

aficionado,-a *adj* **1** *(entusiasta)* keen, fond. **2** *(no profesional)* amateur. ▶ *nm,f* **1** *(entusiasta)* fan, enthusiast. **2** *(no profesional)* amateur.

aficionarse *vpr* to become fond.

afilar *vt* to sharpen.

afinar *vt* **1** *(piano, etc)* to tune. **2** *(puntería)* to sharpen.

afirmación *nf* statement, assertion.

afirmar *vt (aseverar)* to state, say.

aflojar *vt (soltar)* to loosen.

afluente *nm* tributary.

afonía *nf* loss of voice.

afónico,-a *adj* hoarse. • **estar afónico,-a** to have lost one's voice.

afortunado,-a *adj* lucky, fortunate.

África *nf* Africa.

africano,-a *adj-nm,f* African.

afrontar *vt* to face up to.

afuera *adv* outside. ▶ *nf pl* **afueras** outskirts.

agacharse *vpr* **1** *(acuclillarse)* to crouch down; *(inclinarse)* to bend down.

agallas *nf (de pez)* gills.

agarrado,-a *adj* stingy. • **bailar agarrado** to dance cheek to cheek.

agarrar *vt (coger fuerte)* to grab; *(sujetar)* to hold. ▶ *vpr* **agarrarse** to hold on, cling.

agencia *nf* agency. ▪ **agencia de viajes** travel agency; **agencia inmobiliaria** estate agent's.

agenda *nf* **1** *(libro)* diary. **2** *(de direcciones)* address book.

agente *nmf* agent. ■ **agente de policía** police officer.

ágil *adj* agile.

agitar *vt (líquido)* to shake.

aglomeración *nf (acumulación)* agglomeration; *(de gente)* crowd.

agobiar *vt* to overwhelm. ▶ *vpr* **agobiarse** get worked up.

agonía *nf (sufrimiento)* agony, grief; *(de moribundo)* death throes.

agosto *nm* August.

agotado,-a *adj* **1** *(cansado)* exhausted. **2** *(libro)* out of print; *(mercancía)* sold out.

agotar *vt* to exhaust. ▶ *vpr* **agotarse 1** *(cansarse)* to become exhausted. **2** *(acabarse)* to run out; *(existencias)* to be sold out.

agradable *adj* nice, pleasant.

agradar *vi* to please.

agradecer *vt* to thank.

agradecimiento *nm* gratitude, thankfulness.

agrandar *vt* to enlarge.

agravante *nm & nf* **1** *(gen)* added difficulty. **2** JUR aggravating circumstance.

agravarse *vpr* to get worse.

agredir *vt* to attack.

agregar *vt* to add.

agresión *nf* aggression.

agresivo,-a *adj* aggressive.

agresor,-ra *nm,f* aggressor.

agrícola *adj* agricultural.

agricultor,-ra *nm,f* farmer.

agricultura *nf* agriculture, farming.

agridulce *adj* **1** *(gen)* bittersweet. **2** *(salsa)* sweet and sour.

agrio,-a *adj* sour.

agruparse *vpr* **1** *(congregarse)* to group together. **2** *(asociarse)* to associate.

agua *nf* water. ■ **agua con gas** sparkling water; **agua dulce** fresh water; **agua mineral** mineral water; **agua oxigenada** hydrogen peroxide; **agua potable** drinking water; **agua salada** salt water; **agua sin gas** still water; **aguas termales** thermal waters.

aguacate *nm* avocado, avocado pear.

aguacero *nm* heavy shower, downpour.

aguantar *vt* **1** *(sostener)* to hold; *(peso)* to support, bear. **2** *(sufrir - frases afirmativas)* to put up with; *(- frases negativas)* to stand: *no sé cómo aguanta a su marido*, I don't know how she puts up with her husband; *no aguanto a gente como él*, I can't stand people like him. **3** *(contener - respiración)* to hold; *(- risa, lágrimas)* to hold back. ▶ *vpr* **aguantarse** *(resignarse)*: *tendrás que aguantarte*, you'll have to put up with it.

aguardar *vt-vi* to wait (for), await.

aguardiente *nm* liquor, brandy.

aguarrás *nm* turpentine.

agudo,-a *adj* 1 (afilado) sharp. 2 (dolor, acento, ángulo) acute. 3 (ingenioso) witty. 4 (voz) high-pitched.

aguijón *nm* 1 (de animal) sting. 2 (de planta) thorn, prickle.

águila *nf* eagle.

aguja *nf* 1 (de coser, jeringuilla) needle. 2 (de reloj) hand. 3 (de tocadiscos) stylus. 4 (de torre, iglesia) spire, steeple. 5 (de tren) GB point; US switch.

agujero *nm* hole.

agujetas *nf pl* stiffness.

ahí *adv* there. • **por ahí** 1 (lugar) round there. 2 (aproximadamente) more or less.

ahogar *vt* to drown. ► *vpr* **ahogarse** 1 (en agua) to be drowned. 2 (asfixiarse) to choke.

ahora *adv* 1 (en este momento) now. 2 (hace un momento) a moment ago. 3 (dentro de un momento) in a minute, shortly. • **ahora bien** however; **ahora mismo** 1 (en este momento) right now. 2 (enseguida) right away; **de ahora en adelante** from now on; **hasta ahora** until now, so far; **por ahora** for the time being.

ahorcar *vt* to hang.

ahorrar *vt* to save.

ahorros *nm pl* savings.

ahumado,-a *adj* smoked; (bacon) smoky.

aire *nm* 1 (fluido) air. 2 (viento) wind. 3 (aspecto) air, appearance. • **al aire libre** in the open air, outdoors; **tomar el aire** to get some fresh air. ■ **aire acondicionado** air conditioning.

aislamiento *nm* 1 (acción, estado) isolation. 2 (eléctrica) insulation.

aislante *adj* insulating. ► *nm* insulator.

aislar *vt* 1 (apartar) to isolate. 2 (eléctricamente) to insulate.

ajedrez *nm* (juego) chess; (tablero y piezas) chess set.

ajeno,-a *adj* (de otro) another's.

ajillo • **al ajillo** with garlic.

ajo *nm* garlic.

ajustado,-a *adj* 1 (ropa) tight, close-fitting. 2 (resultado, victoria) close.

ajustar *vt* (adaptar) to adjust; (uso técnico) to fit.

al *contr* → a.

ala *nf* wing. ■ **ala delta** hang glider.

alabar *vt* to praise.

alacrán *nm* scorpion.

alambre *nm* wire.

alameda *nf* 1 (bosque) poplar grove. 2 (paseo) avenue.

álamo *nm* poplar.

alargar vt 1 (prenda) to lengthen; (cuerda) to stretch. 2 (prolongar) to prolong, extend. 3 (brazo, mano) to stretch out.

alarma nf alarm. ■ **alarma antirrobo** 1 (para casa) burglar alarm. 2 (para coche) antitheft device; **alarma contra incendios** fire alarm.

alba nf dawn, daybreak.

albañil nm bricklayer.

albaricoque nm apricot.

albergar vt 1 (alojar) to lodge, house. 2 (esperanzas) to cherish. 3 (duda) to harbour.

albergue nm hostel. ■ **albergue juvenil** youth hostel.

albóndiga nf meatball.

albornoz nm bathrobe.

alborotar vt 1 (agitar) to agitate, excite. 2 (sublevar) to incite to rebel.

albufera nf lagoon.

álbum nm album.

alcachofa nf artichoke.

alcalde nm mayor.

alcaldesa nf mayoress.

alcaldía nf 1 (cargo) mayorship. 2 (oficina) mayor's office.

alcance nm 1 (de persona) reach: *fuera del alcance de los niños*, out of children's reach. 2 (de arma, emisora) range. 3 (trascendencia) scope, importance.

alcantarilla nf (cloaca) sewer; (boca) drain.

alcanzar vt 1 (lugar, edad, temperatura) to reach; (persona) to catch up with. 2 (conseguir) to attain, achieve.

alcaparra nf caper.

alcázar nm 1 (fortaleza) fortress. 2 (palacio) palace.

alcoba nf bedroom.

alcohol nm alcohol. • **sin alcohol** non-alcoholic.

alcohólico,-a adj-nm,f alcoholic.

alcornoque nm cork oak.

aldaba nf 1 (llamador) knocker. 2 (pestillo) bolt, crossbar.

aldea nf hamlet, small village.

aleación nf alloy.

alegrar vt to make happy. ► vpr **alegrarse** to be happy, be pleased.

alegre adj 1 (persona - contenta) happy; (- borracha) tipsy. 2 (color) bright.

alegría nf happiness.

alejar vt to move away. ► vpr **alejarse** to go away, move away.

alemán,-ana adj-nm,f German. ► nm **alemán** (idioma) German.

Alemania nf Germany.

alergia nf allergy.

alérgico,-a adj allergic.

alero nm 1 (del tejado) eaves. 2 (de baloncesto) forward.

alerta adv on the alert. ► nf alert.

aleta nf fin.

alfabeto *nm* alphabet.
alfalfa *nf* alfalfa, lucerne.
alfarería *nf* pottery.
alfil *nm* bishop.
alfiler *nm* **1** *(en costura)* pin. **2** *(joya)* brooch.
alfombra *nf* *(grande)* carpet; *(pequeña)* rug.
alga *nf* alga; *(marina)* seaweed; *(de agua dulce)* weed.
álgebra *nf* algebra.
algo *pron* *(en frases afirmativas)* something; *(en frases interrogativas)* anything: **vamos a tomar algo**, let's have something to drink; **¿hay algo que no entiendas?**, is there anything you don't understand? ▶ *adv* *(un poco)* a bit, a little.
● **algo es algo** something is better than nothing.
algodón *nm* cotton. ■ **algodón hidrófilo** cotton wool.
alguien *pron* *(en frases afirmativas)* somebody, someone; *(en frases interrogativas y negativas)* anybody, anyone: **alguien se lo habrá olvidado**, somebody must have left it behind; **¿conoces alguien que hable japonés?**, do you know anyone who speaks Japanese?
algún *adj* → alguno,-a.
alguno,-a *adj* *(en frases afirmativas)* some; *(en frases interrogativas)* any; *(en frases negativas)* no, not … any: **me he**

comprado algunos libros, I've bought some books; **¿tienes alguna idea mejor?**, do you have any better idea?; **sin éxito alguno**, with no success at all; **no vino persona alguna**, nobody came. ▶ *pron* *(en frases afirmativas)* someone, somebody; *(en frases interrogativas)* anybody: **hubo alguno que se quejó**, there was somebody who complained; **puedes quedarte con alguna de estas fotos**, you can keep some of those pictures; **¿alguno sabe la respuesta?**, does anyone know the answer?
alhaja *nf* jewel.
aliado,-a *nm,f* ally.
alianza *nf* **1** *(pacto)* alliance. **2** *(anillo)* wedding ring.
aliarse *vpr* to form an alliance.
alicates *nm pl* pliers.
aliciente *nm* incentive, inducement.
aliento *nm* breath. ● **sin aliento** breathless.
alimentación *nf* **1** *(acción)* feeding. **2** *(comida)* food; *(dieta)* diet.
alimentar *vt* to feed. ▶ *vi* *(servir de alimento)* to be nutritious, be nourishing. ▶ *vpr* **alimentarse** to feed oneself.
alimento *nm* food.
aliñar *vt* *(ensalada)* to dress; *(guiso)* to season.

aliño nm (de ensalada) dressing; (de guiso) seasoning.
alisar vt to smooth.
alistarse vpr to enlist.
aliviar vt 1 (enfermedad, dolor) to relieve. 2 (consolar) to comfort.
alivio nm relief.
allá adv there.
allí adv there. • **por allí** that way.
alma nf soul.
almacén nm warehouse. ► nm pl (**grandes**) **almacenes** department store.
almacenar vt to store.
almeja nf clam.
almendra nf almond. ■ **almendra garapiñada** sugared almond.
almendro nm almond tree.
almíbar nm syrup.
almidón nm starch.
almirante nm admiral.
almohada nf pillow.
almohadón nm cushion.
almorzar vi to have lunch.
almuerzo nm lunch.
alojamiento nm lodging, accommodation.
alojarse vpr to stay.
alpargata nf rope-soled sandal, espadrille.
alpinismo nm mountaineering.
alpinista nmf mountaineer, mountain climber.
alpiste nm birdseed.

alquilar vt 1 (dar en alquiler - casa) to rent out, GB let; (- coche, bicicleta) to hire, rent; (- aparato) to rent. 2 (tomar en alquiler - casa) to rent; (- coche, bicicleta) to hire, rent.
alquiler nm 1 (cesión - de casa) renting, GB letting; (- de coche etc) hire, rental; (- de aparato) rental. 2 (cuota - de casa) rent; (- de coche etc) hire charge; (- de aparato) rental.
alquitrán nm tar.
alrededor adv (gen) around; (cantidad) around, about: **alrededor de veinte**, about twenty. ► nm pl **alrededores** surrounding area sing.
alta nf (a un enfermo) discharge.
altar nm altar.
altavoz nm loudspeaker.
alterar vt to alter, change. ► vpr **alterarse** (enfadarse) to lose one's temper.
altercado nm 1 (discusión) argument. 2 (disturbio) disturbance.
alternar vt-vi (sucederse) to alternate. ► vi (relacionarse) to socialize, mix.
alternativo,-a adj alternative.
alteza nf Highness.
altibajos nm pl ups and downs.
altillo nm (armario) cupboard.
altitud nf height, altitude.
alto,-a adj 1 (gen) high. 2 (persona, edificio, árbol) tall. 3 (so-

nido, voz) loud ► *nm* **alto 1** (*altura*): *Pepe mide dos metros de alto*, Pepe's two metres tall. **2** (*elevación*) height, hillock. **3** (*parada*) halt, stop. ► *adv* **1** (*volar, subir*) high. **2** (*hablar*) loud, loudly.

altura *nf* **1** (*gen*) height. **2** (*persona*) tall: *mide dos metros de altura*, he's two metres tall. **3** (*cosa*) high: *mide dos metros de altura*, it's two metres high. **4** (*altitud*) altitude. ● **a la altura de** next to: *a la altura de la catedral*, next to the cathedral.

alubia *nf* bean.

alucinación *nf* hallucination.

alud *nm* avalanche.

alumbrado *nm* lighting.

alumbrar *vt* (*iluminar - calles, habitación*) to light; (*- monumento, estadio*) to light up, illuminate.

aluminio *nm* aluminium.

alumno,-a *nm,f* (*de colegio*) pupil; (*de universidad*) student.

alza *nf* rise, increase.

alzar *vt* (*levantar - mano, cabeza*) to raise, lift; (*voz*) to raise.

ama *nf*. ■ **ama de casa** housewife.

amabilidad *nf* kindness.

amable *adj* kind, nice.

amainar *vi* to die down.

amanecer *vi* **1** (*hacerse de día*) to dawn. **2** (*clarear*) to get light. ► *nm* dawn, daybreak.

amante *nmf* lover.

amapola *nf* poppy.

amar *vt* to love.

amargo,-a *adj* bitter.

amarillo,-a *adj* yellow. ► *nm* **amarillo** yellow.

amarra *nf* mooring cable. ● **soltar amarras** to cast off.

amasar *vt* **1** (*masa*) to knead; (*cemento*) to mix. **2** (*dinero*) to amass.

amazona *nf* horsewoman.

ámbar *nm* amber.

ambición *nf* ambition.

ambicioso,-a *adj* ambitious.

ambiental *adj* **1** (*contaminación, impacto*) environmental. **2** (*música*) background.

ambiente *nm* **1** (*aire*) air, atmosphere. **2** (*entorno*) environment; (*de casa, ciudad, época*) atmosphere. **3** (*animación*) life, atmosphere.

ambiguo,-a *adj* ambiguous.

ambos,-as *adj-pron* both.

ambulancia *nf* ambulance.

ambulante *adj* itinerant, travelling.

ambulatorio *nm* surgery, clinic.

amenaza *nf* threat. ■ **amenaza de bomba** bomb scare.

amenazar *vt-vi* to threaten.

ameno,-a *adj* (*agradable*) pleasant; (*entretenido*) entertaining.

América *nf* America.

americana *nf* jacket.

americano,-a *adj-nm,f* American.

ametralladora *nf* machine gun.

amígdala *nf* tonsil.

amigo,-a *nm,f* friend.

amistad *nf* friendship.

amnesia *nf* amnesia.

amo *nm* 1 *(señor)* master. 2 *(dueño)* owner.

amoniaco *nm* ammonia.

amontonar *vt* to pile up.

amor *nm* love. • **hacer el amor** to make love. ▪ **amor propio** self-esteem.

amortiguador *nm* shock absorber.

amparar *vt* to protect, shelter. ▶ *vpr* **ampararse en** *(una ley)* to seek protection in.

ampliación *nf* 1 *(de edificio, plazo)* extension. 2 *(de negocio, mercado)* expansion. 3 *(de fotografía)* enlargement.

ampliar *vt* 1 *(edificio, plazo)* to extend. 2 *(negocio, mercado)* to expand. 3 *(fotografía)* to enlarge, blow up.

amplio,-a *adj* 1 *(espacioso)* roomy, spacious. 2 *(margen, gama)* large; *(mayoría)* large.

ampolla *nf* *(en la piel)* blister.

amueblar *vt* to furnish.

amuleto *nm* charm, amulet.

analfabeto,-a *adj-nm,f* illiterate.

analgésico,-a *adj* analgesic. ▶ *nm* **analgésico** analgesic.

análisis *nm* analysis. ▪ **análisis de sangre** blood test.

analizar *vt* to analyse.

anarquía *nf* anarchy.

anatomía *nf* anatomy.

anca *nf* haunch. ▪ **ancas de rana** frogs' legs.

ancho,-a *adj* 1 *(calle, cama, habitación)* wide; *(espalda, cara)* broad. 2 *(prenda)* loose, loose-fitting. ▶ *nm* **ancho** breadth, width. • **de ancho**: *tres metros de ancho*, three metres wide.

anchoa *nf* anchovy.

anchura *nf* breadth, width.

anciano,-a *nm,f* *(hombre)* elderly man; *(mujer)* elderly woman.

ancla *nf* anchor.

anclar *vi* to anchor.

andamio *nm* scaffolding.

andar *vi* 1 *(caminar)* to walk. 2 *(funcionar)* to work, go.

andén *nm* platform.

anécdota *nf* anecdote.

anemia *nf* anaemia.

anestesia *nf* anaesthesia.

anfibio *nm* amphibian.

anfiteatro *nm* amphitheatre.

anfitrión,-ona *nm,f* *(hombre)* host; *(mujer)* hostess.

ángel *nm* angel.

angina *nf* angina. • **tener anginas** to have a sore throat. ▪ **angina de pecho** angina pectoris.

anguila *nf* eel.

angula *nf* elver.

ángulo *nm* 1 *(geometría)* angle. 2 *(rincón)* corner.

angustia *nf* anguish, distress.

anilla *nf* ring.

anillo *nm* ring.

animación *nf* liveliness.

animado,-a *adj* 1 *(persona)* cheerful. 2 *(situación)* animated, lively. 3 *(calle)* full of people.

animal *adj* animal. ▶ *nm* 1 *(ser vivo)* animal. 2 *(persona bruta)* blockhead. ■ **animal doméstico** 1 *(de granja)* domestic animal. 2 *(de compañía)* pet.

animar *vt* 1 *(alentar)* to encourage. 2 *(alegrar - persona)* to cheer up; *(- fiesta, reunión)* to liven up. ▶ *vpr* **animarse** 1 *(alegrarse - persona)* to cheer up; *(- fiesta, reunión)* to liven up. 2 *(decidirse)* to make up one's mind.

ánimo *nm* 1 *(estado emocional)* spirits. 2 *(aliento)* encouragement.

anís *nm* 1 *(planta)* anise. 2 *(bebida)* anisette.

aniversario *nm* anniversary.

ano *nm* anus.

anoche *adv* last night.

anochecer *vi* to get dark. ▶ *nm* nightfall, dusk.

anónimo,-a *adj* anonymous.

anorak *nm* anorak.

anormal *adj* abnormal.

anotar *vt* *(apuntar)* to make a note of, take down.

ansia *nf* *(deseo)* longing.

ansiedad *nf* anxiety.

ante[1] *prep* 1 *(delante de)* before. 2 *(frente a)* in the face of. ● **ante todo** 1 *(primero)* first of all. 2 *(por encima de)* above all.

ante[2] *nm* *(piel)* suede.

anteayer *adv* the day before yesterday.

antebrazo *nm* forearm.

antelación *nf*. ● **con antelación** in advance.

antemano *adv*. ● **de antemano** beforehand, in advance.

antena *nf* 1 *(de aparato)* aerial. 2 *(de animal)* antenna. ■ **antena parabólica** satellite dish.

antepasado *nm* ancestor.

anterior *adj* previous.

antes *adv* 1 *(en el tiempo - previamente)* before; *(- más temprano)* earlier: **te lo he dicho antes**, I told you earlier. 2 *(en el espacio)* before. ● **antes de** before.

antibiótico *nm* antibiotic.

anticiclón *nm* anticyclone, high pressure area.

anticiparse *vpr* 1 *(suceder antes)* to be early. 2 *(adelantarse)* to beat to it.

anticipo *nm* advance payment.

anticonceptivo *nm* contraceptive.

anticongelante *adj-nm* antifreeze.

anticuario *nm* antiquary, antiques dealer.

antídoto *nm* antidote.

antigüedad *nf* 1 *(período)* antiquity. 2 *(edad)*: **una ciudad de tres mil años de antigüedad**, a city which is three thousand years old. ► *nf pl* **antigüedades** *(monumentos)* antiquities; *(objetos)* antiques.

antiguo,-a *adj* 1 *(muy viejo)* ancient. 2 *(viejo)* old. 3 *(anterior)* old, former: **mi antiguo jefe**, my former boss.

antipatía *nf* antipathy, dislike.

antipático,-a *adj* unpleasant.

antirrobo *adj* antitheft.

antivirus *nm* antivirus system.

antojo *nm* 1 *(capricho)* whim; *(de embarazada)* craving. 2 *(en la piel)* birthmark.

antorcha *nf* torch.

anual *adj* annual, yearly.

anular[1] *nm* ring finger.

anular[2] *vt* to annul, cancel.

anunciar *vt* 1 *(notificar)* to announce. 2 *(hacer publicidad de)* to advertise.

anuncio *nm* 1 *(en periódico)* advertisement, advert, ad; *(en televisión, radio)* advertisement, advert, commercial. 2 *(notificación)* announcement.

anzuelo *nm* hook.

añadir *vt* to add.

añejo,-a *adj (vino)* mature.

año *nm* year. • **tener ... años** to be ... years old: **¿cuántos años tienes?**, how old are you? ■ **Año Nuevo** New Year.

aorta *nf* aorta.

apagar *vt* 1 *(fuego)* to extinguish, put out. 2 *(luz)* to turn off. 3 *(aparato)* to turn off, switch off. ► *vpr* **apagarse** *(luz)* to go out.

apagón *nm* power cut, blackout.

aparato *nm* 1 *(máquina)* machine; *(dispositivo)* device. 2 *(electrodoméstico)* appliance; *(televisor, radio)* set. 3 *(de gimnasio)* piece of apparatus. 4 *(para los dientes)* brace; *(audífono)* hearing aid. 5 *(conjunto de órganos)* system.

aparcamiento *nm* 1 *(acción)* parking. 2 *(lugar)* GB car park; US parking lot; *(en la calle)* place to park.

aparcar *vt-vi* to park.

aparecer *vi* 1 *(gen)* to appear; *(objeto perdido)* to turn up. 2 *(dejarse ver)* to show up, turn up.

apariencia *nf* appearance.

apartado,-a *adj* 1 *(lejano)* distant. 2 *(aislado)* isolated, remote. ► *nm* **apartado** section. ■ **apartado de correos** post office box.

apartamento *nm* apartment.

apartar *vt* **1** *(alejar)* to move away. **2** *(poner a un lado)* to set aside. ► *vpr* **apartarse** *(de un lugar)* to move away.

aparte *adv* **1** *(a un lado)* aside, to one side; *(por separado)* apart, separately. **2** *(además)* besides.

apasionante *adj* exciting, fascinating.

apasionar *vt* to excite, fascinate.

apeadero *nm (de trenes)* halt.

apearse *vpr (de caballo)* to dismount; *(de vehículo)* to get off.

apellidarse *vpr* to be called: *¿cómo se apellida usted?*, what's your surname?

apellido *nm* surname, family name.

apenas *adv* **1** *(casi no)* hardly, scarcely. **2** *(casi nunca)* hardly ever.

apéndice *nm* appendix.

apendicitis *nf* appendicitis.

aperitivo *nm* **1** *(bebida)* aperitif. **2** *(comida)* appetizer.

apertura *nf (gen)* opening; *(de temporada, curso académico)* start, beginning.

apetecer *vi*: *me apetece un café*, I feel like a coffee, I fancy a coffee; *¿te apetece ir al cine?*, do you fancy going to the cinema?

apetito *nm* appetite.

apetitoso,-a *adj* appetizing.

apio *nm* celery.

apisonadora *nf* steamroller.

aplanar *vt* to level, make even.

aplastar *vt* to squash, flatten.

aplaudir *vt* to clap, applaud.

aplauso *nm* applause.

aplazar *vt (reunión, acto)* to postpone, put off; *(pago)* to defer.

aplicación *nf* application.

aplicado,-a *adj* **1** *(ciencia)* applied. **2** *(estudiante)* studious, diligent.

aplicar *vt* **1** *(extender)* to apply. **2** *(poner en práctica)* to put into practice.

apoderarse *vpr* to take possession.

apodo *nm* nickname.

aportar *vt* to contribute.

aposento *nm* **1** *(cuarto)* room. **2** *(hospedaje)* lodgings.

aposta *adv* on purpose.

apostar *vt-vi* to bet.

apóstol *nm* apostle.

apoyar *vt* **1** *(reclinar)* to rest, lean. **2** *(basar)* to base, found. **3** *(defender)* to back, support. ► *vpr* **apoyarse** *(basarse)* to be based.

apoyo *nm* support.

apreciar *vt* **1** *(sentir aprecio por)* to regard highly. **2** *(valorar)* to appreciate.

aprecio *nm* esteem, regard.

aprender *vt-vi* to learn.

aprendizaje *nm* learning.
apresurar(se) *vt-vpr* to hurry.
apretar *vt* **1** *(estrechar)* to squeeze. **2** *(tornillo, nudo)* to tighten. **3** *(pulsar - botón)* to press; *(- gatillo)* to pull.
aprieto *nm* fix, awkward situation.
aprisa *adv* quickly.
aprobación *nf (gen)* approval; *(de ley)* passing.
aprobado *nm* pass.
aprobar *vt* **1** *(decisión, plan, préstamo)* to approve. **2** *(comportamiento)* to approve of. **3** *(examen, ley)* to pass.
aprovechar *vt* **1** *(sacar provecho de)* to make good use of. **2** *(emplear)* to use. ► *vpr* **aprovecharse** to take advantage. • **¡que aproveche!** enjoy your meal!
aproximarse *vpr* to approach, draw near.
apto,-a *adj* **1** *(apropiado)* suitable. **2** *(capaz)* capable, able. • **apta para todos los públicos** GB U-certificate; US rated G; **no apta** for adults only.
apuesta *nf* bet.
apuesto,-a *adj* good-looking.
apuntar *vt* **1** *(señalar)* to point at. **2** *(arma)* to aim. **3** *(anotar)* to note down, make a note of. ► *vt-vpr* **apuntar(se)** *(inscribir - en curso)* GB to enrol; US to enroll; *(- en lista)* to put down.
apuntes *nm pl (de clase)* notes.

apuñalar *vt* to stab.
apurar *vt (terminar)* to finish up. ► *vpr* **apurarse** to worry.
apuro *nm* **1** *(dificultad)* predicament, tight spot; *(de dinero)* hardship. **2** *(vergüenza)* embarrassment.
aquel,-lla *adj* that.
aquél,-lla *pron* that one.
aquello *pron: aquello fue lo que más me gustó*, that was what I liked the most; *¿te acuerdas de aquello que me dijiste?*, do you remember what you told me?
aquí *adv* **1** *(lugar)* here. **2** *(tiempo)* now. • **por aquí por favor** this way please.
árabe *adj (gen)* Arab; *(de Arabia)* Arabian; *(alfabeto, número)* Arabic. ► *nmf (persona)* Arab; *(de Arabia)* Arabian. ► *nm (idioma)* Arabic.
arado *nm* plough.
araña *nf (animal)* spider.
arañar(se) *vt-vpr* to scratch.
arañazo *nm* scratch.
arar *vt* to plough.
arbitrar *vt (fútbol, rugby, boxeo)* to referee; *(tenis)* to umpire.
árbitro *nm (en fútbol, rugby, boxeo)* referee; *(en tenis)* umpire.
árbol *nm* tree.
arbusto *nm* shrub, bush.
arca *nf* chest.
arcada *nf* **1** *(de puente)* arcade. **2** *(al vomitar): me dieron arcadas*, I retched.

arcaico,-a *adj* archaic.

archipiélago *nm* archipelago.

archivar *vt* 1 *(ordenar)* to file. 2 INFORM to save.

archivo *nm* 1 *(documento)* file. 2 *(lugar)* archive. ▪ **archivo adjunto** INFORM attachment.

arcilla *nf* clay.

arco *nm* 1 ARQ arch. 2 MAT arc. 3 *(de violín, flecha)* bow. ▪ **arco iris** rainbow.

arder *vi* 1 *(quemarse)* to burn. 2 *(estar muy caliente)* to be boiling hot.

ardilla *nf* squirrel.

ardor *nm* GB ardour; US ardor. ▪ **ardor de estómago** heartburn.

área *nf* 1 *(zona, medida)* area. 2 *(en fútbol)* penalty area.

arena *nf* sand. ▪ **arenas movedizas** quicksand.

arenque *nm* herring. ▪ **arenque ahumado** kipper.

Argentina *nf* Argentina, the Argentine.

argentino,-a *adj-nm,f* Argentinian.

argot *nm* 1 *(popular)* slang. 2 *(técnico)* jargon.

argumento *nm* 1 *(razón)* argument. 2 *(de novela, obra, etc)* plot.

árido,-a *adj* 1 *(tierra)* arid, dry. 2 *(texto, tema)* dry.

arista *nf* edge.

aristócrata *nmf* aristocrat.

aritmética *nf* arithmetic.

arma *nf* weapon, arm. ▪ **arma blanca** knife; **arma de fuego** firearm.

armada *nf* navy.

armadura *nf* 1 *(defensa)* armour. 2 *(armazón)* framework.

armamento *nm* armament.

armar *vt* *(proveer de armas)* to arm. 2 *(ruido, alboroto)* to make.

armario *nm* *(de cocina)* cupboard; *(de ropa)* GB wardrobe; US closet.

armonía *nf* harmony.

armónica *nf* harmonica, mouth organ.

aro *nm* hoop, ring.

aroma *nm* aroma; *(del vino)* bouquet.

arpa *nf* harp.

arpón *nm* harpoon.

arqueología *nf* archaeology.

arquitecto,-a *nm,f* architect.

arquitectura *nf* architecture.

arrancar *vt* 1 *(planta)* to uproot, pull up. 2 *(página)* to tear out. ▶ *vi* 1 *(coche)* to start. 2 *(ordenador)* to boot.

arranque *nm* 1 *(de motor)* starting mechanism: *el motor de arranque*, the starter motor. 2 *(arrebato)* fit.

arrasar *vt* to raze, demolish. ▶ *vi* to sweep the board.

arrastrar *vt* *(llevar por el suelo)* to drag (along), pull (along). ▶ *vpr* **arrastrarse** *(reptar)* to crawl.

arrebato *nm* fit, outburst.

arrecife *nm* reef.

arreglar *vt* 1 (*resolver - conflicto*) to settle; (*- asunto*) to sort out. 2 (*ordenar*) to tidy, tidy up. 3 (*reparar*) to mend, fix up. ▶ *vpr* **arreglarse** (*componerse*) to get ready, dress up; (*cabello*) to do.

arreglo *nm* 1 (*reparación*) repair. 2 (*acuerdo*) agreement. • **con arreglo a** according to.

arrepentirse *vpr* to regret, be sorry.

arrestar *vt* to arrest.

arresto *nm* arrest.

arriar *vt* 1 (*velas*) to lower. 2 (*bandera*) to strike.

arriba *adv* 1 (*dirección*) up; (*encima*) on (the) top. 2 (*situación*) above. 3 (*piso*) upstairs. ▶ *interj* up! • **hacia arriba** upwards.

arriesgado,-a *adj* risky, dangerous.

arriesgar(se) *vt-vpr* to risk.

arrimarse *vpr* to come closer, come nearer.

arrodillarse *vpr* to kneel down.

arrojar *vt* 1 (*tirar*) to throw. 2 (*resultado*) to show.

arroyo *nm* (*río*) stream.

arroz *nm* rice. ▪ **arroz con leche** rice pudding; **arroz integral** brown rice.

arruga *nf* (*en la piel*) wrinkle; (*en la ropa*) crease.

arrugar(se) *vt-vpr* 1 (*piel*) to wrinkle. 2 (*ropa*) to crease. 3 (*papel*) to crumple.

arruinar *vt* to bankrupt, ruin. ▶ *vpr* **arruinarse** to be bankrupt, be ruined.

arsenal *nm* arsenal.

arte *nm* 1 (*gen*) art: **bellas artes**, fine arts. 2 (*habilidad*) craft, skill. ▪ **arte dramático** drama.

artefacto *nm* device.

arteria *nf* artery.

artesanía *nf* 1 (*actividad*) craftsmanship. 2 (*productos*) handicrafts.

artesano,-a *nm,f* craftsman, artisan.

articulación *nf* joint.

artículo *nm* article.

artificial *adj* artificial.

artillería *nf* artillery.

artista *nmf* artist.

artístico,-a *adj* artistic.

artritis *nf* arthritis.

as *nm* ace.

asa *nf* handle.

asado,-a *adj* (*carne*) roast; (*pescado, patata*) baked. ▶ *nm* **asado** roast.

asaltante *nmf* attacker.

asaltar *vt* 1 (*atacar*) to assault, attack. 2 (*robar - banco*) to rob, raid; (*- persona*) to mug.

asalto *nm* 1 (*ataque*) assault, attack. 2 (*robo - de banco*) raid, robbery; (*- a persona*) mugging. 3 (*en boxeo*) round.

asamblea *nf* **1** *(en parlamento)* assembly. **2** *(reunión)* meeting.

asar *vt (carne)* to roast; *(pescado, patata)* to bake.

ascender *vi* **1** *(subir)* to climb. **2** *(sumar)* to amount.

ascenso *nm* **1** *(subida - de temperatura, precio)* rise; *(- de montaña)* ascent. **2** *(- de empleado, equipo)* promotion.

ascensor *nm* GB lift; US elevator.

asco *nm* disgust. • **dar asco** to be disgusting.

asearse *vpr* to wash.

asegurado,-a *nm,f* policy holder.

aseguradora *nf* insurance company.

asegurar *vt* **1** *(coche, casa)* to insure. **2** *(garantizar)* to ensure, guarantee. **4** *(afirmar)* to assure. ▶ *vpr* **asegurarse 1** *(cerciorarse)* to make sure. **2** *(tomar un seguro)* to insure oneself.

aseo *nm* **1** *(limpieza)* cleanliness, tidying up. **2** *(cuarto)* bathroom, toilet.

asequible *adj* accessible: *a un precio asequible*, at a reasonable price.

asesinar *vt* to kill, murder.

asesinato *nm* killing, murder.

asesino,-a *nm,f* killer.

asesorar *vt* to advise, give advice.

asesor,-ra *nm,f* adviser, consultant.

asfalto *nm* asphalt.

asfixia *nf* asphyxia, suffocation.

asfixiarse *vpr* to suffocate.

así *adv* **1** *(de esta manera)* like that, like this, in this way. **2** *(de esa manera)* that way. ▶ *adj* such: *un hombre así*, a man like that, such a man. • **así así** so-so; **así que 1** *(de manera que)* so, therefore. **2** *(tan pronto como)* as soon as; **aun así** even so. **2** *(por así decirlo)* so to speak.

Asia *nf* Asia.

asiático,-a *adj-nm,f* Asian.

asiento *nm* *(silla etc)* seat; *(de bicicleta)* saddle.

asignatura *nf* subject.

asilo *nm* *(amparo)* asylum; *(residencia)* home.

asimilar *vt* to assimilate.

asimismo *adv* **1** *(también)* also. **2** *(de esta manera)* likewise.

asistencia *nf* **1** *(presencia)* attendance. **2** *(público)* audience, public. **3** *(ayuda)* assistance. ▪ **asistencia médica** medical care.

asistente *adj* attending. ▶ *nmf* assistant.

asistir *vi* to attend, be present. ▶ *vt* **1** *(ayudar)* to assist, help. **2** *(cuidar)* to treat.

asma *nf* asthma.

asmático,-a *adj-nm,f* asthmatic.

asno *nm* ass, donkey.

asociación *nf* association.

asociar *vt* to associate. ► *vpr* **asociarse** to form a partnership.

asomar *vi* to appear, show. ► *vpr* **asomarse** *(a ventana)* to lean out; *(a balcón)* to come out. • **"Prohibido asomarse por la ventanilla"** "Do not lean out of the window".

asombrar *vt* to amaze, astonish. ► *vpr* **asombrarse** to be amazed, be astonished.

asombroso,-a *adj* amazing, astonishing.

aspa *nf* 1 *(cruz)* X-shaped cross. 2 *(de molino)* arm; *(de ventilador)* blade.

aspecto *nm* 1 *(apariencia)* look, appearance. 2 *(faceta)* aspect.

áspero,-a *adj* rough, coarse.

aspiración *nf* 1 *(al respirar)* inhalation. 2 *(ambición)* aspiration, ambition.

aspiradora *nf* vacuum cleaner, GB hoover.

aspirante *nmf* candidate.

aspirar *vt* to inhale, breathe in. ► *vi* to aspire to.

aspirina® *nf* aspirin®.

asqueroso,-a *adj* 1 *(sucio)* dirty, filthy. 2 *(desagradable)* disgusting.

asta *nf* 1 *(de bandera)* flagpole. 2 *(cuerno)* horn.

asterisco *nm* asterisk.

astilla *nf* splinter.

astillero *nm* shipyard, dockyard.

astro *nm* star.

astrología *nf* astrology.

astronauta *nmf* astronaut.

astronomía *nf* astronomy.

astucia *nf* *(sagacidad)* astuteness, shrewdness; *(malicia)* cunning.

astuto,-a *adj* *(sagaz)* astute, shrewd; *(malicioso)* cunning.

asumir *vt* 1 *(gen)* to assume, take part on. 2 *(aceptar)* to come to term with, accept.

asunto *nm* 1 *(cuestión)* matter, subject. 2 *(ocupación)* affair, business.

asustar *vt* to frighten. ► *vpr* **asustarse** to be frightened.

atacar *vt* to attack.

atajo *nm* short cut.

atalaya *nf* watchtower.

ataque *nm* 1 *(gen)* attack. 2 *(acceso)* fit. ■ **ataque cardíaco** heart attack; **ataque de nervios** nervous breakdown.

atar *vt* to tie, fasten. ► *vpr* **atarse** to tie up, do up.

atardecer *vi* to get dark, grow dark. ► *nm* evening, dusk.

atascar *vt* to block, obstruct. ► *vpr* **atascarse** 1 *(obstruirse)* to get blocked. 2 *(mecanismo)* to jam.

atasco *nm* traffic jam.

ataúd *nm* coffin.

ateísmo *nm* atheism.

atención *nf* attention. • **prestar atención** to pay attention. ▪ **atención al cliente** customer service.

atender *vt* 1 *(cliente)* to attend to; *(bar, tienda)* to serve: *¿ya la atienden?*, are you being served? 2 *(enfermo)* to take care of, look after. 3 *(llamada)* to answer. ▶ *vi* to pay attention.

atentado *nm* attack, assault.

atentamente *adv (en carta)* sincerely, faithfully.

atentar *vi.* • **atentar contra** ALGN to make an attempt on SB's life.

atento,-a *adj* 1 *(pendiente)* attentive. 2 *(amable)* polite, courteous.

ateo,-a *adj-nm,f* atheist.

aterrizaje *nm* landing.

aterrizar *vt* to land.

ático *nm (buhardilla)* attic; *(piso - último)* top floor; *(- lujoso)* penthouse.

atlántico,-a *adj* Atlantic. • **el (océano) Atlántico** the Atlantic *(Ocean)*.

atlas *nm* atlas.

atleta *nmf* athlete.

atletismo *nm* athletics.

atmósfera *nf* atmosphere.

atmosférico,-a *adj* atmospheric.

atómico,-a *adj* atomic.

átomo *nm* atom.

atracador,-ra *nm,f (de banco)* bank robber; *(en la calle)* mugger.

atracar *vt (robar - banco)* to hold up, rob; *(- persona)* to mug. ▶ *vi (amarrar)* to tie up.

atracción *nf* attraction.

atraco *nm (de banco)* hold-up, robbery; *(de persona)* mugging.

atractivo,-a *adj* attractive. ▶ *nm* **atractivo** *(de persona)* attractiveness, charm; *(de cosa)* attraction.

atraer *vt* to attract.

atragantarse *vpr* to choke.

atrapar *vt* to capture, catch.

atrás *adv* 1 *(posición)* back. 2 *(tiempo)* ago. • **hacia atrás** backwards.

atrasar *vt* 1 *(salida)* to delay. 2 *(reloj)* to put back. ▶ *vi (reloj)* to be slow. ▶ *vpr* **atrasarse** 1 *(tren etc)* to be late. 2 *(quedarse atrás)* to stay behind.

atraso *nm* 1 *(retraso)* delay. 2 *(de reloj)* slowness. 3 *(de país)* backwardness.

atravesar *vt* 1 *(cruzar)* to cross. 2 *(crisis, situación)* to go through.

atreverse *vpr* to dare.

atrevido,-a *adj* 1 *(osado)* daring, bold. 2 *(indecoroso)* risqué.

atribuir *vt* to attribute, ascribe.

atributo *nm* attribute, quality.

atril *nm* lectern.

atrio *nm* **1** *(patio)* atrium. **2** *(vestíbulo)* vestibule.

atropellar *vt* to knock down, run over.

atropello *nm* **1** *(accidente)* running over. **2** *(abuso)* outrage, abuse.

ATS *abr (ayudante técnico sanitario)* medical auxiliary.

atún *nm* tuna.

audaz *adj* audacious, bold.

audición *nf* **1** *(acción)* hearing. **2** *(para obra etc)* audition.

audiencia *nf* **1** *(recepción, público)* audience. **2** *(tribunal)* court.

audífono *nm* hearing aid.

audiovisual *adj* audio-visual.

auditorio *nm* **1** *(público)* audience. **2** *(lugar)* auditorium.

auge *nm* **1** *(del mercado)* boom. **2** *(de fama etc)* peak.

aula *nf* *(en escuela)* classroom; *(en universidad)* lecture hall.

aullido *nm* howl.

aumentar *vt* **1** *(incrementar)* to increase, raise. **2** *(fotos)* to enlarge.

aumento *nm* **1** *(incremento)* rise, increase. **2** *(de foto)* enlargement.

aun *adv* even. • **aun así** even so; **aun cuando** although, even though.

aún *adv* **1** *(en afirmativas, interrogativas)* still: *aún la estoy esperando*, I'm still waiting for her. **2** *(en negativas)* yet: *aún no ha llegado*, he hasn't

arrived yet. **3** *(en comparaciones)* even: *dicen que aún hará más frío*, they say it's going to get even colder.

aunque *conj* **1** *(a pesar de que)* although, even though. **2** *(incluso)* even if. **3** *(pero)* although, though.

auricular *nm* *(de teléfono)* receiver, earpiece. ▶ *nm pl* **auriculares** headphones, earphones.

aurora *nf* dawn.

auscultar *vt* to sound, auscultate.

ausencia *nf* absence.

ausente *adj* absent.

austero,-a *adj* austere.

Australia *nf* Australia.

australiano,-a *adj-nm,f* Australian.

Austria *nf* Austria.

austríaco,-a *adj-nm,f* Austrian.

auténtico,-a *adj* *(cuadro)* authentic, genuine; *(persona, afecto)* genuine; *(piel, joya)* real.

auto *nm* *(coche)* car.

autobús *nm* bus.

autocar *nm* coach.

autoescuela *nf* driving school.

autógrafo *nm* autograph.

automático,-a *adj* automatic.

automóvil *nm* GB car; US automobile.

automovilismo *nm* motoring.

automovilista *nmf* motorist.
autonomía *nf* **1** *(independencia)* autonomy. **2** *(comunidad)* autonomous region.
autónomo,-a *adj* **1** POL autonomous, self-governing. **2** *(trabajador)* self-employed; *(traductor etc)* freelance.
autopista *nf* GB motorway; US expressway; US freeway.
autor, -ra *nm,f* **1** *(de libro)* author, writer; *(de canción)* writer. **3** *(de crimen)* perpetrator.
autoridad *nf* authority.
autorización *nf* authorization.
autorizar *vt* to authorize.
autoservicio *nm* self-service restaurant.
autostop *nm* hitch-hiking. • **hacer autostop** to hitch-hike.
autovía *nf* GB dual-carriageway; US highway.
auxiliar *vt* to help, assist. ► *nmf* assistant. ■ **auxiliar de vuelo** flight attendant.
auxilio *nm* help, assistance.
avalancha *nf* avalanche.
avance *nm* **1** *(progreso, movimiento)* advance. **2** *(pago)* advance payment.
avanzar *vt* to advance, move forward. ► *vi* **1** *(ir hacia adelante)* to advance, to move forward. **2** *(progresar)* to make progress.
avaro,-a *nm,f* miser.

ave *nf* bird.
AVE *abr* **(Alta Velocidad Española)** *Spanish high-speed train.*
avellana *nf* hazelnut.
avena *nf* oats.
avenida *nf* avenue.
aventura *nf* **1** *(suceso)* adventure. **2** *(riesgo)* venture. **3** *(relación amorosa)* affair, love affair.
avergonzarse *vpr* **1** *(por mala acción)* to be ashamed. **2** *(por situación bochornosa)* to be embarrassed.
avería *nf* **1** *(en coche)* breakdown. **2** *(en máquina)* fault.
averiado,-a *adj* **1** *(aparato)* faulty, not working. **2** *(coche)* broken down. • **"Averiado"** "Out of order".
averiarse *vpr* **1** *(coche)* to break. **2** *(máquina)* to malfunction.
averiguar *vt* to find out.
avestruz *nm* ostrich.
avión *nm* plane, GB aeroplane; US airplane.
avioneta *nf* light aircraft.
avisar *vt* **1** *(informar)* to tell. **2** *(advertir)* to warn. **3** *(mandar llamar)* to call for.
aviso *nm* **1** *(información)* notice. **2** *(advertencia)* warning.
avispa *nf* wasp.
axila *nf* armpit.
ayer *adv* yesterday.
ayuda *nf* help, assistance.
ayudante *nmf* assistant.
ayudar *vt* to help, aid, assist.

ayunas *nm pl.* • **en ayunas** without having eaten breakfast.

ayuntamiento *nm* **1** *(corporación)* town council. **2** *(edificio)* town hall.

azada *nf* hoe.

azafata *nf* **1** *(de avión)* flight attendant. **2** *(de congresos)* hostess.

azafrán *nm* saffron.

azar *nm* chance. • **al azar** at random; **por azar** by chance.

azotar *vt* **1** *(con látigo)* to whip. **2** *(golpear)* to beat.

azotea *nf* flat roof.

azúcar *nm & nf* sugar.

azucarero *nm* sugar bowl.

azucena *nf* white lily.

azul *adj-nm* blue.

azulejo *nm* tile.

B

baba *nf (de adulto)* spittle; *(de niño)* dribble.

babero *nm* bib.

babor *nm* port, port side.

bacalao *nm* cod.

bache *nm* **1** *(en carretera)* pothole. **2** *(en el aire)* air pocket. **3** *fig (mal momento)* bad patch.

bacon *nm* bacon.

bacteria *nf* bacterium.

bahía *nf* bay.

bailar *vt-vi* to dance. • **sacar a ALGN a bailar** to ask SB to dance.

bailarín,-ina *nm,f* dancer.

baile *nm* **1** *(danza, fiesta)* dance. **2** *(de etiqueta)* ball.

baja *nf* **1** *(descenso)* fall, drop. **2** *(en guerra)* casualty. **3** *(por enfermedad)* sick leave: **está de baja**, he's off sick. • **darse de baja 1** *(de un club)* to resign. **2** *(en una suscripción)* to cancel.

bajada *nf* **1** *(acción)* descent. **2** *(en carretera etc)* slope. **3** *(de temperatura)* fall, drop.

bajamar *nf* low tide.

bajar *vt* **1** *(de un lugar alto)* to bring down, take down. **2** *(mover abajo)* to lower. **3** *(recorrer de arriba abajo)* to come down, go down. **4** *(voz, radio, volumen)* to lower, to turn down. **5** *(precios)* to reduce. **6** INFORM *(de la red)* to download. ▶ *vi* **1** *(ir abajo - acercándose)* to come down; *(- alejándose)* to go down. **2** *(apearse - de coche)* to get out; *(- de bicicleta, caballo, avión, tren)* to get off. **3** *(reducirse)* to fall, drop, come down. ▶ *vpr* **bajarse 1** *(ir abajo - acercándose)* to come down; *(- alejándose)* to go down. **2** *(apearse - de coche)* to get out; *(- de bicicleta, caballo, avión, tren)* to get off. **3** *(pantalones, falda)* to pull down.

bajo,-a adj **1** *(de poca altura)* low. **2** *(persona)* short. **3** *(inferior)* poor, low: *la clase baja*, the lower classes; *los bajos fondos*, the underworld. ► adv **bajo 1** *(volar)* low. **2** *(hablar)* softly, quietly. ► prep *(gen)* under; *(con temperaturas)* below. ► nm **bajo 1** *(piso)* GB ground floor; US first floor. **2** *(instrumento)* bass. ► nm pl **bajos** GB ground floor; US first floor. • **por lo bajo 1** *(disimuladamente)* on the sly. **2** *(en voz baja)* in a low voice.

bala nf bullet: *un disparo de bala*, a gunshot. • **como una bala** fam like a shot.

balance nm **1** balance, balance sheet. **2** *(resultado)* result.

balancear(se) vi-vpr *(mecerse)* to rock; *(en columpio)* to swing; *(barco)* to roll.

balanza nf **1** *(para pesar)* scales. **2** balance.

balar vi to bleat.

balcón nm balcony.

balda nf shelf.

balde nm *(cubo)* bucket, pail. • **de balde** free, for nothing; **en balde** in vain.

baldosa nf floor tile.

balear adj ▪ **Islas Baleares** Balearic Islands.

ballena nf whale.

ballet nm ballet.

balneario nm spa, health resort.

balón nm ball.

baloncesto nm basketball.

balonmano nm handball.

balonvolea nf volleyball.

balsa nf *(barca)* raft.

bálsamo nm balsam, balm.

bambú nm bamboo.

banana nf banana.

banca nf *(sector)* banking; *(los bancos)* the banks.

bancarrota nf bankruptcy.

banco nm **1** *(institución financiera)* bank. **2** *(asiento)* bench. ▪ **banco de datos** data bank.

banda[1] nf **1** *(de gala)* sash. **2** *(lado)* side. ▪ **banda magnética** magnetic srip; **banda sonora** sound track.

banda[2] nf **1** *(de ladrones)* gang. **2** *(musical)* band.

bandeja nf tray.

bandera nf flag.

bandido,-a nm,f bandit.

bando nm *(facción)* faction, party.

banqueta nf *(taburete)* stool, footstool.

banquete nm banquet, feast. ▪ **banquete de boda** wedding reception.

banquillo nm **1** *(de acusados)* dock. **2** *(en deporte)* bench.

bañador nm *(de mujer)* bathing costume, swimming costume; *(de hombre)* swimming trunks.

bañar vt **1** *(en bañera)* to bath. **2** *(con salsa)* to coat. **3** *(con*

base

licor) to soak. ► *vpr* **bañarse**
(en bañera) to have a bath,
take a bath; *(en el mar, piscina)*
to swim • **"Prohibido bañarse"** "No swimming".

bañera *nf* bath, bathtub.

baño *nm* **1** *(acción)* bath. **2**
(bañera) bath, bathtub. **3** *(capa)* coat, coating. **4** *(sala de
baño)* toilet. **5** *(wáter)* toilet. ► *nm pl* **baños** *(balneario)*
spa *sing*. ■ **baño María** bain-
marie.

bar *nm (cafetería)* café, snack
bar; *(de bebidas alcohólicas)* bar.

baraja *nf* pack, deck.

barajar *vt (naipes)* to shuffle.

barandilla *nf* handrail, banister.

barato,-a *adj* cheap. ► *adv*
barato cheaply, cheap.

barba *nf* beard. • **dejarse
la barba** to grow a beard; **por
barba** each, a head.

barbaridad *nf* **1** *(crueldad)*
cruelty. **2** *(disparate)* piece of
nonsense: *cuesta una barbaridad*, it costs a fortune.

bárbaro,-a *adj* **1** HIST barbar-
ian. **2** *(cruel)* cruel. **3** *fam (grande)* enormous. **4** *fam (espléndido)* tremendous, terrific.

barbería *nf* barber's.

barbilla *nf* chin.

barca *nf* boat.

barco *nm* boat, vessel, ship. ■
barco de vela sailing boat,
yacht.

barómetro *nm* barometer.

barón *nm* baron.

barquero,-a *nm,f (hombre)*
boatman; *(mujer)* boatwoman.

barquillo *nm* wafer.

barra *nf* **1** *(de hierro)* bar. **2** *(de
pan)* loaf. **3** *(de bar, cafetería)*
bar. ■ **barra de labios** lipstick; **barra libre** free bar.

barraca *nf* **1** *(chabola)* shanty.
2 *(de feria)* stall.

barranco *nm* **1** *(precipicio)*
precipice. **2** *(entre montañas)*
gully.

barrendero,-a *nm,f* street
sweeper.

barrer *vt* to sweep.

barrera *nf* barrier. ■ **barrera
de coral** coral reef.

barricada *nf* barricade.

barriga *nf* belly.

barril *nm* barrel, keg.

barrio *nm* GB district, area; US
neighborhood. ■ **barrio bajo**
seedy area; **barrio residencial** residential area.

barro *nm* **1** *(lodo)* mud. **2** *(arcilla)* clay.

barroco,-a *adj* baroque. ►
nm **barroco** baroque.

barrote *nm* **1** *(de celda)* bar. **2**
(de escalera, silla) rung.

basar *vt* to base. ► *vpr* **basarse** to be based.

báscula *nf* scales.

base *nf* **1** *(superficie)* base. **2**
(fundamento) basis. **3** *(componente principal)*: *la base de su*

dieta es la carne, his diet is meat-based; **la base del éxito**, the key to success. ● **a base de**: *un postre hecho a base de leche y huevos*, a pudding made of milk and eggs; *a base de mucho trabajo*, by working hard. ■ **base de datos** database.

básico,-a *adj* basic.

basílica *nf* basilica.

bastante *adj-pron* **1** (*suficiente*) enough, sufficient. **2** (*abundante*) quite a lot. ▶ *adv* **1** enough. **2** (*un poco*) fairly, quite.

bastar *vi* to be sufficient, be enough.

basto,-a *adj* **1** (*grosero*) coarse, rough. **2** (*sin pulimentar*) rough, unpolished.

bastón *nm* stick, walking stick.

basura *nf* GB rubbish; US garbage. ● **tirar algo a la basura** to throw STH away, throw STH in the bin; **sacar la basura** to take out the rubbish.

bata *nf* **1** (*de casa*) dressing gown. **2** (*de trabajo*) overall; (*de médicos etc*) white coat. **3** (*de colegial*) child's overall.

batalla *nf* battle. ● **de batalla** *fam* ordinary, everyday: *zapatos de batalla*, everyday shoes.

bate *nm* bat.

batería *nf* **1** (*de coche*) battery. **2** (*cañones*) battery. **3** (*de conjunto*) drums. ▶ *nmf* drummer. ● **en batería** (*coches*) at an angle to the curb. ■ **batería de cocina** set of pots and pans.

batido *nm* milk shake.

batir *vt* **1** (*huevos*) to beat; (*nata, claras*) to whip. **2** (*alas*) to flap. **5** (*vencer*) to beat, defeat. **6** (*récord*) to break. ▶ *vpr* **batirse** to fight.

batuta *nf* baton.

baúl *nm* trunk.

bautismo *nm* baptism, christening.

bautizar *vt* **1** to baptize, christen. **2** (*poner nombre a*) to name.

bautizo *nm* **1** (*sacramento*) baptism, christening. **2** (*fiesta*) christening party.

baya *nf* berry.

bayeta *nf* cloth.

bazar *nm* bazaar.

bazo *nm* spleen.

bebé *nm* baby.

beber *vt* to drink.

bebida *nf* drink, beverage. ■ **bebida alcohólica** alcoholic drink.

beca *nf* **1** (*ayuda*) grant. **2** (*por méritos*) scholarship.

becerro *nm* calf.

bechamel *nf* béchamel sauce, white sauce.

béisbol *nm* baseball.

belén *nm* nativity scene, crib.

belga *adj-nmf* Belgian.
Bélgica *nf* Belgium.
belleza *nf* beauty.
bello,-a *adj* beautiful.
bellota *nf* acorn.
bendecir *vt* to bless.
bendición *nf* blessing.
beneficiar *vt* to benefit, favour. ► *vpr* **beneficiarse** to benefit from.
beneficio *nm* profit.
beneficioso,-a *adj* beneficial, useful.
benéfico,-a *adj* charitable: *función benéfica*, charity performance.
bengala *nf* flare.
benigno,-a *adj* 1 *(tumor)* benign. 2 *(clima)* mild.
berberecho *nm* cockle.
berenjena *nf* GB aubergine; US eggplant.
bermudas *nf pl* Bermuda shorts.
berro *nm* watercress, cress.
berza *nf* cabbage.
besamel *nf* bechamel sauce, white sauce.
besar *vt* to kiss. ► *vpr* **besarse** to kiss one another.
beso *nm* kiss.
bestia *nf (animal)* beast. ► *nmf (persona)* brute.
besugo *nm* 1 *(pez)* sea bream. 2 *(persona)* idiot.
betún *nm* shoe polish.
biberón *nm* baby bottle.
Biblia *nf* Bible.

bíblico,-a *adj* biblical.
bibliografía *nf* 1 *(en libro)* bibliography. 2 *(de curso)* reading list.
biblioteca *nf* 1 *(edificio)* library. 2 *(mueble)* bookcase, bookshelf.
bicarbonato *nm* bicarbonate.
bíceps *nm* biceps.
bicho *nm* 1 *(insecto)* bug. 2 *(persona)* nasty character: *es un bicho raro*, he's a weirdo.
bici *nf fam* bike.
bicicleta *nf* bicycle: *ir en bicicleta*, to cycle. ■ **bicicleta de carreras** racing bicycle; **bicicleta de montaña** mountain bike; **bicicleta estática** exercise bike.
bidé *nm* bidet.
bidón *nm* 1 *(pequeño)* can. 2 *(grande)* drum.
bien *adv* 1 *(de manera satisfactoria)* well. 2 *(correctamente)* right, correctly. 3 *(debidamente)* properly: *¡pórtate bien!*, behave yourself! 4 *(de acuerdo)*: *¡muy bien!*, O.K., all right. 5 *(mucho)* very; *(bastante)* quite: *es bien sencillo*, it's very simple; *bien tarde*, pretty late. ► *nm* good: *el bien y el mal*, good and evil. ► *adj* well-to-do: *gente bien*, the upper classes. ► *nm pl* **bienes** property, possessions. • **bien que** althoug; **más bien** rather; **si bien** although.

bienestar *nm* well-being, comfort.

bienvenida *nf* welcome. • **dar la bienvenida a** ALGN to welcome SB.

bigote *nm* **1** *(de persona)* moustache. **2** *(de gato)* whiskers.

bikini *nm* bikini.

bilingüe *adj* bilingual.

bilis *nf* bile.

billar *nm* **1** *(juego)* billiards. **2** *(mesa)* billiard table. ▸ *nm pl* **billares** billiard hall.

billete *nm* **1** *(moneda)* note. **2** *(de tren, autobús, sorteo, etc)* ticket: *sacar un billete*, to buy a ticket. ▪ **billete de ida** one-way ticket; **billete de ida y vuelta** GB return ticket; US round-trip ticket.

billetero *nm* wallet.

billón *nm* GB billion; US trillion.

bingo *nm* **1** *(juego)* bingo. **2** *(sala)* bingo hall.

biografía *nf* biography.

biología *nf* biology.

biológico,-a *adj* **1** *(ciclo, madre)* biological. **2** *(alimento)* organic.

biombo *nm* folding screen.

biquini *nm* bikini.

bisagra *nf* hinge.

bisiesto *adj*: *año bisiesto*, leap year.

bisté *nm* steak.

bistec *nm* steak.

bisturí *nm* scalpel.

bisutería *nf* imitation jewellery.

bit *nm* bit.

bizco,-a *adj* cross-eyed.

bizcocho *nm* sponge cake.

blanco,-a *adj* white. ▸ *nm* **blanco 1** *(color)* white. **2** *(objetivo físico)* target. **3** *(hueco)* blank, gap. • **dar en el blanco 1** *(diana)* to hit the mark. **2** *(acertar)* to hit the nail on the head; **quedarse en blanco** *(olvidar)* to forget everything.

blando,-a *adj* **1** *(superficie, madera, queso)* soft; *(carne)* tender. **2** *(persona)* soft.

blanquear *vt* **1** *(poner blanco)* to whiten. **2** *(con cal)* to whitewash. **3** *fam (dinero)* to launder.

bloc *nm* pad, notepad.

bloque *nm* **1** *(de piedra)* block. **2** *(de papel)* pad, notepad. **3** POL bloc. ▪ **bloque de pisos** block of flats.

bloquear *vt* **1** *(camino, entrada)* to block. **2** *(puerto, país)* to blockade. ▸ *vpr* **bloquearse 1** *(quedarse paralizado)* to freeze. **2** *(quedarse en blanco)* to have a blank. **3** *(mecanismo)* to jam.

blusa *nf* blouse.

boa *nf* boa.

bobina *nf* **1** *(carrete)* reel, bobbin. **2** *(eléctrica)* coil.

bobo,-a *adj* silly, foolish. ▸ *nm,f* fool, dunce.

boca nf **1** mouth. **2** (abertura) entrance, opening. • **boca abajo** face down; **boca arriba** face up. ▪ **boca a boca** mouth to mouth resuscitation; **boca del estómago** pit of the stomach.

bocacalle nf side street: *la primera bocacalle a la izquierda*, the first turn to the left.

bocadillo nm **1** (de pan de molde) sandwich. **2** (en barra) roll. **3** (en cómics) speech balloon.

bocata nm **1** fam (de pan de molde) sandwich. **2** (en barra) roll.

bochorno nm **1** (calor) sultry weather, close weather. **2** (vergüenza) embarrassment, shame.

bocina nf horn.

boda nf **1** (ceremonia) marriage, wedding. **2** (fiesta) reception.

bodega nf **1** (de vinos) cellar, wine cellar. **2** (tienda) wine shop. **3** (de barco, avión) hold.

bodegón nm still-life painting.

bofetada nf slap in the face.

boicot nm boycott.

boina nf beret.

bol nm bowl.

bola nf **1** (cuerpo esférico) ball. **2** (de helado) scoop. **3** fam (mentira) fib, lie.

bolera nf bowling alley.

boleto nm (de lotería) ticket; (de quiniela) coupon.

boli nm fam ballpen, Biro®.

bolígrafo nm ballpoint pen, Biro®.

Bolivia nf Bolivia.

boliviano,-a adj-nm,f Bolivian.

bollo nm **1** (dulce) bun. **2** (de pan) roll.

bolo nm skittle, ninepin: *jugar a los bolos*, to go bowling.

bolsa[1] nf bag. ▪ **bolsa de basura** bin liner; **bolsa de viaje** travel bag.

bolsa[2] nf stock exchange.

bolsillo nm pocket.

bolso nm GB handbag; US purse.

bomba[1] nf (explosivo) bomb. • **pasarlo bomba** to have a ball.

bomba[2] nf (para bombear) pump.

bombero,-a nm,f (hombre) firefighter, fireman; (mujer) firefighter, firewoman.

bombilla nf light bulb, bulb.

bombo nm **1** bass drum. **2** (para sorteo) drum.

bombón nm chocolate.

bombona nf cylinder, bottle. ▪ **bombona de butano** butane cylinder.

bondad nf **1** (cualidad) goodness. **2** (afabilidad) kindness: *tenga la bondad de contestar*, be so good as to reply.

bonito,-a *adj* nice, pretty. ►
nm **bonito** *(pez)* tuna, bonito.

bono *nm* **1** bond. **2** *(vale)*
voucher. **3** *(para transporte)*
pass.

bonobús *nm* (multiple journey) bus pass.

boquerón *nm* fresh, anchovy.

borda *nf* gunwale. ● **arrojar
por la borda** to throw overboard.

bordado *nm* embroidering,
embroidery.

bordar *vt* to embroider.

borde[1] *adj fam* nasty.

borde[2] *nm (extremo)* edge; *(de
prenda)* hem; *(de camino)* side;
(de vaso, taza) rim: *al borde
del mar*, beside the sea.

bordillo *nm* kerb.

bordo *nm* board. ● **a bordo**
on board.

borrachera *nf* drunkenness.

borracho,-a *adj* drunk. ►
nm,f drunkard.

borrador *nm* **1** *(de texto)* rough
copy, first draft. **2** *(de pizarra)*
duster.

borrar *vt* **1** *(con goma etc)* to erase,
rub out. **2** INFORM to delete.

borrasca *nf* area of low pressure.

borrego,-a *nm,f (animal)* lamb.

borroso,-a *adj* blurred, hazy.

bosque *nm* forest, wood.

bostezar *vi* to yawn.

bostezo *nm* yawn.

bota[1] *nf (calzado)* boot. ● **ponerse las botas** *(al comer)* to
stuff oneself.

bota[2] *nf (de vino)* wineskin.

botánico,-a *adj* botanical.

botar *vt* **1** *(pelota)* to bounce.
2 *(barco)* to launch. ► *vi (saltar)*
to jump.

bote[1] *nm* small boat. ■ **bote
salvavidas** lifeboat.

bote[2] *nm (salto)* bounce.

bote[3] *nm* **1** *(recipiente)* tin, can;
(para propinas) jar for tips,
box for tips. **2** *(de lotería)*
jackpot.

bote[4] ● **estar de bote en
bote** to be jam-packed.

botella *nf* bottle.

botellín *nm* small bottle.

botijo *nm* drinking jug.

botín *nm* **1** *(de guerra)* booty.
2 *(de ladrones)* loot.

botiquín *nm* **1** *(de medicinas)*
first-aid kit. **2** *(enfermería)*
sick bag.

botón *nm* **1** *(de camisa)* button. **2** *(tecla)* button. ■ **botón
de arranque** starter; **bo-
tón de muestra** sample.

botones *nm (de hotel)* GB bellboy; US bellhop.

bóveda *nf* vault.

boxeador,-a *nm* boxer.

boxear *vi* to box.

boxeo *nm* boxing.

boya *nf* **1** buoy. **2** *(corcho de
pesca)* float.

bragas *nf pl* panties, knickers.

bragueta *nf* fly, flies.

brasa *nf* live coal. ● **a la brasa** barbecued.

Brasil *nm* Brazil.

brasileño,-a *adj-nm,f* Brazilian.

bravo,-a *adj* 1 *(valiente)* brave, courageous. 2 *(fiero)* fierce, ferocious. ► *interj* well done!, bravo!

braza *nf* *(en natación)* breast stroke.

brazo *nm* 1 *(de persona, sillón)* arm. 2 *(de animal)* foreleg.

brecha *nf* 1 *(abertura)* break, opening. 2 *(herida)* gash.

Bretaña *nf*. ■ **Gran Bretaña** Great Britain.

breve *adj* short, brief. ● **en breve** soon, shortly.

bricolaje *nm* do-it-yourself, DIY.

brida *nf* bridle.

brillante *adj* 1 *(luz, color)* bright; *(pelo, calzado)* shiny. 2 *(destacado)* brilliant. ► *nm (diamante)* diamond.

brillar *vi* 1 *(sol, luz, ojos, oro)* to shine. 2 *(sobresalir)* to shine, be outstanding.

brillo *nm* 1 *(resplandor)* shine. 2 *(de estrella)* brightness, brilliance.

brincar *vi* to jump, hop.

brindar *vi* to toast. ► *vt (proporcionar)* to offer: *me brindó su apoyo*, she gave me her support.

brindis *nm* toast.

brisa *nf* breeze.

británico,-a *adj* British. ► *nm,f (hombre)* British man, Briton; *(mujer)* British woman, Briton.

brocha *nf* paintbrush. ■ **brocha de afeitar** shaving brush.

broche *nm* 1 *(cierre)* fastener. 2 *(joya)* brooch.

broma *nf* joke. ● **gastar una broma a** ALGN to play a joke on SB. ■ **broma pesada** practical joke.

bronca *nf* row, quarrel. ● **armar una bronca** to kick up a fuss; **echar una bronca a** ALGN to come down on SB.

bronce *nm* bronze.

bronceado *nm* tan, suntan.

bronceador *nm* suntan lotion.

bronquios *nm pl* bronchial tubes.

bronquitis *nf* bronchitis.

brotar *vi* 1 *(planta)* to sprout, bud. 2 *(hoja)* to sprout, come out. 3 *(agua)* to spring.

brote *nm* 1 *(de planta)* bud, sprout. 2 *(de conflicto, epidemia)* outbreak.

bruja *nf* 1 *(hechicera)* witch, sorceress. 2 *fam (harpía)* old hag.

brujo *nm* wizard, sorcerer.

brújula *nf* compass.

bruma *nf* mist, fog.

brusco,-a *adj* 1 *(persona)* brusque, abrupt. 2 *(movimiento)* sudden.

bruto,-a *adj* **1** *(necio)* stupid, ignorant. **2** *(tosco)* rough, coarse. **3** *(montante, peso)* gross. **4** *(petróleo)* crude.

bucear *vi* to swim under water.

budista *adj-nmf* Buddhist.

buen *adj* → bueno,-a.

bueno,-a *adj* **1** *(gen)* good. **2** *(persona - amable)* kind; *(- agradable)* nice, polite. **3** *(apropiado)* right, suitable. **4** *(grande)* big; *(considerable)* considerable: *un buen número de participantes*, quite a few participants. • **de buenas a primeras** *fam* from the very start; **por las buenas** willingly.

buey *nm* ox.

búfalo *nm* buffalo.

bufanda *nf* scarf.

bufé *nm* buffet. ▪ **bufé libre** self-service buffet.

bufete *nm* **1** *(mesa)* writing desk. **2** *(de abogado)* lawyer's office.

buhardilla *nf* garret, attic.

búho *nm* owl.

buitre *nm* vulture.

bujía *nf* spark plug.

bulevar *nm* boulevard.

bulto *nm* **1** *(tamaño)* volume, size, bulk. **2** *(hinchazón)* swelling, lump. **3** *(fardo)* bundle, pack: *¿cuántos bultos lleva?*, how many pieces of luggage do you have?

buñuelo *nm* **1** *(dulce)* doughnut. **2** *(de bacalao etc)* fritter.

buque *nm* ship, vessel.

burbuja *nf* bubble.

burla *nf* mockery, gibe.

burlar *vt* **1** *(engañar)* to deceive, trick. **2** *(eludir)* to dodge, evade. ▶ *vpr* **burlarse** to mock. • **burlarse de** ALGN to make fun of SB, laugh at SB.

burocracia *nf* bureaucracy.

burro,-a *nm,f* **1** *(asno)* donkey. **2** *(ignorante)* idiot. **3** *(bruto)* brute.

busca *nf* search.

buscador *nm* INFORM search engine.

buscar *vt* *(gen)* to look for, search for; *(en diccionario)* to look up: *ir a buscar algo*, to go and get STH; *vinieron a buscarme a la estación*, they came to pick me up from the station.

búsqueda *nf* search.

busto *nm* bust.

butaca *nf* **1** *(sillón)* armchair. **2** *(en teatro)* seat.

butano *nm* butane.

butifarra *nf* pork sausage.

buzo *nm* diver.

buzón *nm* **1** *(en casa)* GB letter-box; US mailbox. **2** *(en calle)* GB post box; US mailbox. **3** INFORM mailbox. • **echar una carta al buzón** to post a letter. ▪ **buzón de voz** voicemail.

byte *nm* byte.

C

caballa *nf* mackerel.

caballero *nm* **1** *(señor)* gentleman. **2** HIST knight.

caballo *nm* **1** horse. **2** *(en ajedrez)* knight. • **a caballo** on horseback; **montar a caballo** to ride.

cabaña *nf* cabin, hut.

cabecera *nf* **1** *(de periódico)* headline. **2** *(de cama)* bedhead.

cabello *nm* hair. ▪ **cabello de ángel** sweet pumpkin preserve.

caber *vi* to fit: *en esta lata caben diez litros*, this can holds ten litres; *no caben más*, there is no room for any more. • **dentro de lo que cabe** all things considered; **no cabe duda** there is no doubt.

cabestrillo *nm*. • **en cabestrillo** in a sling.

cabeza *nf* head. • **cabeza abajo** upside down; **cabeza arriba** the right way up; **por cabeza** a head, per person. ▪ **cabeza de ajo** head of garlic.

cabida *nf* capacity, room.

cabina *nf* cabin, booth. ▪ **cabina telefónica** phone box.

cable *nm* cable.

cabo *nm* **1** *(gen)* end: *al cabo de un mes*, in a month. **2** *(cuerda)* strand. **3** GEOG cape.

4 *(militar)* corporal. • **de cabo a rabo** from head to tail; **llevar a cabo** to carry out.

cabra *nf* goat.

cabrito *nm* kid.

caca *nf* **1** *fam (excremento)* shit. **2** *(en lenguaje infantil)* poo, poopoo.

cacahuete *nm* peanut.

cacao *nm* **1** *(planta)* cacao. **2** *(polvo, bebida)* cocoa.

cacarear *vi* **1** *(gallina)* to cluck. **2** *(gallo)* to crow.

cacerola *nf* saucepan.

cachalote *nm* cachalot, sperm whale.

cacharro *nm* **1** *(de cocina)* pot. **2** *fam (cosa)* thing, piece of junk.

caché *nm* cache memory.

cachear *vt* to search, frisk.

cacho *nm fam* bit, piece.

cachorro,-a *nm,f (de perro)* puppy; *(de león, tigre)* cub.

cacto *nm* cactus.

cactus *nm* cactus.

cada *adj* **1** *(para individualizar)* each: *tres caramelos para cada uno*, three sweets for each; *cada cual, cada uno*, each one, every one. **2** *(con números, tiempo)* every: *cada cuatro años hay un año bisiesto*, there's a leap year every four years. **3** *(uso enfático)*: *¡dice cada tontería!*, he says such stupid things! • **cada vez más** more and more; **cada vez que** whenever, every time that.

cadáver *nm* corpse, body.

cadena *nf* 1 *(de eslabones, establecimientos)* chain. 2 *(industrial)* line. 3 *(montañosa)* range. 4 *(musical)* music centre. 5 *(de televisión)* channel. 6 *(de radio)* station. ► *nf pl* **cadenas** *(de nieve)* tyre chains. ● **tirar de la cadena del wáter** to flush the toilet.

cadera *nf* hip.

caducar *vi* to expire: *¿cuándo caduca la leche?*, what's the sell-by date on the milk?

caducidad *nf* 1 *(de documento)* expiration, loss of validity. 2 *(de alimento)* best before date.

caer *vi* 1 *(gen)* to fall. 2 *(coincidir fechas)* to be: *el día cuatro cae en jueves*, the fourth is a Thursday. ► *vpr* **caerse** to fall. ● **caer bien**: *me cae bien*, I like her; **caer mal**: *me cae mal*, I don't like him; **caer enfermo,-a** to fall ill; **dejar caer** to drop; **estar al caer** to be about to arrive.

café *nm* 1 *(bebida)* coffee. 2 *(cafetería)* café. ■ **café con leche** white coffee; **café descafeinado** decaffeinated coffee; **café exprés** expresso; **café solo** black coffee.

cafeína *nf* caffeine.

cafetera *nf* coffeepot.

cafetería *nf* cafeteria, café.

caída *nf* 1 *(gen)* fall, falling. 2 *(de tejidos)* body, hang.

caimán *nm* alligator.

caja *nf* 1 *(gen)* box; *(de madera)* chest; *(grande)* crate. 2 *(de bebidas)* case. 3 *(en tienda, bar)* cash desk; *(en supermercado)* checkout; *(en banco)* cashier's desk. ■ **caja de ahorros** savings bank; **caja de cambios** gearbox; **caja fuerte** safe; **caja negra** black box; **caja registradora** cash register.

cajero,-a *nm,f* cashier. ■ **cajero automático** cash dispenser.

cajetilla *nf* packet *(of cigarettes)*.

cajón *nm* drawer.

cal *nf* lime.

cala *nf* cove.

calabacín *nm* GB courgette; US zucchini.

calabaza *nf* pumpkin.

calabozo *nm* 1 *(prisión)* jail. 2 *(celda)* cell.

calado,-a *adj fam* soaked.

calamar *nm* squid. ■ **calamares a la romana** squid fried in batter.

calambre *nm* 1 *(muscular)* cramp. 2 *(eléctrico)* shock, electric shock.

calamidad *nf* calamity, disaster.

calar *vt* 1 *(mojar)* to soak, drench. 2 *fam (intención)* to rumble. ► *vpr* **calarse** 1 *(con* *agua)* to get soaked. **2** *(motor)* to stop, stall.

calavera *nf* skull.

calcetín *nm* sock.

calcio *nm* calcium.

calculadora *nf* calculator.

calcular *vt* to calculate, work out.

cálculo *nm* **1** *(de cantidad, presupuesto)* calculation. **2** *(del riñón, etc)* stone.

caldera *nf* boiler.

calderilla *nf* small change.

caldero *nm* cauldron.

caldo *nm* **1** *(sopa)* broth. **2** *(para cocinar)* stock. ▪ **caldo de cultivo** culture medium.

calefacción *nf* heating. ▪ **calefacción central** central heating.

calendario *nm* calendar.

calentador *nm* heater.

calentar *vt-vi (gen)* to warm up; *(agua, horno, etc)* to heat, heat up.

calidad *nf* quality. ● **en calidad de** as.

cálido,-a *adj* warm.

caliente *adj (ardiendo)* hot; *(templado)* warm.

calificar *vt* **1** *(etiquetar)* to describe. **2** *(dar nota)* to mark, grade.

callado,-a *adj* silent, quiet.

callar(se) *vi-vpr (dejar de hablar)* to stop talking; *(no hablar)* to say nothing, remain silent: *¡cállate!,* shut up!

calle *nf* **1** street, road. **2** *(en atletismo)* lane. ▪ **calle mayor** high street, main street; **calle peatonal** pedestrian street.

callejero *nm* street directory.

callejón *nm.* ▪ **callejón sin salida** cul-de-sac, dead end.

callo *nm (en mano, planta del pie)* callus; *(en dedo del pie)* corn. ▶ *nm pl* **callos** tripe.

calma *nf* calm.

calmante *adj* soothing. ▶ *nm* painkiller.

calmar *vt* **1** *(nervios)* to calm; *(persona)* to calm down. **2** *(dolor)* to relieve, soothe. ▶ *vt-vpr* **calmar(se)** to calm down.

calor *nm (sensación)* heat: *hace calor,* it is hot; *tengo calor,* I feel warm, I feel hot.

caloría *nf* calorie.

caluroso,-a *adj (tiempo)* hot, warm.

calva *nf* bald patch.

calvo,-a *adj (persona)* bald. ▶ *nm,f* bald person.

calzada *nf* road, roadway.

calzado *nm* footwear, shoes.

calzador *nm* shoehorn.

calzarse *vpr* to put one's shoes on. ● **¿qué número calzas?** what size shoes do you take?

calzoncillos *nm pl* underpants, pants.

cama *nf* bed. ▪ **cama de matrimonio** double bed; **cama individual** single bed.

camaleón *nm* chameleon.

cámara *nf* **1** *(fotográfica)* camera. **2** *(del parlamento)* house. **3** *(de rueda)* inner tube. • **a cámara lenta** in slow motion.

camarada *nmf* **1** *(colega)* colleague; *(de colegio)* schoolmate. **2** POL comrade.

camarero,-a *nm,f* **1** *(en bar - hombre)* waiter; *(- mujer)* waitress. **2** *(en barco, - hombre)* steward; *(- mujer)* stewardess.

camarón *nm* shrimp.

camarote *nm* cabin.

cambiar *vt* **1** *(gen)* to change. **2** *(intercambiar)* to exchange, swap. ► *vi* to change. ► *vpr* **cambiarse** to change: *cambiarse de ropa*, to get changed. • **cambiar de** to change: *cambiar de trabajo*, to change jobs.

cambio *nm* **1** *(gen)* change. **2** *(canje)* exchange. **3** *(de divisas)* exchange, rate. **4** *(de tren)* switch. **5** *(de marchas)* gear change. • **a cambio de** in exchange for; **en cambio 1** *(por otro lado)* on the other hand. **2** *(en lugar de)* instead. ■ **cambio automático** *(de coche)* automatic transmission; **cambio de marchas** gearshift.

camello *nm* camel.

camerino *nm* dressing room.

camilla *nf* stretcher.

caminar *vt-vi* to walk.

camino *nm* **1** *(sendero)* path, track. **2** *(ruta)* way.

camión *nm* GB lorry; US truck.

camioneta *nf* van.

camisa *nf* shirt.

camiseta *nf* **1** *(interior)* vest. **2** *(exterior)* T-shirt. **3** *(de deportes)* shirt.

camisón *nm* nightdress, nightgown, nightie.

campamento *nm* camp.

campana *nf* bell. ■ **campana extractora** cooker hood.

campanario *nm* belfry, bell tower.

campanilla *nf* *(úvula)* uvula.

campaña *nf* campaign.

campeonato *nm* championship.

campeón,-ona *nm,f* champion.

campesino,-a *nm,f (que vive en el campo)* country person; *(que trabaja en el campo)* farm worker.

camping *nm* camping site. • **ir de camping** to go camping.

campo *nm* **1** *(gen)* field. **2** *(campiña)* country, countryside; *(paisaje)* countryside. • **ir campo a través** to cut across the fields. ■ **campo de concentración** concentration camp; **campo de fútbol** football pitch, football field; **campo de golf** golf course.

cana *nf* grey hair.
canal *nm* **1** *(artificial)* canal. **2** *(natural, de televisión)* channel.
canapé *nm* *(comida)* canapé.
Canarias *nf pl.* ▪ **islas Canarias** Canary Islands.
canario *nm* *(pájaro)* canary.
canasta *nf* basket.
cancelar *vt* **1** *(anular)* to cancel. **2** *(deuda)* to pay off, settle.
cáncer *nm* **1** *(tumor)* cancer. **2** *(signo)* Cancer.
cancha *nf* court.
canción *nf* song.
candado *nm* padlock.
candidato,-a *nm,f* candidate.
canela *nf* cinnamon.
canelones *nm pl* cannelloni.
cangrejo *nm* crab. ▪ **cangrejo (de río)** crayfish.
canguro *nm* kangaroo. ▶ *nmf* baby-sitter.
canoa *nf* canoe.
cansado,-a *adj* **1** *(fatigado, harto)* tired. **2** *(trabajo, viaje)* tiring, boring.
cansancio *nm* tiredness.
cansar *vt* **1** *(fatigar)* to tire, tire out. **2** *(molestar)* to annoy: *me cansan sus discursos*, I'm fed up with his speeches. ▶ *vi* to be tiring. ▶ *vpr* **cansarse** to get tired.
cantante *nmf* singer.
cantar *vt-vi (gen)* to sing; *(gallo)* to crow.
cante *nm*. ▪ **cante hondo** flamenco.

cantidad *nf* **1** *(volumen)* quantity, amount. **2** *(de dinero)* sum, amount. ▶ *adv fam* a lot: *me gusta cantidad*, I love it.
cantimplora *nf* water bottle.
cantina *nf* **1** *(en fábrica, colegio)* canteen. **2** *(en estación)* buffet, cafeteria.
canto[1] *nm (arte)* singing.
canto[2] *nm* **1** *(borde)* edge. **2** *(piedra)* stone. ▪ **de canto** sideways.
caña *nf* **1** *(planta)* reed. **2** *(tallo)* cane. **3** *(de pescar)* fishing rod. **4** *(de cerveza)* beer, glass of beer. ▪ **caña de azúcar** sugar cane.
cañería *nf* pipe.
cañón *nm* **1** *(de artillería)* cannon. **2** *(de arma)* barrel. **3** GEOG canyon.
caoba *nf* mahogany.
caos *nm* chaos.
capa *nf* **1** *(prenda)* cloak, cape. **2** *(baño)* coat. **3** *(estrato)* layer.
capacidad *nf* **1** *(cabida)* capacity. **2** *(habilidad)* capability, ability.
capaz *adj* capable, able.
capilla *nf (de iglesia)* chapel. ▪ **capilla ardiente** funeral chapel.
capital *nm (dinero)* capital. ▶ *nf (ciudad)* capital.
capitán,-ana *nm,f* captain.
capitel *nm* capital.
capítulo *nm (de libro)* chapter; *(de serie televisiva)* episode.

capó *nm* GB bonnet; US hood.

capote *nm* *(de torero)* cape.

capricho *nm* whim, caprice.

capricornio *nm* Capricorn.

cápsula *nf* capsule.

captar *vt* 1 *(atraer interés, atención)* to capture; *(adeptos)* to attract. 2 *(comprender)* to understand.

capturar *vt* *(persona, animal)* to capture; *(alijo)* to seize.

capucha *nf* hood.

capullo *nm* 1 *(de insectos)* cocoon. 2 *(de flor)* bud.

caqui *nm* *(fruta)* persimmon.

cara *nf* 1 face. 2 *(lado)* side. 3 *(descaro)* cheek, nerve. • **cara a cara** face to face; **cara o cruz** heads or tails; **dar la cara** to take responsibility; **de cara a** opposite, facing; **tener buena cara** to look well; **tener cara de + adj** to look + *adj*; **tener mala cara** to look ill.

caracol *nm* 1 *(de tierra)* snail; *(de mar)* winkle. 2 *(del oído)* cochlea.

caracola *nf* conch.

carácter *nm* 1 *(personalidad, genio)* character: *tiene mucho carácter*, he's got a strong personality. 2 *(condición)* nature: *el proyecto tiene carácter científico*, this project is of a scientific nature. 3 *(de imprenta)* letter. • **tener buen carácter** to be good-natured;

tener mal carácter to be bad-tempered.

característico,-a *adj* characteristic.

carambola *nf* *(billar)* GB cannon; US carom.

caramelo *nm* 1 *(golosina)* GB sweet; US candy. 2 *(azúcar quemado)* caramel.

caravana *nf* 1 *(vehículo)* caravan. 2 *(atasco)* GB tailback; US backup.

carbón *nm* *(mineral)* coal. ■ **carbón vegetal** charcoal.

carbono *nm* carbon.

carburador *nm* GB carburettor; US carburetor.

carburante *nm* fuel.

carcajada *nf* burst of laughter, guffaw.

cárcel *nf* prison, jail.

cardenal[1] *nm* *(de la iglesia)* cardinal.

cardenal[2] *nm* *(hematoma)* bruise.

cardíaco,-a *adj* cardiac, heart.

cardo *nm* *(planta)* thistle

carecer *vi*. • **carecer de algo** to lack STH.

carga *nf* 1 *(mercancías)* load. 2 *(peso)* burden. 3 *(flete)* cargo, freight. 4 *(obligación)* duty. 5 *(explosiva, eléctrica, militar)* charge. 6 *(de pluma, bolígrafo)* refill.

cargamento *nm* *(de tren, camión)* load; *(de avión, barco)* cargo.

cargar vt 1 (vehículo, arma, mercancías) to load. 2 (pluma, encendedor) to fill. 3 (pila) to charge. ► vpr **cargarse** fam (destrozar) to smash, ruin. ● **cargar con** 1 (peso) to carry. 2 (responsabilidad) to take.

cargo nm 1 (puesto) post, position. 2 (gobierno, custodia) charge, responsibility. 3 JUR charge, accusation. ● **hacerse cargo de** 1 (responsabilizarse de) to take charge of. 2 (entender) to take into consideration, realize.

caricatura nf caricature.

caricia nf 1 (a persona) caress, stroke. 2 (a animal) stroke.

caridad nf charity.

caries nf tooth decay, caries.

cariño nm 1 (afecto) love, affection, fondness. 2 (apelativo) darling.

carnaval nm carnival.

carne nf 1 meat. 2 (de persona, fruta) flesh. ● **en carne viva** raw; **ser de carne y hueso** to be only human. ■ **carne asada** roasted meat; **carne de buey** beef; **carne de gallina** goose flesh, goose bumps; **carne picada** mincemeat.

carné nm card. ■ **carné de conducir** driving licence; **carné de identidad** identity card.

carnet nm → carné.

carnicería nf (tienda) butcher's.

caro,-a adj expensive, dear. ► adv **caro** at a high price.

carpa¹ nf (pez) carp.

carpa² nf (toldo) marquee; (de circo) big top.

carpeta nf folder, file.

carpintería nf 1 (labor) carpentry. 2 (taller) carpenter's shop.

carrera nf 1 (competición) race. 2 (estudios) university education. 3 (profesión) career. 4 (trayecto) route. 5 (en las medias) ladder.

carreta nf cart.

carrete nm 1 (de película) roll of film, film. 2 (de hilo, pesca) reel.

carretera nf road. ■ **carretera nacional** GB A road, main road; US state highway.

carril nm lane. ■ **carril bici** GB cycle lane; US bikeway.

carro nm 1 (carreta) cart. 2 (militar) tank. 3 (en supermercado, aeropuerto) trolley. 4 (de máquina de escribir) carriage.

carrocería nf bodywork.

carroza nf 1 (de caballos) coach, carriage. 2 (de carnaval) float.

carruaje nm carriage, coach.

carta nf 1 (documento) letter. 2 (naipe) card. 3 (en restaurante) menu. ■ **carta certificada** registered letter.

cartel nm poster.

cartelera nf 1 (para carteles) GB hoarding; US billboard. 2

(en periódicos) entertainment guide.

cartera *nf* **1** *(monedero)* wallet. **2** *(de colegial)* satchel, schoolbag. **3** *(de ejecutivo)* briefcase; *(sin asa)* portfolio.

carterista *nmf* pickpocket.

cartero,-a *nm,f (hombre)* GB postman; US mailman; *(mujer)* GB postwoman; US mailwoman.

cartilla *nf.* ■ **cartilla de ahorros** savings book; **cartilla del seguro** social security card.

cartón *nm* **1** *(material)* cardboard. **2** *(de cigarrillos, leche)* carton.

casa *nf* **1** *(edificio)* house. **2** *(hogar)* home. ■ **casa adosada** terraced house; **casa de campo** country house; **casa de huéspedes** guesthouse, boarding house; **casa de socorro** first aid post; **casa pareada** semi-detached house.

casarse *vpr* to get married.

cascada *nf* waterfall, cascade.

cascanueces *nm* nutcracker.

cáscara *nf* **1** *(de huevo, nuez)* shell. **2** *(de plátano)* skin. **3** *(de naranja, limón)* peel, rind. **4** *(de grano)* husk.

casco *nm* **1** *(protector)* helmet. **2** *(envase)* empty bottle. **3** *(de barco)* hull. **4** *(de caballo)* hoof. ► *nm pl* **cascos** *(auriculares)* headphones. ■ **casco antiguo** old town; **casco azul** blue beret; **casco urbano** city centre; US downtown area.

caserío *nm* country house.

casero,-a *adj (productos)* homemade. ► *nm,f (dueño - hombre)* landlord; *(- mujer)* landlady.

caseta *nf* **1** *(de feria)* stall. **2** *(de bañistas)* GB bathing hut; US bath house. **3** *(de perro)* kennel.

casete *nm (aparato)* cassette player, cassette recorder. ► *nf (cinta)* cassette *(tape)*.

casi *adv* **1** *(gen)* almost, nearly. **2** *(en frases negativas)* hardly: *casi nunca*, hardly ever.

casilla *nf* **1** *(de casillero)* pigeonhole. **2** *(cuadrícula)* square. **3** *(de formulario)* box.

casino *nm* casino.

caso *nm* case. • **en caso de que** in case; **en ese caso** in that case; **en todo caso** anyhow, at any rate.

caspa *nf* dandruff.

castaña *nf* **1** *(fruto)* chestnut.

castaño,-a *adj* chestnut-coloured; *(pelo)* brown. ► *nm* **castaño** *(árbol)* chestnut tree.

castañuela *nf* castanet.

castellano,-a *adj-nm,f* Castilian. ► *nm* **castellano** *(idioma)* Castilian, Spanish.

castigar *vt* to punish.

castigo *nm* punishment.

castillo *nm* castle.

castor *nm* beaver.

casualidad *nf* chance, coincidence. • **por casualidad** by chance.

catalán,-ana *adj-nm,f* Catalan, Catalonian. ► *nm* **catalán** *(idioma)* Catalan.

catálogo *nm* catalogue.

catarata *nf* 1 *(de agua)* waterfall. 2 *(en ojo)* cataract.

catarro *nm* cold.

catástrofe *nf* catastrophe.

catedral *nf* cathedral.

catedrático,-a *nm,f (de universidad)* professor; *(de instituto)* head of department.

categoría *nf* 1 *(rango)* category. 2 *(nivel)* level.

católico,-a *adj-nm,f* Catholic.

catorce *num* fourteen; *(en fechas)* fourteenth.

cauce *nm* 1 *(de río)* river bed. 2 *(canal)* channel.

caucho *nm* rubber.

caudal *nm* 1 *(de río)* volume of water. 2 *(riqueza)* fortune, wealth.

causa *nf* 1 *(motivo, ideal)* cause. 2 *(proceso)* lawsuit. • **a causa de** because of, on account of.

causar *vt* to cause, bring about.

cautiverio *nm* captivity.

cauto,-a *adj* cautious.

cava *nm (bebida)* cava. ► *nf (bodega)* wine cellar.

cavar *vt* to dig.

caverna *nf* cavern, cave.

caviar *nm* caviar.

cavidad *nf* cavity.

caza *nf* 1 *(acción)* hunting. 2 *(animales)* game. ► *nm (avión)* fighter.

cazadora *nf (chaqueta)* jacket.

cazador,-ra *nm,f* hunter.

cazar *vt* to hunt.

cazo *nm* 1 *(cucharón)* ladle. 2 *(cacerola)* saucepan.

cazuela *nf* casserole.

CD-ROM *nm* CD-ROM.

cebada *nf* barley.

cebo *nm* 1 *(para animales)* food. 2 *(para pescar)* bait.

cebolla *nf* onion.

cebolleta *nf* 1 *(hierba)* chive. 2 *(cebolla)* spring onion.

cebra *nf* zebra.

ceder *vt (dar)* to give. ► *vi* 1 *(rendirse)* to give yield: *cedió a mis peticiones*, she gave in to my requests. 2 *(caerse)* to fall, give way: *las paredes cedieron*, the walls caved in. • **ceder el paso** GB to give way; US to yield.

cedro *nm* cedar.

ceguera *nf* blindness.

ceja *nf* eyebrow.

celda *nf* cell.

celebración *nf* 1 *(fiesta)* celebration. 2 *(de reunión, congreso, etc)* holding.

celebrar *vt* 1 *(festejar)* to celebrate. 2 *(reunión, congreso, etc)* to hold. 3 *(misa)* to say. ► *vpr* **celebrarse** to take place, be held.

célebre *adj* well-known, famous.

celo[1] *nm* **1** *(entusiasmo)* zeal. **2** *(cuidado)* care. ▶ *nm pl* **celos** jealousy. ● **estar en celo** to be on heat, be in season; **tener celos** to be jealous.

celo®[2] *nm* GB Sellotape®; US Scotch tape®.

celofán *nm* Cellophane®.

célula *nf* cell.

cementerio *nm* cemetery, graveyard.

cemento *nm* cement. ■ **cemento armado** reinforced concrete.

cena *nf* dinner, supper.

cenar *vi* to have dinner, have supper. ▶ *vt* to have for dinner, have for supper.

cenicero *nm* ashtray.

ceniza *nf* ash.

censo *nm* census. ■ **censo electoral** electoral roll.

centeno *nm* rye.

centígrado,-a *adj* centigrade.

centímetro *nm* centimetre.

céntimo *nm* cent, centime.

centollo *nm* spider crab.

central *adj* central. ▶ *nf* **1** *(oficina principal)* head office, headquarters. **2** *(eléctrica)* power station.

centralita *nf* switchboard.

céntrico,-a *adj* central: *una calle céntrica*, a street in the centre of town.

centro *nm* **1** *(gen)* GB centre; US center. **2** *(de la ciudad)* town centre; US downtown. ■ **centro comercial** GB shopping centre; US mall.

cepa *nf* *(de vid)* vine.

cepillar(se) *vt-vpr (pelo, zapato, etc)* to brush.

cepillo *nm* brush. ■ **cepillo de dientes** toothbrush.

cera *nf* *(gen)* wax; *(de abeja)* beeswax; *(de oreja)* earwax.

cerámica *nf* ceramics, pottery.

cerca[1] *nf (valla)* fence.

cerca[2] *adv* near, close. ● **cerca de 1** *(cercano a)* near. **2** *(casi)* nearly; **de cerca** close up.

cercano,-a *adj* **1** *(lugar)* nearby. **2** *(tiempo)* near. **3** *(pariente, amigo)* close.

cerda *nf (animal)* sow.

cerdo *nm* **1** *(animal)* pig. **2** *(carne)* pork.

cereal *adj-nm* cereal.

cerebro *nm* brain.

ceremonia *nf* ceremony.

cereza *nf* cherry.

cerilla *nf* match.

cero *nm* **1** zero, nought. **2** nil: *ganamos tres a cero*, we won three-nil. ● **bajo cero** below zero.

cerrado,-a *adj* **1** *(gen)* shut, closed. **2** *(con llave)* locked. **3** *(acento)* broad. **4** *(curva)* sharp.

cerradura *nf* lock.

cerrajero *nm* locksmith.

cerrar vt **1** to close, shut. **2** (con llave) to lock. **3** (grifo, gas) to turn off. **4** (luz) to switch off. **5** (cremallera) to zip (up).

cerrojo nm bolt.

certamen nm competition, contest.

certeza nf certainty.

certificado,-a adj **1** (documento) certified. **2** (envío) registered. ► nm **certificado** (documento) certificate.

cerveza nf beer. ■ **cerveza de barril** GB draught beer; US draft beer.

cesar vi (parar) to cease, stop. ● **sin cesar** nonstop.

césped nm lawn, grass. ● **"Prohibido pisar el césped"** "Keep off the grass".

cesta nf basket.

cesto nm basket.

chabola nf shack.

chacal nm jackal.

chal nm shawl.

chalé nm **1** (gen) house. **2** (en campo, playa) villa.

chaleco nm GB waistcoat; US vest. ■ **chaleco salvavidas** life jacket.

chalet nm chalé.

champán nm champagne.

champiñón nm mushroom.

champú nm shampoo.

chancleta nf GB flip-flop; US thong.

chándal nm track suit, jogging suit.

chantaje nm blackmail.

chapa nf **1** (de metal) sheet. **2** (de madera) panel. **3** (tapón) bottle top. **4** (de coche) bodywork.

chaparrón nm downpour, heavy shower.

chapuzón nm dip.

chaqué nm morning coat.

chaqueta nf jacket.

chaquetón nm winter jacket, three-quarter coat.

charanga nf brass band.

charca nf pool, pond.

charco nm puddle, pool.

charcutería nf pork butcher's shop, delicatessen.

charlar vi to chat, talk.

chárter adj-nm charter.

chasis nm chassis.

chatarra nf **1** (metal) scrap metal. **2** fam (monedas) small change.

chatear vi to chat.

chato,-a adj **1** (nariz) snub. **2** (persona) snub-nosed. **3** (objeto) flat. ► nm **chato** (vaso) small glass.

chaval,-la nm,f kid, youngster; (chico) lad; (chica) lass.

cheque nm GB cheque; US check. ● **extender un cheque** to issue a cheque. ■ **cheque al portador** cheque payable to bearer; **cheque de viaje** traveller's cheque; **cheque en blanco** blank cheque; **cheque sin fondos** dud cheque.

chequeo *nm* checkup.
chichón *nm* bump, lump.
chicle *nm* chewing gum.
chico,-a *nm,f* **1** *(niño)* kid; *(niña)* girl. **2** *(muchacho)* boy, guy; *(muchacha)* girl.
Chile *nm* Chile.
chileno,-a *adj-nm,f* Chilean.
chillar *vi* *(persona)* to scream, yell; *(gritar)* to shout.
chillido *nm* **1** *(de persona)* scream, yell.
chimenea *nf* **1** *(exterior)* chimney. **2** *(hogar)* fireplace. **3** *(de barco)* funnel.
chimpancé *nm* chimpanzee.
chincheta *nf* GB drawing pin; US thumbtack.
chino,-a *adj* Chinese.
chip *nm* INFORM chip.
chipirón *nm* baby squid.
chiquito,-a *adj* tiny, very small. ► *nm* **chiquito** small glass of wine.
chiringuito *nm fam* *(en playa)* bar, restaurant; *(en carretera)* roadside snack bar.
chispa *nf* **1** *(de fuego)* spark. **2** *fig* *(ingenio)* wit.
chiste *nm* joke. ■ **chiste verde** blue joke, dirty joke.
chistera *nf* top hat.
chivato,-a *nm,f fam* *(delator)* informer, GB grass; *(acusica)* GB telltale; US tattletale. ► *nm* **chivato** *(piloto)* warning light.
chocar *vi* **1** *(colisionar)* to collide, crash. **2** *fig* *(sorprender)*

to surprise. **4** *(escandalizar)* to shock. ► *vt (manos)* to shake.
chocolate *nm* chocolate. ■ **chocolate a la taza** drinking chocolate; **chocolate con leche** milk chocolate.
chocolatina *nf* chocolate bar.
chófer *nm* *(particular)* chauffeur; *(de autocar etc)* driver.
chopo *nm* poplar.
choque *nm* collision, crash.
chorizo *nm* spicy pork sausage.
chorro *nm* **1** *(de líquido)* stream, jet. **2** *(de vapor)* jet.
choza *nf* hut.
christmas *nm* Christmas card.
chubasco *nm* heavy shower.
chubasquero *nm* raincoat.
chufa *nf* tiger nut.
chuleta *nf (de carne)* chop.
chulo,-a *adj* **1** *(engreído)* cocky. **2** *fam* *(bonito)* nice. ► *nm,f (presuntuoso)* show-off.
chupar *vt* **1** *(succionar)* to suck. **2** *(lamer)* to lick. **3** *(absorber)* to absorb, soak up.
chupete *nm* GB dummy; US pacifier.
churrería *nf* fritter shop.
churro *nm* **1** *(comida)* fritter. **2** *fam (chapuza)* botch.
chutar *vi* to shoot.
cibercafé *nm* Internet café, cybercafé.
ciberespacio *nm* cyberspace.
cibernética *nf* cybernetics.
cicatriz *nf* scar.

cicatrizar(se) *vt-vpr* to heal.
ciclismo *nm* cycling.
ciclista *nmf* cyclist.
ciclo *nm* 1 *(gen)* cycle. 2 *(de conferencias)* series. 3 *(de películas)* season.
ciclón *nm* cyclone.
ciego,-a *adj (persona)* blind. ► *nm,f (persona)* blind person.
cielo *nm* 1 *(gen)* sky. 2 REL heaven. 3 *(apelativo)* darling.
ciempiés *nm* centipede.
cien *num* a hundred, one hundred. • **cien por cien** a hundred per cent.
ciencia *nf* science. • **a ciencia cierta** with certainty. ▪ **ciencia ficción** science fiction.
científico,-a *adj* scientific. ► *nm,f* scientist.
ciento *num* a hundred, one hundred. • **por ciento** per cent.
cierre *nm* 1 *(de prenda)* fastener. 2 *(de collar, pulsera)* clasp. 4 *(de fábrica)* closure; *(de tienda)* close-down. ▪ **cierre centralizado** central locking.
cierto,-a *adj* 1 *(seguro)* certain, sure. 2 *(verdadero)* true. 3 *(algún)* (a) certain, some: *cierto día*, one day. ► *adv* **cierto** certainly. • **estar en lo cierto** to be right; **por cierto** by the way.
ciervo *nm* deer.
cifra *nf* figure.

cigala *nf* Dublin Bay prawn.
cigarrillo *nm* cigarette.
cigarro *nm* 1 *(cigarrillo)* cigarette. 2 *(puro)* cigar.
cigüeña *nf (ave)* stork.
cilindro *nm* cylinder.
cima *nf* summit, peak.
cimiento *nf* foundation.
cinc *nm* zinc.
cinco *num* five; *(en fechas)* fifth.
cincuenta *num* fifty.
cine *nm* 1 *(lugar)* GB cinema; US movie theater. 2 *(arte)* cinema. ▪ **cine mudo** silent films; **cine negro** film noir.
cinta *nf* 1 *(casete, vídeo)* tape. 2 *(tira)* tape, band; *(decorativa)* ribbon. ▪ **cinta adhesiva** sticky tape; **cinta aislante** insulating tape; **cinta métrica** tape measure; **cinta transportadora** conveyor belt; **cinta virgen** blank tape.
cintura *nf* waist.
cinturón *nm* belt. ▪ **cinturón de seguridad** seat belt, safety belt.
ciprés *nm* cypress.
circo *nm* circus.
circuito *nm* circuit.
circulación *nf* 1 *(de sangre, dinero)* circulation. 2 *(de vehículos)* traffic.
circular *adj* circular. ► *nf (carta)* circular letter. ► *vi* 1 *(sangre)* to circulate. 2 *(trenes, autobuses)* to run; *(coches)* to drive; *(peatones)* to walk.

círculo *nm* circle.

circunferencia *nf* circumference.

circunstancia *nf* circumstance.

ciruela *nf* plum. ▪ **ciruela claudia** greengage; **ciruela pasa** prune.

cirugía *nf* surgery.

cirujano,-a *nm,f* surgeon.

cisne *nm* swan.

cisterna *nf* cistern, tank.

cita *nf* 1 *(para negocios, médico, etc)* appointment. 2 *(con novio, novia)* date. 3 *(mención)* quotation.

citar *vt* 1 *(convocar)* to arrange to meet. 2 *(mencionar)* to quote.

cítricos *nm pl* citrus fruits.

ciudad *nf (grande)* city; *(más pequeña)* town.

ciudadano,-a *nm,f* citizen.

civil *adj* civil.

civilización *nf* civilization.

clandestino,-a *adj* 1 *(actividad, reunión)* clandestine, secret. 2 *(periódico, asociación)* underground.

clara *nf* 1 *(de huevo)* egg white. 2 *(bebida)* shandy.

claridad *nf* clarity, clearness.

clarinete *nm* clarinet. ▶ *nmf* clarinettist.

claro,-a *adj* 1 *(gen)* clear. 2 *(color)* light. 3 *(salsa)* thin. ▶ *adv* **claro** clearly. ▶ *nm (de bosque)* clearing. ▶ *interj* ¡**cla-ro!** of course! • **claro que no** of course not; **claro que sí** of course; **estar claro** to be clear.

clase *nf* 1 *(alumnos)* class. 2 *(lección)* lesson, class. 3 *(aula)* classroom. 4 *(tipo)* type, sort. • **dar clase** to teach. ▪ **clase alta** upper class; **clase baja** lower class; **clase media** middle class; **clase obrera** working class; **clase particular** private class.

clásico,-a *adj* classical.

clasificación *nf* 1 *(ordenación)* classification, sorting. 2 *(deportiva)* league, table.

clasificar *vt* 1 *(ordenar)* to class, classify. 2 *(documentos, cartas)* to sort. ▶ *vpr* **clasificarse** *(deportista)* to qualify.

claustro *nm (de iglesia)* cloister.

cláusula *nf* clause.

clavar *vt* 1 *(sujetar)* to nail. 2 *(a golpes)* to hammer. 3 *(aguja, cuchillo)* to stick.

clave *nf* 1 *(gen)* key. 2 *(de signos)* code.

clavel *nm* carnation.

clavícula *nf* collarbone, clavicle.

clavija *nf (enchufe macho)* plug; *(pata de enchufe)* pin.

clavo *nm* 1 *(de metal)* nail. 2 *(especia)* clove.

claxon *nm* horn, hooter.

cliente *nmf* 1 *(de empresa)* client. 2 *(de tienda)* customer.

clientela *nf* **1** *(de empresa)* clients. **2** *(de tienda)* customers. **3** *(de restaurante)* clientele.

clima *nm* climate.

climatizado,-a *adj* air-conditioned.

clínica *nf* clinic, private hospital.

clip *nm (para papel)* paper clip.

clon *nm* clone.

cloro *nm* chlorine.

club *nm* club.

coartada *nf* alibi.

cobarde *nmf* coward.

cobra *nf* cobra.

cobrador,-ra *nm,f (de autobús - hombre)* conductor; *(- mujer)* conductress.

cobrar *vt (fijar precio por)* to charge; *(cheques)* to cash; *(salario)* to earn. ► *vi* to be paid.

cobre *nm* copper.

cobro *nm* cashing, collection. ▪ **cobro revertido** reverse charge.

cocción *nf (acción de guisar)* cooking; *(en agua)* boiling; *(en horno)* baking.

cocer(se) *vt-vpr (guisar)* to cook; *(hervir)* to boil; *(hornear)* to bake.

coche *nm* **1** *(automóvil)* GB car; US car, automobile. **2** *(de tren, de caballos)* carriage, coach. ▪ **coche cama** sleeping car; **coche de alquiler** hired car.

cochinillo *nm* sucking pig.

cochino,-a *adj (sucio)* filthy. ► *nm,f* **1** *(animal)* pig. **2** *fam (persona)* dirty person.

cocido,-a *adj* cooked; *(en agua)* boiled. ► *nm* **cocido** *(plato)* stew.

cocina *nf* **1** *(lugar)* kitchen. **2** *(gastronomía)* cooking, cuisine. **3** *(aparato)* GB cooker; US stove. ▪ **cocina casera** home cooking; **cocina de mercado** food in season.

cocinar *vt* to cook.

cocinero,-a *nm,f* cook.

coco *nm* coconut.

cocodrilo *nm* crocodile.

cocotero *nm* coconut palm.

cóctel *nm* **1** *(bebida)* cocktail. **2** *(fiesta)* cocktail party.

código *nm* code. ▪ **código de barras** bar code; **código de circulación** highway code; **código postal** GB postcode; US zipcode.

codo *nm* elbow.

codorniz *nf* quail.

cofre *nm* trunk, chest.

coger *vt* **1** *(gen)* to catch. **2** *(tomar)* to take. **3** *(fruta, flor)* to pick.

cogollo *nm* **1** *(de lechuga etc)* heart. **2** *(brote)* shoot.

coherente *adj* coherent.

cohete *nm* rocket.

coincidencia *nf* coincidence.

coincidir *vi* **1** *(fechas, resultados)* to coincide. **2** *(estar de* *acuerdo)* to agree. **3** *(encontrarse)* to meet.

cojear *vi* to limp, hobble.

cojo,-a *adj* lame.

col *nf* cabbage. ▪ **col de Bruselas** Brussels sprout.

cola¹ *nf* **1** *(de animal)* tail. **2** *(fila)* GB queue; US line. • **hacer cola** GB to queue up; US to stand in line.

cola² *nf (pegamento)* glue.

colaborar *vi* **1** *(en tarea)* to collaborate. **2** *(en prensa)* to contribute.

colada *nf* washing.

colador *nm* **1** *(de té, café)* strainer. **2** *(de caldo, alimentos)* colander.

colar *vt (filtrar)* to strain, filter. ▶ *vpr* **colarse 1** *(en un lugar)* to sneak in. **2** *(en una cola)* to push in.

colcha *nf* bedspread.

colchón *nm* mattress.

colchoneta *nf* **1** *(de gimnasio)* mat. **2** *(de playa)* air bed.

colección *nf* collection.

colectivo,-a *adj* collective.

colega *nmf* **1** *(de trabajo)* colleague. **2** *fam (amigo)* GB mate; US buddy.

colegio *nm (escuela)* school. ▪ **colegio electoral** polling station; **colegio mayor** hall of residence; **colegio privado** private school; **colegio público** state school.

cólera¹ *nf (furia)* anger, rage.

cólera² *nm (enfermedad)* cholera.

coleta *nf* pigtail.

colgador *nm* hanger.

colgar *vt* **1** *(cuadro)* to hang, put up; *(colada)* to hang out; *(abrigo)* to hang up. **2** *(teléfono)* to put down.

colibrí *nm* humming bird.

cólico *nm* colic.

coliflor *nf* cauliflower.

colilla *nf* cigarette end, cigarette butt.

colina *nf* hill.

colirio *nm* eyewash.

collar *nm* **1** *(joya)* necklace. **2** *(de animal)* collar.

colmena *nf* beehive.

colmillo *nm* **1** *(de persona)* eye tooth, canine tooth. **2** *(de elefante)* tusk.

colocación *nf* **1** *(acto)* placing. **2** *(situación)* situation. **3** *(empleo)* employment.

colocar *vt* **1** *(situar)* to place, put. **2** *(emplear)* to give a job to.

Colombia *nf* Colombia.

colombiano,-a *adj-nm,f* Colombian.

colon *nm* colon.

colonia¹ *nf (grupo, territorio)* colony. ▶ *nf pl* summer camp.

colonia² *nf (perfume)* cologne.

color *nm* GB colour; US color.

colorete *nm* rouge.

columna *nf* column. ▪ **columna vertebral** spine, spinal column.

columpio *nm* swing.

coma¹ *nf (signo)* comma.

coma² *nm* MED coma.

comandante *nm* **1** *(oficial)* commander, commanding officer. **2** *(graduación)* major.

comando *nm* **1** *(de combate)* commando. **2** INFORM command.

comarca *nf* area, region.

combate *nm* **1** *(lucha)* combat, battle. **2** *(en boxeo)* fight.

combinar *vt (ingredientes, esfuerzos)* to combine. ► *vi (colores)* to match, go with.

combustible *adj* combustible. ► *nm* fuel.

comedia *nf* comedy.

comedor *nm* **1** *(de casa)* dining room. **2** *(de fábrica)* canteen. **3** *(de colegio)* dinning hall.

comentar *vt* **1** *(por escrito)* to comment on; *(oralmente)* to talk about, discuss. **2** *(decir)* to tell.

comentario *nm* remark, comment. ● **sin comentarios** no comment.

comenzar *vt-vi* to begin, start.

comer *vt* to eat. ► *vi* **1** *(alimentarse)* to eat. **2** *(al mediodía)* to have lunch.

comercial *adj* commercial.

comerciante *nmf* **1** *(tendero)* GB shop-keeper; US storekeeper. **2** *(negociante)* trader, dealer.

comerciar *vi* to trade, deal.

comercio *nm* **1** *(ocupación)* commerce, trade. **2** *(tienda)* GB shop; US store. ■ **comercio electrónico** e-commerce.

comestible *adj* edible. ► *nm pl* **comestibles** groceries, food.

cometa *nm (astro)* comet. ► *nf (juguete)* kite.

cometer *vt (crimen)* to commit; *(falta, error)* to make.

cómic *nm* comic.

cómico,-a *adj* comic.

comida *nf* **1** *(comestibles)* food. **2** *(a cualquier hora)* meal. **3** *(a mediodía)* lunch.

comienzo *nm* start, beginning.

comillas *nf pl* inverted commas.

comino *nm* cumin.

comisaría *nf* police station.

comisario *nm* GB superintendent; US captain.

comisión *nf* **1** *(retribución)* commission. **2** *(comité)* committee.

comité *nm* committee.

como *adv* **1** *(lo mismo que)* as: **negro como el tizón**, as dark as night. **2** *(de tal modo)* like: **hablas como un político**, you talk like a politician. **3** *(según)* as: **como dice tu amigo**, as your friend says. **4** *(en calidad de)* as: **como invitado**, as a guest. ► *conj* **1** *(así que)* as soon as. **2** *(si)* if: **como lo vuelvas a hacer ...**, if you do it again … **3** *(porque)* as, since: *como llegamos tarde no pudimos entrar*, since we arrived late we couldn't get in. • **como quiera que** since, as, inasmuch; **como sea** whatever happens, no matter what.

cómo *adv* **1** *(de qué modo)* how: *¿cómo se hace?*, how do you do it? **2** *(por qué)* why: *¿cómo no viniste?*, why didn't you come? • **¿cómo está usted?** **1** *(al conocerse)* how do you do? **2** *(de salud)* how are you?; **¡cómo no!** but of course!, certainly!

comodidad *nf* **1** *(confort)* comfort. **2** *(facilidad)* convenience.

comodín *nm* joker.

cómodo,-a *adj* comfortable, cosy.

compact disc *nm* compact disc.

compacto *adj* compact. ► *nm* compact disc.

compañero,-a *nm,f* **1** *(de tarea)* fellow, mate. **2** *(de trabajo)* colleague. **3** *(pareja)* partner.

compañía *nf* company.

comparación *nf* comparison.

comparar *vt* to compare.

compartimento *nm* compartment.

compartir *vt* to share.

compás *nm* **1** *(instrumento)* compass, a pair of compasses. **2** *(ritmo)* time.

compatible *adj* compatible.

compatriota *nmf* compatriot.

competencia *nf* **1** *(rivalidad)* competition. **2** *(competidores)* competitors. **3** *(habilidad)* competence, ability.

competente *adj* competent, capable.

competición *nf* competition.

competir *vi* to compete.

complejo,-a *adj* complex. ► *nm* **complejo** complex.

complemento *nm* complement. ► *nm pl* **complementos** accessories.

completar *vt* to complete, finish.

completo,-a *adj* **1** *(entero, total)* complete. **2** *(lleno)* full. • **al completo 1** *(lleno)* full up, filled to capacity. **2** *(la totalidad de)* the whole, all of; **por completo** completely.

complicado,-a *adj* complicated, complex.

complicar *vt* to complicate.

cómplice *nmf* accomplice.

componente *adj-nm* component.

componer *vt* **1** *(formar)* to make up. **2** *(música)* to compose; *(poema)* to write, compose.

comportamiento *nm* GB behaviour; US behavior.

comportarse *vpr* to behave.
composición *nf* composition.
compositor,-ra *nm,f* composer.
compota *nf* compote.
compra *nf* purchase, buy. • **hacer la compra** to do the shopping; **ir de compras** to go shopping.
comprador,-ra *nm,f* buyer.
comprar *vt* to buy.
comprender *vt* **1** *(entender)* to understand. **2** *(contener)* to comprise, include.
compresa *nf* **1** *(higiénica)* sanitary towel. **2** *(venda)* compress.
comprimido *nm* tablet.
comprobante *nm* receipt, voucher.
comprobar *vt* to check.
comprometerse *vpr* **1** *(prometer)* to commit oneself. **2** *(novios)* to get engaged.
compromiso *nm* **1** *(obligación)* commitment. **2** *(acuerdo)* agreement. **3** *(cita)* engagement.
compuesto,-a *adj* compound.
computadora *nf* computer.
comulgar *vi* to receive Holy Communion.
común *adj* common. • **por lo común** generally.
comunicación *nf* **1** *(relación)* communication. **2** *(telefónica)* connection.

comunicado *nm* communiqué. • **comunicado de prensa** press release.
comunicar *vi* *(teléfono)* GB to be engaged; US to be busy. ► *vt* **1** *(hacer saber)* to inform. **2** *(unir)* to connect, link.
comunidad *nf* community.
comunión *nf* communion.
comunismo *nm* communism.
comunista *adj-nmf* communist.
con *prep* **1** *(compañía, instrumento, medio)* with: *hay que comerlo con una cuchara*, you have to eat it with a spoon. **2** *(modo, circunstancia)* in, with: *¿vas a salir con ese frío?*, are you going out in this cold?. **3** *(relación)* to: *sé amable con ella*, be kind to her.
conceder *vt* *(dar - préstamo, deseo)* to grant; *(- premio)* to award.
concentración *nf* concentration.
concentrar(se) *vt-vpr* to concentrate.
concepto *nm* concept. • **bajo ningún concepto** under no circumstances; **en concepto de** by way of.
concertar *vt* *(entrevista, cita)* to arrange.
concesión *nf* **1** *(en negociación)* concession. **2** *(de premio)* awarding.
concesionario *nm* dealer.

concha *nf* shell.

conciencia *nf* **1** *(moral)* conscience. **2** *(conocimiento)* awareness. • **a conciencia** conscientiously.

concierto *nm* *(espectáculo)* concert; *(obra)* concerto.

conclusión *nf* conclusion.

concretar *vt* *(precisar)* to specify: *concretar una hora*, to fix a time, set a time.

concreto,-a *adj* **1** *(real)* concrete. **2** *(particular)* specific, definite. • **en concreto 1** *(en particular)* in particular. **2** *(para ser exacto)* to be precise.

concurrido,-a *adj* busy, crowded.

concursante *nmf* contestant, participant.

concursar *vi* to compete.

concurso *nm* *(competición - gen)* competition; *(- de belleza, deportivo)* contest; *(- en televisión)* quiz show.

conde *nm* count.

condecoración *nf* decoration, medal.

condena *nf* sentence.

condenar *vt* **1** *(declarar culpable)* to convict. **2** *(sentenciar)* to sentence.

condesa *nf* countess.

condición *nf* condition. • **a condición de que** on condition that, provided (that).

condimentar *vt* to season, GB flavour; US flavor.

condimento *nm* seasoning, GB flavouring; US flavoring.

conducir *vt* *(guiar)* to lead; *(coche, animales)* to drive; *(moto)* to ride. ▶ *vi* **1** *(dirigir un vehículo)* to drive. **2** *(llevar)* to lead: *esta carretera conduce a Teruel*, this road leads to Teruel.

conducta *nf* conduct.

conducto *nm* **1** *(tubería)* pipe, conduit. **2** *(del cuerpo)* duct.

conductor,-ra *nm,f* driver.

conectar *vt* **1** *(unir)* to connect. **2** *(aparato, luz, etc)* to switch on, turn on.

conejo *nm* rabbit.

conexión *nf* connection.

confección *nf* **1** *(de prendas)* dressmaking. **2** *(elaboración)* making.

conferencia *nf* **1** *(charla)* talk, lecture. **2** *(congreso)* conference. **3** *(llamada telefónica)* long-distance call.

conferenciante *nmf* lecturer.

confesar(se) *vt-vpr* to confess.

confesión *nf* confession.

confianza *nf* **1** *(seguridad)* confidence. **2** *(fe)* trust. **3** *(familiaridad)* familiarity.

confiar *vi* **1 confiar en** ALGN/**algo** *(tener fe)* to trust SB/STH. **2 confiar en + inf** *(estar seguro)* to be confident that, be sure that: *confío en aprobar el examen*, I'm confident that I'll pass the exam.

configuración *nf* INFORM configuration. ■ **configuración por defecto** default settings.

confirmar *vt* to confirm.

confitería *nf* (*bombonería*) GB sweet shop; US candy shop; (*pastelería*) cake shop.

conflicto *nm* conflict.

conformarse *vpr* to resign oneself, be content.

conforme *adj* 1 (*de acuerdo*): **estar conforme**, to agree. 2 (*satisfecho*) satisfied, happy.

confortable *adj* comfortable.

confundir *vt* 1 (*mezclar*) to mix up. 2 (*desconcertar*) to confuse. 3 (*no reconocer*) to mistake. ▶ *vpr* **confundirse** (*equivocarse*) to be mistaken, make a mistake.

confusión *nf* 1 (*desorden*) confusion. 2 (*equivocación*) mistake.

congelado,-a *adj* frozen.

congelador *nm* freezer.

congelar(se) *vt-vpr* to freeze.

congestión *nf* congestion.

congreso *nm* conference, congress.

congrio *nm* conger eel.

conífera *nf* conifer.

conjugación *nf* conjugation.

conjunción *nf* conjunction.

conjuntivitis *nf* conjunctivitis.

conjunto *nm* 1 (*grupo*) group, collection. 2 (*todo*) whole. 3

(*de música - pop*) band, group; (*- clásica*) ensemble. 4 (*prenda*) outfit.

conmigo *pron* with me, to me.

conmoción *nf* (*cerebral*) concussion.

cono *nm* cone.

conocer *vt* 1 (*gen*) to know; (*persona por primera vez*) to meet. 2 (*país, lugar*) to have been to.

conocido,-a *adj* 1 (*reconocible*) familiar. 2 (*famoso*) well-known. ▶ *nm,f* acquaintance.

conocimiento *nm* 1 (*saber*) knowledge. 2 (*conciencia*) consciousness.

conquista *nf* conquest.

conquistador,-ra *nm,f* conqueror.

conquistar *vt* 1 (*con armas*) to conquer. 2 (*victoria, título*) to win. 3 (*ligar con*) to win over.

consciente *adj* conscious.

consecuencia *nf* consequence, result.

conseguir *vt* (*cosa*) to obtain, get; (*objetivo*) to attain, get. ● **conseguir + inf** to manage to + *inf*.

consejero,-a *nm,f* 1 (*asesor*) adviser. 2 POL counsellor.

consejo *nm* (*recomendación*) advice: **te daré un consejo**, I'll give you a piece of advice. ■ **consejo de administración** board of directors; **consejo de ministros** cabinet.

consentir *vt* **1** *(permitir)* to allow, permit, tolerate. **2** *(a un niño)* to spoil.

conserje *nm* **1** *(de hotel, oficina)* porter. **2** *(de escuela)* caretaker.

conservas *nf pl* tinned food, canned food.

conservación *nf* **1** *(de naturaleza, especie)* conservation. **2** *(de alimentos)* preservation.

conservante *nm* preservative.

conservar *vt* **1** *(alimentos)* to preserve. **2** *(calor)* retain. **3** *(guardar)* to keep.

consideración *nf* **1** *(deliberación, atención)* consideration. **2** *(respeto)* regard.

considerar *vt* **1** *(reflexionar)* to consider, think over. **2** *(juzgar)* to consider.

consigna *nf* *(en estación etc)* GB left-luggage office; US check-room.

consigo *pron* *(con él)* with him; *(con ella)* with her; *(con usted, ustedes, vosotros,-as)* with you; *(con ellos,-as)* with them; *(con uno mismo)* with oneself.

consiguiente *adj* consequent. • **por consiguiente** therefore, consequently.

consistir *vi* to consist *(en,* of).

consola *nf* INFORM console.

consolar *vt* to console, comfort.

consomé *nm* consommé, clear soup.

consonante *adj-nf* consonant.

conspiración *nf* conspiracy, plot.

constante *adj* **1** *(invariable)* constant. **2** *(persona)* steadfast. ▪ **constantes vitales** vital signs.

constar *vi* **1** *(consistir en)* to consist (**de**, of). **2** *(ser cierto)*: *me consta que ha llegado*, I am absolutely certain that he has arrived.

constipado *nm* cold.

constitución *nf* constitution.

constituir *vt* to constitute.

construcción *nf* **1** *(acción)* construction, building. **2** *(edificio)* building.

construir *vt* to build, construct.

consuelo *nm* consolation, comfort.

cónsul *nmf* consul.

consulado *nm* **1** *(oficina)* consulate. **2** *(cargo)* consulship.

consulta *nf* **1** *(pregunta)* consultation. **2** *(de médico)* GB surgery; US office.

consultar *vt* *(persona)* to consult; *(libro)* to look it up in.

consumición *nf* *(bebida)* drink.

consumidor,-ra *nm,f* consumer.

consumir *vt* to consume.

contabilidad *nf* **1** *(profesión)* accountancy. **2** *(ciencia)* accountancy, book-keeping.

contacto *nm* **1** *(entre personas, cosas)* contact. **2** *(de coche)* ignition.

contagiar *vt* **1** *(enfermedad)* to transmit, pass on. **2** *(persona)* to infect.

contagioso,-a *adj* contagious.

contaminación *nf (de agua, radiactiva)* contamination; *(atmosférica)* pollution.

contar *vt* **1** *(calcular)* to count. **2** *(explicar)* to tell. ► *vi* to count. • **contar con ALGN** *(confiar)* to count on SB, rely on SB; **contar con algo** *(esperar)* to expect ST.

contemplar *vt-vi* to contemplate.

contener *vt* **1** *(tener dentro)* to contain, hold. **2** *(reprimir)* to contain, hold back.

contenido *nm* content, contents.

contento,-a *adj* happy.

contestación *nf (respuesta)* answer, reply.

contestador *nm.* • **contestador automático** answering machine.

contestar *vt* to answer.

contigo *pron* with you.

contiguo,-a *adj* contiguous, adjoining.

continental *adj* continental.

continente *nm* continent.

continuación *nf* continuation. • **a continuación** next.

continuar *vt-vi* to continue, carry on.

contra *prep* against. • **en contra** against.

contrabando *nm* **1** *(actividad)* smuggling. **2** *(mercancía)* contraband.

contraer *vt* **1** *(gen)* to contract. **2** *(enfermedad)* to catch.

contrario,-a *adj* **1** *(dirección, sentido)* contrary, opposite. **2** *(opinión)* contrary. **3** *(rival)* opposing. ► *nm,f* opponent. • **al contrario** on the contrary.

contrarreloj *adj* against the clock. ► *nf* time trial.

contraseña *nf* password.

contratar *vt* **1** *(servicio etc)* to sign a contract for. **2** *(empleado)* to hire, take.

contrato *nm* contract. • **contrato de alquiler** lease, leasing agreement.

contraventana *nf* shutter.

contribución *nf* **1** *(aportación)* contribution. **2** *(impuesto)* tax.

contribuir *vt-vi* to contribute.

contrincante *nm* opponent.

control *nm* **1** *(dominio)* control. **2** *(verificación)* examination, inspection. • **control remoto** remote control; **control de pasaportes** passport control; **control de policía** police checkpoint.

controlador,-ra *nm,f.* • **controlador,-ra aéreo,-a** air traffic controller.

controlar *vt* to control.

convencer *vt* to convince.

conveniente *adj* **1** *(cómodo)* convenient. **2** *(ventajoso)* advantageous. **3** *(aconsejable)* advisable.

convenio *nm* agreement.

convenir *vi* **1** *(ser oportuno)* to suit. **2** *(ser aconsejable)*: *te conviene descansar*, you should get some rest.

convento *nm (de monjas)* convent; *(de monjes)* monastery.

conversación *nf* conversation.

conversar *vi* to talk.

convertir *vt* to turn into.

convivir *vi* to live together.

convocar *vt* to call.

convocatoria *nf* **1** *(llamamiento)* call. **2** *(examen)* examination, sitting.

coñac *nm* cognac, brandy.

cooperación *nf* cooperation.

cooperar *vi* to cooperate.

coordinación *nf* coordination.

coordinar *vt* to coordinate.

copa *nf* **1** *(recipiente)* glass. **2** *(bebida)* drink. **3** *(de árbol)* top. • **ir de copas** to go (out) drinking; **tomar una copa** to have a drink.

copia *nf* copy. ▪ **copia de seguridad** backup.

copiar *vt* to copy.

copo *nm (de cereal)* flake; *(de nieve)* snowflake.

coral¹ *adj* choral. ▶ *nf* choir.

coral² *nm* coral.

corazón *nm* heart.

corbata *nf* tie.

corcho *nm* cork.

cordero,-a *nm,f* lamb.

cordial *adj* cordial, friendly.

cordillera *nf* mountain range.

cordón *nm (cuerda)* cord, string; *(de zapatos)* lace, shoelace. ▪ **cordón policial** police cordon; **cordón umbilical** umbilical cord.

coreografía *nf* choreography.

córnea *nf* cornea.

córner *nm* corner.

corneta *nf* bugle.

coro *nm (grupo)* choir.

corona *nf* **1** *(de rey)* crown. **2** *(de flores etc)* wreath.

coronel *nm* colonel.

corporación *nf* corporation.

corral *nm (de aves)* yard.

correa *nf* **1** *(de piel)* strap. **2** *(cinturón)* belt. **3** *(de perro)* lead. **4** *(de máquina)* belt.

correcto,-a *adj* **1** *(exacto, adecuado)* correct. **2** *(educado)* polite, courteous.

corredor,-ra *nm,f* **1** *(atleta)* runner. **2** *(ciclista)* cyclist. ▶ *nm* **corredor** corridor.

corregir *vt* to correct.

correo *nm* GB post; US mail. ▶ *nm pl* **correos** *(oficina)* post office. • **echar al correo** GB to post; US to mail; **mandar por correo** GB to post; US to mail. ▪ **correo certificado** GB registered post; US registered mail; **correo electrónico** e-mail, electronic mail: *envíamelo por correo electrónico*, e-mail it to me; **correo urgente** express mail.

correr *vi* **1** *(persona, animal)* to run. **2** *(agua)* to flow. **3** *(tiempo)* to pass. **4** *(darse prisa)* to hurry. ► *vt* **1** *(carrera)* to run. **2** *(deslizar)* to close; *(cortina)* to draw.

correspondencia *nf* **1** *(relación)* correspondence. **2** *(cartas)* GB post; US mail. **3** *(de trenes etc)* connection.

corresponder *vi* **1** *(equivaler)* to correspond. **2** *(pertenecer)* to belong, pertain. **3** *(devolver)* to return.

correspondiente *adj* **1** *(perteneciente)* corresponding. **2** *(respectivo)* respective.

corrida *nf*. ▪ **corrida de toros** bullfight.

corriente *adj* **1** *(frecuente)* common. **2** *(no especial)* ordinary. **3** *(agua)* running. ► *nf* **1** *(masa de agua)* current, stream. **2** *(de aire)* GB draught; US draft. **3** *(eléctrica)* current. **4** *(de arte etc)* current, trend. • **al corriente** up to date; **estar al corriente** to be in the know.

corrupción *nf* corruption.

cortado *nm* coffee with a dash of milk.

cortar *vt* **1** *(gen)* to cut. **2** *(interrumpir)* to cut off, interrupt. **3** *(calle, carretera)* to close. ► *vpr* **cortarse 1** *(herirse)* to cut. **2** *(pelo - por otro)* to have one's hair cut; *(- uno mismo)* to cut one's hair. **3** *(leche)* to sour, curdle.

cortaúñas *nm* nail clipper.

corte¹ *nf* court.

corte² *nm* *(herida, interrupción)* cut. ▪ **corte de pelo** haircut.

cortés *adj* courteous, polite.

cortesía *nf* courtesy, politeness.

corteza *nf* **1** *(de árbol)* bark. **2** *(de pan)* crust. **3** *(de queso)* rind. ▪ **corteza terrestre** earth's crust.

cortina *nf* curtain.

corto,-a *adj* short.

cortocircuito *nm* short circuit.

cortometraje *nm* short (film).

cosa *nf* thing. • **¿alguna cosa más?** anything else?

cosecha *nf* **1** *(acción)* harvest. **2** *(producto)* crop. **3** *(año del vino)* vintage.

cosechar *vt-vi* *(recoger - cosecha)* to harvest, gather; *(- éxitos etc)* to reap.

coser *vt* **1** *(gen)* to sew. **2** *(herida)* to stitch up.

cosmético,-a *adj* cosmetic. ► *nm* **cosmético** cosmetic.

cosquillas *nf pl* tickles, tickling.

cosquilleo *nm* tickling.

costa[1] *nf* coast.

costa[2]. • **a costa de** at the expense of; **a toda costa** at all costs.

costado *nm* side.

costar *vt* 1 *(valer)* to cost. 2 *(esfuerzo, tiempo)* to take. ► *vi* 1 *(al comprar)* to cost. 2 *(ser difícil)* to be difficult.

coste *nm* cost.

costero,-a *adj* coastal, seaside.

costilla *nf* 1 *(de persona, animal)* rib. 2 *(como comida)* cutlet.

costo *nm (precio)* cost.

costumbre *nf* 1 *(hábito)* habit. 2 *(tradición)* custom.

costura *nf* 1 *(cosido)* sewing. 2 *(línea de puntadas)* seam.

cotidiano,-a *adj* daily, everyday.

coto *nm.* ▪ **coto de caza** game preserve.

cotorra *nf (animal)* parrot.

coyote *nm* coyote.

coz *nf* kick.

cráneo *nm* skull, cranium.

cráter *nm* crater.

creación *nf* creation.

crear *vt* 1 *(producir)* to create. 2 *(fundar)* to found, establish.

crecer *vi* 1 *(gen)* to grow. 2 *(corriente, marea)* to rise.

creciente *adj (luna)* crescent.

crecimiento *nm* growth, increase.

crédito *nm* 1 *(al comprar)* credit. 2 *(préstamo)* loan.

creencia *nf* belief.

creer *vi* 1 *(tener fe)* to believe **(en,** in). 2 *(pensar)* to think. ► *vt* 1 *(gen)* to believe. 2 *(pensar)* to think, suppose. • **creo que sí** I think so; **creo que no** I don't think so.

crema *nf* 1 *(nata)* cream. 2 *(natillas)* custard.

cremallera *nf* 1 *(de vestido)* zipper, zip (fastener). 2 *(de máquina)* rack.

cremoso,-a *adj* creamy.

cresta *nf* 1 *(de ola)* crest. 2 *(de gallo)* comb.

cría *nf (cachorro)* baby.

criar *vt* 1 *(educar)* to bring up. 2 *(dar el pecho)* to nurse. 3 *(animales)* to breed.

crimen *nm* 1 *(delito)* crime. 2 *(asesinato)* murder.

criminal *adj-nmf* criminal.

crin *nf* mane.

crisis *nf* 1 *(mal momento)* crisis. 2 *(ataque)* fit, attack.

cristal *nm* glass.

cristalino *nm* crystalline lens.

cristiano,-a *adj-nm,f* Christian.

criterio *nm* 1 *(norma)* criterion. 2 *(juicio)* judgement. 3 *(opinión)* opinion.

crítica *nf* 1 *(juicio, censura)* criticism. 2 *(reseña)* review.

criticar *vt* to criticize.
crítico,-a *adj* critical. ► *nm,f*
  critic.
croar *vi* to croak.
croissant *nm* croissant.
crol *nm* crawl.
cromo *nm* 1 *(metal)* chromium. 2 *(estampa)* picture card.
crónica *nf (en periódico)* article.
crónico,-a *adj* chronic.
cronómetro *nm* stopwatch.
croqueta *nf* croquette.
cross *nm* cross-country race.
cruce *nm* 1 *(acción)* crossing. 2
  (de calles) crossroads. 3 *(de carreteras)* junction.
crucero *nm* 1 *(buque)* cruiser.
  2 *(viaje)* cruise. 3 *(de templo)*
  transept.
crucifijo *nm* crucifix.
crucigrama *nm* crossword.
crudo,-a *adj* 1 *(sin cocer)* raw;
  (poco hecho) underdone. 2 *(color)* off-white. ► *nm* **crudo** *(petróleo)* oil, crude.
cruel *adj* cruel.
crujiente *adj* crunchy.
crujir *vi (puerta)* to creak.
crustáceo *nm* crustacean.
cruz *nf* 1 *(figura)* cross. 2 *(de moneda)* tails.
cruzar *vt* 1 *(río, piernas, animales)* to cross. 2 *(miradas, palabras)* to exchange. ► *vpr*
  cruzarse to pass each other.
cuaderno *nm* 1 *(de notas)* notebook. 2 *(escolar)* exercise book.
cuadra *nf* stable.

cuadrado,-a *adj* square: *diez
metros cuadrados*, ten square
meters. ► *nm* **cuadrado** square.
cuadrilátero *nm* ring.
cuadro *nm* 1 *(pintura)* painting. 2 *(cuadrado)* square. 3
  (diagrama) chart. • **a cuadros**
  1 *(estampado)* checkered. 2 *(camisa)* checked, check.
cual *pron (precedido de artículo
- persona)* who, whom; *(- cosa)*
  which: *la gente a la cual pre-
guntamos dijo que ...*, the
  people whom we asked said
  that ... • **cada cual** everyone,
  everybody; **con lo cual** with
  the result that.
cuál *pron* which one, what.
cualidad *nf* quality.
cualificado,-a *adj* qualified,
  skilled.
cualquier *adj →* cualquiera.
cualquiera *adj* any. ► *pron
(persona indeterminada)* anybody, anyone; *(cosa indeterminada)* any, any one: *cualquiera te lo puede decir*.
• **cualquier cosa** anything;
cualquier otro anyone
else; **cualquiera que** whatever, whichever.
cuando *adv* when. ► *conj* 1
  (temporal) when: *cuando deje
de llover*, when it stops raining. 2 *(condicional)* if: *cuando
ella lo dice...*, if she says so...
• **de (vez en) cuando** now
and then.

cuándo *adv* when.

cuanto,-a *adj (singular)* as much as; *(plural)* as many as. ► *pron (singular)* everything, all; *(plural)* all who, everybody who. ● **cuanto antes** as soon as possible; **en cuanto** as soon as; **en cuanto a** as far as; **unos,-as cuantos,-as** some, a few.

cuánto,-a *adj* **1** *(interrogativo - singular)* how much; *(- plural)* how many. **2** *(exclamativo)* what a lot of. ► *pron (singular)* how much; *(plural)* how many. ► *adv* how, how much: *¡cuánto me alegro!*, I'm so glad!

cuarenta *num* forty.

cuartel *nm* barracks. ■ **cuartel general** headquarters.

cuarto,-a *num* fourth. ► *nm* **cuarto 1** *(parte)* quarter. **2** *(habitación)* room. ■ **cuarto creciente** first quarter; **cuarto menguante** last quarter; **cuarto de baño** bathroom; **cuarto de estar** living room.

cuarzo *nm* quartz.

cuatro *num* four; *(en fechas)* fourth. ● **cuatro por cuatro** four-wheel drive.

cuatrocientos,-as *num* four hundred.

cuba *nf* cask, barrel.

cubalibre *nm (de ron)* rum and coke; *(de ginebra)* gin and coke.

cubano,-a *adj-nm,f* Cuban.

cúbico,-a *adj* cubic.

cubierta *nf* **1** *(tapa)* covering. **2** *(de libro)* jacket. **3** *(de neumático)* GB tyre; US tire. **5** *(de barco)* deck.

cubierto,-a *adj* **1** covered. **2** *(cielo)* overcast. ► *nm* **cubierto 1** *(en la mesa)* place setting. **3** *(menú)* set menu.

cubito *nm.* ■ **cubito (de hielo)** ice cube.

cubo[1] *nm* **1** *(recipiente)* bucket. **2** *(de rueda)* hub. ■ **cubo de la basura** GB dustbin; US garbage can.

cubo[2] *nm (figura)* cube.

cubrir *vt* **1** *(tapar)* to cover. **2** *(puesto, vacante)* to fill.

cucaracha *nf* cockroach.

cuchara *nf* spoon.

cucharilla *nf* teaspoon.

cuchilla *nf* blade. ■ **cuchilla de afeitar** razor blade.

cuchillo *nm* knife.

cucurucho *nm* **1** *(de papel)* cone. **2** *(helado)* cornet, cone.

cuello *nm* **1** *(de persona, animal)* neck. **2** *(de prenda)* collar. **3** *(de botella)* bottleneck. ■ **cuello alto** GB polo neck; US turtleneck; **cuello de pico** V-neck.

cuenta *nf* **1** *(bancaria)* account. **2** *(factura)* bill. ● **darse cuenta de algo** to realize STH; **tener en cuenta** to take into account. ■ **cuenta atrás** countdown.

cuentagotas *nm* dropper.
cuentakilómetros *nm* speedometer.
cuento *nm* short story, tale.
cuerda *nf* 1 *(soga)* rope; *(cordel, de guitarra)* string. 2 *(de reloj)* spring. • **dar cuerda a un reloj** to wind up a watch.
cuerno *nm (de toro)* horn; *(de ciervo)* antler.
cuero *nm* 1 *(de animal)* skin, hide. 2 *(curtido)* leather.
cuerpo *nm* body. • **a cuerpo** without a coat.
cuervo *nm* raven.
cuesta *nf* slope. • **a cuestas** on one's back, on one's shoulders; **cuesta abajo** downhill; **cuesta arriba** uphill.
cuestión *nf* question.
cuestionario *nm* questionnaire.
cueva *nf* cave.
cuidado *nm* 1 *(atención)* care. 2 *(recelo)* worry. ▶ *interj* **¡cuidado!** look out!, watch out! • "**Cuidado con el perro**" "Beware of the dog"; **tener cuidado** to be careful. ■ **cuidados intensivos** intensive care.
cuidar *vt-vi* to look after, take care of.
culebra *nf* snake.
culinario,-a *adj* culinary.
culo *nm* 1 *(trasero)* bottom, backside, GB bum; US butt. 2 *(de recipiente)* bottom.

culpa *nf* 1 *(culpabilidad)* guilt, blame. 2 *(falta)* fault.
culpabilidad *nf* guilt, culpabililiy.
culpable *adj* guilty. ▶ *nmf* offender, culprit.
cultivar *vt* 1 *(terreno)* to cultivate, farm. 2 *(plantas)* to grow.
culto,-a *adj* 1 *(con cultura)* cultured, educated. 2 *(estilo)* refined. ▶ *nm* **culto** worship.
cultura *nf* culture.
cumbre *nf (de montaña)* summit, top. 2 *(reunión)* summit.
cumpleaños *nm* birthday.
cumplir *vt* 1 *(orden)* to carry out. 2 *(compromiso, obligación)* to fulfil. 3 *(promesa)* to keep. 4 *(condena)* to serve. 5 *(años)*: *mañana cumplo veinte años*, I'll be twenty tomorrow.
cuna *nf* GB cot; US crib, cradle.
cuneta *nf* ditch.
cuñado,-a *nm,f (hombre)* brother-in-law; *(mujer)* sister-in-law.
cuota *nf* 1 *(pago)* membership fee, dues. 2 *(porción)* quota, share.
cúpula *nf* cupola, dome.
cura *nm (párroco)* priest. ▶ *nf (curación)* cure.
curación *nf* cure, healing.
curar *vt* 1 *(sanar)* to cure. 2 *(herida)* to dress; *(enfermedad)* to treat. ▶ *vpr* **curarse** *(recuperarse)* to recover, get well.

curiosidad *nf* curiosity.
curioso,-a *adj* **1** *(interesado)* curious, inquisitive. **2** *(indiscreto)* nosy. **3** *(extraño)* strange: *¡qué curioso!*, how strange!
currículum *nm* curriculum (vitae).
curso *nm* **1** *(gen)* course. **2** *(académico)* year. ● **en curso** current.
cursor *nm* cursor.
curva *nf* **1** curve. **2** *(de carretera)* bend.
cutis *nm* skin, complexion.
cuyo,-a *pron* whose, of which. ● **en cuyo caso** in which case.

D

dado *nm* die.
dama *nf* **1** *(señora)* lady. **2** *(en ajedrez)* queen; *(en damas)* king. ► *nf pl* **damas** GB draughts; US checkers. ■ **dama de honor** bridesmaid.
danza *nf* dance.
dañar *vt (cosa)* to damage; *(persona)* to harm.
daño *nm* **1** *(en cosas)* damage. **2** *(en personas)* harm. ● **hacer daño 1** *(doler)* to hurt. **2** *(perjudicar)* to do harm; **hacerse daño** to hurt oneself. ■ **daños y perjuicios** damages.

dar *vt* **1** *(gen)* to give. **2** *(las horas)* to strike. **3** *(película)* to show; *(obra de teatro)* to perform. ► *vi (mirar a)* to look out.
dardo *nm* dart.
dátil *nm* date.
dato *nm* piece of information. ► *nm pl* **datos** *(información)* information; *(informáticos)* data. ■ **datos personales** personal details.
de *prep* **1** *(gen)* of. **2** *(posesión)* 's, s': *el coche de María*, María's car; *los libros de los chicos*, the boys' books. **3** *(materia, tema)*: *una profesora de inglés*, an English teacher. **4** *(origen, procedencia)* from: *es de Navarra*, he's from Navarre. **5** *(descripción)* with, in: *la chica del pelo largo*, the girl with long hair; *el hombre de negro*, the man in black. **6** *(agente)* by: *un libro de Dickens*, a book by Dickens. **7 de + inf** if: *de seguir así, acabarás en la cárcel*, if you continue like this, you'll end up in prison.
debajo *adv* underneath, below. ● **debajo de** under.
debate *nm* debate.
deber *nm (obligación)* duty. ► *vt (dinero)* to owe. ► *aux* **1 deber + inf** *(obligación)* must, to have to; *(recomendación)* should: *debo irme*, I must go;

deberías ir al médico, you should see the doctor. **2 deber de** *(conjetura)* must: *deben de ser las seis*, it must be six o'clock. *nm pl* **deberes** homework.

debido,-a *adj.* • **como es debido** properly; **debido,-a a** due to, owing to.

débil *adj* **1** *(persona)* weak. **2** *(ruido)* faint. **3** *(luz)* dim.

década *nf* decade.

decadencia *nf* decadence.

decente *adj* **1** *(decoroso)* decent. **2** *(honesto)* honest.

decepcionar *vt* to disappoint.

decidir *vt* to decide, settle. ► *vpr* **decidirse** to make up one's mind.

décima *nf* tenth.

decimal *adj-nm* decimal.

décimo,-a *num* tenth. ► *nm* **décimo** lottery ticket.

decir *vt* **1** *(gen)* to say: *dijo que vendría mañana*, he said he'd come tomorrow. **2** *(a alguien)* to tell: *dime lo que piensas*, tell me what you think. • **es decir** that is to say; **querer decir** to mean.

decisión *nf* decision.

declaración *nf* **1** *(afirmación)* statement. **2** *(de guerra, amor)* declaration. • **prestar declaración** *(en juicio)* to give evidence. ■ **declaración de la renta** income tax return.

declarar *vt* **1** *(gen)* to declare: *¿no tiene nada que declarar?*, do you have anything to declare? **2** *(considerar)* to find. ► *vi* *(dar testimonio)* to testify. ► *vpr* **declararse** *(fuego, guerra)* to start, break out.

decoración *nf* decoration.

decorado *nm* scenery, set.

decorar *vt* to decorate.

decreto *nm* decree.

dedal *nm* thimble.

dedicar *vt* to dedicate. ► *vpr* **dedicarse** to devote oneself: *¿a qué te dedicas?*, what do you do?

dedo *nm* *(de la mano)* finger; *(del pie)* toe. • **hacer dedo** to hitchhike. ■ **dedo del corazón** middle finger; **dedo gordo** thumb.

deducir *vt* **1** *(inferir)* to deduce. **2** *(descontar)* to deduct.

defecto *nm* defect, fault.

defectuoso,-a *adj* defective, faulty.

defender *vt* to defend.

defensa *nf* GB defence; US defense. ► *nmf* *(jugador)* defender.

defensor,-ra *adj* defending. ► *nm,f* defender.

déficit *nm* deficit.

definición *nf* definition.

definir *vt* to define.

definitivo,-a *adj* definitive, final.

deformar *vt* to deform.

defraudar vt 1 *(decepcionar)* to disappoint. 2 *(estafar)* to defraud; *(robar)* to steal.

dejar vt 1 *(gen)* to leave. 2 *(permitir)* to let: **déjame entrar**, let me in. 3 *(prestar)* to lend: *¿me dejas tu bici?*, will you lend me your bike?, can I borrow your bike? ► *aux* 1 **dejar de** + *inf*: *deja de gritar*, stop shouting. 2 **no dejar de** + *inf*: *no dejaron de bailar*, they went on dancing. ► *vpr* **dejarse** *(olvidar)* to forget.

delantal nm apron.

delante adv in front. ► *prep* **delante de** in front of. • **de delante** front; **hacia delante** forward; **por delante** ahead.

delantero,-a adj *(rueda)* front; *(pata)* fore. ► nm **delantero** *(deportista)* forward. ▪ **delantero centro** centre forward.

delegación nf 1 *(personas)* delegation. 2 *(sucursal)* branch.

delegar vt to delegate.

deletrear vt to spell.

delfín nm *(animal)* dolphin.

delgado,-a adj thin.

delicado,-a adj 1 *(sensible)* delicate. 2 *(con tacto)* considerate, thoughtful. 3 *(difícil)* difficult.

delicioso,-a adj delicious.

delincuente adj-nmf delinquent.

delito nm offence, crime.

demanda nf 1 *(de producto)* demand. 2 *(legal)* lawsuit.

demandar vt JUR to sue.

demás adj other. ► *pron* the others, the rest. • **por lo demás** otherwise.

demasiado,-a adj *(singular)* too much; *(plural)* too many. ► *adv* **demasiado** *(después de verbo)* too much; *(delante de adjetivo)* too.

democracia nf democracy.

democrático,-a adj democratic.

demonio nm demon, devil.

demostración nf 1 *(muestra)* demonstration. 2 *(prueba)* proof.

demostrar vt 1 *(mostrar)* to demonstrate. 2 *(probar)* to prove.

denegar vt to refuse.

denominación nf denomination.

denominar vt to denominate, name.

denso,-a adj dense.

dentadura nf teeth. ▪ **dentadura postiza** false teeth.

dentífrico nm toothpaste.

dentista nmf dentist.

dentro adv *(gen)* inside; *(de edificio)* indoors. ► *prep* **dentro de** in. • **por dentro** inside.

denuncia nf report, complaint. • **presentar una denuncia** to lodge a complaint.

denunciar *vt (situación)* to condemn; *(delito)* to report.

departamento *nm* department.

dependencia *nf* **1** *(de persona, drogas)* dependence, dependency. **2** *(en edificio)* outbuilding.

depender *vi* to depend.

dependiente,-a *nm,f* sales assistant.

depilar *vt (con cera)* to wax.

deporte *nm* sport.

deportista *nmf (hombre)* sportsman; *(mujer)* sportswoman.

depositar *vt* to deposit.

depósito *nm* **1** *(gen)* deposit. **2** *(almacén)* store. **3** *(receptáculo)* tank. ■ **depósito de gasolina** petrol tank.

depresión *nf* depression.

deprisa *adv* quickly.

derecha *nf* **1** *(dirección)* right. **2** *(mano)* right hand; *(pierna)* right leg. **3** POL right wing. • **a la derecha** to the right: *girar a la derecha*, to turn right.

derecho,-a *adj* **1** *(diestro)* right. **2** *(recto)* straight. ▶ *nm* **derecho 1** *(poder, oportunidad)* right. **2** *(ley)* law. ■ **derechos de autor** copyright.

derramar *vt* **1** *(leche, vino)* to spill. **2** *(sangre, lágrimas)* to shed.

derrapar *vi* to skid.

derretir(se) *vt-vpr* to melt.

derribar *vt* **1** *(edificio)* to demolish. **2** *(avión)* to shoot down.

derrochar *vt* to squander.

derrota *nf* defeat.

derrotar *vt* to defeat.

derrumbarse *vpr (edificio, techo)* to collapse.

desabrochar *vt* to undo, unfasten.

desacuerdo *nm* disagreement.

desafiar *vt* to defy.

desafinar *vi* to be out of tune.

desafío *nm* **1** *(reto)* challenge. **2** *(duelo)* duel.

desagradable *adj* unpleasant.

desagüe *nm* drain.

desalojar *vt* **1** *(persona)* to remove. **2** *(inquilino)* to evict. **3** *(ciudad)* to evacuate. **4** *(edificio)* to clear.

desangrarse *vpr* to bleed to death.

desanimado,-a *adj* despondent.

desapacible *adj* unpleasant.

desaparecer *vi* to disappear, vanish.

desaparición *nf* disappearance.

desaprovechar *vt* to waste.

desarmar *vt* **1** *(quitar armas)* to disarm. **2** *(desmontar)* to dismantle.

desarrollar *vt* **1** *(gen)* to develop. **2** *(realizar)* to carry

out. ► *vpr* **desarrollarse 1**
(*crecer*) to develop. **2** (*ocurrir*)
to take place.
desarrollo *nm* development.
• **en vías de desarrollo** developing.
desastre *nm* disaster.
desatar *vt* to untie.
desatascar *vt* to unblock.
desatornillar *vt* to unscrew.
desayunar *vt* to have something for breakfast. ► *vi* to
have breakfast.
desayuno *nm* breakfast.
desbordar *vt* (*sobrepasar*) to
surpass. ► *vpr* **desbordarse**
(*río*) to overflow.
descafeinado,-a *adj* (*café*)
decaffeinated.
descalificar *vt* **1** (*de un concurso*) to disqualify. **2** (*desprestigiar*) to dismiss.
descalzo,-a *adj* barefoot.
descampado *nm* area of open
ground.
descansar *vi* **1** (*reposar*)
to have a rest. **2** (*apoyarse*) to
rest.
descansillo *nm* landing.
descanso *nm* **1** (*reposo*) rest;
(*en el trabajo*) break. **2** (*en encuentro deportivo*) half time.
descapotable *adj-nm* convertible.
descarga *nf* **1** (*de electricidad*)
discharge. **2** (*de fuego*) discharge, volley. **3** (*en ordenador*)
download.

descargar *vt* **1** (*mercancías*)
to unload. **2** (*en ordenador*) to
download. ► *vpr* **descargarse** (*batería*) to go flat.
descarrilar *vi* to be derailed.
descartar *vt* to rule out.
descendencia *nf* offspring,
children.
descender *vi* **1** (*ir abajo*) to go
down, come down. **2** (*temperatura, índice*) to drop, fall.
descendiente *nmf* descendant.
descenso *nm* **1** (*de escalera,
cumbre*) descent. **2** (*de temperatura, índice*) fall.
descolgar *vt* **1** (*cuadro, cortina*) to take down. **2** (*teléfono*)
to pick up.
descomposición *nf* **1** (*putrefacción*) decomposition, decay. **2** (*diarrea*) GB diarrhoea;
US diarrhea.
desconectar *vt* to disconnect.
desconfiar *vi* to be distrustful.
descongelar *vt* **1** (*comida*) to
thaw. **2** (*nevera*) to defrost.
desconocido,-a *adj* **1** (*no
conocido*) unknown. **2** (*extraño*) strange, unfamiliar. ►
nm,f stranger.
descontento *nm* dissatisfaction.
descorchar *vt* to uncork.
descosido *nm* split seam.
descremado,-a *adj* skimmed.
describir *vt* to describe.

descripción *nf* description.

descubierto,-a *adj* **1** *(sin cubrir)* uncovered; *(sin sombrero)* bareheaded. **2** *(piscina)* outdoor.

descubrimiento *nm* discovery.

descubrir *vt* **1** *(encontrar)* to discover. **2** *(revelar)* to make known. **3** *(averiguar)* to find out.

descuento *nm* discount.

descuido *nm* **1** *(negligencia)* carelessness. **2** *(desliz)* slip, error.

desde *prep* **1** *(lugar)* from: *desde aquí no se ve*, you can't see it from here. **2** *(tiempo)* since: *salen juntos desde junio*, they've been going out together since June. • **desde ahora** from now on; **desde entonces** since then; **desde hace** for: *vivo aquí desde hace cinco años*, I've lived here for five years; **desde luego** of course; **desde que** ever since.

desdoblar *vt* to unfold.

desear *vt* to want.

desechable *adj* disposable.

desechos *nm pl* **1** *(basura)* waste *sing*. **2** *(sobras)* leftovers.

desembarcar *vi* to land.

desembocadura *nf* mouth.

desembocar *vi* **1** *(río)* to flow. **2** *(calle, acontecimiento)* to lead.

desempate *nm* play-off.

desempeñar *vt* **1** *(obligación)* to discharge. **2** *(cargo)* to hold.

desempleo *nm* unemployment.

desencadenar *vt* *(crisis, debate)* to spark. ► *vpr* **desencadenarse** *(tormenta, guerra)* to break out

desenchufar *vt* to unplug.

desenfocado,-a *adj* out of focus.

desengaño *nm* disappointment.

desenlace *nm* **1** *(de aventura)* outcome. **2** *(de libro, película)* ending.

desenterrar *vt* **1** *(objeto escondido)* to unearth. **2** *(cadáver)* to dig up.

desenvolver *vt* to unwrap. ► *vpr* **desenvolverse** **1** *(transcurrir)* to develop. **2** *(espabilarse)* to manage.

deseo *nm* **1** *(anhelo)* wish. **2** *(apetito sexual)* desire.

desequilibrio *nm* imbalance.

desertar *vi* *(soldado)* to desert.

desértico,-a *adj* *(clima, zona)* desert.

desesperación *nf* **1** *(irritación)* exasperation. **2** *(angustia)* desperation.

desesperar *vt* **1** *(irritar)* to exasperate. **2** *(angustiar)* to make despair. ► *vi-vpr* **desesperar(se)** **1** *(irritarse)* to be exasperated. **2** *(angustiarse)* to despair.

desfallecer *vi* to faint.
desfiladero *nm* **1** *(barranco)* gorge. **2** *(paso)* narrow pass.
desfile *nm* parade.
desgracia *nf* *(mala suerte)* misfortune. **2** *(accidente)* mishap. ● **por desgracia** unfortunately.
deshacer *vt* **1** *(gen)* to undo. **2** *(disolver)* to dissolve; *(fundir)* to melt. ► *vpr* **deshacerse 1** *(costura, nudo)* to come undone. **2** *(disolverse)* to dissolve; *(fundirse)* to melt.
deshidratarse *vpr* to get dehydrated.
deshielo *nm* thaw.
deshinchar *vt* to deflate.
desierto *nm* desert.
designar *vt* **1** *(nombrar)* to appoint. **2** *(fijar)* to designate.
desigualdad *nf* **1** *(diferencia)* inequality. **2** *(irregularidad)* unevenness.
desilusión *nf* disappointment.
desinfectante *adj-nm* disinfectant.
desinflar(se) *vt-vpr* to deflate.
desinterés *nm* lack of interest.
deslizar *vt-vi* to slide. ► *vpr* **deslizarse** *(resbalar)* to slip; *(sobre agua)* to glide.
desmayarse *vpr* to faint.
desmayo *nm* fainting fit.
desmontar *vt* *(mueble)* to dismantle. ► *vi* *(del caballo)* to dismount.

desnatado,-a *adj* *(leche)* skimmed; *(yogur)* low-fat.
desnivel *nm* **1** *(desigualdad)* unevenness. **2** *(distancia vertical)* drop.
desnudarse *vpr* to get undressed.
desnudo,-a *adj* naked.
desobedecer *vt* to disobey.
desocupado,-a *adj* **1** *(libre)* free. **2** *(ocioso)* unoccupied. **3** *(desempleado)* unemployed.
desodorante *adj-nm* deodorant.
desorden *nm* disorder.
despachar *vt* **1** *(enviar)* to dispatch. **2** *(despedir)* to sack. **3** *(en tienda)* to serve; *(vender)* to sell.
despacho *nm* *(en oficina)* office; *(en casa)* study.
despacio *adv* slowly.
despedida *nf* goodbye.
despedir *vt* **1** *(lanzar)* to throw. **2** *(del trabajo)* to dismiss. **3** *(decir adiós a)* to say goodbye to. ► *vpr* **despedirse** to say goodbye.
despegar *vt* *(desenganchar)* to detach. ► *vi* *(avión)* to take off.
despegue *nm* takeoff.
despejado,-a *adj* clear.
despejar *vt* *(habitación, calle)* to clear. ► *vi* to clear up. ► *vpr* **despejarse 1** *(tiempo, cielo)* to clear up. **2** *(persona)* to clear one's head.
despensa *nf* pantry.

desperdiciar *vt* to waste.
desperdicios *nm pl* scraps.
desperfecto *nm* slight damage.
despertador *nm* alarm clock.
despertar(se) *vi-vpr* to wake up.
despido *nm* dismissal.
despierto,-a *adj* **1** *(no dormido)* awake. **2** *(espabilado)* lively.
despistado,-a *adj* absent-minded.
despistar *vt* *(desorientar)* to confuse. ► *vpr* **despistarse** **1** *(perderse)* to get lost. **2** *(distraerse)* to get distracted.
desplazar *vt* to move. ► *vpr* **desplazarse** to travel.
desplegar *vt* **1** *(mapa)* to unfold. **2** *(alas)* to spread. **3** *(actividad, cualidad)* to display. **4** *(tropas, armas)* to deploy.
despreciar *vt* **1** *(menospreciar)* to despise. **2** *(rechazar)* to reject.
desprecio *nm* contempt.
desprenderse *vpr* **1** *(soltarse)* to come off. **2** *(deducirse)* to emerge.
desprevenido,-a *adj* unprepared.
después *adv* **1** *(más tarde)* afterwards, later. **2** *(entonces)* then: *y después dijo que sí,* and then he said yes. ► *prep* **después de** *(tras)* after. • **después de todo** after all; **poco después** soon after.

destacar *vt* **1** *(tropas)* to detach. **2** *(resaltar)* to point out.
destapar *vt* **1** *(olla, caja)* to take the lid off. **2** *(botella)* to open.
destierro *nm* exile.
destinar *vt* **1** *(asignar)* to allocate. **2** *(a un puesto)* to post.
destinatario,-a *nm,f* **1** *(de carta)* addressee. **2** *(de mercancías)* consignee.
destino *nm* **1** *(sino)* destiny, fate. **2** *(lugar)* destination. **3** *(empleo)* post. • **con destino a** bound for: *el tren con destino a Bilbao,* the train to Bilbao.
destituir *vt* to dismiss.
destornillador *nm* screwdriver.
destreza *nf* skill.
destrozar *vt* *(edificio, enemigo)* to destroy; *(mueble, cristalera)* to smash; *(planes, vida)* to ruin; *(corazón).*
destrucción *nf* destruction.
destruir *vt* to destroy.
desván *nm* loft, attic.
desventaja *nf* disadvantage.
desvestirse *vt-vpr* to undress.
desviar *vt* **1** *(trayectoria)* to deviate. **2** *(carretera)* to divert. ► *vpr* **desviarse** *(de un camino)* to go off course; *(coche)* to take a detour.
desvío *nm* diversion.
detalle *nm* **1** *(pormenor)* detail. **2** *(delicadeza)* gesture.
detectar *vt* to detect.

detective *nmf* detective.
detener *vt* 1 *(parar)* to stop.
2 *(arrestar)* to arrest. ► *vpr*
detenerse to stop.
detenido,-a *nm,f* prisoner.
detergente *adj-nm* detergent.
deteriorar *vt* to damage. ► *vpr*
deteriorarse to deteriorate.
determinación *nf* 1 *(valor)*
determination. 2 *(decisión)* decision. 3 *(firmeza)* firmness.
determinar *vt* 1 *(decidir)* to
decide. 2 *(fijar)* to determine.
detestar *vt* to detest.
detrás *adv (gen)* behind. ►
prep **detrás de** behind.
deuda *nf* debt.
devolución *nf* 1 *(de dinero
pagado)* refund. 2 *(de artículo
comprado)* return.
devolver *vt* 1 to give back. 2
(vomitar) to vomit.
día *nm* 1 *(gen)* day. 2 *(horas de
luz)* daylight. • **¡buenos días!**
good morning!; **hoy en día**
today, now, nowadays. ■ **día
festivo** holiday; **día laborable** working day; **día libre**
day off.
diabetes *nf* diabetes.
diabético,-a *adj-nm,f* diabetic.
diablo *nm* devil.
diagnosticar *vt* to diagnose.
diagnóstico *nm* diagnosis.
diagonal *adj-nf* diagonal.
diagrama *nm* diagram.
diálogo *nm* dialogue.
diamante *nm* diamond.

diámetro *nm* diameter.
diana *nf (blanco de tiro)* target;
(para dardos) dartboard.
diapositiva *nf* slide.
diario,-a *adj* daily. ► *nm* **diario** 1 *(prensa)* newspaper. 2
(íntimo) diary, journal. • **a diario** every day.
diarrea *nf* GB diarrhoea; US
diarrhea.
dibujar *vt* to draw.
dibujo *nm* 1 *(gen)* drawing. 2
(estampado) pattern. ■ **dibujos animados** cartoons.
diccionario *nm* dictionary.
dicho,-a *adj* said. • **mejor dicho** or rather.
diciembre *nm* December.
dictado *nm* dictation.
dictador *nm* dictator.
dictadura *nf* dictatorship.
dictar *vt* to dictate.
diecinueve *num* nineteen;
(en fechas) nineteenth.
dieciocho *num* eighteen; *(en
fechas)* eighteenth.
dieciséis *num* sixteen; *(en fechas)* sixteenth.
diecisiete *num* seventeen;
(en fechas) seventeenth.
diente *nm* 1 *(de la boca)* tooth.
2 *(de ajo)* clove.
diestro,-a *adj (mano)* right;
(persona) right-handed. ► *nm*
diestro bullfighter.
dieta *nf (régimen)* diet.
dietas *nf pl* expenses allowance.

diez *num* ten; *(en fechas)* tenth.
diferencia *nf* difference.
diferente *adj* different.
diferido,-a *adj* recorded.
difícil *adj* 1 *(costoso)* difficult. 2 *(improbable)* unlikely.
dificultad *nf* difficulty.
difunto,-a *nm,f* deceased.
difusión *nf* 1 *(de luz)* diffusion. 2 *(de noticia)* spreading. 3 *(por radio, televisión)* broadcast.
digerir *vt* to digest.
digestión *nf* digestion.
digital *adj* digital.
digno,-a *adj* 1 *(merecedor)* worthy. 2 *(adecuado)* fitting. 3 *(respetable)* respectable.
diluvio *nm* flood.
dimensión *nf* 1 *(magnitud física)* dimension. 2 *(tamaño)* size.
diminuto,-a *adj* tiny.
dimisión *nf* resignation.
dimitir *vt* to resign.
Dinamarca *nf* Denmark.
dinero *nm* money. ▪ **dinero en efectivo** cash.
dinosaurio *nm* dinosaur.
dintel *nm* lintel.
dioptría *nf* dioptre.
dios *nm* god.
diosa *nf* goddess.
dióxido *nm* dioxide.
diploma *nm* diploma.
diplomático,-a *adj* diplomatic. ▶ *nm,f* diplomat.
diputado,-a *nm,f* deputy.
dirección *nf* 1 *(rumbo)* direction; *(sentido)* way. 2 *(en empresa)* management. 3 *(domicilio)* address. 4 *(de coche)* steering. ▪ **dirección electrónica** e-mail address.
directo,-a *adj* direct. ▪ **en directo** *(transmisión)* live.
director,-ra *nm,f (gerente)* manager. *(de orquesta)* conductor.
dirigente *adj (clase, élite)* ruling. ▶ *nm,f* leader.
dirigir *vt* 1 *(orientar)* to direct. 2 *(negocio)* to manage. 3 *(orquesta)* to conduct. ▶ *vpr* **dirigirse** 1 *(ir)* to go. 2 *(hablar)* to address, speak to.
disciplina *nf* discipline.
disco *nm* 1 *(de música)* record. 2 *(en deporte)* discus. 3 *(de ordenador)* disk. ▪ **disco compacto** compact disc; **disco duro** hard disk.
discoteca *nf* discotheque.
discreto,-a *adj* 1 *(callado)* discreet. 2 *(sobrio)* sober.
discriminación *nf* discrimination.
disculpa *nf* apology.
discurso *nm* speech.
discusión *nf* 1 *(disputa)* argument. 2 *(debate)* discussion.
discutir *vt-vi* 1 *(debatir)* to discuss. 2 *(disputar)* to argue.
diseño *nm* design.
disfraz *nm* 1 *(para cambiar la imagen)* disguise. 2 *(para fiesta)* costume.
disfrutar *vt* to enjoy.

disgusto *nm* upset. • **a disgusto** against one's will.

disimular *vt* (*ocultar*) to hide. ► *vi* (*fingir*) to pretend.

disminuir *vt* to reduce. ► *vi* to decrease, fall.

disparar *vt* **1** (*arma*) to fire. **2** (*balón*) to drive.

disparo *nm* shot.

disponer *vt-vi* (*colocar*) to arrange. ► *vt* (*ordenar*) to order. ► *vi* (*poseer*) to have. ► *vpr* **disponerse** (*prepararse*) to be set to.

disposición *nf* **1** (*actitud*) disposition. **2** (*colocación*) arrangement. • **a su disposición** at your disposal.

dispositivo *nm* device.

disputar *vt* **1** (*discutir*) to dispute. **2** (*partido*) to play.

disquete *nm* diskette.

disquetera *nf* disk drive.

distancia *nf* distance.

distinguir *vt* **1** (*diferenciar*) to distinguish. **2** (*ver*) to see.

distinto,-a *adj* different.

distracción *nf* **1** (*divertimiento*) amusement. **2** (*despiste*) distraction.

distraer *vt* **1** (*divertir*) to keep amused. **2** (*atención*) to distract. ► *vpr* **distraerse 1** (*divertirse*) to keep oneself amused. **2** (*despistarse*) to get distracted.

distribución *nf* **1** (*reparto*) distribution. **2** (*colocación*) arrangement.

distribuir *vt* **1** (*repartir*) to distribute. **2** (*colocar*) to arrange.

diurno,-a *adj* **1** (*curso, autobús*) daytime. **2** (*animal*) diurnal.

diversidad *nf* diversity.

diversión *nf* (*gozo*) fun; (*pasatiempo*) pastime.

diversos,-as *adj pl* several, various.

divertir *vt* to amuse. ► *vpr* **divertirse** to enjoy oneself.

dividir *vt* to divide.

divino,-a *adj* divine.

divisa *nf* foreign currency.

divisar *vt* make out.

división *nf* division.

divorcio *nm* divorce.

divulgar *vt* **1** (*dar a conocer*) to make public. **2** (*propagar*) to spread.

doblar *vt* **1** (*duplicar*) to double. **2** (*plegar*) to fold. **3** (*esquina*) to turn. **4** (*película*) to dub.

doble *adj-nm* double.

doce *num* twelve; (*en fechas*) twelfth.

docena *nf* dozen.

doctor,-ra *nm,f* doctor.

documentación *nf* documentation.

documento *nm* document.

dólar *nm* dollar.

doler *vi* to hurt: *me duele la cabeza*, I've got a headache.

dolor *nm* (*físico, moral*) pain; (*sordo*) ache. ■ **dolor de cabeza** headache; **dolor de es-**

tómago stomachache; **dolor de garganta** sore throat; **dolor de muelas** toothache.

doméstico,-a *adj* domestic.

domicilio *nm* address.

dominar *vt* **1** *(gen)* to dominate. **2** *(tema)* to master.

domingo *nm* Sunday.

dominical *nm* Sunday newspaper.

dominio *nm* **1** *(poder)* control. **2** *(de tema)* mastery. **3** INFORM domain.

dominó *nm* (ficha) domino; *(juego)* dominoes *pl*.

don *nm* (título) don.

donante *nmf* donor.

donde *conj* where.

dónde *pron* where.

dondequiera *adv* wherever.

dorado,-a *adj* (gen) gold; *(color)* golden.

dormir *vi* to sleep. ► *vpr* **dormirse** to go to sleep. • **dormir la siesta** to have a nap.

dormitorio *nm* bedroom.

dorso *nm* back.

dos *num* two; *(en fechas)* second. • **de dos en dos** in twos; **dos puntos** colon.

doscientos,-as *num* two hundred.

dosis *nf* dose.

drama *nm* drama.

dramático,-a *adj* dramatic.

droga *nf* drug. ■ **droga blanda** soft drug; **droga dura** hard drug.

drogadicto,-a *nm,f* drug addict.

droguería *nf* hardware and household goods shop.

dromedario *nm* dromedary.

ducha *nf* shower. • **darse una ducha** to have a shower.

ducharse *vpr* to have a shower.

duda *nf* doubt. • **sin duda** undoubtedly.

dudar *vi* to hesitate. ► *vt* to doubt.

duelo *nm* duel.

duende *nm* elf.

dueño,-a *nm,f* **1** *(propietario)* owner. **2** *(de casa alquilada - hombre)* landlord; *(- mujer)* landlady.

dulce *adj* (comida, bebida) sweet.► *nm* (caramelo) sweet.

duna *nf* dune.

dúo *nm* **1** *(pareja)* duo. **2** *(composición)* duet.

duodécimo,-a *num* twelfth.

dúplex *adj-nm* duplex.

duque *nm* duke.

duquesa *nf* duchess.

duración *nf* duration.

durante *adv* **1** *(a lo largo de un periodo)* for: **durante todo el día**, all day long. **2** *(dentro de un periodo)* during, in: **durante la noche**, during the night, in the night.

durar *vi* to last.

duro,-a *adj* (gen) hard; *(carne)* tough.

E

ébano *nm* ebony.

ebrio,-a *adj* drunk.

eccema *nm* eczema.

echar *vt* 1 *(lanzar)* to throw. 2 *(del trabajo)* to sack. 3 *(correo)* GB to post; US to mail. ► *vi-vpr* **echar(se) a** + *inf* to begin to: *echar a correr*, to run off. ► *vpr* **echarse** *(tenderse)* to lie down. • **echar algo a perder** to spoil STH; **echar de menos** to miss; **echarse atrás** 1 *(inclinarse)* to lean back. 2 *(desdecirse)* to back out.

eclipse *nm* eclipse.

eco *nm* echo.

ecología *nf* ecology.

ecológico,-a *adj* 1 *(gen)* ecological. 2 *(cultivo)* organic.

ecologista *nmf* environmentalist.

economía *nf* 1 *(de un país)* economy. 2 *(ciencia)* economics.

económico,-a *adj* 1 *(de la economía)* economic. 2 *(barato)* economical.

ecuación *nf* equation.

ecuador *nm* equator.

ecuatorial *adj* equatorial.

edad *nf* age: *¿qué edad tiene usted?*, how old are you? ■ **la tercera edad** 1 *(etapa de la vida)* old age. 2 *(gente mayor)* senior citizens.

edición *nf* 1 *(tirada)* edition. 2 *(publicación)* publication. ■ **edición electrónica** electronic publishing.

edificio *nm* building.

editor,-ra *nm,f* 1 *(que publica)* publisher. 2 *(que prepara)* editor. ■ **editor de texto** text editor.

editorial *nm* *(artículo)* editorial, leading article. ► *nf* publishing house.

edredón *nm* quilt. ■ **edredón nórdico** duvet.

educación *nf* 1 *(enseñanza)* education. 2 *(crianza)* upbringing. 3 *(cortesía)* manners.

educado,-a *adj* polite.

educar *vt* *(enseñar)* to educate.

efectivo,-a *adj* *(eficaz)* effective. ► *nm* **efectivo** cash. ► *nm pl* **efectivos** forces.

efecto *nm* 1 *(gen)* effect. 2 *(impresión)* impression. 3 *(pelota)* spin. • **en efecto** indeed; **hacer efecto** to take effect. ■ **efecto invernadero** greenhouse effect; **efectos especiales** special effects; **efectos personales** personal belongings.

efectuar *vt* 1 *(maniobra, investigación, etc)* to carry out. 2 *(pago, viaje, etc)* to make.

efervescente *adj* 1 *(pastilla)* effervescent. 2 *(bebida)* fizzy.

eficaz *adj* 1 *(que surte efecto)* effective. 2 *(eficiente)* efficient.

eficiente *adj* efficient.

egoísta *adj* selfish, egoistic. ▶ *nmf* egoist.

eje *nm* **1** *(en geometría, astronomía)* axis. **2** *(de motor)* shaft. **3** *(de ruedas)* axle.

ejecución *nf* execution.

ejecutar *vt* **1** *(orden)* to carry out. **2** *(programa informático)* to run. **3** *(ajusticiar)* to execute.

ejecutivo,-a *adj-nm,f* executive.

ejemplar *nm* **1** *(obra)* copy. **2** *(espécimen)* specimen.

ejemplo *nm* example. • **por ejemplo** for example, for instance.

ejercer *vt* **1** *(profesión etc)* to practise. **2** *(derecho, poder)* to exercise. **3** *(influencia)* to exert.

ejercicio *nm* **1** *(gen)* exercise. **2** *(financiero)* year. • **hacer ejercicio** to exercise.

ejército *nm* army.

el *det* **1** the: *el coche*, the car. **2** **el + de** the one: *el de tu amigo,-a*, your friend's. **3** **el + que** the one: *el que vino ayer*, the one who came yesterday.

él *pron* **1** *(sujeto - persona)* he; *(- cosa, animal)* it. **2** *(después de preposición - persona)* him; *(- cosa, animal)* it. • **de él** *(posesivo)* his: *es de él*, it's his; **él mismo** himself.

elaborar *vt* to make, manufacture.

elástico,-a *adj* elastic.

elección *nf* **1** *(nombramiento)* election. **2** *(opción)* choice. ▶ *nf pl* **elecciones** elections.

electricidad *nf* electricity.

eléctrico,-a *adj* electric.

electrocutarse *vpr* to be electrocuted.

electrodoméstico *nm* home electrical appliance.

electrónico,-a *adj* electronic.

elefante *nm* elephant.

elegante *adj* elegant.

elegir *vt* **1** *(escoger)* to chose. **2** *(por votación)* to elect.

elemental *adj* elementary.

elemento *nm* element.

elevado,-a *adj* *(edificio)* tall; *(montaña, número)* high.

elevar *vt* to raise. ▶ *vpr* **elevarse** *(ascender - avión)* to climb; *(- globo)* to rise.

eliminación *nf* elimination.

eliminar *vt* **1** *(gen)* to eliminate. **2** *(obstáculo, mancha)* to remove.

ella *pron* **1** *(sujeto - persona)* she; *(- cosa, animal)* it. **2** *(después de preposición - persona)* her; *(- cosa, animal)* it. • **de ella** hers.

ello *pron* it.

ellos,-as *pron* **1** *(sujeto)* they. **2** *(complemento)* them. • **de ellos** theirs: *es de ellas*, it's theirs.

elogio *nm* praise.

embajada *nf* embassy.

embajador,-ra *nm,f* ambassador.

embalaje *nm* packing.

embalar *vt* to pack.

embalse *nm* reservoir.

embarazada *nf* pregnant woman.

embarazo *nm (preñez)* pregnancy.

embarcación *nf* boat.

embarcadero *nm* jetty.

embarcar(se) *vt-vpr* to embark.

embargo *nm* 1 *(incautación de bienes)* seizure. 2 *(prohibición de comercio)* embargo. • **sin embargo** however.

embarque *nm (de personas)* boarding.

emblema *nm* emblem.

emborrachar *vt* to make drunk. ▶ *vpr* **emborracharse** to get drunk.

emboscada *nf* ambush.

embotellamiento *nm (de tráfico)* traffic jam.

embrague *nm* clutch.

embrión *nm* embryo.

embudo *nm* funnel.

embustero,-a *nm,f* liar.

embutido *nm* cold meat.

emergencia *nf* emergency.

emigración *nf* emigration.

emigrante *adj-nmf* emigrant.

emisión *nf* 1 *(de energía, gas)* emission. 2 *(de bonos, acciones)* issue. 3 *(en radio, TV)* broadcast.

emisor *nm* radio transmitter.

emisora *nf* radio station.

emitir *vt* 1 *(sonido, luz, calor)* to emit. 2 *(bonos, acciones)* to issue. 3 *(programa de radio, TV)* to broadcast.

emoción *nf* 1 *(sentimiento)* emotion. 2 *(excitación)* excitement.

emocionante *adj* 1 *(conmovedor)* moving. 2 *(excitante)* exciting.

emocionar *vt* 1 *(conmover)* to move. 2 *(excitar)* to excite. ▶ *vpr* **emocionarse** *(conmoverse)* to be moved.

empacho *nm* indigestion.

empalagoso,-a *adj (dulces)* sickly.

empalme *nm* 1 *(de tuberías, cables)* connection. 2 *(de carreteras, vías)* junction.

empanada *nf* pasty.

empanadilla *nf* pasty.

empañarse *vpr (cristal)* to steam up.

empapar *vt* to soak.

empaquetar *vt* to pack.

emparedado *nm* sandwich.

empaste *nm* filling.

empatar *vi (acabar igualados)* to draw; *(igualar)* to equalize.

empate *nm* tie, draw.

empeine *nm* instep.

empeñar *vt (objeto)* to pawn. ▶ *vpr* **empeñarse** *(insistir)* to insist.

empeño *nm (insistencia)* determination. •

emperador *nm* emperor.

emperatriz *nf* empress.
empezar *vt-vi* to begin, start.
empinado,-a *adj* steep.
empleado,-a *nm,f (gen)* employee; *(oficinista)* clerk. ■
empleadoa de hogar maid.
emplear *vt* to employ.
empleo *nm* 1 *(puesto)* job. 2 *(trabajo)* employment.
empotrado,-a *adj* built-in.
emprender *vt* to undertake.
empresa *nf (compañía)* firm, company.
empresario,-a *nm,f* 1 *(hombre)* businessman; *(mujer)* businesswoman. 2 *(patrón)* employer.
empujar *vt* to push.
empujón *nm* push, shove.
en *prep* 1 *(lugar - gen)* in, at; *(- en el interior)* in, inside; *(- sobre)* on: *en casa*, at home; *en Valencia*, in Valencia; *en el cajón*, in the drawer; *en la mesa*, on the table. 2 *(tiempo - año, mes, estación)* in; *(- día)* on: *en 2004*, in 2004; *en viernes*, on Friday. 3 *(dirección)* into: *entró en su casa*, he went into his house. 4 *(transporte)* by, in: *ir en coche*, to go by car. 5 *(tema, materia)* at, in: *es experto en política*, he's an expert in politics. 6 *(modo)* in: *en voz baja*, in a low voice. • *en seguida* at once, straight away.

enamorado,-a *adj* in love. ►
nm,f lover.
enamorarse *vpr* to fall in love.
enano,-a *adj-nm,f* dwarf.
encabezar *vt* 1 *(en escrito)* to head. 2 *(ser líder)* to lead.
encadenar *vt* 1 *(poner cadenas a)* to chain. 2 *(enlazar)* to link.
encajar *vt-vi* to fit.
encaje *nm (tejido)* lace.
encallar *vi* to run aground
encaminarse *vpr* to head.
encantado,-a *adj (contento)* delighted. • **encantado,-a de conocerle** *fml* pleased to meet you.
encantador,-ra *adj* charming.
encantar *vi*: *me encanta la natación*, I love swimming.
encanto *nm (atractivo)* charm.
encarcelar *vt* to imprison.
encargado,-a *nm,f (responsable)* person in charge; *(de negocio - hombre)* manager; *(- mujer)* manageress.
encargar *vt* 1 *(encomendar)* to entrust. 2 *(solicitar)* to order. ► *vpr* **encargarse** to take charge.
encargo *nm* 1 *(recado)* errand; *(tarea)* job. 2 *(de productos)* order. • **por encargo** to order.
encendedor *nm* lighter.
encender *vt* 1 *(fuego, vela, cigarro)* to light; *(cerilla)* to strike.

2 *(luz, radio, tele)* to turn on, switch on.

encerrar *vt* **1** *(persona - en habitación)* to shut in; *(- en cárcel)* to lock up. **2** *fig (contener)* to contain.

encestar *vi* to score (a basket).

enchufar *vt (aparato)* to plug in.

enchufe *nm (de aparato - hembra)* socket; *(macho)* plug.

encía *nf* gum.

encierro *nm* **1** *(protesta)* sit-in. **2** *(de toros)* bullpen.

encima *adv* **1** *(más arriba)* above; *(sobre)* on top. **2** *(consigo)* on me/you/him *etc*: **ellevas cambio encima?**, do you have any change on you? **3** *(además)* in addition. ● **encima de** on; **por encima 1** *(a más altura)* above. **2** *(de pasada)* superficially; **por encima de** above.

encina *nf* evergreen oak.

encoger(se) *vt-vi-vpr* to shrink.

encontrar *vt* **1** *(hallar)* to find. **2** *(creer)* to think. ► *vpr* **encontrarse 1** *(hallarse)* to be. **2** *(personas)* to meet. **3** *(sentirse)* to feel: **me encuentro bien,** I feel fine; **me encuentro mal,** I feel ill.

encubrir *vt (delito)* to cover up.

encuentro *nm* **1** *(coincidencia)* encounter. **2** *(reunión)* meeting. **3** *(en deporte)* match.

encuesta *nf* survey.

endibia *nf* endive.

endulzar *vt (hacer dulce)* to sweeten.

endurecer(se) *vt-vpr* to harden.

enemigo,-a *adj-nm,f* enemy.

energía *nf* energy. ■ **energía atómica** atomic power; **energía eléctrica** electric power; **energía nuclear** nuclear power; **energía solar** solar power, solar energy.

enero *nm* January.

enfadado,-a *adj* angry.

enfadarse *vpr* to get angry.

enfado *nm* anger.

enfermedad *nf (estado de enfermo)* illness; *(patología específica)* disease.

enfermería *nf* **1** *(profesión)* nursing. **2** *(lugar)* infirmary.

enfermero,-a *nm,f (hombre)* (male) nurse; *(mujer)* nurse.

enfermo,-a *adj* ill, sick. ► *nm,f* sick person.

enfocar *vt* **1** *(con cámara)* to focus on. **2** *(problema etc)* to approach.

enfrentarse *vpr* **1** *(encararse)* to face up. **2** *(pelearse)* to have a confrontation.

enfrente *adv* opposite. ● **enfrente de** opposite.

enfriarse *vpr* **1** *(algo caliente)* to cool down. **2** *(acatarrarse)* catch a cold.

enfurecerse *vpr* to get furious.

enganchar vt (gen) to hook; (animales) to hitch; (vagones) to couple.

engañar vt **1** (gen) to deceive. **2** (mentir) to lie to. **3** (a la pareja) to be unfaithful to.

engaño nm deceit.

engordar vi **1** (persona) to put on weight: *he engordado cinco kilos*, I've put on five kilos. **2** (alimento) to be fattening.

engrasar vt (gen) to lubricate; (con grasa) to grease; (con aceite) to oil.

enhorabuena nf congratulations. • **dar la enhorabuena a ALGN** to congratulate SB.

enigma nm enigma, puzzle.

enjabonar vt to soap.

enjuagar(se) vt-vpr to rinse.

enlace nm **1** (conexión) link. **2** (boda) marriage. **3** (en internet) link.

enlazar vi to connect.

enmienda nf **1** (de error) correction; (de daño) repair. **2** (de texto, ley) amendment.

enojado,-a adj (enfadado) angry; (molesto) annoyed.

enojarse vpr (enfadarse) to get angry; (molestarse) to get annoyed.

enorgullecerse vpr to be proud, feel proud.

enorme adj enormous, huge.

enredadera nf creeper, climbing plant.

enredar vt **1** (enmarañar) to tangle. **2** (dificultar) to complicate. ► vi (hacer travesuras) to get up to mischief. ► vpr **enredarse** (cuerda, pelo) to get tangled.

enriquecerse vpr to get rich.

enrollado,-a adj fam (persona) cool.

enrollar vt to roll up. ► vpr **enrollarse** fam (hablar) to go on and on. • **enrollarse con ALGN** to get off with SB.

ensalada nf salad.

ensaladera nf salad bowl.

ensaladilla nf. ■ **ensaladilla rusa** Russian salad.

ensanchar vt (agrandar) to widen; (prenda) to let out

ensanche nm **1** (de carretera) widening. **2** (de ciudad) new development.

ensayar vt (obra de teatro) to rehearse; (música) to practise.

ensayo nm **1** (de obra de teatro) rehearsal; (de música) practice. **2** (prueba) test, trial. **3** (literario) essay. ■ **ensayo general** dress rehearsal.

enseguida adv at once, straight away.

enseñanza nf **1** (educación) education. **2** (docencia) teaching.

enseñar vt **1** (en escuela etc) to teach. **2** (mostrar) to show.

ensuciar(se) vt-vpr to get dirty.

entablar vt (conversación) to start; (amistad) to strike up.

entender vt 1 (comprender) to understand. 2 (opinar) to consider. ► vi to know: **¿tú entiendes de motores?**, do you know anything about engines? ► vpr **entenderse** fam (llevarse bien) to get along well together. • **dar a entender que …** to imply that …

entendido,-a nm,f expert.

enterarse vpr 1 (averiguar) to find out. 2 (darse cuenta) to notice. 3 (comprender) to understand.

entero,-a adj (completo) whole.

enterrar vt to bury.

entidad nf 1 (organismo) body. 2 (ente, ser) entity. ■ **entidad bancaria** bank.

entierro nm 1 (acto) burial. 2 (ceremonia) funeral.

entonación nf intonation.

entonces adv then.

entorno nm environment.

entorpecer vt (dificultar) to obstruct, hinder.

entrada nf 1 (acción) entrance, entry. 2 (lugar) entrance. 3 (en espectáculo - billete) ticket; (admisión) admission. 4 (pago inicial) down payment. ► nf pl **entradas** receding hairline. • **"Prohibida la entrada"** "No admittance".

entrañable adj beloved.

entrañas nf pl entrails.

entrar vi 1 (ir adentro) to come in, go in. 2 (en una sociedad etc) to join. 3 (encajar) to fit. 4 (en fase, etapa) to enter. 5 (venir): **me entraron ganas de llorar**, I felt like crying.

entre prep 1 (dos términos) between; (más de dos términos) among. 2 (sumando) counting: **entre niños y adultos somos doce**, counting children and adults, there are twelve of us. • **entre tanto** meanwhile.

entreacto nm interval.

entrecot nm entrecôte.

entrega nf (acción) handing over; (de mercancía) delivery.

entregar vt 1 (dar) to hand over; (deberes, solicitud) to hand in. 2 (mercancía) to deliver.

entremés nm hors d'oeuvre.

entrenador,-ra nm,f trainer, coach.

entrenamiento nm (acción) training; (sesión) training session.

entrenar(se) vt-vpr to train.

entresuelo nm mezzanine.

entretanto adv meanwhile.

entretener vt 1 (divertir) to entertain. 2 (distraer) to distract. ► vpr **entretenerse 1** (retrasarse) to be late. 2 (divertirse) keep oneself amused.

entretenido,-a adj 1 (divertido) entertaining. 2 (complicado) timeconsuming.

entretenimiento *nm* entertainment.

entrevista *nf* interview.

entusiasmar *vt* to excite: *me entusiasma la ópera*, I love opera. ► *vpr* **entusiasmarse** to get enthusiastic.

entusiasmo *nm* enthusiasm.

enumerar *vt* to enumerate.

enunciado *nm* statement.

envasar *vt* (*en paquete*) to pack; (*en botella*) to bottle; (*en lata*) to can, tin. • **envasado,-a al vacío** vacuum-packed.

envase *nm* (*recipiente*) container; (*botella*) bottle.

envejecer *vt* (*dar aspecto viejo*) to make look older. ► *vi* (*hacerse viejo*) to grow old.

envenenamiento *nm* poisoning.

envenenarse *vpr* to poison oneself.

enviado,-a *nm,f.* ■ **enviado,-a especial** special correspondent.

enviar *vt* to send.

envidia *nf* envy.

envío *nm* 1 (*acción*) sending. 2 (*remesa*) consignment; (*de mercancía*) dispatch, shipment. ■ **envío contra reembolso** cash on delivery.

envolver *vt* 1 (*cubrir*) to wrap. 2 (*rodear*) to surround. 3 (*implicar*) to involve.

enyesar *vt* (*pierna, brazo*) to put in plaster.

epidemia *nf* epidemic.

episodio *nm* episode.

época *nf* 1 (*período*) time, period. 2 (*del año*) season.

equilibrio *nm* balance. • **mantener el equilibrio** to keep one's balance; **perder el equilibrio** to lose one's balance.

equipaje *nm* luggage, baggage. • **hacer el equipaje** to pack, do the packing. ■ **equipaje de mano** hand luggage.

equipo *nm* 1 (*de personas, jugadores*) team. 2 (*equipamiento*) equipment. 3 (*ordenador*) machine.

equivalente *adj-nm* equivalent.

equivaler *vi* 1 (*ser igual*) to be equivalent. 2 (*significar*) to be tantamount.

equivocación *nf* mistake, error.

equivocarse *vpr* 1 (*no tener razón*) to be mistaken, be wrong. 2 (*cometer un error*) to make a mistake.

era *nf* (*período*) era, age.

erguirse *vpr* to straighten up.

erigir *vt* to erect. ► *vpr* **erigirse** to establish oneself.

erizo *nm* hedgehog. ■ **erizo de mar** sea urchin.

ermita *nf* hermitage.

erosión *nf* erosion.

erótico,-a *adj* erotic.

errar *vt* (*objetivo, disparo*) to miss; (*pronóstico*) to get wrong.

error *nm* mistake, error. • **por error** by mistake.

eructo *nm* belch.

erupción *nf* **1** *(volcánica)* eruption. **2** *(cutánea)* rash.

esbozo *nm (dibujo)* sketch.

escabeche *nm* pickle.

escafandra *nf* diving suit.

escala *nf* scale. • **a escala** scale; **hacer escala 1** *(avión)* to stop over. **2** *(barco)* to put in.

escalador,-ra *nm,f* climber.

escalar *vt* to climb.

escalera *nf* **1** *(de edificio)* stairs. **2** *(portátil)* ladder. **3** *(naipes)* run. ▪ **escalera de caracol** spiral staircase; **escalera mecánica** escalator.

escalerilla *nf (de barco)* gangway; *(de avión)* steps.

escalofrío *nm* shiver.

escalón *nm (peldaño)* step.

escalope *nm* escalope.

escama *nf* scale.

escándalo *nm* **1** *(acto inmoral)* scandal. **2** *(alboroto)* racket.

escanear *vt* to scan.

escáner *nm* scanner.

escapada *nf* **1** *fam (viaje)* quick trip. **2** *(en ciclismo)* breakaway.

escapar(se) *vi-vpr (lograr salir)* to escape; *(irse corriendo)* to run away. ▶ *vpr* **escaparse 1** *(gas etc)* to leak out. **2** *(autobús etc)* to miss.

escaparate *nm* shop window.

escape *nm* **1** *(huida)* escape. **2** *(de gas etc)* leak. **3** *(de coche)* exhaust.

escarabajo *nm* beetle.

escarcha *nf* frost.

escarola *nf* GB curly endive; US escarole.

escaso,-a *adj* scarce, scant.

escayola *nf* plaster.

escayolar *vt* to put in plaster.

escena *nf* **1** *(gen)* scene. **2** *(escenario)* stage.

escenario *nm* **1** *(en teatro)* stage. **2** *(de suceso)* scene.

escéptico,-a *adj* GB sceptical; US skeptical.

esclavo,-a *nm,f* slave.

esclusa *nf (de canal)* lock; *(compuerta)* sluice gate.

escoba *nf* broom.

escobilla *nf* **1** *(gen)* brush. **2** *(de coche)* windscreen wiper blade.

escocer *vi (herida)* to smart.

escocés,-a *adj* Scottish. ▶ *nm,f (persona)* Scot.

Escocia *nf* Scotland.

escoger *vt* to choose.

escolar *adj* school.

escolta *nmf* escort.

escombros *nm pl* rubble.

esconder(se) *vt-vptr* to hide.

escopeta *nf* shotgun.

escorpión *nm* scorpion.

escote[1] *nm (de vestido)* low neckline.

escote[2]. • **pagar a escote** to share the expenses.

escotilla *nf* hatchway.

escozor *nm (picor)* irritation, smarting.

escribir *vt-vi* to write. ► *vpr* **escribirse 1** *(dos personas)* to write to each other. **2** *(palabra)* to spell: *se escribe con "j"*, it's spelt with a "j".

escrito,-a *adj* written. ● **por escrito** in writing.

escritor,-ra *nm,f* writer.

escritorio *nm* **1** *(mueble)* writing desk. **2** INFORM desktop.

escrupuloso,-a *adj* **1** *(cuidadoso)* scrupulous. **2** *(aprensivo)* finicky, fussy.

escuadra *nf* **1** *(instrumento)* square. **2** *(de soldados)* squad.

escuchar *vt* **1** *(atender)* to listen to. **2** *(oír)* to hear.

escudo *nm* shield.

escuela *nf* school.

escultor,-ra *nm,f (hombre)* sculptor; *(mujer)* sculptress.

escultura *nf* sculpture.

escupir *vi* to spit.

escurridor *nm* **1** *(colador)* colander. **2** *(de platos)* dish rack.

escurrir *vt (platos)* to drain; *(ropa)* to wring out. ► *vpr* **escurrirse** *(resbalarse)* to slip.

ese,-a *adj* that.

ése,-a *pron* that one.

esencial *adj* essential.

esfera *nf* **1** *(figura)* sphere. **2** *(de reloj)* face.

esforzarse *vpr* to try hard.

esfuerzo *nm* effort.

esgrima *nf* fencing.

esguince *nm* sprain.

eslabón *nm* link.

eslip *nm* briefs, underpants.

eslogan *nm* slogan.

esmalte *nm* enamel. ■ **esmalte de uñas** nail polish, nail varnish.

esmeralda *nf* emerald.

esmerarse *vpr* to do one's best.

esmoquin *nf* GB dinner jacket; US tuxedo.

eso *pron* that.

esófago *nm* GB oesophagus. US esophagus.

espacial *adj (cohete etc)* space; *(en física)* spatial.

espacio *nm* **1** *(sitio)* space. **2** *(de tiempo)* period. **3** *(en radio, televisión)* programme. ■ **espacio aéreo** air space.

espada *nf* sword.

espaguetis *nm pl* spaghetti.

espalda *nf* **1** *(parte del cuerpo)* back. **2** *(en natación)* backstroke.

espantapájaros *nm* scarecrow.

espantar *vt* **1** *(asustar)* to frighten, scare. **2** *(ahuyentar)* to frighten away.

espantoso,-a *adj* **1** *(terrible)* frightful, dreadful. **2** *(muy feo)* hideous, frightful.

español,-la *adj* Spanish. ► *nm,f (persona)* Spaniard. ► *nm* **español** *(idioma)* Spanish.

esparadrapo *nm* GB sticking plaster; US Band-Aid.

espárrago *nm* asparagus.

esparto *nm* esparto grass.

especia *nf* spice.

especial *adj* special.

especialidad *nf* GB speciality; US specialty.

especie *nf* 1 *(de animales, plantas)* species. 2 *(tipo)* kind, sort.

específico,-a *adj* specific.

espectáculo *nm* 1 *(escena)* spectacle, sight. 2 *(de TV, radio etc)* show.

espectador,-ra *nm,f* 1 *(en un estadio)* spectator. 2 *(en teatro, cine)* member of the audience; *(de televisión)* viewer.

espejo *nm* mirror. ▪ **espejo retrovisor** rear-view mirror.

espera *nf* wait.

esperanza *nf* hope. • **perder la esperanza** to lose hope. ▪ **esperanza de vida** life expectancy.

esperar *vt* 1 *(aguardar)* to wait for, await. 2 *(confiar)* to hope for, expect: *espero que sí*, I hope so. 3 *(bebé)* to expect. ▶ *vi* to wait.

esperma *nm* sperm.

espeso,-a *adj* thick.

espía *nmf* spy.

espiga *nf* *(de trigo)* ear; *(de flor)* spike.

espina *nf* 1 *(de planta)* thorn. 2 *(de pez)* fishbone. ▪ **espina dorsal** spine, backbone.

espinacas *nf pl* spinach *sing.*

espinilla *nf* 1 *(tibia)* shinbone. 2 *(grano)* blackhead.

espiral *adj-nf* spiral.

espíritu *nm* spirit.

espléndido,-a *adj* 1 *(magnífico)* splendid, magnificent. 2 *(generoso)* lavish.

esponja *nf* sponge.

espontáneo,-a *adj* spontaneous.

esposas *nf pl* handcuffs.

esposo,-a *nm,f* spouse; *(hombre)* husband; *(mujer)* wife.

espuela *nf* spur.

espuma *nf* *(de mar)* foam; *(de olas)* surf; *(de jabón)* lather; *(de cerveza)* froth. ▪ **espuma de afeitar** shaving foam.

espumadera *nf* skimmer.

espumoso,-a *adj* *(vino)* sparkling.

esquela *nf* death notice.

esqueleto *nm* skeleton.

esquema *nm* *(plan)* outline; *(gráfica)* diagram.

esquí *nm* 1 *(tabla)* ski. 2 *(deporte)* skiing. ▪ **esquí acuático** water-skiing.

esquiar *vi* to ski.

esquimal *adj-nmf* Eskimo.

esquina *nf* corner. • **a la vuelta de la esquina** just around the corner; **doblar la esquina** to turn the corner.

esquivar *vt* 1 *(persona)* to avoid. 2 *(golpe)* to dodge.

estable *adj* stable, steady.

establecer vt to establish. ▶
vpr **establecerse** to settle.
establecimiento nm (local)
establishment; (tienda) shop.
establo nm stable.
estación nf 1 (del año) season. 2 (de tren) station. ▪ **estación de esquí** ski resort;
estación de servicio service station.
estacionarse vt-vpr to park.
estadio nm stadium.
estadística nf statistics.
estado nm 1 (gen) state. 2
(médico) condition. • **estar
en mal estado** 1 (alimento)
to be off. 2 (carretera) to be in
poor condition; **estar en estado** to be pregnant. ▪ **estado civil** marital status.
estafar vt 1 (timar) to swindle. 2 (defraudar) to defraud.
estalactita nf stalactite.
estalagmita nf stalagmite.
estallar vi 1 (bomba) to explode. 2 (neumático, globo)
to burst. 3 (rebelión, guerra) to
break out.
estancarse vpr 1 (líquido) to
stagnate. 2 (proceso) to come
to a standstill.
estancia nf 1 (permanencia)
stay. 2 (aposento) room.
estanco nm tobacconist's.
estándar adj-nm standard.
estanque nm pool, pond.
estante nm (gen) shelf; (para
libros) bookcase.

estantería nf shelves.
estaño nm tin.
estar vi to be. ▶ aux **estar** +
inf to be: **estar comiendo**, to
be eating.
estatua nf statue.
estatura nf height.
este adj-nm east.
este,-a adj this.
éste,-a pron this one.
estela nf (de barco) wake; (de
avión) GB vapour trail; US vapor trail.
estelar adj 1 (sideral) stellar.
2 (actuación, elenco) star.
estepa nf steppe.
estéreo adj stereo.
estéril adj sterile.
esternón nm sternum.
esteticista nmf beautician.
estético,-a adj GB aesthetic;
US esthetic.
estetoscopio nm stetho-
scope.
estilo nm 1 (gen) style. 2 (en
natación) stroke. • **estilo de
vida** way of life, lifestyle.
estilográfica nf fountain pen.
estimado,-a adj 1 (apreciado)
esteemed. 2 (valorado) val-
ued. • **estimada señora** (en
carta) Dear Madam; **estimado señor** (en carta) Dear Sir.
estimar vt 1 (apreciar) to esteem; (objeto) to value. 2 (juzgar) to consider.
estímulo nm 1 stimulus. 2
(aliciente) encouragement.

estirar(se) *vt-vpr* to stretch.

estival *adj* summer.

esto *pron* this.

estofado *nm* stew.

estómago *nm* stomach.

estorbar *vt* **1** *(dificultar)* to hinder. **2** *(molestar)* to annoy. ► *vi* to get in the way.

estornudo *nm* sneeze.

estos,-as *adj pl* these.

éstos,-as *pron* these.

estragón *nm* tarragon.

estrangular *vt* to strangle.

estrategia *nf* strategy.

estrechar *vt* **1** *(calle)* to narrow; *(vestido)* to take in. **2** *(abrazar)* to embrace. • **estrechar la mano** to shake hands.

estrecho,-a *adj* **1** *(gen)* narrow; *(vestido, zapatos)* tight. **2** *(amistad etc)* close. ► *nm* **estrecho** straits.

estrella *nf* star. ▪ **estrella de mar** starfish.

estrellarse *vpr* to crash, smash.

estrenar *vt* **1** *(gen)* to use for the first time; *(ropa)* to wear for the first time. **2** *(obra de teatro)* to open; *(película)* to release.

estreno *nm* **1** *(de cosa)* first use. **2** *(de obra de teatro)* first night, opening night; *(de película)* premiere.

estreñimiento *nm* constipation.

estrés *nm* stress.

estribillo *nm* *(de canción)* chorus.

estribo *nm* stirrup. • **perder los estribos** to lose one's head.

estribor *nm* starboard.

estricto,-a *adj* strict.

estrofa *nf* stanza.

estropajo *nm* scourer.

estropear *vt* **1** *(máquina)* to damage, break. **2** *(plan etc)* to spoil, ruin. ► *vpr* **estropearse** **1** *(máquina)* to break down. **2** *(comida)* to go off.

estructura *nf* structure.

estruendo *nm* great noise, din.

estuario *nm* estuary.

estuche *nm* case, box.

estudiante *nmf* student.

estudiar *vt-vi* to study.

estudio *nm* **1** *(gen)* study. **2** *(apartamento, oficina; de cine, televisión)* studio. ► *nm pl* **estudios** studies, education.

estufa *nf* heater.

estupendo,-a *adj* wonderful.

estúpido,-a *adj* stupid. ► *nm,f* idiot.

etapa *nf* **1** *(gen)* stage. **2** *(en competición)* leg, stage.

eterno,-a *adj* eternal, everlasting.

ético,-a *adj* ethical.

etiqueta *nf* **1** *(rótulo)* label. **2** *(formalidad)* etiquette.

eucalipto *nm* eucalyptus.

euforia *nf* euphoria, elation.

euro *nm* euro.

Europa *nf* Europe.

europeo,-a *adj-nm,f* European.

evacuar *vt* to evacuate.

evadir *vt (capital)* to evade. ▶ *vpr* **evadirse** *(escaparse)* to escape.

evaluar *vt* to evaluate, assess.

evaporar(se) *vt-vpr* to evaporate.

evasión *nf* escape.

eventual *nmf* casual worker, temporary worker.

evidencia *nf* obviousness.

evidente *adj* evident, obvious.

evitar *vt* to avoid.

evolución *nf (gen)* evolution; *(de enfermedad)* development; *(de enfermo)* progress.

evolucionar *vi (gen)* to evolve; *(enfermedad)* to develop; *(enfermo)* progress.

exacto,-a *adj* exact, accurate.

exagerar *vt-vi* to exaggerate.

examen *nm* exam, examination. ▪ **examen de conducir** driving test; **examen médico** check-up, medical.

examinar *vt* 1 *(estudiante)* to examine. 2 *(considerar)* to look into, consider.

excavar *vt (gen)* to dig; *(en arqueología)* to excavate.

excelente *adj* excellent.

excepción *nf* exception.

excepcional *adj* exceptional.

excepto *adv* except, apart from.

exceso *nm (demasía)* excess; *(de mercancía)* surplus. ▪ **exceso de equipaje** excess baggage; **exceso de velocidad** speeding.

excitar *vt* 1 *(gen)* to excite. 2 *(emociones)* to stir up.

exclamación *nf* exclamation.

exclusivo,-a *adj* exclusive.

excursión *nf* excursion, outing.

excursionista *nmf (turista)* tripper; *(a pie)* hiker.

excusa *nf* excuse.

exhaustivo,-a *adj* exhaustive, thorough.

exhibición *nf* 1 *(exposición)* exhibition. 2 *(de película)* showing.

exhibir *vt (mostrar)* to exhibit, put on, show.

exigente *adj* demanding.

exigir *vt (pedir)* to demand; *(necesitar)* to require, demand.

exilio *nm* exile.

existencia *nf* existence. ▶ *nf pl* **existencias** inventory, stocks. ● **en existencia** in stock.

existir *vi* 1 *(ser real)* to exist. 2 *(haber)* to be.

éxito *nm* success. ● **tener éxito** to be successful.

exótico,-a *adj* exotic.
expedición *nf* **1** *(viaje, grupo)* expedition. **2** *(envío)* shipping.
expedir *vt* **1** *(documento)* to issue. **2** *(carta, paquete)* to dispatch.
experiencia *nf* experience.
experimentar *vt* **1** *(probar)* to test. **2** *(sentir)* to experience; *(cambio)* to undergo.
experimento *nm* experiment.
experto,-a *adj-nm,f* expert.
explicación *nf* explanation.
explicar *vt* to explain.
explorador,-ra *nm,f* explorer.
explorar *vt* to explore.
explosión *nf* explosion.
explosivo *nm* explosive.
explotación *nf* exploitation.
explotar *vt (sacar provecho de)* to exploit; *(mina)* to work; *(tierra)* to cultivate. ► *vi (explosionar)* to explode.
exponer *vt* **1** *(explicar)* to explain. **2** *(mostrar)* to show.
exportación *nf* export.
exportar *vt* to export.
exposición *nf* **1** *(de arte)* exhibition. **2** *(de fotografía)* exposure.
expresar(se) *vt-vpr* to express (oneself).
expresión *nf* expression.
expreso *nm (tren)* express train, express.
exprimir *vt* to squeeze.
expulsar *vt* **1** *(gen)* to expel. **2** *(jugador)* to send off.

expulsión *nf* **1** *(gen)* expulsion. **2** *(de jugador)* sending off.
exquisito,-a *adj* delicious.
extender *vt* **1** *(gen)* to extend. **2** *(cheque)* to make out. **3** *(mantequilla, pintura)* to spread.
extensión *nf* **1** *(gen)* extension. **2** *(dimensión)* extent.
exterior *adj* **1** *(de fuera)* exterior, outer. **2** *(extranjero)* foreign. ► *nm* exterior, outside.
externo,-a *adj* external, outward. • **"Para uso externo"** "External use only".
extinción *nf* extinction.
extintor *nm* fire extinguisher.
extra *adj* **1** *(adicional)* extra. **2** *(superior)* top. ► *nmf (actor)* extra. ► *nm* **1** *(gasto)* extra expense. **2** *(plus)* bonus.
extracto *nm* **1** *(substancia)* extract. **2** *(resumen)* summary. ■ **extracto de cuenta** statement of account.
extraer *vt* to extract.
extranjero,-a *adj* foreign. ► *nm,f* foreigner. • **vivir en el extranjero** to live abroad.
extraño,-a *adj* **1** *(raro)* strange. **2** *(desconocido)* alien, foreign.
extraordinario,-a *adj* extraordinary.
extraviado,-a *adj* missing, lost.
extremo,-a *adj* extreme. ► *nm* **extremo** **1** *(límite)* extreme; *(punta)* end. **2** *(en deporte)* wing.

F

fa *nf (nota)* F.

fábrica *nf* factory.

fabricar *vt (crear)* to make; *(en fábrica)* to manufacture.

fabuloso,-a *adj* fabulous.

fachada *nf* façade, front.

fácil *adj* easy.

facilitar *vt* **1** *(simplificar)* to make easy. **2** *(proporcionar)* to provide.

factor *nm* factor.

factoría *nf* factory.

factura *nf* bill.

facturar *vt* **1** *(cobrar)* to invoice; *(vender)* to have a turnover of. **2** *(equipaje)* to check in.

facultad *nf* **1** *(capacidad)* faculty. **2** *(de universidad)* faculty.

faena *nf* **1** *(tarea)* job. **2** *fam (mala pasada)* dirty trick.

faisán *nm* pheasant.

faja *nf (de mujer)* girdle.

fajo *nm (de billetes)* wad.

falda *nf* **1** *(prenda)* skirt. **2** *(regazo)* lap. **3** *(ladera)* slope. ▪ **falda pantalón** culottes.

fallar[1] *vt (tiro, penalty)* to miss. ▶ *vi (no funcionar)* to fail.

fallar[2] *vt (premio)* to award.

fallecimiento *nm* death.

fallo[1] *nm* **1** *(error)* mistake; *(fracaso)* failure. **2** *(defecto)* fault.

fallo[2] *nm* **1** *(de tribunal)* judgement. **2** *(premio)* awarding.

falsedad *nf* **1** *(hipocresía)* falseness. **2** *(mentira)* falsehood.

falsificar *vt* to forge.

falso,-a *adj* false, untrue.

falta *nf* **1** *(carencia)* lack, shortage. **2** *(ausencia)* absence. **3** *(error)* mistake: *falta de ortografía*, spelling mistake. **4** *(delito menor)* misdemeanour. **5** *(en fútbol)* foul; *(en tenis)* fault. ● **hacer falta** to be necessary: *no hace falta preguntar*, there is no need to ask; **sin falta** without fail. ▪ **falta de educación** bad manners.

faltar *vi* **1** *(cosa)* to be missing; *(persona)* to be absent. **2** *(haber poco)* to be needed: *me falta azúcar*, I haven't got enough sugar. **3** *(no acudir)* to miss. **4** *(quedar)* to be left: *faltan dos semanas para el examen*, there are two weeks to go till the exam. ● **¡no faltaba más!** *(por supuesto)* of course!

fama *nf* *(renombre)* fame, renown. ● **tener buena fama** to have a good name; **tener mala fama** to have a bad name.

familia *nf* **1** *(parientes)* family. **2** *(prole)* children.

famoso,-a *adj* famous.

fan *nf* fan.

fanático,-a *adj-nm,f* fanatic.

fango *nm (barro)* mud.

fantasía *nf* fantasy.

fantasma *nm (espectro)* ghost.
fantástico,-a *adj* fantastic.
faringe *nf* pharynx.
farmacéutico,-a *adj* pharmaceutical. ▶ *nm,f (de farmacia)* GB chemist; US druggist, pharmacist.
farmacia *nf (tienda)* GB chemist's; US drugstore, pharmacy.
faro *nm* 1 *(torre)* lighthouse. 2 *(en coche)* headlight.
farol *nm (de luz)* lantern; *(farola)* streetlamp, streetlight.
farola *nf* streetlight, streetlamp.
fascículo *nm* part, GB instalment; US installment.
fascinante *adj* fascinating.
fase *nf* 1 *(etapa)* stage. 2 *(en física)* phase.
fastidiar *vt* 1 *(molestar)* to annoy, bother. 2 *(dañar)* to hurt. ▶ *vpr* **fastidiarse** *(aguantarse)* to put up with: *si no le gusta que se fastidie,* if he doesn't like it that's tough.
fatal *adj* 1 *(inexorable)* fateful. 2 *(mortal)* deadly, fatal. 3 *fam (muy malo)* awful, terrible. ▶ *adv fam* badly, terribly: *me siento fatal,* I feel awful.
fatiga *nf (cansancio)* fatigue.
fauna *nf* fauna.
favor *nm* GB favour; US favor. ● **por favor** please;
favorable *adj* GB favourable; US favorable; *(condiciones)* suitable.

favorecer *vt* 1 *(ayudar)* GB to favour; US to favor. 2 *(agraciar)* to suit.
favorito,-a *adj-nm,f* GB favourite; US favorite.
fax *nm* fax. ● **enviar por fax** to fax.
fe *nf* faith. ● **de buena fe** in good faith.
febrero *nm* February.
fecha *nf* 1 *(día, mes, etc)* date. 2 *(día)* day. ● **hasta la fecha** to date. ■ **fecha de caducidad** best before date: *"Fecha de caducidad...",* "Best before...".
fecundación *nf* fertilization. ■ **fecundación in vitro** in vitro fertilization.
federación *nf* federation.
felicidad *nf* happiness. ● **¡felicidades!** congratulations!
felicitación *nf (tarjeta)* greetings card.
felicitar *vt* to congratulate.
feliz *adj* 1 *(contento)* happy. 2 *(acertado)* fortunate.
felpa *nf* felt.
felpudo *nm* doormat.
femenino,-a *adj (gen)* feminine; *(sexo)* female.
fenomenal *adj* 1 *(extraordinario)* phenomenal. 2 *fam (fantástico)* fantastic, terrific.
fenómeno *nm* 1 *(hecho)* phenomenon. 2 *(prodigio)* genius.
feo,-a *adj* ugly.
féretro *nm* coffin.

feria *nf* **1** *(exhibición)* fair. **2** *(fiesta)* fair, festival. ■ **feria de muestras** trade fair.

fermentar *vi* to ferment.

feroz *adj* fierce, ferocious.

ferretería *nf* *(tienda)* hardware store.

ferrocarril *nm* GB railway; US railroad.

fértil *adj* fertile.

fertilizante *nm* fertilizer.

festejo *nm* *(celebración)* celebration.

festival *nm* festival.

festivo,-a *adj* **1** *(alegre)* festive. **2** *(agudo)* witty.

fiable *adj* reliable.

fiambre *nm* cold meat.

fiambrera *nf* lunch box.

fianza *nf* **1** *(depósito)* deposit, security. **2** *(para acusado)* bail. ● **bajo fianza** on bail.

fiar *vt* to sell on credit. ▶ *vpr* **fiarse** to trust.

fibra *nf* GB fibre; US fiber.

ficción *nf* fiction.

ficha *nf* **1** *(tarjeta)* index card; *(datos)* file. **2** *(de máquina)* token. **3** *(en juegos)* counter; *(de ajedrez)* piece, man; *(de dominó)* domino.

fichar *vt* **1** *(anotar)* to put on an index card, put on a file. **2** *(futbolista etc)* to sign up. ▶ *vi* *(al entrar)* to clock in; *(al salir)* to clock out. ● **estar fichado,-a por la policía** to have a police record.

fichero *nm* **1** *(de ordenador)* file. **2** *(archivo)* card index.

fidelidad *nf* **1** *(lealtad)* fidelity. **2** *(exactitud)* accuracy.

fideo *nm* noodle.

fiebre *nf* fever. ● **tener fiebre** GB to have a temperature; US to have a fever.

fiel *adj* **1** *(leal)* faithful. **2** *(exacto)* accurate.

fieltro *nm* felt.

fiera *nf* **1** *(animal)* wild animal. **2** *(persona)* beast, brute. **3** *(genio)* wizard.

fiesta *nf* **1** *(día festivo)* holiday. **2** *(celebración)* party. ■ **la fiesta nacional** bullfighting.

figura *nf* figure.

figurarse *vpr* *(imaginarse)* to imagine.

fijador *nm* *(laca)* hair-spray, hair gel; *(gomina)* hair gel.

fijar *vt* **1** *(sujetar)* to fix, fasten. **2** *(pegar)* to stick. **3** *(establecer)* to set. ▶ *vpr* **fijarse** **1** *(darse cuenta)* to notice. **2** *(poner atención)* to pay attention.

fijo,-a *adj* **1** *(sujeto)* fixed, fastened. **2** *(permanente)* fixed, permanent.

fila *nf* **1** *(línea)* line. **2** *(en cine, clase)* row. ● **en fila india** in single file.

filete *nm* *(de carne, pescado)* fillet; *(solomillo)* sirloin.

filial *adj-nf* *(empresa)* subsidiary.

filmar *vt* *(gen)* to film; *(escena, película)* to shoot.

filo *nm* edge.

filosofía *nf* philosophy.

filósofo,-a *nm,f* philosopher.

filtro *nm* filter.

fin *nm* **1** *(final)* end. **2** *(objetivo)* purpose, aim. • **a fin de** in order to; **a fin de que** so that; **al fin y al cabo** when all's said and done; **en fin** anyway; **¡por fin!** at last! ■ **fin de año** New Year's Eve; **fin de semana** weekend.

final *adj* final. ► *nm (conclusión)* end. ► *nf (en competición)* final.

finalizar *vt-vi* to end, finish.

financiar *vt* to finance.

finanzas *nm pl* finances.

finca *nf* property, estate. ■ **finca urbana** building.

fingir *vt* to feign.

fino,-a *adj* **1** *(gen)* fine. **2** *(alimento)* fine, choice. **3** *(educado)* refined, polite. ► *nm* **fino** *(vino)* dry sherry. • **no estar fino** *(de salud)* **1** not to be feeling well. **2** *(agudo, centrado)* not to be on the ball.

firma *nf* **1** *(autógrafo)* signature. **2** *(acto)* signing. **3** *(empresa)* firm.

firmar *vt* to sign.

firme *adj* firm, steady.

fiscal *adj* fiscal. ► *nmf* GB public prosecutor; US district attorney.

física *nf* physics.

físico,-a *adj* physical.

flaco,-a *adj* skinny.

flan *nm* caramel custard, crème caramel.

flash *nm* flash.

flato *nm* stitch.

flauta *nf* flute. ■ **flauta dulce** recorder.

flecha *nf* arrow.

flemón *nm* gumboil, abscess.

flequillo *nm* GB fringe; US bangs *pl*.

flexible *adj* flexible.

flexo *nm* anglepoise lamp.

flojo,-a *adj* **1** *(suelto)* loose. **2** *(débil)* weak.

flor *nf* flower.

floreciente *adj* flourishing.

florero *nm* vase.

floristería *nf* florist's.

flota *nf* fleet.

flotador *nm* **1** *(para pescar)* float. **2** *(de niño)* rubber ring.

flotar *vi* to float.

flote *nm.* • **salir a flote** **1** *(recuperarse)* to get back on one's feet. **2** *(descubrirse)* to emerge.

fluido,-a *adj* **1** *(sustancia)* fluid. **2** *(lenguaje)* fluent. ► *nm* **fluido** fluid. ■ **fluido eléctrico** current.

flúor *nm* fluorine.

fluorescente *adj* fluorescent. ► *nm* fluorescent light.

foca *nf (animal)* seal.

foco *nm* **1** *(centro)* centre, focal point. **2** *(en fotografía, física)* focus. **3** *(lámpara)* spotlight.

folleto nm (prospecto) leaflet; (explicativo) instruction leaflet; (turístico) brochure.

fomentar vt (industria, turismo) to promote; (desarrollo, ahorro) to encourage.

fonda nf 1 (para comer) restaurant. 2 (para alojarse) guest house.

fondo nm 1 (parte más baja) bottom. 2 (parte más lejana) end, back. 3 (segundo término) background. ▶ nm pl **fondos** (dinero) funds. • **a fondo** thoroughly; **en el fondo** deep down, at heart. ▪ **fondo del mar** sea bed.

fontanero,-a nm,f plumber.

footing nm jogging.

forestal adj forest.

forma nf 1 (figura) form, shape. 2 (manera) way. 3 (condiciones físicas) form. • **de forma que** so that; **de todas formas** anyway; **estar en forma** to be fit. ▪ **forma de pago** method of payment; **forma física** physical fitness.

formación nf 1 (gen) formation. 2 (educación) training.

formal adj 1 (serio) serious. 2 (cumplidor) reliable, dependable.

formalidad nf (trámite) formality.

formar vt 1 (gen) to form. 2 (educar) to educate; (en técnicas) to train.

formatear vt to format.

formidable adj (maravilloso) wonderful.

fórmula nf formula.

formulario nm (documento) form.

forofo,-a nm,f fan.

forrar vt 1 (por dentro) to line. 2 (por fuera) to cover. ▶ vpr **forrarse** fam (de dinero) to make a packet.

forro nm 1 (interior) lining. 2 (funda) cover.

fortaleza nf 1 (vigor) strength. 2 (castillo) fortress.

fortuna nf 1 (suerte) luck. 2 (capital) fortune.

forzar vt to force.

fosa nf 1 (sepultura) grave. 2 (hoyo) pit. ▪ **fosas nasales** nostrils.

fósforo nm 1 (elemento) phosphorus. 2 (cerilla) match.

fósil nm fossil.

foso nm (gen) pit; (de castillo etc) moat.

foto nf fam photo. • **hacer una foto** to take a photo.

fotocopia nf photocopy.

fotografía nf 1 (proceso) photography. 2 (retrato) photograph.

fotógrafo,-a nm,f photographer.

fracaso nm failure.

fractura nf fracture.

frágil adj 1 (delicado) fragile. 2 (débil) frail.

fragmento *nm* **1** *(pedazo)* fragment. **2** *(literario)* passage.

fraile *nm* friar.

frambuesa *nf* raspberry.

francés,-esa *adj* French. ► *nm,f (persona)* French person. ► *nm* **francés** *(idioma)* French.

Francia *nf* France.

franela *nf* flannel.

franja *nf* band, strip.

franquear *vt (carta)* to frank. • **a franquear en destino** postage paid.

franqueo *nm* postage.

frasco *nm* flask.

frase *nf* **1** *(oración)* sentence. **2** *(expresión)* phrase.

fraterno,-a *adj* fraternal, brotherly.

fraude *nm* fraud. ■ **fraude fiscal** tax evasion.

frecuencia *nf* frequency.

frecuente *adj* **1** *(repetido)* frequent. **2** *(usual)* common.

fregadero *nm* kitchen sink.

fregar *vt* **1** *(lavar)* to wash. **2** *(frotar)* to scrub. **3** *(suelo)* to mop. • **fregar los platos** to do the washing up.

fregona *nf (utensilio)* mop.

freidora *nf* fryer.

freír *vt* to fry.

frenar *vt-vi* to brake.

freno *nm* **1** *(de vehículo)* brake. **2** *(de caballería)* bit.

frente *nm* front. ► *nf (de cara)* forehead. ► *adv* **frente a** in front of, opposite. • **al frente de** at the head of; **frente a frente** face to face.

fresa *nf* strawberry plant.

fresco,-a *adj* **1** *(gen)* cool. **2** *(comida)* fresh. **3** *(desvergonzado)* cheeky, shameless. ► *nm* **fresco** **1** *(frescor)* fresh air. **2** *(pintura)* fresco. • **hacer fresco** to be chilly.

fresno *nm* ash tree.

fresón *nm* large strawberry.

frialdad *nf* coldness.

fricción *nf* **1** *(gen)* friction. **2** *(friega)* rubbing.

frigorífico *nm* refrigerator, fridge.

frío,-a *adj* cold. ► *nm* **frío** cold. • **hacer frío** to be cold; **tener frío, pasar frío** to be cold.

frito,-a *adj (comida)* fried. ► *nm pl* **fritos** fried food *sing*.

frontal *adj* **1** *(choque)* head-on. **2** *(oposición)* direct.

frontera *nf (geográfica)* frontier; *(entre países)* border.

frotar *vt* to rub.

frustración *nf* frustration.

fruta *nf* fruit. ■ **fruta del tiempo** seasonal fruit.

frutal *nm* fruit tree.

frutería *nf* fruit shop.

frutero *nm* fruit bowl.

fruto *nm* fruit. ■ **frutos secos 1** *(almendras etc)* nuts. **2** *(pasas etc)* dried fruit.

fuego *nm* **1** *(gen)* fire. **2** *(lumbre)* light. **3** *(fogón de cocina)* burner, ring. • **a fuego lento 1** (*cocinar*) on a low flame. **2** (*al horno*) in a slow oven. • **¿me da fuego?** have you got a light? ▪ **fuegos artificiales** fireworks.

fuente *nf* **1** (*manantial*) spring. **2** (*artificial*) fountain. **3** (*recipiente*) serving dish. **4** (*de información*) source.

fuera *adv* **1** (*gen*) out, outside. **2** (*en otro lugar*) away; (*en el extranjero*) abroad. • **fuera de combate** knocked out. ▪ **fuera de juego** offside.

fuerte *adj* **1** (*gen*) strong. **2** (*intenso*) severe. **3** (*sonido*) loud. **4** (*golpe*) heavy. ► *nm* (*fortificación*) fort.

fuerza *nf* strength. • **a la fuerza** by force. ▪ **fuerza de voluntad** willpower **fuerzas del orden** police force.

fuga *nf* **1** (*escapada*) escape. **2** (*de gas, líquido*) leak.

fugarse *vpr* to flee, escape.

fumador,-ra *adj* smoking. ► *nm,f* smoker.

fumar(se) *vt-vi-vpr* to smoke. • "**No fumar**" "No smoking".

función *nf* **1** (*gen*) function. **2** (*espectáculo*) performance. • **en función de** according to.

funcionamiento *nm* operation, working.

funcionar *vi* to work. • "**No funciona**" "Out of order".

funcionario,-a *nm,f* civil servant.

funda *nf* **1** (*flexible*) cover. **2** (*rígida*) case. ▪ **funda de almohada** pillowcase.

fundación *nf* foundation.

fundador,-ra *nm,f* founder.

fundamental *adj* fundamental.

fundamento *nm* basis, grounds.

fundar *vt* **1** (*crear*) to found; (*erigir*) to raise. **2** (*basar*) to base, found.

fundir *vt* **1** (*un sólido*) to melt. **2** (*metal*) to cast; (*hierro*) to smelt. **3** (*bombilla, plomos*) to blow.

funeral *nm* **1** (*entierro*) funeral. **2** (*ceremonia*) memorial service.

funicular *nm* funicular railway.

furgoneta *nf* van.

furioso,-a *adj* furious.

fusible *nm* fuse.

fusil *nm* rifle.

fusilar *vt* (*ejecutar*) to shoot.

fusión *nf* **1** (*de metales*) fusion; (*de hielo*) thawing. **2** (*de empresas*) merger.

fútbol *nm* football, soccer.

futbolín *nm* GB table football, US table soccer.

futbolista *nmf* footballer, football player, soccer player.

futuro,-a *adj* future. ► *nm* futuro future.

G

gabardina *nf* raincoat.

gacela *nf* gazelle.

gafas *nf pl* glasses. ■ **gafas de sol** sunglasses.

gaita *nf* bagpipes.

gajo *nm (de naranja)* section.

gala *nf (espectáculo)* show: *cena de gala*, gala dinner; *traje de gala*, evening dress.

galardón *nm* award.

galaxia *nf* galaxy.

galería *nf* gallery. ■ **galería de arte** art gallery; **galerías comerciales** GB shopping arcade *sing*; US mall.

Gales (País de) *nm* Wales.

galés,-a *adj* Welsh. ► *nm,f (hombre)* Welshman; *(mujer)* Welshwoman. ► *nm* **galés** *(idioma)* Welsh.

galgo *nm* greyhound.

gallego,-a *adj-nm,f* Galician. ► *nm* **gallego** *(idioma)* Galician.

galleta *nf* GB biscuit; US cookie. ■ **galleta salada** cracker.

gallina *nf (ave)* hen.

gallinero *nm* **1** *(corral)* henhouse. **2** *(en teatro)* the gods.

gallo *nm* **1** *(ave)* cock, rooster. **2** *(nota falsa)* false note.

galón *nm (distintivo)* stripe.

galopar *vi* to gallop.

gama *nf (variedad)* range.

gamba *nf* prawn.

gamberro,-a *nm,f* hooligan.

gamo *nm* fallow deer.

gana *nf* wish, desire: *el equipo jugó sin ganas*, the team played half-heartedly. ● **de buena gana** willingly; **de mala gana** reluctantly; **dar la gana** to want, like: *no me da la gana*, I don't want to; **tener ganas de** to want, feel like.

ganadería *nf* **1** *(cría)* livestock farming. **2** *(ganado)* livestock.

ganado *nm* livestock.

ganador,-ra *nm,f* winner.

ganancia *nf* gain, profit.

ganar *vt* **1** *(premio, concurso)* to win. **2** *(dinero)* to earn. **3** *(a un contrincante)* to beat. ● **salir ganando** to do well.

gancho *nm* hook.

ganga *nf* bargain.

gangrena *nf* gangrene.

gángster *nm* gangster.

ganso *nm* goose; *(macho)* gander.

garaje *nm* garage.

garantía *nf* guarantee.

garbanzo *nm* chickpea.

garganta *nf* **1** throat. **2** *(desfiladero)* gorge.

garra *nf (de león, oso, etc)* claw; *(de águila, halcón, etc)* talon.

garrafa *nf* container.

gas *nm* gas.

gasa *nf* gauze.

gaseosa *nf* fizzy lemonade.

gaseoso,-a adj 1 (estado) gaseous. 2 (bebida) carbonated, fizzy.

gasoil nm diesel, diesel oil.

gasóleo nm diesel, diesel oil.

gasolina nf GB petrol; US gas, US gasoline. • **echar gasolina** to put some petrol in. ■ **gasolina normal** two-star petrol; **gasolina sin plomo** lead-free petrol; **gasolina súper** four-star petrol.

gasolinera nf GB petrol station; US gas station.

gastar vt 1 (dinero) to spend. 2 (usar) to use.

gasto nm 1 (de dinero) expenditure, expense. 2 (de agua, luz) consumption. • **con todos los gastos pagados** all expenses paid.

gastronomía nf gastronomy.

gatear vi to crawl.

gatillo nm (de arma) trigger.

gato,-a nm,f (animal) cat. ► nm gato (de coche) jack. • **a gatas** on all fours.

gaviota nf gull.

gazpacho nm cold tomato soup.

gel nm gel.

gelatina nf 1 (sustancia) gelatine. 2 (de fruta) jelly.

gemelo,-a adj-nm,f (hermano) twin. ► nm gemelo (músculo) calf muscle. ► nm pl gemelos 1 (de camisa) cufflinks. 2 (prismáticos) binoculars.

gen nm gene.

generación nf generation.

general adj general. ► nm (oficial) general. • **en general** in general; **por lo general** generally.

generar vt to generate.

género nm 1 (clase) sort: *es único en su género*, it's unique of its kind. 2 (gramatical) gender. 3 (especie) genus. 4 (en literatura) genre. 5 (tela) cloth. 6 (producto) article. ■ **géneros de punto** knitwear.

generoso,-a adj generous.

genético,-a adj genetic.

genial adj brilliant.

genio nm 1 (carácter) temper: *Paco tiene mal genio*, Paco is bad tempered. 2 (persona) genius. 3 (criatura imaginaria) genie.

gente nf people.

gentileza nf 1 (elegancia) grace. 2 (cortesía) politeness. • **por gentileza de** by courtesy of.

gentío nm crowd.

genuino,-a adj genuine, real.

geografía nf geography.

geología nf geology.

geometría nf geometry.

geranio nf geranium.

gerente nmf (hombre) manager; (mujer) manager, manageress.

germen nm germ.

gerundio nm gerund.

gesticular *vi* to gesticulate.

gestión *nf* 1 *(negociación)* negotiation. 2 *(de negocio)* administration, management. 3 *(trámite)* step.

gesto *nm* 1 *(gen)* gesture. 2 *(con la cara)* expression.

gestor,-ra *nm,f* agent.

gestoría *nf* business agency.

gigante,-a *adj-nm,f* giant.

gimnasia *nf* gymnastics. • **hacer gimnasia** to exercise, work out. ▪ **gimnasia rítmica** rhythmic gymnastics.

gimnasio *nm* gym(nasium).

ginebra *nf* gin.

ginecólogo,-a *nm,f* gynaecologist.

gira *nf (artística)* tour.

girar *vi* 1 *(dar vueltas)* to rotate, revolve; *(rápidamente)* to spin. 2 *(torcer)* to turn: **gira a la derecha**, turn right. 3 *(conversación)* to deal with.

girasol *nm* sunflower.

giro *nm* 1 *(vuelta)* turn. 2 *(de dinero, postal)* money order. 3 *(frase idiomática)* turn of phrase.

gitano,-a *adj-nm,f* gypsy.

glaciar *nm* glacier.

glándula *nf* gland.

global *adj* total.

globo *nm* 1 *(esfera)* globe, sphere. 2 *(de aire)* balloon. ▪ **globo ocular** eyeball; **globo terráqueo** globe.

glóbulo *nm* 1 globule. 2 *(en sangre)* corpuscle.

gloria *nf* 1 *(triunfo, honor)* glory. 2 *(fama)* fame.

glorieta *nf* 1 *(rotonda)* roundabout. 2 *(en jardín)* arbour, bower.

glorioso,-a *adj* glorious.

glucosa *nf* glucose.

gobernar *vt (país)* to govern.

gobierno *nm (de país)* government.

gol *nm* goal. • **marcar un gol** to score a goal.

golf *nm* golf.

golfo *nm (bahía)* gulf.

golondrina *nf* swallow.

golosinas *nf* GB sweets; US candy *sing.*

goloso,-a *adj* sweet-toothed.

golpe *nm* 1 *(porrazo)* blow, knock. 2 *(ruido)* knock, bang. 3 *(en coche)* bump. 4 *(desgracia)* blow. • **de golpe** suddenly; **no dar golpe** not to do a thing. ▪ **golpe de Estado** coup d'état.

golpear *vt* to hit.

goma *nf* 1 *(material)* rubber. 2 *(de borrar)* GB rubber; US eraser. 3 *(tira elástica)* elastic band.

gomina *nf* hair gel.

gordo,-a *adj* 1 *(persona, cara)* fat. 2 *(libro, jersey)* thick. 3 *(accidente, problema)* serious. ► *nm* **gordo** *(en lotería)* first prize, jackpot.

gorila *nm* gorilla.

gorra *nf (con visera)* cap; *(de bebé)* bonnet. • **de gorra** *fam* free.

gorrión *nm* sparrow.

gorro *nm* **1** *(de lana)* hat. **2** *(de bebé)* bonnet.

gota *nf* **1** *(de líquido)* drop. **2** *(enfermedad)* gout.

gotera *nf* leak.

gótico,-a *adj* Gothic.

gozar *vi* to enjoy oneself.

grabación *nf* recording.

grabado *nm* **1** *(técnica)* engraving, print. **2** *(ilustración)* picture.

grabadora *nf* recorder.

grabar *vt* **1** *(en piedra)* to engrave. **2** *(sonido, imagen)* to record. **3** INFORM to save.

gracia *nf* **1** *(donaire)* gracefulness. **2** *(encanto)* charm. **3** *(chiste)* joke. ● **dar las gracias a** ALGN to thank SB; **gracias a** thanks to; **hacer gracia** to be funny; **¡muchas gracias!** thank you very much!

gracioso,-a *adj* funny.

grada *nf* **1** *(peldaño)* step. **2** *(asiento)* row of seats.

grado *nm* degree.

graduable *adj* adjustable.

graduación *nf* **1** *(acción)* adjustment. **2** *(militar)* rank.

graduar *vt* **1** *(regular)* to adjust. **2** *(ordenar)* to grade. ● **graduarse la vista** to have one's eyes tested.

gráfico,-a *adj* graphic. ▶ *nm* **gráfico** graph. ■ **gráfico de barras** bar chart.

gragea *nf* pill.

gramática *nf* grammar.

gramo *nm* gram, gramme.

gran *adj* → grande.

granada *nf* **1** *(fruta)* pomegranate. **2** *(bomba)* grenade.

granate *adj-nm (color)* maroon.

grande *adj* **1** *(de tamaño)* big, large. **2** *(de número, cantidad)* large. **3** *(de importancia)* great.

granel *adv.* **a granel** *(sólidos)* loose, in bulk; *(líquidos)* in bulk.

granero *nm* granary, barn.

granizada *nf* hailstorm.

granizado *nm* iced drink.

granizar *vi* to hail.

granizo *nm* hail.

granja *nf* farm.

granjero,-a *nm,f* farmer.

grano *nm* **1** *(de arroz)* grain; *(de café)* bean. **2** *(en la piel)* spot, pimple.

grapa *nf* **1** *(para papel)* staple. **2** *(bebida)* grappa.

grapadora *nf* stapler.

grasa *nf* **1** *(comestible)* fat. **2** *(lubricante, suciedad)* grease.

gratinar *vt* to brown under the grill.

gratis *adv* free.

gratuito,-a *adj* free.

grava *nf* **1** *(piedras)* gravel. **2** *(piedra machacada)* broken stone.

grave *adj* **1** *(accidente, enfermedad)* serious: **está muy grave**, she's very seriously ill. **2** *(situación)* difficult. **3** *(voz)* deep, low.

gravedad *nf* **1** *(de la Tierra)* gravity. **2** *(importancia)* seriousness.

Grecia *nf* Greece.

griego,-a *adj-nm,f* Greek. ► *nm* **griego** *(idoma)* Greek.

grieta *nf* crack, crevice.

grifo *nm* GB tap; US faucet.

grillo *nm* *(insecto)* cricket.

gripe *nf* flu, influenza.

gris *adj-nm* GB grey; US gray.

gritar *vi* *(gen)* to shout; *(chillar)* to cry out, scream.

grito *nm* **1** *(gen)* shout. **2** *(de dolor)* cry. **3** *(de miedo)* scream. • **ser el último grito** to be the latest fashion.

grosella *nf* redcurrant. ■ **grosella silvestre** gooseberry.

grosero,-a *adj* **1** *(vulgar)* coarse, rough. **2** *(maleducado)* rude.

grosor *nm* thickness.

grúa *nf* **1** crane. **2** *(para averías)* breakdown van; *(por mal aparcamiento)* tow truck. • **"No aparcar, se avisa grúa"** "Any vehicles parked here will be towed away".

grueso,-a *adj* **1** *(objeto)* thick. **2** *(persona)* fat, stout.

grumete *nm* cabin boy.

grumo *nm* **1** *(de salsa)* lump. **2** *(de sangre)* clot.

gruñido *nm* **1** *(de cerdo)* grunt. **2** *(de perro)* growl.

grupo *nm* group. ■ **grupo de noticias** newsgroup.

gruta *nf* cave.

guante *nm* glove.

guantera *nf* glove compartment.

guapo,-a *adj* *(hombre)* good-looking; *(mujer)* pretty, beautiful.

guarda *nmf* *(vigilante)* guard; *(de zoo)* keeper. ■ **guarda de seguridad** security guard; **guarda jurado** armed security guard.

guardabarros *nm* mudguard.

guardabosque *nmf* forest ranger.

guardaespaldas *nm* bodyguard.

guardameta *nmf* goalkeeper.

guardar *vt* **1** *(en su sitio)* to put away. **2** *(mantener)* to keep. **3** *(para otra ocasión)* to save. **4** INFORM to save. • **guardar cama** to stay in bed; **guardar silencio** to remain silen.

guardarropa *nm* *(en museo, discoteca)* cloakroom.

guardería *nf* crèche, nursery.

guardia *nmf* *(vigilante)* guard. ► *nf* **1** *(servicio)* turn of duty. **2** *(tropa)* guard. • **estar de guardia** to be on duty. ■ **guardia urbana** local police.

guarida *nf* **1** *(de animales)* den. **2** *(de personas)* hideout.

guarnición *nf* **1** *filete con guarnición de patatas fritas*, steak with chips. **2** *(militar)* garrison.

guarro,-a adj **1** (sucio) dirty, filthy. **2** (indecente) disgusting, revolting.

guay adj fam great.

guerra nf war.

guerrillero,-a nm,f guerrilla.

guía nmf (persona) guide. ▶ nf (libro) guidebook: *una guía de Madrid*, a guide to Madrid. ■ **guía telefónica** telephone directory.

guiar vt (instruir, orientar) to guide, lead: *nos guió por la ciudad*, he took us round the city.

guinda nf cherry.

guindilla nf red pepper.

guiñar vt to wink.

guiñol nm puppet theatre.

guión nm **1** hyphen. **2** (de discurso) notes. **3** (de película) script.

guionista nmf scriptwriter.

guiri nmf arg foreigner.

guirnalda nf garland.

guisado,-a adj cooked, prepared. ▶ nm **guisado** stew.

guisante nm pea.

guisar vt (cocinar) to cook; (carne, pescado) to stew.

guiso nm stew.

güisqui nm whisky.

guitarra nf guitar. ■ **guitarra eléctrica** electric guitar.

guitarrista nmf guitarist.

gusano nm (de tierra) worm; (de mariposa) caterpillar. ■ **gusano de seda** silkworm.

gustar vi to like: *me gusta*, I like it; *le gusta leer*, she likes reading. ● **gustar más** to prefer: *¿cuál te gusta más?*; **cuando guste** fml whenever you want.

gusto nm **1** (sentido) taste. **2** (sabor) flavour: *no le noto el gusto*. **3** (placer) pleasure: *tenemos el gusto de invitarles a la boda*, we are pleased to invite you to the wedding. ● **con mucho gusto** with pleasure; **dar gusto** to be nice; **estar a gusto** to feel comfortable; **tanto gusto** pleased to meet you.

H

haba nf broad bean.

haber aux to have. ▶ nm **1** (cuenta corriente) credit. **2** (posesiones) property. ● **haber de** to have to, must: *he de salir*, I have to go out; **hay** there is/there are: *hay dos habitaciones*, there are two bedrooms; **hay que** you have to: *hay que tener mucho cuidado*, you have to be very careful.

hábil adj **1** (diestro) skilful. **2** (despabilado) clever.

habilidad nf skill.

habitación *nf* **1** *(cuarto)* room. **2** *(dormitorio)* bedroom.

habitante *nmf* inhabitant.

hábito *nm* habit.

habitual *adj* **1** *(normal)* usual. **2** *(cliente, visitante)* regular.

habla *nf* **1** *(facultad)* speech. **2** *(idioma)* language.

hablar *vi* **1** *(gen)* to talk. **2** *(en situaciones formales)* to speak. ► *vt* *(idioma)* to speak. • **¡ni hablar!** certainly not!

hacer *vt* **1** *(crear, producir, causar)* to make: *hacer la comida,* to make lunch. **2** *(actividad, estudios, trayecto)* to do: *hacer los deberes,* to do one's homework; *hicimos 250 km,* we did 250 km. ► *vi* *(tiempo meteorológico)* to be: *hace calor,* it's hot. ► *vpr* **hacerse** *(convertirse en)* to become, turn, get. • **hace 1** *(tiempo pasado)* ago: *compré la moto hace tres años,* I bought the bike three years ago. **2** *(tiempo que dura)* for: *tengo la moto desde hace tres años,* I've had the bike for three years.

hacha *nf* axe.

hacia *prep* **1** *(dirección)* towards. **2** *(tiempo)* about, around.

hacienda *nf* *(finca)* estate. ■ **hacienda pública** public funds, public finances.

hada *nf* fairy. ■ **hada madrina** fairy godmother.

halcón *nm* falcon.

hallar *vt* to find. ► *vpr* **hallarse** *(estar)* to be.

hamaca *nf* hammock.

hambre *nf* **1** *(apetito)* hunger. **2** *(escasez)* famine. • **tener hambre** to be hungry.

hamburguesa *nf* hamburger.

harina *nf* flour.

harto,-a *adj* **1** *(repleto)* full. **2** *fam (cansado)* fed up.

hasta *prep* **1** *(tiempo)* until, till: *hasta ahora,* until now. **2** *(lugar)* as far as: *te acompañaré hasta la iglesia,* I'll go with you as far as the church. ► *conj* even: *hasta mi hermano pequeño podría hacerlo,* even my little brother could do it. • **¡hasta luego!** see you later!; **hasta que** until.

haya *nf* *(árbol)* beech.

hazaña *nf* deed, exploit.

hebilla *nf* buckle.

hechizo *nm* spell, charm.

hecho,-a *adj* *(manufacturado)* made. ► *nm* **hecho 1** *(realidad)* fact. **2** *(suceso)* event. • **bien hecho** *(bistec)* well done; **de hecho** in fact.

hectárea *nf* hectare.

helada *nf* frost.

heladería *nf* GB ice-cream parlour; US ice-cream parlor.

helado *nm* ice cream.

helar *vi* to freeze.

helecho *nm* fern.

hélice *nf* propeller.

helicóptero *nm* helicopter.

hembra *nf* female.
hemisferio *nm* hemisphere.
hemorragia *nf* GB haemorrhage; US hemorrhage.
heredar *vt* to inherit.
hereditario,-a *adj* hereditary.
herencia *nf* **1** *(bienes)* inheritance. **2** *(genética)* heredity.
herida *nf (con arma)* wound; *(en accidente)* injury.
herido,-a *adj (con arma)* wounded; *(en accidente)* injured.
herir *vt (con arma)* to wound; *(en accidente)* to injure.
hermano,-a *nm,f (hombre)* brother; *(mujer)* sister.
hermoso,-a *adj* beautiful.
hernia *nf* hernia, rupture.
héroe *nm* hero.
heroína *nf* **1** *(mujer)* heroine. **2** *(droga)* heroin.
herradura *nf* horseshoe.
herramienta *nf* tool.
herrero *nm* blacksmith.
hervir *vt-vi* to boil.
hidratante *adj* moisturizing.
hidroavión *nm* seaplane.
hidrógeno *nm* hydrogen.
hiedra *nf* ivy.
hielo *nm* ice.
hiena *nf* hyaena, hyena.
hierba *nf* **1** *(césped, pasto)* grass. **2** *(para cocinar)* herb.
hierbabuena *nf* mint.
hierro *nm* iron. ▪ **hierro colado** cast iron; **hierro forjado** wrought iron.

hígado *nm* liver.
higiene *nf* hygiene.
higo *nm* fig. ▪ **higo chumbo** prickly pear.
higuera *nf* fig tree.
hijo,-a *nm,f (chico)* son; *(chica)* daughter; *(sin especificar)* child.
hilera *nf* row.
hilo *nm* **1** *(de coser)* thread. **2** *(lino)* linen. **3** *(telefónico)* wire. ▪ **hilo musical** piped music.
himno *nm* hymn. ▪ **himno nacional** national anthem.
hincar *vt* to drive in.
hincha *nmf* fan, supporter.
hinchar *vt* to inflate, blow up.
hinchazón *nf* swelling.
hipermercado *nm* hypermarket.
hípico,-a *adj (club)* riding.
hipo *nm* hiccups.
hipócrita *nmf* hypocrite.
hipódromo *nm* racetrack, racecourse.
hipopótamo *nm* hippopotamus.
hipoteca *nf* mortgage.
hispano,-a *adj* **1** *(de España)* Spanish, Hispanic. **2** *(de América)* Spanish-American. ► *nm,f (de América)* Spanish American; US Hispanic.
hispanoamericano,-a *adj* Spanish American.
histérico,-a *adj* hysterical.
historia *nf* **1** *(estudio del pasado)* history. **2** *(relato)* story.
historial *nm (médico)* record.

histórico,-a *adj* historical.
hobby *nm* hobby.
hockey *nm* hockey. ■ **hockey sobre hielo** ice hockey; **hockey sobre hierba** hockey.
hogar *nm* home. • **sin hogar** homeless.
hoguera *nf* bonfire.
hoja *nf* 1 *(de planta)* leaf. 2 *(de papel, metal)* sheet. 3 *(de libro)* page. 4 *(de cuchillo)* blade. ■ **hoja de afeitar** razor blade.
hojalata *nf* tin.
hojaldre *nm & nf* puff pastry.
hola *interj* hello!, hi!
Holanda *nf* Holland.
holandés,-esa *adj* Dutch. ► *nm,f* Dutch person. ► *nm* **holandés** *(idioma)* Dutch.
hombre *nm* man. ■ **hombre de negocios** businessman.
hombro *nm* shoulder.
homenaje *nm* tribute, homage.
homicidio *nm* homicide, murder.
homogéneo,-a *adj* homogeneous.
homosexual *adj-nmf* homosexual.
hondo,-a *adj* deep.
honesto,-a *adj* honest.
hongo *nm (planta)* fungus; *(como comida)* mushroom.
honor *nm* GB honour; US honor.
honrado,-a *adj* honest.
hora *nf* 1 *(60 minutos)* hour. 2 *(tiempo)* time: *¿qué hora es?*, what time is it?; *¿tiene hora, por favor?*, have you got the time? 3 *(cita)* appointment: *mañana tengo hora con el dentista*, I have an appointment with the dentist for tomorrow. • **de última hora** last-minute: *noticias de última hora*, breaking news. ■ **hora punta** 1 *(tráfico)* rush hour. 2 *(electricidad, teléfonos)* peak time; **horas de oficina** business hours; **horas extras** overtime.
horario *nm* 1 *(de trenes, clases)* timetable. 2 *(de trabajo, consulta)* hours. ■ **horario de atención al público** opening hours.
horca *nf* gallows.
horizontal *adj* horizontal.
horizonte *nm* horizon.
hormiga *nf* ant.
hormigón *nm* concrete. ■ **hormigón armado** reinforced concrete.
hormigueo *nm* prickling sensation.
hormona *nf* hormone.
horno *nm* 1 *(de cocina)* oven. 2 *(de fábrica)* furnace. • **al horno** 1 *(manzana, patata, pescado)* baked. 2 *(pollo)* roast.
horóscopo *nm* horoscope.
horquilla *nf* hairgrip.
horrible *adj* horrible, dreadful.
horror *nm* 1 *(miedo)* horror. 2 *fam (muchísimo)* an awful lot.

horroroso,-a *adj* **1** *(atroz)* horrible. **2** *(malísimo)* dreadful.

hortalizas *nf pl* vegetables.

hortensia *nf* hydrangea.

hospedarse *vpr* to stay.

hospital *nm* hospital.

hospitalidad *nf* hospitality.

hostal *nm* small hotel.

hostelería *nf* hotel and catering industry.

hostia *nf* **1** *(oblea)* host. **2** *fam (golpe)* thump. ► *interj* **¡hostia!** *fam (enfado)* damn it!, bugger!; *(sorpresa)* bloody hell!

hotel *nm* hotel.

hoy *adv* **1** *(día)* today. **2** *(actualmente)* now. • **hoy en día** nowadays; **hoy por hoy** at the present time.

hoyo *nm* hole.

hoz *nf* sickle.

hucha *nf* money box.

hueco *nm* hollow.

huelga *nf* strike. ▪ **huelga de celo** work-to-rule.

huella *nf* **1** *(de pie)* footprint; *(de animal, máquina)* track. **2** *(vestigio)* trace, sign. ▪ **huella dactilar** fingerprint.

huérfano,-a *adj-nm,f* orphan.

huerta *nf* *(de verduras)* vegetable garden; *(de frutales)* orchard.

huerto *nm* *(de verduras)* vegetable garden; *(de frutales)* orchard.

hueso *nm* **1** *(del cuerpo)* bone. **2** *(de aceituna, cereza)* stone.

huésped,-da *nm,f* guest.

huevo *nm* egg. ▪ **huevo duro** hard-boiled egg; **huevo escalfado** poached egg; **huevo estrellado** fried egg; **huevo frito** fried egg; **huevo pasado por agua** soft-boiled egg; **huevos revueltos** scrambled eggs.

huida *nf* escape, flight.

huir *vi* **1** *(escapar)* to escape, flee. **2** *(evitar)* to avoid STH: *huir de algo*, to avoid STH.

humanidad *nf* humanity.

humanitario,-a *adj* humanitarian.

humano,-a *adj* human.

humedad *nf* **1** *(en la atmósfera)* humidity. **2** *(en pared, suelo)* damp.

húmedo,-a *adj* **1** *(tiempo, clima)* humid. **2** *(pelo, tierra)* damp.

humilde *adj* humble.

humillar *vt* to humiliate, humble.

humo *nm* smoke.

humor *nm* **1** *(ánimo)* mood. **2** *(gracia)* GB humour; US humor. ▪ **humor negro** black comedy.

hundir *vt* **1** *(gen)* to sink. **2** *(mano, puñal)* to plunge. ► *vpr* **hundirse 1** *(gen)* to sink. **2** *(edificio)* to collapse. **3** *(empresa)* to go under. **4** *(bolsa, precio)* to plummet.

huracán *nm* hurricane.

I

ida *nf.* • **billete de ida** GB single; US one-way ticket; **billete de ida y vuelta** GB return ticket; US round-trip ticket.

idea *nf* idea.

ideal *adj-nm* ideal.

idéntico,-a *adj* identical.

identificar *vt* to identify.

ideología *nf* ideology.

idioma *nm* language.

idiota *nmf* idiot.

ídolo *nm* idol.

idóneo,-a *adj* suitable, fit.

iglesia *nf* church.

ignorancia *nf* ignorance.

ignorar *vt (no saber)* not to know, be ignorant of.

igual *adj* 1 *(idéntico)* the same. 2 *(en jerarquía)* equal. ► *nm (signo)* equals sign. ► *adv* 1 *(quizá)* maybe: **igual no vienen**, they may not come. 2 *(de la misma manera)* the same: **piensan igual**, they think the same. • **dar igual** not to matter; **es igual** it doesn't matter; **igual de...** as... as: **soy igual de alto que tú**, I'm as tall as you.

ilegal *adj* illegal.

ileso,-a *adj* unharmed, unhurt.

iluminación *nf* lighting.

iluminar *vt* to light up, illuminate.

ilusión *nf* 1 *(esperanza)* hope. 2 *(imagen falsa)* illusion. • **hacerle ilusión algo a** ALGN: **me hace mucha ilusión que vengas**, I'm really looking forward to you coming.

ilustración *nf* illustration.

ilustre *adj* illustrious, distinguished.

imagen *nf* 1 *(gen)* image. 2 *(en televisión)* picture.

imaginación *nf* imagination.

imaginar(se) *vt-vpr* to imagine.

imán *nm* magnet.

imbécil *nmf* idiot, imbecile.

imitación *nf* 1 *(copia)* imitation. 2 *(parodia)* impression.

imitar *vt* 1 *(copiar)* to imitate, copy. 2 *(gestos)* to mimic; *(como diversión)* to do an impression of, GB take off.

impaciente *adj* impatient.

impar *adj* odd.

imparcial *adj* impartial.

impasible *adj* impassive.

impedir *vt* 1 *(imposibilitar)* to prevent. 2 *(dificultar)* to impede, hinder.

imperativo *nm* imperative.

imperdible *nm* safety pin.

imperfecto,-a *adj (defectuoso)* flawed, imperfect. ► *nm* **imperfecto** imperfect, imperfect tense.

imperio *nm* empire.

impermeable *adj* waterproof. ► *nm* raincoat.

impersonal *adj* impersonal.
implantar *vt* 1 *(corazón, cabello)* to implant. 2 *(reforma)* to introduce.
implicar *vt (conllevar)* to imply.
imponer *vt* 1 *(castigo, tarea)* to impose. 2 *(respeto, miedo)* to inspire. ► *vpr* **imponerse** 1 *(hacerse obedecer)* to impose one's authority. 2 *(vencer)* to win.
importación *nf* import. ● **de importación** imported.
importancia *nf* importance.
importante *adj* important.
importar *vi* 1 *(tener importancia)* to matter: *no me importa*, I don't care. 2 *(molestar)* to mind: *¿te importaría cerrar la ventana?*, would you mind closing the window? ► *vt* to import. ● **no importa** it doesn't matter.
importe *nm* 1 *(coste)* cost. 2 *(cantidad)* amount.
imposible *adj* impossible.
impotente *adj* impotent.
imprenta *nf* 1 *(arte)* printing. 2 *(taller)* printer's, printing house.
imprescindible *adj* essential, indispensable.
impresión *nf* 1 *(sensación)* impression. 2 *(de texto)* printing.
impresionante *adj* impressive, striking.
impresionar *vt* 1 *(causar admiración a)* to impress. 2 *(conmover)* to touch, move.

impreso,-a *adj* printed. ► *nm* **impreso** *(formulario)* form.
impresora *nf* printer. ■ **impresora de chorro de tinta** inkjet printer; **impresora láser** laser printer.
imprevisto,-a *adj* unforeseen, unexpected.
imprimir *vt* to print.
improbable *adj* improbable.
improvisar *vt-vi* to improvise.
imprudente *adj (irreflexivo)* imprudent, rash; *(al conducir)* careless, reckless.
impuesto *nm* tax, duty. ■ **impuesto sobre el valor añadido (IVA)** value added tax *(VAT)*; **impuesto sobre la renta** income tax.
impulso *nm* 1 *(deseo súbito)* impulse, urge. 2 *(fuerza, velocidad)* momentum. 3 *(estímulo)* boost.
inadmisible *adj* unacceptable.
inaguantable *adj* intolerable, unbearable.
inalámbrico,-a *adj* cordless.
inauguración *nf* opening, inauguration.
inaugurar *vt* to open, inaugurate.
incapaz *adj* 1 *(no capaz)* incapable. 2 *(incompetente)* incompetent.
incendiar *vt* to set on fire, set fire to. ► *vpr* **incendiarse** to catch fire.

incendio *nm* fire. ▪ **incendio provocado** arson.

incentivo *nm* incentive.

incesante *adj* incessant, unceasing.

incidente *nm* incident.

incierto,-a *adj* 1 *(dudoso)* uncertain, doubtful. 2 *(desconocido)* unknown.

incinerar *vt (basura)* to incinerate; *(cadáver)* to cremate.

incisivo *nm (diente)* incisor.

incitar *vt* to incite

inclinación *nf* 1 *(pendiente)* slant, slope. 2 *(tendencia)* inclination.

inclinar *vt (ladear)* to tilt; *(cuerpo)* to bow; *(cabeza)* to nod.

incluir *vt* to include.

incluso *adv-conj-prep* even.

incógnita *nf* 1 unknown quantity. 2 *(misterio)* mystery.

incoherencia *nf* incoherence.

incoloro,-a *adj* colourless.

incómodo,-a *adj* 1 *(gen)* uncomfortable. 2 *(molesto)* awkward.

incomunicado,-a *adj* 1 *(aislado)* isolated; *(por la nieve)* cut off. 2 *(preso)* in solitary confinment.

inconfundible *adj* unmistakable.

inconsciente *adj* unconscious.

inconveniente *nm (desventaja)* drawback; *(dificultad)* problem.

incorporar *vt* to incorporate. ► *vpr* **incorporarse 1** *(levantarse)* to sit up. **2** *(a puesto, regimiento)* to join.

incorrecto,-a *adj* incorrect.

increíble *adj* incredible, unbelievable.

incremento *nm* increase.

incubadora *nf* incubator.

incurable *adj* incurable.

indecente *adj* indecent.

indeciso,-a *adj* indecisive.

indefenso,-a *adj* defenceless.

indefinido,-a *adj* 1 *(impreciso)* undefined, vague. 2 *(ilimitado)* indefinite.

indemnización *nf* 1 *(acción)* indemnification. 2 *(compensación)* compensation, indemnity.

independencia *nf* independence.

independiente *adj* independent.

indicación *nf* 1 *(señal)* sign. 2 *(observación)* hint.

indicador *nm (gen)* indicator; *(uso técnico)* gauge.

indicar *vt* to indicate, show.

indicativo,-a *adj-nm* indicative.

índice *nm* 1 *(gen)* index. 2 *(dedo)* index finger, forefinger. ▪ **índice de precios al consumo** retail price index.

indicio *nm* sign, indication.

indiferente *adj* indifferent.

indígena *adj-nmf* native.

indigente *nmf* destitute person.

indigestión *nf* indigestion.

indignar *vt* to infuriate, make angry. ► *vpr* **indignarse** to become annoyed.

indio,-a *adj-nm,f* Indian.

indiscreto,-a *adj* **1** *(falto de discreción)* indiscreet. **2** *(falto de tacto)* tactless.

indispensable *adj* indispensable, essential.

indispuesto,-a *adj* indisposed, unwell.

individual *adj (gen)* individual; *(habitación, cama)* single.

individuo *nm* person, individual.

indulto *nm* pardon.

indumentaria *nf* clothing, clothes.

industria *nf* industry.

industrial *adj* industrial.

inercia *nf* inertia.

inesperado,-a *adj* unexpected.

inevitable *adj* inevitable, unavoidable.

infalible *adj* infallible.

infancia *nf* childhood.

infantería *nf* infantry. ■ **infantería de marina** marines.

infantil *adj* **1** *(libro, enfermedad)* children's. **2** *(educación, población)* child.

infarto *nm* heart attack.

infección *nf* infection.

infeccioso,-a *adj* infectious.

infectar *vt* to infect.

infeliz *adj* unhappy.

inferior *adj* **1** *(gen)* lower. **2** *(en calidad)* inferior.

infierno *nm* hell.

infinitivo *nm* infinitive.

infinito,-a *adj* infinite.

inflación *nf* inflation.

inflamable *adj* inflammable.

inflamación *nf* inflammation.

inflar *vt* **1** *(globo, neumático)* to inflate, blow up. **2** *(hechos, noticias)* to exaggerate.

influencia *nf* influence.

influir *vi* to influence.

información *nf* **1** *(datos)* information. **2** *(oficina)* information desk. **3** *(noticias)* news.

informal *adj* **1** *(ambiente, reunión)* informal. **2** *(ropa)* casual.

informar *vt* to inform.

informática *nf* computer science, computing.

informático,-a *adj* computer, computing. ► *nm,f* computer expert.

informativo,-a *adj* informative. ► *nm* **informativo** news bulletin.

informe *nm* report.

infracción *nf (fiscal, de circulación)* GB offence; US offense; *(de ley)* infraction, infringement.

infusión *nf* infusion: *infusión de manzanilla*, camomile tea; *infusión de menta*, mint tea.

ingeniero,-a *nm,f* engineer.

ingenioso,-a *adj (inteligente)* ingenious, clever; *(con chispa)* witty.

ingenuo,-a *adj* naïve, ingenuous.

ingerir *vt* to consume, ingest.

Inglaterra *nf* England.

ingle *nf* groin.

inglés,-esa *adj* English. ▶ *nm,f (persona)* English person. ▶ *nm* **inglés** *(idioma)* English.

ingrediente *nm* ingredient.

ingresar *vt* 1 *(dinero)* to deposit, pay in. 2 *(paciente)* to admit. ▶ *vi (en colegio)* to enter; *(en club etc)* to become a member; *(en hospital)* to be admitted to.

ingreso *nm* 1 *(en organización)* entry. 2 *(en hospital, club, etc)* admission. 3 *(en cuenta bancaria)* deposit. ▶ *nm pl* **ingresos** income.

inicial *adj-nf* initial.

iniciar *vt* 1 *(introducir)* to initiate. 2 *(empezar)* to begin.

iniciativa *nf* initiative.

inicio *nm* beginning, start.

injusto,-a *adj* unjust, unfair.

inmediato,-a *adj* 1 *(reacción, respuesta)* immediate. 2 *(lugar)* next to, adjoining.

inmenso,-a *adj* immense.

inmigrante *adj-nmf* immigrant.

inmigrar *vi* to immigrate.

inmobiliaria *nf* GB estate agency; US real estate agency.

inmóvil *adj* still, motionless.

inmueble *nm* building.

inmunidad *nf* immunity.

innovación *nf* innovation.

inocente *adj* 1 *(libre de culpa)* innocent. 2 *(ingenuo)* naïve. 3 *(no culpable)* not guilty, innocent. ▶ *nmf (no culpable)* innocent person.

inodoro *nm* toilet.

inofensivo,-a *adj* inoffensive, harmless.

inoxidable *adj (gen)* rustproof; *(acero)* stainless.

inquietar(se) *vt-vpr* to worry.

inquieto,-a *adj* 1 *(agitado)* restless. 2 *(preocupado)* worried, anxious.

inquilino,-a *nm,f* tenant.

inscribirse *vpr* 1 *(en colegio)* to enrol. 2 *(en club, organización)* to join. 3 *(en concurso)* to enter.

inscripción *nf* 1 *(grabado)* inscription. 2 *(registro)* enrolment, registration.

insecticida *adj-nm* insecticide.

insecto *nm* insect.

inseguro,-a *adj* 1 *(falto de confianza)* insecure. 2 *(peligroso)* unsafe.

insertar *vt* to insert.

inservible *adj* useless, unusable.

insignia *nf (distintivo)* badge.

insignificante *adj* insignificant.

insinuar *vt* to insinuate, hint.
insípido,-a *adj* insipid.
insistir *vi* to insist.
insolación *nf* sunstroke.
insólito,-a *adj* unusual.
insomnio *nm* insomnia.
inspección *nf* inspection.
inspector,-ra *nm,f* inspector.
inspiración *nf* inspiration.
inspirar *vt* 1 *(aspirar)* to inhale, breathe in. 2 *(infundir)* to inspire.
instalación *nf* installation. ► *nf pl* **instalaciones** *(recinto)* installations; *(servicios)* facilities.
instalar *vt* to install. ► *vpr* **instalarse** to settle.
instantánea *nf* snapshot.
instantáneo,-a *adj* 1 *(repuesta, reacción)* instantaneous. 2 *(éxito, resultado, café)* instant.
instante *nm* moment, instant. • **al instante** immediately.
instinto *nm* instinct.
institución *nf* institution, establishment.
instituto *nm* 1 *(organismo)* institute. 2 *(de enseñanza)* GB secondary school; US high school. ■ **instituto de belleza** beauty salon.
instrucción *nf* education. ► *nf pl* **instrucciones** instructions.
instrumento *nm* instrument.
insuficiencia *nf* lack, shortage. ■ **insuficiencia cardíaca** heart failure; **insuficien-**

cia respiratoria respiratory failure.
insultar *vt* to insult.
insulto *nm* insult.
intacto,-a *adj* intact.
integración *nf* integration.
integral *adj* 1 *(total)* comprehensive. 2 *(sin refinar - pan, harina)* wholemeal; *(- arroz)* brown.
íntegro,-a *adj* 1 *(completo)* whole, entire. 2 *(honrado)* honest, upright.
intelectual *adj-nmf* intellectual.
inteligencia *nf* intelligence.
inteligente *adj* intelligent, clever.
intención *nf* intention.
intensidad *nf* *(gen)* intensity; *(de viento)* force.
intenso,-a *adj* *(gen)* intense; *(dolor)* acute.
intentar *vt* to try, attempt.
intento *nm* attempt, try.
intercambio *nm* exchange.
interés *nm* interest.
interesante *adj* interesting.
interesar *vi* to interest.
interferencia *nf* interference.
interfono *nm* intercom.
interior *adj* 1 *(jardín, patio)* interior. 2 *(estancia, piso)* inner. 3 *(bolsillo)* inside. 4 *(comercio, política)* domestic, internal. 5 *(mar, desierto)* inland. ► *nm* 1 *(parte interna)* inside, inner part. 2 *(de país)* interior.

interjección *nf* interjection.

intermedio,-a *adj* **1** *(nivel)* intermediate. **2** *(tamaño)* medium. ▶ *nm* **intermedio** intermission, interval.

intermitente *nm* GB indicator; US turn signal.

internacional *adj* international.

internauta *nmf* Net user.

interno,-a *adj* internal.

interpretación *nf* **1** *(explicación)* interpretation. **2** *(actuación)* performance. **3** *(traducción)* interpreting.

interpretar *vt (obra, pieza)* to perform; *(papel)* to play; *(canción)* to sing.

intérprete *nmf* **1** *(traductor)* interpreter. **2** *(actor, músico)* performer.

interrogación *nf (signo)* question mark.

interrogar *vt* **1** *(testigo)* to question. **2** *(sospechoso)* to interrogate, question.

interrumpir *vt* to interrupt.

interruptor *nm* switch.

interurbano,-a *adj (transporte)* intercity; *(llamada)* long-distance.

intervalo *nm* **1** *(de tiempo)* interval. **2** *(de espacio)* gap.

intervención *nf* **1** *(gen)* intervention. **2** *(operación)* operation. **3** *(discurso)* speech.

intervenir *vi* to take part. ▶ *vt (paciente)* to operate on.

intestino *nm* intestine.

íntimo,-a *adj* **1** *(secreto, ambiente)* intimate. **2** *(vida)* private. **3** *(amistad)* close.

intoxicación *nf* poisoning.

intranet *nm* intranet.

intriga *nf* **1** *(maquinación)* intrigue. **2** *(de película etc)* plot.

introducción *nf* introduction.

introducir *vt (meter)* to put in, insert. ▶ *vpr* **introducirse** to enter, get in.

intruso,-a *nm,f* intruder.

intuición *nf* intuition.

inundación *nf* flood(ing).

inútil *adj* useless.

invadir *vt* to invade.

inválido,-a *adj (persona)* disabled, handicapped.

invasión *nf* invasion.

invención *nf* invention.

inventar *vt* to invent.

invento *nm* invention.

invernadero *nm* greenhouse, hothouse.

invernal *adj* wintry, winter.

inversión *nf (de dinero, tiempo)* investment.

inverso,-a *adj* inverse.

invertir *vt* **1** *(orden)* to invert. **2** *(dinero, tiempo)* to invest.

investigación *nf* **1** *(policial, judicial)* investigation, inquiry. **2** *(científica, académica)* research.

investigar *vt* **1** *(indagar)* to investigate. **2** *(estudiar)* to do research on.

invierno *nm* winter.
invisible *adj* invisible.
invitación *nf* invitation.
invitado,-a *nm,f* guest.
invitar *vt* to invite: *déjame que te invite a un café*, let me buy you a coffee.
inyección *nf* injection.
ir *vi* **1** *(gen)* to go. **2** *(camino etc)* to lead. **3** *(funcionar)* to work. ▶ *aux* **1** **ir + a + infin**: *voy a salir*, I'm going out. **2** **ir + ger**: *vas mejorando*, you're getting better; *fuimos corriendo*, we ran. ▶ *vpr* **irse** *(marcharse)* to go away, leave.
ira *nf* anger, rage, wrath.
iris *nm* iris.
Irlanda *nf* Ireland. ▪ **Irlanda del Norte** Northern Ireland.
irlandés,-esa *adj* Irish. ▶ *nm,f* *(hombre)* Irishman; *(mujer)* Irish woman. ▶ *nm* **irlandés** *(idioma)* Irish.
irónico,-a *adj* ironic.
irregular *adj* irregular.
irritar *vt* to irritate, annoy.
isla *nf* island.
istmo *nm* isthmus.
Italia *nf* Italy.
italiano,-a *adj-nm,f* Italian.
itinerario *nm* itinerary, route.
izar *vt* to hoist.
izquierda *nf* **1** *(dirección)* left: *gira a la izquierda*, turn left. **2** *(mano)* left hand; *(pierna)* left leg. **3** POL left wing.
izquierdo,-a *adj* left.

J

jabalí *nm* wild boar.
jabón *nm* soap.
jabonera *nf* soapdish.
jacinto *nm* hyacinth.
jaleo *nm* *(alboroto)* racket, din.
jamás *adv* never; *(con superlativos)* ever: *jamás he escrito un libro*, I have never written a book; *el mejor libro que jamás se haya escrito*, the best book ever written.
jamón *nm* ham. ▪ **jamón de York** boiled ham; **jamón serrano** cured ham.
jaque *nm* check. ▪ **jaque mate** checkmate.
jaqueca *nf* migraine, headache.
jarabe *nm* syrup.
jardín *nm* garden. ▪ **jardín de infancia** nursery school.
jardinero,-a *nm,f* gardener.
jarra *nf* GB jug; US pitcher. ▪ **jarra de cerveza** beer mug.
jarro *nm* GB jug; US pitcher.
jarrón *nm* vase.
jaula *nf* cage.
jefe,-a *nm,f* *(superior)* boss; *(de departamento)* head; *(de tribu)* chief. ▪ **jefe de estación** station master; **jefe de Estado** Head of State.
jerarquía *nf* **1** *(gradación)* hierarchy. **2** *(categoría)* rank.

jergón *nm* straw mattress.

jeringuilla *nf* syringe.

jeroglífico *nm* **1** *(texto antiguo)* hieroglyph. **2** *(juego)* rebus.

jersey *nm* sweater, pullover, GB jumper.

jilguero *nm* goldfinch.

jinete *nm* rider, horseman.

jirafa *nf* giraffe.

jornada *nf* day.

joroba *nf (deformidad)* hump.

joven *adj* young. ► *nmf (hombre)* youth, young man; *(mujer)* girl, young woman.

joya *nf* jewel, piece of jewellery.

joyería *nf (tienda)* jewellery shop, jeweller's.

joyero *nm* jewel case, jewel box.

juanete *nm* bunion.

jubilación *nf* **1** *(acción)* retirement. **2** *(dinero)* pension.

jubilado,-a *nm,f* retired person.

jubilarse *vpr* to retire.

judía *nf (planta)* bean. ■ **judía blanca** haricot bean; **judía pinta** kidney bean; **judía verde** French bean, green bean.

judicial *adj* judicial.

judío,-a *adj* Jewish. ► *nm,f* Jew.

juego *nm* **1** *(para entretenerse)* game. **2** *(acto)* play. **3** *(en tenis)* game. **4** *(de apuestas)* gambling. **5** *(conjunto de piezas)* set. ● **a juego** matching; **hacer juego** to match.

juerga *nf fam* binge, rave-up.

jueves *nm* Thursday.

juez *nmf* judge. ■ **juez de banda** linesman; **juez de línea** linesman.

jugada *nf (en ajedrez)* move; *(en billar)* shot; *(en dardos)* throw.

jugador,-ra *nm,f* **1** *(en deportes, juegos)* player. **2** *(apostador)* gambler.

jugar *vt-vi* **1** *(gen)* to play. **2** *(apostar)* to bet.

jugo *nm* juice.

juguete *nm* toy.

juguetería *nf* toy shop.

juicio *nm* **1** *(facultad)* judgement. **2** *(sensatez)* reason, common sense. **3** *(proceso)* trial, lawsuit. ● **a mi juicio** in my opinion.

julio *nm* July.

jungla *nf* jungle.

junio *nm* June.

junta *nf* **1** *(reunión)* meeting. **2** *(conjunto de personas)* board, committee.

juntar *vt (unir)* to put together; *(piezas)* to assemble. ► *vpr* **juntarse** *(reunirse)* to get together.

junto,-a *adj* together. ► *adv.* ● **junto a** near, close to; **junto con** together with.

jurado *nm* **1** *(tribunal)* jury. **2** *(en concurso)* panel of judges, jury.

juramento *nm (promesa)* oath.
jurar *vt-vi* to swear.
justicia *nf* justice.
justificar *vt* to justify.
justo,-a *adj* **1** *(con justicia)* fair, just. **2** *(apretado)* tight. **3** *(exacto)* exact: **me dio el dinero justo**, she gave me the right money. **4** *(escaso)*: **me queda el dinero justo**, I've just got enough money left. ► *adv* **justo** exactly, precisely.
juvenil *adj-nmf (en deporte)* under 18.
juventud *nf* **1** *(edad)* youth. **2** *(conjunto de jóvenes)* young people, youth.
juzgado *nm* court.
juzgar *vt* **1** *(gen)* to judge. **2** *(en tribunal)* to try.

K

karaoke *nm* karaoke.
kárate *nm* karate.
kart *nm* go-cart.
kilo(gramo) *nm* kilo(gram).
kilométrico *nm* runabout ticket.
kilómetro *nm* kilometre, kilometer.
kiosko *nm* → quiosco.
kiwi *nm* kiwi.
Kleenex® *nm* Kleenex®, tissue.

L

la¹ *det* the.
la² *pron (persona, ella)* her; *(usted)* you; *(cosa, animal)* it.
la³ *nm (nota musical)* la, A.
labio *nm* lip.
labor *nf* **1** *(trabajo)* task. **2** *(de costura)* needlework; *(de punto)* knitting.
laborable *adj* working.
laboratorio *nm* laboratory.
labrador,-ra *nm,f* farm worker.
labrar *vt (tierra, metal)* to work.
laca *nf (para pelo)* hair lacquer, hair spray.
lácteo,-a *adj* dairy, milk.
ladera *nf* slope, hillside.
lado *nm* side. • **al lado** close by, near by; **al lado de** next to, beside.
ladrar *vi* to bark.
ladrillo *nm* brick.
ladrón,-ona *nm,f* thief.
lagartija *nf (wall)* lizard.
lagarto *nm* lizard.
lago *nm* lake.
lágrima *nf* tear.
laguna *nf* pool.
lamentar *vt* to regret, be sorry about.
lamer *vt* to lick.
lámpara *nf* lamp.
lamparón *nm* stain.
lana *nf* wool. • **de lana** woollen.

lancha *nf* launch.

langosta *nf* **1** *(crustáceo)* lobster. **2** *(insecto)* locust.

langostino *nm* prawn, king prawn.

lanza *nf* *(en torneo)* lance; *(arrojadiza)* spear.

lanzadera *nf* shuttle.

lanzamiento *nm* **1** *(de objeto)* throwing. **2** *(de cohete, producto)* launch. ▪ **lanzamiento de disco** the discus; **lanzamiento de jabalina** the javelin.

lanzar *vt* **1** *(tirar)* to throw. **2** *(cohete, nave, producto)* to launch.

lapa *nf* limpet.

lápida *nf* tombstone.

lápiz *nm* pencil. ▪ **lápiz de labios** lipstick.

largo,-a *adj* long. ▶ *nm* **largo** length: *tiene dos metros de largo*, it's two metres long. ● **a lo largo de** along, throughout.

largometraje *nm* feature film, full-length film.

laringe *nf* larynx.

larva *nf* larva.

las *det* the. ▶ *pron (ellas)* them; *(ustedes)* you.

láser *nm* laser.

lástima *nf* pity, shame.

lastimarse *vpr* to get hurt.

lata *nf* **1** *(envase)* tin, can. **2** *fam (fastidio)* bore, nuisance. ● **dar la lata** to annoy; **en lata** canned, tinned.

lateral *adj* lateral, side.

latido *nm* beat.

látigo *nm* whip.

latir *vi* to beat.

latitud *nf* latitude.

latón *nm* brass.

laurel *nm* **1** *(árbol)* bay tree. **2** *(hoja)* bay leaf.

lava *nf* lava.

lavabo *nm* **1** *(pila)* washbasin. **2** *(cuarto de baño)* bathroom. **3** *(público)* toilet.

lavadora *nf* washing machine.

lavandería *nf* laundry. ▪ **lavandería automática** GB launderette; US laundromat.

lavaplatos *nm* → lavavajillas.

lavar *vt* **1** *(manos, ropa)* to wash. **2** *(platos)* to wash. **3** *(limpiar)* to clean. ▶ *vpr* **lavarse** to have a wash, get washed.

lavavajillas *nm* **1** *(máquina)* dishwasher. **2** *(líquido)* washing-up liquid.

laxante *adj-nm* laxative.

lazo *nm* **1** *(lazada)* bow. **2** *(nudo)* knot.

le *pron* **1** *(objeto directo)* him; *(usted)* you. **2** *(objeto indirecto - a él)* him; *(- a ella)* her; *(a cosa, animal)* it; *(a usted)* you.

leal *adj* loyal, faithful.

lección *nf* lesson.

leche *nf* milk. ▪ **leche condensada** condensed milk;

leche descremada skimmed milk; **leche en polvo** powdered milk; **leche entera** whole milk.

lechón *nm* sucking pig.

lechuga *nf* lettuce.

lechuza *nf* barn owl.

lector *nm* reader.

lectura *nf* **1** *(acción)* reading. **2** *(textos)* reading matter.

leer *vt* to read.

legal *adj* legal.

legaña *nf* sleep.

legendario,-a *adj* legendary.

legislación *nf* legislation.

legislativo,-a *adj* legislative.

legislatura *nf* term of office.

legítimo,-a *adj* legitimate.

legumbre *nf* pulse.

lejano,-a *adj* distant.

lejía *nf* bleach.

lejos *adv* far, far away.

lencería *nf* **1** *(de mujer)* underwear, lingerie. **2** *(tienda)* lingerie shop.

lengua *nf* **1** *(en la boca)* tongue. **2** *(idioma)* language. **3** *(de tierra)* strip. ▪ **lengua materna** mother tongue.

lenguado *nm* sole.

lenguaje *nm* **1** *(gen)* language. **2** *(habla)* speech.

lengüeta *nf* *(de zapato)* tongue.

lente *nm & nf* lens. ▪ **lentes de contacto** contact lenses.

lenteja *nf* lentil.

lentilla *nf* contact lens.

lento,-a *adj* slow.

leña *nf* firewood.

leñador,-ra *nm,f* woodcutter.

leño *nm* log.

león,-ona *nm,f* *(macho)* lion; *(hembra)* lioness.

leopardo *nm* leopard.

leotardos *nm pl* thick tights.

lepra *nf* leprosy.

les *pron* **1** *(objeto indirecto - a ellos)* them; *(- a ustedes)* you. **2** *(objeto directo - ellos)* them; *(- ustedes)* you.

lesión *nf* injury.

lesionarse *vpr* to injure oneself, get injured.

letra *nf* **1** *(del alfabeto)* letter. **2** *(de imprenta)* type. **3** *(escritura)* handwriting. **4** *(de canción)* lyrics, words. ▪ **letra de cambio** bill of exchange, draft.

letrero *nm* sign, notice.

levadura *nf* yeast.

levantar *vt* **1** *(alzar)* to raise; *(bulto, trampilla)* to lift. **2** *(construir)* to erect, build. **3** *(sanción, embargo)* to lift. ▶ *vpr* **levantarse 1** *(ponerse de pie)* to rise, stand up. **2** *(de la cama)* to get up, rise.

leve *adj* **1** *(ligero)* light. **2** *(poco importante)* slight, trifling.

léxico,-a *adj* lexical.

ley *nf* *(gen)* law; *(del parlamento)* act, bill.

leyenda *nf* legend.

liar *vt* **1** *(cigarrillo)* to roll. **2** *(confundir)* to confuse.

libélula *nf* dragonfly.

liberación nf (de país) liberation; (de preso, rehén) freeing, release.

liberar vt (país) to liberate; (preso, rehén) to free, release.

libertad nf freedom, liberty. ▪ **libertad bajo fianza** bail.

libra nf (moneda, peso) pound.

libre adj free. ● **libre de impuestos** tax-free, duty-free.

librería nf 1 (tienda) bookshop. 2 (estantería) bookcase.

libreta nf notebook.

libro nm book. ▪ **libro de bolsillo** paperback; **libro de consulta** reference book; **libro de reclamaciones** complaints book; **libro de texto** textbook.

licencia nf 1 (documento) licence, permit. 2 (permiso) permission.

licenciado,-a nm,f graduate.

lícito,-a adj licit, lawful.

licor nm liqueur.

licuadora nf liquidizer.

líder nmf leader.

lidiar vt (toros) to fight.

liebre nf hare.

liga nf 1 (para media) garter. 2 (en política, deporte) league.

ligamento nm ligament.

ligar vt (salsa) to thicken. ▶ vi fam (conquistar) to pick up.

ligero,-a adj 1 (liviano) light. 2 (leve) slight. 3 (frívolo) flippant, thoughtless. ● **a la ligera** hastily.

light adj 1 (comida) low-calorie; (refresco) diet. 2 (tabaco) light.

lija nf sandpaper.

lila adj-nf lilac.

lima¹ nf (utensilio) file.

lima² nf (fruta) lime.

limitar vt to limit. ▶ vi to border.

límite nm 1 (tope) limit. 2 (frontera) boundary, border.

limón nm lemon.

limonada nf lemonade.

limosna nf alms. ● **pedir limosna** to beg.

limpiabotas nm bootblack.

limpiacristales nmf-nm window cleaner.

limpiaparabrisas nm GB windscreen wiper; US windshield wiper.

limpiar vt 1 (gen) to clean. 2 (con paño) to wipe.

limpio,-a adj 1 (gen) clean. 2 (persona) neat, tidy.

lince nm (animal) lynx.

línea nf 1 (gen) line. 2 (tipo) figure. ● **cuidar la línea** to watch one's weight; **en línea** on-line. ▪ **línea aérea** airline; **línea continua** solid white line; **línea férrea** railway line.

lingote nm ingot.

lino nm 1 (tela) linen. 2 (planta) flax.

linterna nf torch.

lío nm 1 (embrollo) mess, muddle. 2 (problema) trouble.

liquidación *nf* **1** *(de deuda)* settlement. **2** *(de mercancías)* clearance sale.

líquido,-a *adj* liquid. ► *nm* líquido liquid.

lírico,-a *adj* lyrical.

lirio *nm* iris.

liso,-a *adj* **1** *(superficie)* smooth, even. **2** *(pelo)* straight. **3** *(color)* plain.

lista *nf* list. ■ **lista de correo** mailing list; **lista de espera 1** *(gen)* waiting list. **2** *(para avión)* standby.

listado *nm* INFORM listing.

listín *nm* telephone directory.

listo,-a *adj* **1** *(preparado)* ready. **2** *(inteligente)* clever, smart.

litera *nf* *(en dormitorio)* bunk bed; *(en barco)* bunk; *(en tren)* couchette.

literatura *nf* literature.

litoral *nm* coast.

litro *nm* GB litre; US liter.

llaga *nf* ulcer, sore.

llama¹ *nf* *(de fuego)* flame. ● **en llamas** ablaze.

llama² *nf* *(animal)* llama.

llamada *nf* **1** *(telefónica)* phone call. **2** *(a la puerta)* knock; *(con timbre)* ring. ■ **llamada a cobro revertido** GB reverse-charge call; US collect call.

llamar *vt* **1** *(gen)* to call. **2** *(por teléfono)* to phone, call, ring. ► *vi (a la puerta)* to knock; *(al timbre)* to ring. ► *vpr* **llamarse**

to be called, be named: *¿cómo te llamas?*, what's your name?; *me llamo Juan*, my name is Juan.

llano,-a *adj (plano)* flat.

llanta *nf* rim.

llanto *nm* crying, weeping.

llanura *nf* plain.

llave *nf* **1** *(de puerta etc)* key. **2** *(herramienta)* spanner. ● **cerrar con llave** to lock. ■ **llave de contacto** ignition key; **llave de paso 1** *(del agua)* stopcock. **2** *(del gas)* mains tap; **llave inglesa** adjustable spanner; **llave maestra** master key.

llavero *nm* key ring.

llegada *nf* **1** *(gen)* arrival. **2** *(en deportes)* finishing line.

llegar *vi* **1** *(gen)* to arrive, reach. **2** *(alcanzar)* to reach: *¿llegas al estante?*, can you reach the shelf? **3** *(ser suficiente)* to be enough: *no me llega el dinero*, I haven't got enough money.

llenar *vt* gen) to fill (up); *(formulario)* to fill in. ► *vi* to be filling. ► *vpr* **llenarse** *(de gente)* to get crowded.

lleno,-a *adj* **1** *(gen)* full. **2** *(de gente)* crowded.

llevar *vt* **1** *(transportar)* to carry. **2** *(prenda)* to wear, have on. **3** *(acompañar)* to take; *(conducir, guiar)* to lead: *te llevaré al zoo*, I'll take you to the zoo. **4** *(libros, cuentas)* to

keep. **5** *(dirigir)* to be in charge of, manage, run. ▶ *vpr*
llevarse 1 *(coger)* to take. **2** *(premio)* to win. **3** *(estar de moda)* to be fashionable. **4** *(entenderse)* to get on.
llorar *vi* **1** *(persona)* to cry, weep. **2** *(ojos)* to water.
llover *vi* to rain.
llovizna *nf* drizzle.
lluvia *nf* rain.
lo *det* the. ▶ *pron (él)* him; *(usted)* you; *(cosa, animal)* it.
lobo,-a *nm,f (macho)* wolf; *(hembra)* she-wolf.
local *adj* local. ▶ *nm* premises.
localidad *nf* **1** *(pueblo)* village; *(ciudad)* town. **2** *(asiento)* seat. **3** *(entrada)* ticket. • **"No hay localidades"** "Sold out".
loción *nf* lotion.
loco,-a *adj* mad, crazy.
locomotora *nf* engine, locomotive.
locura *nf* madness, insanity.
locutor,-ra *nm,f* announcer.
lodo *nm* mud, mire.
lógico,-a *adj* logical.
lograr *vt* **1** *(trabajo, beca)* to get, obtain. **2** *(objetivo)* to attain, achieve.
lomo *nm* **1** *(de animal)* back. **2** *(de cerdo)* loin. **3** *(de libro)* spine.
lona *nf* canvas.
loncha *nf* slice.
longaniza *nf* pork sausage.
longitud *nf* **1** *(largo)* length. **2** *(geográfica)* longitude.

loro *nm* parrot.
los *det* the. ▶ *pron (ellos)* them; *(ustedes)* you.
lote *nm* **1** *(de productos)* lot. **2** *(en informática)* batch.
lotería *nf* lottery.
lubina *nf* bass.
lucha *nf* **1** *(pelea)* fight, struggle. **2** *(deporte)* wrestling.
luchar *vi* **1** *(pelear)* to fight. **2** *(como deporte)* to wrestle.
luciérnaga *nf* glow-worm.
luego *adv* **1** *(más tarde)* later. **2** *(después de algo)* then. ▶ *conj* therefore, then.
lugar *nm* **1** *(sitio)* place. **2** *(posición)* position. • **en lugar de** instead of.
lujo *nm* luxury. • **de lujo** luxury.
luna *nf* **1** *(astro)* moon. **2** *(cristal - de ventana)* window pane; *(- de vehículo)* windscreen. ■ **luna de miel** honeymoon; **luna llena** full moon.
lunar *adj* lunar. ▶ *nm* **1** *(en la piel)* mole; *(postizo)* beauty spot. **2** *(en tejido)* spot, polka-dot.
lunes *nm* Monday.
lupa *nf* magnifying glass.
luto *nm* mourning.
luz *nf* **1** *(gen)* light. **2** *fam (electricidad)* electricity. • **dar a luz** to give birth to. ■ **luces de carretera** full-beam headlights; **luces de cruce** dipped headlights; **luces de posición** sidelights.

M

macarrones *nm pl* macaroni.

macedonia *nf* fruit salad.

maceta *nf* plant pot, flowerpot.

macho *nm* 1 *(animal)* male. 2 *(pieza)* male piece, male part.

macizo,-a *adj* 1 *(sólido)* solid; *(fuerte)* well-built. ► *nm* **macizo** *(montañoso)* massif.

madera *nf* 1 *(gen)* wood; *(para la construcción)* timber.

madre *nf* mother.

madrina *nf* 1 *(de bautizo)* godmother. 2 *(de boda)* matron of honour.

madrugada *nf* 1 *(después de medianoche)* early morning. 2 *(alba)* dawn. • **de madrugada** in the small hours.

madrugar *vi* to get up early.

madurar *vt (fruta)* to ripen. ► *vi* to mature.

maduro,-a *adj* 1 *(persona)* mature. 2 *(fruta)* ripe.

maestro,-a *nm,f* teacher.

magdalena *nf* sponge cake.

magia *nf* magic.

magistrado,-a *nm,f* judge.

magnetófono *nm* tape recorder.

magnífico,-a *adj* magnificent, splendid.

mago,-a *nm,f* magician, wizard.

mahonesa *nf* mayonnaise.

maíz *nm* maize; US corn.

majestad *nf* majesty.

mal *adj* 1 *(desagradable, adverso)* bad. 2 *(enfermo)* ill. ► *adv* badly, wrong. • **menos mal que...** thank goodness...

maldición *nf* curse.

maldito,-a *adj fam* damned, bloody.

maleducado,-a *adj* rude, bad-mannered.

malentendido *nm* misunderstanding.

malestar *nm* 1 *(incomodidad)* discomfort. 2 *fig (inquietud)* uneasiness.

maleta *nf* suitcase, case. • **hacer la maleta** to pack.

maletero *nm (de coche)* GB boot; US trunk.

maletín *nm* briefcase.

maleza *nf* weeds.

malgastar *vt (tiempo)* to waste; *(dinero)* squander.

malherido,-a *adj* seriously injured.

malhumor *nm* bad temper.

malla *nf* 1 *(red)* mesh. 2 *(prenda)* leotard.

Mallorca *nf* Majorca.

malo,-a *adj* 1 *(perjudicial, imperfecto)* bad. 2 *(malvado)* wicked. • **estar malo,-a** to be ill.

maltratar *vt (animal)* to illtreat, mistreat; *(persona)* to batter.

malva *adj-nm (color)* mauve.

malvado,-a *nm,f* villain.

mama *nf (de mujer)* breast; *(de animal)* udder.

mamá *nf fam* mum(my).

mamar *vi (niño)* to suck.

mamífero *nm* mammal.

mampara *nf* screen.

manada *nf (de elefantes)* herd; *(de lobos)* pack.

manantial *nm* spring.

mancha *nf (de sangre, aceite, comida)* stain; *(de bolígrafo)* mark; *(en la piel)* spot.

manchar *vt-vi* to stain. ► *vpr* **mancharse** to get dirty.

manco,-a *adj* one-handed.

mandar *vt* **1** *(ordenar)* to order. **2** *(enviar)* to send.

mandarina *nf* mandarin, tangerine.

mandíbula *nf* jaw.

mando *nm* **1** *(autoridad)* command. **2** *(para mecanismos)* control. ▪ **mando a distancia** remote control.

manecilla *nf (de reloj)* hand.

manejable *adj* manageable, easy-to-handle.

manejar *vt* to handle, operate.

manera *nf* way, manner. • **de manera que** so that; **de ninguna manera** by no means; **de todas maneras** anyway, in any case. ▪ **manera de ser** character, the way SB is.

manga *nf* sleeve.

mango¹ *nm (asa)* handle.

mango² *nm (fruta)* mango.

manguera *nf* hose.

manía *nf* **1** *(ojeriza)* dislike. **2** *(obsesión)* mania.

manicomio *nm* mental hospital.

manifestación *nf* **1** *(de protesta etc)* demonstration. **2** *(expresión)* manifestation. **3** *(declaración)* statement, declaration.

manifestar *vt (opinión)* to express, state; *(sentimiento)* to show. ► *vpr* **manifestarse** *(en la calle)* to demonstrate.

manilla *nf (de reloj)* hand.

manillar *nm* handlebars.

maniobra *nf* manoeuvre.

manipular *vt* to manipulate.

maniquí *nm (muñeco)* dummy. ► *nmf (modelo)* model.

manivela *nf* crank.

manjar *nm* delicacy.

mano *nf* **1** *(de persona)* hand. **2** *(de pintura etc)* coat. • **dar la mano** *(saludar)* to shake hands; **de segunda mano** secondhand. ▪ **mano de obra** labour.

manojo *nm* bunch.

mansión *nf* mansion.

manso,-a *adj* tame, docile.

manta *nf* **1** *(para abrigarse)* blanket. **2** *(pez)* manta ray. ▪ **manta de viaje** travelling rug.

manteca *nf* fat. ▪ **manteca de cacao** cocoa butter; **manteca de cerdo** lard.

mantecado *nm* Christmas cake.

mantel *nm* tablecloth.

mantener *vt* 1 *(conservar)* to keep. 2 *(guardar)* to store. 3 *(sostener)* to support, hold up. 4 *(ideas)* to defend.

mantenimiento *nm* maintenance.

mantequilla *nf* butter.

manual *adj-nm* manual.

manuscrito *nm* manuscript.

manzana *nf* 1 *(fruta)* apple. 2 *(de casas)* block.

manzanilla *nf* 1 *(flor)* camomile. 2 *(infusión)* camomile tea. 3 *(vino)* manzanilla sherry.

manzano *nm* apple tree.

mañana *nf (parte del día)* morning. ► *nm (porvenir)* tomorrow, the future. ► *adv* tomorrow. • **hasta mañana** see you tomorrow; **pasado mañana** the day after tomorrow.

mapa *nm* map.

maquillaje *nm* make-up.

máquina *nf* machine. ■ **máquina de afeitar** razor, shaver; **máquina de escribir** typewriter; **máquina de fotos** camera; **máquina tragaperras** slot machine.

maquinilla *nf*. ■ **maquinilla de afeitar** razor.

mar *nm & nf* 1 *(gen)* sea. 2 *fam* very, a lot: *lo pasamos la mar de bien*, we had a great time. • **en alta mar** on the high seas; **hacerse a la mar**

to put out to sea. ■ **mar adentro** out to sea.

maravilloso,-a *adj* wonderful, marvellous.

marca *nf* 1 *(señal)* mark, sign. 2 *(de comestibles, productos del hogar)* brand; *(de otros productos)* make. 3 *(récord)* record. • **de marca** top-quality: *ropa de marca*, designer clothes. ■ **marca de fábrica** trademark; **marca registrada** registered trademark.

marcador *nm* scoreboard.

marcar *vt* 1 *(señalar)* to mark. 2 *(hacer un tanto)* to score. 3 *(a otro jugador)* to mark. 4 *(pelo)* to set. 5 *(al teléfono)* to dial.

marcha *nf* 1 *(caminar)* march. 2 *(partida)* departure. 3 *(música)* march. • **a marchas forzadas** against the clock; **salir de marcha** to go out. ■ **marcha atlética** walking race; **marcha atrás** reverse gear.

marcharse *vpr* to leave. • **¡marchando!** coming up!

marchitarse *vt-vpr* to wither.

marco *nm* frame.

marea *nf* tide. ■ **marea alta** high tide; **marea baja** low tide; **marea negra** oil slick.

mareado,-a *adj* 1 *(con náuseas)* sick. 2 *(aturdido)* dizzy, giddy. 3 *(borracho)* tipsy.

marearse *vpr (sentir náuseas)* to get sick; *(sentirse aturdido)* to feel dizzy.

mareo *nm* **1** *(con náuseas)* sickness. **2** *(aturdimiento)* dizziness.

marfil *nm* ivory.

margarina *nf* margarine.

margarita *nf* daisy.

margen *nm & nf* **1** *(gen)* margin. **2** *(extremidad)* border, edge. **3** *(de río)* bank.

marginar *vt* to leave out.

marido *nm* husband.

marinero *nm* sailor.

marino,-a *adj* marine. ► *nm* **marino** seaman.

marioneta *nf* puppet, marionette.

mariposa *nf* butterfly.

mariquita *nf* ladybird.

marisco *nm* shellfish, seafood.

marisma *nf* salt marsh.

marisquería *nf* seafood restaurant.

marítimo,-a *adj* maritime.

mármol *nm* marble.

marrón *adj-nm* brown.

martes *nm* Tuesday.

martillo *nm* hammer.

mártir *nmf* martyr.

marzo *nm* March.

mas *conj* but.

más *adv* **1** *(gen)* more: *más pequeño*, smaller; *más caro*, more expensive, dearer; *¿no quieres más?*, don't you want more? **2** *(superlativo)* most: *el más caro*, the most expensive; *el más pequeño*, the smallest. **3** *(de nuevo)* anymore: *no voy más a ese sitio*, I'm not going there anymore. **4** *(con pronombre)* else: *¿algo más?*, anything else? ► *pron* more. ► *nm (signo)* plus. • **de más** spare, extra; **más bien** rather; **más o menos** more or less; **ni más ni menos** no less; **por más (que)** however much.

masa *nf* **1** *(de volumen)* mass. **2** *(de pan)* dough.

masaje *nm* massage.

máscara *nf* mask.

mascarilla *nf* **1** *(cosmética)* face pack. **2** *(de médico)* face mask.

masculino,-a *adj* **1** *(no femenino)* male. **2** *(para hombres)* men's. **3** *(sustantivo)* masculine.

masticar *vt-vi* to masticate, chew.

mástil *nm* **1** mast. **2** *(de bandera)* flagpole.

mata *nf (arbusto)* bush. ■ **mata de pelo** mop of hair.

matadero *nm* slaughterhouse, abattoir.

matamoscas *nm (insecticida)* flykiller; *(pala)* flyswatter.

matar *vt-vi* to kill.

matasellos *nm* postmark.

mate *adj (sin brillo)* matt.

matemáticas *nf pl* mathematics.

materia *nf* **1** *(sustancia)* matter. **2** *(asignatura)* subject. ■ **materia prima** raw material.

material *adj-m* material. ■
material de oficina office
equipment.

materno,-a *adj* maternal: *le-che materna*, mother's milk.

matiz *nm* **1** *(color)* shade, tint.
2 *fig (variación)* nuance.

matorral *nm* bushes, thicket.

matrícula *nf* **1** *(en curso)* registration. **2** *(número)* registration
number; *(placa)* GB number
plate; US licence plate. ■ **matrícula de honor** honours.

matricular(se) *vt-vpr* to register, enrol.

matrimonio *nm* **1** *(ceremonia, institución)* marriage. **2**
(pareja) married couple.

maullido *nm* miaow.

maxilar *adj* maxillary. ► *nm*
jaw.

máximo,-a *adj* maximum.

mayo *nm* May.

mayonesa *nf* mayonnaise.

mayor *adj* **1** *(comparativo)* big-
ger, greater, larger; *(persona)*
older; *(hermanos, hijos)* elder.
2 *(superlativo)* biggest, great-
est, largest; *(persona)* oldest;
(hermanos, hijos) eldest. • **al
por mayor** wholesale.

mayordomo *nm* butler.

mayoría *nf* majority, most. ■
mayoría de edad adulthood.

mayorista *nmf* wholesaler.

mayúscula *nf* capital letter.

mazapán *nm* marzipan.

mazorca *nf* cob.

me *pron* **1** *(como objeto)* me. **2**
(reflexivo) myself.

mecánico,-a *adj* mechani-
cal. ► *nm,f* mechanic.

mecanismo *nm* mechanism.

mecanógrafo,-a *nm,f* typist.

mecedora *nf* rocking chair.

mecha *nf* **1** *(de vela)* wick. **2**
(de bomba) fuse. ► *nf pl* **me-
chas** *(en el pelo)* highlights.

mechero *nm* lighter.

mechón *nm* lock.

medalla *nf* medal.

media *nf* *(promedio)* average.
► *fpl* **medias** *(hasta la cintura)* tights; *(hasta la pierna)*
stockings.

mediano,-a *adj* **1** *(de tamaño)*
middle-sized. **2** *(de calidad)*
average, medium.

medianoche *nf* midnight.

mediante *adj* by means of.

medicamento *nm* medicine.

medicina *nf* medicine.

médico,-a *adj* medical. ► *nm,f*
doctor, physician.

medida *nf* **1** *(unidad)* measure.
2 *(disposición)* measure, step. •
a medida que as; **hecho a
medida** made-to-measure.

medio,-a *adj* **1** *(mitad)* half. **2**
(intermedio) middle. **3** *(promedio)* average. ► *nm* **medio 1**
(mitad) half. **2** *(centro)* middle.
► *adv* half. ► *nm pl* **medios**
means. • **a medias 1** *(sin terminar)* half done, half fin-
ished. **2** *(entre dos)* between

the two: *lo pagamos a medias*, we went halves on it.
■ **media pensión** half board; **medio ambiente** environment; **medio de transporte** means of transport; **medios de comunicación** the mass media.

mediocre *adj* mediocre.

mediodía *nm* **1** *(las doce)* noon, midday. **2** *(hora del almuerzo)* lunchtime.

medir *vt* **1** *(tomar medidas)* to measure. **2** *(calcular)* to gauge.

médula *nf* marrow. ■ **médula espinal** spinal cord.

medusa *nf* jellyfish.

megáfono *nm* megaphone, loudspeaker.

mejilla *nf* cheek.

mejillón *nm* mussel.

mejor *adj-adv* **1** *(comparativo)* better. **2** *(superlativo)* best. ● **a lo mejor** perhaps, maybe; **mejor dicho** rather; **tanto mejor** so much the better.

mejorar *vt* to improve. ▶ *vi-vpr* **mejorar(se)** **1** *(reponerse)* to recover, get better. **2** *(el tiempo)* to clear up.

melena *nf* **1** *(de persona)* long hair. **2** *(de león, caballo)* mane.

mellizo,-a *adj-nm,f* twin.

melocotón *nm* peach.

melodía *nf* melody.

melón *nm* melon.

membrana *nf* membrane.

membrete *nm* letterhead.

membrillo *nm* *(dulce)* quince jelly.

memoria *nf* **1** *(gen)* memory. **2** *(informe)* report. ▶ *nf pl* **memorias** *(biografía)* memoirs. ● **de memoria** by heart.

mencionar *vt* to mention.

mendigo,-a *nm,f* beggar.

mendrugo *nm* hard crust of bread.

menestra *nf* vegetable stew.

menisco *nm* meniscus.

menopausia *nf* menopause.

menor *adj* **1** *(comparativo)* smaller, lesser; *(persona)* younger. **2** *(superlativo)* smallest, least; *(persona)* youngest. ▶ *nmf* **menor (de edad)** minor. ● **al por menor** retail.

Menorca *nf* Minorca.

menos *adj* **1** *(comparativo - con incontables)* less; *(- con contables)* fewer. **2** *(superlativo - con incontables)* the least; *(con contables)* the fewest. ▶ *adv* **1** *(comparativo - con incontables)* less; *(- con contables)* fewer. **2** *(superlativo - con incontables)* the least; *(con contables)* the fewest. **3** *(para hora)* to: *las tres menos cuarto*, a quarter to three. ▶ *prep (excepto)* except, but. ▶ *nm* minus. ● **a menos que** unless; **al menos** at least; **por lo menos** at least.

mensaje *nm* message.

menstruación *nf* menstruation.

mensual *adj* monthly.
menta *nf* mint.
mental *adj* mental.
mente *nf* mind.
mentir *vi* to lie, tell lies.
mentira *nf* lie.
mentiroso,-a *nm,f* liar.
mentón *nm* chin.
menú *nm* menu.
menudo,-a *adj* **1** *(pequeño)* small, tiny. **2** fine: *¡menudo lío!,* what a fine mess! • **a menudo** often, frequently.
meñique *nm* little finger.
mercadillo *nf* market, street market.
mercado *nm* market. ■ **mercado de valores** stock-market.
mercancía *nf* goods.
mercería *nf* *(tienda)* GB haberdasher's; US notions store.
merecer(se) *vt-vi* to deserve.
merendar *vi* to have an afternoon snack, have tea.
merendero *nm* picnic spot.
merengue *nm* meringue.
merienda *nf* afternoon snack, tea.
mérito *nm* merit, worth.
merluza *nf* *(pescado)* hake.
mermelada *nf* *(de cítricos)* marmalade; *(de otras frutas)* jam.
mero *nm* *(pez)* grouper.
mes *nm* month.
mesa *nf* *(de salón, comedor)* table; *(de despacho)* desk. • **poner la mesa** to set the table;

quitar la mesa to clear the table.
meseta *nf* tableland, plateau.
mesilla *nf* small table. ■ **mesilla de noche** bedside table.
mesón *nm* inn, tavern.
mestizo,-a *adj* of mixed race, half-breed.
meta *nf* **1** *(portería)* goal; *(de carreras)* finishing line. **2** *fig (objetivo)* aim, goal.
metal *nm* metal.
metálico,-a *adj* metallic. • **pagar en metálico** to pay cash.
meter *vt* **1** *(introducir)* to put. **2** *(punto)* to score. ► *vpr* **meterse 1** *(entrar)* to get in. **2** *(entrometerse)* to interfere, meddle. • **meterse con** ALGN **1** *(burlarse)* to tease SB. **2** *(atacar)* to pick on SB.
método *nm* methodl.
metralleta *nf* submachine gun.
metro[1] *nm* *(medida)* metre.
metro[2] *nm* *(transporte)* GB underground, tube; US subway.
mexicano,-a *adj-nm,f* Mexican.
México *nm* Mexico.
mezcla *nf* **1** *(acción - de razas, colores)* mixing; *(- de cafés, tabacos)* blending. **2** *(producto - de razas, colores)* mixture; *(- de cafés, tabacos)* blend.
mezclar *vt* **1** *(razas, colores)* to mix; *(cafés, tabacos)* blend. **2** *(desordenar)* to mix up.

mezquita *nf* mosque.

mi¹ *adj* my.

mi² *nm (nota)* E.

mí *pron* **1** me. **2** *(mí mismo,-a)* myself.

michelín *nm fam* spare tyre.

microbio *nm* microbe.

micrófono *nm* microphone.

microondas *nm* microwave.

microscopio *nm* microscope.

miedo *nm* fear. • **tener miedo** to be afraid.

miel *nf* honey.

miembro *nm* **1** *(socio)* member. **2** *(extremidad)* limb.

mientras *conj* **1** while. **2** *(condición)* as long as, while. ▶ *adv* meanwhile. • **mientras tanto** meanwhile, in the meantime.

miércoles *nm* Wednesday.

mierda *nf* shit.

miga *nf* crumb.

migración *nf* migration.

migraña *nf* migraine.

mil *num* thousand.

milagro *nm* miracle.

milenio *nm* millenium.

milímetro *nm* millimetre.

militar *adj* military. ▶ *nm* military man, soldier. ▶ *vi* POL to be a militant.

milla *nf* mile.

millón *nm* million.

mimar *vt* to spoil.

mimbre *nm* wicker.

mina *nf* **1** *(gen)* mine. **2** *(de lápiz)* lead.

mineral *adj-nm* mineral.

miniatura *nf* miniature.

minifalda *nf* miniskirt.

mínimo,-a *adj (gasto)* minimal; *(cantidad, temperatura)* minimum. • **como mínimo** at least.

ministerio *nm* ministry; US department.

ministro,-a *nm,f* minister.

minoría *nf* minority.

minorista *nmf* retailer.

minúscula *nf* small letter.

minusválido,-a *adj* handicapped, disabled.

minutero *nm* minute hand.

minuto *nm* minute.

mío,-a *adj* my, of mine. ▶ *pron* mine.

miope *adj* short-sighted.

miopía *nf* shortsightedness, myopia.

mirada *nf* look.

mirador *nm* viewpoint.

mirar *vi* **1** *(ver)* to look at. **2** *(observar)* to watch.

mirilla *nf* peephole.

misa *nf* mass.

miseria *nf* **1** *(desgracia)* misery. **2** *(pobreza)* extreme poverty.

misil *nm* missile.

misión *nf* mission.

mismo,-a *adj* **1** *(igual)* same. **2** *(enfático - propio)* own; *(- uno mismo)* oneself: *lo haré yo mismo*, I'll do it myself. ▶ *pron* same. ▶ *adv* right: *aquí mismo*, right here.

misterio *nm* mystery.

mitad *nf* **1** half: *la mitad de una botella*, half a bottle. **2** *(en medio)* middle: *en mitad de la carretera*, in the middle of the road.

mitin *nm* rally.

mito *nm* myth.

mocasín *nm* loafer, moccasin.

mochila *nf* rucksack, backpack.

moco *nm* mucus.

moda *nf* fashion. • **pasado de moda** old-fashioned.

modales *nm pl* manners.

modelo *adj-nm* model. ▶ *nmf* fashion model.

módem *nm* modem.

moderar *vt* to moderate.

moderno,-a *adj* modern.

modesto,-a *adj* modest.

modificar *vt* to modify,.

modista *nmf (que confecciona)* dressmaker; *(que diseña)* fashion designer.

modo *nm* manner, way. • **de cualquier modo** anyway; **de ningún modo** by no means; **de todos modos** anyhow, in any case; **en cierto modo** to a certain extent.

módulo *nm* module.

moflete *nm fam* chubby cheek.

moho *nm* mould.

mojar *vt (empapar)* to wet; *(humedecer)* to dampen.

molde *nm* mould.

moler *vt (café)* to grind.

molestar *vt-vi* to disturb, bother. ▶ *vpr* **molestarse 1** *(tomarse el trabajo)* to bother. **2** *(ofenderse)* to get upset.

molestia *nf (incomodidad)* nuisance, bother. **2** *(dolor)* slight pain, discomfort. • **"Rogamos disculpen las molestias"** "We apologize for any inconvenience".

molido,-a *adj (café)* ground.

molinillo *nm* grinder, mill.

molino *nm* mill.

molusco *nm* mollusc.

momento *nm* **1** *(gen)* moment, instant. **2** *(época)* time. • **de momento** for the time being; **por el momento** for the time being.

momia *nf* mummy.

monaguillo *nm* altar boy.

monarquía *nf* monarchy.

monasterio *nm* monastery.

mondadientes *nm* toothpick.

moneda *nf* **1** *(unidad monetaria)* currency, money. **2** *(pieza)* coin.

monedero *nm* purse.

monitor,-ra *nm,f (profesor)* instructor. ▶ *nm* monitor *(pantalla)* monitor.

monja *nf* nun.

monje *nm* monk.

mono,-a *adj (bonito)* pretty, cute. ▶ *nm* **mono 1** *(animal)* monkey. **2** *(prenda)* overalls.

monopatín *nm* skateboard.

monótono,-a *adj* monotonous.

monstruo *nm* monster.

montacargas *nm* GB goods lift; US freight elevator.

montaje *nm* **1** *(de aparato, mueble)* assembly. **2** *(de película)* cutting, editing. **3** *(de obra teatral)* staging.

montaña *nf* mountain. ■ **montaña rusa** big dipper.

montañismo *nm* mountain climbing, mountaineering.

montar *vi* **1** *(a vehículo)* to mount, get on. **2** *(caballo, bicicleta)* to ride. ► *vt* **1** *(cabalgar)* to ride. **2** *(nata)* to whip; *(claras)* whisk. **3** *(máquinas)* to assemble. **4** *(negocio, exposición)* to set up. **5** *(película)* to edit, mount. **6** *(obra de teatro)* to stage.

monte *nm* mountain, mount.

montón *nm* **1** *(pila)* heap, pile. **2** *fam (gran cantidad)* loads great quantity.

montura *nf (de gafas)* frame.

monumento *nm* monument.

moño *nm (de pelo)* bun.

moqueta *nf* fitted carpet.

mora *nf* **1** *(de moral)* mulberry. **2** *(zarzamora)* blackberry.

morado,-a *adj* dark purple. ► *nm* **morado** **1** *(color)* dark purple. **2** *(golpe)* bruise.

moral *adj* moral. ► *nf* **1** *(reglas)* morality, morals. **2** *(ánimo)* morale, spirits.

morcilla *nf* black pudding.

morder *vt-vi* to bite.

mordisco *nm* bite.

moreno,-a *adj* dark. ► *nm* **moreno** suntan. ● **ponerse moreno** to tan.

morir(se) *vi-vpr* to die.

moro,-a *adj* **1** *(norteafricano)* Moorish. **2** *(musulmán)* Moslim.

morro *nm* **1** *fam (de persona)* mouth, lips. **2** *(de animal)* snout, nose.

morsa *nf* walrus.

mortadela *nf* mortadella.

mortal *adj* **1** *(persona)* mortal. **2** *(mortífero)* lethal.

mortero *nm* mortar.

mosaico *nm* mosaic.

mosca *nf* fly.

moscardón *nm* blowfly.

mosquearse *vpr* *fam (enfadarse)* to get cross.

mosquito *nm* mosquito.

mostaza *nf* mustard.

mosto *nm* grape juice.

mostrador *nm* counter. ■ **mostrador de facturación** check-in desk.

mostrar *vt (enseñar)* to show. ► *vpr* **mostrarse** to be: *se mostró muy interesado*, he was very interested.

mote *nm* nickname.

motín *nm* riot.

motivar *vt* **1** *(causar)* to cause, give rise to. **2** *(estimular)* to motivate.

motivo *nm* **1** *(causa)* motive, reason. **2** *(de dibujo, música)* motif. • **con motivo de** on the occasion of.

moto *nf fam* motorbike.

motocicleta *nf* motorbike.

motor,-ra *adj* motor. ► *nm* **motor** *(no eléctrico)* engine; *(eléctrico)* motor. ▪ **motor de búsqueda** search engine.

motora *nf* small motorboat.

motorista *nmf* motorcyclist.

mover(se) *vt-vpr* to move.

móvil *adj* movable, mobile. ► *nm* **1** *(teléfono)* mobile (phone), cellular phone. **2** *(motivo)* motive, inducement.

movimiento *nm* movement.

mozo,-a *nm* **1** *(de hotel)* buttons. **2** *(de estación)* porter.

muchacho,-a *nm,f (chico)* boy, lad; *(chica)* girl, lass.

muchedumbre *nf* crowd.

mucho,-a *adj* **1** *(frases afirmativas - singular)* a lot of, much; *(- plural)* a lot of, many. **2** *(frases negativas e interrogativas - singular)* much; *(- plural)* many. ► *pron (singular - frases afirmativas)* a lot, much; *(- frases negativas e interrogativas)* much; *(plural)* many. ► *adv* **mucho 1** *(gen)* a lot: *lo siento mucho*, I'm very sorry. **2** *(comparaciones)* much. **3** *(mucho tiempo)* a long time. **4** *(frecuentemente)* often, much.

mudanza *nf* removal.

mudarse *vpr* **1** *(gen)* to change. **2** *(de residencia)* to move.

mudo,-a *adj* dumb.

mueble *nm* piece of furniture.

mueca *nf* grimace.

muela *nf* tooth.

muelle[1] *nm (en puerto)* dock.

muelle[2] *nm (resorte)* spring.

muerte *nf* death.

muerto,-a *adj* dead. ► *nm,f* dead person. • **estar muerto de hambre** to be starving.

muestra *nf* **1** *(ejemplar)* sample. **2** *(señal)* proof, sign.

muestrario *nm* collection of samples.

mujer *nf* **1** woman. **2** *(esposa)* wife. ▪ **mujer de la limpieza** cleaning lady.

mulato,-a *adj-nm,f* mulatto.

muleta *nf* crutch.

mulo,-a *nm,f (macho)* mule; *(hembra)* she-mule.

multa *nf* fine.

multinacional *adj-nf* multinational.

múltiple *adj* **1** *(numeroso)* multiple. **2** *(muchos)* many, a number of.

multiplicar(se) *vt-vpr* to multiply.

multitud *nf* multitude, crowd.

mundial *adj* world(wide). ► *nm* world championship.

mundo *nm* world. • **todo el mundo** everybody.

municipal *adj* municipal.

municipio *nm* municipality.

muñeca *nf* **1** *(del brazo)* wrist. **2** *(juguete)* doll.

muñeco *nm* **1** *(monigote)* dummy. **2** *(juguete)* doll. ▪ **muñeco de nieve** snowman; **muñeco de peluche** soft toy.

mural *adj-nm* mural.

muralla *nf* wall.

murciélago *nm* bat.

murmurar *vi* to murmur.

muro *nm* wall.

muscular *adj* muscular.

músculo *nm* muscle.

museo *nm* museum.

musgo *nm* moss.

música *nf* music. ▪ **música de fondo** background music.

músico,-a *adj* musical. ▶ *nm,f* musician.

muslo *nm* thigh.

musulmán,-ana *adj-nm,f* Muslim, Moslem.

mutuo,-a *adj* mutual.

muy *adv* very.

N-Ñ

nabo *nm* turnip.

nácar *nm* mother-of-pearl.

nacer *vi* **1** *(persona, animal)* to be born. **2** *(río)* to rise.

nacimiento *nm* **1** *(de persona, animal)* birth. **2** *(de río)* source.

nación *nf* nation.

nacional *adj* **1** *(bandera, equipo, seguridad)* national. **2** *(productos, mercados, vuelos)* domestic.

nada *pron* nothing, not... anything. ▶ *adv* not at all: **no es nada fácil**, it isn't at all easy. • **como si nada** as if nothing had happened; **–de nada** –don't mention it.

nadar *vi* to swim.

nadie *pron* nobody, not... anybody.

naipe *nm* card.

nana *nf* lullaby.

naranja *nf* orange.

naranjada *nf* orangeade.

narcótico *nm* narcotic.

nariz *nf* nose.

narración *nf* **1** *(acción)* narration, account. **2** *(relato)* story.

nata *nf* **1** *(para montar)* cream. **2** *(de leche hervida)* skin.

natación *nf* swimming.

natal *adj* of birth. ▪ **ciudad natal** home town.

natillas *nf pl* custard.

nativo,-a *adj-nm,f* native.

natural *adj* **1** *(color, estado, gesto)* natural. **2** *(fruta, flor)* fresh. **3** *(yogur)* plain.

naturaleza *nf* nature.

naufragio *nm* *(de barco)* shipwreck.

náusea *nf* nausea, sickness. • **sentir náuseas/tener náuseas** to feel sick.

náutico,-a *adj* nautical.

navaja *nf* **1** *(cuchillo)* pen-knife, pocketknife. **2** *(molusco)* razor-shell. ▪ **navaja de afeitar** razor.

nave *nf* **1** *(barco)* ship. **2** *(de iglesia)* nave. ▪ **nave espacial** spaceship; **nave industrial** industrial building.

navegador *nm* browser.

navegar *vi* to navigate, sail. ● **navegar por Internet** to surf the Net.

Navidad *nf* Christmas: *¡Feliz Navidad!*, Merry Christmas!

necesario,-a *adj* necessary.

neceser *nm* GB toilet bag; US toilet kit.

necesidad *nf* **1** *(falta)* need. **2** *(cosa esencial)* necessity. ● **hacer sus necesidades** to relieve oneself.

necesitar *vt* to need. ● **"Se necesita camarero"** "Waiter required".

negar *vt* **1** *(acusación, afirmación)* to deny. **2** *(permiso, solicitud)* to refuse. ▶ *vpr* **negarse** to refuse.

negativo,-a *adj* negative.

negociación *nf* negotiation.

negociar *vi* **1** *(comerciar)* to trade, deal. **2** *(hablar)* to negotiate.

negocio *nm* **1** *(comercio, actividad)* business. **2** *(transacción)* deal, transaction.

negro,-a *adj* **1** *(color, raza, pelo)* black. **2** *(tono, ojos, piel)* dark. ▶ *nm* **negro** *(color)* black.

nervio *nm* nerve.

nervioso,-a *adj* nervous.

neto,-a *adj* net.

neumático *nm* GB tyre; US tire.

neutro,-a *adj* **1** *(neutral)* neutral. **2** *(género)* neuter.

● **nevada** *nf* snowfall.

nevar *vi* to snow.

nevera *nf* fridge, refrigerator.

ni *conj* **1** *(en doble negación)* neither… nor: *no tengo tiempo ni dinero*, I have got neither time nor money. **2** *(ni siquiera)* not even: *ni por dinero*, not even for money.

nido *nm* nest.

niebla *nf* fog.

● **nieto,-a** *nm,f* *(gen)* grandchild; *(niño)* grandson; *(niña)* granddaughter.

nieve *nf* snow.

ningún *adj* → ninguno,-a.

ninguno,-a *adj* no, not… any. ▶ *pron* **1** *(hablando de varias personas o cosas)* none: *ninguno de nosotros vio nada*, none of us saw anything. **2** *(hablando de dos personas o cosas)* neither: *ninguno de los dos funciona*, neither of them works. **3** *(nadie)* nobody, no one: *ninguno lo vio*, nobody saw it, no one saw it.

niñera *nf* nursemaid, nanny.

niño,-a *nm,f* (gen) child; (chico) boy; (chica) girl; (bebé) baby.

níspero *nm* medlar.

nivel *nm* 1 (en una escala, jerarquía) level. 2 (calidad) standard.

no *adv* 1 no, not. 2 (prefijo) non: **la no violencia**, nonviolence. ▶ *nm* no. • **..., ¿no?** *tag question*: **lo viste, ¿no?**, you saw it, didn't you?

noble *adj* noble.

noche *nf* night. • **buenas noches** 1 (saludo) good evening. 2 (despedida) good night; **esta noche** tonight; **por la noche** at night.

nochebuena *nf* Christmas Eve.

nochevieja *nf* New Year's Eve.

noción *nf* notion.

nocivo,-a *adj* harmful.

nogal *nm* walnut tree.

nómada *nmf* nomad.

nombre *nm* 1 (gen) name. 2 (sustantivo) noun. • **en nombre de** on behalf of. ■ **nombre de pila** first name, Christian name; **nombre y apellidos** full name.

nómina *nf* (sueldo) pay.

noria *nf* (de feria) big wheel.

norma *nf* rule.

normal *adj* 1 (común, usual) normal. 2 (nada especial) ordinary.

norte *adj-nm* north.

nos *pron* 1 (complemento) us. 2 (reflexivo) ourselves. 3 (recíproco) each othe.

nosotros,-as *pron* 1 (sujeto) we. 2 (complemento, con preposiciones) us.

nota *nf* 1 (anotación) note. 2 (calificación) GB mark; US grade. 3 (cuenta) bill. 4 (musical) note.

notar *vt* 1 (percibir) to notice. 2 (sentir) to feel. • **se nota que...** you can see that....

notario,-a *nm,f* notary.

noticia *nf* news: **una noticia**, a piece of news.

novato,-a *nm,f* novice, beginner.

novecientos,-as *num* nine hundred.

novedad *nf* 1 (cosa nueva) novelty. 2 (cambio) change.

novela *nf* novel.

noveno,-a *num* ninth.

noventa *num* ninety.

noviazgo *nm* engagement.

noviembre *nm* November.

novio,-a *nm,f* 1 (chico) boyfriend; (chica) girlfriend. 2 (prometido - chico) fiancé; (- chica) fiancée. 3 (en boda - hombre) bridegroom; (- mujer) bride.

nube *nf* cloud.

nublado,-a *adj* cloudy, overcast.

nuboso,-a *adj* cloudy.

nuca *nf* nape of the neck.

nuclear *adj* nuclear.
núcleo *nm* nucleus.
nudillo *nm* knuckle.
nudo *nm* knot.
nuera *nf* daughter-in-law.
nuestro,-a *adj* our, of ours.
▶ *pron* ours.
nueve *num* nine; *(en fechas)* ninth.
nuevo,-a *adj* new. • **de nuevo** again.
nuez *nf* walnut. ■ **nuez de Adán** Adam's apple; **nuez moscada** nutmeg.
nulo,-a *adj* invalid.
numerar *vt* to number.
número *nm* **1** *(gen)* number. **2** *(de zapatos)* size.
nunca *adv* **1** *(en negativa)* never. **2** *(en interrogativa)* ever. • **casi nunca** hardly ever; **nunca más** never again.
nutria *nf* otter.
nutritivo,-a *adj* nutritious, nourishing.
ñoqui *nm* gnocchi.
ñu *nm* gnu.

O

o *conj* or. • **o... o...** either... or.; **o sea** that is to say.
oasis *nm* oasis.
obedecer *vt* to obey.
obediente *adj* obedient.

obeso,-a *adj* obese.
obispo *nm* bishop.
objetivo,-a *adj* objective. ▶ *nm* **objetivo 1** *(fin)* aim, goal. **2** *(de ataque)* target. **3** *(lente)* lens.
objeto *nm* object.
oblicuo,-a *adj* oblique.
obligación *nf* obligation.
obligar *vt* to oblige, force.
obligatorio,-a *adj* compulsory, obligatory.
obra *nf* **1** *(de arte, ingeniería)* work; *(de literatura)* book; *(de teatro)* play. **2** *(acto)* deed. **3** *(edificio en construcción)* building site. ▶ *nf pl* **obras** *(en casa)* building work; *(en la calle)* roadworks. ■ **obra maestra** masterpiece.
obrero,-a *nm,f* worker.
obsequio *nm* gift.
observación *nf* observation.
observar *vt* **1** *(mirar)* to observe. **2** *(notar)* to notice.
obsesión *nf* obsession.
obstáculo *nm* obstacle, hindrance.
obstante. • **no obstante** however, nevertheless.
obstruirse *vpr* to get blocked up.
obtener *vt* to obtain.
obús *nm* shell.
obvio,-a *adj* obvious.
oca *nf* goose.
ocasión *nf* **1** *(momento)* occasion. **2** *(oportunidad)* opportu-

nity, chance. **3** *(ganga)* bargain. **• de ocasión 1** *(segunda mano)* secondhand. **2** *(barato)* bargain.

ocaso *nm* sunset.

occidental *adj* western.

occidente *nm* the West.

océano *nm* ocean.

ochenta *num* eighty.

ocho *num* eight; *(en fechas)* eighth.

ochocientos,-as *num* eight hundred.

ocio *nm (tiempo libre)* leisure.

octavo,-a *num* eighth.

octubre *nm* October.

oculista *nmf* oculist.

ocultar *vt* to hide.

ocupación *nf* occupation.

ocupado,-a *adj* **1** *(persona)* busy. **2** *(asiento)* taken; *(aseos, teléfono)* engaged.

ocupar *vt* **1** *(conquistar)* to occupy. **2** *(llenar)* to take up.

ocurrir *vi* to happen, occur. ► *vpr* **ocurrirse**: *no se le ocurrió preguntar*, it didn't occur to her to ask.

odiar *vt* to hate.

odio *nm* hatred.

odontólogo,-a *nm,f* dental surgeon, odontologist.

oeste *nm* west.

ofender *vt* to offend.

ofensiva *nf* offensive.

oferta *nf* **1** *(propuesta, ganga)* offer. **2** *(en concurso)* bid, tender. **• de oferta** on offer.

oficial *adj* official. ► *nm* **1** *(militar)* officer. **2** *(empleado)* clerk. **3** *(obrero)* journeyman.

oficina *nf* office.

oficinista *nmf* office worker.

oficio *nm (trabajo manual especializado)* trade; *(profesión)* profession.

ofimática *nf* office automation.

ofrecer *vt* **1** *(dar - premio, trabajo)* to offer; *(- banquete, fiesta)* to hold. **2** *(presentar - posibilidad)* to give; *(- dificultad)* to present.

oído *nm* **1** *(sentido)* hearing. **2** *(órgano)* ear.

oír *vt* to hear.

ojal *nm* buttonhole.

ojeras *nm pl* bags under the eyes.

ojo *nm* **1** *(órgano)* eye. **2** *(agujero)* hole. **• a ojo** at a rough guess. **■ ojo de buey** porthole; **ojo de la cerradura** keyhole.

ola *nf* wave.

oleaje *nm* swell.

óleo *nm (material)* oil paint; *(cuadro)* oil painting.

oler *vt-vi* to smell. **• olerse algo** to suspect STH.

olfato *nm* sense of smell.

oliva *nf* olive.

olivo *nm* olive tree.

olla *nf* pot. **■ olla a presión** pressure cooker.

olmo *nm* elm.

olor *nm* smell.
olvidar *vt* 1 *(gen)* to forget. 2 *(dejar)* to leave.
olvido *nm (lapsus)* oversight.
ombligo *nm* navel.
once *num* eleven; *(en fechas)* eleventh.
onceavo,-a *num* eleventh.
onda *nf* wave.
ondear *vi (bandera)* to flutter.
opaco,-a *adj* opaque.
opción *nf* option.
ópera *nf* opera.
operación *nf* operation.
operador,-ra *nm,f* operator. ■ **operador turístico** tour operator.
operar *vt* to operate.
opinar *vt* to think. ► *vi* to express an opinion.
opinión *nf (juicio)* opinion. • **cambiar de opinión** to change one's mind.
oponer *vt (resistencia)* to offer. ► *vpr* **oponerse** 1 *(estar en contra)* to oppose. 2 *(ser contrario)* to be opposed.
oportunidad *nf* 1 *(ocasión)* opportunity. 2 *(ganga)* bargain. 3 *(conveniencia)* advisability.
oposición *nf* 1 *(enfrentamiento)* opposition. 2 *(examen)* competitive examination.
oprimir *vt* 1 *(tecla, botón)* to press. 2 *(persona, pueblo)* to oppress.
optativo,-a *adj* optional.

óptica *nf* 1 *(tienda)* optician's. 2 *(ciencia)* optics.
optimismo *nm* optimism.
opuesto,-a *adj* opposite.
oración *nf* 1 *(rezo)* prayer. 2 *(frase)* clause, sentence.
orador,-ra *nm,f* speaker.
oral *adj* oral. • **por vía oral** to be taken orally.
orangután *nm* orangutan.
órbita *nf* 1 *(de satélite)* orbit. 2 *(de ojo)* socket.
orca *nf* killer whale.
orden *nm (disposición)* order. ► *nf* 1 *(mandato, asociación)* order. 2 *(judicial)* warrant. • **del orden de** GB in the order of; US on the order of. ■ **orden del día** agenda; **orden público** law and order.
ordenado,-a *adj* tidy.
ordenador *nm* computer. ■ **ordenador portátil** laptop.
ordenar *vt* 1 *(arreglar)* to put in order; *(habitación)* to tidy up. 2 *(mandar)* to order.
ordeñar *vt* to milk.
ordinario,-a *adj* 1 *(corriente)* ordinary. 2 *(grosero)* vulgar, common.
orégano *nm* oregano.
oreja *nf* ear.
organigrama *nm (de empresa)* organization chart; *(de procedimiento, sistema)* flow chart.
organismo *nm* 1 *(ser viviente)* organism. 2 *(entidad pública)* organization, body.

organización *nf* organization.

organizar *vt* to organize.

órgano *nm* organ.

orgullo *nm* pride.

orgulloso,-a *adj* proud.

orientación *nf* **1** *(dirección)* orientation. **2** *(guía)* guidance.

oriental *adj* eastern.

orientar *vt* **1** *(dirigir)* to orientate. **2** *(guiar)* to guide. ► *vpr* **orientarse 1** *(encontrar el camino)* to find one's way about.

oriente *nm* east.

orificio *nm* orifice.

origen *nm* origin: *de origen español*, of Spanish extraction.

original *adj-nm* original.

orilla *nf* **1** *(borde)* edge. **2** *(del río)* bank; *(del mar)* shore.

orina *nf* urine.

orinal *nm* *(de adulto)* chamber pot; *(de niño)* potty.

oro *nm* gold.

orquesta *nf* **1** *(clásica, sinfónica)* orchestra. **2** *(banda)* dance band.

orquídea *nf* orchid.

ortiga *nf* nettle.

ortografía *nf* spelling.

oruga *nf* caterpillar.

os *pron* **1** *(complemento directo)* you. **2** *(complemento indirecto)* to you. **3** *(reflexivo)* yourselves. **4** *(recíproco)* each other.

oscuridad *nf* darkness.

oscuro,-a *adj* **1** *(lugar, color)* dark. **2** *(origen, explicación)* obscure. • **a oscuras** in the dark.

oso *nm* bear. ■ **oso de peluche** teddy bear; **oso hormiguero** anteater.

ostentar *vt* **1** *(exhibir)* to flaunt. **2** *(poseer)* to hold.

ostra *nf* oyster.

otoño *nm* GB autumn; US fall.

otorgar *vt* *(conceder)* to grant; *(premio)* to award.

otro,-a *adj* **1** *(con sustantivo en singular)* another; *(precedido de determinante o adjetivo posesivo)* other: *vino otra persona en su lugar*, another person came in his place; *la otra silla era más cómoda*, the other chair was more confortable. **2** *(con sustantivo en plural)* other: *entre otras cosas*, amongst other things. ► *pron* **1** *(singular)* another, another one. **2 el otro, la otra** *(cosa, persona)* the other one. **3 los otros, las otras** *(cosa)* the other ones, the others; *(personas)* the others. • **otro tanto** as much.

ovación *nf* ovation.

ovalado,-a *adj* oval.

ovario *nm* ovary.

oveja *nf* sheep

óvulo *nm* ovule.

oxidado,-a *adj* rusty.

oxígeno *nm* oxygen.

oyente *nmf* *(de la radio)* listener. ► *nm pl* **oyentes** audience.

ozono *nm* ozone. ■ **capa de ozono** ozone layer.

P

pabellón *nm* **1** *(edificio - aislado)* block, section; *(- anexo en feria)* pavilion. **2** *(de la oreja)* outer, ear. ▪ **pabellón deportivo** sports hall.

paciencia *nf* patience.

paciente *adj-nmf* patient.

pacífico,-a *adj* peaceful.

pacto *nm* pact, agreement.

padecer *vt-vi* to suffer.

padre *nm* father. ▪ **padre de familia** family man.

padrenuestro *nm* Lord's Prayer.

padrino *nm* **1** *(de bautizo)* godfather. **2** *(de boda)* best friend.

paella *nf* paella.

paga *nf* pay; *(de niños)* pocket money. ▪ **paga extra** bonus.

pagar *vt* *(compra, entrada)* to pay for; *(sueldo, alquiler, cuenta)* to pay; *(deuda)* to pay off.

página *nf* page. ▪ **páginas amarillas** yellow pages.

pago *nm* payment. ▪ **pago por visión** pay per view.

país *nm* country.

paisaje *nm* **1** *(terreno)* landscape. **2** *(vista)* scenery.

paja *nf* straw.

pajarería *nf* pet shop.

pajarita *nf* **1** *(lazo)* bow tie. **2** *(de papel)* paper bird.

pájaro *nm* bird. ▪ **pájaro carpintero** woodpecker.

pala *nf* **1** *(para cavar)* spade. **2** *(de pelota)* bat.

palabra *nf* word. ● **tener la palabra** to have the floor. ▪ **palabra clave** keyword.

palabrota *nf* swearword.

palacio *nm* palace. ▪ **palacio de congresos** conference centre; **palacio de deportes** sports centre.

paladar *nm* palate.

palanca *nf* lever. ▪ **palanca de cambio** gear lever, gearstick.

palangana *nf* washbasin.

palco *nm* box. ▪ **palco de autoridades** royal box.

pálido,-a *adj* pale.

palillo *nm* **1** *(mondadientes)* toothpick. **2** *(de tambor)* drumstick. ▪ **palillos chinos** chopsticks.

paliza *nf* **1** *(zurra)* beating, thrashing. **2** *(derrota)* defeat. **3** *fam* *(pesadez)* bore.

palma *nf* **1** *(planta)* palm tree. **2** *(de la mano)* palm.

palmera *nf* palm tree.

palo *nm* **1** *(vara)* stick. **2** *(mástil)* mast. ● **a palo seco** on its own. ▪ **palo de golf** golf club.

paloma *nf* dove, pigeon.

palomitas *nf pl* popcorn.

palpitación *nf* palpitation.

pamela *nf* sun hat.

pan *nm* *(alimento)* bread; *(hogaza)* round loaf; *(barra)* French loaf. ▪ **pan de molde** sliced bread; **pan integral** wholemeal bread; **pan rallado** breadcrumbs.

pana *nf* corduroy.

panadería *nf* bakery, baker's.

panal *nm* honeycomb.

pancarta *nf* placard.

páncreas *nm* pancreas.

panda *nm* panda.

pandereta *nf* small tambourine.

panel *nm* panel.

panfleto *nm* pamphlet.

pánico *nm* panic.

panorama *nm* panorama, view.

pantalla *nf* 1 *(gen)* screen. 2 *(de lámpara)* shade.

pantalón *nm* trousers. ■ **pantalón corto** shorts (trousers); **pantalón vaquero** jeans.

pantano *nm (de fango)* marsh; *(embalse)* reservoir.

pantera *nf* panther.

pantorrilla *nf* calf.

pañal *nm* GB nappy ; US diaper.

paño *nm* 1 *(tela)* cloth, material. 2 *(trapo para polvo)* duster. ■ **paño de cocina** tea cloth, tea towel.

pañuelo *nm* 1 *(para sonarse)* handkerchief. 2 *(complemento)* scarf. ■ **pañuelo de papel** tissue.

papa *nm (pontífice)* pope.

papá *nm fam* dad, daddy. ■ **Papá Noel** Father Christmas.

papagayo *nm* parrot.

papel *nm* 1 *(material)* paper. 2 *(hoja)* piece of paper, sheet of paper. 3 *(en obra, película)* role, part. ■ **papel de aluminio** aluminium foil; **papel de fumar** cigarette paper; **papel de lija** sandpaper; **papel de plata** silver paper, tinfoil; **papel higiénico** toilet paper; **papel pintado** wallpaper.

papelera *nf* 1 *(en oficina)* wastepaper basket. 2 *(en la calle)* GB litter bin; US litter basket.

papelería *nf* stationer's.

paperas *nf pl* mumps.

papilla *nf* 1 *(para enfermo)* pap. 2 *(para bebé)* baby food.

paquete *nm (de libros, ropa)* package, parcel; *(de tabaco, folios, galletas)* packet; *(de azúcar, harina)* bag. ■ **paquete postal** parcel.

par *adj* even. ► *nm (pareja)* pair. ● **a la par 1** *(al mismo tiempo)* at the same time. **2** *(juntos)* together; **de par en par** wide open; **sin par** matchless.

para *prep* **1** *(finalidad)* for, to, in order to: *para ahorrar dinero*, (in order) to save money. **2** *(dirección)* for, to: *el tren para Toledo*, the train to Toledo; *para adelante*, forwards; *para atrás*, backwards. **3** *(tiempo, fechas límites)* by: *déjalo para luego*, leave it for later. ● **para en-**

tonces by then; **para que** in order that, so that; **¿para qué?** what for?

parabrisas *nm* GB windscreen; US windshield.

paracaídas *nm* parachute.

parachoques *nm (de coche)* GB bumper; US fender.

parada *nf* **1** *(gen)* stop. **2** DEP save. ■ **parada de taxis** GB taxi stand; US cab stand.

parado,-a *adj* **1** *(quieto)* still, motionless. **2** *(desempleado)* unemployed. ● **salir bien/mal parado de algo** to come off well/badly out of STH.

parador *nm* hotel.

paraguas *nm* umbrella. ■ **paraíso fiscal** tax haven.

paraje *nm* spot, place.

paralelo,-a *adj* parallel.

parálisis *nf* paralysis. ■ **parálisis cerebral** cerebral palsy.

paralítico,-a *adj-nm,f* paralytic.

paralizarse *vpr* **1** *(miembro)* to be paralysed. **2** *(actividad)* to come to a standstill.

parapente *nm (deporte)* paragliding; *(paracaídas)* paraglider.

parar(se) *vt-vi-vpr (gen)* to stop. ● **ir a parar** to end up; **sin parar** nonstop, without stopping.

pararrayos *nm* lightning conductor.

parásito *nm* parasite.

parche *nm* patch.

parchís *nm* GB ludo; US Parcheesi®.

parcial *adj* partial. ▶ *nm (examen)* mid-term exam.

parecer *vi* **1** *(por cómo se percibe)* to seem; *(por su aspecto externo)* to look. **2** *(opinar)* to think: *si te parece bien…*, if it's all right with you… **3** *(aparentar)* to look as if: *parece que va a llover*, it looks as if it's going to rain. ▶ *vpr* **parecerse 1** to look alike, be alike: *Hugo y su hermano se parecen*, Hugo and his brother look alike. **2** to look like: *Hugo se parece a su padre*, Hugo looks like his father. ▶ *nm (opinión)* opinion. ● **al parecer** apparently.

parecido,-a *adj* similar.

pared *nf* wall.

pareja *nf* **1** *(gen)* pair. **2** *(de personas)* couple. **3** *(de baile, compañero)* partner. ● **hacer buena pareja** to be two of a kind. ■ **pareja de hecho** unmarried couple.

parentesco *nm* kinship, relationship.

paréntesis *nm* **1** *(signo)* parenthesis, bracket. **2** *(pausa)* break, interruption. ● **entre paréntesis** in brackets.

pariente,-a *nm,f* relative.

parir *vi* to give birth.

parking *nm (público)* GB car-park; US parking lot; *(particular)* garage: *una plaza de parking*, a parking space.

parlamento *nm* parliament.

paro *nm* **1** *(desempleo)* unemployment. **2** *(interrupción)* stoppage. **3** *(dinero)* unemployment benefitt. • **estar en el paro** to be out of work, unemployed. ▪ **paro cardiaco** cardiac arrest.

párpado *nm* eyelid.

parque *nm* park. ▪ **parque de atracciones** funfair; **parque infantil** children's playground; **parque natural** nature reserve; **parque temático** theme park; **parque zoológico** zoo.

parqué *nm* parquet.

parra *nf* grapevine.

párrafo *nm* paragraph.

parrilla *nf* grill. • **a la parrilla** grilled. ▪ **parrilla de salida** starting grid.

parrillada *nf* mixed grill.

parte *nf* **1** *(gen)* part. **2** *(en contrato)* party. **3** *(de un partido)* half. • **a partes iguales** in equal shares; **de parte de** on behalf of, from; **¿de parte de quién?** who's calling?; **en ninguna parte** nowhere; **por todas partes** everywhere; **por una parte...**, **por otra** on the one hand..., on the other hand... ▪ **parte**

facultativo medical report; **parte meteorológico** weather report.

participación *nf* **1** *(colaboración)* participation. **2** *(de lotería)* share.

participante *nmf* participant.

participar *vi (tomar parte)* to take part, participate. ▶ *vt (notificar)* to notify, inform.

participio *nm* participle.

partícula *nf* particle.

particular *adj* **1** *(específico)* particular. **2** *(especial)* special. **3** *(privado)* private. • **sin otro particular** yours faithfully.

partida *nf* **1** *(salida)* departure, leave. **2** *(documento)* certificate. **3** *(de juego)* game.

partidario,-a *nm,f* supporter.

partido *nm* **1** *(grupo)* party, group. **2** *(partida)* game, match. • **sacar partido de** to profit from; **tomar partido** to take sides. ▪ **partido amistoso** friendly match.

partir *vt* **1** *(separar)* to divide, split. **2** *(romper)* to break, crack. ▶ *vi (irse)* to leave, set out, set off. ▶ *vpr* **partirse** to split up, break up. • **a partir de hoy** from today onwards.

partitura *nf* score.

parto *nm* (child)birth, delivery. ▪ **parto provocado** induced labour; **parto sin dolor** painless childbirth.

pasa *nf* raisin.

pasadizo *nm* passage.

pasado,-a *adj* **1** *(anterior)* past, gone by: *el lunes pasado*, last Monday. **2** *(último)* last. **3** *(carne)* overdone. ▶ *nm* **pasado** *(momento anterior)* past; *(de un verbo)* past tense. • **pasadas las...** after...; **las... pasadas** gone...: *son las cuatro pasadas*, it's gone four.

pasaje *nm* **1** *(billete)* ticket, fare. **2** *(pasajeros)* passengers *pl.* **3** *(calle)* passage, alley. **4** *(de texto)* passage.

pasajero,-a *adj* passing. ▶ *nm,f* passenger.

pasamanos *nm* handrail.

pasamontañas *nm* balaclava.

pasaporte *nm* passport.

pasar *vi* **1** *(gen)* to pass. **2** *(entrar)* to come in, go in. **3** *(cesar)* to come to an end. **4** *(límite)* to exceed: *pasa de la edad que piden*, he is over the age they are asking for. **5** *(ocurrir)* to happen. **6** *fam (mostrar poco interés)* not to be bothered. ▶ *vt* **1** *(entregar)* to pass. **2** *(página)* to turn. **3** *(límite)* to go beyond. **4** *(aventajar)* to surpass, beat. **5** *(adelantar)* to overtake. **6** *(tiempo)* to spend. ▶ *vpr* **pasarse** **1** *(excederse)* to go too far, exaggerate. **2** *(pudrirse)* to go off. **3** *(ir)* to go by,

walk past. • **pasar por** to be considered; **pasarlo bien/mal** to have a good/bad time; **¿qué pasa?** what's the matter?, what's wrong?

pasarela *nf (de barco)* walkway; *(de modelos)* catwalk.

pasatiempo *nm* pastime, hobby.

Pascua *nf (cristiana)* Easter; *(judía)* Passover. ▶ *nf pl* **Pascuas** Christmas.

pase *nm* **1** *(gen)* pass, permit. **2** *(de película)* showing.

pasear *vt* to walk. ▶ *vi-vpr* **pasear(se)** to go for a walk.

paseo *nm* **1** *(a pie)* walk, stroll; *(en coche)* drive; *(en bici, a caballo)* ride. **2** *(calle)* avenue, promenade. • **dar un paseo** to go for a walk. ■ **paseo marítimo** sea front, promenade.

pasillo *nm (de casa)* corridor; *(de avión)* aisle.

pasión *nf* passion.

pasivo,-a *adj* passive. ▶ *nm* **pasivo** liabilities.

paso *nm* **1** *(al caminar)* step, footstep. **2** *(camino)* passage, way. • **a dos pasos** just round the corner; **abrirse paso** to force one's way through; **"Ceda el paso"** "Give way"; **de paso 1** by the way: *me pilla de paso al trabajo*, it's on my way to work. **2** in passing: *lo dijo de paso*, he mentioned it in passing; **estar de paso** to

be passing through; **"Prohibido el paso"** "No entry".
■ **paso a nivel** level crossing; **paso de cebra** zebra crossing; **paso de peatones** pedestrian crossing; **paso elevado** flyover; **paso subterráneo** subway.

pasta nf 1 *(masa)* paste; *(de pan)* dough. 2 *(fideos, macarrones, etc)* pasta. 3 *(pastelito)* cake. 4 fam *(dinero)* dough, money. ■ **pasta dentífrica** toothpaste; **pastas de té** biscuits.

pastar vt-vi to pasture, graze.

pastel nm 1 *(tipo bizcocho)* cake; *(de fruta)* pie, tart. 2 *(colores, etc)* pastel.

pastelería nf cake shop, patisserie.

pastilla nf 1 *(medicamento)* tablet, pill. 2 *(de jabón)* cake, bar.

pasto nm pasture.

pastor,-ra nm,f *(hombre)* shepherd; *(mujer)* shepherdess.

pata[1] nf 1 *(gen)* leg. 2 *(garra)* paw. 3 *(pezuña)* hoof. ● **a cuatro patas** on all fours; **a la pata coja** hopping; **meter la pata** fam to put one's foot in it; **patas arriba** upside down. ■ **patas de gallo** crow's feet.

pata[2] nf *(ave)* female duck.

patada nf kick.

patata nf potato. ■ **patatas fritas 1** *(de bolsa)* GB crisps;

US potato chips. 2 *(de sartén)* GB chips; US French fries.

paté nm paté.

patente adj patent, evident. ▶ nf patent.

paterno,-a adj paternal.

patín nm 1 skate. 2 *(de agua)* pedalo. ■ **patines de ruedas** roller skates; **patines en línea** rollerblades.

patinaje nm skating. ■ **patinaje artístico** figure skating; **patinaje sobre hielo** ice skating.

patinar vi 1 *(con patines)* to skate. 2 *(vehículo)* to skid.

patinazo nm *(con el coche)* skid.

patinete nm scooter.

patio nm 1 *(de casa)* courtyard. 2 *(de escuela)* playground. ■ **patio de butacas** GB stalls; US orchestra.

pato nm duck.

patria nf homeland.

patrimonio nm heritage, patrimony. ■ **patrimonio de la humanidad** world heritage.

patriotismo nm patriotism.

patrocinar vt to sponsor.

patrón,-ona nm,f 1 *(santo)* patron saint. 2 *(jefe)* employer, boss. 3 *(de barco)* skipper. ▶ nm **patrón 1** *(de modista)* pattern. 2 *(modelo)* standard.

patrulla nf patrol.

pausa nf pause.

pavo nm turkey. ■ **pavo real** peacock.

payaso *nm* clown.

paz *nf* peace. • **dejar en paz** to leave alone; **hacer las paces** to make up, make it up.

peaje *nm* toll.

peatón *nm* pedestrian.

peca *nf* freckle.

pecado *nm* sin.

pecera *nf* (*redonda*) fishbowl; (*rectangular*) aquarium, fish tank.

pecho *nm* **1** (*tórax*) chest. **2** (*de mujer - busto*) bust; (*- seno*) breast. • **dar el pecho** to breast-feed.

pechuga *nf* breast.

peculiar *adj* peculiar.

pedal *nm* pedal.

pedazo *nm* piece, bit. • **hacer pedazos** to break to pieces.

pedestal *nm* pedestal.

pediatra *nmf* pediatrician.

pedido *nm* order. • **hacer un pedido** to place an order.

pedir *vt* **1** (*gen*) to ask for. **2** (*mendigar*) to beg. **3** (*mercancías, en restaurante*) to order: *¿qué has pedido de postre?*, what did you order for dessert?

pedo *nm fam* (*ventosidad*) fart. • **estar pedo** *fam* to be drunk.

pega *nf fam* (*dificultad*) snag.

pegamento *nm* glue.

pegar¹ *vt* **1** (*adherir - gen*) to stick; (*- con pegamento*) to glue. **2** (*arrimar*) to put. ► *vi* (*combi-*

nar) to match: *ese color no pega en el salón*, that colour doesn't look right in the living room. ► *vpr* **pegarse** (*adherirse*) to stick.

pegar² *vt* **1** (*golpear*) to hit. **2** (*dar*) to give: *deja ya de pegar gritos*, stop shouting. ► *vpr* **pegarse** (*golpearse*) to hit each other.

pegatina *nf* sticker.

peinado *nm* hair style.

peinar *vt* (*con peine*) to comb; (*con cepillo*) to brush. ► *vpr* **peinarse** to comb one's hair.

peine *nm* comb.

peladilla *nf* sugared almond.

pelar *vt* **1** (*fruta, verdura*) to peel. **2** (*persona*) to cut SB's hair. ► *vpr* **pelarse 1** (*perder piel*) to peel. **2** (*cortarse el pelo*) to get one's hair cut.

peldaño *nm* step.

pelea *nf* fight, quarrel.

pelear(se) *vi-vpr* **1** (*gen*) to fight, quarrel. **2** (*a golpes*) to come to blows.

peletería *nf* fur shop, furrier's.

pelícano *nm* pelican.

película *nf* film. ▪ **película de acción** adventure film; **película de miedo** horror film; **película de suspense** thriller; **película del oeste** western; **película muda** silent movie.

peligro *nm* danger.

peligroso,-a adj dangerous.
pelirrojo,-a adj red-haired. ▶ nm,f redhead.
pellizco nm pinch.
pelo nm 1 (gen) hair. 2 (de barba) whisker. 3 (de animal) coat, fur. • **no tener pelos en la lengua** to speak one's mind; **por los pelos** by the skin of one's teeth; **tomarle el pelo a** ALGN to pull SB's leg; **venir a pelo** to be just what SB needs.
pelota nf ball. • **en pelotas** fam naked; **hacer la pelota a** ALGN fam to suck up to SB. ▪ **pelota vasca** pelota.
pelotón nm squad.
peluca nf wig.
peluche nm plush.
peluquería nf hairdresser's.
peluquín nm hairpiece.
pelusa nf fluff.
pelvis nf pelvis.
pena nf 1 (tristeza) grief, sorrow. 2 (lástima) pity. 3 (castigo) penalty, punishment. • **valer la pena** to be worth while.
penalti nm penalty.
pendiente adj 1 (por resolver) pending. 2 (deuda) outstanding. 3 (atento): **estaba pendiente de todos los detalles**, none of the details escaped him, he missed nothing. ▶ nf slope. ▶ nm earring.
pene nm penis.

penetrar vt 1 (atravesar) to penetrate. 2 (líquido) to permeate.
península nf peninsula.
pensamiento nm 1 (idea, facultad) thought. 2 (mente) mind. 3 (flor) pansy.
pensar vt-vi to think. • **¡ni pensarlo!** no way!, don't even think about it!; **sin pensar** without thinking.
pensión nf 1 (dinero) pension. 2 (residencia) boarding house. ▪ **media pensión** half board; **pensión completa** full board; **pensión de jubilación** retirement pension.
pensionista nmf pensioner.
pentágono nm pentagon.
pentagrama nm stave, staff.
penúltimo,-a adj-nm,f penultimate.
peña nf (roca) rock.
peón nm 1 (trabajador) unskilled labourer. 2 (en damas) man. 3 (en ajedrez) pawn.
peor adj-adv 1 (comparativo) worse. 2 (superlativo) worst.
pepinillo nm gherkin.
pepino nm cucumber.
pepita nf 1 (de fruta) seed, pip. 2 (de metal) nugget.
pequeño,-a adj 1 (de tamaño) little, small. 2 (de edad) young, small: **tengo dos hermanos pequeños**, I have to younger brothers.• **de pequeño,-a** as a child.

pera *nf* pear.

percance *nm* mishap.

percatarse *vpr* to notice.

percebe *nm* goose barnacle.

percha *nf* (*individual*) hanger; (*de gancho*) coat hook.

perchero *nm* (*en la pared*) clothes rack; (*de pie*) coat stand.

percibir *vt* (*notar*) to perceive.

perdedor,-ra *nm,f* loser.

perder *vt* 1 (*gen*) to lose. 2 (*malgastar*) to waste. 3 (*tren, avión etc*) to miss. ▶ *vi* 1 (*salir derrotado*) to lose. 2 (*empeorar*) to go downhill. ▶ *vpr* **perderse** 1 (*extraviarse*) to go astray, get lost. 2 (*acontecimiento*) to miss.

pérdida *nf* 1 (*extravío*) loss. 2 (*de tiempo, dinero*) waste. 3 (*escape*) leak. • **no tener pérdida** to be easy to find: *no tiene pérdida*, you can't miss it.

perdido,-a *adj* 1 (*gen*) lost: *objetos perdidos*, lost property. 2 (*desperdiciado*) wasted.

perdigón *nm* pellet.

perdiz *nf* partridge.

perdón *nm* 1 (*indulto*) pardon. 2 (*de pecado*) forgiveness. • **con perdón** if you'll pardon the expression; **pedir perdón** to apologize; **¡perdón!** sorry!; **¿perdón?** pardon?, sorry?

perdonar *vt* 1 (*error, ofensa*) to forgive. 2 (*deuda*) to let off. 3 (*excusar*) to excuse.

perdurar *vt* to last, endure.

peregrino,-a *nm,f* pilgrim.

perejil *nm* parsley.

perenne *adj* perennial, perpetual: *árbol de hoja perenne*, evergreen tree.

pereza *nf* laziness, idleness.

perfección *nf* perfection.

perfecto,-a *adj* 1 (*ideal*) perfect. 2 (*rematado*) complete: *un perfecto desconocido*, a complete stranger.

perfil *nm* profile.

perforar *vt* 1 (*gen*) to perforate. 2 (*uso técnico*) to drill, bore.

perfume *nm* perfume, scent.

perfumería *nf* perfumery, perfume shop.

periferia *nf* 1 (*gen*) periphery. 2 (*afueras*) outskirts.

perilla *nf* goatee.

perímetro *nm* perimeter.

periódico,-a *adj* periodic. ▶ *nm* **periódico** newspaper.

periodista *nmf* journalist.

periodo *nm* period.

periquito *nm* parakeet.

periscopio *nm* periscope.

perito *nm* expert.

perjudicar *vt* to damage, harm.

perjudicial *adj* damaging, harmful.

perjuicio *nm* (*moral*) injury; (*material*) damage.

perla *nf* (*joya*) pearl. ▪ **perla cultivada** cultured pearl.

permanecer *vi* to remain.
permanente *adj* permanent, lasting. ► *nf (del pelo)* perm. • **hacerse la permanente** to have one's hair permed.
permiso *nm* **1** *(autorización)* permission. **2** *(documento)* permit. **3** *(soldado)* leave. • **con su permiso** if you'll excuse me. ■ **permiso de conducir** driving licence.
permitir *vt* to permit, allow, let. ► *vpr* **permitirse** to take the liberty of.
pero *conj* but.
peroné *nm* fibula.
perpendicular *adj-nf* perpendicular.
perra *nf* bitch.
perro *nm* dog. • **"Cuidado con el perro"** "Beware of the dog". ■ **perro callejero** stray dog; **perro guardián** guard dog.
persecución *nf* **1** *(seguimiento)* pursuit. **2** *(represión)* persecution.
perseguir *vt* **1** *(delincuente, presa)* to pursue, chase. **2** *(pretender)* to be after.
persiana *nf (gen)* blind; *(enrollable)* roller blind; *(de tablas)* shutter.
persistente *adj* persistent.
persona *nf* person: *una persona, dos personas*, one person, two people. ■ **persona mayor** adult, grown-up.

personaje *nm* **1** *(en libro, etc)* character. **2** *(persona famosa)* celebrity.
personal *adj* personal. ► *nm* personnel, staff.
personalidad *nf* **1** *(carácter)* personality. **2** *(persona famosa)* public figure.
perspectiva *nf* **1** *(gen)* perspective. **2** *(posibilidad)* prospect. **3** *(vista)* view.
persuadir *vi* to persuade, convince.
pertenecer *vi* to belong
pertenencias *nf pl* belongings.
pértiga *nf* pole.
perverso,-a *adj* perverse.
pesa *nf* weight: *hacer pesas*, to do weight training.
pesadilla *nf* nightmare.
pesado,-a *adj* **1** *(gen)* heavy. **2** *(aburrido)* dull, tiresome, boring.
pésame *nm* condolences, expression of sympathy. • **dar el pésame** to offer one's condolences.
pesar *vt-vi* **1** *(gen)* to weigh. ► *vi* **1** *(tener mucho peso)* to be heavy. **2** *(sentir)* to be sorry, regret. ► *nm* **1** *(pena)* sorrow, grief. **2** *(arrepentimiento)* regret. • **a pesar de** in spite of, despite.
pesca *nf* fishing. ■ **pesca de arrastre** trawling; **pesca submarina** underwater fishing.

pescadería *nf* fishmonger's, fish shop.

pescadilla *nf* small hake.

pescado *nm* fish.

pescador *nm* fisherman.

pescar *vi* to fish.

pesebre *nm* (de Navidad) crib.

pesimista *adj* pessimistic. ▶ *nmf* pessimist.

pésimo,-a *adj* very bad.

peso *nm* **1** (gen) weight. **2** (balanza) scales, balance. **3** DEP shot: *lanzamiento de peso*, shot put; *levantamiento de peso*, weight-lifting. fishing boat.

pestaña *nf* **1** (del ojo) eyelash. **2** (de cartón) flap.

peste *nf* **1** (epidemia) plague. **2** (mal olor) stink, stench.

pestillo *nm* bolt.

pétalo *nm* petal.

petanca *nf* petanque.

petardo *nm* (cohete) banger.

petición *nf* request.

petirrojo *nm* robin.

peto *nm* bib.

petróleo *nm* oil, petroleum.

petrolero *nm* oil tanker.

pez *nm* fish.

pezón *nm* nipple.

pezuña *nf* hoof.

pianista *nmf* pianist.

piano *nm* piano: *yo toco el piano*, I can play the piano. ■ **piano de cola** grand piano.

piar *vi* to chirp.

piara *nf* herd of pigs.

pica *nf* **1** (lanza) pike. **2** (de toros) goad.

picado,-a *adj* **1** (ajo, cebolla) chopped; (carne) minced. **2** (mar) choppy. **3** (vino) sour. **4** (diente) decayed. **5** fam (ofendido) offended. ● **caer en picado** to plummet.

picadura *nf* **1** (de mosquito, serpiente) bite; (de abeja, avispa) sting. **2** (tabaco) cut tobacco.

picante *adj* **1** (sabor) hot, spicy. **2** (pícaro) spicy, naughty.

picaporte *nm* **1** (llamador) door knocker. **2** (pomo) door handle.

picar *vt* **1** (mosquito, serpiente) to bite; (abeja, avispa) to sting. **2** (algo de comer) to nibble. **3** (cebolla, patata, etc) to chop; (carne) to mince; (hielo) to crush. ▶ *vi* **1** (sentir escozor) to itch. **2** (tomar algo de comer) to nibble. **3** (estar picante) to be spicy. ▶ *vpr* **picarse 1** (fruta) to begin to rot. **2** (diente) to begin to decay. **3** (mar) to get choppy. **4** (enfadarse) to take offense.

pícaro,-a *adj* **1** (malicioso) mischievous. **2** (astuto) sly, crafty.

pichón *nm* young pigeon.

picnic *nm* picnic.

pico *nm* **1** (de ave) beak. **2** (de montaña) peak. **3** (herramienta) pick, pickaxe. **6** (cantidad) small surplus: *tres mil y pico*, three thousand odd.

picor *nm* itch.

picotear *vt* **1** *(ave)* to peck at. **2** *(persona)* to nibble.

pie *nm* **1** foot: *fuimos a pie*, we went on foot; *con los pies descalzos*, barefoot. **2** *(de página)* bottom. **3** *(de columna, lámpara)* base, stand. ● **al pie de la letra** literally; **dar pie a** to give occasion for; **ponerse de pie** to stand up. ■ **pie de atleta** athlete's foot; **pie plano** flat foot.

piedad *nf* **1** *(devoción)* piety. **2** *(compasión)* pity, mercy.

piedra *nf* **1** *(gen)* stone. **2** *(de mechero)* flint. ■ **piedra pómez** pumice stone; **piedra preciosa** precious stone.

piel *nf* **1** *(de persona)* skin. **2** *(de animal - gen)* skin; *(- de vaca, elefante)* hide; *(- de foca, zorro, visón)* fur. **3** *(cuero - tratado)* leather; *(- sin tratar)* pelt. **4** *(de fruta - gen)* skin; *(- de naranja, manzana, patata)* peel. ■ **piel de gallina** goose pimples.

pienso *nm* fodder.

pierna *nf* leg.

pieza *nf* piece. ■ **pieza de recambio** spare part.

pigmento *nm* pigment.

pijama *nm* pyjamas.

pila *nf* **1** *(eléctrica)* battery. **2** *(de bautismo)* font.

píldora *nf* pill.

pillar *vt* *(atrapar)* to catch; *(atropellar)* to run over. ▶ *vpr*

pillarse to catch : *me he pillado el dedo con la puerta*, I caught my finger in the door.

pilotar *vt* *(avión)* to pilot; *(coche)* to drive.

piloto *nmf* *(de avión, barco)* pilot; *(de coche)* driver. ▶ *nm* *(luz - de coche)* tail light, rear light; *(- de aparato)* pilot light. ▶ *adj* pilot: *piso piloto*, show flat. ■ **piloto automático** automatic pilot.

pimentón *nm* paprika.

pimienta *nf* pepper.

pimiento *nm* pepper. ■ **pimiento morrón** sweet pepper.

pinar *nm* pine grove.

pincel *nm* brush, paintbrush.

pinchadiscos *nmf fam* DJ, disc jockey.

pinchar *vt* **1** *(con objeto punzante)* to prick. **2** *(rueda)* to puncture. **3** *(globo, pelota)* to burst. **4** *fam* *(teléfono)* to tap. ▶ *vpr* **pincharse 1** *(persona)* to prick oneself. **2** *(rueda)* to puncture. **3** *(globo, pelota)* to burst.

pinchazo *nm* **1** *(punzada)* prick. **2** *(de rueda)* puncture, flat.

pincho *nm* **1** *(espina)* thorn, prickle. **2** *(aperitivo)* tapa, bar snack. ■ **pincho moruno** kebab.

ping-pong® *nm* ping-pong®.

pingüino *nm* penguin.

pino *nm* pine tree.

pintada *nf* piece of graffiti.

pintalabios *nm* lipstick.

pintar *vt* to paint. ► *vpr* **pintarse** to make up one's face.

pintaúñas *nm* nail varnish.

pintor,-ra *nm,f* painter.

pintoresco,-a *adj* picturesque.

pintura *nf* 1 *(arte)* painting. 2 *(color, bote)* paint. 3 *(cuadro)* picture.

pinza *nf* 1 *(de cangrejo)* claw. 2 *(para la ropa)* peg. ► *nf pl* **pinzas** *(de cocina)* tongs; *(de manicura)* tweezers.

piña *nf* 1 *(fruta)* pineapple. 2 *(de pino)* pine cone.

piñón *nm (de pino)* pine nut.

piojo *nm* louse.

pionero,-a *adj* pioneering.

pipa¹ *nf (de tabaco)* pipe.

pipa² *nf* 1 *(de fruta)* pip, seed. 2 *(de girasol)* sunflower seeds.

piragua *nf* canoe.

pirámide *nf* pyramid.

pirata *nm* pirate.

piropo *nm* compliment.

pirueta *nf* pirouette, caper.

piruleta *nf* lollipop.

pirulí *nm* lollipop.

pisada *nf* 1 *(acción)* footstep. 2 *(huella)* footprint.

pisapapeles *nm* paperweight.

pisar *vt* to tread on, step on.

piscina *nf* swimming-pool.

piso *nm* 1 *(planta, suelo)* floor. 2 *(vivienda)* flat, apartment.

pista *nf* 1 *(rastro)* trail, track. 2 *(indicio)* clue. 3 *(de atletismo)* track; *(de tenis)* court; *(de esquí)* slope, ski run. 4 *(de circo)* ring. 5 *(de aterrizaje)* runway. ▪ **pista de baile** dance floor.

pistacho *nm* pistachio.

pistola *nf* pistol.

pistón *nm* piston.

pitar *vi (con silbato)* to blow a whistle; *(con claxon)* to hoot. ► *vt (abuchear)* to boo at.

pitido *nm* whistle.

pitillera *nf* cigarette case.

pitillo *nm* cigarette.

pito *nm* whistle.

pizarra *nf* 1 *(roca)* slate. 2 *(de escuela)* blackboard.

pizca *nf* bit, jot: *una pizca de sal*, a pinch of salt.

pizza *nf* pizza.

placa *nf* 1 *(lámina)* plate. 2 *(inscrita)* plaque. 3 *(de policía)* badge. 4 *(de cocinar)* plate.

placer *nm* pleasure.

plaga *nf* plague, pest.

plan *nm* plan, project. ▪ **plan de estudios** syllabus.

plancha *nf* 1 *(de metal)* plate, sheet. 2 *(para planchar)* iron.

planchar *vt (gen)* to iron; *(traje, pantalón)* to press.

planear *vt* to plan. ► *vi (avión)* to glide.

planeta *nm* planet.

planificar *vt* to plan.

plano,-a *adj* flat, even. ► *nm* **plano** 1 *(mapa)* plan, map. 2

(en filmación) shot. ■ **primer plano** *(foto)* close-up.

planta *nf* **1** *(gen)* plant. **2** *(del pie)* sole. **3** *(piso)* floor. ■ **planta baja** ground floor.

plantación *nf* plantation.

plantar *vt (en tierra)* to plant; *(semilla)* to sow. ● **dejar a ALGN plantado** to keep SB waiting indefinitely.

plantear *vt* **1** *(problema)* to set out. **2** *(pregunta)* to pose, raise. ► *vpr* **plantearse 1** *(pensar)* to think about. **2** *(cuestión)* to arise.

plantilla *nf* **1** *(de zapato)* insole. **2** *(patrón)* model, pattern. **3** *(personal)* staff.

plasma *nm* plasma.

plástico,-a *adj* plastic. ► *nm* **plástico** plastic.

plata *nf* silver.

plataforma *nf* platform. ■ **plataforma de lanzamiento** launchpad; **plataforma petrolífera** oil rig.

plátano *nm* **1** *(fruta)* banana. **2** *(árbol)* plane tree.

platea *nf* stalls.

platillo *nm* **1** *(plato)* saucer. **2** *(de balanza)* pan. **3** *(instrumento)* cymbal. ■ **platillo volante** flying saucer.

plato *nm* **1** *(gen)* dish. **2** *(en comida)* course. ● **lavar los platos** to do the washing-up, wash up.

plató *nm* set.

playa *nf* beach.

playeras *nf pl* gym shoes.

plaza *nf* **1** *(de pueblo, ciudad)* square. **2** *(mercado)* marketplace. **3** *(sitio)* space. **4** *(asiento)* seat. **5** *(empleo)* position, post. ■ **plaza de toros** bullring; **plaza mayor** main square.

plazo *nm* **1** *(de tiempo)* period. **2** *(pago)* instalment. ● **a plazos** by instalments.

plegable *adj* folding.

plegar *vt* to fold.

pleito *nm* litigation, lawsuit.

pleno,-a *adj* full, complete.

pliegue *nm* **1** *(doblez)* fold. **2** *(en ropa)* pleat.

plomo *nm* **1** *(metal)* lead. **2** *(de la luz)* fuse: *se fundieron los plomos*, the fuses blew.

pluma *nf* **1** *(de ave)* feather. **2** *(de escribir)* quill pen; *(estilográfica)* fountain pen.

plumero *nm* feather duster.

plural *adj-nm* plural.

población *nf* **1** *(habitantes)* population. **2** *(ciudad)* city, town; *(pueblo)* village. ■ **población activa** working population.

poblado,-a *adj* **1** *(zona)* populated. **2** *(barba)* thick. ► *nm* **poblado** settlement.

pobre *adj* poor.

pobreza *nf* poverty.

pocilga *nf* pigsty.

poco,-a *adj (singular)* little, not much; *(plural)* few, not many. ▶ *pron (singular)* little; *(plural)* not many. ▶ *adv* little, not much. • **dentro de poco** soon, presently; **hace poco** not long ago; **poco a poco** little by little; **por poco** nearly.

podar *vt* to prune.

poder *vt* 1 *(gen)* can. 2 *(tener permiso para)* can, may: *¿puedo fumar?*, may I smoke? 3 *(en conjeturas)* may, might: *puede que esté enfermo*, he may be ill, he might be ill. ▶ *nm (capacidad, facultad)* power. • **no poder con** not to be able to cope with; **no poder más** to be unable to do more; **¿se puede?** may I come in?

podio *nm* podium.

podrido,-a *adj* rotten.

poema *nm* poem.

poesía *nf* 1 *(género)* poetry. 2 *(poema)* poem.

poeta *nmf* poet.

poetisa *nf* poetess.

polar *adj* polar.

polémico,-a *adj* polemic.

polen *nm* pollen.

policía *nf* police. ▶ *nmf (hombre)* policeman; *(mujer)* policewoman.

polideportivo *nm* sports centre.

polígono *nm* polygon. ▪ **polígono industrial** industrial estate.

polilla *nf* moth.

política *nf* 1 *(ciencia)* politics: *se dedica a la política*, he's into politics. 2 *(método)* policy.

político,-a *adj* politic. ▶ *nm,f* politician.

póliza *nf* certificate, policy.

polizón *nm* stowaway.

pollería *nf* poultry shop.

pollo *nm* chicken. ▪ **pollo asado** roast chicken.

polo *nm* 1 *(gen)* pole. 2 *(helado)* GB ice lolly ; US Popsicle®. 3 *(jersey)* polo shirt.

polvo *nm* 1 *(en aire, muebles)* dust. 2 *(en farmacia, cosmética)* powder. • **estar hecho polvo** *fam* to be knackered. ▪ **polvos de talco** talcum powder.

pólvora *nf* gunpowder.

polvorón *nm* crumbly shortcake.

pomada *nf* cream.

pomelo *nm* grapefruit.

pomo *nm* knob, handle.

pómulo *nm* cheekbone.

ponche *nm* punch.

poner *vt* 1 *(gen)* to place, put, set. 2 *(instalar)* to install. 3 *(encender)* to turn on, put on. 4 *(huevos)* to lay. 5 *(estar escrito)* to say: *¿qué pone en ese letrero?*, what does that sing say? 6 *(establecer)* to open: *han puesto un bar*, they've opened a bar. 7 *(programa, película)* to show. 8 **poner +**

adj to make: *me pone enfermo*, he makes me sick. ▸ *vpr*
ponerse 1 *(sombrero, ropa)* to put on. **2** *(sol)* to set. **3** *(volverse)* to become, get, turn. **4** *(al teléfono - cogerlo)* to answer the phone; *(- acudir)* to come to the phone: *dígale que se ponga*, tell her to come to the phone. ● **ponerse a + inf** to start to + inf.

popa *nf* stern.

popular *adj* popular.

por *prep* **1** *(causa)* because of: *llegaron tarde por la nieve*, they were late because of the snow; *lo hice por ti*, I did it for you. **2** *(tiempo)* at, in; *(duración)* for: *por la noche*, at night; *vino por poco tiempo*, he didn't stay for long. **3** *(lugar)* along, in, on, by, up, down: *iremos por la autopista*, we'll go by motorway. **4** *(medio, agente)* by: *por avión*, by air. **5** *(distribución)* per: *cinco por ciento*, five per cent. **6** *(en multiplicación)* times. **9** *(medidas)* by: *mide tres metros por dos*, it measures three metres by two. ● *¿por qué?* why?; **por supuesto** of course; **por tanto** therefore.

porcelana *nf* **1** *(material)* porcelain. **2** *(vajilla)* china.

porcentaje *nm* percentage.

porche *nm* porch.

porción *nf* **1** *(parte)* portion, part. **2** *(cuota)* share.

poro *nm* pore.

porque *conj* because.

porquería *nf* dirt, filth.

porra *nf* cudgel, club.

portaaviones *nm* aircraft carrier.

portada *nf* **1** *(de libro)* title page. **2** *(de revista)* cover. **3** *(de periódico)* front page. **4** *(de disco)* sleeve.

portador,-ra *nm,f (de virus)* carrier. ● **páguese al portador** pay the bearer.

portaequipajes *nm* luggage rack.

portal *nm* **1** *(entrada)* doorway; *(vestíbulo)* entrance hall. **2** *(de Internet)* portal.

portarse *vpr* to behave, act.

portátil *adj* portable. ▸ *nm (ordenador)* laptop, portable.

portavoz *nmf (gen)* spokesperson.

portería *nf* **1** *(de edificio)* porter's lodge. **2** *(en fútbol)* goal.

portero,-a *nmf* **1** *(de edificio)* doorkeeper, porter. **2** *(guardameta)* goalkeeper. ■ **portero automático** entry phone.

porvenir *nm* future.

posada *nf* lodging-house, inn.

posar *vi* to pose. ▸ *vpr* **posarse 1** *(pájaro)* to alight, perch, sit. **2** *(sedimento)* to settle.

posdata *nf* postscript.

poseer *vt* to own, possess.

posesión *nf* possession.

posesivo,-a *adj* possessive

posibilidad *nf* possibility.

posible *adj* possible. • **hacer todo lo posible** to do one's best.

posición *nf* position.

positivo,-a *adj* positive.

poso *nm* **1** *(de mineral)* sediment. **2** *(de café, vino)* dregs.

posponer *vt* to postpone, delay, put off.

postal *adj* postal. ► *nf* postcard.

poste *nm* post.

póster *nm* poster.

posterior *adj* **1** *(de atrás)* back, rear. **2** *(más tarde)* later.

postre *nm* dessert.

postura *nf* **1** *(posición)* posture, position. **2** *(actitud)* attitude, stance.

potable *adj* drinkable.

potaje *nm* stew.

potencia *nf* power.

potente *adj* powerful.

potro,-a *nm,f* colt, foal. ► *nm* **potro** *(para gimnasia)* vaulting horse.

pozo *nm* **1** *(de agua, petróleo)* well. **2** *(en mina)* shaft.

práctica *nf* practice. ► *nf pl* **prácticas** training.

practicar *vt* **1** *(idioma, profesión)* to practice. **2** *(deporte)* to play, do. ► *vi* to practice.

práctico,-a *adj* practical.

pradera *nf* prairie.

prado *nf* meadow.

precaución *nf* precaution. • **conducir con precaución** to drive carefully.

precedente *adj* preceding, prior, foregoing. ► *nm* precedent. • **sin precedentes** unprecedented.

precinto *nm* seal.

precio *nm* price. ■ **precio de fábrica** factory price; **precio de venta al público** retail price.

precioso,-a *adj* **1** *(valioso)* precious. **2** *(bello)* beautiful.

precipicio *nm* precipice.

precipitación *nf* **1** *(prisa)* rush, haste, hurry. **2** *(lluvia)* precipitation.

precipitarse 1 *(apresurarse)* to be hasty. **2** *(obrar sin reflexión)* to act rashly.

precisión *nf* precision,.

preciso,-a *adj* **1** *(exacto)* precise, exact, accurate. **2** *(necesario)* necessary.

precocinado,-a *adj* precooked.

precoz *adj* **1** *(niño)* precocious. **2** *(envejecimiento, eyacualción)* premature.

predecir *vt* to predict, foretell.

predicar *vt* to preach.

predicción *nf* prediction. ■ **predicción meteorológica** forecast.

predominio *nm* predominance.

preferencia *nf* preference. • **tener preferencia** *(al volante)* to have right of way.

preferir *vt* to prefer.

prefijo *nm* prefix; *(telefónico)* code.

pregunta *nf* question.

preguntar *vt* to ask. ► *vpr* **preguntarse** to wonder.

prehistoria *nf* prehistory.

prejuicio *nm* prejudice.

prematuro,-a *adj* premature.

premiar *vt* 1 *(otorgar premio a)* to award a prize to. 2 *(recompensar)* to reward.

premio *nm* 1 *(en concurso, sorteo)* prize. 2 *(recompensa)* reward. ▪ **premio gordo** jackpot.

prenda *nf* 1 *(de vestir)* garment. 2 *(garantía)* pledge.

prender *vt* 1 *(agarrar)* to seize. 2 *(sujetar)* to attach. ► *vi* *(fuego etc)* to catch.

prensa *nf* press. ▪ **prensa amarilla** gutter press; **prensa del corazón** gossip magazines.

prensar *vt* to press.

preocupar(se) *vt-vpr* to worry.

preparación *nf* preparation.

preparado,-a *adj* ready, prepared.

preparar *vt* to prepare. ► *vpr* **prepararse** to get ready.

preparativos *nm pl* preparations, arrangements.

preposición *nf* preposition.

presa *nf* 1 *(cosa prendida)* prey. 2 *(embalse)* dam.

presencia *nf* presence. ▪ **buena presencia** smart appearance.

presenciar *vt (asistir)* to be present at; *(contemplar)* to witness.

presentación *nf* 1 *(gen)* presentation. 2 *(de personas)* introduction.

presentador,-ra *nm,f* presenter, host.

presentar *vt* 1 *(gen)* to present. 2 *(mostrar)* to display, show. 3 *(personas)* to introduce. ► *vpr* **presentarse** *(comparecer)* to present oneself; *(candidato)* to stand.

presente *adj-nm* present. • **tener presente** to bear in mind.

preservar *vt (proteger)* to protect; *(conservar)* to preserve.

preservativo *nm* condom.

presidencia *nf* 1 *(de nación)* presidency. 2 *(en reunión)* chairmanship.

presidente,-a *nm,f* 1 *(de nación, club, etc)* president. 2 *(en reunión - hombre)* chairman; *(- mujer)* chairwoman.

presidir *vt* 1 *(nación)* to be president of. 2 *(reunión)* to chair.

presión *nf* pressure. ▪ **presión arterial** blood pressure.

presionar vt 1 (apretar) to press. 2 (coaccionar) to put pressure on.

preso,-a nm,f prisoner.

préstamo nm (acción) lending; (dinero) loan.

prestar vt 1 (dejar prestado) to lend, loan; (pedir prestado) to borrow. 2 (servicio) to do, render. 3 (ayuda) to give. 4 (atención) to pay. ► vpr **prestarse 1** (ofrecerse) to lend oneself. 2 (dar motivo) to cause.

prestigio nm prestige.

presumir vi to be vain, be conceited.

presupuesto nm (cálculo anticipado) estimate; (coste) budget.

pretender vt 1 (querer) to want to. 2 (intentar) to try to.

prevenir vt 1 (prever) to prevent. 2 (advertir) to warn.

previo,-a adj previous.

previsión nf forecast.

previsto,-a adj: su llegada está prevista para las cinco, he is expected to arrive at five; había previsto todo, she had thought of everything. • según lo previsto according to plan.

prima nf bonus. 2 → primo,-a.

primavera nf spring.

primer num → primero,-a.

primera nf 1 (clase) first class. 2 (marcha) first gear

primero,-a num first. ► adv **primero** first. • **a primeros de mes** at the beginning of the month. ■ **primeros auxilios** first aid.

primitivo,-a adj primitive.

primo,-a adj 1 (materia) raw. 2 (número) prime. ► nm,f cousin.

princesa nf princess.

principal adj main, chief. ► nm (piso) first floor.

príncipe nm prince.

principiante,-a nm,f beginner.

principio nm 1 (inicio) beginning, start. 2 (norma) principle. • **al principio** at first; **en principio** in principle.

prioridad nf priority.

prisa nf hurry. • **darse prisa** to hurry, hurry up; **tener prisa** to be in a hurry.

prisión nf (lugar) prison, jail. • **en prisión preventiva** remanded in custody.

prisionero,-a nm,f prisoner.

prismáticos nm pl binoculars.

privado,-a adj private.

privar vt 1 (despojar) to deprive. 2 (prohibir) to forbid. ► vpr **privarse** to do without.

privilegio nm privilege.

proa nf prow, bow.

probabilidad nf probability.

probable adj probable, likely.

probador nm changing room.

probar vt 1 (demostrar) to prove. 2 (comprobar) to try, test. 3 (vino, comida) to taste, try. 4 (prendas) to try on.

problema *nm* problem.

procedencia *nf* **1** *(de persona, producto)* origin, source. **2** *(de tren)* point of departure.

procedente *adj* coming.

proceder *vi (venir de)* to come.

procedimiento *nm* procedure, method.

procesar *vt* **1** *(dato, texto)* to process. **2** JUR to prosecute.

procesión *nf* procession.

proceso *nm* **1** *(gen)* process. **2** JUR trial.

proclamar *vt* to proclaim. ▶ *vpr* **proclamarse**: *se proclamó campeona*, she won the championship.

procurar *vt (intentar)* to try.

producción *nf* production.

producir *vt* **1** *(gen)* to produce. **2** *(causar)* to cause. ▶ *vpr* **producirse** to happen.

productividad *nf* productivity.

producto *nm* product.

productor,-ra *adj* productive. ▶ *nm,f* producer.

profesión *nf* profession.

profesional *adj-nmf* professional.

profesor,-ra *nm,f* teacher; *(de universidad)* lecturer.

profundidad *nf* depth.

profundo,-a *adj* **1** *(agujero, piscina)* deep. **2** *(pensamiento, misterio, etc)* profound.

programa *nm* GB programme; US program.

programación *nf* programming.

programador,-ra *nm,f* INFORM programmer.

programar *vt* GB to programme; US to program.

progresar *vi* to progress.

progreso *nm* progress.

prohibición *nf* prohibition, ban.

prohibir *vt (gen)* to forbid; *(por ley)* to prohibit, ban.

prolongar *vt (en el tiempo)* to prolong; *(de longitud)* to extend.

promedio *nm* average.

promesa *nf* promise.

prometer *vt* to promise.

prometido,-a *nm,f (hombre)* fiancé; *(mujer)* fiancée. • **estar prometidos** to be engaged.

promoción *nf* **1** *(gen)* promotion. **2** *(curso)* class, year.

pronombre *nm* pronoun.

pronóstico *nm* **1** *(gen)* forecast. **2** *(médico)* prognosis.

pronto *adv* **1** *(inmediatamente)* soon. **2** *(rápidamente)* quickly. **3** *(temprano)* early. • **de pronto** suddenly; ¡**hasta pronto!** see you soon!; **tan pronto como…** as soon as…

pronunciar *vt* **1** *(palabra)* to pronounce. **2** *(discurso)* to make.

propaganda *nf* **1** POL propaganda. **2** *(anuncios)* advertising.

propiedad nf **1** *(derecho)* ownership. **2** *(objeto)* property. • **hablar con propiedad** to speak properly.

propietario,-a nm,f owner.

propina nf tip.

propio,-a adj **1** *(perteneciente)* own: *en defensa propia*, in self-defence. **2** *(indicado)* proper, appropriate. **3** *(particular)* typical, peculiar: *es muy propio de él*, it's very typical of him. **4** *(mismo - él)* himself; *(- ella)* herself; *(- cosa, animal)* itself: *el propio autor*, the author himself.

proponer vt to suggest, propose.

proporción nf proportion.

proporcionar vt to supply, give.

propósito nm intention. • **a propósito** *(adrede)* on purpose.

propuesta nf proposal.

prórroga nf **1** *(de un plazo)* extension. **2** *(en deporte)* GB extra time; US overtime.

prosa nf prose.

prospecto nm *(de propaganda)* leaflet; *(de medicina)* directions for use.

prosperar vi to prosper, thrive.

protagonista nmf **1** *(de película)* main character, leading role. **2** *(de suceso)* major figure. **3** *(actor principal)* star.

protección nf protection.

proteger vt to protect.

proteína nf protein.

protesta nf protest.

protestar vi **1** to protest. **2** *(quejarse)* to complain.

provecho nm profit, benefit. • **¡buen provecho!** enjoy your meal!

proveedor,-ra nm,f supplier, purveyor.

provenir vi to come.

proverbio nm proverb, saying.

provincia nf province.

provisional adj provisional.

provisto,-a adj provided.

provocar vt **1** *(irritar)* to provoke. **2** *(causar)* to cause.

próximo,-a adj **1** *(cercano)* near, close. **2** *(siguiente)* next: *el mes próximo*, next month.

proyección nf **1** *(gen)* projection. **2** *(de película)* screening.

proyectil nm projectile.

proyecto nm **1** *(plan)* plan. **2** *(estudio, esquema)* project. ■ **proyecto de ley** bill.

prudente adj *(sabio)* sensible, wise, prudent; *(cuidadoso)* careful.

prueba nf **1** *(demostración)* proof. **2** *(examen)* test. **3** *(deportiva)* event. **4** *(de delito)* evidence. • **hacer la prueba** to try; **poner a prueba** to put to the test. ■ **prueba de alcoholemia** breath test.

psicología nf psychology.

psiquiatra *nmf* psychiatrist.
publicar *vt* to publish.
publicidad *nf* 1 *(difusión)* publicity. 2 *(anuncios)* advertising.
público,-a *adj* public. ► *nm* **público** *(espectadores)* audience.
puchero *nm* cooking pot.
pudrirse *vt-vpr* 1 *(gen)* to rot. 2 *(comida)* to go bad.
pueblo *nm* village, small town.
puente *nm* 1 bridge. 2 *(fiesta)* long weekend. ■ **puente aéreo** shuttle service; **puente de mando** bridge.
puerro *nm* leek.
puerta *nf* door. ■ **puerta de embarque** boarding gate.
puerto *nm* 1 *(de mar - pequeño)* harbour; *(- grande)* port;. 2 *(de montaña)* mountain pass. 3 INFORM port. ■ **puerto deportivo** marina.
pues *conj* 1 *(ya que)* since, as. 2 *(por lo tanto)* then, therefore. 3 *((enfático)* well: *pues bien*, well then; *¡pues claro!*, of course!.
puesta *nf*. ■ **puesta a punto** tuning; **puesta de sol** sunset; **puesta en marcha** 1 *(de vehículo)* starting. 2 *(de proyecto)* implementation.
puesto *nm* 1 *(lugar)* place. 2 *(de mercado)* stall; *(de feria etc)* stand. 3 *(empleo)* position, post. ● **puesto que** since.
pulga *nf* flea.

pulgar *nm* thumb.
pulmón *nm* lung.
pulmonía *nf* pneumonia.
pulpo *nm* octopus.
pulsar *vt* to press.
pulsera *nf* bracelet.
pulso *nm* pulse. ● **echar un pulso** to arm-wrestle; **tener buen pulso** to have a steady hand.
pulverizador *nm* spray, atomizer.
puma *nm* puma.
punta *nf* *(extremo - de dedo, lengua)* tip; *(- de aguja, cuchillo, lápiz)* point. ● **sacar punta a** *(lápiz)* to sharpen.
puntería *nf* aim.
punto *nm* 1 *(gen)* point. 2 *(de puntuación)* GB full stop; US period. 3 *(en costura, cirugía)* stitch. ● **en punto** sharp, on the dot; **estar en su punto** to be just right; **hasta cierto punto** up to a certain point. ■ **punto de encuentro** meeting point; **punto de vista** point of view; **punto muerto** 1 *(cambio de marchas)* neutral. 2 *(en negociaciones)* impasse, deadlock; **punto y aparte** full stop, new paragraph; **punto y coma** semicolon; **puntos suspensivos** US suspension points.
puntuación *nf* 1 *(en ortografía)* punctuation. 2 *(en competición)* scoring; *(total)* score.

puntual *adj* punctual.
puñado *nm* handful.
puñal *nm* dagger.
puñetazo *nm* punch.
puño *nm* 1 *(mano)* fist. 2 *(de prenda)* cuff.
pupila *nf* pupil.
pupitre *nm* desk.
puré *nm* purée. ■ **puré de patatas** mashed potatoes.
puro,-a *adj* 1 *(sin mezclar)* pure. 2 *(mero)* sheer, mere. ► *nm* **puro** cigar.
pus *nm* pus.
puzzle *nm* puzzle.

Q

que[1] *pron* 1 *(sujeto - persona)* who, that; *(- cosa)* that, which. 2 *(complemento - persona)* whom, who; *(cosa)* that, which. 3 *(complemento - de tiempo)* when; *(- de lugar)* where.
que[2] *conj* 1 *(después de verbos)* that. 2 *(con comparativos)* than: *es más alto que su padre*, he is taller than his father.
qué *pron* what? ► *adj* 1 *(en exclamativas)* how, what: *¡qué bonito!*, how nice! 2 *(en interrogativas)* which?
quebrar *vi* to go bankrupt.
quedar *vi* 1 *(faltar)* to remain, be left. 2 *(sentar)* to

look: *te queda muy bien*, it suits you. 3 *(estar situado)* to be: *¿por dónde queda tu casa?*, whereabouts is your house? ► *vpr* **quedarse** to remain, stay, be.
queja *nf* 1 *(protesta)* complaint. 2 *(de dolor)* moan, groan.
quejarse *vpr* 1 *(protestar)* to complain. 2 *(gimiendo)* to moan, groan.
quemadura *nf* 1 *(gen)* burn. 2 *(de agua hirviendo)* scald.
quemar *vt* 1 *(gen)* to burn. 2 *(incendiar)* to set on fire. ► *vi (estar muy caliente)* to be burning hot. ► *vpr* **quemarse** 1 to burn oneself. 2 *(al sol)* to get burnt.
querer *vt* 1 *(amar)* to love. 2 *(desear)* to want.
querido,-a *adj* dear, beloved.
queso *nm* cheese.
quiebra *nf* bankruptcy.
quien *pron* 1 *(sujeto)* who. 2 *(complemento)* who, whom. 3 *(indefinido)* whoever, anyone who.
quién *pron* 1 *(sujeto)* who. 2 *(complemento)* who, whom. ● *¿de quién?* whose?
quienquiera *pron* whoever.
quieto,-a *adj* still.
quilla *nf* keel.
química *nf* chemistry.
químico,-a *adj* chemical.
quince *num* fifteen; *(en fechas)* fifteenth.

quiniela nf football pools.

quinientos,-as num five hundred.

quinto,-a num fifth.

quiosco nm kiosk. ▪ **quiosco de periódicos** newspaper stand.

quirófano nm operating theatre.

quiste nm cyst.

quitamanchas nm stain remover.

quitanieves nm snowplough.

quitar vt to remove, take out, take off. ► vpr **quitarse 1** (apartarse) to move away. **2** (desaparecer) to go away, come out: *se me han quitado las ganas*, I don't feel like it any more. **3** (ropa) to take off. • **de quita y pon** detachable.

quizá adv perhaps, maybe.

quizás adv perhaps, maybe

R

rábano nm radish.

rabia nf **1** (enfermedad) rabies. **2** (enfado) rage, fury.

rabo nm tail

racha nf **1** (de viento) gust. **2** (período): *una buena racha*, a run of good luck.

racimo nm bunch.

ración nf **1** (porción) portion. **2** (parte que toca) share.

racional adj rational.

racista adj-nmf racist.

radar nm radar.

radiactivo,-a adj radioactive.

radiador nm radiator.

radical adj-nmf radical.

radio[1] nm **1** (de círculo) radius. **2** (de rueda) spoke.

radio[2] nf (medio) radio.

radio[3] nm **1** (hueso) radius. **2** (elemento químico) radium.

radiocasete nm radio-cassette.

radiografía nf **1** (técnica) radiography. **2** (imagen) X-ray.

ráfaga nf **1** (de viento) gust. **2** (de disparos) burst.

raíl nm rail.

raíz nf root. • **a raíz de** as a result of. ▪ **raíz cuadrada** square root.

rallado,-a adj grated. • **pan rallado** breadcrumbs.

rallar vt to grate.

rama nf branch.

rambla nf (paseo) boulevard, avenue.

ramillete nm bouquet.

ramo nm **1** (de flores) bunch. **2** (ámbito) field, section.

rampa nf ramp.

rana nf frog.

rancho nm (granja) ranch.

rango nm rank, class.

ranura nf **1** (canal) groove. **2** (para monedas, fichas) slot.

rapaz *nf (ave)* bird of prey.

rape *nm (pez)* angler fish.

rápido,-a *adj* quick, fast. ▶ *nm pl* **rápidos** *(del río)* rapids.

raptar *vt* to kidnap.

raqueta *nf* 1 racket. 2 *(para nieve)* snowshoe.

raro,-a *adj* 1 *(poco común)* rare. 2 *(peculiar)* odd, strange. • **raras veces** seldom.

rascacielos *nm* skyscraper.

rascar *vt* to scratch.

rasgo *nm* 1 *(línea)* stroke. 2 *(facción)* feature. 3 *(peculiaridad)* characteristic. • **a grandes rasgos** in outline.

rasguño *nm* scratch.

raso *nm (tejido)* satin. • **al raso** in the open air.

raspa *nf (de pescado)* bone.

raspar *vt (rascar)* to scrape; *(quitar rascando)* to scrape off.

rastrillo *nm* rake.

rastro *nm* 1 *(pista)* trail. 2 *(señal)* trace. 3 *(mercado)* flea market.

rata *nf* rat.

ratero,-a *nm,f* pickpocket.

ratificar *vt* to ratify.

rato *nm (momento)* while. • **pasar el rato** to kill time.

ratón *nm* mouse.

raya¹ *nf* 1 *(línea)* line. 2 *(de color)* stripe: *a rayas*, striped. 3 *(del pantalón)* crease. 4 *(del pelo)* parting. • **pasarse de la raya** to overstep the mark; **tener a raya** to keep within bounds.

raya² *nf (pez)* skate.

rayado,-a *adj* 1 *(con rayas)* striped. 2 *(disco)* scratched.

rayar *vt* 1 *(líneas)* to draw lines on, line, rule. 2 *(superficie)* to scratch.

rayo *nm* 1 *(de luz)* ray, beam. 2 *(en el cielo)* flash of lightning. ▪ **rayo de sol** sunbeam.

raza *nf* 1 *(humana)* race. 2 *(animal)* breed.

razón *nf* reason. • **no tener razón** to be wrong; **"Razón aquí"** "Enquire within"; **tener razón** to be right.

razonable *adj* reasonable.

re *nm (nota)* D; *(en solfeo)* re, ray.

reacción *nf* reaction.

reaccionar *vi* to react.

reactor *nm* 1 *(nuclear etc)* reactor. 2 *(avión)* jet plane.

real¹ *adj (auténtico)* real.

real² *adj (regio)* royal.

realidad *nf* reality. • **en realidad** really, in fact.

realización *nf (de tarea)* carrying out; *(de propósito)* achievement.

realizar *vt* 1 *(propósito, sueño)* to realize. 2 *(tarea)* to accomplish, carry out, do.

reanimar(se) *vt-vpr* to revive.

reanudar *vt* to renew, resume.

rebaja *nf* reduction. ▶ *nf pl* **rebajas** sales.

rebajar *vt* 1 *(precio, coste)* to reduce; *(color)* to tone down. 2 *(nivel)* to lower.

rebanada *nf* slice.

rebaño *nm (de cabras)* herd; *(de ovejas)* flock.

rebasar *vt* to exceed.

rebeca *nf* cardigan.

rebelde *nmf* rebel.

rebelión *nf* rebellion, revolt.

rebobinar *vt* to rewind.

rebotar *vi (balón)* to bounce.

rebote *nm* rebound.

rebozar *vt (con pan rallado)* to coat in breadcrumbs; *(con huevo)* to batter.

rebuznar *vi* to bray.

recado *nm* **1** *(mensaje)* message. **2** *(encargo)* errand.

recaída *nf* relapse.

recambio *nm (de maquinaria)* spare part, spare; *(de pluma, bolígrafo)* refill.

recapacitar *vi* to reflect.

recargable *adj (mechero)* refillable; *(batería)* rechargable.

recargar *vt* **1** *(arma)* to reload; *(mechero)* to refill; *(batería)* to recharge. **2** *(sobrecargar)* to overload.

recargo *nm* extra charge.

recaudación *nf (dinero)* takings.

recaudar *vt (impuestos)* to collect; *(dinero)* to raise.

recepción *nf* reception.

recepcionista *nmf* receptionist.

receptor *nm* TV receiver.

receta *nf* **1** *(médica)* prescription. **2** *(culinaria)* recipe.

rechazar *vt* to reject, turn down.

rechazo *nm* rejection.

rechoncho,-a *adj* chu

recibidor *nm* entrance hall.

recibimiento *nm* reception, welcome.

recibir *vt* **1** *(carta, señal, etc)* to get, receive. **2** *(persona)* to meet.

recibo *nm* **1** *(resguardo)* receipt. **2** *(factura)* invoice, bill.

reciclable *adj* recyclable.

reciclar *vt* **1** *(materiales)* to recycle. **2** *(profesionales)* to retrain.

recién *adv* recently, newly: *pan recién hecho*, freshly baked bread. • **"Recién pintado"** "Wet paint". ▪ **recién casados** newlyweds; **recién nacido** newborn baby.

reciente *adj* recent.

recinto *nm (gen)* premises; *(cerrado)* enclosure.

recipiente *nm* container.

recíproco,-a *adj* reciprocal.

recital *nm* recital.

recitar *vt* to recite.

reclamación *nf* **1** *(demanda)* claim, demand. **2** *(queja)* complaint, protest.

reclamar *vt (pedir)* to demand. ▶ *vi (quejarse)* to complain.

recluso,-a *nm,f* prisoner.

recluta *nm* **1** *(voluntario)* recruit. **2** *(obligado)* conscript.

recobrar(se) *vt-vpr* to recover.

recogedor *nm* dustpan.
recoger *vt* **1** *(coger del suelo)* to pick up. **2** *(ordenar)* to clear up. **3** *(ir a buscar persona)* to fetch, pick up.
recolectar *vt* *(cosecha)* to harvest; *(dinero)* to collet.
recomendación *nf* recommendation.
recomendar *vt* to recommend.
recompensa *nf* reward, recompense.
reconocer *vt* **1** *(gen)* to recognize. **2** *(a paciente)* to examine. **3** *(un error)* to admit.
reconocimiento *nm* **1** *(gen)* recognition. **2** *(chequeo médico)* examination, check up
reconstruir *vt* to reconstruct.
récord *adj-nm* record. • **batir un récord** to break a record.
recordar *vt-vi* to remember.
recorrer *vt* to travel round.
recorrido *nm* **1** *(trayecto)* journey. **2** *(distancia)* distance travelled.
recortar *vt* to cut (out).
recorte *nm* **1** *(de periódico)* press clipping. **2** *(de presupuesto)* cut.
recreativo,-a *adj* recreational.
recreo *nm* **1** *(entretenimiento)* recreation, amusement. **2** *(en la escuela)* playtime.
recta *nf* **1** *(línea)* straight line. **2** *(en carretera)* straight (piece of road). • **recta final** final straight.

rectángulo *nm* rectangle.
rectificar *vt* to rectify.
recto,-a *adj* **1** *(derecho)* straight. **2** *(honesto)* just, honest. ► *nm* **recto** rectum. ► *adv* straight on.
recuadro *nm* box.
recuento *nm* recount.
recuerdo *nm* **1** *(imagen mental)* memory. **2** *(regalo)* souvenir. ► *nm pl* **recuerdos** *(saludos)* regards; *(en carta)* best wishes.
recuperar(se) *vt-vpr* to recover.
recurrir *vi* *(acogerse - a algo)* to resort to; *(- a alguien)* to turn to. ► *vt* *(una sentencia)* to appeal against.
recurso *nm* **1** *(medio)* resort. **2** JUR appeal. ► *nm pl* **recursos** resources, means.
red *nf* **1** *(de pesca, Internet)* net. **2** *(sistema)* network.
redacción *nf* **1** *(escrito)* composition. **2** *(oficina)* editorial office. **3** *(redactores)* editorial staff.
redactor,-ra *nm,f* editor.
redada *nf* raid.
redondear *vt* *(cantidad)* to round off; *(por encima)* to round up; *(por debajo)* to round down.
redondo,-a *adj* **1** *(circular)* round. **2** *(perfecto)* perfect, excellent: *un negocio redondo*, an excellent business deal. ► *nm* **redondo** *(de carne)* topside. • **a la redonda** around.

reducir vt (disminuir) to reduce. ► vi (al conducir) to change down.
reembolso nm (pago) reimbursement; (devolución) refund. • **contra reembolso** cash on delivery.
reemplazar vt to replace.
referencia nf reference.
referirse vpr (aludir) to refer: *¿a qué te refieres?*, what do yo mean?
refinar vt to refine.
reflejar vt to reflect.
reflejo nm 1 (imagen) reflection. 2 (destello) gleam. ► mpl **reflejos** 1 (reacción) reflexes. 2 (en el pelo) highlights.
reflexionar vt to reflect.
reflexivo,-a adj (verbo etc) reflexive.
reforma nf 1 (cambio) reform. 2 (de edificio) alteration: *"Cerrado por reformas"*, "Closed for alterations".
refrán nm proverb, saying.
refrescar vt 1 (bebida) to cool, chill. 2 (memoria) to refresh. ► vi (tiempo) to turn cool: *por la noche refresca*, the nights are cold. ► vpr **refrescarse** 1 (tomar el fresco) to take a breath of fresh air. 2 (con agua) to freshen up.
refresco nm soft drink.
refrigerador nm fridge.
refuerzos nm pl (tropas) reinforcements.

refugiado,-a adj-nm,f refugee.
refugiarse vpr to take refuge.
refugio nm shelter, refuge.
regadera nf watering can.
regalar vt to give: *me lo han regalado*, they gave it to me, it was a present.
regaliz nm liquorice.
regalo nm gift, present. • **de regalo** free.
regar vt 1 (plantas) to water. 2 (terreno) to irrigate. 3 (calle) to hose down.
regata nf regatta.
regate nm dribble.
régimen nm 1 (de comida) diet. 2 (político) régime. • **estar a régimen** to be on a diet.
regimiento nm regiment.
región nf region.
registrar vt 1 (inspeccionar) to search, inspect. 2 (datos) to register.
registro nm 1 (inspección) search, inspection. 2 (inscripción) registration. 3 (oficina) registry; (libro) register.
regla nf 1 (norma) rule. 2 (instrumento) ruler. 3 (menstruación) period. • **en regla** in order; **por regla general** as a rule.
reglamento nm regulations.
regresar vi to return, come back, go back.
regreso nm return.
regular adj 1 (habitual) regular. 2 (pasable) so-so, average. ► vt to regulate.

rehén *nmf* hostage.

rehusar *vt* to refuse, decline.

reina *nf* queen.

reinar *vi* to reign.

reincidir *vi* to relapse.

reino *nm* kingdom, reign.

reintegro *nm* 1 *(de dinero de cuenta)* withdrawal. 2 *(de dinero pagado)* reimbursement.

reír(se) *vi-vpr* to laugh.

reivindicar *vt (derecho)* to demand, claim; *(propiedad)* to claim; *(atentado)* to claim responsability for.

reja *nf* grille.

rejilla *nf* 1 *(de ventilación)* grille. 2 *(de chimenea)* grate.

relación *nf* 1 *(gen)* relation. 2 *(listado)* list. 3 *(de pareja)* relationship. ■ **relaciones públicas** public relations.

relacionar *vt (vincular)* to relate, connect. ► *vpr* **relacionarse** *(tener amistad)* to get acquainted.

relajación *nf* relaxation.

relajarse *vpr* to relax.

relámpago *nm* flash of lightning.

relativo,-a *adj* relative.

relato *nm* story, tale.

relevar *vt (sustituir)* to relieve.

relevo *nm* 1 *(acto, persona)* relief. 2 DEP relay. ● **tomar el relevo** to take over.

relieve *nm* relief. ● **poner de relieve** to emphasize.

religión *nf* religion.

religioso,-a *adj* religious.

reliquia *nf* relic.

rellano *nm* landing.

rellenar *vt* 1 *(volver a llenar)* to refill. 2 *(cuestionario)* to fill in. 3 *(ave)* to stuff; *(pastel)* to fill.

relleno *nm (de aves)* stuffing; *(de pasteles)* filling.

reloj *nm (de pared, mesa)* clock; *(de pulsera)* watch. ● **contra reloj** against the clock. ■ **reloj de arena** hourglass; **reloj de sol** sundial; **reloj despertador** alarm clock; **reloj digital** 1 *(de pulsera)* digital watch. 2 *(de pared, mesa)* digital clock.

relojería *nf (tienda)* watchmaker's shop.

remar *vi* to row.

rematar *vt* 1 *(acabar)* to finish off. 2 DEP *(con cabeza)* to head; *(con pie)* to shoot.

remate *nm* 1 *(final)* end. 2 DEP *(con cabeza)* header; *(con pie)* shot.

remedio *nm* 1 *(medicamento)* remedy, cure. 2 *(solución)* solution.

remesa *nf (de mercancías)* consignment, shipment.

remite *nm* sender's name and address.

remitente *nmf* sender.

remitir *vt* 1 *(enviar)* to remit, send. 2 *(tormenta)* to abate; *(fiebre)* to go down.

remo *nm* 1 *(pala)* oar; *(de canoa)* paddle. 2 *(deporte)* rowing.

remojo *nm* soaking. • **poner algo en remojo** to leave STH to soak.

remolacha *nf* beetroot. ■ **remolacha azucarera** sugar beet.

remolcar *vt* to tow.

remolino *nm* 1 *(de agua)* whirlpool; *(de aire)* whirlwind. 2 *(de pelo)* GB tuft; US cowlick.

remolque *nm* trailer. • **a remolque** in tow.

remontar *vt* 1 *(río)* to go up. 2 *(superar)* to overcome. ▶ *vpr* **remontarse** *(datar)* to go back, date back.

remordimiento *nm* remorse.

remoto,-a *adj* remote.

remover *vt* 1 *(líquido, salsa)* to stir. 2 *(tierra)* to turn over. 3 *(tema)* to bring up again.

renacuajo *nm* tadpole.

rencor *nm* rancour.

rendido,-a *adj* worn out, exhausted.

rendija *nf* crack.

rendimiento *nm* 1 *(de máquina)* output. 2 *(de persona)* performance.

rendir *vt* *(producir)* to yield, produce. ▶ *vt-vi* *(dar fruto)* to pay. ▶ *vpr* **rendirse** to surrender.

reno *nm* reindeer.

renovar *vt* 1 *(contrato, actividad)* to renew. 2 *(casa)* to renovate.

renta *nf* 1 *(ingresos)* income. 2 *(beneficio)* interest. 3 *(alquiler)* rent. ■ **renta per cápita** per capita income.

rentable *adj* profitable.

renunciar *vt* 1 *(dejar)* to give up; *(abandonar)* to abandon; *(rechazar)* to refuse. 2 *(dimitir)* to resign.

reñir *vi* *(discutir)* to quarrel, argue. ▶ *vt* *(reprender)* to scold.

reparación *nf* *(arreglo)* repair.

reparar *vt* *(arreglar)* to repair, mend.

repartir *vt* 1 *(distribuir)* to deliver. 2 *(entregar)* to give out; *(correo)* to deliver.

reparto *nm* 1 *(gen)* delivery. 2 *(actores)* cast.

repasar *vt* 1 *(lección, texto)* to revise, go over. 2 *(máquina, cuenta)* to check.

repelente *adj* repellent.

repente *nm*. • **de repente** suddenly.

repercusión *nf* repercussion.

repertorio *nm* repertoire.

repetición *nf* repetition.

repetidor *nm* relay, booster station.

repetir *vt-vi* to repeat.

repisa *nf* shelf.

repleto,-a *adj* full up.

réplica *nf* 1 *(respuesta)* answer. 2 *(copia)* replica.

repollo *nm* cabbage.

reportaje *nm* *(en televisión)* report; *(prensa)* feature.

reportero,-a *nm,f* reporter.
reposar *vt-vi* to rest.
reposo *nm* rest. • **dejar en reposo** to leave to stand.
repostar *vi (coche)* to fill up, get some petrol; *(avión)* to refuel.
repostería *nf* confectionery.
representación *nf* 1 *(imagen, sustitución)* representation. 2 *(teatral)* performance. 3 *(delegación)* delegation.
representante *nmf* representative.
representar *vt* 1 *(ilustrar, sustituir)* to represent. 2 *(obra de teatro)* to perform. 3 *(edad)* to look: *no representa esa edad*, she doesn't look that age.
reprimir *vt* to repress.
reproche *nm* reproach.
reproducir(se) *vt-vpr* to reproduce.
reptar *vi* to crawl.
reptil *nm* reptile.
república *nf* republic.
repuesto *nm* spare part.
repugnante *adj* repugnant.
reputación *nf* reputation.
requesón *nm* cottage cheese.
requisito *nm* requisite.
resaca *nf* hangover.
resbalar(se) *vi-vpr* 1 *(deslizarse)* to slide. 2 *(sin querer)* to slip.
resbalón *nm* slip.
rescatar *vt* 1 *(salvar)* to rescue. 2 *(recuperar)* to recover.

rescate *nm* 1 *(de persona)* rescue. 2 *(dinero)* ransom.
resentimiento *nm* resentment.
reserva *nf* 1 *(de plazas)* booking, reservation. 2 *(provisión)* reserve. 3 *(vino)* vintage. 4 *(de animales)* reserve. ► *nmf* *(deportista)* reserve, substitute. • **sin reservas** unreservedly, wholeheartedly.
reservar *vt (plazas)* to book, reserve. ► *vpr* **reservarse** *(conservarse)* to save oneself.
resfriado *nm (con congestión)* cold; *(poco importante)* chill.
resfriarse *vpr* to catch a cold.
resguardo *nm (recibo)* receipt.
residencia *nf* residence. ■ **residencia de ancianos** residential home; **residencia de estudiantes** GB hall of residence; US dormitory.
residir *vi* 1 *(habitar)* to reside, live. 2 *(radicar)* to lie: *es ahí donde reside el problema*, that's where the problem lies.
residuo *nm* residue. ■ **residuos radiactivos** radioactive waste.
resignarse *vpr* to resign.
resina *nf* resin.
resistencia *nf* 1 *(de material)* resistance. 2 *(de persona)* endurance. 3 *(oposición)* reluctance, opposition.
resistente *adj* resistant.

resistir vt **1** (no ceder, aguantar) to withstand. **2** (tolerar) to stand, bear. ► vpr **resistirse 1** (negarse) to refuse. **2** (forcejear) to resist. **3** (oponerse) to offer resistance.

resolver vt (problema) to solve.

respaldo nm **1** (de asiento) back. **2** (apoyo) support, backing.

respectivo,-a adj respective.

respecto nm. • **al respecto** on the matter, about; **con respecto a** with regard to, regarding.

respetar vt to respect.

respeto nm respect.

respiración nf breathing. ▪ **respiración boca a boca** mouth-to-mouth resuscitation.

respirar vi to breathe.

responder vt-vi to answer, reply.

responsabilidad nf responsibility.

responsable adj responsible.

respuesta nf (contestación) answer, reply; (reacción) response.

resta nf substraction.

restablecerse vpr (recuperarse) to recover, get better.

restante adj remaining.

restar vt to subtract.

restauración nf **1** (de muebles etc) restoration. **2** (hostelería) catering.

restaurante nm restaurant.

resto nm **1** (lo que queda) rest. **2** (en matemáticas) remainder. ► nm pl **restos** (gen) remains; (de comida) leftovers.

resultado nm result.

resultar vi **1** (funcionar) to work. **2** (ocurrir, ser) to turn out to be. **3** (salir) to come out: **resultar herido**, to be wounded. • **resulta que** it turns out that.

resumen nm summary. • **en resumen** in short.

resumir vt to summarize.

retablo nm altarpiece.

retina nf retina.

retirada nf retreat, withdrawal.

retirar vt (apartar) to withdraw. ► vpr **retirarse 1** (tropas) to retreat. **2** (apartarse) to withdraw. **3** (jubilarse) to retire.

retiro nm **1** (jubilación) retirement. **2** (pensión) pension.

reto nm challenge.

retocar vt to touch up.

retorcer vt (doblar) to twist. ► vpr **retorcerse** (de dolor) to writhe; (de risa) to double up.

retorno nm return.

retransmisión nf broadcast.

retransmitir vt to broadcast.

retrasar vt **1** (salida, proceso) to delay, put off. **2** (reloj) to put back. ► vi-vpr **retrasar-(se) 1** (ir atrás) to fall behind.

2 *(llegar tarde)* to be late. **3** *(reloj)* to be slow.

retraso *nm* **1** *(de tiempo)* delay. **2** *(subdesarrollo)* backwardness.

retrato *nm* **1** portrait. **2** *(foto)* photograph. ▪ **retrato robot** identikit picture, photofit picture.

retrete *nm* toilet, lavatory.

retroceder *vi* to go back.

retrovisor *nm* rear-view mirror.

reúma *nm* rheumatism.

reunión *nf* meeting.

reunir(se) *vt-vpr (personas)* to meet; *(cosas)* to get together.

revelado *nm* developing.

revelar *vt* **1** *(descubrir)* to reveal. **2** *(fotos)* to develop.

reventar(se) *vt-vpr (estallar)* to burst.

reventón *nm* **1** *(de tubería)* burst. **2** *(de neumático)* blowout.

reverencia *nf (saludo - de hombre)* bow; *(- de mujer)* curts(e)y.

revés *nm* **1** *(reverso)* back, reverse. **2** *(bofetada)* slap. **3** *(contrariedad)* misfortune. **4** *(en tenis etc)* backhand. • **al revés 1** *(todo lo contrario)* on the contrary. **2** *(en orden inverso)* the other way round. **3** *(lo de dentro fuera)* inside out. **4** *(lo delantero detrás)* back to front. **5** *(boca abajo)* upside down, the wrong way up.

revisar *vt (teoría, edición)* to revise; *(cuenta)* to check.

revisión *nf (de teoría, edición)* revision. ▪ **revisión médica** checkup.

revisor,-ra *nm,f* ticket inspector. ▪ **revisor ortográfico** spellchecker.

revista *nf* **1** *(publicación)* magazine, review. **2** *(espectáculo)* revue.

revolcarse *vpr* to roll about.

revolución *nf* revolution.

revólver *nm* revolver.

revolver *vt* **1** *(remover)* to stir; *(agitar)* to shake. **2** *(desordenar)* to mess up.

revuelta *nf (revolución)* revolt, riot.

revuelto *m* scrambled eggs.

rey *nm* king. ▪ **los Reyes Magos** the Three Kings, the Three Wise Men.

rezagarse *vpr* to fall behind.

rezar *vi* to pray.

riachuelo *nm* stream.

riada *nf* flood.

ribera *nf* **1** *(de río)* bank. **2** *(de mar)* seashore.

rico,-a *adj* **1** *(gen)* rich. **2** *(sabroso)* tasty, delicious.

ridículo,-a *adj* ridiculous.

riego *nm* irrigation, watering. ▪ **riego sanguíneo** blood circulation.

riel *nm* rail.

rienda *nf (brida)* rein.

riesgo *nm* risk, danger.

rifar vt to raffle.
rifle nm rifle.
rígido,-a adj rigid.
rigor nm GB rigour, US rigor.
rima nf rhyme.
rímel nm mascara.
rincón nm corner.
rinoceronte nm rhinoceros.
riña nf 1 (pelea) fight. 2 (discusión) quarrel.
riñón nm kidney.
río nm rive. • **río abajo** downstream; **río arriba** upstream.
risa nf laugh.
ritmo nm 1 (compás) rhythm. 2 (velocidad) pace, speed.
rito nm rite.
rival nmf rival.
rizado,-a adj curly.
rizo nm curl.
robar vt (banco, persona) to rob; (objeto) to steal ; (casa) to burgle, break into.
roble nm oak tree.
robo nm (a banco, persona) robbery; (de objeto) theft; (en casa) burglary.
robot nm robot.
roca nf rock.
roce nm 1 (señal - en superficie) scuff mark; (- en piel) chafing mark. 2 (contacto físico) light touch.
rocío nm dew.
rodaja nf slice.
rodaje nm 1 (de película) filming, shooting. 2 (de vehículo) running-in.

rodar vi (dar vueltas) to roll, turn. ► vt 1 (película) to shoot. 2 (coche) to run in.
rodear vt 1 (cercar) to surround, encircle. 2 (desviarse) to make a detour.
rodeo nm 1 (desvío) detour. 2 (elusión) evasiveness.
rodilla nf knee.
roedor nm rodent.
rogar vt 1 (suplicar) to beg. 2 (pedir) to ask, request.
rojo,-a adj red. ► nm **rojo** red.
rollo nm 1 (de tela, papel) roll. 2 fam (aburrimiento) drag, bore, pain.
románico,-a adj-mn Romanesque.
romántico,-a adj-nm,f romantic.
rombo nm rhombus.
romero nm rosemary.
rompecabezas nm 1 (juego) puzzle. 2 (problema) riddle.
rompeolas nm breakwater.
romper(se) vt-vpr (gen) to break; (papel, tela) to tear; (cristal) to smash. ► vt (relaciones) to break off.
ron nm rum.
roncar vi to snore.
ronda nf 1 (patrulla) patrol. 2 (de policía) beat. 3 (de bebidas, cartas) round.
rondar vt-vi 1 (vigilar) to patrol. 2 (merodear) to prowl around. 3 (cifra) to be about.
ronquido nm snore, snoring.

ropa *nf* clothes. ■ **ropa interior** underwear.

rosa *adj-nm* (*color*) pink. ► *nf* (*flor*) rose.

rosado *adj-nm* (*vino*) rosé.

rosal *nm* rosebush.

rosca *nf* (*de tuerca*) thread.

roscón *nm* ring-shaped roll or cake.

rosquilla *nf* doughnut.

rostro *nm fml* face.

roto,-a *adj* broken.

rotonda *nf* roundabout.

rótula *nf* knee-cap.

rotulador *nm* felt-tip pen.

rótulo *nm* **1** (*etiqueta*) label. **2** (*letrero*) sign. **3** (*anuncio*) poster, placard.

rotura *nf* **1** (*de objeto*) breakage. **2** (*de hueso*) fracture.

roulotte *nf* caravan.

rozadura *nf* scratch.

rozar *vt-vi* (*tocar ligeramente*) to touch, brush. ► *vt* (*raer*) to rub against: *el zapato me rozaba*, my shoe was rubbing.

rubéola *nf* German measles, rubella.

rubí *nm* ruby.

rubio,-a *adj* (*hombre*) blond; (*mujer*) blonde.

ruborizarse *vpr* to blush.

rúbrica *nf* **1** (*firma*) flourish. **2** (*título*) title.

rueda *nf* (*de vehículo*) wheel. ■ **rueda de recambio** spare wheel.

ruedo *nm* bullring.

ruego *nm* request.

rugby *nm* rugby.

rugir *vi* to roar.

ruido *nm* noise.

ruina *nf* ruin: *al borde de la ruina*, on the brink of ruin; *el edificio amenazaba ruina*, the building was about to collapse. ► *nf pl* **ruinas** ruins. ■ **en ruinas** in ruins.

ruiseñor *nm* nightingale.

rulo *nm* (*para pelo*) curler.

rumba *nf* rumba.

rumbo *nm* course, direction. ■ **con rumbo a** bound for; **sin rumbo** aimlessly.

rumiante *adj-nm* ruminant.

rumor *nm* **1** (*noticia, voz*) GB rumour; US rumor. **2** (*murmullo*) murmur.

rumorearse *vi* GB to be rumoured; US to be rumored.

rupestre *adj* (*planta*) rock; (*pintura*) cave.

ruptura *nf* **1** (*de acuerdo*) breaking. **2** (*de relación*) breaking-off; (*de matrimonio*) break-up.

rural *adj* rural, country.

Rusia *nf* Russia.

ruso,-a *adj* Russian. ► *nm,f* (*persona*) Russian. ► *nm* **ruso** (*idioma*) Russian.

rústico,-a *adj* rustic.

ruta *nf* route.

rutina *nf* routine.

rutinario,-a *adj* monotonous.

S

sábado *nm* Saturday.
sabana *nf* savannah.
sábana *nf* sheet.
saber *nm* knowledge. ► *vt-vi (conocer)* to know. ► *vt* **1** *(poder)* can: **sabe tocar el piano**, she can play the piano. **2** *(tener noticias de)* to hear: **hace mucho que no sé nada de ellos**, I haven't heard anything from them for ages. **3** *(enterarse)* to find out: **cuando supe que era su cumpleaños...**, when I found out it was her birthday... ► *vi (tener sabor a)* to taste. ● **a saber** *fml* namely; **hacer saber** to inform; **saber mal a ALGN**: **le supo mal que se fueran sin ella**, she was upset that they went without her; **que yo sepa** as far as I know.
sabio,-a *adj* learned, wise.
sable *nm* sabre.
sabor *nm* **1** *(gusto)* taste. **2** *(gusto añadido)* GB flavour, US flavor. ● **tener sabor** to taste.
sabroso,-a *adj* tasty.
sacacorchos *nm* corkscrew.
sacapuntas *nm* pencil sharpener.
sacar *vt* **1** *(poner fuera)* to take out. **2** *(extraer)* to extract, pull out: **fui al dentista a** **sacarme una muela**, I went to the dentist to have a tooth out. **3** *(moda)* to introduce, bring out: **han sacado un nuevo disco**, they have brought out a new record. **4** *(entrada, pasaporte)* to get: **he sacado las entradas para el concierto**, I've bought the tickets for the concert. **5** *(tenis)* to serve; *(fútbol - al principio)* to kick off; *(durante el partido)* to take the kick. ● **sacar adelante 1** *(proyecto)* to carry out. **2** *(hijos)* to bring up.
sacarina *nf* saccharine.
sacerdote *nm* priest.
saciar *vt (hambre)* to satiate; *(sed)* to quench.
saco *nm* **1** *(bolsa)* sack, bag. **2** *(contenido)* sackful, bagful. ■ **saco de dormir** sleeping bag.
sacramento *nm* sacrament.
sacrificarse *vpr* to make sacrifices.
sacrificio *nm* sacrifice.
sacudir *vt (agitar)* to shake.
safari *nm* safari.
sagrado,-a *adj* **1** *(religioso)* holy. **2** *(que merece respeto)* sacred.
sal *nf* **1** *(condimento)* salt. **2** *(gracia)* wit. ■ **sal de mesa** table salt; **sales de baño** bath salts.
sala *nf* **1** *(habitación)* room. **2** *(sala de estar)* living room. **3** *(de hospital)* ward. **4** *(de tribu-*

nal) courtroom. **5** *(cine)* cinema. ■ **sala de espera** waiting room; **sala de estar** living room; **sala de fiestas** nightclub, discotheque.

salado,-a *adj* **1** *(con sal)* salted. **2** *(con demasiada sal)* salty. **3** *(no dulce)* savoury.

salamandra *nf* salamander.

salar *vt* to salt.

salario *nm* salary, wages.

salchicha *nf* sausage.

salchichón *nm* salami.

saldo *nm* **1** *(de una cuenta)* balance. **2** *(liquidación)* sale.

salero *nm* *(recipiente)* saltcellar.

salida *nf* **1** *(acto)* departure. **2** *(de personas)* exit, way out; *(de aire, gas)* vent; *(de agua)* outlet. **3** *(de autopista)* exit. **4** DEP start. **5** *(excursión)* trip, outing. ■ **salida de emergencia** emergency exit; **salida del sol** sunrise; **salida nula** false start; **salidas internacionales** international departures; **salidas nacionales** domestic departures.

salir *vi* **1** *(ir de dentro para afuera)* to go out. **2** *(venir de dentro para fuera)* to come out. **3** *(partir)* to leave: *el autobús sale a las tres,* the bus leaves at three. **4** *(aparecer)* to appear: *salir en los periódicos,* to be in the newspapers. **5** *(resultar)* to turn out, to be: *la tortilla te ha salido perfec-*

ta, the omelette has turned out perfect. **6** *(del trabajo, colegio)* to leave, come out. **7** *(producto)* to come out, be released. **8** *(sol)* to rise. ► *vpr* **salirse 1** *(soltarse, desviarse)* to come off. **2** *(líquido)* to leak, leak out. ● **salir a** ALGN to take after SB; **salir adelante** to be successful; **salir con** ALGN to go out with SB; **salir ganando con algo** to do well out of STH; **salir perdiendo** to lose out.

saliva *nf* saliva.

salmón *nm* salmon.

salmonete *nm* red mullet.

salón *nm* **1** *(en casa)* living room, lounge. **2** *(público)* hall. ■ **salón de actos** assembly hall; **salón de belleza** beauty salon, beauty parlour; **salón recreativo** amusement arcade.

salpicadero *nm* dashboard.

salpicar *vt* to splash.

salpicón *nm*. ■ **salpicón de marisco** seafood salad.

salsa *nf* **1** sauce. **2** *(baile)* salsa.

salsera *nf* gravy boat.

saltamontes *nm* grasshopper.

saltar *vi* **1** *(botar)* to jump. **2** *(al agua)* to dive. **3** *(desprenderse)* to come off. ► *vt (valla etc)* to jump (over). ► *vpr* **saltarse 1** *(ley etc)* to ignore. **2** *(omitir)* to skip, miss out.

salto nm 1 (gen) jump. 2 (de trampolín) dive. • **dar un salto** to jump. ▪ **salto con pértiga** pole vault; **salto de agua** waterfall, falls pl; **salto de altura** high jump; **salto de cama** negligée; **salto de esquí** ski-jump; **salto de longitud** long jump; **salto mortal** somersault.

salud nf health. ▶ interj **¡salud!** (al brindar) cheers!; (al estornudar) bless you!

saludar vt-vi to say hello to. • **le saluda atentamente 1** (si no conocemos el nombre) yours faithfully. **2** (si conocemos el nombre) yours sincerely.

saludo nm 1 (gen) greeting. 2 (entre militares) salute. ▶ nm pl **saludos** best wishes.

salvación nf salvation.

salvaje adj (gen) wild; (pueblo) savage, uncivilized. ▶ nmf savage.

salvamanteles nm table mat.

salvamento nm rescue.

salvar vt to save, rescue. ▶ vpr **salvarse** (sobrevivir) to survive. • **¡sálvese quien pueda!** every man for himself!

salvavidas nm life belt.

salvo prep except, except for. • **estar a salvo** to be safe and sound; **ponerse a salvo** to reach safety; **salvo que** unless.

san adj → santo,-a.

sanción nf 1 (multa) fine. 2 (castigo) sanction: **una sanción de cuatro partidos**, a four-game suspension.

sandalia nf sandal.

sandía nf watermelon.

sándwich nm sandwich.

sangrar vt-vi to bleed.

sangre nf blood. • **a sangre fría** in cool blood. ▪ **sangre fría** sangfroid, calmness.

sangría nf (bebida) sangria.

sanidad nf public health.

sanitarios nm pl bathroom fittings.

sano,-a adj healthy. • **sano y salvo** safe and sound.

santo,-a adj 1 (lugar, vida, misa) holy. 2 (con nombre) Saint. 3 (para enfatizar) blessed: **todo el santo día**, the whole day long. ▶ nm,f saint.

sapo nm toad.

saque nm 1 (tenis) service. 2 (fútbol) kick-off. ▪ **saque de banda** throw-in; **saque de esquina** corner.

sarampión nm measles pl.

sardina nf sardine.

sargento nm sergeant.

sarpullido nm rash.

sartén nf GB frying pan; US skillet.

sastre,-a nm,f (hombre) tailor; (mujer) dressmaker.

satélite nm satellite.

satén nm satin.

satisfacción nf satisfaction.

satisfacer *vt* to satisfy.
satisfecho,-a *adj* satisfied.
sauce *nm* willow. ▪ **sauce llorón** weeping willow.
sauna *nf* sauna.
saxofón *nm* saxophone.
sazonar *vt* to season.
se¹ *pron* **1** *(reflexivo - a él mismo)* himself; *(- a ella misma)* herself; *(- a usted mismo)* yourself; *(- a ellos mismos)* themselves; *(- a ustedes mismos)* yourselves. **2** *(recíproco)* one another, each other, each other. **3** *(en pasivas e impersonales): se dice que…,* it is said that…; *se suspendió el partido,* the match was postponed; *se habla español,* Spanish spoken.
se² *pron (objeto indirecto - a él)* him; *(- a ella)* her; *(cosa)* it; *(- a usted/ustedes)* you; *(- a ellos/ellas)* them.
secador *nm* dryer. ▪ **secador de pelo** hair-dryer.
secadora *nf* clothes-dryer, tumble-dryer.
secar *vt (pelo, ropa, piel)* to dry; *(lágrimas, vajilla)* to wipe.
sección *nf* **1** *(división)* section. **2** *(en tienda, oficina)* department.
seco,-a *adj* **1** *(no mojado)* dry. **2** *(frutos, flores)* dried. **3** *(golpe, ruido)* sharp. • **a secas** simply, just; **en seco** sharply, suddenly.
secretaría *nf* secretary's office.

secretario,-a *nm,f* secretary: *secretario,-a de dirección,* executive secretary.
secreto,-a *adj* secret. ▶ *nm* **secreto** secret.
secta *nf* sect.
sector *nm* **1** *(zona)* area. **2** *(de la industria)* sector.
secuela *nf* consequence.
secuencia *nf* sequence.
secuestro *nm* **1** *(de persona)* kidnapping. **2** *(de avión)* high-jacking.
secundario,-a *adj* secondary.
sed *nf* thirst. • **tener sed** to be thirsty.
seda *nf* silk. ▪ **seda dental** dental floss.
sedal *nm* fishing line.
sedante *adj-nm* sedative.
sede *nf* **1** *(de organización)* headquarters; *(de empresa)* head office. **2** *(del gobierno)* seat. **3** *(de acontecimiento)* venue.
seducir *vt* to seduce.
segar *vt* to reap.
segmento *nm* segment.
seguido,-a *adj* **1** *(acompañado)* followed. **2** *(consecutivo)* consecutive: *dos días seguidos,* two days running. ▶ *adv* straight on. • **en seguida** at once, immediately.
seguidor,-ra *nm,f* follower.
seguir *vt* **1** *(gen)* to follow. **2** *(continuar)* to continue. ▶ *vi* **1** *(proseguir)* to go on: *siga to-*

do recto hasta la plaza, go straight on until you get to the square. **2** *(permanecer)* to remain: *siguió de pie*, he remained standing. **3** *(estar todavía)* to be still: *sigue enfermo*, he's still sick.

según *prep (de acuerdo con)* according to. ► *adv* **1** *(depende de)* depending on: *según lo que digan*, depending on what they say. **2** *(como)* just as: *todo quedó según estaba*, everything stayed just as it was. **3** *(a medida que)* as: *según iban entrando se les daba una copa*, as they came in they were given a drink.

segundero *nm* second hand.

segundo,-a *num* second. ► *nm* **segundo** second.

seguridad *nf* **1** *(contra accidentes)* safety. **2** *(contra robos, ataques)* security. **3** *(certeza)* certainty. **4** *(confianza)* confidence. ● **con toda seguridad** definitely. ■ **Seguridad Social** National Health Service.

seguro,-a *adj* **1** *(físicamente)* safe. **2** *(estable)* secure. **3** *(fiable)* reliable: *un método muy seguro*, a very reliable method. **4** *(cierto)* definite: *aún no es seguro que venga*, it's not definite that he's coming yet. **5** *(convencido)* confident, sure, certain: *estoy seguro de que no va a defraudarnos*, I'm

sure he won't let us down. ► *nm* **seguro 1** *(contrato, póliza)* insurance. **2** *(mecanismo)* safety catch, safety device. ► *adv (sin duda)* for sure, definitely: *lo sé seguro*, I know for sure. ● **seguro que...** I bet...

seis *num* six; *(en fechas)* sixth. ● **son las seis** it's six o'clock.

seiscientos,-as *num* six hundred.

seísmo *nm* earthquake.

selección *nf* selection. ■ **selección nacional** national team.

seleccionar *vt* to select.

selecto,-a *adj*: *un club selecto*, an exclusive club; *vinos selectos*, fine wines, choice wines; *ante un público selecto*, before a selected audience.

sellar *vt* to seal.

sello *nm* **1** *(de correos)* stamp. **2** *(de estampar, precinto)* seal. **3** *(distintivo)* hallmark. ■ **sello discográfico** record label.

selva *nf* jungle.

semáforo *nm* traffic lights.

semana *nf* week. ■ **Semana Santa** Easter.

semanal *adj* weekly.

semanario *nm* weekly magazine.

sembrar *vt (con semillas)* to sow; *(con plantas)* to plant.

semejante *adj (parecido)* similar. ► *nm* fellow being.

semen *nm* semen.

semestre *nm* six-month period, semester.

semifinal *nf* semifinal.

semilla *nf* seed.

senado *nm* senate.

senador,-ra *nm,f* senator.

sencillo,-a *adj* **1** *(fácil)* simple. **2** *(persona)* natural, unaffected.

sendero *nm* path.

seno *nm* *(pecho)* breast.

sensación *nf* **1** *(percepción)* feeling. **2** *(efecto)* sensation.

sensacional *adj* sensational.

sensato,-a *adj* sensible.

sensibilidad *nf* sensitivity.

sensible *adj* sensitive.

sentar *vi* **1** *(comida)* to agree: *el chocolate no me sienta bien*, chocolate doesn't agree with me. **2** *(ropa)* to suit: *esa corbata te sienta bien*, that tie suits you. **3** *(hacer efecto)* to do: *un poco de aire fresco te sentará bien*, a bit of fresh air will do you good. ► *vpr* **sentarse** to sit down.

sentencia *nf* *(condena)* sentence. • **dictar sentencia** to pass sentence.

sentido *nm* **1** *(vista, oído, etc)* sense. **2** *(dirección)* direction: *una calle de sentido único*, a one-way street. **3** *(juicio)* consciousness. **4** *(significado)* meaning. • **perder el sentido** to faint; **recobrar el sentido** to regain consciousness;

tener sentido to make sense. ▪ **sentido común** common sense; **sentido del humor** sense of humour.

sentimiento *nm* feeling.

sentir *vt* **1** *(lamentar)* to regret. **2** *(oír)* to hear. ► *vt-vpr* **sentir(se)** to feel. • **¡lo siento!** I'm sorry!; **sentirse mal** to feel ill.

seña *nf* sign. ► *nf pl* **señas** address. • **hacer señas** to signal, gesture.

señal *nf* **1** *(indicio)* sign. **2** *(marca)* mark. **3** *(signo)* signal. **4** *(por teléfono)* tone: *no había señal*, there was no dialling tone. ▪ **señal de tráfico** road sign.

señalar *vt* **1** *(indicar)* to show. **2** *(marcar)* to mark: *señálalo en rojo*, mark it in red. **3** *(hacer notar)* to point to. **4** *(con el dedo)* to point at.

señor *nm* **1** *(hombre)* man; *(caballero)* gentleman. **2** *(en tratamientos)* sir; *(delante de apellido)* Mr: *el señor Pérez*, Mr Pérez.

señora *nf* **1** *(mujer)* woman; *(dama)* lady. **2** *(esposa)* wife. **4** *(en tratamientos)* madam; *(delante de apellido)* Mrs: *la señora Gómez*, Mrs Gómez; *señoras y señores*, ladies and gentlemen.

señorita *nf* **1** *(mujer joven)* young lady. **2** *(delante de ape-*

llido) Miss: *la señorita López*, Miss López. **3** *(profesora)* teacher.

separación *nf* **1** *(acción)* separation. **2** *(espacio)* gap.

separar *vt* to separate. ▶ *vpr* **separarse** *(de una persona)* to separate, split up.

sepia *nf* cuttlefish.

septiembre *nm* September.

séptimo,-a *num* seventh.

sepultar *vt* to bury.

sepultura *nf* grave.

sequía *nf* drought.

ser *vi* **1** *(gen)* to be. **2** *(pertenecer)* to belong: *el cuadro es de Picasso*, the painting is by Picasso. **3** *(material)* to be made of: *la mesa es de madera*, the table is made of wood. ▶ *aux* to be. ● **a no ser que** unless; **a poder ser** if possible; **de no ser por ...** had it not been for ...; **érase una vez** once upon a time; **es más** furthermore; **sea como sea** in any case. ■ **ser humano** human being; **ser vivo** living creature.

sereno,-a *adj* calm.

serial *nm* serial.

serie *nf* series.

serio,-a *adj* **1** *(persona, enfermedad)* serious. **2** *(formal)* reliable.

serpiente *nf* snake. ■ **serpiente de cascabel** rattlesnake.

serrar *vt* to saw.

serrín *nm* sawdust.

servicio *nm* **1** *(atención)* service. **2** *(criados)* servants. **3** *(juego)* set. **4** *(tenis)* serve, service. **5** *(retrete)* toilet. ■ **servicio a domicilio** home delivery service; **servicio militar** military service.

servidor *nm* INFORM server.

servilleta *nf* napkin, serviette.

servir *vt* **1** *(comida)* to serve: *¿ya le sirven?*, are you being served? **2** *(bebida)* to pour: *¿te sirvo yo?*, shall I pour? ▶ *vi* **1** *(ser útil)* to be useful. **2** *(trabajar)* to serve. ▶ *vpr* **servirse 1** *(comida)* to help oneself: *sírvase usted mismo*, help yourself. **2** *(utilizar)* to use. ● **servir de** to be used as; **servir para** to be used for.

sesenta *num* sixty.

sesión *nf* **1** *(reunión)* session, meeting. **2** *(de película)* showing.

seso *nm* brain, brains.

seta *nf* mushroom; *(no comestible)* toadstool.

setecientos,-as *num* seven hundred.

setenta *num* seventy.

setiembre *nm* September.

seto *nm* hedge.

sexo *nm* sex.

sexto,-a *num* sixth.

short *nm* shorts.

si[1] *conj* if. ● **si bien** although; **si no** otherwise.

si² *nm (nota musical)* ti, si, B.

sí¹ *pron (él)* himself; *(ella)* herself; *(cosa)* itself; *(uno mismo)* oneself; *(plural)* themselves.

sí² *adv* 1 *(en respuestas)* yes. 2 *(sustituye al verbo)*: **ella no irá, pero yo sí**, she won't go, but I will. ▶ *nm* yes

sida *nm* AIDS.

sidra *nf* cider.

siempre *adv* always. ● **para siempre** forever; **siempre que** whenever; **siempre y cuando** provided, as long as.

sien *nf* temple.

sierra *nf* 1 *(herramienta)* saw. 2 *(cordillera)* mountain range.

siesta *nf* siesta, afternoon nap.

siete *num* seven; *(en fechas)* seventh. ▶ *nm (rasgón)* tear.

sifón *nm (bebida)* soda water.

sigla *nf* acronym.

siglo *nm* century.

significado *nm* meaning.

significar *vt* to mean.

signo *nm (señal)* sign.

siguiente *adj* following, next.

sílaba *nf* syllable.

silbar *vi* 1 *(con los labios, viento)* to whistle. 2 *(abuchear)* to hiss.

silbato *nm* whistle.

silbido *nm* whistle.

silencio *nm* silence. ● **guardar silencio** to keep quiet.

silicona *nf* silicone.

silla *nf* chair. ▪ **silla de montar** saddle.

sillín *nm* saddle.

sillón *nm* armchair.

silueta *nf* 1 *(contorno)* silhouette. 2 *(figura)* figure: **te realza la silueta**, it shows off your figure.

silvestre *adj* wild.

símbolo *nm* symbol.

simétrico,-a *adj* symmetric.

similar *adj* similar.

simpático,-a *adj* nice.

simple *adj* 1 *(sencillo)* simple. 2 *(puro)* mere: **con una simple llamada**, with just a phone call.

simultáneo,-a *adj* simultaneous.

sin *prep* 1 *(gen)* without. 2 *(por hacer)*: **está sin planchar**, it has not been ironed. ● **sin embargo** however.

sincero,-a *adj* sincere.

sindicato *nm* trade union.

sinfonía *nf* symphony.

singular *adj* 1 *(único)* singular, single. 2 *(excepcional)* extraordinary. 3 *(raro)* peculiar.

siniestro *nm (accidente)* accident. ● **fue declarado siniestro total** it was declared a write-off.

sino *conj* but.

sinónimo *nm* synonym.

sintético,-a *adj* synthetic.

síntoma *nm* symptom.

sintonizar *vt* to tune in to.

sinvergüenza *nmf* cheeky devil.

siquiera *conj.* • **ni siquiera** not even.

sirena *nf* 1 *(alarma)* siren. 2 *(ninfa)* mermaid.

sirviente,-a *nm,f* servant.

sistema *nm* system.

sitio *nm* 1 *(lugar)* place. 2 *(espacio)* space, room.

situación *nf* situation.

situar *vt* to place, locate.

sobaco *nm* armpit.

soborno *nm* 1 *(acción)* bribery. 2 *(regalo)* bribe.

sobra *nf* excess, surplus. ► *nf pl* **sobras** leftovers. • **de sobra** more than enough.

sobrar *vi* 1 *(quedar)* to be left over. 2 *(sin aprovechar)* to be more than enough. 3 *(estar de más)* to be superfluous.

sobre *prep* 1 *(encima)* on, upon: *el jarrón está sobre la mesa*, the vase is on the table. 2 *(por encima)* over, above: *el helicóptero volaba sobre la ciudad*, the helicopter flew over the city. 3 *(acerca de)* on, about: *hablar sobre algo*, to talk about STH. 4 *(alrededor de)* around, about: *llegaré sobre las once*, I'll get there at about eleven o'clock. ► *nm* 1 *(de carta)* envelope. 2 *(envoltorio)* packet: *sopa de sobre*, packet soup. 3 *(paquete pequeño)* sachet: *sobre de azúcar*, sachet of sugar. • **sobre todo** above all, especially.

sobremesa *nf* *(charla)* after-lunch chat; *(hora)* afternoon.

sobresaliente *nm* *(calificación)* A, first

sobresalir *vi* 1 *(destacarse)* to stand out. 2 *(estar saliente)* to stick out 3 *(abultar)* to protrude.

sobrevivir *vi* to survive.

sobrino,-a *nm,f* *(chico)* nephew; *(chica)* niece.

sobrio,-a *adj* sober, temperate.

social *adj* social.

sociedad *nf* society. ■ **sociedad anónima** GB limited company; US incorporated company; **sociedad limitada** private limited company.

socio,-a *nm,f* 1 *(de un grupo)* member. 2 *(de empresa)* partner.

sociología *nf* sociology.

socorrer *vt* to help, aid.

socorrista *nmf* life-saver, lifeguard.

socorro *nm* help, aid, assistance. ► *interj* ¡**socorro!** help! • **pedir socorro** to ask for help.

soda *nf* soda water.

sofá *nm* sofa, settee.

software *nm* software.

soga *nf* rope.

soja *nf* soya bean.

sol[1] *nm* 1 *(astro)* sun. 2 *(luz)* sunlight, sunshine. • **tomar el sol** to sunbathe.

sol² nm (nota) sol, G.
solapa nf 1 (de chaqueta) lapel. 2 (de sobre, libro) flap.
solar¹ adj solar.
solar² nm (terreno) plot.
soldado nm soldier.
soldar vt (unir) to weld; (con estaño) to solder.
soledad nf 1 (estado) solitude. 2 (sentimiento) loneliness.
solemne adj solemn.
soler vi 1 (presente) be in the habit of doing: *soler hacer*, to usually do. 2 (pasado): *solía ir a correr*, he used to go running.
solicitar vt 1 (pedir) to request. 2 (trabajo) to apply for.
solidaridad nf solidarity.
sólido,-a adj solid.
solitario,-a adj 1 (sin compañía) solitary. 2 (sentimiento) lonely. 3 (lugar) deserted. ► nm **solitario** solitaire.
sólo adv only.
solo,-a adj 1 (sin compañía) alone: *vive sola*, she lives alone. 2 (solitario) lonely: *se siente muy solo*, he feels very lonely. 3 (único) one, single: *una sola persona*, one single person. ► nm **solo** 1 fam (café) black coffee. 2 (canción) solo. • **a solas** alone, in private.
solomillo nm sirloin.
soltar vt 1 (dejar suelto) to let go of. 2 (poner en libertad) to set free, release. 3 (desatar)

to undo, unfasten. ► vpr **soltarse** 1 (desatarse) to come undone. 2 (desprenderse) to come off.
soltero,-a nm,f (hombre) bachelor; (mujer) single woman.
solución nf solution.
solucionar vt to solve.
sombra nf 1 (lugar sin sol) shade. 2 (silueta) shadow. ■ **sombra de ojos** eye shadow.
sombrero nm hat.
sombrilla nf parasol, sunshade.
someter vt 1 (subyugar) to subdue. 2 (exponer) to subject: *someter algo a prueba*, to put STH to test. ► vpr **someterse** 1 (rendirse) to surrender: *el país tuvo que someterse al invasor*, the country had to surrender to the invasor. 2 (tratamiento etc) to undergo.
somier nm (de muelles) spring mattress; (de láminas) slats.
somnífero nm sleeping pill.
sonajero nm rattle.
sonámbulo,-a adj-nm,f sleepwalker.
sonar vi 1 (con timbrazos) to ring; (con campanadas) to strike; (con pitido) to beep. 2 (ponerse en marcha) to go off. 3 (conocer vagamente) to sound familiar: *su cara me suena*, her face is familiar. ► vpr **sonarse** to blow one's nose.

sonda nf probe.
sondeo nm poll.
sonido nm sound.
sonreír vi to smile.
sonrisa nf smile.
soñar vt-vi to dream.
sopa nf soup.
sopera nf soup tureen
soplar vi to blow.
soportar vt 1 (sostener) to support. 2 (aguantar) to put up with: ¿cómo lo soportas?, how can you put up with him? 3 (tolerar) to stand: no soporto a esta chica, I can't stand this girl.
soprano nmf soprano.
sorbete nm sorbet.
sorbo nm sip.
sordo,-a adj 1 (persona) deaf. 2 (sonido, dolor) dull.
sordomudo,-a adj deaf and dumb. ▶ nm,f deaf mute.
sorprendente adj surprising.
sorprender vt to surprise.
sorpresa nf surprise.
sortear vt 1 (echar a suertes) to draw lots for; (rifar) to raffle. 2 (obstáculos) to get round.
sorteo nm (de lotería) draw; (rifa) raffle.
sortija nf ring.
soso,-a adj 1 (sin sabor) tasteless. 2 (sin sal): está soso, it needs salt. 3 (aburrido) dull.
sospecha nf suspicion.
sospechar vt to suspect.

sospechoso,-a nm,f suspect.
sostén nm 1 (apoyo) support. 2 (prenda) bra, brassiere.
sostener vt 1 (aguantar) to support, hold up. 2 (sujetar) to hold. 3 (conversación, reunión) to have. 4 (opinión) to maintain, affirm.
sótano nm 1 (usado como almacén) cellar. 2 (en casa) basement.
stop nm stop sign.
su adj (de él) his; (de ella) her; (de usted/ustedes) your; (de ellos) their; (de animales, cosas) its.
suave adj 1 (piel, tela, color, voz) soft. 2 (superficie) smooth. 3 (brisa, persona) gentle. 4 (clima, sabor, detergente) mild.
suavizante nm 1 (para ropa) fabric softener. 2 (para pelo) conditioner.
subasta nf auction.
subcampeón,-ona nm,f runner-up.
subida nf 1 (ascenso) ascent; (a montaña) climb. 2 (pendiente) slope. 3 (aumento) rise.
subir vi 1 (a coche) to get in; (a tren, autobús, avión) to get on. 2 (aumentar) to rise. ▶ vt 1 (escalar) to climb. 2 (mover arriba) to carry up, take up. 3 (incrementar) to put up. ▶ vpr **subirse** 1 (a coche) to get in; (a tren, autobús, avión) to get on; (a caballo) to mount. 2

(trepar) to climb. **3** *(elevar)* to pull up: **súbete los calcetines**, pull your socks up.

submarinismo *nm* scuba diving.

submarino *nm* submarine

subrayar *vt* **1** *(con una línea)* to underline. **2** *(recalcar)* to emphasize.

subsidio *nm* subsidy, aid. ■ **subsidio de desempleo** unemployment benefit.

subterráneo,-a *adj* subterranean, under-ground.

suburbano,-a *adj* suburban.

suburbio *nm* *(barrio pobre)* slums; *(barrio de las afueras)* suburb.

subvención *nf* subsidy, grant.

suceder *vi* **1** *(acontecer)* to happen, occur. **2** *(seguir)* to follow. **3** *(sustituir)* to succeed.

sucesivo,-a *adj* consecutive, successive. ● **en lo sucesivo** from now on.

suceso *nm* **1** *(hecho)* event, happening. **2** *(incidente)* incident.

sucesor,-ra *nm,f* **1** *(en un puesto)* successor. **2** *(heredero)* heir; *(heredera)* heiress.

suciedad *nf* dirt.

sucio,-a *adj* dirty.

sucursal *nf* branch office.

Sudamérica *nf* South America.

sudamericano,-a *adj* South American.

sudar *vi* to sweat.

sudor *nm* sweat.

sudoroso,-a *adj* sweating.

suegro,-a *nm,f* *(hombre)* father-in-law; *(mujer)* mother-in-law.

suela *nf* sole.

sueldo *nm* salary, pay.

suelo *nm* **1** *(en la calle)* ground; *(de interior)* floor. **2** *(tierra)* soil.

suelto,-a *adj* *(no sujeto)* loose; *(desatado)* undone. ▶ *nm* **suelto** *(cambio)* small change.

sueño *nm* **1** *(ganas de dormir)* sleepiness: **tengo mucho sueño**, I'm very sleepy. **2** *(lo soñado)* dream.

suero *nm* **1** *(de la sangre)* serum. **2** *(solución salina)* saline solution.

suerte *nf* **1** *(fortuna)* luck. **2** *(azar)* chance: **fur la suerte la que me llevó hasta ti**, it was fate that led me to you. ● **tener suerte** to be lucky; **tener mala suerte** to be unlucky.

suéter *nm* sweater.

suficiente *adj-pron* enough.

sufrir *vt* **1** *(padecer)* to suffer. **2** *(ser sujeto de)* to have; *(operación)* to undergo: **sufrir un accidente**, to have an accident.

sugerir *vt* to suggest.

suicidarse *vpr* to commit suicide.

suicidio *nm* suicide.

sujetador *nm* bra, brassiere.

sujetar *vt* 1 *(agarrar)* to hold. 2 *(fijar)* to fix, secure.

sujeto,-a *adj (fijo)* fastened. ► *nm* **sujeto** 1 *(de verbo)* subject. 2 *(persona)* fellow.

suma *nf* sum, amount.

sumar *vt* to add up.

sumergir *vt (meter en líquido)* to put in; *(con fuerza)* to plunge; *(rápidamente)* to dip. ► *vpr* **sumergirse** *(submarinista)* to go underwater, dive; *(submarino)* to dive.

suministrar *vt* to provide, supply.

suministro *nm* supply.

súper *nm* 1 *fam (supermercado)* supermarket. 2 *(gasolina)* four-star petrol.

superar *vt* 1 *(exceder)* to surpass, exceed. 2 *(obstáculo etc)* to overcome. 3 *(récord)* to break. 4 *(prueba)* to pass.

superficie *nf* surface.

superior *adj* 1 *(de arriba)* upper. 2 *(mayor)* greater. 3 *(mejor)* superior.

supermercado *nm* supermarket.

superviviente *nmf* survivor.

suplemento *nm* supplement.

suplente *adj-nmf* substitute.

suplicar *vt* to beg.

suponer *vt* 1 *(creer)* to suppose. 2 *(dar por sentado)* to assume. 3 *(acarrear)* to entail.

supositorio *nm* suppository.

suprimir *vt (noticia)* to suppress; *(ley, impuestos)* to abolish; *(palabras, texto)* to delete.

supuesto,-a *adj* 1 *(falso)* supposed, assumed. 2 *(presunto)* alleged. • **por supuesto** of course.

sur *adj-nm* south.

surgir *vi* to arise, appear.

surtido *nm* assortment.

surtidor *nm* 1 *(fuente)* fountain. 2 *(chorro)* jet, spout. ■ **surtidor de gasolina** petrol pump.

suscribir *vt* 1 *(contrato)* to sign. 2 *(opinión)* to subscribe. ► *vpr* **suscribirse** *(a una revista)* to subscribe to.

suscripción *nf* subscription.

suspender *vt* 1 *(aplazar)* to postpone. 2 *(examen)* to fail. 3 *(cancelar)* to suspend.

suspense *nm* suspense.

suspensión *nf* 1 *(de coche)* suspension. 2 *(cancelación)* suspension.

suspenso *nm* fail.

suspiro *nm* sigh.

sustancia *nf* substance.

sustantivo *nm* noun.

sustitución *nf* 1 *(transitoria)* substitution. 2 *(permanente)* replacement.

sustituir *vt* 1 *(transitoriamente)* to substitute. 2 *(permanentemente)* to replace.

susto *nm* fright, scare.

tallarines

suyo,-a *adj (de él)* of his; *(de ella)* of hers; *(de usted/ustedes)* yours; *(de ellos)* theirs. ▶ *pron (de él)* his; *(de ella)* hers; *(de usted/ustedes)* yours; *(de ellos,-as)* theirs.

T

tabaco *nm* 1 *(planta, hoja)* tobacco. 2 *(cigarrillos)* cigarettes: *el tabaco es malo para la salud,* smoking damages your health. ■ **tabaco negro** black tobacco; **tabaco rubio** Virginia tobacco.

tábano *nm* horsefly.

taberna *nf* pub, bar.

tabique *nm* partition wall. ■ **tabique nasal** nasal bone.

tabla *nf* 1 *(de madera pulida)* board; *(de madera basta)* plank. 2 *(índice)* table. ▶ *nf pl* **tablas** *(ajedrez)* stalemate, draw. ■ **tabla de planchar** ironing board; **tabla de surf** surfboard; **tabla de windsurf** sailboard.

tablero *nm* board. ■ **tablero de ajedrez** chessboard.

tableta *nf* 1 *(de chocolate)* bar. 2 *(pastilla)* tablet.

tablón *nm* plank. ■ **tablón de anuncios** notice board.

taburete *nm* stool.

tachar *vt* to cross out.

taco *nm* 1 *(para calzar)* wedge. 2 *(para tornillo)* Rawlplug®. 3 *(de entradas)* book; *(de billetes)* wad. 4 *(de billar)* cue. 5 *(de jamón, etc)* cube, piece. 6 *(en botas de fútbol)* stud. 7 *fam (palabrota)* swearword.

tacón *nm* heel.

táctica *nf* tactics.

tacto *nm* 1 *(sentido)* touch. 2 *(textura)* feel. 3 *(delicadeza)* tact.

tal *adj* such: *en tales condiciones,* in such conditions; *tal día,* such and such a day; *te llamó un tal García,* someone called García phoned you. ▶ *pron (cosa)* something; *(persona)* someone, somebody. • **con tal de que** so long as, provided; **¿qué tal?** how are things?; **tal como** just as; **tal cual** just as it is; **tal vez** perhaps, maybe.

taladro *nm (herramienta)* drill; *(barrena)* gimlet.

talar *vt* to fell, cut down.

talco *nm* talc.

talento *nm* talent.

talla *nf* 1 *(estatura)* height; *(altura moral etc)* stature. 2 *(de prenda)* size: *¿qué talla usas?,* what size are you? 3 *(escultura)* carving, sculpture. • **dar la talla** *(ser competente)* to measure up.

tallarines *nm pl* noodles.

taller nm **1** (de artesano, profesional) workshop. **2** (de pintor) studio. **3** (industrial) factory. ■ **taller de coches** garage.

tallo nm stem, stalk.

talón nm **1** (de pie, calzado) heel. **2** (cheque) GB cheque; US check.

tamaño nm size.

también adv also, too, as well.

tambor nm **1** (instrumento) drum. **2** (de lavadora) drum. **3** (de detergente) drum, giant size pack.

tampoco adv neither, nor, not… either.

tampón nm **1** (de entintar) inkpad. **2** (absorbente) tampon.

tan adv **1** so; (después de sustantivo) such: **no quiero una moto tan grande**, I don't want such a big motorbike; **¡son unos chicos tan malos!**, they are such naughty boys. **2** (con adjetivos o adverbios) so: **no comas tan deprisa**, don't eat so quickly. **3** (comparativo) as… as: **es tan alto como tú**, he's as tall as you are. **4** (consecutivo) so: **pasó tan deprisa que no lo vi**, he went by so fast that I didn't see him. ● **tan sólo** only.

tanda nf **1** (conjunto) batch, lot. **2** (serie) series, course. **3** (turno) shift.

tanque nm tank.

tanto,-a adj **1** (con incontables) so much; (con contables) so many. **2** (en comparaciones - incontables) as much; (- contables) as many. **3** (en cantidades aproximadas) odd: **tiene treinta y tantos años**, he's thirty something. ▶ pron (incontables) so much; (contables) so many. ▶ adv **1** (cantidad) so much. **2** (tiempo) so long. **3** (frecuencia) so often. ▶ nm **1** (punto) point. **2** (cantidad imprecisa) so much, a certain amount. ● **a las tantas** very late; **estar al tanto** (saber) to be informed; **no es para tanto** it's not that bad; **por lo tanto** therefore; **¡y tanto!** oh, yes!, certainly! ■ **tanto por ciento** percentage.

tapa nf **1** (cubierta - de caja, olla) lid; (-de tarro) top. **2** (de libro) cover. **3** (de comida) appetizer, savoury.

tapar vt **1** (cubrir) to cover. **2** (abrigar) to wrap up. **3** (cerrar - olla, tarro) to put the lid on; (- botella) to put the top on. **4** (ocultar) to hid; (vista) to block. ▶ vpr **taparse** (cubrirse) to cover oneself; (abrigarse) to wrap up.

tapete nm table runner.

tapia nf **1** (cerca) garden wall. **2** (muro) wall.

tapicería nf upholstery.

tapiz nm tapestry.

tapón *nm* **1** *(de goma, vidrio)* stopper; *(de botella)* cap, cork; *(de lavabo, bañera)* plug. **2** *(en baloncesto)* block.

taquilla *nf* **1** *(de tren etc)* ticket office, booking office; *(de teatro, cine)* box-office. **2** *(en vestuario, colegio)* locker.

tardar *vt* *(emplear tiempo)* to take: *tardé tres años*, it took me three years. ► *vi (demorar)* to take long: *se tarda más en tren*, it takes longer by train.

tarde *nf* **1** *(hasta las seis)* afternoon. **2** *(después de las seis)* evening. ► *adv* lat. • **llegar tarde** to be late; **más tarde** later; **¡buenas tardes!** **1** *(más temprano)* good afternoon. **2** *(hacia la noche)* good evening.

tarea *nf* task, job.

tarifa *nf* **1** *(precio)* tariff, rate; *(en transporte)* fare. **2** *(lista de precios)* price list.

tarjeta *nf* card. • **pagar con tarjeta** to pay by credit card. ■ **tarjeta de embarque** boarding card; **tarjeta de visita 1** *(personal)* GB visiting card; US calling card. **2** *(profesional)* business card; **tarjeta telefónica** phone card; **tarjeta postal** postcard.

tarro *nm (recipiente)* jar, pot.

tarta *nf (pastel)* cake; *(de hojaldre)* tart, pie.

tartamudo,-a *nm,f* stutterer, stammerer.

tartera *nf* lunch box.

tasa *nf* **1** *(precio)* fee, charge. **2** *(impuesto)* tax. **4** *(índice)* rate.

tasca *nf* bar, pub.

tatuaje *nm* tattoo.

taxi *nm* taxi, cab.

taxímetro *nm* taximeter, clock.

taxista *nmf* taxi driver, cab driver.

taza *nf* **1** *(recipiente)* cup. **2** *(de retrete)* bowl.

tazón *nm* bowl.

te *pron* **1** *(complemento directo)* you; *(complemento indirecto)* you, for you. **2** *(reflexivo)* yourself.

té *nm* tea: *té con limón*, lemon tea.

teatro *nm* **1** *(sala)* theatre. **2** *(género)* drama. • **hacer teatro** to play, act.

tebeo *nm* comic.

techo *nm* ceiling. • **los sin techo** the homeless.

tecla *nf* key.

teclado *nm* keyboard.

técnica *nf* **1** *(tecnología)* technics, technology. **2** *(habilidad)* technique, method.

técnico,-a *adj* technical. ► *nm,f* technician.

tecnología *nf* technology.

teja *nf (en tejado)* tile.

tejado *nm* roof.

tejanos *nm pl* jeans.

tejido *nm* **1** *(tela)* fabric, material. **2** *(en anatomía)* tissue.

tejón *nm* badger.

tela *nf* **1** *(tejido)* material, fabric, cloth; *(retal)* piece of material. **2** *(cuadro)* painting.

telaraña *nf* cobweb, spider's web.

tele *nf fam* telly, TV.

telecomunicaciones *nf pl* telecommunications.

telediario *nm* news.

teleférico *nm* cable car.

telefonista *nmf* telephone operator.

teléfono *nm* **1** *(aparato)* telephone, phone. **2** *(número)* phone number. • **contestar al teléfono** to answer the phone; **estar hablando por teléfono** to be on the phone; **llamar a** ALGN **por teléfono** to phone SB, ring SB. ▪ **teléfono inalámbrico** cordless telephone; **teléfono móvil** mobile phone; **teléfono público** public phone.

telegrama *nm* telegram, cable.

telenovela *nf* soap opera.

telesilla *nf* chair lift.

telespectador,-ra *nm,f* viewer.

telesquí *nm* ski lift.

teletexto *nm* Teletext®.

televisar *vt* to televise.

televisión *nf* **1** *(sistema)* television. **2** *fam (aparato)* television set. • **ver la televisión** to watch television.

televisor *nm* television set.

télex *nm* telex.

telón *nm* curtain.

tema *nm* **1** *(asunto)* subject. **2** *(canción)* song. ▪ **tema de actualidad** current affair.

temblar *vi* **1** *(de frío)* to shiver; *(de miedo)* to tremble. **2** *(voz)* to quiver.

temblor *nm* tremor, shudder. ▪ **temblor de tierra** earthquake.

temer *vt* to fear, be afraid of.

temor *nm* fear.

temperamento *nm* temperament, nature.

temperatura *nf* temperature.

tempestad *nf* storm.

templado,-a *adj (agua, comida)* lukewarm; *(clima, temperatura)* mild, temperate.

templo *nm* temple.

temporada *nf* **1** *(en artes, deportes, moda)* season. **2** *(período)* period, time: *voy a pasar una temporada en casa de mis abuelos*, I'm going to live with my grandparents for a time. ▪ **temporada alta** high season; **temporada baja** low season.

temporal *adj* temporary. ▸ *nm* storm.

temprano *adv* early.

tenazas *nf pl* pincers; *(para el fuego)* tongs.

tendedero nm (cuerda) clothes-line; (lugar) drying place.

tendencia nf tendency, inclination.

tender vt 1 (puente) to build; (vía, cable) to lay. 2 (ropa, colada) to hang out. 3 (mano) to stretch out, hold out. 4 (emboscada, trampa) to lay. ▶ vi to tend. ▶ vpr **tenderse** (tumbarse) to lie down.

tendero,-a nm,f shopkeeper.

tendón nm tendon, sinew.

tenedor nm fork.

tener vt 1 (posesión) to have, have got. 2 (coger) to take: **ten esto**, take this. 3 (sensación, sentimiento) to be, feel: **tengo calor**, I'm hot; **tengo hambre**, I'm hungry; **tengo sed**, I'm thirsty. 4 (edad, tamaño) to be: **tiene diez años**, he's ten, he's ten years old. 5 (celebrar) to hold: **tener una reunión**, to hold a meeting. ▶ aux **tener que** 1 (obligación- a otra persona) to have to. 2 (- a uno mismo) must.

teniente nm lieutenant. ■ **teniente de alcalde** deputy mayor.

tenis nm tennis. ■ **tenis de mesa** table tennis.

tenista nmf tennis player.

tenor nm (cantante) tenor.

tensión nf 1 (gen) tension. 2 (sanguínea) pressure. ■ **tensión arterial** blood pressure.

tenso,-a adj 1 (cable, cuerda) taut. 2 (persona, músculo) tense. 3 (relaciones) strained.

tentación nf temptation.

tentáculo nm tentacle.

tentativa nf attempt.

teñir vt to dye.

teoría nf theory.

terapia nf therapy.

tercer num → tercero,-a.

tercero,-a num third. ■ **tercera edad** old age.

tercio nm one third.

terciopelo nm velvet.

terco,-a adj obstinate, stubborn.

terminal adj terminal. ▶ nf 1 (gen) terminal. 2 (de autobuses) terminus.

terminar vt-vi (acabar) to finish. ▶ vi (ir a parar) to end up, end. ▶ vpr **terminarse** 1 (finalizar) to finish, be over. 2 (agotarse) to run out: **se nos ha terminado el papel**, we've run out of paper.

término nm 1 (final) end, finish. 2 (plazo, palabra) term. ● **en otros términos** in other words; **en primer término** in the foreground; **en términos generales** generally speaking; **poner término a algo** to put an end to STH; **por término medio** on average. ■ **término municipal** district.

termita nf termite.

termo *nm* thermos (flask).

termómetro *nm* thermometer.

termostato *nm* thermostat.

ternera *nf* veal.

ternero,-a *nm,f* calf.

ternura *nf* tenderness.

terraplén *nm* embankment.

terraza *nf* 1 (*balcón*) terrace. 2 (*azotea*) roof terrace. 3 (*de un café*): **en la terraza de un bar**, outside a bar.

terremoto *nm* earthquake.

terreno *nm* 1 (*tierra*) piece of land, ground; (*solar*) plot, site. 2 (*superficie*) terrain. 3 (*de cultivo*) soil; (*campo*) field. 4 (*ámbito*) field, sphere. ▪ **terreno de juego** pitch.

terrestre *adj* 1 (*vida, transporte*) land, terrestrial. 2 (*animal, vegetación*) land.

terrible *adj* terrible, awful.

territorio *nm* territory.

terrón *nm* lump.

terror *nm* terror.

terrorismo *nm* terrorism.

tertulia *nf* gathering. ▪ **tertulia televisiva** talk show.

tesis *nf* thesis.

tesoro *nm* 1 (*cosas de valor*) treasure. 2 (*del Estado*) treasury, exchequer.

test *nm* test. ▪ **test de embarazo** pregnancy test.

testamento *nm* will, testament. • **hacer testamento** to make one's will.

testículo *nm* testicle.

testificar *vt-vi* to testify.

testigo *nmf* witness. ▶ *nm* DEP baton.

testimonio *nm* testimony. ▪ **falso testimonio** perjury.

tetera *nf* teapot.

tetilla *nf* (*de biberón*) teat.

tetina *nf* teat.

tetrabrik *nm* carton.

textil *adj* textile.

texto *nm* text.

ti *pron* you.

tía *nf* (*pariente*) aunt.

tibia *nf* tibia, shinbone.

tibio,-a *adj* tepid, lukewarm.

tiburón *nm* shark.

tic *nm* tic, twitch.

tiempo *nm* 1 (*período, momento*) time. 2 (*meteorológico*) weather. 3 (*parte de partido*) half. 4 (*gramatical*) tense. • **a tiempo** in time; **al mismo tiempo** at the same time; **del tiempo** 1 (*fruta*) in season. 2 (*bebida*) at room temperature; **¿qué tiempo hace?** what's the weather like? ▪ **tiempo libre** spare time; **tiempo muerto** time out.

tienda *nf* 1 GB shop; US store. 2 (*de campaña*) tent. ▪ **tienda de comestibles** grocer's.

tierno,-a *adj* 1 (*blando*) tender, soft. 2 (*reciente*) fresh.

tierra *nf* 1 (*superficie sólida*) land. 2 (*terreno cultivado*) soil, land. 3 (*sustancia*) earth, soil. **4** *(zona de origen)*: **en mi tierra**, where I come from. **5** *(suelo)* ground. **6 la Tierra** *(planeta)* the Earth. • **tierra adentro** inland; **tomar tierra** to land. ■ **tierra firme** terra firma.

tieso,-a *adj* **1** *(rígido)* stiff, rigid. **2** *(erguido)* upright, erect.

tiesto *nm* flowerpot.

tifón *nm* typhoon.

tigre *nm* tiger.

tijeras *nf pl* scissors.

tila *nf* lime-blossom tea.

timar *vt* to swindle.

timbre *nm* **1** *(de la puerta)* bell. **2** *(sello)* stamp. • **llamar al timbre** to ring the bell.

tímido,-a *adj* shy.

timo *nm* swindle, fiddle.

timón *nm* *(de barco)* rudder.

tímpano *nm* eardrum.

tinta *nf* ink.

tinte *nm* **1** *(colorante)* dye. **2** *(tintorería)* dry-cleaner's.

tinto,-a *adj* *(vino)* red. ► *nm* **tinto** red wine.

tintorería *nf* dry-cleaner's.

tío *nm* *(pariente)* uncle.

tiovivo *nm* merry-go-round, roundabout.

típico,-a *adj* typical.

tipo *nm* **1** *(clase)* sort, kind. **2** *(de interés, etc)* rate. **3** *(de hombre)* build, physique; *(de mujer)* figure.

tira *nf* strip. • **la tira** *fam* a lot, loads.

tirada *nf* **1** *(impresión)* print run. **2** *(jugada)* throw. • **de una tirada** in one go.

tirado,-a *adj* **1** *fam (precio)* dirt cheap. **2** *fam (problema, examen)* dead easy. • **dejar tirado a ALGN** to leave SB in the lurch.

tirador *nm* *(de puerta)* knob; *(de cajón)* handle.

tirantes *nm pl* **1** *(de vestido)* straps. **2** *(de pantalón)* GB braces; US suspenders.

tirar *vt* **1** *(lanzar)* to throw; *(tiro)* to fire; *(bomba)* to drop. **2** *(dejar caer)* to drop. **3** *(desechar)* to throw away. **4** *(derribar)* to knock down; *(casa, árbol)* to pull down; *(vaso, botella)* to knock over. ► *vi* **1** *(cuerda, puerta)* to pull: **tira de la cadena**, pull the chain. **2** *(en juegos)*: **tira tú**, it's your turn, it's your go. **3** *fam (funcionar)* to work, run. **4** *(disparar)* to shoot. ► *vpr* **tirarse** *(lanzarse)* to throw oneself. ■ **tira y afloja** give and take.

tirita® *nf* GB plaster; US Band-aid®.

tiritar *vi* to shiver, shake.

tiro *nm* **1** *(lanzamiento)* throw. **2** *(disparo, ruido)* shot. **3** *(herida)* bullet wound. **4** *(de caballos)* team. **5** *(de chimenea)* draught. • **a tiro 1** *(de arma)* within range. **2** *(a mano)* within reach; **sentar como**

un tiro a ALGN 1 (comida) to not agree with SB. 2 (comentario) to make SB really upset. ■ **tiro al blanco** target shooting; **tiro con arco** archery.

tirón nm 1 (acción) tug: *sufrió un tirón en un músculo*, he pulled a muscle. 2 (robo) bagsnatching. • **de un tirón** fam in one go.

tiroteo nm shooting.

títere nm puppet, marionette.

titular adj appointed, official. ▶ nmf 1 (en deporte) first-team player. 2 (de cuenta, pasaporte) holder. ▶ nm (de prensa) headline. ▶ vpr **titularse** (obra, película) to be called.

título nm 1 (gen) title. 2 (académico) degree; (diploma) certificate, diploma. 4 (acción) bond, security.

tiza nf chalk.

toalla nf towel.

toallero nm towel rail.

tobillo nm ankle.

tobogán nm slide.

tocadiscos nm record player.

tocador nm (mueble) dressing table. ■ **tocador de señoras** powder room.

tocar vt 1 (gen) to touch. 2 (hacer sonar - instrumento, canción) to play; (- timbre) to ring; (- bocina) to blow, honk; (- campanas) to strike. ▶ vi 1 (corresponder) to be one's turn: *¿a quién le toca ahora?*, whose turn is it now? 2 (caer en suerte) to win.

tocino nm 1 (grasa) lard. 2 (carne) bacon.

todavía adv 1 (tiempo -en frases afirmativas) still; (-en frases negativas) yet. 2 (para reforzar) even: *esto todavía te gustará más*, you'll enjoy this even more.

todo,-a adj 1 (gen) all. 2 (por completo) whole: *participó toda la clase*, the whole class took part. 3 (cada) every: *todos los veranos*, every summer. 4 (enfático) quite. ▶ pron 1 **todo** (sin exclusión) all, everything. 2 **todos,-as** everybody, everyone. ▶ adv all. • **del todo** completely; **estar en todo** to be really with it; **todos nosotros/ vosotros/ ellos** all of us/you/ them.

todoterreno nm all-terrain vehicle.

toldo nm awning.

tolerancia nf tolerance.

tolerar vt to tolerate.

toma nf 1 (acción) taking. 2 (dosis) dose. 3 (captura) capture. 4 (grabación) recording. 5 (de imágenes) take. ■ **toma de contacto** initial contact; **toma de corriente** power point; **toma de posesión** takeover; **toma de tierra** GB earth wire; US ground wire.

tomar vt **1** (gen) to take. **2** (comida, bebida, baño) to have: *¿quieres tomar algo?*, would you like a drink? ► vpr **tomarse** (vacaciones, comentario) to take. • **tomarla con** ALGN to have it in for SB; **tomar por** to take for.

tomate nm tomato. • **ponerse como un tomate** to go as red as a beetroot.

tómbola nf tombola.

tomillo nm thyme.

tomo nm volume.

ton. • **sin ton ni son** without rhyme or reason.

tonel nm barrel, cask.

tonelada nf ton.

tónica nf **1** (bebida) tonic. **2** (tendencia) tendency, trend.

tónico nm tonic.

tono nm **1** (de sonido, voz) tone. **2** (de color) shades. • **a tono con** in tune with; **bajar el tono** to lower one's voice; **subir el tono** to speak louder.

tontería nf **1** (dicho, hecho) silly thing, stupid thing. **2** (insignificancia) little thing.

tonto,-a adj silly.

tope nm **1** (límite) limit, end. **2** (objeto) stop: *el tope de la puerta*, the doorstop. • **a tope** fam (lleno) packed. **2** (al máximo) flat out.

tópico nm commonplace, cliché. • **de uso tópico** for external use.

topo nm mole.

toquilla nf shawl.

tórax nm thorax.

torbellino nm whirlwind.

torcedura nf sprain.

torcer vt **1** (cuerda, brazo) to twist. **2** (inclinar) to slant. ► vi (girar) to turn: *tuerce a la derecha*, turn right. ► vpr **torcerse 1** to sprain: *se torció el tobillo*, she sprained her ankle. **2** (plan) to fall through.

tordo nm (pájaro) thrush.

torear vt-vi (toro) to fight.

torero,-a nm,f bullfighter.

tormenta nf storm.

tornado nm tornado.

torneo nm tournament.

tornillo nm screw.

torniquete nm tourniquet.

torno nm (de carpintero) lathe; (de alfarero) potter's wheel. • **en torno a 1** (alrededor de) around. **2** (acerca de) about, concerning.

toro nm bull.

torpe adj (patoso) clumsy.

torre nf **1** (de edificio) tower. **2** (de ajedrez) rook, castle. ■ **torre de control** control tower.

torrente nm torrent.

torrija nf French toast.

torta nf **1** (dulce) cake. **2** fam (bofetón) slap. • **ni torta** not a thing; **pegarse una torta** to give oneself a bump.

tortazo nm **1** (bofetón) slap. **2** (golpe) thump.

tortícolis *nf* stiff neck.

tortilla *nf* omelette. ▪ **tortilla de patatas** Spanish omelette; **tortilla francesa** plain omelette.

tórtola *nf* dove.

tortuga *nf* 1 *(de tierra)* GB tortoise; US turtle. 2 *(marina)* turtle.

tortura *nf* torture.

tos *nf* cough. ▪ **tos ferina** whooping cough.

toser *vi* to cough.

tostada *nf* piece of toast.

tostadora *nf* toaster.

tostar *vt (pan)* to toast; *(café)* to roast.

total *adj-nm* total.

tóxico,-a *adj* toxic.

trabajador,-ra *adj* hardworking. ▸ *nm,f* worker.

trabajar *vi-vt* to work.

trabajo *nm* 1 *(gen)* work. 2 *(tarea)* task, job. 3 *(empleo)* job. 4 *(para clase)* essay, project. ▪ **trabajos manuales** handicrafts.

tracción *nf* traction. ▪ **tracción delantera/trasera** front/rear-wheel drive.

tractor *nm* tractor.

tradición *nf* tradition.

tradicional *adj* traditional.

traducción *nf* translation. ▪ **traducción automática** machine translation; **traducción simultánea** simultaneous translation.

traducir *vt* to translate.

traductor,-ra *nm,f* translator.

traer(se) *vt-vpr* to bring. ● **traerse algo entre manos** to be busy with STH; **me trae sin cuidado** I couldn't care less; **traérselas** *fam* to be really difficult.

traficante *nmf* dealer, trafficker.

tráfico *nm* traffic.

tragaperras *nf* slot machine.

tragar(se) *vt-vpr* 1 *(comida, medicina)* to swallow. 2 *(creer)* to fall for it.

tragedia *nf* tragedy.

trago *nm* 1 *(sorbo)* swig. 2 *(bebida)* drink. ● **echar un trago** to have a drink; **pasar un mal trago** to have a bad time of it.

traicionar *vt* to betray.

traidor,-ra *nm,f* traitor.

tráiler *nm* 1 *(película)* trailer. 2 *(vehículo)* GB articulated lorry; US trailer truck.

traje *nm* 1 *(de hombre)* suit. 2 *(de mujer)* dress. ▪ **traje de baño** bathing suit, bathing costume; **traje de etiqueta** evening dress; **traje de luces** bullfighter's costume; **traje espacial** spacesuit.

trama *nf* 1 *(textil)* weft, woof. 2 *(argumento)* plot.

tramar *vt (preparar)* to plot: *estarán tramando algo*, they must be up to something.

trámite *nm* **1** *(paso)* step. **2** *(negociación)* procedures. **3** *(formalismo)* formality: **es puro trámite**, it's purely a formality.

tramo *nm* **1** *(de carretera)* stretch, section. **2** *(de escalera)* flight.

trampa *nf* **1** *(para cazar)* trap. **2** *(engaño)* trap, trick. • **hacer trampas** to cheat.

trampolín *nm* **1** *(de piscina)* springboard, diving board. **2** *(de esquí)* ski jump.

tramposo,-a *nm,f* cheat.

tranquilidad *nf* **1** *(paz)* quiet, piece. **2** *(calma)* calm.

tranquilizante *nm* tranquillizer.

tranquilizar(se) *vt-vpr (alguien nervioso)* to calm down; *(alguien preocupado)* to set one's mind at rest.

tranquilo,-a *adj* **1** *(persona, voz, mar)* calm. **2** *(lugar, momento)* quiet, peaceful. • **dejar a ALGN tranquilo** to leave SB alone; **¡tranquilo! 1** *(cálmate)* take it easy! **2** *(no te preocupes)* don't worry!

transatlántico,-a *adj* transatlantic. ▶ *nm* **transatlántico** liner.

transbordador *nm* ferry. ▪ **transbordador espacial** space shuttle.

transbordo *nm (de pasajeros)* change; *(de equipajes)* transfer. • **hacer transbordo** to change.

transcurrir *vi* to pass, elapse.

transeúnte *nmf* passer-by.

transferencia *nf* transfer.

transformador *nm* transformer.

transformar(se) *vt-vpr* to change.

transfusión *nf* transfusion.

transición *nf* transition.

transistor *nm* transistor.

transitivo,-a *adj* transitive.

tránsito *nm* **1** *(tráfico)* traffic. **2** *(acción)* passage, transit.

transmisión *nf* **1** *(gen)* transmission. **2** *(de radio etc)* broadcast.

transmisor,-ra *adj* transmitting. ▶ *nm,f* transmitter.

transmitir *vt* **1** *(gen)* to transmit. **2** *(por radio etc)* to broadcast.

transparencia *nf* **1** *(gen)* transparency. **2** *(diapositiva)* slide.

transparentarse *vpr (blusa, vestido)* to show through.

transparente *adj* transparent.

transpirar *vi* to perspire.

transportar *vt (gen)* to transport; *(en barco)* to ship.

transporte *nm* transport.

transportista *nmf* haulier.

tranvía *nm* GB tram; US streetcar.

trapecio *nm (de circo, gimnasia)* trapeze.

trapecista *nmf* trapeze artist.
trapo *nm (paño)* cloth. ► *nm pl* **trapos** clothes. ■ **trapo de cocina** tea towel; **trapo de polvo** duster.
tráquea *nf* trachea.
tras *prep* **1** *(después de)* after: *día tras día*, day after day. **2** *(detrás de)* behind: *se escondió tras la puerta*, she hid behind the door.
trasero,-a *adj* back, rear.
trasladar *vt* **1** *(desplazar)* to move. **2** *(de cargo etc)* to transfer. ► *vpr* **trasladarse 1** *(persona)* to go. **2** *(mudarse)* to move.
traslado *nm* **1** *(mudanza)* move. **2** *(de cargo)* transfer.
trasnochar *vi* to stay up late.
traspasar *vt* **1** *(atravesar)* to go through, pierce. **2** *(negocio,jugador)* to transfer. ● **"Se traspasa"** "For sale".
traspaso *nm* **1** *(de negocio)* sale. **2** *(de jugador, competencias)* transfer. **3** *(precio)* takeover fee.
trasplante *nm* transplant.
trastero *nm* lumber room.
trasto *nm (cosa)* piece of junk. ► *nm pl* **trastos** *(utensilios)* tackle.
trastorno *nm* **1** disruption; *(molestia)* inconvenience. **2** *(enfermedad)* disorder.
tratado *nm* **1** *(pacto)* treaty. **2** *(estudio)* treatise.

tratamiento *nm* **1** *(gen)* treatment. **2** *(título)* title, form of address. ■ **tratamiento de textos** word processing.
tratar *vt* **1** *(gen)* to treat. **2** *(asunto, relación)* to deal with. ► *vi (relacionarse)* to be acquainted. ► *vpr* **tratarse 1** *(ser cuestión)* to be about: *tratándose de ti...*, seeing as it's you... **2** *(tener relación)* to be friendly with. ● **tratar de 1** *(intentar)* to try to. **2** *(dirigirse a)* to address as: *nos tratamos de usted*, we address each other as "usted". **3** *(versar)* to be about.
trato *nm* **1** *(de personas)* manner, treatment. **2** *(contacto)* contact. **3** *(acuerdo)* agreement. **4** *(comercial)* deal. ● **cerrar un trato** to close a deal; **¡trato hecho!** it's a deal! ■ **malos tratos** ill-treatment.
través *nm.* ● **a través de 1** *(mediante)* through. **2** *(de un lado a otro)* across.
travesía *nf* **1** *(viaje)* voyage, crossing. **2** *(calle)* street.
trayecto *nm* **1** *(distancia)* distance, way. **2** *(recorrido)* route: *¿el autobús cubría el trayecto Madrid-Burgos*, the bus was doing the Madrid-Burgos run. **3** *(viaje)* journey: *el trayecto entre Barcelona y Mallorca*, the journey between Barcelona and Majorca.

trayectoria *nf* **1** *(recorrido)* trajectory. **2** *(evolución)* line, course. ▪ **trayectoria profesional** career.

trébol *nm* **1** *(hierba)* clover. **2** *(naipes)* club.

trece *num* thirteen; *(en fechas)* thirteenth.

tregua *nf* **1** MIL truce. **2** *(descanso)* respite, rest.

treinta *num* thirty; *(en fechas)* thirtieth.

tremendo,-a *adj* **1** *(terrible)* terrible, dreadful. **2** *(muy grande)* tremendous.

tren *nm* **1** *(ferrocarril)* train. **2** *(ritmo)* speed, pace: *a este tren no llegaremos*, we won't get there at this speed. ▪ **tren de cercanías** suburban train; **tren de aterrizaje** undercarriage; **tren de lavado** car wash.

trenza *nf* GB plait; US braid.

trepar *vt-vi* to climb.

tres *num* three; *(en fechas)* third. ▪ **tres en raya** noughts and crosses.

trescientos,-as *num* three hundred.

tresillo *nm* three-piece suite.

triángulo *nm* triangle.

tribu *nf* tribe.

tribuna *nf* **1** *(plataforma)* platform, rostrum. **2** stand.

tribunal *nm* **1** *(gen)* court. **2** *(de examen)* board of examiners.

triciclo *nm* tricycle.

trigo *nm* wheat.

trillizo,-a *nm,f* triplet.

trimestre *nm* **1** *(académico)* term. **2** *(tres meses)* quarter.

trinchar *vt* to carve.

trinchera *nf* trench.

trineo *nm* *(de perros)* sleigh; *(para jugar)* sledge.

trío *nm* trio.

tripa *nf* **1** *(estómago)* stomach. **2** *(panza)* belly.

triple *adj-nm* triple. • **el triple** three times. ▪ **triple salto** triple jump.

tripulación *nf* crew.

tripulante *nmf* crew member.

tripular *vt* to man.

triste *adj* sad.

tristeza *nf* sadness.

triturar *vt* *(ajo, verdura)* to crush; *(-papel)* to shred.

triunfar *vi* **1** *(tener éxito)* to succeed. **2** *(ganar)* to win.

triunfo *nm* **1** *(victoria)* triumph, victory; *(en deportes)* win. **2** *(éxito)* success. **3** *(naipes)* trump.

trocear *vt* to cut up.

trofeo *nm* trophy.

trombón *nm* trombone.

trompa *nf* **1** *(instrumento)* horn. **2** *(de elefante)* trunk.

trompeta *nf* trumpet.

tronco *nm* trunk.

trono *nm* throne.

tropa *nf* troops, soldiers.

tropezar(se) *vi-vpr* to trip.

tropical *adj* tropical.

trote *nm* *(de caballo)* trot.

trozo *nm* piece, chunk.
trucha *nf* trout.
truco *nm* trick. • **coger el truco** to get the knack.
trueno *nm* thunderclap, clap of thunder.
tu *adj* your.
tú *pron* you.
tuberculosis *nf* tuberculosis.
tubería *nf (de agua)* pipe; *(de gas, petróleo)* pipeline.
tubo *nm* tube. ■ **tubo de ensayo** test tube; **tubo de escape** exhaust pipe; **tubo digestivo** alimentary canal.
tuerca *nf* nut.
tuerto,-a *adj* one-eyed.
tulipán *nm* tulip.
tumba *nf* **1** *(mausoleo)* tomb. **2** *(fosa)* grave.
tumbarse *vpr* to lie down.
tumbona *nf (de playa)* deckchair; *(para tumbarse)* lounger.
tumor *nm* tumour.
túnel *nm* tunnel. ■ **túnel de lavado** car wash.
túnica *nf* tunic.
tupé *nm* quiff.
turbina *nf* turbine.
turbio,-a *adj* cloudy.
turismo *nm* **1** *(actividad)* tourism. **2** *(industria)* tourist trade, tourist industry. **3** *(coche)* car.
turista *nmf* tourist.
turístico,-a *adj* tourist.
turnarse *vpr* to take turns.

turno *nm* **1** *(en cola, lista)* turn. **2** *(de trabajo)* shift.
turrón *nm* nougat.
tutor,-ra *nm,f* **1** JUR guardian. **2** *(profesor)* tutor.
tuyo,-a *adj* of yours. ► *pron* yours.

U

u *conj* or.
UCI *abr (Unidad de Cuidados Intensivos)* Intensive Care Unit, ICU.
úlcera *nf* ulcer.
último,-a *adj* **1** *(gen)* last. **2** *(más reciente)* latest: *las últimas noticias*, the latest news. **3** *(más alejado)* furthest; *(de más abajo)* bottom, lowest; *(de más arriba)* top; *(de más atrás)* back: *vive en el último piso*, he lives on the top floor. **4** *(definitivo)* final: *mi última oferta*, my final offer. • **a la última** up to date; **estar en las últimas 1** *(moribundo)* to be at death's door. **2** *(arruinado)* to be down and out; **por último** finally.
ultramarinos *nm pl (tienda)* grocer's; *(comestibles)* groceries.
umbral *nm* threshold.
un,-a *det a*, an. ► *adj* one.
unanimidad *nf* unanimity.

undécimo,-a *num* eleventh.

único,-a *adj* **1** *(solo)* only. **2** *(extraordinario)* unique.

unidad *nf* **1** unit. **2** *(cohesión)* unity.

uniforme *adj (velocidad, ritmo)* uniform; *(temperatura, superficie)* even. ► *nm* uniform.

unión *nf* union.

unir *vt* **1** *(juntar)* to join. **2** *(enlazar)* to link.

universal *adj* universal.

universidad *nf* university.

universitario,-a *adj* university. ► *nm,f (en curso)* university student; *(con título)* university graduate.

universo *nm* universe.

uno,-a *adj (número)* one. ► *pron* **1** one. **2** *(impersonal)* one, you: *en estos casos, uno no sabe qué hacer*, you don't know what to do in these situations. ► *nm (número)* one; *(en fechas)* first. ► *adj pl* **unos,-as 1** some. **2** *(aproximado)* about, around: *seremos unos veinte*, there will be around twenty of us. • **de uno en uno** one by one; **es la una** it's one o´clock.

untar *vt (crema, pomada)* to smear; *(mantequilla, queso)* to spread.

uña *nf* nail.

urbanización *nf* **1** *(proceso)* urbanization. **2** *(conjunto residencial)* housing development, housing estate.

urbano,-a *adj* urban.

urgencia *nf* **1** *(prisa)* urgency. **2** *(asunto)* emergency. ► *nf pl* **urgencias** casualty.

urgente *adj* **1** *(llamada, asunto)* urgent. **2** *(carta)* express.

urna *nf* **1** *(para votar)* ballot box. **2** *(para cenizas)* urn. **3** *(para objetos valiosos)* glass case.

urraca *nf* magpie.

urticaria *nf* rash.

usado,-a *adj* **1** *(gastado)* worn out, old. **2** *(de segunda mano)* secondhand, used.

usar *vt* **1** *(utilizar)* to use. **2** *(prenda)* to wear. • **de usar y tirar** disposable.

uso *nm* **1** *(utilización)* use. **2** *(de prenda)* wearing: *es obligatorio el uso del cinturón de seguridad*, seat belts must be worn.

usted *pron fml* you.

usual *adj* usual, customary.

usuario,-a *nm,f* user.

utensilio *nm* **1** *(de cocina)* utensil. **2** *(herramienta)* tool.

útero *nm* uterus.

útil *adj* useful.

utilización *nf* use.

utilizar *vt* to use, utilize.

uva *nf* grape.

UVI *abr (Unidad de Vigilancia Intensiva)* ICU, intensive care unit.

V

vaca *nf* **1** *(animal)* cow. **2** *(carne)* beef.

vacaciones *nf pl* holiday, holidays. ● **estar de vacaciones** to be on holiday; **irse de vacaciones** to go on holiday.

vacante *nf* vacancy.

vaciar *vt* **1** *(recipiente)* to empty. **2** *(contenido)* to pour away, pour out.

vacilar *vi* to hesitate.

vacío,-a *adj* **1** *(recipiente, lugar)* empty. **2** *(no ocupado)* unoccupied. ► *nm* **vacío 1** *(abismo)* void, emptiness. **2** *(en física)* vacuum. ● **envasado al vacío** vacuum-packed.

vacuna *nf* vaccine.

vacunar *vt* to vaccinate.

vado *nm* **1** *(de río)* ford. **2** *(en calle)* garage entrance. ■ **"Vado permanente"** "Keep clear".

vagabundo,-a *nm,f* tramp.

vagina *nf* vagina.

vago,-a¹ *nm,f* idler, loafer.

vago,-a² *adj (impreciso)* vague.

vagón *nm* **1** *(para pasajeros)* GB carriage, coach; US car. **2** *(para mercancías)* GB wagon, goods van; US boxcar, freight car. ■ **vagón restaurante** restaurant car.

vaho *nm* vapour, steam. ► *nm pl* **vahos** MED inhalation.

vaina *nf* **1** *(de espada)* sheath, scabbard. **2** *(de guisante, judía)* pod.

vainilla *nf* vanilla.

vaivén *nm* swaying, swinging.

vajilla *nf* **1** *(gen)* dishes, crockery. **2** *(juego completo)* dinner service.

vale *nm (de compra)* voucher. ► *interj* OK, all right.

valer *vi* **1** *(tener valor)* to be worth. **2** *(costar)* to cost: *¿cuánto vale?*, how much is it? **3** *(ser válido)* to be valid. **4** *(servir)* to be useful, be of use: *no vale para director*, he's no use as a manager. ● **no vale** it's no good; **vale más...** it's better...: *más te vale no llegar tarde*, you'd better not arrive late.

válido,-a *adj* valid.

valiente *adj* brave.

valioso,-a *adj* valuable.

valla *nf* **1** *(cerca)* fence, barrier. **2** *(en atletismo)* hurdle. ■ **valla publicitaria** GB hoarding; US billboard.

valle *nm* valley.

valor *nm* **1** *(gen)* value. **2** *(precio)* price. **3** *(coraje)* courage, valour. ► *nm pl* **valores** *(financieros)* securities, bonds. ● **¡qué valor!** what a nerve!; **sin ningún valor** worthless, worth nothing.

valorar *vt* to value.

válvula *nf* valve.

vampiro *nm* vampire.

vanguardia *nf* **1** *(en arte etc)* avant-garde. **2** MIL vanguard.

vano,-a *adj* **1** *(inútil)* vain, useless. **2** *(ilusorio)* illusory, futile. • **en vano** in vain.

vapor *nm* vapour, steam. • **al vapor** steamed.

vaquero *nm* GB cowherd; US cowboy. ▶ *nm pl* **vaqueros** jeans.

variable *adj* variable.

variante *nf (carretera)* bypass.

variar *vt-vi* to vary, change. • **para variar** for a change.

varicela *nf* chickenpox.

variedad *nf* variety. ▶ *nf pl* **variedades** *(espectáculo)* variety show.

varilla *nf* **1** *(palito)* stick, rod. **2** *(de paraguas)* rib.

varios,-as *adj (algunos)* some, several.

variz *nf* varicose vein.

varón *nm* male, man.

vasija *nf* vessel.

vaso *nm* **1** *(de cristal)* glass. **2** *(de papel, plástico)* cup. **3** *(sanguíneo)* vessel.

vasto,-a *adj* vast, immense.

vatio *nm* watt.

vaya *interj* **1** well! **2** *(con sustantivos)* what a...: **¡vaya casa!**, what a house!

vecino,-a *nm,f* **1** *(de edificio, calle)* neighbour. **2** *(habitante - de barrio)* resident; *(- de ciudad)* inhabitant.

veda *nf* close season.

vegetación *nf* vegetation.

vegetal *adj-nm* plant.

vegetariano,-a *adj-nm,f* vegetarian.

vehículo *nm* vehicle.

veinte *num* twenty; *(en fechas)* twentieth.

vejez *nf* old age.

vejiga *nf* bladder.

vela¹ *nf (de cera)* candle. • **pasar la noche en vela** to have a sleepless night.

vela² *nf (de barco)* sail.

velada *nf* evening.

velarse *vpr (fotografía)* to fog.

velatorio *nm* wake, vigil.

velero *nm* sailing boat.

veleta *nf* weathercock.

vello *nm* hair.

velo *nm* veil.

velocidad *nf* **1** *(rapidez)* speed, velocity. **2** *(marcha)* gear.

velódromo *nm* cycle track.

veloz *adj* fast, quick, swift.

vena *nf* vein.

vencedor,-ra *nm,f* winner.

vencer *vt* **1** *(derrotar)* to beat. **2** *(militarmente)* to defeat. ▶ *vi* **1** *(gen)* to win. **2** *(deuda)* to fall due.

venda *nf* bandage.

vendaje *nm* bandaging.

vendar *vt* to bandage.

vendedor,-ra *nm,f (hombre)* salesman; *(mujer)* saleswoman.

vender *vt* to sell. • **"Se vende"** "For sale".

vendimia *nf* grape harvest.
veneno *nm* (*químico, vegetal*) poison; (*de animal*) venom.
venenoso *adj* poisonous.
venganza *nf* revenge.
vengarse *vpr* to take revenge.
venir *vi* 1 (*gen*) to come. 2 (*estar*) to be: *mi teléfono viene en la guía*, my phone number is in the book. • **venir bien** to be suitable: *¿te viene bien esta tarde?*, does this afternoon suit you?; **venir mal** not to be convenient: *a esa hora me viene mal*, that time isn't convenient; **venirse abajo** 1 (*edificio*) to collapse, fall down. 2 (*persona*) to go to pieces; **¡venga!** come on!
venta *nf* 1 (*transacción*) sale, selling. 2 (*hostal*) roadside inn. • **"En venta"** "For sale".
ventaja *nf* advantage.
ventana *nf* window. • **doble ventana** double-glazed window.
ventanilla *nf* 1 (*de coche, sobre*) window. 2 (*de cine*) box office.
ventilador *nm* fan.
ventilar *vt* (*habitación, ropa*) to air.
ventisca *nf* snowstorm, blizzard.
ventosa *nf* sucker.
ver *vt* 1 (*percibir, mirar*) to see. 2 (*televisión*) to watch. ▶ *vpr* **verse** (*con ALGN*) to meet,

see each other: *nos vemos bastante a menudo*, we see each other quite often. • **a ver** let's see; **hacer ver algo** to pretend STH; **¡hay que ver!** would you believe it!; **no poder ver** not to be able to stand: *no puede ver a su vecino*, she can't stand her neighbour; **véase** see.
veraneante *nmf* summer resident.
veranear *vi* to spend the summer.
veraneo *nm* summer holiday.
verano *nm* summer.
veras *adv.* • **de veras** really, truly.
verbena *nf* (*fiesta*) dance.
verbo *nm* verb.
verdad *nf* 1 truth. 2 (*confirmación*): *es bonita, ¿verdad?*, she's pretty, isn't she? • **de verdad** 1 (*en serio*) really. 2 (*como debe ser*) real.
verdadero,-a *adj* true, real.
verde *adj* 1 (*color, tela, ojos*) green. 2 (*fruta*) unripe. 3 *fam* (*chiste*) blue, dirty. ▶ *nm* (*color*) green. • **poner verde a ALGN** *fam* to run SB down.
verdulería *nf* greengrocer's.
verdura *nf* vegetables *pl*.
veredicto *nm* verdict.
vergüenza *nf* 1 (*culpabilidad*) shame. 2 (*bochorno*) embarrassment.

verificar *vt* to verify.

verja *nf* railing.

vermut *nm* vermouth.

verruga *nf* wart.

versión *nf* version. • **en versión original** in the original language.

verso *nm* verse.

vértebra *nf* vertebra.

vertebral *adj* vertebral.

vertedero *nm* dump, tip.

vertical *adj-nf* vertical.

vértice *nm* vertex.

vértigo *nm* vertigo.

vesícula *nf* vesicle.

vespa® *nf* scooter.

vestíbulo *nm* hall.

vestido *nm* dress. ▪ **vestido de noche** evening dress; **vestido de novia** wedding dress.

vestimenta *nf* clothes.

vestir *vt* 1 (*llevar*) to wear. 2 (*a alguien*) to dress. ► *vpr* **vestirse** to get dressed.

vestuario *nm* 1 (*ropa*) wardrobe, clothes. 2 (*camerino*) dressing room; (*en gimnasio etc*) changing room.

veterano,-a *adj-nm,f* veteran.

veterinario,-a *nm,f* GB veterinary surgeon, vet; US veterinarian.

vez *nf* 1 (*ocasión*) time. 2 (*turno*) turn. • **a la vez** at the same time; **a veces** sometimes; **alguna vez** 1 (*en afirmación*) sometimes. 2 (*en pre-*

gunta) ever; **de vez en cuando** from time to time; **dos veces** twice; **en vez de** instead of; **muchas veces** often; **otra vez** again; **rara vez** seldom, rarely; **tal vez** perhaps, maybe.

vía *nf* 1 (*camino*) road, way; (*calle*) street. 2 (*de tren - raíl*) track, line; (*- andén*) platform. • **por vía oral** to be taken orally. ▪ **vía de acceso** slip road; **vía pública** thoroughfare; **vías respiratorias** respiratory tract.

viable *adj* viable.

viajante *nm* commercial traveller.

viajar *vi* to travel.

viaje *nm* journey, trip. • **¡buen viaje!** have a good journey!; **estar de viaje** to be away; **irse de viaje** to go on a journey, go on a trip. ▪ **viaje de novios** honeymoon.

viajero,-a (*pasajero*) passenger. (*aventurero*) traveller.

víbora *nf* viper.

vibrar *vi* to vibrate.

viceversa *adv* vice versa.

vicio *nm* 1 (*corrupción*) vice, corruption. 2 (*mala costumbre*) bad habit.

víctima *nf* victim.

victoria *nf* 1 (*en enfrentamiento, batalla*) victory, triumph. 2 (*en partido*) win.

vid *nf* vine.

vida *nf* **1** *(de ser vivo)* life. **2** *(medios)* living: *se gana la vida como escritor,* he earns a living as a writer. • **en mi/tu/su/la vida** never.

vídeo *nm* video. • **grabar algo en vídeo** to tape STH.

videocámara *nf* camcorder.

videocasete *nm* video cassette.

videoclip *nm* video.

videoclub *nm* video shop.

videojuego *nm* video game.

vidriera *nf* *(obra artística)* stained glass window.

vidrio *nm* glass.

viejo,-a *adj (persona)* old, aged; *(cosa)* old. ► *nm,f (hombre)* old man; *(mujer)* old woman. • **hacerse viejo** to get old.

viento *nm* wind

vientre *nm* belly, abdomen.

viernes *nm* Friday.

viga *nf* **1** *(de madera)* beam, rafter. **2** *(de acero)* girder.

vigente *adj* in use, in force.

vigilante *nmf (hombre)* watchman; *(mujer)* watchwoman.

vigilar *vt-vi* **1** *(ir con cuidado)* to watch. **2** *(con armas)* to guard.

vigor *nm* vigou. • **en vigor** in force.

villa *nf* **1** *(casa)* villa. **2** *(pueblo)* small town.

villancico *nm* Christmas carol.

vinagre *nm* vinegar.

vinagreras *nf pl* cruet stand.

vinagreta *nf* vinaigrette.

vino *nm* wine. ■ **vino blanco** white wine; **vino de Jerez** sherry; **vino rosado** rosé wine; **vino tinto** red wine.

viña *nf* vineyard.

viñedo *nm* vineyard.

viñeta *nf* **1** *(dibujo)* cartoon. **2** *(tira)* comic strip.

violar *vt* **1** *(acuerdo, derecho)* to violate. **2** *(persona)* to rape.

violencia *nf* violence.

violento,-a *adj* violent.

violeta *adj-nm (color)* violet. ► *nf (flor)* violet.

violín *nm* violin.

violinista *nmf* violinist.

violonchelo *nm* cello.

virgen *adj* **1** *(persona)* virgin. **2** *(cinta)* blank. **3** *(en estado natural)* unspoiled. ► *nf* virgin.

virtual *adj* virtual.

virtud *nf* virtue.

viruela *nf* smallpox.

virus *nm* virus.

visado *nm* visa.

vísceras *nf pl* viscera.

visera *nf (de gorra)* peak; *(de casco)* visor.

visible *adj* visible.

visión *nf* sight, vision. • **ver visiones** to dream, see things.

visita *nf* **1** *(acción)* visit. **2** *(visitante)* visitor, guest.

visitante *nmf* visitor.

visitar *vt* **1** *(ir a casa de)* to visit. **2** *(enfermo)* to see.

voluntad

visón nm mink.

víspera nf 1 (día anterior) day before. 2 (de fiesta) eve.

vista nf 1 (sentido) sight, vision. 2 (panorama) view. • **con vistas a 1** (jardín, calle) overlooking. 2 (beneficios, resultados) with a view to; **conocer de vista** to know by sight; **estar a la vista** to be evident; **hasta la vista** good-bye, so long; **salta a la vista que...** it is obvious that...

visto,-a adj seen. • **por lo visto** as it seems; **ser lo nunca visto** to be unheard of. ■ **visto bueno** approval.

vitamina nf vitamin.

vitrina nf 1 (en casa) glass cabinet, display cabinet. 2 (de exposición) glass case, showcase. 3 (escaparate) shop window.

viudo,-a nm,f (hombre) widower; (mujer) widow.

viva interj hurrah!

víveres nm pl food, provisions.

vivero nm 1 (de plantas) nursery. 2 (de peces) fish farm.

vivienda nf 1 (alojamiento) housing, accommodation. 2 (morada) home; (- casa) house; (- piso) flat.

viviente adj living, alive.

vivir vi to live. ► vt (pasar) to live through: *los que vivieron la guerra*, those

who lived through the war. • **vivir de** to live on: *vive de su pensión*, she lives on her pension.

vivo,-a adj 1 (con vida) alive, living. 2 (color) bright, vivid. 3 (animado) lively. • **en vivo** (programa) live.

vocabulario nm vocabulary.

vocación nf vocation.

vocal adj vocal. ► nf (letra, sonido) vowel. ► nmf (de comité) member.

vodka nm vodka.

volante nm 1 (de vehículo) steering wheel. 2 (documento) note: *pedí un volante para el médico de la piel*, I asked to be referred to the skin specialist.

volar vi to fly. ► vt (hacer explotar) to blow up. • **volando** in a rush: *tuve que desayunar volando*, I had to eat my breakfast in a hurry.

volcán nm volcano.

volcar vt to knock over. ► vi to overturn. ► vpr **volcarse** (entregarse) to devote oneself.

voleibol nm volleyball.

voltereta nf somersault.

volumen nm volume. • **bajar/subir el volumen** to turn the volume down/up. ■ **volumen de negocios** turnover.

voluntad nf 1 (de decidir) will. 2 (propósito) intention, purpose. 3 (deseo) wish.

voluntario,-a *adj* voluntary. ► *nm,f* volunteer.

volver *vt* **1** *(dar vuelta a)* to turn (over); *(hacia abajo)* to turn upside down; *(de fuera a dentro)* to turn inside out. **2** *(convertir)* to turn, make: *me vuelve loco*, he drives me mad. ► *vi (regresar)* to come back, go back. ► *vpr* **volverse 1** *(darse la vuelta)* to turn (round): *se volvió hacia mí*, he turned towards me. **2** *(convertirse)* to turn, become: *se ha vuelto loco*, he's gone mad. ∎ **volver en sí** to recover consciousness, come round; **volverse atrás** to back out.

vomitar *vi* to vomit, be sick.

vosotros,-as *pron* you. ∎ **vosotros,-as mismos,-as** yourselves.

votación *nf (*vote, voting.

votar *vi* to vote.

voto *nm* vote.

voz *nf* **1** *(gen)* voice. **2** *(grito)* shout: *no me des esas voces*, don't shout! ∎ **a media voz** in a whisper; **en voz alta** aloud; **en voz baja** in a low voice.

vuelo *nm* flight. ∎ **vuelo sin motor** gliding.

vuelta *nf* **1** *(giro)* turn: *da una vuelta a la llave*, give the key one turn. **2** *(en un circuito)* lap. **3** *(paseo a pie)* walk, stroll: *ir a dar una vuelta*, to go for a walk. **4** *(paseo en coche)* drive. **5** *(regreso)* return: *la vuelta la haremos en tren*, we'll come back by train. **6** *(dinero de cambio)* change: *quédese con la vuelta*, keep the change. ∎ **a la vuelta** on the way back; **dar la vuelta 1** *(alrededor)* to go round. **2** *(girar)* to turn round. **3** *(de arriba abajo)* to turn upside down. **4** *(de dentro a fuera)* to turn inside out; **estar de vuelta** to be back. ∎ **vuelta al mundo** round-the-world trip; **vuelta ciclista** cycle race.

vuestro,-a *adj* your, of yours. ► *pron* yours.

vulgar *adj* **1** *(grosero)* vulgar. **2** *(corriente)* common, general.

W-X

Walkman® *nm* Walkman®.

wáter *nm fam* toilet.

waterpolo *nm* water polo.

W.C. *abr (retrete)* WC, toilet.

web *nf* **1** *(sitio)* website. **2** *(página)* webpage.

whisky *nm* whisky; *(irlandés)* whiskey.

windsurf *nm* windsurfing.

xenofobia *nf* xenophobia.

xilófono *nm* xylophone.

Y

y *conj* **1** *(gen)* and. **2** *(con hora)* past: *son las tres y cuarto*, it's a quarter past three. **3** *(con números)*: *cuarenta y cuatro*, forty-four.

ya *adv* **1** *(con pasado)* already: *ya lo sabía*, I already knew. **2** *(con presente)* now: *es preciso actuar ya*, it is vital that we act now. **3** *(ahora mismo)* immediately, at once. **4** *(luego)* later: *ya veremos*, we'll see. **5** *(uso enfático)*: *ya lo sé*, I know; *ya entiendo*, I see. • **ya no** not any more, no longer; **ya que** since.

yacimiento *nm* bed, deposit. ▪ **yacimiento arqueológico** archaeological site.

yate *nm* *(a motor)* pleasure cruiser; *(de vela)* yacht.

yegua *nf* mare.

yema *nf* **1** *(de huevo)* yolk. **2** *(del dedo)* fingertip.

yerno *nm* son-in-law.

yeso *nm* **1** *(mineral)* gypsum. **2** *(en construcción)* plaster.

yo *pron* **1** *(sujeto)* I. **2** *(objeto, con preposición)* me. • **yo mismo** myself.

yoga *nm* yoga.

yogur *nm* yoghurt.

yóquey *nm* jockey.

yugular *adj-nf* jugular.

yunque *nm* anvil.

Z

zafiro *nm* sapphire.

zamarra *nf* sheepskin jacket.

Zambia *nf* Zambia.

zambullirse *vpr* to dive.

zanahoria *nf* carrot.

zancada *nf* stride.

zancadilla *nf* *(para caer)* trip.

zanja *nf* ditch, trench.

zapatería *nf* shoe shop.

zapatilla *nf* slipper. ▪ **zapatillas de deporte** trainers.

zapato *nm* shoe. ▪ **zapatos de tacón** high-heeled shoes.

zar *nm* tsar, czar.

zarpa *nf* paw.

zarpar *vi* to set sail.

zarza *nf* bramble, blackberry bush.

zarzamora *nf* *(planta)* blackberry bush; *(fruto)* blackberry.

zócalo *nm* skirting board.

zona *nf* area, zone. ▪ **zona azul** pay-and-display parking area; **zona verde** park.

zoo *nm* zoo.

zoología *nf* zoology.

zoológico *nm* zoo.

zorro,-a *nm,f* *(animal)* fox.

zueco *nm* clog.

zumbido *nm* **1** *(de insecto)* buzzing. **2** *(de motor)* humming.

zumo *nm* juice.

zurda *nf* *(mano)* left hand.

zurdo,-a *adj* left-handed.

Monetary Units/
Unidades monetarias

Country / País	Name / Nombre	Symbol / Símbolo
THE AMERICAS / LAS AMÉRICAS		
Argentina	peso	$
Bahamas	dollar / dólar bahameño	B$
Barbados	dollar / dólar de Barbados	$
Belize / Belice	dollar / dólar	$
Bolivia	peso	$B
Brazil / Brasil	cruzeiro / nuevo cruzeiro	$; Cr$
Canada / Canadá	dollar / dólar canadiense	$
Chile	peso* / peso chileno*	$
Colombia	peso	$; P
Costa Rica	colon / colón	₡; ¢
Cuba	peso	$
Dominican Republic / República Dominicana	peso	RD$
Ecuador	sucre	S/
El Salvador	colon / colón	₡; ¢
Guatemala	quetzal	Q; Q
Guyana	dollar / dólar guayanés	G$
Haiti / Haití	gourde	₲; G; Gde
Honduras	lempira	L
Jamaica	dollar / dólar jamaicano	$
Mexico / México	peso	$

* The Chilean monetary unit, the escudo, was replaced by the peso in 1975.

* El escudo, la unidad monetaria chilena, fue reemplazado por el peso en 1975.

Country / País	Name / Nombre	Symbol / Símbolo
Nicaragua	cordoba / córdoba	C$
Panama / Panamá	balboa	B/
Paraguay	guarani / guaraní	Ø; G
Peru / Perú	sol	S/; $
Puerto Rico	dollar / dólar	$
Suriname / Surinam	guilder / gulder de Surinam	g
Trinidad and Tobago / Trinidad y Tabago	dollar / dólar trinitario	TT$
United States / Estados Unidos	dollar / dólar	$
Uruguay	peso	$
Venezuela	bolivar / bolívar	B

Weights and Measures

Metric System

Unit	Abbreviation	Approximate U.S. Equivalent	
LENGTH			
1 millimeter	mm	0.04	inch
1 centimeter	cm	0.39	inch
1 meter	m	39.37	inches
		1.094	yards
1 kilometer	km	3,281.5	feet
		0.62	mile
AREA			
1 square centimeter	sq cm (cm²)	0.155	square inch
1 square meter	m²	10.764	square feet
		1.196	square yards
1 hectare	ha	2.471	acres
1 square kilometer	sq km (km²)	247.105	acres
		0.386	square mile
VOLUME			
1 cubic centimeter	cu cm (cm³)	0.061	cubic inch
1 stere	s	1.308	cubic yards
1 cubic meter	m³	1.308	cubic yards
CAPACITY (Liquid Measure)			
1 deciliter	dl	0.21	pint
1 liter	l	1.057	quarts
1 dekaliter	dal	2.64	gallons
MASS AND WEIGHT			
1 gram	g, gm	0.035	ounce
1 dekagram	dag	0.353	ounce
1 hectogram	hg	3.527	ounces
1 kilogram	kg	2.2046	pounds
1 quintal	q	220.46	pounds
1 metric ton	MT, t	1.1	tons

Pesas y medidas

Sistema métrico

Unidad	Abreviatura	Equivalente aproximado del sistema estadounidense	
LONGITUD			
1 milímetro	mm	0,04	pulgada
1 centímetro	cm	0,39	pulgada
1 metro	m	39,37	pulgadas
		1,094	yardas
1 kilómetro	Km	3.281,5	pies
		0,62	milla
ÁREA			
1 centímetro cuadrado	cm²	0,155	pulgada cuadrada
1 metro cuadrado	m²	10,764	pies cuadrados
		1,196	yardas cuadradas
1 hectárea	ha	2,471	acres
1 kilómetro cuadrado	Km²	247,105	acres
		0,386	milla cuadrada
VOLUMEN			
1 centímetro cúbico	cm³	0,061	pulgadas cúbicas
1 metro cúbico	m³	1,308	yardas cúbicas
CAPACIDAD (Medida líquida)			
1 decilitro	dl	0,21	pinta
1 litro	l	1,057	quarts
1 decalitro	Dl	2,64	galones
MASA Y PESO			
1 gramo	g	0,035	onza
1 decagramo	Dg	0,353	onza
1 hectogramo	Hg	3,527	onzas
1 kilogramo	Kg	2,2046	libras
1 quintal métrico	q	220,46	libras
1 tonelada métrica	t	1,1	toneladas

U.S. Customary Weights and Measures /
Unidades de pesas y medidas estadounidenses

Linear measure / Medida de longitud

1 foot / pie	=	12 inches / pulgadas
1 yard / yarda	=	36 inches / pulgadas
	=	3 feet / pies
1 rod	=	5½ yards / yardas
1 mile / milla	=	5,280 feet / 5.280 pies
	=	1,760 yards / 1.760 yardas

Liquid measure / Medida líquida

1 pint / pinta	=	4 gills
1 quart / quart líquido	=	2 pints / pintas
1 gallon / galón	=	4 quarts / quarts líquidos

Area measure / Medida de superficie

1 square foot / pie cuadrado	=	144 square inches / pulgadas cuadradas
1 square yard / yarda cuadrada	=	9 square feet / pies cuadrados
1 square rod / rod cuadrado	=	30¼ square yards / yardas cuadradas
1 acre	=	160 square rods / rods cuadrados
1 square mile / milla cuadrada	=	640 acres

Dry measure / Medida árida

1 quart	=	2 pints / pintas áridas
1 peck	=	8 quarts
1 bushel	=	4 pecks

Some useful measures / Unas medidas útiles
Quantity / Cantidad

1 dozen / docena	=	12 units / unidades
1 gross / gruesa	=	12 dozen / docenas

Electricity / Electricidad

charge / carga	=	coulomb / culombio
power / potencia	=	watt / vatio
		kilowatt / kilovatio
resistance / resistencia	=	ohm / ohmio
strength / fuerza	=	ampere / amperio
voltage / voltaje	=	volt / voltio

Numbers/Numerales

Cardinal Numbers		Números cardinales	Cardinal Numbers		Números cardinales
zero	0	cero	twenty	20	veinte
one	1	uno	twenty-one	21	veintiuno
two	2	dos	twenty-two	22	veintidós
three	3	tres	twenty-three	23	veintitrés
four	4	cuatro	twenty-four	24	veinticuatro
five	5	cinco	twenty-five	25	veinticinco
six	6	seis	twenty-six	26	veintiséis
seven	7	siete	twenty-seven	27	veintisiete
eight	8	ocho	twenty-eight	28	veintiocho
nine	9	nueve	twenty-nine	29	veintinueve
ten	10	diez	thirty	30	treinta
eleven	11	once	forty	40	cuarenta
twelve	12	doce	fifty	50	cincuenta
thirteen	13	trece	sixty	60	sesenta
fourteen	14	catorce	seventy	70	setenta
fifteen	15	quince	eighty	80	ochenta
sixteen	16	dieciséis	ninety	90	noventa
seventeen	17	diecisiete	one hundred	100	cien, ciento
eighteen	18	dieciocho	five hundred	500	quinientos
nineteen	19	diecinueve	one thousand	1000	mil

219

Numbers / Numerales

Ordinal Numbers		Números ordinales	
1st	first	1.º, 1.ª	primero, -a
2nd	second	2.º, 2.ª	segundo, -a
3rd	third	3.º, 3.ª	tercero, -a
4th	fourth	4.º, 4.ª	cuarto, -a
5th	fifth	5.º, 5.ª	quinto, -a
6th	sixth	6.º, 6.ª	sexto, -a
7th	seventh	7.º, 7.ª	séptimo, -a
8th	eighth	8.º, 8.ª	octavo, -a
9th	ninth	9.º, 9.ª	noveno, -a
10th	tenth	10.º, 10.ª	décimo, -a
11th	eleventh	11.º, 11.ª	undécimo, -a
12th	twelfth	12.º, 12.ª	duodécimo, -a
13th	thirteenth	13.º, 13.ª	decimotercero, -a / decimotercio, -a
14th	fourteenth	14.º, 14.ª	decimocuarto, -a
15th	fifteenth	15.º, 15.ª	decimoquinto, -a
16th	sixteenth	16.º, 16.ª	decimosexto, -a
17th	seventeenth	17.º, 17.ª	decimoséptimo, -a
18th	eighteenth	18.º, 18.ª	decimoctavo, -a
19th	nineteenth	19.º, 19.ª	decimonoveno, -a / decimonono, -a
20th	twentieth	20.º, 20.ª	vigésimo, -a
21st	twenty-first	21.º, 21.ª	vigésimo (-a) primero (-a)
22nd	twenty-second	22.º, 22.ª	vigésimo (-a) segundo (-a)
30th	thirtieth	30.º, 30.ª	trigésimo, -a
40th	fortieth	40.º, 40.ª	cuadragésimo, -a
50th	fiftieth	50.º, 50.ª	quincuagésimo, -a
60th	sixtieth	60.º, 60.ª	sexagésimo, -a
70th	seventieth	70.º, 70.ª	septuagésimo, -a
80th	eightieth	80.º, 80.ª	octogésimo, -a
90th	ninetieth	90.º, 90.ª	nonagésimo, -a
100th	hundredth	100.º, 100.ª	centésimo, -a

Temperature/
La temperatura

**Fahrenheit and Celsius /
Grados Fahrenheit y grados Celsius**

To convert Fahrenheit to Celsius, subtract 32 degrees, multiply by 5, and divide by 9.

Para convertir grados Fahrenheit a grados Celsius (centígrados), réstese 32 grados, multiplíquese por 5 y divídase por 9.

$$104°F - 32 = 72 \times 5 = 360 \div 9 = 40°C$$

To convert Celsius to Fahrenheit, multiply by 9, divide by 5, and add 32 degrees.

Para convertir grados Celsius (centígrados) a grados Fahrenheit, multiplíquese por 9, divídase por 5 y agréguese 32 grados.

$$40°C \times 9 = 360 \div 5 = 72 + 32 = 104°F$$

At sea level, water boils at
Al nivel del mar, se hierve el agua a } 212°F / 100°C

Water freezes at
Se congela el agua en } 32°F / 0°C

Average human temperature
Temperatura promedia del ser humano } 98.6°F / 37°C

**Some normal temperatures in the Americas /
Algunas temperaturas normales en las Américas**

	Winter / Invierno	Summer / Verano
North of the equator / Al norte del ecuador		
Churchill, Manitoba	-11°F / -23.9°C	63°F / 17.2°C
Montreal, Quebec	22°F / -5.6°C	79°F / 26.1°C
Anchorage, Alaska	12°F / -11.1°C	58°F / 14.4°C
Chicago, Illinois	24°F / -4.4°C	75°F / 23.9°C
New York, New York	32°F / 0°C	77°F / 25°C
Dallas, Texas	45°F / 7.2°C	86°F / 30°C
Los Angeles, California	57°F / 13.9°C	73°F / 22.8°C
Phoenix, Arizona	51°F / 10.6°C	94°F / 34.4°C
Tegucigalpa, Honduras	50°F / 10°C	90°F / 32°C
South of the equator / Al sur del ecuador		
Tierra del Fuego, Argentina	32°F / 0°C	50°F / 10°C
Sao Paulo, Brazil	57.2°F / 14°C	69.8°F / 21°C
Montevideo, Uruguay	55.4°F / 13°C	71.6°F / 22°C
Buenos Aires, Argentina	52.3°F / 11.3°C	73.8°F / 23.2°C
Lima, Peru	59°F / 15°C	77°F / 25°C

Abbreviations Most Commonly Used in Spanish

A	Aprobado (*in examinations*)	c.ª	compañía
		c/a.	cuenta abierta
a	área	cap.	capítulo
(a)	alias	C.C.	corriente
AA.	autores		continua
ab.	abad	cénts.	céntimos
abr.	abril	cf.	compárese
A.C., A. de C.	Año de Cristo	C.G.S.	cegesimal
		Cía., cía.	compañía
admón.	administración	C.M.B., c.m.b.	cuya mano beso
adm.ᵒʳ	administrador		
afmo., affmo.	afectísimo	comis.ᵒ	comisario
		comp.ª	compañía
afto.	afecto	comps.	compañeros
ago.	agosto	Const.	Constitución
a la v/	a la vista	corrte.	corriente
a.m.	ante meridiem, antes del mediodía	C.P.B., c.p.b.	cuyos pies beso
		cps.	compañeros
anac.	anacoreta	cs.	cuartos; céntimos
ap.	aparte; apóstol		
apdo.	apartado	cta.	cuenta
art., art.ᵒ	artículo	cte.	corriente
att.ᵒ, atto.	atento	c/u	cada uno
		C.V.	caballo (*or* caballos) de vapor
B	beato; Bueno (*in examinations*)		
Barna.	Barcelona		
B.L.M., b.l.m.	besa la mano; besa las manos	D.	Don
		D.ª	Doña
B.L.P., b.l.p.	besa los pies	descto.	descuento
		d/f., d/fha.	días fecha
bto.	bulto; bruto		
		dha., dho., dhas., dhos.	dicha, dicho, dichas, dichos
c.	capítulo		
c/	caja; cargo; contra	dic.	diciembre
C.A.	corriente alterna		

dls.	dólares	Hno.,	Hermano,
dna.,	docena, docenas	Hnos.	Hermanos
dnas.		HP., H.P.	caballo (*or*
d/p.	días plazo		caballos) de
Dr., dr.	Doctor		vapor
dra., dro.,	derecha,		
dras.,	derecho,	ib., ibíd.	ibidem (en el
dros.	derechas,		mismo lugar)
	derechos	íd.	idem
dupdo.	duplicado	i. e.	id est (*that is*)
d/v.	días vista	it.	item
		izq.ª, izq.º	izquierda,
E	este (*east*)		izquierdo
E.M.	Estado Mayor		
E.M.G.	Estado Mayor	J.C.	Jesucristo
	General	jul.	julio
ENE	estenordeste	jun.	junio
ene.	enero		
E.P.D.	en paz descanse	L/	letra
E.P.M.	en propia mano	L.	ley; libro
ESE	estesudeste	Ldo., ldo.	licenciado
etc.	etcétera	lín.	línea
		liq.	liquidación
f.ª, fact.ª	factura	líq.º	líquido
f/	fardo(s)		
f.a.b.	franco a bordo	M.	Maestro;
F.C., f.c.	ferrocarril		Majestad;
fcos.	francos		Merced
feb., febr.	febrero	m.	minuto,
F.E.M.,	fuerza		minutos;
f.e.m.	electromotriz		mañana
fha., fho.	fecha, fecho	m/	mes; mi, mis;
f.º, fol.	folio		mío, míos
fra.	factura	mar.	marzo
fund.	fundador	m/cta.	mi cuenta
		merc.	mercaderías
		m/f.	mi favor
g/	giro	milés.	milésimas
gde.	guarde	m/L.	mi letra
gobno.	gobierno	m/o.	mi orden
gob.ʳ	gobernador	m/p.	mi pagaré
gral.	general	m/r.	mi remesa
gte.	gerente	Mtro.	Maestro

m.a.	muchos años	p. ej.	por ejemplo
M.S.	manuscrito	P.O., p.o.	por orden
		PP.	Padres
N	norte; Notable *(in examinations)*	P.P., p.p.	porte pagado; por poder
n.	noche	p. pd.º, ppdo.	próximo pasado
n/	nuestro, nuestra		
N. B.	nota bene	pral.	principal
n/cta.	nuestra cuenta	pralte.	principalmente
NE	nordeste	prof.	profesor
NNE	nornoreste	pról.	prólogo
NNO	nornoroeste	prov.ª	provincia
NO	noroeste	próx.º	próximo
nov., novbre.	noviembre	P.S.	Post Scriptum
		ps.	pesos
núm., núms.	número, números	P.S.M.	por su mandato
nto.	neto	pta., ptas.	peseta, pesetas
ntra., ntro., ntras., ntros.	nuestra, nuestro, nuestras, nuestros	pte.	parte; presente
		pza.	pieza
O	oeste	Q.B.S.M., q.b.s.m.	que besa su mano
o/	orden	Q.B.S.P., q.b.s.p.	que besa sus pies
oct.	octubre	Q.D.G., q.D.g.	que Dios guarde
ONO	oesnoroeste	q.e.g.e.	que en gloria esté
OSO	oessudoeste	q.e.p.d.	que en paz descanse
P.	Papa; padre; pregunta	q.e.s.m.	que estrecha su mano
P.A., p.a.	por ausencia; por autorización	qq.	quintales
		q.s.g.h.	que santa gloria haya
pág., págs.	página, páginas		
paq.	paquete	R.	respuesta; Reprobado *(in examinations)*
Part.	Partida		
Patr.	Patriarca	Rbi.	Recibí
pbro.	presbítero	R.D.	Real Decreto
p/cta.	por cuenta	R.I.P.	Requiescat in pace (descanse en paz)
P.D.	posdata		

Rl., Rls.	real, reales *(royal)*	SSE	sudsudeste
		SSO	sudsudoeste
rl., rls.	real, reales *(coin)*	S.S.S.,	su seguro
r.p.m.	revoluciones por minuto	s.s.s.	servidor
		SS. SS.	seguros servidores
S.	San, Santo; sur; Sobresaliente *(in examinations)*	Sta.	Santa; Señorita
		Sto.	Santo
		suplte.	suplente
s/	su, sus; sobre	tit., tit.º	título
S.ª	Señora	tpo.	tiempo
s/c.	su cuenta	trib.	tribunal
S.C., s.c.	su casa		
s/cta.	su cuenta	U., Ud.	usted
S.D.	Se despide	Uds.	ustedes
SE	sudeste		
sep., sept., sepbre.	septiembre	V.	usted; Venerable; Véase
serv.º	servicio		
serv.ᵒʳ	servidor	V	versículo
s. e. u o.	salvo error u omisión	vencimto.	vencimiento
		vers.º	versículo
sigte.	siguiente	vg., v.g.,	verbigracia
Sn.	San	v. gr.	
SO	sudoeste	Vmd., V.	vuestra merced; usted
S.ʳ, Sr.	Señor		
Sra., Sras.	Señora, Señoras	V.º B.º	Visto bueno
Sres.	Señores	vol.	volumen; voluntad
Sría.	Secretaría		
sria., srio.	secretaria, secretario	vols.	volúmenes
		VV.	ustedes
Srta.	Señorita		
S. S.ª	Su Señoría		

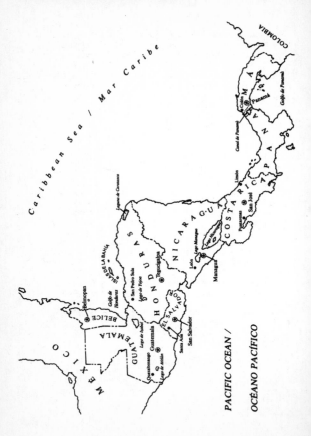

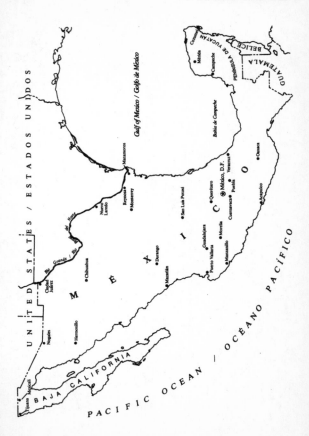

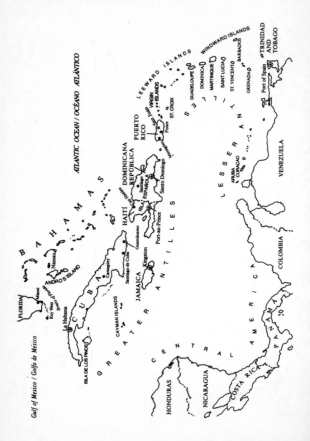

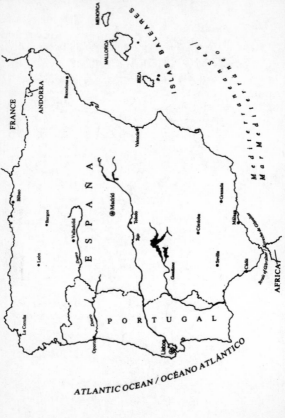

MENORCA

MALLORCA

IBIZA

ISLAS BALEARES

FRANCE

ANDORRA

Barcelona

Valencia

Bilbao

Burgos

León

Valladolid

● Madrid

Toledo

Tajo

Granada

● Córdoba

Málaga

ESPAÑA

Sevilla

Duero

Guadalquivir

Estrecho de Gibraltar

Cádiz

Strait of Gibraltar

AFRICA

La Coruña

Oporto

Duero

PORTUGAL

Lisboa

Mediterráneo

Mar Mediterráneo

ATLANTIC OCEAN / OCÉANO ATLÁNTICO